LEARNING
WEB TECHNOLOGIES

Jim Maivald
Cheryl Brumbaugh-Duncan

Boston • Columbus • Indianapolis • New York • San Francisco
Amsterdam • Cape Town • Dubai • London • Madrid • Milan • Munich
Paris • Montreal • Toronto Delhi • Mexico City • Sao Paulo • Sydney
Hong Kong • Seoul • Singapore • Taipei • Tokyo

Printed in the United States of America. This publication is protected by copyright, and permission should be obtained from the publisher prior to any prohibited reproduction, storage in a retrieval system, or transmission in any form or by any means, electronic, mechanical, photocopying, recording, or otherwise. For information regarding permissions, request forms and the appropriate contacts, please visit www.pearsoned.com/permissions to contact the Pearson Education Rights and Permissions Department.

Unless otherwise indicated herein, any third party trademarks that may appear in this work are the property of their respective owners and any references to third party trademarks, logos or other trade dress are for demonstrative or descriptive purposes only. Such references are not intended to imply any sponsorship, endorsement, authorization, or promotion of Pearson Education Inc. products by the owners of such marks, or any relationship between the owner and Pearson Education Inc. or its affiliates, authors, licensees or distributors.

330 Hudson Street, New York, NY 10013

Hardcover ISBN 10:   0-13-442744-0

Hardcover ISBN 13: 978-0-13-442744-7

Pearson

1   16

Contents

Contents

Contents

Introduction

Learning Web Technologies gives you an in-depth introduction to Adobe Dreamweaver and other web design and development technologies. This book supports the Creative Cloud versions of the Adobe Dreamweaver application. Adobe Creative Cloud gives you access to the most up-to-date tools and features for all Adobe applications.

Adobe® Dreamweaver® CC is an industry standard for web design and development excellence. Its powerful web programming features and intuitive interface make it easy to learn and simple to use for both beginners and professionals. Whether you are a web designer or an experienced HTML programmer, producing web pages or online content with Adobe Dreamweaver and its tools enable you to achieve professional-quality results.

How the Book Is Organized

Learning Web Technologies consists of 15 Chapters. Chapters 1–4 provide an overview of Web technologies by covering an introduction to the Internet and World Wide Web, HTML basics, CSS basics, and an introduction to Dreamweaver and the Dreamweaver workspace. Chapters 5–10 cover how to create webpage layout, format, and navigation as well as webpage structure for supporting computer full screen displays, tablets, and mobile phone screen sizes. Chapters 11–15 cover how to insert images, multimedia, web animation, and video, as well as including other web programming languages for advanced interactivity in a webpage. Each chapter contains multiple exercises that introduce a number of web technologies features. You will learn and practice these features as you complete other real-world projects through the end-of-chapter Critical Thinking Project and the Online Portfolio Builder websites.

Chapters are structured to make the learning process simple and enjoyable. Each chapter begins with a listing of the topics that will be covered, followed by an overview of why those topics are important.

Chapter Overview

In this chapter, you'll learn how to do the following:

- Examine the chosen page design and evaluate the use of the predefined layouts provided by Dreamweaver
- Work with the Visual Media Query interface
- Create a new layout using the BootStrap framework
- Modify the layout structure to use HTML5 semantic elements

Each chapter presents the concepts and skills through a written introduction to the skills or features, and then follows this up with hands-on exercises focused on guided learning for mastering these skills and features. All exercises are introduced so you know what you are going to accomplish in the following steps. Numbered steps make it easy for you to complete each part of the project. Frequent illustrations show you how to select settings, as well as show you results you can use to check your progress. Icons included in the steps help you identify the correct tool to use for the current task.

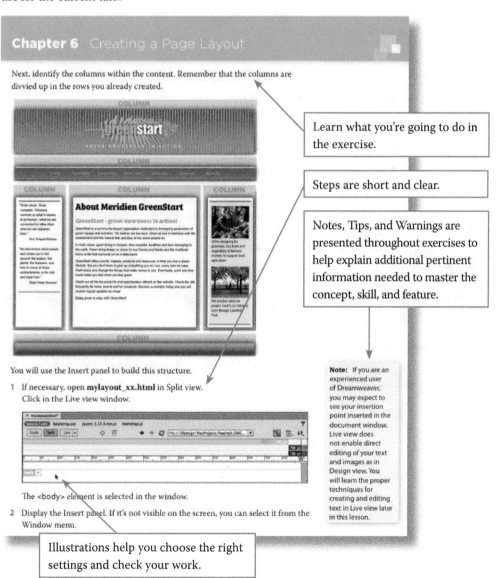

Learn what you're going to do in the exercise.

Steps are short and clear.

Notes, Tips, and Warnings are presented throughout exercises to help explain additional pertinent information needed to master the concept, skill, and feature.

Illustrations help you choose the right settings and check your work.

Softskills features cover a variety of subjects related to the study of web technologies, preparation for a career in web design and development, and the skills and qualities a person needs to be a successful employee. Many of these features are included in the Critical Thinking Project at the end of the chapter, and allow you to explore the feature through further research, writing, and designing. Softskills topics include employability skills; history of web and web technologies; principles and elements of graphic design; web design certificates and education; legal and ethical issues; communication, teamwork, and leadership; cyber safety; entrepreneurial and public relations opportunities; and how to give and receive constructive criticism.

Interpersonal communications

The process of interacting with others, exchanging information with each other and understanding each other.

Emotional intelligence:

The ability to perceive and understand emotions and to use that knowledge to guide your own behavior as well as respond to others.

Working with Others

Unless you work completely by yourself, your success on the job depends on working well—and communicating well— with others: coworkers and teammates, supervisors and managers, vendors and service providers, and customers and clients. This ongoing process of interacting with others, exchanging information and meaning, and achieving understanding is called **interpersonal communication**. People who are good at it typically have what experts call **emotional intelligence**—the ability to perceive and understand emotions and to use that knowledge to guide their own behavior and respond to others. Research by experts such as psychologist Daniel Goldman has shown that emotional intelligence is as important to good leadership and effective teamwork as are more traditionally valued skills and capacities.

Each chapter concludes with review questions designed to remind you of the most important skills and features you have learned and a section of objective questions to test your knowledge of the lesson's key points. Review questions are both multiple choice and essay questions.

End-of-Chapter Activities

Multiple Choice Questions

Directions: Choose the correct answer for each question.

1. What is the typical layout of a mockup web page design?
   a. Nav, Header, Content, Footer
   b. Content, Header Nav, Footer
   c. Header, Nav, Content, Footer
   d. Header, Content, Nav, Footer

2. The position-assist interface does what?
   a. Determines whether the element is inserted before, after, or nested in the page or HTML element.
   b. Quickly access the HTML code of the active element.
   c. Makes placeholder text editable.
   d. Shows the CSS style rules attached to an element.

3. True of False: Dreamweaver will remember any customizations your make to the workspace interface.
   a. True
   b. False

4. The CSS Designer is very useful for what?
   a. Creating and linking style sheets
   b. Creating style rules
   c. Troubleshooting CSS rule conflicts
   d. All of the above

5. How many link properties are there for formatting hypertext links in a web page?
   a. 4
   b. 5
   c. 3
   d. 6

6. In the CSS Designer, how do you know which style sheet contains the active style rule?
   a. The aMedia window displays the style sheet in red.
   b. The Selectors window displays the style sheet in a blue highlight
   c. The Show Set option displays the style sheet in bold
   d. The Sources window displays the style sheet in bold

Two hands-on projects, the Critical Thinking Project and the Online Portfolio Builder, at the end of each chapter give you another chance to practice the skills you have learned. The Critical Thinking Project allows you to practice what you learn in the chapter and challenges you to complete a project on your own or with minimal instruction. The Online Portfolio Builder allows you to apply the concepts, skills, and features to create your own online portfolio.

Critical Thinking Project – Working with Pre-Defined Layouts

This project has you working with Pre-defined layouts that are included in Dreamweaver to help you get started with a page design.

1. On your computer create a local root folder as directed by your teacher. Name the folder **layouts_xx**. Open this folder and create a new folder. Name the folder **images**.

2. Open Dreamweaver and define a new site.

Online Portfolio Builder – Create a Bootstrap Layout for your Portfolio Site

Using the mockup sketch of your site that you created in Lesson 5 Online Portfolio Builder project, create a custom Bootstrap page layout to start converting the mockup to HTML. Think about design principles, in particular Alignment, as you analyze the mockup and determine the rows and columns that occure naturally in the design. These rows and columns will translate to HTML elements and you are building the framework for these elements in this project.

1. Analyze your mockup sketch of your Online Portfolio website's home page that you created in Lesson 5. Draw lines that identify the basic page layout components. Label these on the sketch.

Working with Data and Solution Files

As you work through the exercises and projects in this book, you'll be creating, opening, and saving files. Keep the following instructions in mind:

* All chapters have a Datafiles folders and they contain the files, folders, and documents that you need to complete the exercise or project. Inside the Datafiles folders are other folders that match up with either the chapter exercise or Critical Thinking Project that you are going to complete for the chapter. The Datafiles folder contains just the website files you need to get started on the exercise or project.

* Most exercises will require you to open a data file to begin the exercise. These files are found in the Datafiles folder and the Chapter exercise folder and called out by name in the step-by-step instruction. Additional files may be required to complete some steps; they are generally given a name that relates to their content, such as **Roses.jpg**.

* You will be directed to include the initials of your first and last name to the folder associated with the exercise or project so you can easily locate your files if you have to share a computer. The folder names will appear in the text with two *xx*'s to stand for your initials; i.e., **layouts_xx.**

* Follow your teacher's directions for where to access and save the files on a network, local computer hard drive, or portable storage device such as a USB drive.

GETTING STARTED

Adobe® Dreamweaver® CC is the industry-leading
web-authoring program. Whether you create websites
for others for a living or plan to create one for your
own business, Dreamweaver offers all the tools you
need to get professional-quality results.

TinyURLs

At several points in the book, we reference external information available on the Internet. The **uniform resource locators (URLs)** for this information are often long and unwieldy, so we have provided custom TinyURLs in many places for your convenience. Unfortunately, the TinyURLs sometimes expire over time and no longer function. If you find that a TinyURL doesn't work, look up the actual URL provided in the appendix.

Prerequisites

Before using *Web Technologies*, you should have a working knowledge of your computer and its operating system. Be sure you know how to use the mouse, standard menus, and commands, and also how to open, save, and close files. If you need to review these techniques, see the printed or online documentation included with your Windows or Mac operating system.

Conventions Used in This book

Working in Dreamweaver means you'll be working with code. We have used several conventions in the following chapters and exercises to make working with the code in this book easier to follow and understand.

Code Font

In many instructions, you will be required to enter **HTML** code, **CSS** rules, and properties and other **code-based markup**. To distinguish the markup from the instructional text, the entries will be styled with a code font, like this:

Examine the following code `<h1>Heading goes here</h1>`

In instances where you must enter the markup yourself, the entry will be formatted in color, like this:

Insert the following code `<h1>Heading goes here</h1>`

Uniform Resource Locators (URLs)

The web address for a web resource such as a web site. The URL specifies the location of the web resource on a network and also how to retrieve it. A common form of a URL is a web address that uses HTTP or HTTPS - for example http://www.mywebsite.com. You can also use URLs for File Transfer Protocol (FTP), email - (mailto), or to access a database on the Web using JDBC. There also are other types of URL but these are the most popular.

HTML

HTML stands for HypterText Markup Language is the standard programming language for the World Wide Web. It is the backbone programming language of the web. Today it is combined with CSS and Javascript to create interactive, dynamic webpages.

CSS

CSS stands for Cascading Style Sheets and is used to format and control the display of an HTML document. Today HTML, CSS, and JavaScript are cornerstones for the development of a webpage or web content.

Strikethrough

In several exercises, you will be instructed to delete markup that already exists within the webpage or style sheet. In those instances, the targeted references will be identified with strikethrough formatting, like this:

Delete the following values:

```
margin: 10px 20px 10px 20px;
background-image: url(images/fern.png), url(images/stripe.png);
```

Be careful to delete only the identified markup so that you achieve the following result:

```
margin: 10px 10px;
background-image: url(images/fern.png);
```

Missing Punctuation

HTML code, CSS markup, and **JavaScript** often require the use of various punctuation, such as periods (.), commas (,) and semicolons (;), among others, and can be damaged by their incorrect usage or placement. Consequently, periods and other punctuation expected in a sentence or paragraph may be omitted from an instruction or hyperlink whenever it may cause confusion or a possible error, as in the following two instructions:

Enter the following code: `<h1>Heading goes here</h1>`

Type the following link: `http://adobe.com`

Element References

Within the body of descriptions and exercise instructions, elements may be referenced by name or by class or id attributes. When an element is identified by its tag name, it will appear as <h1> or h1. When referenced by its class attribute, the name will appear with a leading period (.) in a code-like font, like this: `.content` or `.sidebar1`. References to elements by their id attribute will appear with a leading hash (#) and in a code font, like this: `#top`. This practice matches the way these elements appear in Dreamweaver's tag selector interface.

Code-Based Markup

Computer programming code used to instruct a software to display text or media using predefined actions. In the case of HTML, these predefined actions are tags. An HTML code-based markup tag typically is comprised of both an opening and closing tag that is encased in brackets - <>. For instance, to bold the sentence "Put your text here." on a web page you would use Put your text here..

JavaScript

A programing language that is another cornerstone for the development of a webpage along with HTML and CSS.

Windows vs. OS X Instructions

In most cases, Dreamweaver performs identically in both Windows and OS X. Minor differences exist between the two versions, mostly due to platform-specific issues out of the control of the program. Most of these are simply differences in keyboard shortcuts, how dialogs are displayed, and how buttons are named. In most cases, screen shots were made in the OS X version of Dreamweaver and may appear differently from your own screen.

Where specific commands differ, they are noted within the text. Windows commands are listed first, followed by the OS X equivalent, such as Ctrl+C/Cmd+C. Common abbreviations are used for all commands whenever possible, as follows:

WINDOWS	OS X
Control = Ctrl	Command = Cmd
Alternate = Alt	Option = Opt

As chapters proceed, instructions may be truncated or shortened to save space, with the assumption that you picked up the essential concepts earlier in the chapter. For example, at the beginning of a chapter you may be instructed to "press Ctrl+C/Cmd+C." Later, you may be told to "copy" text or a code element. These should be considered identical instructions.

If you find you have difficulties in any particular task, review earlier steps or exercises in that chapter. In some cases if an exercise is based on concepts covered earlier, you will be referred back to the specific chapter.

Additional Resources

For comprehensive information about program features and tutorials, refer to these resources:

Adobe Dreamweaver Learn & Support: helpx.adobe.com/dreamweaver (accessible in Dreamweaver by choosing Help > Help And Support > Dreamweaver Support Center) is where you can find and browse tutorials, help, and support on Adobe.com.

Dreamweaver Help: helpx.adobe.com/dreamweaver/topics.html is a reference for application features, commands, and tools (press F1 or choose Help > Help And Support > Dreamweaver Online Help). You can also download Help as a PDF document optimized for printing at helpx.adobe.com/pdf/dreamweaver_reference.pdf.

Chapter 1

THE INTERNET AND WORLD WIDE WEB

Chapter Overview

In this chapter, you'll learn how to do the following:

- Compare the Internet to the World Wide Web
- Describe the history and hardware that makes up the Internet
- Understand the organization of the Internet
- Distinguish the Internet from a WAN
- List organizations that manage the Internet
- Understand the various documents and resources that make up the World Wide Web
- Compare and contrast the Internet and the telephone system
- List and explore careers for managing the Internet and the web
- Distinguish between Internet Protocol addresses and domain names
- Explain how domain names are organized
- Identify the different parts of a URL
- Describe how to find an owner of a domain name

The Internet and World Wide Web

Before beginning to learn Dreamweaver CC it is a good idea to take a step back and really understand how the Internet and the World Wide Web work.

The terms Internet and World Wide Web are used interchangeably today but the "Internet" is not a term **synonymous** with "World Wide Web" — The two are entirely different entities but reliant on each other for global functionality, interactivity and communications.

> **Synonymous**
>
> The same or equivalent in meaning.

The Internet is a series of networks connected to each other by systems similar to our telephone networks: copper wires, fiber-optic cables, and wireless connections, as well as billions and millions of computers and connectivity hardware like servers, computers, routers, and modems make up the Internet. The Internet is the hardware backbone for the World Wide Web.

The World Wide Web, often referred to as WWW or the web, is the collection of web resources, webpages and websites, email, and applications that can be accessed online. The Web is made up of documents and other resources, such as applications, videos, animations, and audio. These web resources are stored on servers and accessible via a URL or web address like http://www.youtube.com. The web runs on top of the Internet.

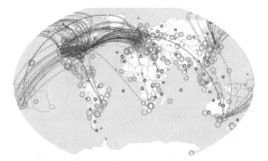

Today, the Internet includes millions of servers and connection all over the globe.

The Internet: A Network of Networks

The Internet connects people all over the world through a huge network of computer systems and servers. The U.S. government and university researchers began the Internet to share information. Since then, it has turned into one of the most exciting inventions in history.

As more and more people use the Internet, the demand for user-friendly online services has also grown and created new business opportunities. Additionally, electronic mail and instant messaging services have changed the way people meet and stay in touch with one another. People online can work together on projects in different locations, sharing information as if they were in the same office.

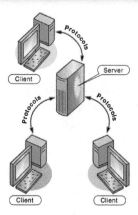

Like many networks, the Internet is made up of connected client and server computers that use protocols to communicate.

History of the Internet

In the 1960s, people were working on ideas that later became the Internet. In 1969, the first four major computer centers in the United States were linked. By 1973, the network was international. In 1983, the Internet protocols went online for the first time. Two major groups worked on the development of the Internet: the United States military and university researchers.

United States Military: In the 1960s, the United States government wanted to find a way to communicate in the event of a disaster or military attack. The military began to work on a system that would operate even if some communication connections were destroyed. The Defense Advanced Research Projects Agency (DARPA) of the U.S. Department of Defense focused on computer networking and communications. In 1968, this research led to a network of connected computer centers called the Advanced Research Projects Agency Network (ARPANET).

University Researchers: With the military's leadership and funding, DARPA formed computing research centers at universities across the United States. From 1969 through 1987, the number of computers on the network increased from 4 to more than 10,000. These connections created the networks that became the Internet.

Organization of the Internet

The Internet is a global **WAN**, a network of networks. It connects everything from single computers to large networks. The Internet can even connect computers that run different operating systems. This ability to share information with almost any computer makes the Internet a powerful tool for communication. The Internet is made up of three important parts: **servers**, **clients**, and **protocols**. These three components make up what is called a client-server architecture.

Client

Clients are the computers that request services from a server. When you connect to the Internet, the computer you use is considered a client. Like other networks, the Internet uses protocols—the sets of rules that allow clients and servers to communicate. Client is one component of the client-server architecture.

Server

A computer or computer program that serves up information based on requests it receives from other client computers or software on the network. Internet servers are the computers that provide services to other computers by way of the Internet. These services include processing e-mail, storing webpages, or helping send files from one computer to another. Common servers used today are web servers, mail servers, database servers, print servers, file servers, gaming servers and application servers. Servers are the other component of the client-server architecture.

Protocols

A group of rules that regulate the format of information that is accessible via the Internet.

Is the Internet a WAN?

There are three key differences between the Internet and other WANs.

- **Type of Access:** The Internet is public, while WANs are typically private.

- **Degree of Security:** While the Internet is becoming more secure, it is still not as secure as a private WAN connection. As data travels through the Internet, snoops and eavesdroppers on the public networks through which the data moves sometimes try to access it. A private WAN is more secure because it is more likely that only the organization that owns it has access to it. Internet users must take security measures on their own, such as installing firewalls and using antivirus and antimalware programs.

- **Types of Information:** On the Internet, information is transmitted in the form of webpages and other types of files. A WAN is used for more than just browsing webpages. It provides access to network resources, such as printers, file servers, and databases.

Internet Management

Who owns the Internet? The truth is, no specific organization or government does. Many organizations are responsible for different parts of the network. Here are some examples:

- The World Wide Web Consortium (W3C) issues standards related to the World Wide Web, like HTML standards.

- Internet Engineering Task Force (IETF) is a large international community of network designers, operators, vendors, and researchers. This group is concerned with the future structure and smooth operation of the Internet. Like many organizations that set computing standards, the IETF is "open," meaning any interested person can participate.

- Internet Corporation for Assigned Names and Numbers (ICANN) is a nonprofit corporation with a variety of responsibilities, including the management of domain names.

- Web Standards Project (WaSP) is a coalition that supports standards for simple, affordable access to web technologies.

- Freedom of the Internet – one advantage to the open quality of the Internet is the ability to share information. Anyone can make an idea or opinion accessible to anyone else.

- Pitfalls of the Internet - there are pitfalls to this open organization. People can post whatever point of view or information they want, even if it can sometimes be misleading or false. It is up to the users of the Internet to think critically about the information they find. If you have a question about anything you find on the Internet, ask an adult you trust about it.

Voting on the Internet? According to the Federal Election Commission, the Internet is not ready for U.S. citizens to vote on it. Safeguarding the privacy, security, and reliability of the voting process is important to ensuring a free democratic election.

While there have been some experiments with Internet voting, experts agree that it will be a long time before it is used in general elections. The Internet, however, can improve some parts of the election process. For example, the technology is in place for secure overseas military voting. Also, registration databases and vote totals can be sent over the Internet, saving time and money.

In what other ways might you use the Internet to find out more about politics?

The World Wide Web

The World Wide Web is a huge collection of **hypertext** documents called web pages. In a hypertext document, certain words or pictures can serve as hyperlinks. A hyperlink is a link to another document on the World Wide Web.

Standard pages of text are considered linear, which means you read through the page from top to bottom. Hypertext, however, is non-linear. As you are reading through a webpage, you can click on hyperlinks to move through multiple layers of information.

Hyperlinks: Usually hyperlinks appear underlined, in a different color, or highlighted. Sometimes there are buttons or images that can be clicked. When you move your mouse over a hyperlink, the pointer changes to an icon of a hand. You can click this hyperlink item to be transferred to another document.

URLs: When you click a hyperlink, the web browser retrieves and displays the document connected to that hyperlink. How does this work? Every document has a unique address, called a uniform resource locator (URL), which tells exactly where the document is located on the Internet. A hyperlink instructs the browser to go to the URL for that document.

Note: Did you know that you could get a traffic report about the Internet? Like the traffic reports you may hear on television or on the radio during rush hour, the Internet Traffic Report monitors the flow of data around the world.

visit www.internettrafficreport.com to see how the Internet traffic is in your neighborhood.

Hypertext

Text displayed in a document that has hyperlinks that allow the user to interact with the page by clicking a hyperlink to display a new page or new data.

Electronic Mail

For many Internet users, electronic mail, or e-mail, has replaced traditional mail and telephone services. E-mail is fast and easy. If you organize your e-mail addresses into groups, you can broadcast, or send, a message to a group in just one step.

E-mail Pros and Cons: E-mail is not free, and it's not instantaneous. However, you do not pay to send each e-mail, as you would a letter. The cost of your e-mail service is included in the fee you pay your Internet service provider or online service provider. In most cases, it takes minutes or more for an e-mail message to reach its destination. But it costs the same and takes approximately the same amount of time to send a message to someone in your own city as it does to send a message halfway around the world.

Transferring Files

File Transfer Protocol (FTP) lets you transfer files on the Internet. With an FTP client, you can transfer files from an FTP server to your computer in an operation called downloading. In uploading, you transfer files from the client to the server.

FTP can transfer both text files and binary files. Binary files are program files, graphics, pictures, music or video clips, and documents. Once you've stored a file on an FTP server, you can share the URL so that others can download the file from the server, as well. The file remains on the server until you delete it. When you transfer a file as an e-mail attachment you must save the file on your computer or it will be deleted when you delete the message. E-mail is considered a more secure method, however, because only the recipient of the e-mail message has access to the attached files.

Telnet is an older protocol, which lets users access files on remote computers. Telnet has largely been replaced by SSH and SSH2, which are encrypted, and therefore more secure than Telnet.

Of course, when you upload or download files you are transferring them between your computer and an Internet, or **cloud server**. Most web sites have buttons or links to make it easy to upload and download files, or you may use your browser's File > Open and File > Save As commands.

Cloud Server

A server that hosts web applications that requires a user to have an account and a login to that account. Once logged in, the user can access the application. This type of server enables users to use any computer or mobile device to access the application – all they need is an Internet connection. Google Docs is a good example of a Cloud Server and Cloud computing. The company that manages the server is responsible for all server upgrades and functionality. For a business, this could save them thousands of dollars in hardware costs for upgrading their servers.

File Transfer Issues

Computer Viruses: It's important to exercise caution when downloading files from the Internet, especially program files. Files are commonly used to transmit viruses. A **virus** is a program created to damage computers and networks. The damage caused may be minor or serious, such as altering or destroying data. It's a good idea to check all downloaded files for viruses before saving them. Most anti-virus programs will do this for you automatically. You should update your anti-virus program regularly to be protected from the newest viruses. The Windows operating system helps by giving a security warning when a download is about to begin. You may want to review the advice provided by clicking the What's the Risk? link.

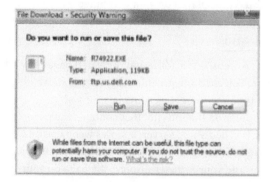

The File Download – Security Warning from Windows. If you trust the source of the file, click Run or Save.

File Compression: The larger a file is, the more time it takes to travel over a network. File compression is a way of reducing file size so it can travel more quickly over a network. If you are sending a large file, it is important to compress it. It can also be convenient to compress multiple files into one when you are sending them to someone in an e-mail attachment. Some compressed files are set to decompress automatically. Others must be decompressed using decompression software. The most widely used compression software for a Windows system is WinZip®. Macintosh computers use a program called StuffItTM to compress files and a utility called StuffIt Expander to decompress files.

Domains and IP Addresses

Have you ever wondered why does data magically display when you type in a web address? Do you know what a domain is or what is an IP Address? How does a

ISP

Short for Internet Service Provider, is a Web Hosting company that has a server connected to the Internet. Their business is to host Web sites and provide email services. Some provide Internet service as well as offer other higher end connectivity products.

browser know how to find and then display a webpage? These are important questions and before you start creating websites, you need to know more about how the web works.

To understand how a data request is sent on the Internet, it might be helpful to compare the process to taking a road trip. Recall that when you request a webpage through your web browser, the request travels by local connections—like streets in a town— to your ISP's local POP. From there, your **ISP** sends your request to a regional backbone—a type of data highway.

Your webpage request then travels to a Network Access Point or **NAP**, which is like a freeway. As your request nears its destination, it moves off the information freeway. It travels back through other regional highways and local roads until its trip is complete and the webpage you requested is displayed on your computer screen.

Understanding How the Web Works

A webpage is a document on the web. A website is a collection of related pages, which are connected using hyperlinks. You click a hyperlink to browse, or move, from one page to another. When you type a URL or click a link in your web browser, it sends a request to the computer on the Internet that contains the page identified by the URL. That computer is called a web server. It stores webpages and responds to requests from web browsers. When the server receives your request, it sends the document to your computer, and your browser displays the page on your screen.

Most websites have a primary page called the home page or index page, which appears when you first enter the site's URL. A URL can also identify a specific page on a website.

A - Domain name, B - Protocol, C - Folder name, D - Path to document on web server, E - Resource File Name
The parts of a URL

Protocol: The first part of a URL specifies the protocol required to access the document. Web documents use http://, indicating that the file should be retrieved using hypertext transfer protocol (HTTP). Some URLs might have other protocols, such as ftp, which shows that the file should be retrieved with file transfer protocol. Another protocol, telnet, allows for access to remote computers. Still another protocol, mailto, lets you click an e-mail address link on a webpage to automatically start your e-mail client with the address entered in the To: field.

Domain Name: The next part of a URL, such as www.fbi.gov, is the domain name of the server that stores the website. This part of the URL usually takes you to the site's home page.

Path: The remainder of a URL, if any, defines the path to the document's location on the web server. Like any computer, a web server stores files in folders, so the path lists the folder and subfolders, if any, containing the desired document. Thus, a URL such as http://www.fbi.gov/employment/ identifies a folder named "employment" on the site's web server.

Resource File Name: At the end of a URL, you may see the name of a file—the specific web resource for which you are looking. The resource may be an HTML document or a webpage, a video clip, a text file, or another type of resource. The file name extension identifies the type of resource.

Domain Names

Each computer that connects to the Internet has to be uniquely identified. To do this, every computer is assigned a four-part number separated by periods called the **Internet Protocol (IP) address**. For example, the IP address for your computer might be 123.257.91.7. The administrator of the network to which your computer connects assigns your IP address. You can locate your computer's IP address by visiting http://www.whatsmyip.org/ in a browser from your computer or by checking your computers network settings.

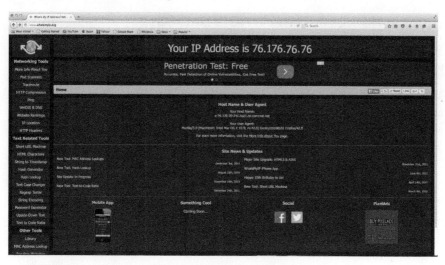

WhatsMyIP.org is a great site for identifying any computer's IP address.

Domain name

A domain name identifies one or more IP addresses and is used to locate information on the Internet. For example, an Internet server computer's domain name might be whitehouse.gov, but its numeric IP address might be 206.166.48.45. The domain name and the IP address are simply two ways to identify the same computer on the Internet.

Top-Level Domains

Every domain name has a suffix or domain extension that tells which type of organization registered the name. The most common domains are .com (commercial), .edu (education), .org (nonprofit organizations), .gov (government), .mil (military), and .net (network organizations). These are called **top-level domains**. New top-level domain names such as .biz (business) and .museum (arts and culture) are coming online to meet the growing demand for new classifications. Top-level domain country codes are two letter codes that identify the country where the site is located. For example, "us" is the country code for the United States.

If a company has Internet access, it can start its own website. But first it has to get a **domain name**. Which **top-level** domain name(s) listed below do you think would be most appropriate for Jarrett's company?

- .org
- .gov
- .edu
- .com
- .mil

Acquiring a Domain Name

When starting to develop a website, you need to acquire a domain name first. This process involves you or your ISP contacting a registering organization like ehost.com or 1and1.com, which then contacts **InterNIC**.

When you register a domain name, you are setting up the domain on a special server called a **Domain Name System (DNS)** server, which matches the domain name to the correct IP address. InterNIC is a service organization that maintains a central database of domain names in the United States. Other countries maintain their own network information centers. This information establishes the home for your domain on the Internet.

Domain Names and the WHOIS Database

Within the Domain Name System, each computer on the Internet must have a unique name, or the browser would not know which server it needs to access.

The central database of domain names is called the **WHOIS database.** You can look up information about the owner and servers of a certain domain on this database by visiting http://www.whois.com.

Use Whols.com to research domain names and see who owns a domain.

Software as a Service

In the past, people and companies would purchase software programs and install them on their local computers or networks. Now, more and more applications are stored on a cloud server and can be accessed on the Internet. Instead of purchasing a program outright, you purchase a subscription that allows you to log in and use the software. Accessing applications this way is call **Software as a Service (SAAS)**. With SAAS, the applications are kept on the software company's network instead of on the client computer, leaving more storage space available on the client. The software company maintains the software and keeps it up-to-date. Customers can log in from any location making it possible for them to work at the office, at home, or while traveling.

Determining Your Career Path

There are an overwhelming number of available career opportunities. How can you possibly identify the ones that might be of interest to you? The 16 career clusters—developed by the National Association of State Directors of Career Technical Education Consortium or NASDCTEC. Visit their website at www.careertech.org. This is a good place to start as they can help you identify types of careers and specific jobs as well as help you pick out the ones that you might find interesting. They

InterNIC

The organization responsible for maintaining the list of the registered domain names is the InterNIC. When you register a domain name, you pay an accredited registrar to insert an entry into a directory of all the domain names and their corresponding computers on the Internet. An Accredited Registrar Directory provides a listing of accredited domain name registrars available on the InterNIC website.

Domain Name System (DNS)

DNS is a naming system at the server level that associates a domain name with an IP address. This creates a digital index of the domain name and its IP address and associates the IP address with the hosting server. This is like the white pages of a telephone book with the person's name being similar to the domain and the phone number is similar to the IP address.

also show you the educational and skill requirements you might need and the path you might take to achieve the career of your dreams.

Common Skills and Traits of a Successful Employee

When you consider a career, it is important to think about whether or not you are willing to meet its requirements. If you do not live up to your responsibilities at work, you will soon be looking for a new job. What are some ways you show that you can or cannot meet responsibilities?

- Showing up late and leaving early
- Letting co-workers do your job
- Skipping meetings
- Cooperating with co-workers
- Always trying your best
- Making sure you have the training you need to complete your work
- Communicating effectively both verbally and nonverbally

How can researching the requirements of a job help you avoid problems at work?

Identifying Careers through Job-Related Activities

Even if you do not hold a full- or part-time job, the tasks you do and activities in which you are involved on a daily basis can help you identify the career clusters that best match your interests, skills, aptitudes, and values. For example:

- Helping a younger sibling with his homework might lead you to a career in the Education & Training career cluster.
- Volunteering at a local park or zoo might mean you are cut out for a career in the Agriculture, Food & Natural Resources career cluster.
- Taking photos for your school newspaper could prepare you for a career in the Arts, Audio/Video Technology & Communications career cluster.

Think about the job-related activities you perform at home, in school, and in the community. How can they help you identify the career cluster(s) best suited to you?

Exploring Careers in Information Technology and Web

Information Technology is a general term that can be associated with the career clusters for the Internet and the World Wide Web. Both offer many different types of jobs and careers. Since the Internet is made up of computer networks, there are many jobs that allow you to focus on the network hardware, architecture, schematics, and analysis. Here are a few jobs for working on computer networks linking into the Internet:

- Network Administrator
- Network Architect
- Network Programmer/Analyst
- Network/Information Systems Manager
- Network Systems Engineer
- Network Service Technician
- Information Technology (IT) Application Developer

If you want to focus more on websites, webpages, or applications on the World Wide Web, you could explore these jobs:

- Webmaster
- WordPress Developer
- Graphic Designer
- Search Engine Optimization (SEO) Manager
- Web Content Specialist
- Web Software Developer
- Website Sections Editor
- Web Technical Producer
- Web Promotions Specialist
- Social Media Manager
- Web Editorial Assistant
- Website Copy Editor
- Java Developer
- Cascading Style Sheet (CSS) Developer
- Graphical User Interface (GUI) Programmer

Web Advertising

Careers in advertising aren't new, but careers in web advertising are. Candidates for jobs in online advertising still need traditional art, marketing, and advertising skills. But they also need strong business and technical skills that will let them use the powerful tools of the web to attract customers' attention to the product's message.

Research Internet and web careers by going to www.monster.com and searching in the **Jobs** section for a few of the Internet or web jobs by using keywords of:

- Information technologies
- Web Development or Web Design
- Internet
- Networks
- Social Media
- Search Engine Optimization or SEO

Identify different jobs that you might have an interest. Read through the various Monster.com job listings to identify duties, tasks, and educational requirements of the job.

End-of-Chapter Activities

Review Questions

Directions: Choose the correct answer for each question.

1. What is the highlighted text or graphic in a website that directs browser to another URL?
   a. Hypertext
   b. Hyperlink
   c. Protocol
   d. Web text

2. What is the software that finds and lists information that matches criteria?
   a. Hyperlink
   b. URL
   c. Search Engine
   d. Portal

3. What is the term for computer that requests services from a server?
   a. Internet client
   b. Internet service provider
   c. Internet
   d. Portal

4. Which method allows you to determine your computer's IP address?
   a. Check you Network Settings
   b. Visit WhatsMyIP.org
   c. None of the above
   d. Both A & B work

5. What is the term for the address of documents on the web?
   a. Protocol
   b. IP Address
   c. WAN
   d. Uniform Resource Locator or URL

6. What is a vast network of connected computers called?
   a. Internet
   b. Internet client
   c. Internet server
   d. Portal

7. What is the general term for a company that provides access to the Internet?
   a. Internet client
   b. Google
   c. Search Engine
   d. Internet service provider

8. What is the general term for an Internet service that provides a guide to Internet content?
   a. WAN
   b. Portal
   c. Cloud Computing
   d. LAN

9. What is the name of the organization responsible for maintaining the list of the registered domain names?
   a. Google
   b. Microsoft
   c. InterNIC
   d. W3C

10. Who is the governing organization for the World Wide Web?
    a. Google
    b. Microsoft
    c. InterNIC
    d. W3C

Essay Questions

Directions: Respond to each question by writing your answers in complete sentences and paragraphs. Be thorough in your answers.

1. Compare the Internet to the World Wide Web.

2. There are certain common skills and traits that help anyone perform a job successfully. Please identify these skills and traits and discuss why they are necessary for good job performance.

3. Describe the History of the Internet.

4. Describe the hardware that makes up the Internet.

5. Compare and contrast e-mail and the telephone system.

6. List jobs for the Internet and identify job duties, tasks and educational requirements for each job?

7. List careers for the World Wide Web and identify job duties, tasks and educational requirements for each job.

8. Describe the process of acquiring a domain name.

9. Describe the role of the World Wide Web Consortium (W3C).

10. Describe the cloud and how it works.

Web Technologies Book Project

Integrated into this book in each chapter is a project that requires you to create a Portfolio website. A Portfolio website is an online presentation of your work and accomplishments. In today's world, you have to have an online presence. This includes your own website as well as all your social media sites. When applying for a job, one of the first things an employer will do is search your name on the web to find out more about you. So it is very important that you start now creating the online image that you want to present to the world.

You will create the Portfolio website from scratch without any data or source files being supplies. Your portfolio website will focus on your work and information about you that you think an employer will want to know or that sets you apart from the competition. As you progress through this book, you will build and develop the Portfolio website chapter by chapter and upon completion of the book, you will have a fully developed, functioning website that showcases you and your skills and talents.

Online Portfolio Builder — Gather Information

To begin your portfolio website, you need to start by gathering the information that you want to highlight in your site. This could be graphics, Web site, illustrations, drawings, paintings and artwork that you have created or it can be jobs, sports, opportunities, skills, honors and acknowledgements that you have attained or been awarded. Then identify the ones that are your best efforts or showcase your skills and talents. All of the work in your online portfolio should be your best effort. A good number to shoot for is about fifteen and each should represent a successful design solution, work skill, or accomplishment.

1. Begin by identifying and gathering your best designs, projects, accomplishments and/or honors.

2. Take digital pictures of any traditional artworks, like paintings or pottery.

3. Optimize and compress in physical file size your digitized pictures so that they download easily and quickly from a website. Optimizing web graphics is covered later in this book in Chapter 11, "Working with Images".

4. Identify and write any verbal or textual information that you want to include in the site.

5. If you have a personal logo or brand that you use for promoting yourself, gather these items for the site.

6. Include your resume. If you have not already, you need to develop a resume. Be complete and accurate. Be sure to list any licenses or certificates that you have earned. Include an objective specific to the job for which you plan to apply. Use action words to describe your experience and skills. Use formatting that is professional and easy to read.

Once you have your material identified, you can then start developing your Portfolio website. These items give you a good idea of what your site will be about as well as items that you might be missing and still need to find or create.

This process of gathering your portfolio pieces is the same as what you would use with a client that hires you to develop their company website. You start the process by having the client gather all pictures, videos, text, documents, and graphics they want in the site. You also need to get a copy of their company logo and company colors so you can integrate their company brand into the new website. Identify items that might be missing for the site and communicate these to the clients so they know what to keep looking for or to develop for the site.

Critical Thinking — Client Server Architecture

In groups of three or four students explain by writing an essay about client-server applications and describe the process of client-server transactions. Identify the advantages and disadvantages of client-side processing as well as identify security issues related to client-side processing. Create a diagram of the flow of information in the client-server architecture.

Information Technology and Web Careers Class Activity

Has anyone ever asked you what you want to be when you grow up? Did you answer firefighter or doctor? Did you answer artist or president of the United States? These are all good careers. However, they are not the right careers for everyone. If you choose a career that interests you and that makes use of your skills and abilities, you are more likely to be happy and satisfied with your work.

Why do people work? Ask ten people that question, and you are likely to get ten different answers! Yes, people work to make money. They also work to feel pride and satisfaction, to stay busy, and because it can be fun. The average person spends between 40 and 50 hours a week at work. If that work is enjoyable and rewarding, that person is going to be happier in all areas of life.

In two groups, take a few minutes to select and write down a career in either the Information Technology or Web career clusters without the other group knowing what you have picked. Take turns asking the other group "Yes" or "No" questions about their career, until you can guess what it is. As a class, discuss the skills and abilities you might need for the careers each group picked, and what it would be like to work in those careers.

Chapter 2

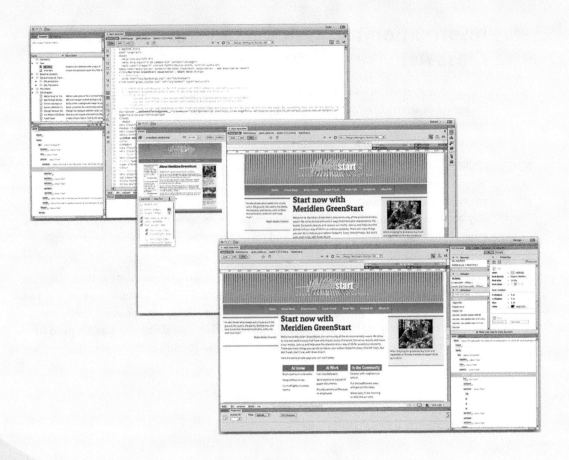

CUSTOMIZING YOUR WORKSPACE

Dreamweaver offers a customizable and easy-to-use WYSIWYG HTML editor that doesn't compromise on power and flexibility. You'd probably need a dozen programs to perform all the tasks that Dreamweaver can do—and none of them would be as fun to use.

Chapter Overview

In this chapter, you'll familiarize yourself with the Dreamweaver CC (2015.1 release) program interface and learn how to do the following:

- Use the program Welcome screen
- Switch document views
- Work with panels
- Select a workspace layout
- Adjust toolbars
- Personalize preferences
- Create custom keyboard shortcuts
- Use the Property inspector
- Use the Extract workflow

Touring the Workspace

Dreamweaver is the industry-leading Hypertext Markup Language (HTML) editor, with good reasons for its popularity. The program offers an incredible array of design and code-editing tools. Dreamweaver offers something for everyone.

Coders love the range of enhancements built into the Code view environment, and developers enjoy the program's support for a variety of programming languages and code hinting. Designers marvel at seeing their text and graphics appear in an accurate What You See Is What You Get (WYSIWYG) depiction as they work, saving hours of time previewing pages in browsers. Novices certainly appreciate the program's simple-to-use and power-packed interface. No matter what type of user you are, if you use Dreamweaver you don't have to compromise.

A	Menu bar	F	Workspace menu	K	Assets panel	P	Code view
B	Document tab	G	Files panel	L	Behaviors panel	Q	Tag selectors
C	Referenced files interface	H	CC Libraries panel	M	Design/Live views	R	Property inspector
D	Document toolbar	I	CSS Designer	N	Scrubber		
E	New Features	J	Insert panel	O	Coding toolbar		

The Dreamweaver interface features a vast array of user-configurable panels and toolbars. Take a moment to familiarize yourself with the names of these components.

You'd think a program with this much to offer would be dense, slow, and unwieldy, but you'd be wrong. Dreamweaver provides much of its power via dockable panels and toolbars that you can display or hide and arrange in innumerable combinations to create your ideal workspace. In most cases, if you don't see a desired tool or panel, you'll find it in the Window menu.

This chapter introduces you to the Dreamweaver interface and gets you in touch with some of the power hiding under the hood.

Using the Welcome Screen

The Dreamweaver Welcome screen provides quick access to recent pages, easy creation of a range of page types, and a direct connection to several key Help topics. The Welcome screen appears when you first start the program or when no other documents are open. The Welcome screen has gotten a facelift in the last few versions and deserves a quick review to check out what it offers. For example, it now has four main tabs: Create, New Features, Getting Started, and Tips & Techniques. Click the name of the tab to access these features.

Create

If the Create tab looks familiar it's because it has been around in one form or another for many versions of Dreamweaver. As it has always done, it provides instant access to a list of up to your last ten files. At this moment, your screen may not display any filenames at all if you have not used Dreamweaver previously. Choosing a file from this list is a quick alternative to choosing File > Open when you want to edit an existing page.

In addition to recent documents, the Create tab enables you to create up to eight different web file types with a single click, including HTML, CSS, JavaScript, and PHP, as well as predefined starter templates and site setup interfaces.

New Features

When you select New Features in the Welcome screen, you see a list of the most recent features that have been added to the program. Click one of the topics and get a video- or text-based overview of these new tools and workflows. This tab is updated dynamically as new features are added to Dreamweaver.

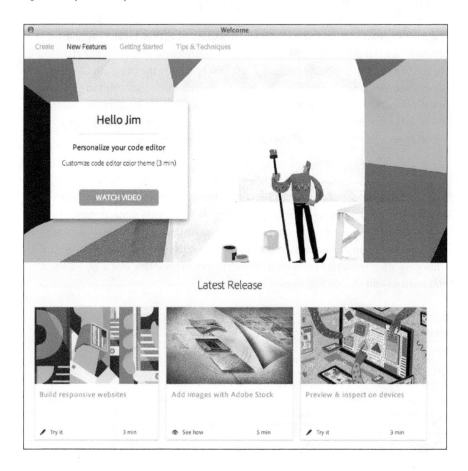

Getting Started

Select Getting Started to access quick tutorials that can get you up and running in various basic techniques and workflows in Dreamweaver. Learn how to create a new layout or style it with CSS. Sample files and assets can be downloaded within each tutorial as needed.

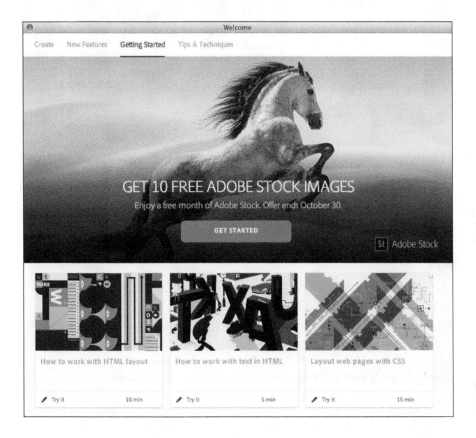

Tips & Techniques

For more advanced tutorials, check out Tips & Techniques. Learn how to create a responsive website, preview your new designs on your favorite mobile devices, or access web fonts.

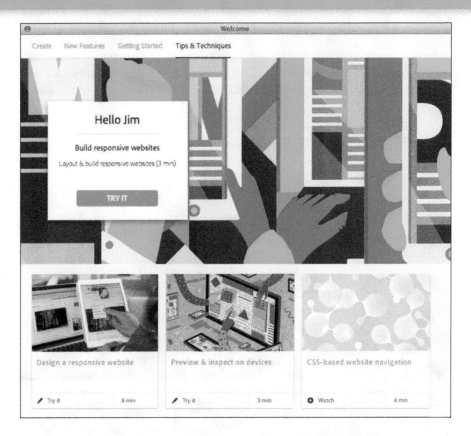

You may use the Welcome screen at any time while working in this book. When you've completed the chapters, you may prefer not to use the Welcome screen or even to see it. If so, you can close it by clicking the Close icon at the top of the screen. To bring back the Welcome screen, select Help > Welcome.

Exploring New Feature Guides

Another new enhancement to Dreamweaver CC (2015.1 release) is the New Feature **guides**, which will pop up from time to time as you access various features. The pop-ups will call your attention to new features or **workflows** that have been added to the program and provide handy tips to help you get the most out of them.

Guides

Horizontal and vertical lines that display when certain features are selected. Guides help you align multiple items.

Workflow

The order of activities that you use when you complete a task.

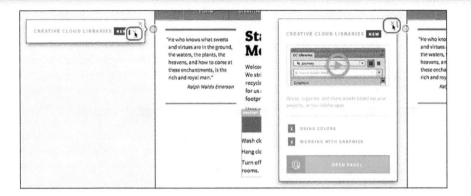

When a tip appears, you can reveal the entire content by clicking the pop-up. You can then close the pop-up by clicking the Close icon ✕ in the upper-right corner of each tip. When you close the tip, it will not appear again. If desired, you can display the tips again by resetting the option in **Preferences**.

Preferences

Dreamweaver is configured with pre-determined preferences for its operation. You can access these Preferences by choosing Edit, Preferences(PC)/ Dreamweaver CC, Preferences(Mac) from the menu bar and then change them to accommodate your workflow

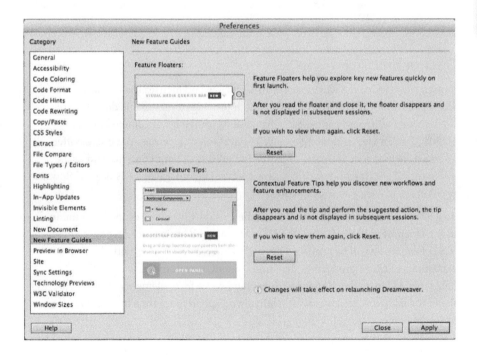

Switching and Splitting Views

Dreamweaver offers dedicated environments for coders and designers as well as a new option that allows you to work with Photoshop mockups.

Code View

Code view focuses the Dreamweaver workspace exclusively on the HTML code and a variety of code-editing productivity tools. To access Code view, click the Code view button in the Document toolbar.

Code view

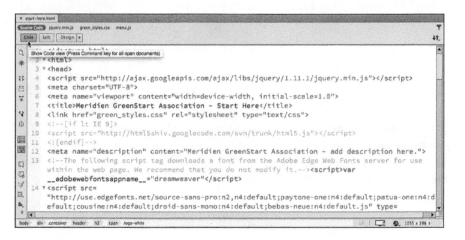

WYSIWYG editor

Acronym for 'What You See Is What You Get' which indicates that what you see on the screen, the layout of text and graphics, is what you will get in your final document. This could be a printed document, a Web page or a presentation. In regards to Dreamweaver, the WYSIWYG editor is used in the Design view.

CSS

Acronym for Cascading Style Sheet. CSS is used to format HTML documents.

CSS3

The latest release of CSS that has many more formatting properties that can be applied to HTML.

Design View

Design view shares the workspace with Live view and focuses the Dreamweaver workspace on its **WYSIWYG editor**, which provides a reasonable depiction of the webpage as it would appear in a browser. With the advancements in **CSS** and HTML, Design view is no longer as WYSIWYG as it once was. But it does offer an interface that speeds up the creation and editing of your content. And at the moment, it's also the only way to access certain Dreamweaver tools or workflows, as you will see in the upcoming chapters.

To activate Design view, choose it from the Design/Live views drop-down menu in the Document toolbar. Most HTML elements and basic cascading style sheets (CSS) formatting will be rendered properly within Design view, with the major exceptions of **CSS3** properties, dynamic content, interactivity, such as link behaviors, video, audio, **jQuery widgets**, and some form elements. This may be the first version of Dreamweaver in which you spend more time in Live view than in Design view.

jQuery Widget

A software application that allows access to a javascript library of Web functionality that is designed to work with HTML. The jQuery library contains advanced functionality like printing, navigating, events, and animation that would take hours of coding to re-create. You can easily insert this pre-created functionality into your HTML Web page.

Design view

Dynamic effects

Animated effects that can change to reflect the end users interaction with the webpage. A dynamic webpage changes in appearance and functionality which is different than a static webpage which always displays the same layout of information.

Elements

an HTML component used in coding a webpage. Most elements are created through HTML tags like the [H1] tag which creates a Heading 1 headline in an HTML document.

Classes

Used in CSS to uniquely identify an HTML element. For instance, if you create a class selector to format all [H1] tags to be bold and red, anytime you add an [H1] tag to your webpage, it will automatically be formatted bold and red.

Live View

Live view is the new default workspace of Dreamweaver CC. It speeds up the process of developing modern websites by allowing you to *visually* create and edit webpages and web content in a browser-like environment, and it supports and previews most **dynamic effects** and interactivity.

To use Live view, choose it from the Design/Live views drop-down menu in the Document toolbar. When Live view is activated, most HTML content will function as it would in an actual browser, allowing you to preview and test most dynamic applications and behaviors.

In previous versions of Dreamweaver, the content in Live view was not editable. This has all changed. You can now edit text, add and delete **elements**, create **classes** and **ids**, and even style elements, all in the same window. It's like working on a live webpage right inside Dreamweaver.

Live view is integrally connected to the CSS Designer, allowing you to create and edit advanced CSS styling and build fully responsive webpages without having to switch views or waste time previewing the page in a browser.

Live view

Ids

Used in CSS to uniquely identify an individual HTML element. For instance, you create n ID selector to format just one paragraph in a webpage and not affect any other HTML element. This type of a CSS selector only applies to one item or element in an HTML document.

Split View

Split view provides a composite workspace that gives you access to both the design and the code simultaneously. Changes made in either window update in the other in real time.

To access Split view, click the Split view button in the Document toolbar. Dreamweaver splits the workspace horizontally by default. When using Split view, you can display the Code view with either Live or Design view.

Split view (horizontal)

Note: Split view can pair Code view with either Design or Live view.

If desired, you can also split the screen vertically by selecting the Split Vertically option on the View menu. When the window is split, Dreamweaver also gives you options for how the two windows display. You can put the code window on the top, bottom, left, or right. You can find all these options in the View menu. Most screen shots in the book that show Split view show Design or Live view at top or left.

Split view (vertical)

Live Source Code

Live Source Code is an HTML code-troubleshooting display mode available whenever Live view is activated. To access Live Source Code, activate Live view and then click the Live Source Code icon <> at the top of the document window. While active, Live Source Code displays the HTML code as it would appear in a live browser on the Internet.

The code window will interactively render changes to the elements, **attributes**, and styling as you interact with the content in the page. You can see this interaction by changing the width of the screen using the Scrubber until the horizontal navigation menu collapses to an icon. When you click the icon to open the menu, in Code view you will see that a class attribute of open is added to the menu interactively. The class is then removed when you close the menu. Without the live source code, you would not be able to see this interaction and behavior.

Be aware that while Live Source Code is active, you will not be able to edit the HTML code, although you can still modify external files, such as linked style sheets.

> **Attributes**
>
> Characteristics of HTML elements that can be controlled or formatted. For instance you can change the [H1] tag to a different font, color, size, and style. Each of these are attributes of the [H1] tag.

Live Source Code mode

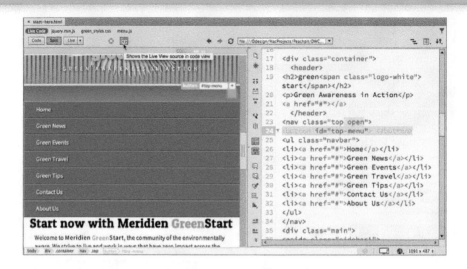

Inspect Mode

Inspect mode is a CSS troubleshooting display mode available whenever Live view is activated. It is integrated with the CSS Designer and allows you to identify CSS styles applied to content within the page by moving the mouse insertion point over elements within the webpage. Clicking an element freezes the focus on that item.

The Live view window highlights the targeted element and displays the pertinent CSS rules applied or inherited by that element. You can access Inspect mode at any time by clicking the Live view button whenever an HTML file is open and then clicking the Inspect icon ⊙ at the top of the document window.

Inspect mode

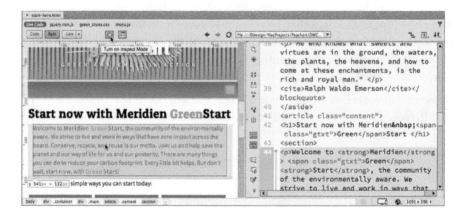

Working with Panels

Although you can access most commands from the menus, Dreamweaver scatters much of its power in user-selectable panels and toolbars. You can display, hide, arrange, and **dock** panels at will around the screen. You can even move them to a second or third video display if you desire.

Dock

Attaching a panel to another Workspace element. You can dock a panel to any panel group.

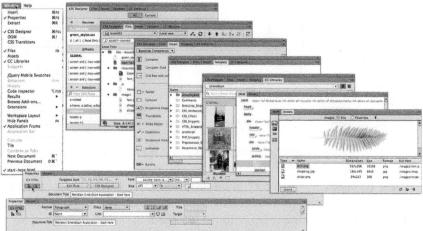

Standard panel grouping

The Window menu lists all the panels available in the program. If you do not see a desired panel on the screen, choose it from the Window menu. A checkmark appears next to its name in the menu to indicate that the panel is open. Occasionally, one panel may lie behind another on the screen and be difficult to locate. In such situations, simply choose the desired panel from the Window menu and the panel will rise to the top of the stack.

Minimizing Panels

To create room for other panels or to access obscured areas of the workspace, you can minimize or expand individual panels in place. To minimize a standalone panel, double-click the tab containing the panel name. To expand the panel, click the tab once.

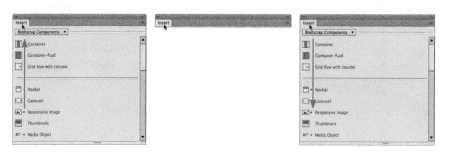

Minimizing a panel by double-clicking its tab

You can also minimize one panel within a stack of panels individually by double-clicking its tab. To open the panel, click once on its tab.

Minimizing one panel in a stack using its tab

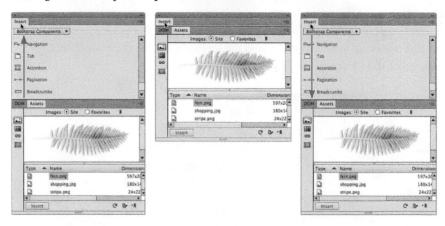

To recover more screen real estate, you can minimize panel groups or stacks down to icons by double-clicking the title bar. You can also minimize the panels to icons by clicking the double arrow icon ▶▶ in the panel title bar. When panels are minimized to icons, you access any of the individual panels by clicking its icon or button. The selected panel will appear on the left or right of the icon, wherever room permits.

Collapsing a panel to icons or buttons

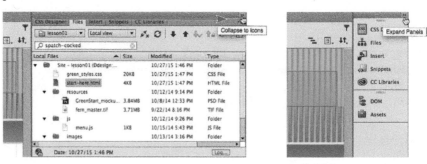

Closing Panels and Panel Groups

Each panel or panel group may be closed at any time. You can close a panel or panel group in several ways; the method often depends on whether the panel is floating, docked, or grouped with another panel.

To close an individual panel that is docked, right-click in the panel tab and choose Close from the context menu. To close an entire group of panels, right-click any tab in the group and choose Close Tab Group.

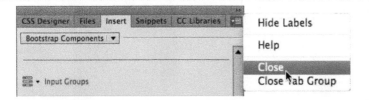

To close a **floating panel** or panel group, click the Close icon ✖ that appears in the left corner of the title bar of the panel or panel group. To reopen a panel, choose the panel name from the Window menu. Reopened panels will sometimes appear undocked. Feel free to dock them as desired.

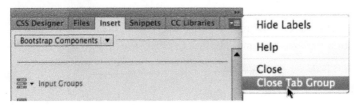

Floating panel

A panel that is not grouped or docked to another Workspace element.

Dragging

You can reorder a panel tab by dragging it to the desired position within the group.

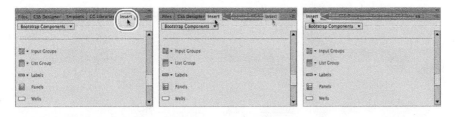

Dragging a tab to change its position

Floating

A panel that is grouped with other panels can be floated separately. To float a panel, drag it from the group by its tab.

Pulling a panel out by its tab

To reposition panels, groups, and stacks in the workspace, simply drag them by the title bar. To pull out a single panel group when it's docked, grab it by the tab bar.

Dragging a whole docked panel group to a new position

Grouping, Stacking, and Docking

You can create custom groups by dragging one panel into another. When you've moved the panel to the correct position, Dreamweaver highlights the area, called the *drop zone*, in blue. Release the mouse button to create the new group.

Creating new groups

In some cases, you may want to keep both panels visible simultaneously. To stack panels, drag the desired tab to the top or bottom of another panel. When you see the blue drop zone appear, release the mouse button.

Creating panel stacks

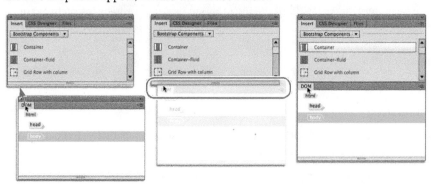

Floating panels can be docked to the right, left, or bottom of the Dreamweaver workspace. To dock a panel, group, or stack, drag its title bar to the edge of the window on which you wish to dock. When you see the blue drop zone appear, release the mouse button.

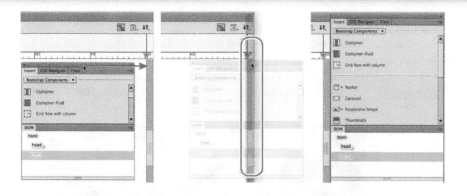

Docking panels

Selecting a Workspace Layout

A quick way to customize the program environment is to use one of the prebuilt workspaces in Dreamweaver. These workspaces have been optimized by experts to put the tools you need at your fingertips.

Dreamweaver CC (2015.1 release) includes five prebuilt workspaces: Beginner, Code, Default, Design, and Extract. To access these workspaces, choose them from the Workspace menu located at the upper-right side of the program window.

Beginner Workspace

The Beginner workspace simplifies the program interface by focusing on the bare essentials. It provides the new user a good balance between design and code, with a minimum number of panels displayed.

Beginner workspace

Code Workspace

Users who work mostly with code will want to use the Code workspace, because it optimizes the panels and windows to provide an effective workspace for coding.

Code workspace

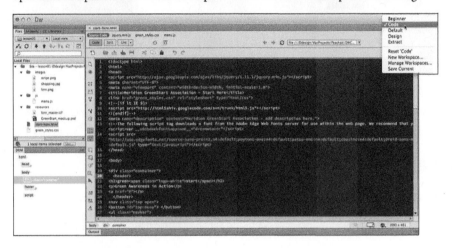

Default Workspace

The Default workspace maximizes the document window and emphasizes the power provided by various panels, such as CC Libraries, Snippets, Insert, and CSS Designer.

Default workspace

Design Workspace

The Design workspace focuses the available screen real estate on the Design and Live view window. Design is the default workspace for screen shots in this book.

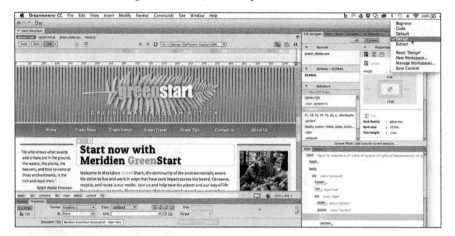

Design workspace

Extract Workspace

The Extract workspace provides a direct connection to the online interface for extracting CSS styles and image assets from **Photoshop mockups** uploaded to Creative Cloud. You can upload PSD files directly from Dreamweaver or post them in the Creative Cloud app or website once you are logged in to your account.

Photoshop mockups
Webpage designs/layouts that you create using layers in Photoshop.

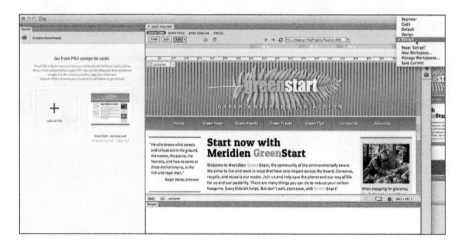

Extract workspace

Working with Extract

Extract is a new workflow that has been added to Dreamweaver CC (2015.1 release). It allows you to create CSS styles and image assets from a

Photoshop-based mockup. You can create your webpage design using text and linked or embedded image layers and post the file to **Creative Cloud**, where Dreamweaver can access the styles, colors, and images to help you build your basic site design.

Build your design in Photoshop using text, images, and effects stored in layers.

Post your file to your Creative Cloud online folder right inside Dreamweaver.

Access the various layers from the Extract panel inside Dreamweaver, copy styles and text, and even download image assets.

If you have an Adobe ID, try these features yourself by uploading **GreenStart_mockup.psd**, in the chapter01 resources folder, to your **Creative Cloud account** online folder. If you teacher and school allows this, go to helpx.adobe.com/creative-cloud/help/sync-files.html to learn how to upload files to your Creative Cloud account.

Adjusting Toolbars

Some program features are so handy you may want them available all the time in toolbar form. Two of the toolbars—Document and Standard—appear horizontally at the top of the document window. The Coding toolbar, however, appears vertically, but only in the Code view window. You can display the desired toolbar by choosing it from the View menu. You can also display the toolbar by simply right-clicking the top of the document window and choosing the desired toolbar from the context menu.

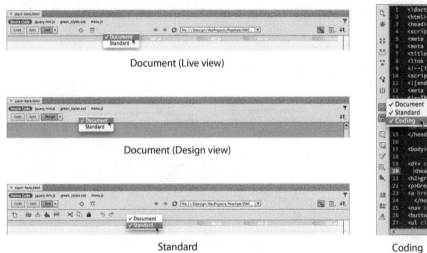

Document (Live view)

Document (Design view)

Standard

Coding

Personalizing Dreamweaver

As you continue to work with Dreamweaver, you'll devise your own optimal workspace of panels and toolbars for each activity. You can store these configurations in a custom workspace of your own naming.

Saving a Custom Workspace

To save a custom workspace, first create your desired configuration of panels, choose New Workspace from the Workspace menu, and then give it a custom name.

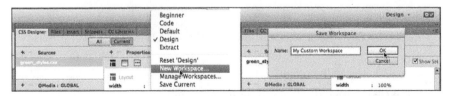

Saving a custom workspace

Editing Preferences

In addition to the ability to order and arrange the program's panels and toolbars, Dreamweaver's Preferences dialog provides advanced customizations for many functions and workflows. There are way too many options to cover in this chapter, but let's make one adjustment to give you a taste of the types of things you can do.

1   Click the Code view button at the top of the document window.

Dreamweaver is sporting a new dark color scheme in Code view. Some designers love it; some hate it. You can change it completely, or merely tweak it, right in Preferences.

2   In Windows, select Edit > Preferences.
    In the Mac OS, select Dreamweaver CC > Preferences.

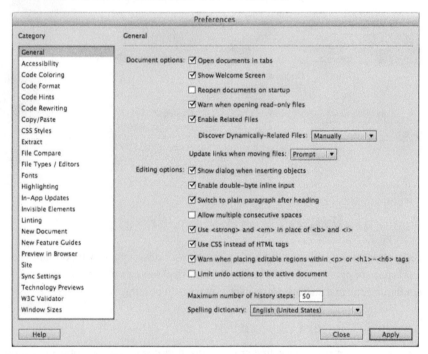

The Preferences dialog appears.

3   Select the Code Coloring category.

As you see from the dialog, Dreamweaver gives you fine control over various aspects of the code-editing interface. For example, you can change the colors one by one or select a theme and change them all at once.

4   Select Classic from the Theme drop-down menu.

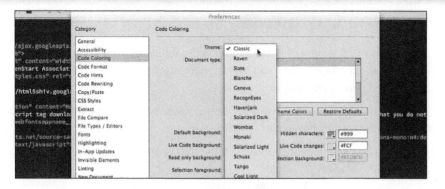

The colors assigned to each item change. This scheme is the traditional color scheme of previous versions of Dreamweaver. At the moment, the changes have happened only in the dialog.

5   Click Apply in the lower-right corner of the dialog.

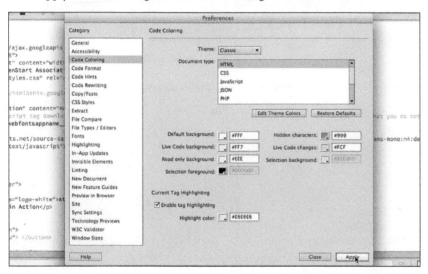

The Code window behind the dialog has changed to match the Classic color scheme. You can use this scheme as you work through the upcoming chapters. It is the default scheme used for all the code-based screen shots in the book. But feel free to use any of the predefined schemes or make your own.

6   Click Close.

Saved preferences persist from session to session and through each workspace.

Creating Custom Keyboard Shortcuts

Another powerful feature of Dreamweaver is the ability to create your own **keyboard shortcuts** as well as edit existing ones. Keyboard shortcuts are loaded and preserved independently of workspaces.

Is there a command you can't live without that doesn't have a keyboard shortcut or that uses one that's inconvenient? Create one of your own. Try this:

Note: The default keyboard shortcuts are locked and cannot be edited. But you can duplicate the set, save it under a new name, and modify any shortcut within that custom set.

1 Choose Edit > Keyboard Shortcuts (Windows) or Dreamweaver CC > Keyboard Shortcuts (Mac OS).

2 Click the Duplicate Set icon to create a new set of shortcuts.

3 Enter a name in the Name Of Duplicate Set field. Click OK.

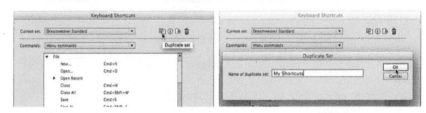

Keyboard Shortcuts

Keystrokes that automatically apply a function or process in Dreamweaver. For example, you can create a new HTML page by pressing Control+N (PC)/ Command+N (Mac) from your keyboard.

4 Choose Menu Commands from the Commands pop-up menu.

5 In the Commands window, choose File > Save All.

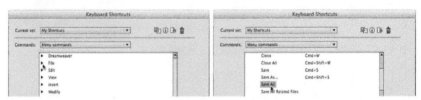

Note that the Save All command does not have an existing shortcut, although you'll use this command frequently in Dreamweaver.

6 Insert the insertion point in the Press Key field. Press Ctrl+Alt+S/Cmd+Opt+S.

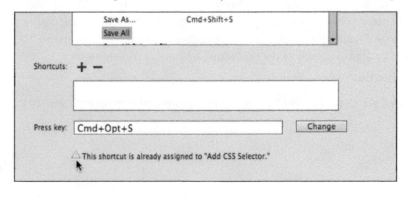

Note the error message indicating that the keyboard combination you chose is already assigned to a command. Although we could reassign the combination, let's choose a different one.

7   Press Ctrl+Alt+Shift+S/Ctrl+Cmd+S.

This combination is not currently being used, so let's assign it to the Save All command.

8   Click the Change button.

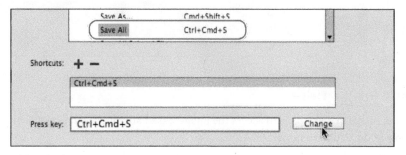

The new shortcut is now assigned to the Save All command.

9   Click OK to save the change.

You have created your own keyboard shortcut—one you can use in upcoming chapters.

Using the Property Inspector

One tool vital to your workflow is the Property inspector. In the built-in Dreamweaver workspaces, the Property inspector typically appears at the bottom of the workspace. If it is not visible in your program interface, you can display it by selecting Window > Properties and then dock it to the bottom of the document window as described earlier. The Property inspector is **context-driven** and adapts to the type of element you select.

Using the HTML Tab

Insert the insertion point into any text content on your page and the Property inspector provides a means to quickly assign some basic HTML codes and formatting. When the HTML button is selected, you can apply heading or paragraph tags as well as bold, italics, bullets, numbers, and indenting, among other formatting and attributes. The Document Title **metadata field** is also available in the Property inspector when Design view is active. Enter your desired Document Title in this field, and Dreamweaver adds it automatically to the document <head> section.

Context driven

Dynamically displays different options based on the item or element that is selected by the user.

Metadata Field

A field that contains data that describes one or more aspects of that data. Metadata is used to provide more information about data so that tracking and working with it is easier.

HTML Property
inspector

Using the CSS Tab

Click the CSS button to quickly access commands to assign or edit CSS formatting.

CSS Property inspector

Image Properties

Select an image in a webpage to access the image-based attributes and formatting controls of the Property inspector.

Image Property
inspector

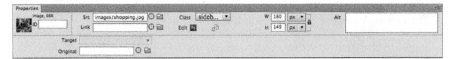

Table Properties

To access table properties, insert your insertion point in a table and then click the table tag selector at the bottom of the document window.

Table Property inspector

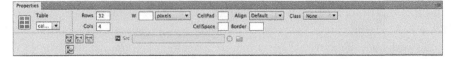

Using the Related Files Interface

Webpages are often built with multiple external files providing styling and programming assistance. Dreamweaver enables you to see all the files linked to, or referenced by, the current document by displaying the filenames in the Related Files interface at the top of the document window. This interface displays the name of any external file and will actually display the contents of each file—if it's available—when you simply select the filename in the display.

The Related Files
interface lists all
external files linked
to a document.

To view the contents of the referenced file, click the name. If you are in Live or Design view, Dreamweaver splits the document window and shows the contents of the selected file in the Code view window. If the file is stored locally, you'll even be able to edit the contents of the file when it's selected.

Use the Related Files interface to edit locally stored files.

To view the HTML code contained within the main document, click the Source Code option in the interface.

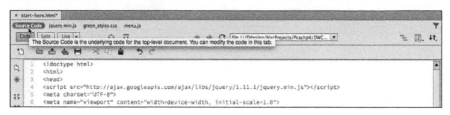

Choose the Source Code option to see the contents of the main document.

Using Tag Selectors

One of the most important features of Dreamweaver is the tag selector interface that appears at the bottom of the document window. This interface displays the tags and element structure in any HTML file pertinent to the insertion point of, or selection by, the insertion point. The display of tags is hierarchical, starting at the document root at the left of the display and listing each tag or element in order based on the structure of the page and the selected element.

Child Element

Any HTML element that is nested inside another HTML element. The nested element is referred to as a child element and the nesting HTML element is the parent element.

The display in the tag selector interface mimics the structure of the HTML code based on your selection.

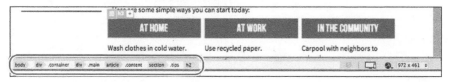

The tag selectors also enable you to select any of the elements displayed by simply clicking a tag. When a tag is selected, all the content and **child elements** contained within that tag are also selected.

Use the tag selectors to select elements.

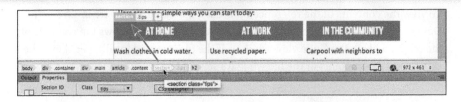

The tag selector interface is closely integrated with the CSS Designer panel. You may use the tag selectors to help you style content or to cut, copy, paste, and delete elements.

The tag selector is closely integrated with the styling and editing of elements.

Using the CSS Designer

The CSS Designer has been greatly improved in Dreamweaver CC (2015.1 release). Along with its visual method of creating, editing, and troubleshooting CSS styling, CSS Designer has gained new productivity enhancements for copying and pasting CSS styles from one rule to another. You can also decrease or increase the specificity of new selector names by pressing the up or down arrow keys, respectively.

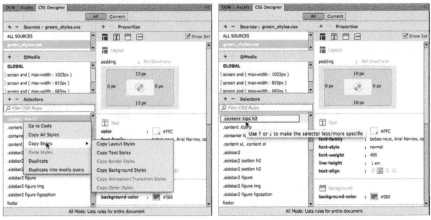

Copy and paste styles from one rule to another.

Make selectors more or less specific by using the arrow keys.

The CSS Designer panel consists of four windows: Sources, @Media, Selectors, and Properties.

Sources

The Sources window allows you to create, attach, define, and remove internal embedded and external linked style sheets.

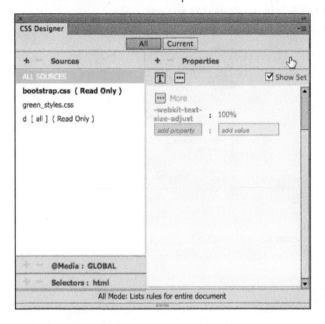

@Media

The @Media window is used to define **media queries** to support various types of media and devices.

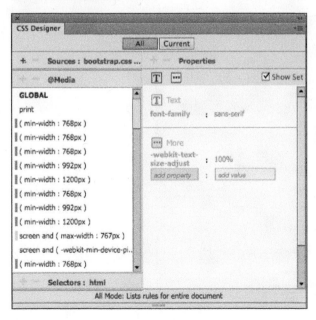

Media Queries

A logical expression that has a true or false criteria. For instance, in web design a media query is used to identify the screen display size so that the correct HTML code that was designed for that screen size is displayed.

Selectors

The Selectors window is used to create and edit the CSS rules that format the components and content of your page. Once a selector, or rule, is created you define the formatting you wish to apply in the Properties window.

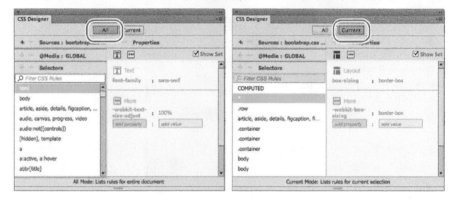

In addition to allowing you to create and edit CSS styling, the CSS Designer can also be used to identify styles already defined and applied, and to troubleshoot issues or conflicts with these styles.

Properties

The Properties window features two basic modes. By default, the Properties window displays all available CSS properties in a list, organized in five categories: Layout ▇, Text T, Borders ☐, Background ▇, and More ⋯. You can scroll down the list and apply styling as desired.

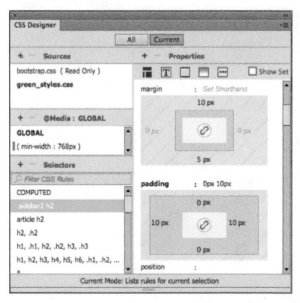

The second mode can be accessed by selecting Show Set at the upper-right edge of the window. In this mode, the Properties pane will then filter the list down to only the properties actually applied to the rule chosen in the Selectors window. In either mode, you can add, edit, or remove style sheets, media queries, rules, and properties.

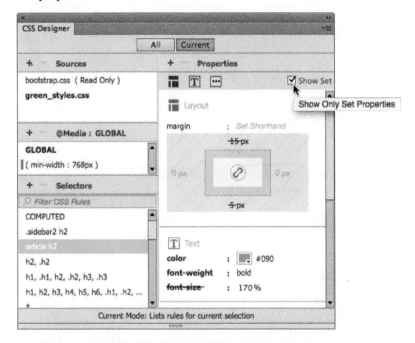

Selecting the Show Set option limits the property display to only the properties that are styled.

The Properties pane also features a COMPUTED option that displays the aggregated list of styles applied to the selected element. The COMPUTED option will appear anytime you select an element or component on the page. When you're creating any type of styling the code created by Dreamweaver complies with industry standards and best practices.

The COMPUTED option collects in one place all styles applied to the selection.

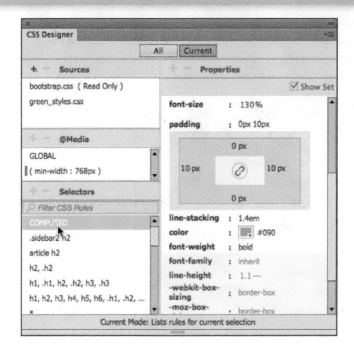

All and Current Modes

In Dreamweaver CC (2015.1 release), the CSS Designer has two new buttons, All and Current, that enable specific functions and workflows within the panel.

When the All button is selected, the panel allows you to create and edit CSS style sheets, media queries, rules, and properties. When the Current button is selected, the CSS troubleshooting functions are enabled, allowing you to inspect individual elements and assess existing styling properties applied to a selected element. In this mode, you are able to edit existing properties, but you're not allowed to add new style sheets, media queries, or rules. This interaction works the same way in all document views modes.

When the Current button is selected, the CSS Designer displays all styling associated with a selected element.

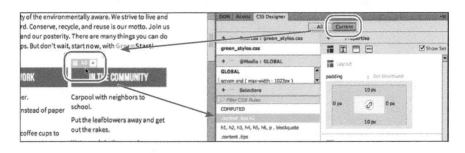

In addition to using the CSS Designer, you may also create and edit CSS styling manually within Code view while taking advantage of many productivity enhancements, such as code hinting and auto completion.

Using the Visual Media Query Interface (VMQ)

A new addition to Dreamweaver CC (2015.1 release) is the Visual Media Query (VMQ) interface. Appearing above the document window, the VMQ interface allows you to visually inspect and interact with existing media queries, as well as create new ones on the fly using a simple point-and-click interface.

Open any webpage that is formatted by a style sheet with one or more media queries, and the VMQ interface will appear above the document window, displaying color-coded bars that specify the type of media query that has been defined. Media queries using only a max-width specification will be displayed in green. Media queries using only a min-width specification will be displayed in purple. Ones that use both will be displayed in blue.

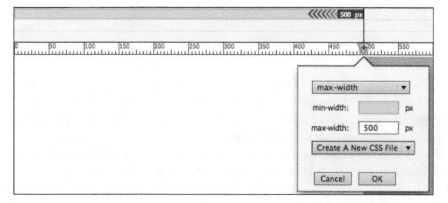

Max-width media query in the VMQ interface

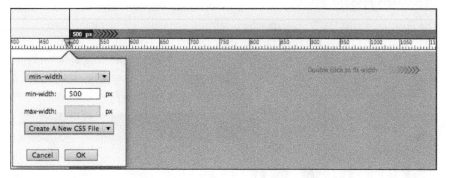

Min-width media query in the VMQ interface

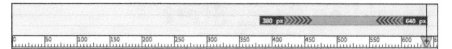

Media using both max-width and min-width specifications

Using the DOM Viewer

The DOM Viewer is another new tool introduced recently that has already been improved in Dreamweaver CC (2015.1 release). It allows you to view the Document Object Model (DOM) to quickly examine the structure of your layout as well as interact with it to select and move existing elements and to insert new ones by drag and drop.

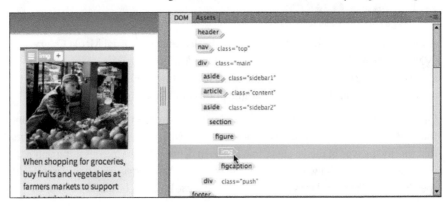

Using the Heads-up Displays

The movement toward Live view as the default Dreamweaver workspace has driven the development of new methods for editing and managing HTML elements. In Dreamweaver CC (2015.1 release), you will see a handful of new heads-up displays (HUDs) whenever you are working in Live view. All of them, except the Text HUD, allow you to add class or id attributes to the selected element and then insert references to the class or id in your CSS style sheets and media queries.

Position Assist HUD

Nest

In reference to HTML, you nest an element when you place it inside another element.

The Position Assist HUD allows you to control how elements and components are inserted in Live view.

The Position Assist HUD appears whenever new elements are being inserted in Live view, using either the Insert menu or Insert panel. Typically, the Position Assist HUD will offer the options Before, After, Wrap, and **Nest**. Depending on what type of element is selected and what item is targeted by the insertion point, one or more of the options may be grayed out.

Before | After | Wrap | Nest

Start now with
Meridien GreenStart

Element HUD

The Element HUD appears whenever you select an element in Live view. When an element is selected in Live view, you can change the selection focus by pressing the up and down arrow keys; the Element HUD will then highlight each element in the page, in turn, based on its position in the HTML structure.

The Element HUD enables you to quickly apply classes, ids, and links, as well as basic formatting.

Image HUD

The Image HUD provides access to the image source, alt text, width and height attributes as well as a field to add a hyperlink.

The Image HUD gives you quick access to the image source and allows you to add hyperlinks.

Text HUD

The Text HUD appears whenever you select a portion of text in Live view. The Text HUD allows you to apply bold <strong>, italic <em>, and hyperlink <a> markup to the text.

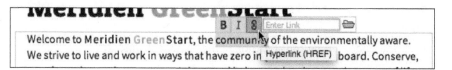

The Text HUD lets you apply bold, italics, and hyperlink markup to selected text.

Linting Support

Dreamweaver CC (2015.1 release) provides live code error checking. Linting support is enabled by default in Preferences, which means the program monitors your code writing and flags errors in real time. The errors will be displayed in the new Output panel. Double-click the error message and Dreamweaver will jump to the error in the Code view window.

Enabling Linting support in Preferences to check your HTML code for errors.

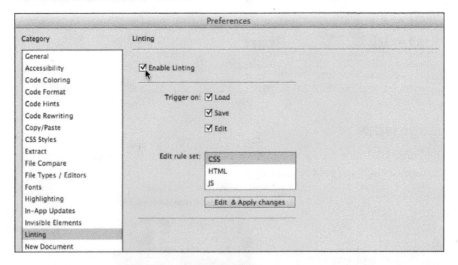

Linting checks the file for coding errors in real time.

Introducing Emmet

Emmet is a new feature in Dreamweaver CC (2015.1 release) that allows you to supercharge your code-writing tasks. By entering shorthand characters and operators, Emmet enables you to create whole blocks of code with just a few keystrokes. To experience the power of Emmet, try this:

1 Select File > Open. Select **emmet-test.html** in the chapter01 folder and click Open.

2 Click the Code view button at the top of the document window. Insert the insertion point in the <body> section.

3 Type div and press the Tab key.

A full `<div></div>` element is created. The insertion point should appear within it.

4   Type p*5 and press Tab.

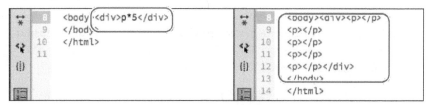

Five `<p>` elements are created inside the `<div>`. Emmet also allows you to combine these operations to save even more time.

5   Select the `div` tag selector.
    Press Delete to remove the content.

    The code created in steps 3 and 4 should be deleted.

6   Type div>p*5 and press Tab.

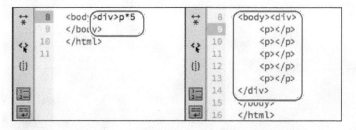

A `<div>` and five nested `<p>` elements are created all at once. Emmet can also generate placeholder text along with the HTML if desired.

7   Press Ctrl+Z/Cmd+Z to undo step 6.

    The shorthand div>p*5 reappears, replacing the `<div>` and five `<p>` elements.

8   Edit the shorthand phrase as highlighted:
    div>p(lorem)*5. Press Tab.

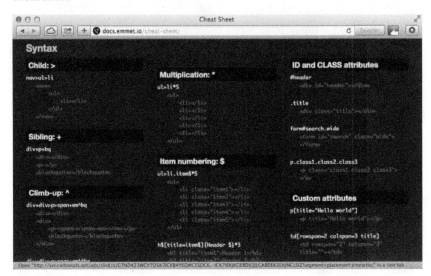

Lorem Ipsum

Nonsense text that can be added to a webpage as a placeholder for the actual text you will add later in your development process.

This time, the `<div>` and five nested `<p>` elements appear with **lorem ipsum** placeholder text. You can see how Emmet can make dreary code-writing tasks much faster and even fun.

Check out http://emmet.io to learn more about Emmet.

Check out http://docs.emmet.io/cheat-sheet/ for a handy Emmet shorthand cheat sheet.

Exploring, Experimenting, and Learning

The Dreamweaver interface has been carefully crafted over many years to make the job of webpage design and development fast and easy. Feel free to explore and experiment with various menus, panels, and options to create the ideal workspace and keyboard shortcuts to produce the most productive environment for your own purposes. You'll find the program endlessly adaptable, with power to spare for any task.

Defining a Dreamweaver Site

In the course of completing this book instruction, you will create webpages from scratch and use existing files and resources that your teacher gives you. The resulting webpages and assets make up what's called your **local site**. When you are ready to upload your site to the Internet (see Chapter 15, "Publishing to the Web"), you publish your completed files to a web host server, which then becomes your **remote site**. The folder structures and files of the local and remote sites are usually mirror images of one another.

The first step is to define your local site:

1 Launch Adobe Dreamweaver CC (2015.1 release) or later.

2 Open the Site menu. The Site menu provides options for creating and managing standard Dreamweaver sites.

3 Choose New Site.

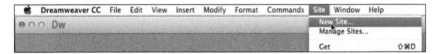

To create a standard website in Dreamweaver, you need only name it and select the local site folder. Site names typically relate to a specific project or client and appear in the Files panel. This name is intended for your own purposes, so there are no limitations to the name you can create. Use a name that clearly describes the purpose of the website. For the purposes of this book, use the name that your teacher instructs you to use.

4 Type chapter01 or the name for the new site as indicated by your teacher, in the Site Name field.

5   Next to the Local Site Folder field, click the Browse for Folder icon 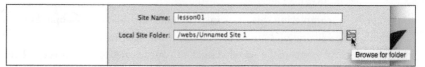.

6   The Choose Root Folder dialog appears. Navigate to the folder that contains the lesson files, and click Select(PC)/Choose(Mac).

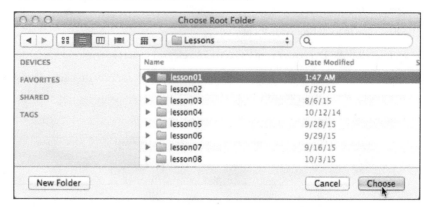

Note: The folder that contains the image assets will be referred to throughout the book as the site default images folder or the default images folder.

You could click Save at this time and begin working on your new website, but we'll add one more piece of handy information.

7   Click the arrow ▶ next to the Advanced Settings category to reveal the categories listed there. Select Local Info.

Although it's not required, a good policy for site management is to store different file types in separate folders. For example, many websites provide individual folders for images, PDFs, videos, and so on. Dreamweaver assists in this endeavor by including an option for a Default Images folder. Later, as you insert images from other places on your computer, Dreamweaver will use this setting to automatically move the images into the site structure.

8   Next to the Default Images Folder field, click the Browse for Folder icon . When the dialog opens, navigate to the appropriate images folder for that lesson or site and click Select(PC)/Choose(Mac). The path to the images folder appears in the Default Images Folder field. The next step would be to enter your site domain name in the Web URL field.

9   In the Web URL field enter http://green-start.org for the lessons in this book, or
enter a website URL as instructed by your teacher.

You've entered all the information required to begin your new site. In
subsequent lessons, you'll add more information to enable you to upload files to
your remote and testing servers.

10 In the Site Setup dialog, click Save.

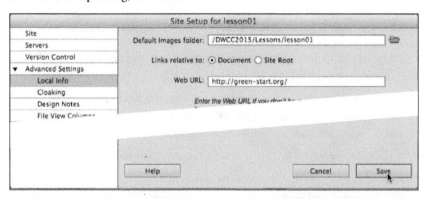

Note: Resource
folders for images
and other assets
should always be
contained within the
main site root folder.

The Site Setup dialog closes.

In the Files panel, the new site name appears in the site list drop-down menu.
As you add more site definitions, you can switch between the sites by selecting
the appropriate name from this menu.

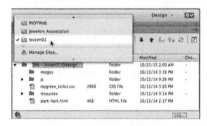 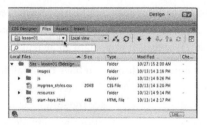

Note: The Web URL
is not needed for
most static HTML
sites, but it's required
for working with
sites using dynamic
applications or to
connect to databases
and a testing server.

Whenever a site is selected or modified, Dreamweaver will build, or rebuild,
a cache of every file in the folder. The cache identifies relationships between
the webpages and the assets within sites, and will assist you whenever a file is
moved, renamed, or deleted to update links or other referenced information.

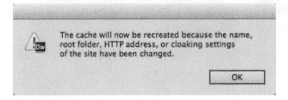

The cache will now be recreated because the name, root folder, HTTP address, or cloaking settings of the site have been changed.

OK

11 Click OK.

Setting up a site is a crucial first step in beginning any project in Dreamweaver. Knowing where the site root folder is located helps Dreamweaver determine link pathways and enables many site-wide options, such as orphaned-file checking and Find and Replace.

Career Search Skills

Note: In addition to completing an application form, some employers require applicants to take a test as part of the application process. For example, a personality test might help identify if someone is honest. Other tests are used for specific jobs.

- A cashier might be asked to take a basic math test.
- A customer support representative might be asked to take a problem-solving test.
- A computer technician might be asked to demonstrate a repair.

You can ask a potential employer if you will be expected to take any tests so that you can be prepared.

Employability skills also include the ability to prepare and organize the materials you will need for a job search. Every job search requires the following:

- A **resume**, which is a written summary of your work-related skills, experience, and education. It should be brief and to the point, printed on white paper, true and accurate and have no typographical, grammatical, or spelling errors.
- A **cover letter**, which is a letter of introduction that you send with a resume.
- A list of **references** that includes the names and contact information of people who know you and your qualifications and who are willing to speak about you too potential employers.
- A **portfolio** of your work. This can be a portfolio website or a physical collection of your projects or work.

You will also be expected to fill out an **application form**— sometimes online and sometimes on paper. Application forms require you to enter specific information about your education and past employment, including dates and locations. As with your resume, it is important to be truthful and accurate.

If an employer thinks you have the qualifications for the job, you will be invited for a **job interview**. A preliminary interview may be by phone but almost all employers will expect a face-to-face meeting. The interview is an opportunity for you and the interviewer to ask questions and decide if the position is right for you. You should prepare for the interview by researching the company and the position and practicing the answers to questions you think the employer might ask. You should also prepare a few questions that you can ask the employer.

After an interview, it is important to write a thank-you note to the employer to show your interest in the position. You should also be prepared to follow-up with a phone call or e-mail.

Recognizing the Value of School

Finishing school is an investment in your future. Most companies will not hire an employee who has not graduated from high school, and many will not hire an employee who has not graduated from college. If a company does hire dropouts, it usually pays them less than it pays graduates.

School also provides an opportunity to prepare for a career. Core subjects such as reading, writing, and math are vital for the career search process.

Science, social studies, music, art, technology, and sports all help you gain knowledge and build skills you will need to succeed at work, such as teamwork, leadership, and problem-solving. School clubs and organizations such as Skills USA also help you build skills for future success.

Employers value employees who graduate from high school and earn a college degree.

Developing a Personal Academic Plan

A **personal academic plan** is a document that you use to set goals for the things you want to accomplish in school. Some schools call it a personal career plan. Some things that you might put in your plan include:

- Yearly academic goals
- Assessment of your skills, knowledge, and experience
- Assessment of factors that will contribute to your success
- Assessment of factors that might interfere with your success
- Basic skills assessment

Participate in Lifelong Learning

Lifelong learning means continually acquiring new knowledge and skills through-out the course of your life. Education and training are not limited to learning new skills for the workplace. You should consider educational opportunities to enrich your life at home, with friends, and in your community. Understanding and using technology can help you achieve lifelong learning. It provides access to online information and helps you stay informed about current events and other topics.

Researching Your Career

Local and global trends can impact career plans and life goals in almost all career fields. You can use the Internet to monitor trends to help you stay prepared so you can adjust your plans and goals.

With your teacher's permission, research local and global trends that you think might impact your choice of career. Which of the following trends would most likely impact a career in a Web Technology profession?

- population shifts from rural areas to cities
- local food movements
- new wireless networking systems
- discovery of a new planet

Employment trends influence the number of available jobs in a certain industry as well as where the jobs are. A **trend** is a general move in a certain direction. An employment trend is one way the job market is changing over time. Many factors influence employment trends, including economic factors and even cultural trends. For example, a shift from using personal computers to using smart phones impacts employment in the information technology industry.

- Technology itself has a strong influence on employment and job outlook. It creates new jobs, replaces old jobs, and changes the way some people perform their existing jobs. Understanding the function and use of technology in the modern workplace is an essential skill in many professions.

- The development of new technology such as mobile phones and handheld devices creates new jobs in areas such as application development, sales, and research and development.

- The trend toward smaller computers has shifted the manufacturing of systems from desktops to notebooks and tablets.

- Improvements in robotics have made it possible to use robots in positions that people once held, such as on automobile assembly lines.

- Electronic record keeping in healthcare has changed the way medical professionals enter patient information, order prescriptions, and access patient records.

- The trend toward storing information and applications on the Internet instead of on local computers has eliminated the need for some information technology managers at large companies.

- The trend toward using video conferencing instead of traveling to meetings impacts travel agents, hotel workers, and people who work in restaurants where travelers might eat.

Role of Certifications in a Web Technology Profession

Based on the job you are interested in the web technology profession, there are certifications that you must attain to show that you are proficient and trained in that profession. Since there are many different areas in webpage technology professions like HTML, Javascript, PHP, or CSS, you need research the required certifications for a web designer and developer in that area.

Adobe offers the more widely recognized certifications available today. Adobe Authorized Training Centers offer instructor-led courses and training on Adobe products that prepare you to become an Adobe Certified Expert. There are three different certifications:

- Adobe Single Product certification

- Adobe Specialist certification

- Adobe Master certification

Visit training.adobe.com/certification/overview.html for a description of each certification. A directory of AATCs is available at training.adobe.com/trainingpartners.

Developing a Portfolio

Some academic plans include a **portfolio**. A portfolio is a collection of information and documents that show the progress you make in school and in your career planning. It helps you stay on track to achieve your educational and career goals. A portfolio may be an actual folder that holds printed documents and other materials, or it may be electronic and stored on a computer. Some things to include in a portfolio are examples of achievement such as an essay you are proud of, and awards or certificates of accomplishment. Based on your academic plans and the career cluster you thinking of entering, your portfolio items will differ from others in your class. For instance if you are an artist you'll want to include drawings, paintings, sketches, comics or cartoons that you have created in your portfolio. Throughout this book, you will develop an online portfolio.

Developing a Resume

In today's job market, employers are looking for candidates who can step in and start producing results quickly. By crafting a persuasive, professional résumé with clear evidence of skills and accomplishments, you take the first step in convincing recruiters you are that kind of employee. A resume is one of the most important writing projects in your entire career.

What's your story? Thinking about where you've been and where you want to go will help focus your job search. Writing or updating your resume is a great opportunity to step back and think about where you've been and where you'd like to go. Do you like the path you're on, or is it time for a change? Are you focused on a particular field, or do you need some time to explore?

You might find it helpful to think about the "story of you," the things you are passionate about, your skills, your ability to help an organization reach its goals, the path you've been on so far, and the path you want to follow in the future. Think in terms of an image or a theme you'd like to project. Are you academically gifted? An effective leader? A well-rounded professional with wide-ranging talents? A creative problem solver? A technical wizard? Writing your story is a valuable planning exercise that helps you think about where you want to go and how to present yourself to target employers.

End-of-Chapter Activities

Review Questions

Directions: Choose the correct answer for each question.

1. Where can you access the command to display or hide any panel?
   a. File menu
   b. Window menu
   c. Files panel
   d. Property inspector

2. Where can you find the Codes, Split, Design , and Live View buttons?
   a. Files Panel
   b. Property inspector
   c. Menu bar
   d. Document toolbar

3. What can be saved in a workspce?
   a. Position of panels
   b. Panel groupings
   c. Location and size of Property Inspector
   d. Location and size of Design/Code views
   e. All of the above
   f. None of the above

4. Do workspaces also load keyboard shortcuts?
   a. True
   b. False
   c. Dreamweaver does not have any keyboard shortcuts

5. What new features have been added to the CSS Designer?
   a. Copy and paste CSS styles from one rule to another
   b. Decrease or increase the specificity of new selector names by pressing the up or down arrow keys
   c. COMPUTED option
   d. All of the above
   e. A & B only

6. How do you minimize a panel grouping?
   a. Double-click its title bar
   b. Double-click a panel tab in the panel grouping
   c. Click and drag the lower-right corner of the panel grouping
   d. All of the above
   e. None of the above

7. If you are new to Dreamweaver, what prebuilt workspace should you use to get started?
   a. Default
   b. Beginner
   c. Code
   d. Design
   e. Extract

8. What is the Extract workspace used for in Dreamweaver?
   a. Creating a webpage from scratch
   b. Creating the CSS styles and image assets from a Photoshop-based mockup
   c. Creating a webpage from a Microsoft Word Document
   d. Creating a webpage from a text (.txt) document

9. What type of certification does Adobe offer through their Authorized Training Centers?
   a. Adobe Single Product certification
   b. Adobe Specialist certification
   c. Adobe Master certification
   d. None of the above
   e. All of the above

10. What are some items that you can include in your portfolio
   a. Essays, Awards, Certifications
   b. Test scores
   c. Absentee Reports
   d. Subject Grades

Essay Questions

Directions: Respond to each question by writing your answers in complete sentences and paragraphs. Be thorough in your answers.

1. What happens in the Property inspector when you insert the insertion point into various elements on the webpage?

2. What can you do with the DOM viewer?

3. Describe a HUD and provide an example of its use.

4. What is the difference between the Design and Live views?

5. What is the Code View used for when creating a webpage?

6. Describe the process of creating and reorganizing a panel group.

7. What is the Inspect mode used for in Dreamweaver?

8. What is the advantage of the Split view when compared to either Code view or Design view?

9. Describe 5 examples of the functionality that the Welcome Screen offers for creating a webpage.

10. What are the differences between a resume and a portfolio?

Online Portfolio Builder – Organize Your Information

Throughout this book you will create a portfolio website to promote yourself to future employers. To do this you must first gather the content for your portfolio website. If you are an artist, this could be sketches, paintings, drawings, and digital graphic media. If you are looking for a more tradition occupation like business or office management, these could projects you've worked on in school, essays, letters or documents you have created, and your resume. If you are interested in the Web technology profession field, this could be the websites you have created, social media sites you have developed, websites you have optimized for Search Engine Optimization (SEO), Web graphics, or mobile applications you have developed. Any of these require you to gather and digitize your portfolio items for display in a webpage. Also start to gather and/or create your text and verbiage for describing your skills and your portfolio items. You can use any word processor or text editor for creating a digital format for your text and verbiage. If you save the document in text (.txt) format, it can be easily imported or copied into Dreamweaver.

Save and organize all digitized files in folders on a Flash drive, Thumb Drive or external storage device as instructed by your teacher so you can bring your identified portfolio items to class.

It is important to save your portfolio items in a separate folder outside of your website folder. This allows you to keep an original document for all these items prior to importing, optimizing and/or embedding them into your webpage. Follow these steps, to organize your gathered portfolio items:

1. Digitize your portfolio items by scanning or taking a photo of them with your digital camera or mobile phone.

2. In a word processing application like Microsoft Word or Google Docs, create and save any text verbiage to text (.txt) format as instructed by your teacher. Make sure you name your files using your initials at the end of the file, like painting_xx.txt where the xx is replaced with your initials.

3. To organize these digitized documents, create a new folder on the computer or external device as instructed by your teacher. In this example, you create a new folder at the desktop level by right-clicking in a blank area of your desktop and then choosing New Folder from the context menu that displays.

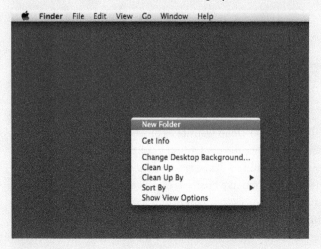

4. Rename the folder to "Portfolio Items" by highlighting the Untitled Folder name under the folder icon and delete it by pressing the Delete key on your keyboard. Then type "Portfolio Items" to rename the folder.

5. Open the new Portfolio Items folder by double-clicking it.

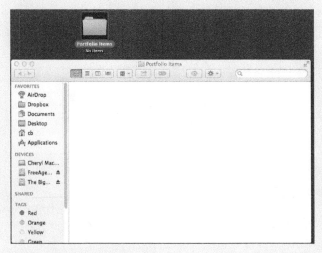

6. Next create the folders to hold your portfolio items. In the Portfolio Items window that displays, right-click and choose New Folder from the context menu that displays.

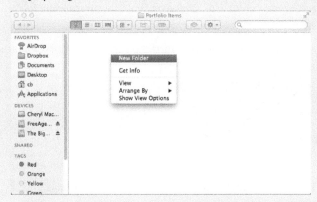

7. Repeat step 2 and rename the folder to "text".

8. Create the other folders you might need based on the types of portfolio items you have gathered. Try to create folders that will hold multiple items and name them appropriately for the type of files they will contain.

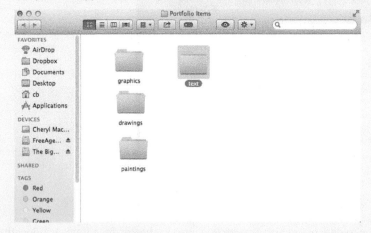

9. With your folders set up you can now start to gather, copy/paste, save, and organize your portfolio items. Place, move, copy/paste, or save these in the appropriate folder in the Portfolio Items folder.

10. Next you'll create the local root directory for your portfolio site. Create a new folder in the location your teacher instructs

11. Rename the new folder to "myPortfolio_xx". Replace the xx with your initials.

12. Open this folder by double-clicking it and create another new folder for the graphics you will use in your website.

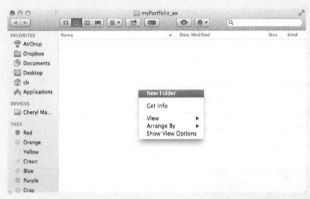

13. Rename this folder "images".

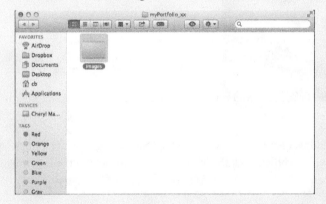

You have now create your local root directory that will hold all the files that make up your portfolio Web site.

Note: Moving Files Between Devices: It has never been easier to transfer and/or move files between devices. You can share your camera digital files with your computer, printer, cell phone, or mobile tablet through a variety of techniques. You can use a cable to physically link the two devices in preparation to transfer the files or you can use wireless technology, like Blue Tooth, to transfer your files. You can also upload the files to a cloud location and access them easily from another device. Refer to your device's operations manual for more instructions on how to move files. You can also check out other techniques by searching the Internet with the keywords of "move digital files between devices" to see other instruction on moving your files between devices.

Critical Thinking – Review Project

In this review project you will review skills covered in this chapter by setting up the Dreamweaver workspace for your workflow and defining your portfolio website. Remember the first step to developing any website is to set up your workspace and then define your site.

1. Open Dreamweaver as instructed by your teacher.

2. The Welcome screen displays. Create a new document by click the Open a new HTML5 document by clicking New Document.

A – New Document

3. The New Document window display with the New Document category active. Click the HTML document type and then click the None tab. Click to set the the Document Type to HTML5 and then click Create. A new HTML5 document is created.

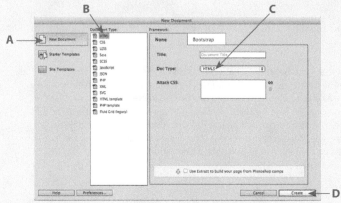

A – New Document, **B** - HTML, **C** – HTML5, **D** - Create

4. Set your workspace to the a pre-built workspace click the Workspace menu and choose the Design workspace.

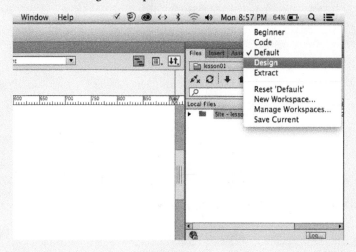

Note: The pre-built workspaces of Beginner or Design are good workspaces to use when first learning Dreamweaver.

5. Click the Properties tab of the Property inspector to make this active.

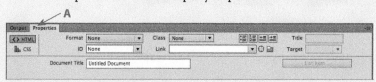

A – Properties tab

6. Switch to the Design view by clicking the Design/Live views drop-down menu and choosing Design.

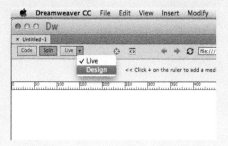

7. Now Switch to the Code view by clicking the Code view button.

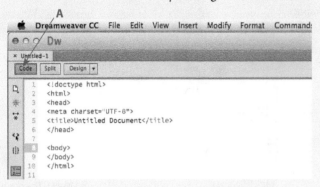

A-Code view

8. Switch back to the Split view by clicking the Split view button.

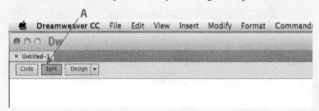

A-Split view

9. Make the Code window display vertically by choosing View>Split Vertically.

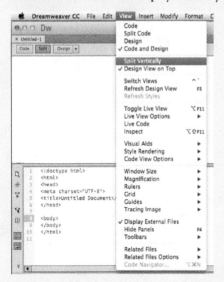

10. Move the Code Window to display on the left of the Design view. Choose View>Design View on Left. Notice that by default the Design View on Left is a default preference setting and it is checked. When you choose it from the menu, the check mark is removed indicating that this setting is no longer active.

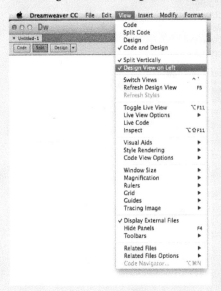

11. Adjust the size of the Code window by placing your insertion point on the vertical border between the Code window and the Design window. Your insertion point becomes a double-arrow tool. Click and drag left to decrease the size of the Code window.

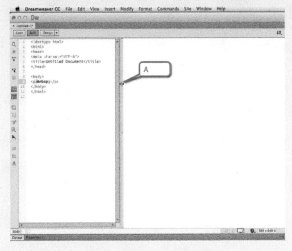

A – Double-Arrow tool

12. Save this custom workspace layout by selecting the Workspace menu and choosing New Workspace.

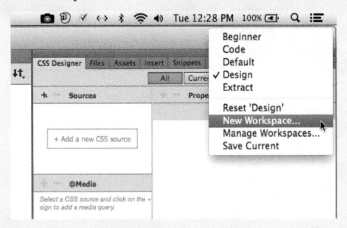

13. In the Save Workspace window, type My Workspace and click OK.

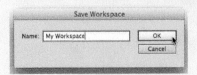

14. Click the Files panel tab to make this panel active.

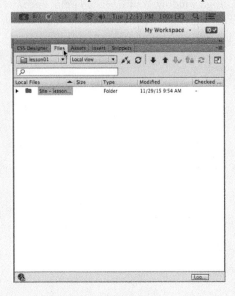

15. Click the CSS Designer tab to make this panel active.

16. Click the Current button in the CSS Designer panel to make this view active.

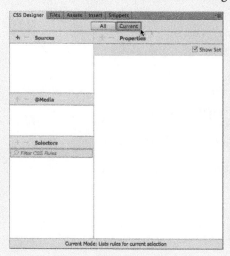

17. Open Emmet by selecting File>Open and then click emmet-test.html in the Lesson01 folder. Click Open to open Emmet.

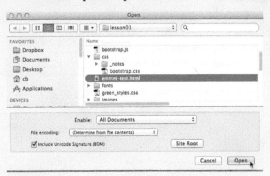

18. Type h1 and again press Tab to create the opening and closing tags for the <h1> tag.

19. Add a couple of <h2> tags by typing h2*2 and then press Tab.

Note: The code for the Heading 1 tag is <h1> and <h2> is the Heading 2 tag

20. Click the Untitled-1 document tab to switch to that document.

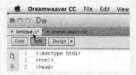

21. Close both documents by selecting File>Close All.

22. Do not save these documents by clicking the Don't Save button in the Save window.

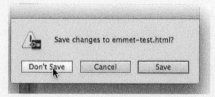

Critical Thinking Activity

This lesson covered information about developing your resume and your portfolio. Write a paragraph description of what a resume is and what information (education, skills, jobs, duties, honors, achievements, awards) that you would emphasize in your resume. Write another paragraph that describes what a portfolio is and what you will include in your portfolio.

Chapter 3

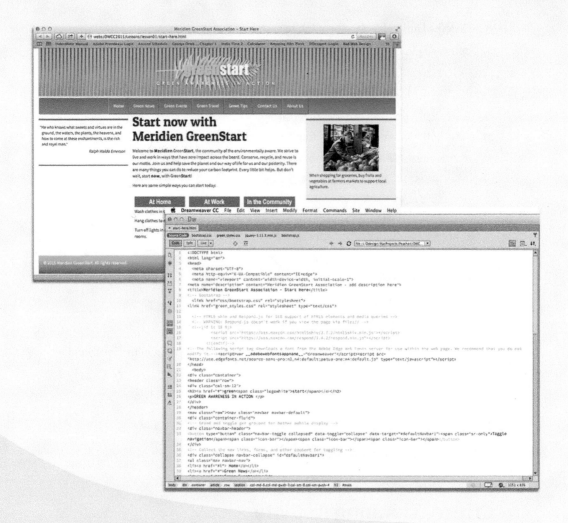

HTML BASICS

HTML is the backbone of the web, the skeleton of your webpage. Like the bones in your body, it is the structure and substance of the Internet, although it is usually unseen except by the web designer. Without it, the web would not exist. Dreamweaver has many features that help you access, create, and edit HTML code quickly and effectively.

Chapter Overview

In this chapter, you'll familiarize yourself with HTML and learn:

- What HTML is and where it came from
- Frequently used HTML tags
- How to insert special characters
- What semantic web design is and why it's important
- New features and capabilities in HTML5

What is HTML?

"What other programs can open a Dreamweaver file?"

This question was asked by an actual student in a Dreamweaver class; although it might seem obvious to an experienced developer, it illustrates a basic problem in teaching and learning web design. Most people confuse the program with the technology. They assume that the extension .htm or .html belongs to Dreamweaver or Adobe. Designers are used to working with files ending with extensions, such as .ai, .psd, .indd, and so on; it's just a part of their jobs. They have learned over time that opening these file formats in a different program may produce unacceptable results or even damage the file.

On the other hand, the goal of the web designer is to create a webpage for display in a browser. The power and/or functionality of the originating program has little bearing on the resulting browser display, because the display is all contingent on the HTML code and how the browser interprets it. Although a program may write good or bad code, it's the browser that does all the hard work.

The web is based on HyperText Markup Language (HTML). The language and the file format don't belong to any individual program or company. In fact, it is a *non*-proprietary, plain-text language that can be edited in any text editor, in any operating system, on any computer. Dreamweaver is, in part, an HTML editor, although it is also much more than this. But to maximize the potential of Dreamweaver, you first need to have a good understanding of what HTML is and what it can (and can't) do. This chapter is intended as a concise primer on HTML and its capabilities. It will be a helpful foundation for understanding Dreamweaver.

Where did HTML Begin?

As discussed in Chapter 1, HTML and the first browser were invented in 1989 by Tim Berners-Lee, a computer scientist working at the CERN (Conseil Européen pour la Recherche Nucléaire, which is French for European Council for Nuclear Research) particle physics laboratory in Geneva, Switzerland. He intended the technology as a means for sharing technical papers and information via the fledgling Internet that existed at the time. He shared his HTML and browser inventions openly as an attempt to get the scientific community at large and others to adopt them and engage in the development themselves. The fact that he did not copyright or try to sell his work started a trend for openness and camaraderie on the web that continues to this day.

The language that Berners-Lee created over 25 years ago was a much simpler construct of what we use now, but HTML is still surprisingly easy to learn and master. At the time of this writing, HTML is now at version 5, officially adopted as of October 2014. It consists of over 120 *tags*, such as html, head, body, h1, p, and so on.

The tag is inserted between less-than (<) and greater-than (>) angle brackets, as in <p>, <h1>, and <table>. These tags are used to identify, or *mark up*, text and graphics to enable a browser to display them in a particular way. HTML code is considered properly *balanced* when the markup features both an opening (<...>) and a closing (</...>) tag, such as <h1>...</h1>.

When two matching tags appear this way, they are referred to as an *element*; an element entails any contents contained within the two tags, as well. Empty, or void, elements, like the horizontal rule, can be written in an abbreviated fashion using only one tag, such as <hr/>, essentially opening and closing the tag at the same time. In HTML5, empty elements can also be validly expressed without the closing slash, such as <hr>.

Some elements are used to create page structures, others to structure and format text, and yet others to enable interactivity and programmability. Even though Dreamweaver obviates the need for writing most of the code manually, the ability to read and interpret HTML code is still a recommended skill for any burgeoning web designer. Sometimes it's the only way to find an error in your webpage. The ability to understand and read code may also become an essential skill in other fields as more information and content is created and disseminated via mobile devices and Internet-based resources.

Basic HTML Code Structure

Here you see the basic structure of a webpage:

Basic HTML Code Structure

You may be surprised to learn that the only text from this code that displays in the web browser is "Welcome to my first webpage." The rest of the code creates the page structure and text formatting. Like an iceberg, most of the content of the actual webpage remains out of sight.

Note: If you are dead set against learning how to read and write good HTML, you should check out Adobe Muse. This program allows you to create professional-looking webpages and complete websites using point-and-click techniques in a graphical user interface similar to Adobe InDesign while never exposing you to the code running behind the scenes.

Note: Go to the book's online resources at Peachpit. com for bonus hands-on exercises to gain some vital skills and experience writing and editing HTML code. See the "Getting Started" section at the beginning of the book for more details.

Note: Revealing Webpage HTML Code: You can view the code the makes up a Web page in any browser by right-clicking in a blank area of the page and choosing View Source or View Page Source from the context menu. The menu command that is displayed is based on the browser being used but all browsers will let you view the backend HTML.

Frequently Used HTML Elements

HTML code elements serve specific purposes. Tags can create distinct objects, apply formatting, identify logical content, or generate interactivity. Tags that make their own space on the screen and stand alone are known as *block* elements; the ones that perform their duties within the flow of another tag are known as *inline* elements. Some elements can also be used to create *structural* relationships within a page, like stacking content in vertical columns or collecting several elements together in logical groupings. Structural elements can behave like block or inline elements or do their work entirely invisible to the user.

HTML Tags

The following table shows some of the most frequently used HTML tags. To get the most out of Dreamweaver and your webpages, it helps to understand the nature of these elements and how they are used. Remember that some tags can serve multiple purposes.

Table 2.1 Frequently used HTML tags

TAG	DESCRIPTION
`<!--...-->`	Comment. Designates an HTML comment. Allows you to add notes within the HTML code that are not displayed within the browser.
`<a>`	Anchor. The basic building block for a hyperlink.
`<blockquote>`	Quotation. Creates a standalone, indented paragraph.
`<body>`	Designates the document body. Contains the visible portions of the webpage content.
` `	Break. Inserts a line break without creating a new paragraph.
`<div>`	Division. Used to divide webpage content into discernible sections.
`<em>`	Emphasis. Adds semantic emphasis. Displays as italics by default in most browsers and readers.
`<form>`	Designates an HTML form. Used for collecting data from users.
`<h1>` to `<h6>`	Headings. Creates headings. Implies semantic value. Default formatting is bolded.
`<head>`	Designates the document head. Contains code that performs background functions, such as meta tags, scripts, styling, links, and other information not overtly visible to site visitors.
`<hr>`	Horizontal Rule. Empty element that generates a horizontal line.
`<html>`	Root element of most webpages. Contains the entire webpage, except in certain instances where server-based code must load before the opening `<html>` tag.
`<iframe>`	Inline Frame. A structural element that can contain another document.
`<img>`	Image. Provides the source reference to display an image.
`<input>`	Input element for a form such as a text field.
`<li>`	List Item. The content of an HTML list.

TAG	DESCRIPTION
`<link>`	Designates the relationship between a document and an external resource.
`<meta>`	Metadata. Additional information provided for search engines or other applications.
`<ol>`	Ordered List. Defines a numbered list. List items display in a numbered sequence.
`<p>`	Paragraph. Designates a standalone paragraph.
`<script>`	Script. Contains scripting elements or points to an internal or external script.
`<span>`	Designates a document section. Provides a means to apply special formatting or emphasis to a portion of an element.
`<strong>`	Strong. Adds semantic emphasis. Displays as bold by default in most browsers and readers.
`<style>`	Style. Embedded or inline reference for CSS styling.
`<table>`	Designates an HTML table.
`<td>`	Table Data. Designates a table cell.
`<textarea>`	Designates a multi-line text input element for a form.
`<th>`	Table Header. Identifies a cell as containing a header.
`<title>`	Title. Contains the metadata title reference for the current page.
`<tr>`	Table Row. Structural element that delineates one row of a table from another.
`<ul>`	Unordered List. Defines a bulleted list. List items display with bullets by default.

HTML Character Entities

Entities exist for every letter and character. If a symbol can't be entered directly from the keyboard, it can be inserted by typing the name or numeric value listed in the following table:

Note: Some entities can be created using either a name or a number, as in the copyright symbol, but named entities may not work in all browsers or applications. So either stick to numbered entities or test the specific named entities before you use them.

Table 2.2 HTML character entities

CHARACTER	DESCRIPTION	NAME	NUMBER
©	Copyright	&copy;	&#169;
®	Registered trademark	&reg;	&#174;
™	Trademark		&#153;
•	Bullet		&#149;
–	En dash		&#150;
—	Em dash		&#151;
	Nonbreaking space		

Go to www.w3schools.com/html/html_entities.asp to see a complete list of entities.

What's New in HTML5

Every new version of HTML has made changes to both the number and purpose of the tags that make up the language. HTML 4.01 consisted of approximately 90 tags. HTML5 has removed some of those HTML 4 tags from its specification altogether, and some new ones have been adopted or proposed.

Changes to the list usually revolve around supporting new technologies or different types of content models, as well as removing features that were bad ideas or ones infrequently used. Some changes simply reflect customs or techniques that have been popularized within the developer community over time. Other changes have been made to simplify the way code is created, to make it easier to write and faster to **disseminate**.

Disseminate
To spread around or disperse to all.

HTML5 Tags

The Table 2.3 shows some of the important new tags in HTML5. The specification features nearly 50 new tags in total, while at least 30 old tags were **deprecated**. As we move through the exercises of this book, you will learn how to use many of these new HTML5 tags as appropriate to help you understand their intended role on the web. Take a few moments to familiarize yourself with these tags and their descriptions.

Deprecated
To become less in value or to become less important."

Go to www.w3schools.com/tags/default.asp to see the complete list of HTML5 elements.

Table 2.3 Important new HTML5 tags

TAG	DESCRIPTION
<article>	Designates independent, self-contained content, which can be distributed independently from the rest of the site.
<aside>	Designates sidebar content that is related to the surrounding content.
<audio>	Designates multimedia content, sounds, music, or other audio streams.
<canvas>	Designates graphics content created using a script.
<figure>	Designates a section of standalone content containing an image or video.
<figcaption>	Designates a caption for a <figure> element.
<footer>	Designates a footer of a document or section.
<header>	Designates the introduction of a document or section.
<hgroup>	Designates a set of <h1> to <h6> elements when a heading has multiple levels.
<nav>	Designates a section of navigation.

TAG	DESCRIPTION
`<section>`	Designates a section in a document.
`<source>`	Designates media resources for media elements, a child element of video, or audio elements. Multiple sources can be defined for browsers that do not support the default file type.
`<video>`	Designates video content, such as a movie clip or other video streams.

Importance of Web Standards

The W3C sets the standards for HTML and CSS. It is made up of volunteers that are industry experts in the area of web design and development. Some are programmers, some are designers, others are HTML and/or CSS coders. These people look at where the web is now and where it should go based on popular trends in business and the way people use and interact with the web. From these insights and ideas, standards are developed for controlling HTML and CSS as well as other Web programming languages. Visit this site for a complete list of web standards:

http://www.w3.org/standards/

Because the web is basically a free entity, many designers and developers are very liberal with their use of HTML. In fact, prior to HTML5, the all mighty **DIV tag** was used to help segment and layout a webpage. No two designers used the same names or organization for their webpages. This worked for many years but as we developed and started using more mobile devices, like smart phones and tablets, it became increasing difficult to find any commonality in code structure. This is one reason why HTML 5 was created by the W3C, to create a common structure and uniform semantic meaning for HTML code. Now you can use the <section> tag to create a section and then include in that section its own headings and articles using the H1 – H6 tags and the <article> tag.

Another value of having web standards is that it helps web designers and developers create websites that are consistent in the backend code and therefore also in the frontend (browser) display. This helps the browser developers, like Microsoft or Firefox, to create a browser that consistantly interprets the HTML and CSS code as well as displays the Web page quicker and more accurately as the web developer intended.

Semantic Web Design

Many of the changes to HTML were made to support the concept of **semantic web design**. This movement has important ramifications for the future of HTML, its usability, and the interoperability of websites on the Internet. At the moment, each webpage stands alone on the web. The content may link to other pages and sites,

DIV tag

A container created in HTML that can contain HTML elements and page data and assets. DIV tags are used to create structure and areas in a webpage layout.

Note: You will find as you work with HTML that each browser has its own interpretation of the HTML tags. For instance, the [H1] tag in one browser might be set to display in a 14 point font whereas in another browser this might be 16 points. Each browser has its own rules for how to display all the HTML tags and CSS rules.

Semantic Web Design

Designing for the web following the W3C standards that provide a framework for common webpage content and protocols.

Coherent

Consistent and logically connected.

but there's really no way to combine or collect the information available on multiple pages or multiple sites in a **coherent** manner. Search engines do their best to index the content that appears on every site, but much of it is lost due to the nature and structure of old HTML code.

HTML was initially designed as a presentation language. In other words, it was intended to display technical documents in a browser in a readable and predictable manner. If you look carefully at the original specifications of HTML, it looks like a list of items you would put in a college research paper: headings, paragraphs, quoted material, tables, numbered and bulleted lists, and so on.

The element list in the first version of HTML basically identified how the content would be displayed. These tags did not convey any intrinsic meaning or significance. For example, using a heading tag displayed a particular line of text in bold, but it didn't tell you what relationship the heading had to the following text or to the story as a whole. Is it a title or merely a subheading?

The Internet before HTML looked more like MS DOS or the OS X Terminal application. There was no formatting, no graphics, and no user-definable color.

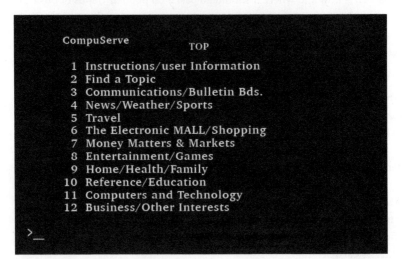

HTML5 has added a significant number of new tags to help us add semantic meaning to our markup. Tags, such as <header>, <footer>, <article>, and <section>, allow you for the first time to identify specific content without having to resort to additional attributes. The result is simpler code and less of it. But most of all, the addition of semantic meaning to your code allows you and other developers to connect the content from one page to another in new and exciting ways—many of which haven't even been invented yet. It's truly a work in progress.

New Techniques and Technology

HTML5 has also revisited the basic nature of the language to take back some of the functions that over the years have been increasingly handled by third-party plug-in applications and programming.

If you are new to web design, this transition will be painless because you have nothing to relearn, no bad habits to break. If you already have experience building webpages and applications, this book will guide you safely through some of these waters and introduce the new technologies and techniques in a logical and straightforward way. But either way, you don't have to trash all your old sites and rebuild everything from scratch.

Valid HTML 4 code will remain valid for the foreseeable future. HTML5 was intended to make web design easier by allowing you to do more with less work. So let's get started!

See www.w3.org/TR/2014/WD-html5-20140617 to learn more about HTML5.

See www.w3.org to learn more about W3C.

Keywords and Keyword Phrases

Keywords words and keyword phrases describe the site content. For instance if you are creating a website for a company that sells designer tennis shoes you could used these keywords and keyword phrases for the site:

- Tennis shoes
- Athletic shoes
- Designer tennis shoes
- Designer athletic shoes
- Custom designed tennis shoes
- Custom designed athletic

Keywords are important because search engines scan and index them, creating the links that bring visitors to your site. The keywords you add to your webpages help search engines to index a site in their databases.

Using the <meta> Tag to Add Keywords

The <meta> tag records information about the current page and supplies information such as keywords that search engines use to identify your page. This tag does not require a closing tag and appears in HTML code as <meta> in the <head> section of the webpage.

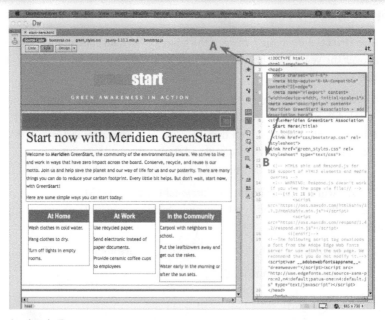

A - <head> Tag

B - <meta> Tags

This page has a four meta tags.

To add keyword meta data to a webpage, choose Insert>HTML>Keywords from the menu bar.

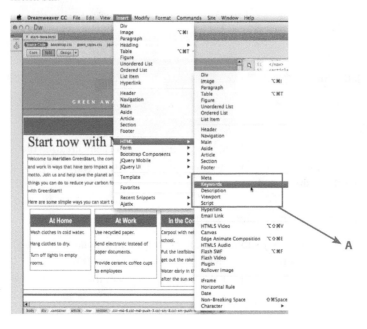

A-Meta data menu choices

In the Keywords window type the keywords you want to set for your site and click OK.

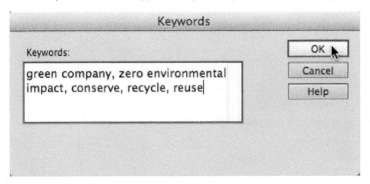

Look in the <head> section of the page code to see your new keywords.

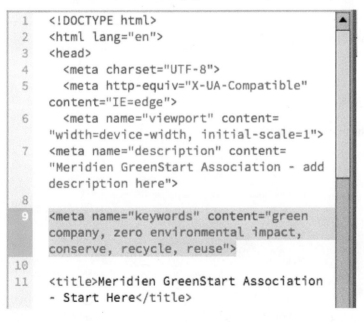

```
1   <!DOCTYPE html>
2   <html lang="en">
3   <head>
4     <meta charset="UTF-8">
5     <meta http-equiv="X-UA-Compatible"
    content="IE=edge">
6     <meta name="viewport" content=
    "width=device-width, initial-scale=1">
7   <meta name="description" content=
    "Meridien GreenStart Association - add
    description here">
8
9   <meta name="keywords" content="green
    company, zero environmental impact,
    conserve, recycle, reuse">
10
11  <title>Meridien GreenStart Association
    - Start Here</title>
```

End-of-Chapter Activities

Review Questions

Directions: Choose the correct answer for each question.

1. What is the backbone of the web?
   a. CSS
   b. browsers
   c. HTML
   d. PHP

2. What is used to interpret an HTML page?
   a. World Wide Web
   b. Browser
   c. Property Inspector
   d. Internet

3. Who invented HTML and the first browser?
   a. Tim Berners-Lee
   b. Mark Zuckerberg
   c. Steven Spielberg
   d. Steve Jobs

4. How many tags are used in HTML5?
   a. Under 100
   b. Exactly 25
   c. Over 750
   d. Over 120

5. In HTML, there are two matching tags, an opening tag and a closing tag, the content between these tags is called what?
   a. An element
   b. An attribute
   c. Just a tag
   d. None of these above

6. Tags that make their own space on a webpage are called what?
   a. Attributes
   b. Block elements
   c. Inline elements
   d. CSS

7. What tag creates a line break in an HMTL page?
   a. `<a>` Anchor tag
   b. `<em>` Emphasis tag
   c. `<h1>` Heading1 tag
   d. `<br>` Break tag

8. What tag designates the document head area of an HTML page?
   a. `<html>` Root Element tag
   b. `<iframe>` Inline frame tag
   c. `<head>` Head tag
   d. `<img>` Image tag

9. What is the numeric value for the Trademark sign?
   a. `&#169`
   b. `&#153`
   c. `&#149`
   d. ` `

10. What is new in HTML5?
    a. New tags
    b. Tags with semantic meaning
    c. Tags and code that takes back some of the functions that was handled by third party plugins and programming
    d. All of the above
    e. None of the above

Essay Questions

Directions: Respond to each question by writing your answers in complete sentences and paragraphs. Be thorough in your answers.

1. What programs can open HTML files?

2. What does a markup language do?

3. HTML is composed of how many code elements?

4. What are the three main parts of most webpages?

5. What is the difference between block and inline elements?

6. When was HTML5 adopted and what are some of the obstacles for full support?

7. Why is it important to have Internet programming standards?

8. What does the `<article>` tag bring to a webpage that was missing in other versions of HTML?

9. What functionality does the <canvas> tag offer in web design.

10. List four tags that are depreciated in HTML5.

Online Portfolio Builder – Use Effective Keywords

One of the most important aspects of creating a new website is to identify keywords that will help potential visitors find your site using a search engine. Keyword research is an important strategy for creating a new website.

Think about your goals in creating your online portfolio site. Identify five or six words that you think will bring visitors to your site. These could be keywords or keyword phrases that identify your artwork in your portfolio site, or the documents, honors or awards you have chosen to include in your site. Use the Internet to search for information using those keywords. What kind of sites do you find? Are the words you identified the ones that will be most effective in bringing people to your site? Revise your list of keywords and create a summary report of the top five sites in your topic area. Share your list with the class to find out how they might search for your site differently.

Critical Thinking Project – Using HTML5 to Create a Webpage

In this project you examine the books example website for HTML5 tags and code as well as create a keyword <meta> tag.

1. Open Dreamweaver and define a site for Chapter03/DataFiles as instructed by your teacher.

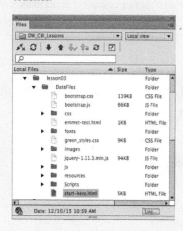

2. Choose the Default workspace. This workspace will be used throughout this book.

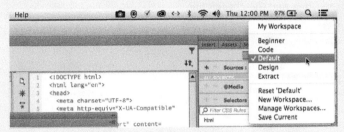

3. Click the Files panel tab to make it active and open the start-here.html page by double-clicking it.

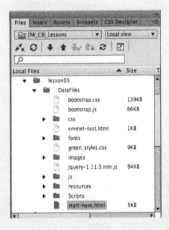

Note: The start-here.html webpage is a preview of the site that is used throughout the book as the example site in the chapter instruction.

4. In the Code view find the DOCTYPE tag in line 1. This is the code that declares this page an HTML5 page. Then find the <head> tag.

A - Root or <DOCTYPE> tag

B - <head> tag

5. Find the opening <body> tag.

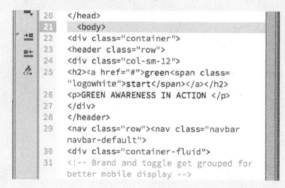

6. Scroll down to find the closing </body> tag. All code contained in the <body> tag is what is displayed in a browser and is what the visitor sees.

```
       "js/jquery-1.11.3.min.js"></script>
103
104        <!-- Include all compiled plugins
       (below), or include individual files as
       needed -->
105        <script src="js/bootstrap.js">
       </script>
106     </body>
107  </html>
```

7. In the Code view window, click to set the insertion point after the closing tag of the description <meta> tag and press Return(Mac)/Enter(PC) to create a blank line.

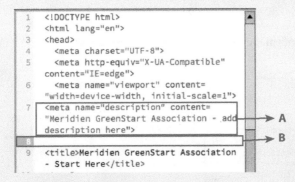

```
1   <!DOCTYPE html>
2   <html lang="en">
3   <head>
4     <meta charset="UTF-8">
5     <meta http-equiv="X-UA-Compatible"
    content="IE=edge">
6     <meta name="viewport" content=
    "width=device-width, initial-scale=1">
7   <meta name="description" content=          ➤ A
    "Meridien GreenStart Association - add
    description here">
8                                               ➤ B
9   <title>Meridien GreenStart Association
    - Start Here</title>
```

A – Description <meta> tag

B – Blank line

By inserting your insertion point in the code and creating a blank line, you are directing Dreamweaver to insert the next code at this location

8. To insert keywords at this location in the code, choose Insert>HTML>Keywords from the menu bar.

9. Type these keywords in the Keywords dialog box, separating keywords with commas as shown in the figure below. Click OK.

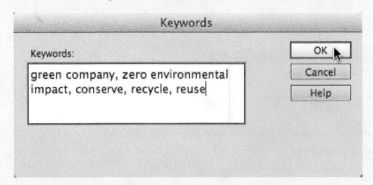

10. In the Code View window, confirm that the new keyword <meta> tag was added to your code.

```
1   <!DOCTYPE html>
2   <html lang="en">
3   <head>
4     <meta charset="UTF-8">
5     <meta http-equiv="X-UA-Compatible"
    content="IE=edge">
6     <meta name="viewport" content=
    "width=device-width, initial-scale=1">
7     <meta name="description" content=
    "Meridien GreenStart Association - add
    description here">
8     <meta name="keywords" content="green
    company, zero environmental impact,
    conserve, recycle, reuse">
9     <title>Meridien GreenStart Association
    - Start Here</title>
```

11. Find the following semantic HTML tags in the Code view window.
    a. <header>
    b. <section>
    c. <article>
    d. <aside>
    e. <figure>
    f. <footer>

12. Save the document as **start-here_xx.html** with xx being your initials as instructed by your teacher.

Chapter 4

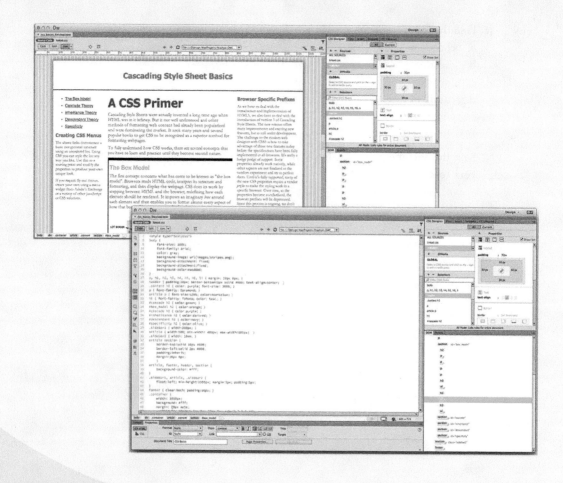

CSS BASICS

Cascading style sheets control the look and feel of a webpage. The language and syntax of CSS is complex, powerful, and endlessly adaptable. It takes time and dedication to learn and years to master, but a modern web designer can't live without it.

Chapter Overview

In this chapter, you'll familiarize yourself with CSS and learn:

- CSS (cascading style sheets) terms and terminology

- The difference between HTML and CSS formatting

- How the cascade, inheritance, descendant, and specificity theories affect the way browsers apply CSS formatting

- New features and capabilities of CSS3

What is CSS?

HTML was never intended to be a design medium. Other than allowing for bold and italic, version 1 lacked a standardized way to load fonts or format text. Formatting commands were added along the way—up to version 3 of HTML—to address these limitations, but these changes still weren't enough. Designers resorted to various tricks to produce the desired results. For example, they used HTML tables to simulate multicolumn and complex layouts for text and graphics, and they used images when they wanted to display typefaces other than Times or Helvetica.

HTML-based formatting was so misguided a concept that it was **deprecated** from the language less than a year after it was formally adopted in favor of cascading style sheets (CSS). CSS avoids all the problems of HTML formatting, while saving time and money too. Using CSS lets you strip the HTML code down to its essential content and structure and then apply the formatting separately, so you can more easily tailor the webpage to specific applications.

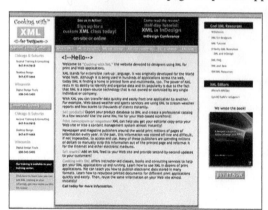 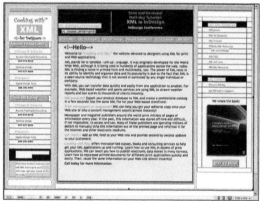

By adding **cell padding** and **margins** to the table structure in Dreamweaver (left), you can see how this webpage relies on tables and images to produce the final design (right).

Cell Padding

The space around the inside of a rectangular or box area.

Margins

The space around the outside boundary of a rectangular or box area.

HTML vs. CSS Formatting

When comparing HTML-based formatting to CSS-based formatting, it's easy to see how CSS produces vast efficiencies in time and effort. In the following exercise, you'll explore the power and **efficacy** of CSS by editing two webpages, one formatted by HTML and the other by CSS.

1 Launch Dreamweaver, if it's not currently running.

2 As instructed by your teacher, define a new site for the Chapter04/DataFiles folder.

3 Choose File > Open.

4 Open **html_form.html** from the Chapter04/dataFiles folder as instructed by your teacher.

5 Click the Split view button. If necessary, choose View > Split Vertically to split Code and Live view windows vertically, side by side.

Each element of the content is formatted individually using the deprecated `<font>` tag. Note the attribute `color="blue"` in each `<h1>` and `<p>` element.

6 Replace the word `"blue"` with `"green"` in each line in which it appears. If necessary, click in the Live view window to update the display.

The text displays in green now in each line where you changed the color value. As you can see, formatting using the **obsolete** `<font>` tag is not only slow but prone to error too. Make a mistake, like typing greeen or geen, and the browser will ignore the color formatting entirely.

7 Open **css_form.html** from the Chapter04/DataFiles folder as instructed by your teacher.

8 If it's not currently selected, click the Split view button.

Efficacy
The ability to create a desired effect or result.

Note: Dreamweaver usually defaults to Live view when you open or create a new page. If not, you may select it from the Document toolbar using the Live/Design drop-down menu.

Deprecated
Means that the tag has been removed from future support in HTML but may still be honored by current browsers and HTML readers.

Note: HTML will ignore any code that it does not understand. It skips any code it does not understand and moves to the next line of code.

Obsolete
No longer relevant or current.

The content of the file is identical to the previous document, except that it's formatted using CSS. The code that formats the HTML elements appears in the <head> section of this file. Note that the code contains only two color:blue; attributes.

9   In the code h1 { color: blue; } select the word blue and type green to replace it. If necessary, click in the Live view window to update the display.

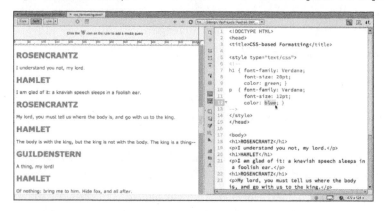

Productivity Enhancements

Techniques or skills the increase the productivity and/or speed to complete a task.

In Live view, all the heading elements display in green. The paragraph elements remain blue.

10 Select the word blue in the code p { color: blue; } and type green to replace it. Click in the Live view window to update the display.

In Live view, all the paragraph elements have changed to green.

In this exercise, CSS accomplished the color change with two simple edits, whereas the HTML <font> tag required you to edit every line. Are you beginning to understand why the W3C deprecated the <font> tag and developed cascading style sheets? This exercise highlights just a small sampling of the formatting power and **productivity enhancements** offered by CSS that can't be matched by HTML alone.

Note: You might be wondering if you are limited to just basic colors, like green, red, blue. There is an entire hexadecimal system for representing millions of colors that you can use instead of the basic color names.

HTML Defaults

Since the very beginning, HTML tags came right out of the box with one or more default formats, characteristics, or behaviors. So even if you did nothing, much of your text would already be formatted in a certain way in most browsers. One of the essential tasks in mastering CSS is learning and understanding these defaults. Let's take a look.

Note: The Code and Live view windows can be swapped top to bottom, left to right by selecting the option under the View menu. See Chapter 2, "Customizing Your Workspace," for more information.

1   Open **html_defaults.html** from the Chapter04/DataFiles folder as instructed by your teacher. If necessary, select Live view to preview the contents of the file.

The file contains a range of HTML headings and text elements. Each element exhibits basic styling for traits such as size, font, and spacing, among others.

2   Switch to Split view. If necessary, choose View > Split Vertically to split Code and
    Live view windows side by side. In the Code view window, locate the <head>
    section and try to identify any code that may be formatting the HTML elements.

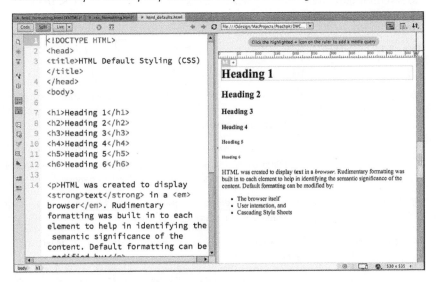

A quick look will tell you that there is no **overt styling information** in the file, yet
the text still displays different kinds of formatting. So where does the formatting
come from? And more importantly, what are the settings being used?

The answer is: It depends. In the past, HTML 4 elements drew characteristics
from multiple sources. The W3C, the web standards organization that establishes
Internet specifications and protocols, created a default style sheet. You can find this
document at www.w3.org/TR/CSS21/sample.html. It defines the standard formatting and behaviors of all HTML elements. This was the style sheet that all browser
vendors used to base their default rendering of HTML elements. But that was before
HTML5.

HTML5 Defaults

The last decade has seen a consistent movement on the web to separate "content"
from its "styling." At the time of this writing, the concept of "default" formatting
in HTML seems to be dead. According to specifications adopted by WC3 in 2014,
there are no default styling standards for HTML5 elements. If you look for a default
style sheet for HTML5 on w3.org, like the one noted for HTML 4, you won't find
one. There are no public moves to change this relationship, and for the time being,
browser manufacturers are still honoring and applying HTML 4 default styling to
HTML5-based webpages. Confused? Join the club.

The ramifications could be dramatic and wide-reaching. Some day, in the not too
distant future, HTML elements may not display any formatting at all by default.

Overt styling information

Visible code for styling
the HTML elements.

Note: If the current
trends continue,
the lack of an
HTML5 default style
sheet makes the
development of your
own site standards
even more important.

This doesn't seem to be an imminent danger; HTML5-based webpages continue to display the same default styling we've come to expect from the HTML 4 defaults.

To save time and give you a bit of a head start, here is a table of some of the most common defaults:

Table 3.1 Common HTML defaults

ITEM	DESCRIPTION
Background	In most browsers, the page background color is white. The background of the elements <div>, <table>, <td>, <th>, and most other tags are transparent.
Headings	Headings <h1> through <h6> are bold and align to the left. The six heading tags apply differing font size attributes, with <h1> the largest and <h6> the smallest. Sizes may vary between browsers.
Body text	Outside of a table cell, paragraphs—<p>, <li>, <dd>, <dt>—align to the left and start at the top of the page.
Table cell text	Text within table cells, <td>, aligns horizontally to the left and vertically to the center.
Table header	Text within header cells, <th>, aligns horizontally and vertically to the center (this is not standard across all browsers).
Fonts	Text color is black. Default typeface and font is specified and supplied by the browser (or by browser defaults specified by the manufacturer, which can be overridden by the user applying preference settings in the browser itself).
Margins	Spacing external to the element border/boundary is handled by margins. Many HTML elements feature some form of margin spacing. Margins are often used to insert additional space between paragraphs and to indent text, as in lists and blockquotes.
Padding	Spacing within the box border is handled by padding. According to the default HTML 4 style sheet, no elements feature default padding.

Browser Antics

The next task is to identify the browser (and its version) that is displaying the HTML. That's because browsers frequently differ (sometimes dramatically) in the way they interpret, or **render**, HTML elements and CSS formatting. Unfortunately, even different versions of the same browser can produce wide variations from identical code.

The best practice is to build and test your webpages to make sure they work properly in the browsers employed by the majority of web users—especially the browsers preferred by your own visitors. The breakdown of browser use of your own visitors can differ quite a bit from the norm. They also change over time, especially now as more and more people abandon desktop computers in favor of tablets and smartphones. In July 2014, the W3C published the following statistics identifying the most popular browsers:

Render

Generating an image for display.

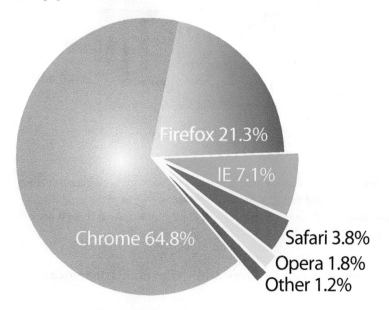

Although it's nice to know which browsers are the most popular among the general public, it's crucial that before you build and test your pages you identify the browsers your target audience uses.

Note: There are free and paid software on the Internet that allow you to view the display of a webpage in multiple browsers. This is called cross browser compatibility. You can visit http://netrenderer.com/index.php to see a free program that displays the same webpage in different versions of Internet Explorer. Search the Internet with the keywords of "cross browser compatibility" for other programs that display a webpage in multiple browsers and versions of these browsers. These programs can be a web designers best friend.

Although this chart shows the basic breakdown in the browser world, it obscures the fact that multiple versions of each browser are still being used. This is important to know because older browser versions are less likely to support the latest HTML and CSS features and effects. To make matters more complicated, these statistics show trends for the Internet overall, but the statistics for your own site may vary wildly.

CSS Box Model

Browsers normally read the HTML code, interpret its structure and formatting, and then display the webpage. CSS does its work by stepping between HTML and the browser, redefining how each element should be rendered. It imposes an imaginary box around each element and then enables you to format almost every aspect of how that box and its contents are displayed.

The box model is a programmatic construct imposed by HTML and CSS that enables you to format, or redefine, the default settings of any HTML element.

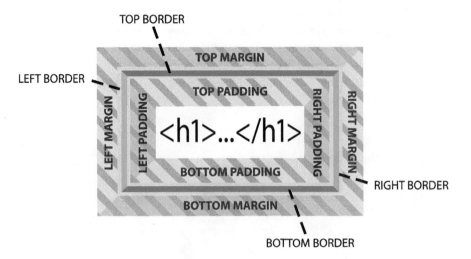

CSS permits you to specify fonts, line spacing, colors, borders, background shading and graphics, margins, and padding, among other things. Most of the time these boxes are invisible, and although CSS gives you the ability to format them it doesn't require you to do so.

1 Launch Dreamweaver, if necessary.
   Open **boxmodel.html** from the Chapter04/DataFiles folder as instructed by your teacher.

2 If necessary, click the Split view button to divide the workspace between the Code view and Live view windows.

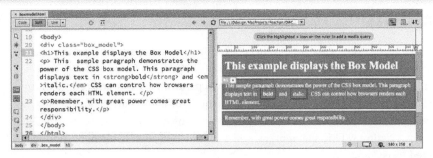

The file's sample HTML code contains a heading and two paragraphs with sample text formatted to illustrate some of the properties of the CSS box model. The text displays visible borders, background colors, margins, and padding. To see the real power of CSS, sometimes it's helpful to see what the page would look like without CSS.

3 Switch to Design view.
Choose View > Style Rendering > Display Styles to disable style rendering.

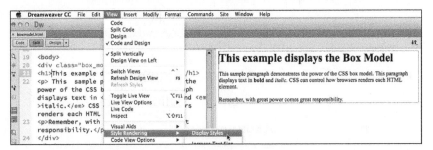

Dreamweaver now displays the page without any applied styling. A basic **tenet** in web standards today is the separation of the *content* (text, images, lists, and so on) from its *presentation* (formatting). Although the text now is not wholly unformatted, it's easy to see the power of CSS to transform HTML code. Whether formatted or not, this illustrates the importance in the *quality* of your content. Will people still be enthralled by your website if all the wonderful formatting were pulled away?

4 Choose View > Style Rendering > Display Styles to enable the CSS rendering in Dreamweaver again.

The working specifications found at www.w3.org/TR/css3-box describe how the box model is supposed to render documents in various media.

Note: The style rendering command is only available in Design view.

Tenet
A belief or doctrine or principle that is generally believed to be true.

Formatting Text

Inline style

A CSS style that is applied to an HTML element with the style attribute directly in the line of code of the HTML element.

Embedded style

A CSS style rule that is embedded in the <style> HTML element in the <head> tag of the webpage.

These sample rules demonstrate some typical constructions used in selectors and declarations. The way the selector is written determines how the styling is applied and how the rules interact with one another.

Linked style

Linked style is a stye rule that is contained in a separate stylesheet document from the webpage.

Cascade

The order and placement of rules in the CSS style sheet or on the webpage and how these rules affect the styling and formatting of HTML elements.

Inheritance

How an HTML element can be affected by one or more rules at the same time. This includes rules of the same name as well as rules that format parent elements.

You can apply CSS formatting in three ways: **inline**, **embedded** (in an internal style sheet), or **linked** (via an external style sheet). A CSS formatting instruction is known as a rule. A rule consists of two parts—a *selector* and one or more *declarations*. The selector specifies what element, or combination of elements, is to be formatted; declarations contain the styling information. CSS rules can redefine any existing HTML element, as well as define two custom element modifiers, named "class" and "id."

A rule can also combine selectors to target multiple elements at once or to target specific instances within a page where elements appear in unique ways, such as when one element is nested within another.

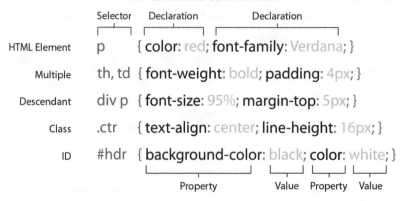

Applying a CSS rule is not a simple matter of selecting some text and applying a paragraph or character style, as in Adobe InDesign or Adobe Illustrator. CSS rules can affect single words, paragraphs of text, or combinations of text and objects. A single rule can affect an entire webpage, a single paragraph, or just a few words or letters. Basically, anything that has an HTML tag on it can be styled, and there is even an HTML tag specifically intended to style content that has no tag.

Many factors come into play in how a CSS rule performs its job. To help you better understand how it all works, the exercises in the following sections illustrate four main CSS concepts, which I'll refer to as theories: **cascade**, **inheritance**, **descendant**, and **specificity**.

Descendant

CSS rules that target format and styling to specific HTML elements based on their position relative to other elements on the webpage.

Specificity

Specificity determines what formatting to apply when two or more rules conflict by giving certain rules higher priority based on order (cascade), proximity, inheritance, and descendant relationships.

CSS Rule Syntax: Write or Wrong

CSS is a powerful adjunct to HTML. It has the power to style and format any HTML element, but the language is sensitive to even the smallest typo or syntax error. Miss a period, comma, or semicolon and you may as well have left the code out of your page entirely.

For example, take the following simple rule:

```
p { padding: 1px;
    margin: 10px; }
```

It applies both padding and margins to the paragraph <p> element.

This rule can also be written properly without spacing as:

```
p{padding:1px;margin:10px;}
```

The spaces and line breaks used in the first example are unnecessary, merely accommodations for the humans who may write and read the code. The browsers and other devices processing the code do not need them. But the same cannot be said of the various punctuation marks sprinkled throughout the CSS.

Use parentheses ( ) or brackets [ ] instead of braces { }, and the rule (and perhaps your entire style sheet) is useless. The same goes for the use of colons ":" and semicolons ";" in the code.

Can you catch the error in each of the following sample rules?

```
p { padding; 1px: margin; 10px: }
p { padding: 1px; margin: 10px; ]
p { padding 1px, margin 10px, }
```

Similar problems can arise in the construction of compound selectors too. For example, putting a space in the wrong place can change the meaning of a selector entirely.

The rule `article.content { color: #F00 }` formats the <article> element and all its children in this code structure:

```
<article class="content"><p>…</p></article>
```

On the other hand, the rule `article .content { color: #F00 }` would ignore the previous HTML structure altogether, and format only the <p> element in the following code:

```
<article class="content"><p class="content">…</p></article>
```

A tiny error can have dramatic and far-reaching repercussions. To keep their CSS and HTML functioning properly, good web designers keep their eyes peeled for any little error, misplaced space, or punctuation mark. As you work through the following exercises, keep a careful eye on all the code for any similar errors. As mentioned in the "Getting Started" section, some instructions in this book may omit an expected period or other punctuation in a sentence when including it might cause confusion or possible errors.

Cascade Theory

The cascade theory describes how the order and placement of rules in the style sheet or on the page affects the application of styling. In other words, if two rules conflict, which one wins out? Let's take a look at how cascade influences CSS formatting.

1 Open the **css_basics.html** file from the Chapter04/DataFiles folder as instructed by your teacher. Then switch to the Split view if necessary.

The file contains a complete HTML page with various elements, headings, paragraphs, lists, and links that are currently formatted only by default HTML styling.

Tip: Dreamweaver CC (2015.1 release) will open most files in Live view by default. In the following exercises be aware that certain commands will only function in Design view. Be prepared to switch between Live and Design view as necessary.

2 Save the file as **mycss_basics_xx.html** in the site root folder as instructed by your teacher.

Dreamweaver creates a copy of the file using the new name and displays two tabs at the top of the document window. Since the original file is still open it could cause confusion during the following exercises. Let's close the original file.

3 Select the document tab for the **css_basics.html** file. Choose File > Close.

The **mycss_basics.html** file should be the only one open.

4 Click the Split view button, if necessary, and observe the <head> section in the Code view window for any CSS rules.

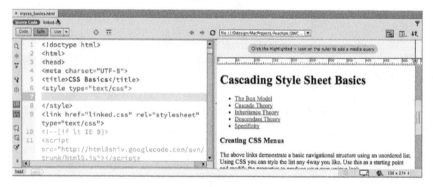

Note that the code contains a <style> section but no CSS rules.

5 Insert the cursor between the <style> and </style> tags.

6 Type h1 { color:gray; } and, if necessary, click in the Live view window to refresh the display.

Note: As you type the rule markup, Dreamweaver provides code hints as it did with the HTML code in Chapter 3. Feel free to use these hints to speed up your typing, or simply ignore them and continue typing.

The h1 headings throughout the page now display in gray. The rest of the text still displays the default formatting. Congratulations, you wrote your first CSS rule.

7   In Code view, insert the insertion point at the end of the rule created in step 6. Press Enter/Return to create a new line.

8   Type `h1 { color:red; }` and click in the Live view window, if necessary, to refresh the display.

```
 4    <meta charset="UTF-8">
 5    <title>CSS Basics</title>
 6    <style type="text/css">
 7    h1 { color:gray; }
 8    h1 { color:red; }
 9    </style>
10    <link href="linked.css" rel="stylesheet"
```

Cascading Style Sheet Basics

- The Box Model
- Cascade Theory
- Inheritance Theory
- Descendant Theory
- Specificity

The h1 headings now display in red. The styling of the new rule supersedes the formatting applied by the first. It's important to understand that the two rules are identical except that they apply different colors: red or gray. Both rules want to format the same elements, but only one will be honored.

It's clear the second rule won, but why? In this case, the second rule is the last one declared, making it the *closest* one to the actual content. Whether intentional or not, a style applied by one rule may be overridden by declarations in a subsequent rule.

9   Select the rule `h1 { color: gray; }`

10 Choose Edit > Cut.

11 Insert the insertion point at the end of the rule `h1 { color: red; }` and press Enter/Return to insert a new line.

12 Choose Edit > Paste or press Ctrl+V/Cmd+V.

The rule applying the gray color now appears last. You have switched the order of the rules.

13 If necessary, click in the Live view window to refresh the preview display.

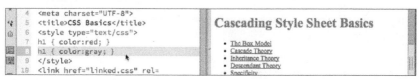

```
 4    <meta charset="UTF-8">
 5    <title>CSS Basics</title>
 6    <style type="text/css">
 7    h1 { color:red; }
 8    h1 { color:gray; }
 9    </style>
10    <link href="linked.css" rel=
```

Cascading Style Sheet Basics

- The Box Model
- Cascade Theory
- Inheritance Theory
- Descendant Theory
- Specificity

The h1 headings display in gray again. *Cascade* applies to styles whether the rules are embedded in the webpage or located in a separate external, linked style sheet.

14 Select **linked.css** in the Related Files interface.

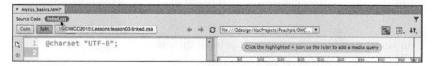

When you select the name of referenced file, the contents of that file appear in the Code view window. If the file is stored on a local hard drive, Dreamweaver allows you to edit the contents without actually opening the file itself.

15 Insert the insertion point in line 2. Type `h1 { color:orange; }` and press Ctrl+S/Cmd+S to save the file. Click in the Design view window to refresh the display.

The h1 headings now display in orange.

16 Select Source Code in the Related Files interface. Locate the `<link>` reference for **linked.css** in the `<head>` section.

The `<link>` element appears after the `<style>` element. Based strictly on cascade, this means that any rule that appears in the linked file will supersede duplicate rules in the embedded sheet.

17 Click the line number for the external CSS `<link>` reference to select the entire reference. Drag the entire `<link>` reference above the `<style>` element. Click in the Live view window to refresh the display.

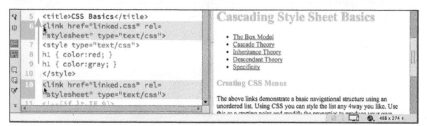

The headings revert to gray.

18 Select File > Save All.

As you can clearly see, the order and *proximity* of the rules within the markup are powerful factors in how CSS is applied. When you try to determine which

CSS rule will be honored and which formatting will be applied, browsers typically honor the following order of hierarchy, with number 4 being the most powerful:

1. Browser defaults.

2. External or embedded style sheets. If both are present, the one declared last **supersedes** the earlier entry in conflicts.

3. Inline styles (within the HTML element itself).

4. Styles with the value attribute `!important` applied.

Note: `!important` is an attribute you can append to any CSS value to make it supersede values set by other equivalent rules. It can trump cascade, inheritance, and sometimes even more specific rules.

Supersede
Take the place of or come before.

Inheritance Theory

The inheritance theory describes how an element can be affected by one or more rules at the same time. Inheritance can affect rules of the same name as well as rules that format parent elements—ones that contain other elements. Let's take a look at how inheritance influences CSS formatting.

1 If necessary, open the **mycss_basics_xx.html** file from the Chapter04/DataFiles folder as instructed by your teacher. In Split view, observe the HTML code.

The webpage contains headings, paragraphs, lists, and HTML5 semantic elements formatted by HTML defaults, as well as CSS rules created in the previous exercise.

2 Insert the insertion point after the rule h1 { `color: gray;` } in the embedded style sheet. Press Enter/Return to insert a new line.

3 Type h1 { `font-family:Arial;` } and click in the Live view window to refresh the display.

```
6   <link href="linked.css" rel=
    "stylesheet" type="text/css">
7   <style type="text/css">
8   h1 { color:red; }
9   h1 { color:gray; }
10  h1 { font-family:Arial; }
11  </style>
```

Cascading Style Sheet Basics

- The Box Model
- Cascade Theory
- Inheritance Theory
- Descendant Theory
- Specificity

The h1 elements appear in Arial and gray. The other content remains formatted by default styling.

Now there are four CSS rules that format <h1> elements. Can you tell, by looking at the Live view window, which of the rules is formatting the <h1> text? If you said *two* of them, you're the winner.

At first glance, you may think that the rules formatting <h1> elements are separate from each other. And technically, that's true. But if you look closer, you'll see that the new rule doesn't contradict the others. It's not resetting the color attribute as you did in the previous exercise; it's declaring a new, additional attribute. In other words, since both rules do something different, both will be honored, or inherited, by the h1 element. All <h1> elements will be formatted as gray *and* Arial.

Far from being a mistake or an unintended consequence, the ability to build rich and elaborate formatting using multiple rules is one of the most powerful and complex aspects of cascading style sheets.

4   Insert the insertion point after the last h1 rule. Insert a new line in the code.

5   Type h2 { font-family:Arial; color:gray; } and click in the Live view window to refresh the display.

The h2 element appears in Arial and gray; it originally displayed in a serif font in black.

6   After the h2 rule, type the following code:

```
h3 { font-family:Arial; color:gray; }
p { font-family:Arial; color:gray; }
li { font-family:Arial; color:gray; }
```

```
"stylesheet" type="text/css">
 7   <style type="text/css">
 8   h1 { color:red; }
 9   h1 { color:gray; }
10   h1 { font-family:Arial; }
11   h2 { font-family:Arial; color:gray; }
12   h3 { font-family:Arial; color:gray; }
13   p { font-family:Arial; color:gray; }
14   li { font-family:Arial; color:gray; }
15   </style>
16   <!--[if lt IE 9]>
```

A CSS Primer

Cascading Style Sheets were actually invented a long time ago when HTML was in its infancy. But it was not well understood and other methods of formatting web content had already been popularized and were dominating the market. It took many years and several popular books to get CSS to be recognized as a superior method for formatting webpages.

To fully understand how CSS works, there are several concepts that you have to learn and practice until they become second nature.

The Box Model

7   If necessary, refresh the Live view window display by clicking in it or clicking the Refresh button in the Properties panel.

All the elements now display the same styling, but it took six rules to format the entire page.

Although CSS styling is far more efficient than the obsolete HTML-based method, inheritance can help you optimize your styling chores even more. For example, all the rules include the statement { font-family:Arial; color:gray; }. Redundant code like this should be avoided whenever possible. It adds to the amount of code in each webpage as well as to the time it takes to download and process it. By using inheritance, sometimes you can create the same effect with a single rule. One way to make your styling more efficient is to apply formatting to a *parent* element instead of to the elements themselves.

8   Create a new line in the <style> section and type the following code:

```
article { font-family: Arial; color: gray; }
```

If you look through the code, you will see that the <article> tag contains much, but not all, of the webpage content. Let's see what happens if we delete some of our CSS rules.

9   Select and delete the rule:
    ~~h2 { font-family: Arial; color: gray; }~~
    Refresh the Live view window display.

```
 8  h1 { color:red; }
 9  h1 { color:gray; }
10  h1 { font-family:Arial; }
11
12  h3 { font-family:Arial; color:gray; }
13  p { font-family:Arial; color:gray; }
14  li { font-family:Arial; color:gray; }
15  article { font-family: Arial; color:
    gray; }
16  </style>
17  <!--[if lt IE 9]>
18  <script
```

The Box Model

The first concept concerns what has come to be known as "the box model". Browsers reads HTML code, interpret its structure and formatting, and then display the webpage. CSS does its work by stepping between HTML and the browser, redefining how each element should be rendered. It imposes an imaginary box around each element and then enables you to format almost every aspect of how that box and its contents are displayed.

TOP BORDER

TOP MARGIN

LEFT BORDER

TOP PADDING

488 x 274

The h2 elements appearing within the <article> element remain formatted as gray Arial. The other h2 element down the page and outside the <article> now appears in HTML default styling.

10 Select and delete all h1 rules. Don't forget the one in the **linked.css** file. Refresh the Live view display.

    The h1 elements contained within the <article> element continue to be styled. Those outside the <article> element have also reverted to the HTML defaults. Since the rule targets only the <article> element, only the elements contained within it are styled.

11 Select and delete the rules formatting h3, p, and li.
    Refresh the Live view display.

```
 7  <style type="text/css">
 8
 9
10
11
12
13
14  |
15  article { font-family: Arial; color: gray; }
16  </style>
17  <!--[if lt IE 9]>
18  <script
```

Block elements by default:

- Occupy the full width of the screen or their parent element, unless an alternative width is specified.
- Stack on top of other block elements, regardless of their width.
- Dimensions are calculated by adding up width, height, padding, borders and margins.
- Will expand vertically to the height of its content, plus any padding.
- Include div, h1-h6, p, li, among others.

Inline elements by default:

As in step 10, any content contained in the <article> tag remains formatted, while content elsewhere has reverted.

This is the way inheritance works. You could simply recreate the rules to format the other content, but there's a simpler alternative. Instead of adding additional CSS rules, can you figure out a way to use inheritance to format all the content on the page the same way? A hint: Look carefully at the entire structure of the webpage.

Did you think about using the <body> element? If so, you win again. The <body> element contains all the visible content on the webpage and therefore is the parent of all of it.

Tip: In this particular page, you could also use the <div> element to achieve the same result. But since <div> is a frequently used element, it might pose unpredictable conflicts in the future. Since webpages have only one <body> element, it is definitely the preferred target.

Note: Dreamweaver frequently edits externally linked files. Use Save All whenever changes on your page may affect multiple files in your site.

12 Change the rule selector from `article` to `body` and delete any blank lines. Choose File > Save All. Refresh the Live view display, if necessary.

```
 6   <link href="linked.css" rel="stylesheet"
     type="text/css">
 7   <style type="text/css">
 8   body { font-family: Arial; color: gray; }
 9   </style>
10   <!--[if lt IE 9]>
```

Block elements by default:

- Occupy the full width of the screen or their parent element, unless an alternative width is specified.
- Stack on top of other block elements, regardless of their width.
- Dimensions are calculated by adding up width,

Once again, all the text displays in gray Arial. By using inheritance, only one rule is needed to format all the content instead of six. You'll find that the <body> element is a popular target for setting various default styles.

Descendant Theory

Inheritance provides a means to apply styling to multiple elements at once, but CSS also provides the means to target styling to specific elements.

The descendant theory describes how formatting can target particular elements based on their position relative to others. This technique involves the creation of a selector name that identifies a specific element, or elements, by combining multiple tags, as well as id and class attributes. Let's take a look at how descendant selectors influence CSS formatting.

1 If necessary, open the **mycss_basics_xx.html** file from the Chapter04/DataFiles folder as instructed by your teacher. In Split view, observe the structure of the HTML content.

The page contains headings and paragraphs in various HTML5 structural elements, such as `article`, `section`, and `aside`. The rule body `{font-family:Arial; color: gray; }` applies a default font and color to the entire page. In this exercise, you will learn how to create descendant CSS rules to target styling to specific elements in context.

2 In Code view, insert the insertion point at the end of the body rule. Press Enter/ Return to insert a new line.

Note: Step 3 assumes you have Garamond installed on your computer. If it is not, select another serif style font, like Times.

3 Type `p { font-family:Garamond; }` and refresh the Live view display.

```
     type="text/css">
 7   <style type="text/css">
 8   body { font-family: Arial; color: gray; }
 9   p { font-family:Garamond; }
10   </style>
11   <!--[if lt IE 9]>
```

Cascade Theory

The cascade theory describes how the order and placement of rules in the style sheet or on the page affects the application of styling. In other words, if two rules conflict, which one wins out? The basic concept is that the rule closest to the element

All p elements on the page display in Garamond. The rest of the page continues to be formatted as before.

By creating a selector using the p tag, the font formatting has been overridden for all p elements no matter where they appear. You may be thinking that since the p rule appears *after* the body rule, this type of styling simply relates to the cascade order. Let's try an experiment to see if that's true.

4 Click the line number for the p rule.

Drag the p rule above the body rule.

Refresh the Live view display.

```
      type="text/css">
  7   <style type="text/css">
  8   p { font-family:Garamond; }
  9   body { font-family: Arial; color: gray; }
 10   </style>
 11   <!--[if lt IE 9]>
```

Cascade Theory

The cascade theory describes how the order and placement of rules in the style sheet or on the page affects the application of styling. In other words, if two rules conflict, which one wins out? The basic concept is that the rule closest to the element

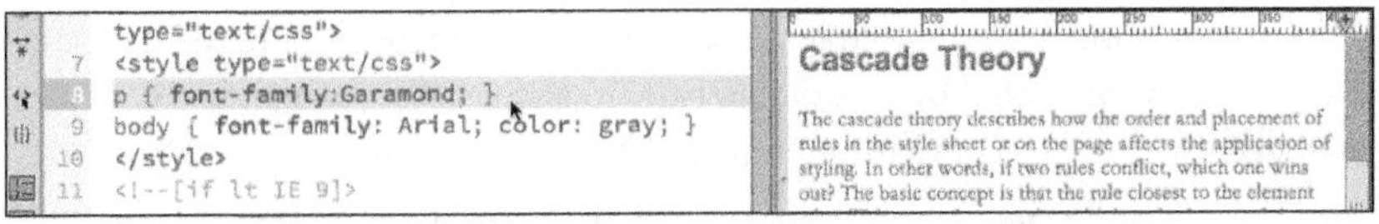

The p rule now appears above the body rule, but the styling did not change.

If the styling of p elements were determined simply by cascade, you would expect the headings to revert to gray Arial. Yet here, the styling is unaffected by changing the order of the rules. Instead, by using a more specific tag name in the selector, the new p rule becomes more powerful than the generic body rule. By properly combining two or more tags in the selector, you can craft the CSS styling on the page in even more sophisticated ways.

Note: We will examine the role of specificity later in this chapter.

5 Create a new line after the p rule.

On the new line, type:

```
article p { font-size:120%; color:darkblue; }
```

By adding a p tag immediately after `article` in the selector, you are telling the browser to format only p elements that are children, or *descendants*, of `article` elements. Remember, a *child* element is one contained or nested within another element.

6 If necessary, refresh the Live view display.

```
      ="text/css">
  7   <style type="text/css">
  8   p { font-family:Garamond; }
  9   article p { font-size:120%; color:darkblue; }
 10   body { font-family: Arial; color: gray; }
 11   </style>
 12   <!--[if lt IE 9]>
 13   <script
      src="http://html5shiv.googlecode.com/svn/trun
      k/html5.js"></script>
```

A CSS Primer

Cascading Style Sheets were actually invented a long time ago when HTML was in its infancy. But it was not well understood and other methods of formatting web content had already been popularized and were dominating the market. It took many years and several popular books to get CSS to be recognized as a superior method for formatting webpages.

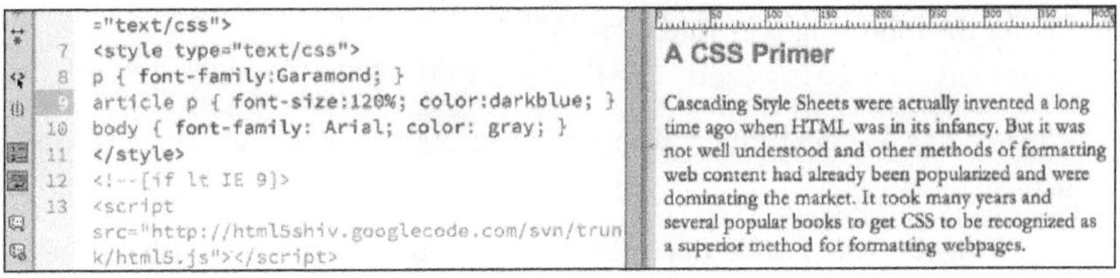

All paragraphs appearing within the `<article>` element now display in dark blue, 120 percent larger than the other paragraph text on the page.

7 Choose File > Save All.

Although it may be hard to understand at this moment, the styling in other rules—both body and p—are still being inherited by the newly formatted paragraphs. But wherever two or more rules conflict, a descendant selector will win over any less specific styling.

CSS class and ID attribute

Both are a type of CSS selector and they can be applied to any individual HTML element. The class selector is represented with a period prior to the selector name - .redBold, whereas the ID is represented with a # prior to the selector name - #redBold.

Using Classes and Ids

So far, you've learned that you can create CSS rules that format specific HTML elements and ones that can target specific HTML element structures or relationships. In some instances, you may want to apply unique formatting to an element that is already formatted by an existing rule. In such cases, you can use **CSS classes or id attributes** to target that element.

In **mycss_basic_xx.html**, all h1 elements are formatted identically regardless of where they appear in the layout. In the following exercise, you'll use classes and ids to differentiate the styling among the headings.

1 Insert a new line after the rule `article p`.
   Type `h1 { font-family:Tahoma; color:teal; }` and refresh the display.

```
    ="text/css">
 7  <style type="text/css">
 8  p { font-family:Garamond; }
 9  article p { font-size:120%; color:darkblue; }
10  h1 { font-family:Tahoma; color:teal; }
11  body { font-family: Arial; color: gray; }
12  </style>
13  <!--[if lt IE 9]>
14  <script
    src="http://html5shiv.googlecode.com/svn/trun
```

Cascading Style Sheet Basics

- The Box Model
- Cascade Theory
- Inheritance Theory
- Descendant Theory
- Specificity

All h1 headings now display in the color teal and the font Tahoma.

Although it's tagged identically to the other h1 headings, "A CSS Primer" is the main heading in the `<article>` element. To make it stand out from the other headings, you can use the class attribute assigned to its parent to target it for special formatting.

2 Create the following new rule:
   `.content h1 { color:red; font-size:300%; }`

The heading "A CSS Primer" displays in red, 300 percent larger than the body text.

In CSS syntax, the period (.) refers to a *class* attribute, and the hash (#) means *id*. By adding `.content` to the selector, you have targeted the styling only to h1 elements in `<article class="content">`.

In the same way, you can assign custom styling to the subheadings (h2). You can use the id attributes of each `<section>`.

3 Create the following rules:

   `#box_model h2 { color:orange; }`
   `#cascade h2 { color:purple; }`
   `#inheritance h2 { color:darkred; }`
   `#descendant h2 { color:navy; }`
   `#specificity h2 { color:olive; }`

4 To understand these new CSS rules better and how they work, you need to look at the names of the various elements in the HTML Document. Click your insertion point in the Cascade Theory heading in the HTML document and look at the tag selector. It reflects the flow of HTML elements down to the ID selector #cascade which is h2.

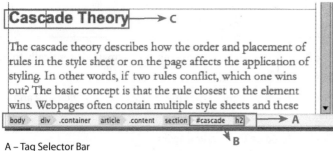

A – Tag Selector Bar
B – ID Name assigned to heading
C – Heading with Insertion point

5 Repeat step 4 for the headings: Inheritance Theory, Descendent Theory, Specificity. Each of these headings HTML code and elements match the CSS style rule that you created in Step 3.

6 Choose File > Save All.

If necessary, refresh the display.

All the h2 headings now display unique colors.

What's important to understand here is that no formatting or additional attributes have been added to any of the headings themselves. They are being formatted based solely on their position within the structure of the code.

Understanding Descendant Selectors

CSS formatting can be very confusing for designers coming from the print world. Print designers are accustomed to applying styles directly to text and objects, one at a time. In some cases, styles can be based on one another, but this relationship is intentional. In print-based styling, it's impossible for one paragraph or character style to affect another unintentionally. On the other hand, in CSS, the chance of one element's formatting overlapping or influencing another's happens all the time.

It may be helpful to think of it as if the elements were formatting themselves. When you use CSS properly, the formatting is not intrinsic to the element but to the entire page and to the way the code is structured. The following exercise will help you understand this concept.

1 In Code view, click the line number for the "The Box Model" heading (approximately line 50).

2 Choose Edit > Copy or press Ctrl+C/Cmd+C.

3 Insert the insertion point at the end of the h2 element "Cascade Theory" (approximately line 81) and create a new line.

4 Choose Edit > Paste or press Ctrl+V/Cmd+V and then refresh the display.

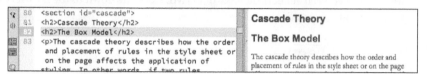

```
80  <section id="cascade">
81  <h2>Cascade Theory</h2>
82  <h2>The Box Model</h2>
83  <p>The cascade theory describes how the order
    and placement of rules in the style sheet or
    on the page affects the application of
    styling  In other words  if two rules
```

Cascade Theory

The Box Model

The cascade theory describes how the order and
placement of rules in the style sheet or on the page

The heading "The Box Model" appears following and formatted identically to the heading "Cascade Theory."

5 Insert the insertion point at the end of the "Inheritance Theory" heading and create a new line.

6 Press Ctrl+V/Cmd+V to paste the heading again.

The heading matches the styling of the "Inheritance Theory" heading.

As you can see, the formatting of the heading in the original instance does not travel with the text. That's the point of separating content from presentation—you can insert the content anywhere and it will adopt the formatting native to that position. It even works in reverse.

7 In Code view, select and copy the "Inheritance Theory" heading.

8 Insert the insertion point after the original "The Box Model" heading and press Ctrl+V/Cmd+V.

The heading appears and adopts the same styling as "The Box Model."

Once again, the pasted text matches the formatting applied to the other h2 element within the <article>, ignoring its original styling altogether. Now that you've seen how descendant theory works there's no need for the extra headings.

9 Choose File > Revert. Click Yes to revert the file to the previously saved version.

The ability to separate the content from its presentation is an important concept in modern web design. It allows you great freedom in moving content from page to page and structure to structure without worrying about the effects of residual or latent formatting. Since the formatting doesn't reside with the element itself, the content is free to adapt instantly to its new surroundings.

Specificity Theory

Bane

The nemesis or dread.

Conflicts between two or more rules are the **bane** of most web designers' existence and can waste hours of time in troubleshooting CSS formatting errors. In the past, designers would have to spend hours manually scanning style sheets and rules one by one trying to track down the source of styling errors.

Specificity describes how browsers determine what formatting to apply when two or more rules conflict. Some refer to this as *weight*—giving certain rules higher priority based on order (cascade), proximity, inheritance, and descendant relationships. One way to make it easier to see a selector's weight is by giving numeric values to each component of its name. For example, each HTML tag gets 1 point, each class gets 10 points, each id gets 100 points, and inline style attributes get 1000 points. By adding up the component values of one selector, its specificity can be calculated and compared to another. The higher specific weight wins.

Note: Don't confuse CSS weight with code weight.

As you have learned in this chapter, CSS rules often don't work alone. They may style more than one HTML element at a time and may overlap or inherit styling from one another. Each of the theories described so far has a role to play in how CSS styling is applied through your webpage and across your site. When the style sheet is loaded, the browser will use the following hierarchy—with number 4 being the most powerful—to determine how the styles are applied, especially when rules conflict:

1. Cascade

2. Inheritance

3. Descendant structure

4. Specificity

Of course, knowing this hierarchy doesn't help much when you are faced with a CSS conflict on a page with dozens or perhaps hundreds of rules and multiple style sheets. Luckily, Dreamweaver has several tools that can help you in this endeavor. The first one we'll look at is named Code Navigator.

Calculating Specificity

Can you do the math? Look at the following list of selectors and see how they add up. Now look through the list of rules you created in the previous exercises in **mycss_basics.html.** Can you determine the weight of each of those selectors and figure out which rule is more specific on sight?

* (wildcard)	{}	0 + 0 + 0 + 0 =	0 points
h1	{}	0 + 0 + 0 + 1 =	1 point
ul li	{}	0 + 0 + 0 + 2 =	2 points
.class	{}	0 + 0 + 10 + 0 =	10 points
.class h1	{}	0 + 0 + 10 + 1 =	11 points
a:hover	{}	0 + 0 + 10 + 1 =	11 points
#id	{}	0 + 100 + 0 + 0 =	100 points
#id.class	{}	0 + 100 + 10 + 0 =	110 points
#id.classh1	{}	0 + 100 + 10 + 1 =	111 points
`style=" "`	{}	1000 + 0 + 0 + 0 =	1000 points

Code Navigator

Code Navigator is an editing tool within Dreamweaver that allows you to instantly inspect an HTML element and assess its CSS-based formatting. When activated, it displays all the embedded and externally linked CSS rules that have some role in formatting a selected element, and it lists them in the order of their cascade application and specificity. Code Navigator works in all Dreamweaver-based document views.

1 If necessary, open the **mycss_basics_xx.html** file from the Chapter04/DataFiles folder as instructed by your teacher. In Split view, observe the CSS code and the structure of the HTML content. Then, note the appearance of the text in the Live view window.

The page contains headings, paragraphs, and lists in various HTML5 structural elements, such as `article`, `section`, and `aside`, styled by CSS rules you created in the previous exercises.

2 In Live view, insert the insertion point in the "A CSS Primer" heading.

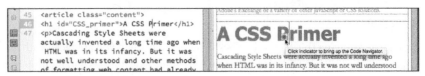

When Code Navigator is enabled, after a moment, an icon that looks like a ship's wheel appears. This icon provides access to Code Navigator.

3 Click the Code Navigator icon. If the Code Navigator does not appear automatically, right-click the heading and choose Code Navigator from the context menu or press Ctrl+Alt+N(PC)/Cmd+Opt+N(Mac).

A small window appears, displaying a list of three CSS rules that apply to this heading.

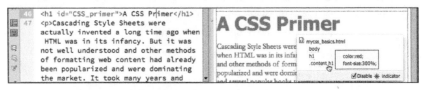

If you position the insertion point over each rule in turn, Dreamweaver displays any properties formatted by the rule and their values. The rule with the highest specificity (most powerful) is at the bottom of the list.

Unfortunately, Code Navigator doesn't show styling applied via inline styles, so you'll have to check for these types of properties separately and calculate the effect of inline styles in your head. Otherwise, the sequence of rules in the list indicates both their cascade order and their specificity.

When rules conflict, rules farther down in the list override rules that are higher up. Remember that elements may inherit styling from one or more rules, and default styling—that is not overridden—may still play a role in the final presentation. Unfortunately, Code Navigator doesn't display what, if any, default styling characteristics may still be in effect.

The `.content h1` rule appears at the bottom of the Code Navigator window, indicating that its specifications are the most powerful ones styling this element. But many factors can influence which of the rules may win. Sometimes the specificity of two rules is identical; then, it's simply the order (cascade) in which rules are declared in the style sheet that determines which one is actually applied.

As you saw earlier, changing the order of rules can often affect how the rules work. There's a simple exercise you can perform to determine whether a rule is winning because of cascade or specificity.

Note: Code Navigator doesn't display inline CSS rules. Since most CSS styling is not applied this way, it's not much of a limitation, but you should still be aware of this blind spot as you work with Code Navigator.

4   In the Code view window, click the line number for the `.content h1` rule.

5   Drag the rule to the top of the embedded style sheet.

6   Click in the Live view window to refresh the display.

The styling did not change.

7   Insert the insertion point into the text of the `<h1>` element "A CSS Primer" and activate Code Navigator.

Although the rule was moved to the top of the style sheet, the order of the rules in Code Navigator did not change. The `.content h1` selector has a specificity higher than either the body or h1 selectors. In this instance, it would win no matter where it was placed in the code. But specificity can change by simply modifying the selector.

8   Select and delete the ~~.content~~ class notation from the `.content h1` selector.

9   Click in the Live view window to refresh the display.

Did you notice how the styling changed? The "A CSS Primer" heading reverted to the color teal, and the other h1 headings scaled to 300 percent. Do you know why this happened?

10 Insert the insertion point in the "A CSS Primer" heading and activate Code Navigator.

By removing the class notation from its selector, it now has equal value to the other h1 rule, but since it is the first one declared, it loses precedence by virtue of its cascade position.

11 Using Code Navigator, examine and compare the rules applied to the headings "A CSS Primer" and "Creating CSS Menus."

The Code Navigator shows the same rules applied to both.

By removing the `.content` class from the selector, the rule no longer targets only h1 headings in the `<article class="content">` element; it's now styling all h1 elements on the page.

12 Choose Edit > Undo to restore the `.content` class to the h1 selector. Refresh the Live view display.

All the headings return to their previous styling.

13 Insert the insertion point in the heading "Creating CSS Menus" and activate Code Navigator.

The heading is no longer styled by the `.content` h1 rule.

14 Choose File > Save All.

Is it starting to make more sense? Don't worry, it will—over time. Until that time, just remember that the rule appearing last in Code Navigator has the most influence on any particular element.

CSS Designer

Code Navigator was introduced in Dreamweaver CS4 and has been an invaluable aid for troubleshooting CSS formatting. Yet the latest tool in Dreamweaver's CSS arsenal is much more than a good troubleshooting tool. CSS Designer not only displays all the rules that pertain to any selected element but also allows you to create and edit CSS rules at the same time.

When you use Code Navigator, it shows you the relative importance of each rule, but you still have to access and assess the effect of all the rules to determine the final effect. Since some elements can be affected by a dozen or more rules, this can be a daunting task for even a veteran web coder. CSS Designer eliminates this pressure altogether by providing a Properties window that computes the final CSS display for you. And best of all, unlike Code Navigator, CSS Designer can even compute the effects of inline styles too.

1   If necessary, open the **mycss_basics_xx.html** file from the Chapter04/DataFiles folder as instructed by your teacher and switch to the Split view.

2   If necessary, choose Window > CSS Designer to display the panel.

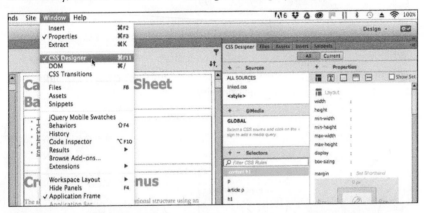

The CSS Designer panel features four windows: Sources, @Media, Selectors, and Properties. Feel free to adjust the heights and widths of the windows as needed. The panel is also responsive: It will even take advantage of the extra screen space, if you drag out the edge, by splitting into two columns.

3   Insert the insertion point in the heading "A CSS Primer."

The CSS Designer has two basic modes: *All* and *Current*. When the All mode is engaged, the panel allows you to review and edit all existing CSS rules and create new rules. In Current mode, the panel allows you to identify and edit the rules and styling already applied to a selected element.

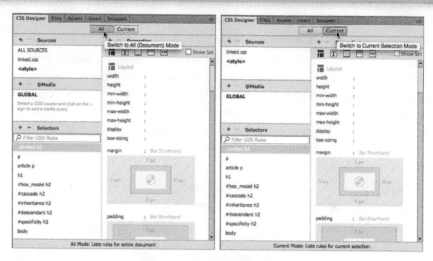

4   If necessary, click the Current button in the CSS Designer panel.

When the Current mode is active the panel displays the CSS rules that are affecting the heading. In the CSS Designer, the most powerful rules appear at the top of the Selectors window, the opposite of Code Navigator.

5   Click the rule `.content h1` in the Selectors panel.

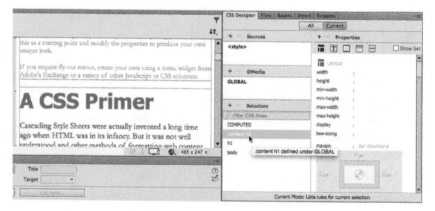

By default, the Properties window of CSS Designer displays a list of properties that you can style for this element. The list is not exhaustive, but it contains most of the properties you will need.

Showing a seemingly endless list of properties can be confusing as well as inefficient. For one thing, it makes it difficult to differentiate the properties assigned from those that aren't. Luckily, CSS Designer allows you to limit the display to only the properties currently applied to the selected element.

6   Click the Show Set option in the CSS Designer panel menu to enable it, if necessary.

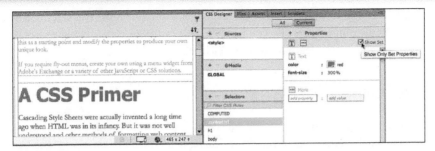

When Show Set is enabled, the Properties panel shows only the items that have been set in that rule.

7 Select each rule that appears in the Selectors window and observe the properties of each. To see the expected result of all the rules combined, select the COMPUTED option.

The COMPUTED option analyzes all the CSS rules affecting the element and generates a list of properties that should be displayed by browsers or HTML readers. By displaying a list of pertinent CSS rules and then computing how the CSS should render, the CSS Designer does Code Navigator one step better. But it doesn't stop there. Whereas Code Navigator allows you to select a rule to edit it in Code view, the CSS Designer lets you edit the CSS properties right inside the panel itself. Best of all, CSS Designer can even compute and edit *inline* styles too.

8 Select COMPUTED in the Selectors window. In the Properties window, change the `color` property from `red` to `purple`. Press Enter/Return to complete the change.

Tip: Click to edit the text-based color name. You can also select colors by using the color picker.

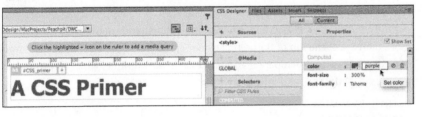

The heading displays in purple. What you may not have noticed is that the change you made was actually entered directly in the rule that contributed the styling.

9 In the Code view window, scroll to the embedded style sheet and examine the `.content h1` rule.

As you can see, the color was changed within the code and added to the proper rule.

10 Save all files.

The CSS Designer is a mixture of Code Navigator and Dreamweaver's old CSS Styles panel. In upcoming exercises, you'll get the chance to experience all aspects of the CSS Designer as you learn more about cascading style sheets.

Multiples, Classes, and Ids

By taking advantage of the cascade, inheritance, descendant, and specificity theories, you can target formatting to almost any element anywhere on a webpage. But CSS offers a few more ways to optimize and customize the formatting and increase your productivity even further.

Applying Formatting to Multiple Elements

To speed things up, CSS allows you to apply formatting to multiple elements at once by listing each in the selector, separated by commas. For example, the formatting in these rules:

```
h1 { font-family:Verdana; color:gray; }
h2 { font-family:Verdana; color:gray; }
h3 { font-family:Verdana; color:gray; }
```

can also be expressed like this:

```
h1, h2, h3 { font-family:Verdana; color:gray; }
```

CSS Shorthand

Although Dreamweaver will write most of the CSS rules and properties for you, at times you will want, or need, to write your own. All properties can be written out fully, but many can also be written using a shorthand method. Shorthand does more than make the job of the web designer easier; it reduces the total amount of code that has to be downloaded and processed. For example, when all properties of margins or padding are identical, such as:

```
margin-top:10px;
margin-right:10px;
margin-bottom:10px;
margin-left:10px;
```

the rule can be shortened to `margin:10px;`

When the top and bottom and left and right margins or padding are identical, like this:

```
margin-top:0px;
margin-right:10px;
margin-bottom:0px;
margin-left:10px;
```

it can be shortened to `margin:0px 10px;`

But even when all four properties are different, like this:

```
margin-top:20px;
margin-right:15px;
margin-bottom:10px;
margin-left:5px;
```

they can be shortened to `margin:20px 15px 10px 5px;`

In these three examples, you can see clearly how much code can be saved using shorthand. There are way too many references and shorthand techniques to cover here. To get a full description, check out www.w3.org/community/webed/wiki/CSS_shorthand_reference.

In the following exercises, I'll use common shorthand expressions wherever possible; see if you can identify them as we go.

Creating Class Attributes

Frequently, you will want to create unique formatting to apply to objects, paragraphs, phrases, words, or even individual characters appearing within a webpage. To accomplish this, CSS allows you make your own custom attributes, named class and id.

Class attributes may be applied to any number of elements on a page, whereas id attributes should appear only once per page. If you are a print designer, think of classes as being similar to a combination of Adobe InDesign's paragraph, character, table, and object styles all rolled into one. Class and id names can be a single word, an abbreviation, any combination of letters and numbers, or almost anything, but they may not contain spaces. In HTML 4, ids could not start with a number. There don't seem to be any similar restrictions in HTML5, but for backward compatibility you should probably avoid starting class and id names with numbers.

Although there's no strict rule or guideline on how to create them, classes should be more general in nature, and ids should be more specific. Everyone seems to have an opinion, but at the moment there is no absolutely right or wrong answer. However, most agree that they should be descriptive, such as `"co-address"` or `"author-bio"` as opposed to `"left-column"` or `"big-text"`. This will especially help to improve your site analytics. The more sense Google and other search engines can make of your site's structure and organization, the higher your site will rank in the search results.

To declare a CSS class selector, insert a period before the name within the style sheet, like this:

```
.content
.sidebar1
```

Then, apply the CSS class to an entire HTML element as an attribute, like this:

```
<p class="intro">Type intro text here.</p>
```

Or to individual characters or words using the <span> tag, like this:

```
<p>Here is <span class="copyright">some text</span> formatted
differently.</p>
```

Creating Id Attributes

HTML designates id as a unique attribute. Therefore, any id should be assigned to no more than one element per page. In the past, many web designers used id attributes to style or identify specific components within the page, such as the header, the footer, or specific articles. With the advent of HTML5 elements—header, footer, aside, article, and so on—the use of id and class attributes for this purpose became less necessary. But ids can still be used to identify specific text elements, images, and tables to assist you in building powerful hypertext navigation within your page and site. You will learn more about using ids this way in Chapter 12, "Working with Navigation."

To declare an id attribute in a CSS style sheet, insert a number sign, or hash mark, before the name, like this:

```
#cascade
#box_model
```

Here's how you apply the CSS id to an entire HTML element as an attribute:

```
<div id="cascade">Content goes here.</div>
<div id="box_model">Content goes here.</div>
```

Or to a portion of an element:

```
<p>Here is <span id="copyright">some text</span> formatted
differently.</p>
```

CSS3 Overview and Support

In the previous exercise, the last two properties both seemed to apply a drop shadow to the main content container. Did you notice that one used a -webkit- prefix? This notation is a temporary accommodation for certain browsers as they implement new CSS3 properties. CSS3 is relatively new to the web design arena and many of the older browsers do not support the new CSS3 rules and attributes. But by using the -webkit- prefix, you can help these older browsers understand CSS3 and how to display them in that browser. The specifications provide some amazing, and long-needed, new features for styling the modern web.

The Internet doesn't stand still for long. Technologies and standards are evolving and changing constantly. The members of the W3C have been working diligently to adapt the web to the latest realities, such as powerful mobile devices, large flat-panel displays, and HD images and video—all of which seem to get better and cheaper every day. This is the urgency that currently drove the development of HTML5 and CSS3.

Many of these new standards have not been officially defined yet and browser vendors are implementing them in varying ways. But don't worry. The latest version of Dreamweaver has been updated to take advantage of the latest changes, and it provides many new features based on these evolving standards. This includes ample support for the current mix of HTML5 elements and CSS3 formatting. As new features and capabilities are developed, you can count on Adobe to add them to the program as quickly as possible using Creative Cloud.

As you work through the chapters that follow, you will be introduced to and actually implement many of these new and exciting techniques in your own sample pages.

CSS3 Features and Effects

CSS3 has over two dozen new features. Many are ready now and have been implemented in all the modern browsers; others are still experimental and are supported less fully. Among the new features, you will find

- Rounded corners and border effects
- Box and text shadows
- Transparency and translucency
- Gradient fills
- Multicolumn text elements

You can implement all these features and more via Dreamweaver today. The program will even assist you in building vendor-specific markup when necessary. To give you a quick tour of some of the coolest features and effects brewing, I've provided a sample of CSS3 styling in a separate file.

1   Open the **css3_demo.html** file from the Chapter04/DataFiles folder as instructed by your teacher. Display the file in Split view and observe the CSS and HTML code.

Some of the new effects can't be previewed directly in Design view. You'll need to use Live view or an actual browser to get the full effect.

2 If necessary, activate Live view to preview all the CSS3 effects.

The file contains a hodgepodge of features and effects that may surprise and even delight you—but don't get too excited. Although many of these features are already supported in Dreamweaver and will work fine in modern browsers, there's still a lot of older hardware and software out there that can turn your dream site into a nightmare. And there's at least one additional twist.

Some of the new CSS3 features have not been standardized, and certain browsers may not recognize the default markup generated by Dreamweaver. In these instances, you may have to include specific vendor commands to make them work properly. Like the box shadow in the previous exercise, these commands are preceded by a vendor prefix, such as –ms–, –moz–, and –webkit–. If you look carefully in the code of the demo file, you'll be able to find examples of these within the CSS markup.

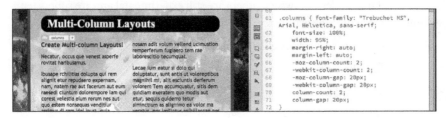

End-of-Chapter Activities

Review Questions

Directions: Choose the correct answer for each question.

1. In the early days of HTML, the default HTML stylesheet enabled browsers to render a display of what HTML elements?
   a. Headings
   b. Font size
   c. Font type
   d. Line spacing
   e. All of the above
   f. A and D only

2. It is a good idea to identify the browser of the website's target audience.
   a. True
   b. False

3. What browser is used the most today?
   a. Safari
   b. Firefox
   c. Chrome
   d. Internet Explorer

4. The box model is what?
   a. A plastic model
   b. An imaginary rectangle that is imposed around all HTML elements
   c. A CSS3 rule
   d. An HTML element

5. CSS allows you to format what?
   a. Fonts and line spacing
   b. Colors, borders and backgrounds
   c. Shading, graphics, margins and padding
   d. All of these above
   e. Just b. and c.

6. Which view is best to use for seeing the CSS formatting applied to a webpage?
   a. Live View
   b. Design View
   c. Code View
   d. Code Navigator

7. When there is a conflict between two rules, which of the following carries more weight for determining the style to use?
   a. Embedded stylesheets
   b. Linked stylessheets
   c. A selector
   d. Inline styles

8. How does the Cascade theory determine which style rule to use if there is a conflict between two style rules?
   a. Formatting is determined based on a particular element location based on other elements around it
   b. Formatting is determined based on order, proximity, inheritance, and descendant relationships of the style rules
   c. Formatting is determined based on the order and placement of rules in the style sheet or on the webpage
   d. All of the above

9. Which style rule is correctly coded?
   a. h1 {margin: 10px, color:blue; font-family:Palatino;}
   b. h1 {margin: 10px; color:blue; font-family:Palatino;}
   c. h1 [margin:10px; color:blue; font-family:Palatino;]
   d. h1 {margin; 10px; color:blue; font-family:Palatino;}

10. All browsers render HTML and CSS the same.
    a. True
    b. False

Essay Questions

Directions: Respond to each question by writing your answers in complete sentences and paragraphs. Be thorough in your answers.

1. CSS and CSS3 are new trends in web development, how have they affected how web pages are developed?

2. Should you use HTML-based formatting? Explain your answer.

3. What does CSS impose on each HTML element?

4. True or False - If you do nothing, HTML elements will feature no formatting or structure? Explain your answer.

5. What four "theories" affect the application of CSS formatting?

6. What is the difference between block and inline elements?

7. True or false: CSS3 features are all experimental, and you shouldn't use them at all.

8. Summarize some of the new features that CSS3 brings to web design.

9. What are some of the new challenges that web designers now face due to the rapidly changing technologies in our world today?

10. How can you apply multiple style properties to a group of HTML elements in one line of code? Please provide an example of this code.

Online Portfolio Builder – Identify Your Web Site Audience and Target Browser

You should have gathered your information for your online portfolio website from the previous Chapter Online Portfolio Builder exercises. The next step is to identify your target audience and the target browser that your audience will use the most. You need to do a little research on who will be looking at your site. Will this be colleges, businesses, art and graphic design companies?

Write an essay that identifies your target audience and why you think these people will be interested in your online portfolio. Then research their area of business and what browser you think they will use the most. Your website needs to cater to this audience and the target browser so that you can effectively communicate your talents and skills to the largest number of potential visitors of your site.

Critical Thinking Project – CSS in Practice

Work through the following exercise to apply CSS to HTML5.

1. Open css_practice.html from the Chapter 04/Datafiles as instructed by your teacher.

2. Save the file as **css_practice_xx.html** in the location your teacher indicates.

3. Click the Split view button to view both the page and the code. Scroll to the top of the Code view and confirm that this page is an HTML5 page. Click the Design view button and choose Live view.

4. Find the embedded style sheet in the <head> area of the Web page. Review the CSS style rules. Find the closing </head> tag to confirm where the <head> area ends. Find the opening <body> tag and scroll down to the bottom of the Code view and find the closing </body> tag.

5. Find line 65 in the Code view. Notice that this contains an HTML deprecated <font> tag that makes the line display in a font-family of Verdana, font-size of 3 and gray. Highlight the words "wash clothes in cold water". Look in the Live view for where these words fall in the page layout. Notice that they look the same as the other bullet points, same font, same color. Change the color gray to red by deleting the word **gray** and then type in **red** in the Code view. Click in the Live view to make it active and confirm that the first bullet point becomes red.

6. Delete the <font> depreciated tag by deleting the opening <font> tag and style properties up to the text of "Wash clothes in cold water", don't delete this text. Then delete the closing font tag at the end of this text. All you should see for line 73 in Code view is:

   <li>Wash clothes in cold water</li>

7. Again, click in the Live view to make it active and notice that CSS style rule in line 11 for the <li> tag has taken over the formating for this text – all bullets have the same format.

8. Now change the color for the <h1> tags in the CSS embedded stylesheet. Locate line 16 in the Code view and change the color attribute to blue by deleting the color **teal** and typing **blue** in the code. Click in the Live view to make it active and notice that all the <h1> heading become blue.

9. To understand the default stylesheet used by earlier versions of HTML (as well as HTML5) first look at line 11 in Code view. Notice that all <p> tags (paragraph) and <h1>, <h2>, <h3> tags (headings 1 – 3) as well as the <li> tags (line item) are formatted with a grouped CSS rule that separates each selector rule with a comma and then defines the style properties.

   To see the default HTML stylesheet apply both an <h4> and <h5> tag to the first quote on the page that displays in the left sidebar. Since there is not a style rule for either the <h4> and <h5> tag , you'll see the default stylesheet take over with the formatting for this quote. Change the code in line 75 and 76 to the following:

*"We have forgotten how to be good guests, how to walk
lightly on the earth as its other creatures do."*
Barbara Ward

10. Click in the Live view to make it active and notice that the first quote displays larger than the other quotes and the author name becomes smaller.

11. Explore the CSS box model by adding margin and padding space to the right sidebar. Find the ID style rule **#book** in line 38. Notice that this rule only has a top margin of 5 pixels applied. Click at the end of line 39 and press Enter/Return to create a new line in the code. Type the following code to apply other Box model settings for formating this book information in the page:

   margin-left: 10px;

   margin-right: 10px;

   margin-bottom: 5px;

   padding-top: 5px;

   padding-bottom: 5px;

12. Click in the Live view to make it active and notice that the book information now displays with new left and right margins as well as more padding at the top and the bottom of the information.

13. To see an example of the Cascade theory of CSS, find the two **header** selectors rules - the first is in line 12 and the second rule is in line 54. The second **header** rule formats the <header> tag on the HTML page. Highlight the second **header** rule in line 54 and cut it out by choosing Edit>Cut. Click at the beginning of line 12 to set your insertion point and press Enter/Return to create a blank line. Paste the second **header** rule in the blank line by choosing Edit>Paste. Your code should now look like this:

   header { padding:10px; border-bottom:10px solid #060; }

   header { padding:30px; border-bottom:2px solid #000; text-align:center; }

   Click in the Live view to make it active and notice that the green bottom border under the header area is now gone and there is more margin spacing both on the top and bottom of the header text. Highlight the rule that you pasted in line 12 and cut it out again. Paste it after the second header rule. Click in the Live view to see the changes. Now the header displays as it did before.

14. To see an example of the Inheritance theory of CSS, look at the properties in the opening **body** tag rule in line 8. Notice that the font-family is declared to be Arial. In the Live view, click to set your insertion point in the Green Tips heading. Examine the flow of tags in the Tag Selector. Notice that the name of this <div> tag is #tips. Review the style rules again in the Code view and notice that there is not a **#tips** selector rule controling the font in this area. Therefore, this area of the page inherits the font-family of Arial from the **body** selector rule. Lets add a new style rule to override the inherited Arial font of this area. Click at the end of the code in line 11 and press Enter/Return to create a new line of code. Then type this code into the blank line:

#tips {font-family: Times; }

Click in the Live view to see the changes. The bullets in the Tips area now are in the font-family of Times due to the new style rule for the Tips area.

15. To see an example of the Descendant theory, look at the font-family and font color declared in the opening **body** selector rule in line 8 – Arial and gray. Now look at the **p** selector rule in line 16. This rule declares the font to be Garamond and orange. Look at the far right sidebar in the Live view. The **#book** selector displays these properties – Garamond and orange. This looks like it is just the Cascade theory working but highlight the **p** selector rule in line 16 and cut it out. Click your insertion point infront of the **body** selector rule in line 8 and press Enter/Return to create a new line of code. Paste the **p** selector rule above the **body** selector rule and notice that the text in the #book div does not become Arial and gray, it stays Garamond and orange. This is because the p selector rule is more specific than the body selector rule and controls the font-family and color.

16. To understand the Specificity theory you need to use the Code Navigator and the CSS Designer. These tools help you understand which rules are more specific than the others when multiple rules are applied to an HTML element. In the Live view, click in the "CSS in Practice" heading. After a moment, an icon that looks like a ship's steering wheel appears. Click this icon to access to Code Navigator. If you do not see this icon, right-click in the heading and choose Code Naviagtor from the context menu. You'll see a window with a list of all the CSS rules applied to this heading. Then position the insertion point over each rule in the window to see the properties of each rule. The property at the bottom of the list is the most powerful and each one above it is one degree less powerful.

The CSS Designer is a bit more powerful for showing specificity. Open the CSS Designer panel if it is not already open by choosing Window>CSS Designer. If this panel is already open, click the panel tab to make it active. Click in the same "CSS in Practice" heading and look at the listing of rules. The rule at the top of the list is the most powerful and other rules below it are one degree less powerful than this top rule.

17. Save your HTML document and close it as instructed by your teacher.

WEB DESIGN BASICS

Whether you use thumbnails and wireframes,
Photoshop, or just a vivid imagination, Dreamweaver
can quickly turn your design concepts into complete,
standards-based CSS layouts.

Chapter Overview

In this chapter, you'll learn the following:

- The basics of webpage design
- How to create page thumbnails and wireframes
- How to use Photoshop to generate site image assets automatically

Developing a New Website

Before you begin any web design project for yourself or for a client, you need to answer these important questions:

- What is the purpose of the website?
- Who is your audience?
- How do they get there?
- What type of devices will be connecting to your site?
- What is the typical Internet speed of your visitors?
- Any colors or color palettes that need to be used or would be best to use?

What is the Purpose of the Website?

Will the website sell or support a product or service? Is your site for entertainment or games? Will you provide information or news? Will you need a shopping cart or database? Do you need to accept credit card payments or electronic transfers? Knowing the purpose of the website tells you what type of content you'll be developing and working with and what types of technologies you'll need to incorporate.

Who is the Audience?

Is the audience adults, children, seniors, professionals, hobbyists, men, women, everyone? Knowing *who* your audience will be is vital to the overall design and functionality of your site. A site intended for children probably needs more animation, interactivity, and bright, engaging colors. Adults will want serious content and in-depth analysis. Seniors may need larger type and other accessibility enhancements.

A good first step is to check out the competition. Is there an existing website performing the same service or selling the same product? Are they successful? You don't have to mimic others just because they're doing the same thing. Look at Google and Yahoo—they perform the same basic service, but their site designs couldn't be more different from one another.

How Do They Get Here?

This sounds like an odd question when speaking of the Internet. But just as with a brick-and-mortar business, your online customers can come to you in a variety of ways. For example, are they accessing your site on a desktop computer, laptop, tablet, or cellphone? Are they using high-speed Internet, wireless, or dial-up service? What browser are they most likely to use, and what is the size and resolution of the display? These answers will tell you a lot about what kind of experience your customers will expect. Dial-up and cellphone users may not want to see a lot of graphics or video, whereas users with large flat-panel displays and high-speed connections may demand as much bang and sizzle as you can send at them.

So where do you get this information? Some you'll have to get through painstaking research and demographic analysis. Some you'll get from educated guesses based on your own tastes and understanding of your market. But a lot of it is actually available on the Internet itself. W3Schools, for one, keeps track of tons of statistics regarding access and usage, all updated regularly:

- w3schools.com/browsers/browsers_stats.asp provides information about browser statistics.

- w3schools.com/browsers/browsers_os.asp gives the breakdown on operating systems. In 2011, they started to track the usage of mobile devices on the Internet.

- w3schools.com/browsers/browsers_display.asp lets you find out the latest information on the resolution, or size, of screens using the Internet. ,

If you are redesigning an existing site, your web-hosting service itself may provide valuable statistics on historical traffic patterns and even the visitors themselves. If you host your own site, you can incorporate third-party tools, such as **Google Analytics** and **Adobe Omniture**, into your code to do the tracking for you for free or for a small fee.

Google Analytics

Web master tool offered through Google provides web analytics, measurement, and optimization technologies.

Adobe Omniture

Web master tool from Adobe that provides web analytics, measurement, and optimization technologies.

Analytics provides comprehensive statistics on the visitors to your site. Google Analytics, pictured here, is a popular choice.

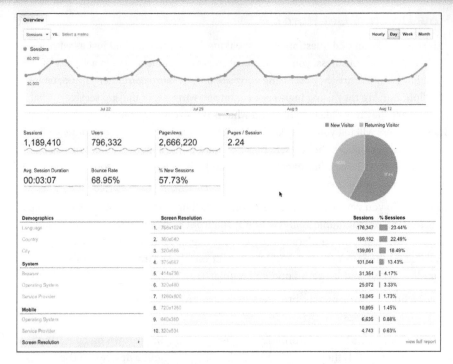

As of the fall of 2015, Windows still dominates the Internet (80 to 85 percent), with most users favoring Google Chrome (60 percent), followed by Firefox (21 percent), with various versions of Internet Explorer (7 percent) a distant third. The vast majority of browsers (99 percent) are set to a resolution higher than 1024 pixels by 768 pixels. If it weren't for the rapid growth in usage of tablets and smartphones for accessing the Internet, these statistics would be great news for most web designers and developers. But designing a website that can look good and work effectively for both flat-panel displays and cellphones is a tall order.

Responsive Web Design

Each day, more people are using cellphones and other mobile devices to access the Internet. Some people may use them to access the Internet more frequently than they use desktop computers. This presents a few nagging challenges to web designers. For one thing, cellphone screens are a fraction of the size of even the smallest flat-panel display. How do you cram a two- or three-column page design into a meager 300 to 400 pixels? Another problem is that mobile device manufacturers have dropped support for **Flash-based content** on their devices.

Until recently, web design usually required that you target an optimum size (height and width in pixels) for a webpage and then build the entire site on these specifications. Today, that scenario is becoming a rare occurrence. Now, you are presented with the decision to either build a site that can adapt to displays of multiple different dimensions (responsive) or build two or more separate websites to support desktop *and* mobile users at the same time (adaptive).

Your own decision will be based in part on the content you want to provide and on the capabilities of the devices accessing your pages. Building an attractive website that supports video, audio, and other dynamic content is hard enough without throwing in a **panoply** of different display sizes and device capabilities. The term *responsive web design* was coined, in a book of the same name (2011), by a Boston-based web developer named Ethan Marcotte; he describes the notion of designing pages that can adapt to multiple screen dimensions automatically. As you work through the following chapters, you will learn many techniques for responsive web design and implement them in your site and asset design.

Flash-based content

Movies and interactive SWF files that were created with Adobe Flash.

Panoply

A wide array and/or multiple impressive displays.

Many of the concepts of print design are not applicable to the web, because you are not in control of the user's experience. A page carefully designed for a typical flat panel is basically useless on a cellphone.

Color Theory and Web Design

Note: Learn More About Color Associations

To learn more about color associations visit this site - http://joehallock.com/edu/COM498/associations.html

Site map

Flow charge of pages in a website and the flow of information.

Company brand

Image created of a company based on their message, product and services, logo, tag line or slogan, company colors and mascot. Company brand is derived from these items and is a promise to their customers. Simply put, company brand is how others perceive the company.

Choosing the colors for a site is one of the first steps after creating your **site map** and wireframe. Many times the client or customer that you are creating the site for will have a logo and **company brand** already established and you will need to use their company colors for the site. Gather this information from the customer.

Exploring color theory is an interesting area and a science in itself. As a web designer, knowing about color theory is also important. Color theory involves how colors work or interact with each other as well as the analysis of the emotions or feelings that colors invoke when we look at them. There are warm colors like red, yellow and orange, as well as cool colors like green and blue. These colors each communicate an association with a human emotion or feeling. For instance, blue and white communicate trust. Red can be associated with hunger, love, and anger. Black can be associated with power or high quality as well as doom or evil. Orange is associated with value and less expensive.

Understanding color theory and color associations is important when you create a website design as the colors used with invoke or reinforce the site message. For example, look at the colors used for many of the fast food companies, like McDonalds or Burger King or Subway. What colors are used in their company brand, i.e. their logos, signage, appearance of their restaurant. Do you see lots of red and yellow? Both red and yellow can be associated with hunger. To apply this to web design, if you are creating a site for a food product or restaurant, you'll want to use colors of red or yellow. Colors create a feeling or mood and are a very important part of a site's design.

Choosing a Color Scheme

The next step and tool for creating a website is to identify a color scheme for your site. Typically you will want to have about five colors in a website color scheme. These colors are used for creating a consistent design for the site as a whole and for each page. Think about your audience and the site message to help you decide on your color scheme. For instance if this site is for children, you could use primary colors in your color scheme. Or if the site promotes conservation, you would use earthy colors, greens and browns. Choose colors that work well together for your site.

Adobe offers a product, Adobe Kuler, to help you make your color scheme. You can access Adobe Kuler by going to this URL - http://www.kuler.adobe.com.

The Adobe Kuler site lets you create a color scheme based on color rules. The rules are based on how colors are displayed on a color wheel. A color wheel presents colors based on the primary colors of yellow, red and blue.

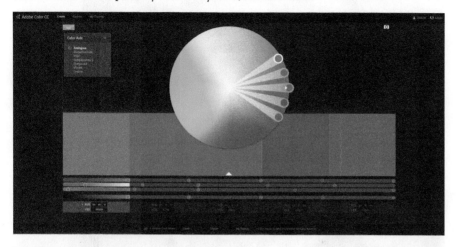

Mixing any other colors cannot create these three colors. That is why they are called primary colors. The secondary colors are the colors that are created by mixing two of the primary colors. For instance red mixed with blue creates purple.

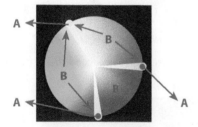

A - colors

B- Secondary colors

Kuler uses the following color rules for creating color schemes:

- Analogous: Color rule that uses colors that are adjacent to each other on the color wheel. One color is identified as the dominant color and the other colors are used to enrich the color scheme.

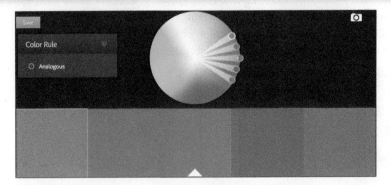

- Monochromatic: This color rule is based on a single color and variations in lightness and saturation of that color.

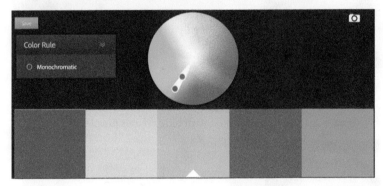

- Triad: This color rule uses three colors that are equally spaced around the color wheel.

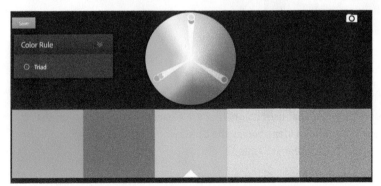

- Complementary: Color rule based on two colors that are opposite of each other on the color wheel. This rule can create colors that really clash with each other so the rule of thumb is to use a warm color with a cool color.

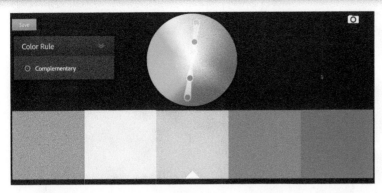

- Compound: This color rule uses two complementary color schemes together and creates the riches color palettes.

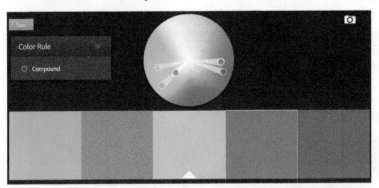

- Shades: Color rule that uses one single color and other colors are created by adding various amounts of black to that color. This rule is often confused with tints and tones. You can create a tint color scheme by adding various amounts of white to the single color or a color scheme based on tone or hue by adding various amounts of gray to the single color.

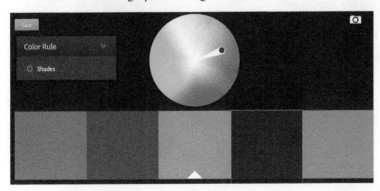

- Custom: This color rule uses a image that you upload to Adobe Kuler website. Click the Camera icon in the upper right corner of Adobe Kuler and then follow the prompts to upload the image.

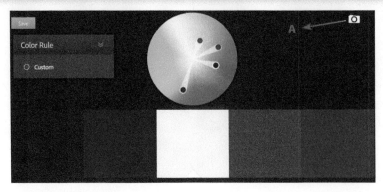

A- Upload an Image

Once you have this uploaded, you can then choose the colors from your image based on Color Mood or custom colors that you choose for your color scheme.

Note: You need to have an Adobe ID if you want to save any of your color schemes that you create otherwise you can write the hexadecimal number or RGB value down and recreate these colors in Dreamweaver using these numbers or values.

A- Color Mood

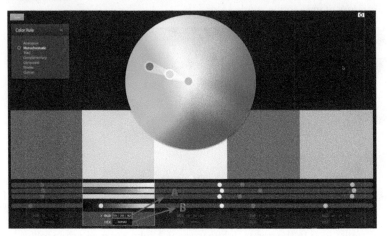

Note: Kuler and Adobe Photoshop

Adobe includes the Adobe Kuler functionality in Photoshop CC allowing you to create your color schemes with Photoshop CC too.

A – RGB Values

B - Hexadecimal Value

Scenario

For the purposes of this book, you'll be working to develop a website for Meridien GreenStart, a fictitious community-based organization dedicated to green investment and action. This website will offer a variety of products and services and require a broad range of webpage types, including dynamic pages using technologies such as jQuery, which is a form of JavaScript.

Your customers come from a wide demographic that includes all ages and education levels. They are people who are concerned about environmental conditions and who are dedicated to conservation, recycling, and the reuse of natural and human resources.

Your marketing research indicates that most of your customers use desktop computers or laptops, connecting via high-speed Internet services. You can expect to get 20 to 30 percent of your visitors exclusively via cellphone and other mobile devices, and much of the rest will be using mobile from time to time.

To simplify the process of learning Dreamweaver, we'll focus on creating a fixed-width site design first. In Chapter 8, "Designing for Mobile Devices," you'll learn how to adapt your fixed-width design to work with smartphones and tablets.

Working with Thumbnails and Wireframes

After you have nailed down the answers to the three questions about your website purpose, **customer demographic**, and access model, the next step is to determine how many pages you'll need, what those pages will do, and finally, what they will look like. The process of using thumbnails and wireframes can also be referred to as storyboarding a site.

> **Customer demographic**
>
> Social, geographic and behavior data about people.

Creating Thumbnails

Many web designers start by drawing thumbnails with pencil and paper. Think of thumbnails as a graphical shopping list of the pages you'll need to create for the website. The first page of a web site is called the home page. The home page is the first page displayed when a web site is accessed. The home page typically includes an easy-to-locate navigation panel with links to all secondary pages in the site. The navigation bar provides links to all secondary pages in your site as well as a link back to the home page and typically matches with the secondary level pages of the site. Thumbnails can also help you work out the basic navigation structure for the site. Draw lines between the thumbnails showing how your navigation will connect them.

> **Note:** The home page is the first page that opens in a web site. This page usually gives general information about the site and includes links to other pages in the site.

Most sites are divided into levels. Typically, the first level of the site is comprised of the home page and other pages that have a direct link to them from all pages in the site, for instance a Contact Us form. The second level of the site is mad up the pages that the visitor can reach direcly from the home page. The third level includes pages you can reach only through specific actions or from specific locations, say from a shopping cart or product detail page.

Thumbnails list the pages that need to be built and how they are connected to each other.

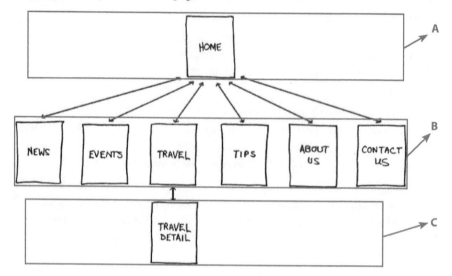

A – First Level

B – Second Level

C – Third Level

Planning a Webpage Design

Dreamweaver is an application that encourages creativity, and it gives you considerable support and assistance as you work to bring your ideas to life. Before jumping in and starting a site design, however, you may want to consider some design guidelines that can help turn out professional-quality pages.

An effective website not only looks good, but also conveys a message and is easy to use. A successful web developer uses the principles of design, color theory, and organization to communicate useful information quickly and efficiently. They focus on the page design and layout as well as the content to be presented. The content must be informative and easily understood. The site interface must be easy to use as well as consistent in navigation and page layout. Knowing how to use the available web development tools will help you plan, design, create, publish, and maintain a successful website.

Coming up with a website design can often be challenging and many designers look at other similar sites for inspiration. This requires searching the web and evaluating other sites in terms of their design, color, layout, navigation, site functionality, and how they present products, services and the site's message.

Evaluating Search Results

Learning how to search and evaluate the information that you access is very important for making wise decisions. The web provides access to valuable and fascinating information. You have the world at your fingertips. Be aware that some sites post inaccurate or deceptive information. It is up to each user to evaluate search results and the content of a website for accuracy and validity.

Most search engines list results based on popularity, or the number of hits a site receives, which means the most popular sites are at the top of the list. But, the most popular site may not be the most accurate.

Also, search engines accept advertising and sponsored links, which means companies pay for their links to be placed at the top of the list. Most sites label sponsored links and ads so you can easily identify them. They may be relevant but you should be aware that they are paying for placement.

Evaluating a Website

When evaluating a website, first look at the content on the page and ask yourself the following questions:

- Is the organization that runs the site well-respected?
- Are there references or sources listed on the site? If so, are they valid and authoritative?
- Is the author identified or anonymous?
- Is the text biased or is it balanced, accurate, up to date, and objective?
- Is the grammar and spelling on the site correct?
- Can you find the same information on a different site?

Think about these questions and come up with others you that you can use for evaluating the content presented in a website.

Learn to use Google more effectively

Google's Inside Search offers the tips and techniques you need in order to get the best research results in the least amount of time. Go to http://real-timeupdates.com/bce7. Under "Students," click on "Learn More."

Try these 100 serious search tools - This list is billed as "100 serious tools for academic search," but most are great tools for general business research, too. Go to http://real-timeupdates.com

The Importance of Design

A website's design can make or break the business. A well-designed site encourages visitors to stay in the site and use the site's services. A poorly designed site can drive visitors away, resulting in loss of potential sales.

Before you begin creating a site, answering three key questions can help you make choices about the look, feel, and content of your site:

- **Who:** Know who will be visiting your site.

- **What:** Know what the purpose of your site is.

- **How:** Determine how you'll know when you reach the site goals you have set.

Many web developers also seek inspiration for designing a website from other sites that are similar in content. For instance, if you have a client that wants a website to advertise their construction business, a logical place to start is by evaluating other construction company websites. Using the web Favorites or Bookmark feature of you browser helps you start saving sites that you like based on their design, navigation, page layout, and/or content.

Here is a list of other important design and content questions that can help guide the development of a website.

- **Know your audience**: Who will be visiting your site? Thinking through what they expect to see— and then surpassing their expectations—will ensure a successful browsing experience for users.

- **Name your pages well:** Search engines pick up the titles you use—the title of your site as well as page titles. Make your titles clear and easy to understand.

- **Be consistent**: Consistency in color, graphics, and placement helps your visitor understand your site.

- **Make your site easy to navigate:** When visitors come to your website, they should be able to tell from your home page how to get around your site and find the features they need.

- **Pay attention to connection speed:** If it takes too long to download your website, your visitors will not return. Time is valuable, both theirs *and* yours.

- **Keep it simple:** Clean lines and clear, easy-to-read content are features you always should keep in mind when building your site.

Note: Did you Know?

Many website developers use the three-click-rule when designing the navigation scheme for a website. The three-click-rule states that visitors should be able to find the information they need with no more than three clicks. It is based on the belief that people will become frustrated or angry after three clicks and then leave the website to try to find the information somewhere else. Recently, however, studies have shown that in fact people are willing to go as high as 25 clicks before abandoning a site. But it is always wise to create navigation in a site that quickly presents the information your visitors want to access with the least amount of effort and clicks.

- **Be unique:** When you copy another designer's site ideas, you are not only plagiarizing but also limiting your own ideas and site potential.

- **Take it easy:** Resist the temptation to overdo your site by loading it up with large image files or media objects. The more you add, the more you may affect your site download times. And visitors love fast-loading sites.

- **Respect your visitors:** Make sure your site looks professional from the very first moment it is online. Don't fall into the habit of posting a "construction guy" graphic or similar icon to notify your visitors that your site is under construction. If your visitors are visiting your site for information, when they don't find what they are looking for, they likely will look elsewhere.

Creating a Page Design

Once you've figured out what your site needs in terms of pages, products, and services, you can then turn to what those pages will look like. Make a list of components you want or need on each page, such as headers and footers, navigation, and areas for the main content and the sidebars (if any). Put aside any items that won't be needed on every page. What other factors do you need to consider? If mobile devices are going to be an important consideration of your design identity, will any of the components be required or optional for these devices? Although many components can be simply resized for mobile screens, some will have to be completely redesigned or reimagined.

1. Header (includes banner and logo)
2. Footer (copyright info)
3. Horizontal navigation (for internal reference, i.e., Home, About Us, Contact Us)
4. Main content (one-column with chance of two or more)

Identifying the essential components for each page helps you create a page design and structure that will meet your needs.

Do you have a company logo, business identity, graphic imagery, or color scheme you want to match or complement? Do you have publications, brochures, or current advertising campaigns you want to emulate? It helps to gather them all in one place so you can see everything all at once on a desk or conference table. If you're lucky, a theme will rise organically from this collection.

Desktop or Mobile

Once you've created your checklist of the components that you'll need on each page, sketch out several rough layouts that work for these components. Depending on your target visitor demographics, you may decide to focus on a design that's optimized for desktop computers or one that works best on tablets and smartphones.

Most designers settle on one basic page design that is a compromise between flexibility and sizzle. Some site designs may naturally lean toward using more than one basic layout. But resist the urge to design each page separately. Minimizing the number of page designs may sound like a major limitation, but it's key to producing a professional-looking site that's easy to manage. It's the reason why some professionals, like doctors and airline pilots, wear uniforms. Using a consistent page design, or template, conveys a sense of professionalism and confidence to your visitor. While you're figuring out what your pages will look like, you'll have to address the size and placement of the basic components. Where you put a component can drastically affect its impact and usefulness.

In print, designers know that the upper-left corner of a layout is considered one of the "power positions," a place where you want to locate important aspects of a design, such as a logo or title. This is because in western culture we read from left to right, top to bottom. The second power position is the lower-right corner, because this is the last thing your eyes will see when you're finished reading.

Unfortunately, in web design this theory doesn't hold up for one simple reason: You can never be certain how the user is seeing your design. Are they on a 20-inch flat panel or a 2-inch cellphone?

In most instances, the only thing you can be certain of is that the user can see the upper-left corner of any page. Do you want to waste this position by slapping the company logo here? Or make the site more useful by slipping in a navigation menu? This is one of the key predicaments of the web designer. Do you go for design sizzle, workable utility, or something in between?

Creating Wireframes

After you pick the winning design, wireframing is a fast way to work out the structure of each page in the site. A wireframe is like a thumbnail, but bigger, that sketches out each page and fills in more details about the components, such as actual link names and main headings, but with minimal design or styling. This step helps to catch or anticipate problems before you smack into them when working in the code.

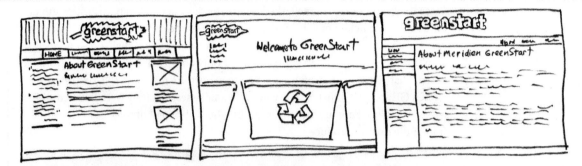

Wireframes allow you to experiment with page designs quickly and easily without wasting time with code.

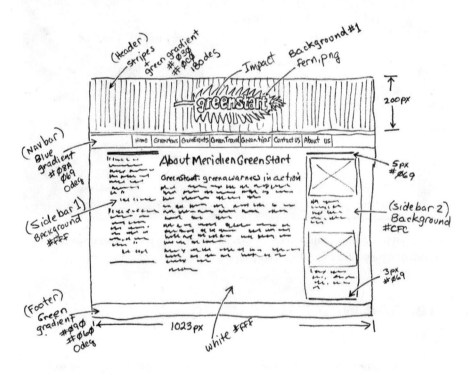

The wireframe for the final design should identify all components and include specific information about content, color, and dimensions.

Once the basic concepts are worked out, many designers take an extra step and create a full-size mockup or "proof of concept" using a program like Adobe Photoshop or even Illustrator. It's a handy thing to do because you'll find that some clients just aren't comfortable giving an approval based only on pencil sketches. The advantage here is that all these programs allow you to export the results to full-size images (JPEG, GIF, or PNG) that can be viewed in a browser as if they were finished webpages. Such mockups are as good as seeing the real thing but may take only a fraction of the time to produce.

In some cases, creating a mockup in Adobe Photoshop, Adobe Fireworks, or Adobe Illustrator can save hours of tedious coding to receive a needed approval.

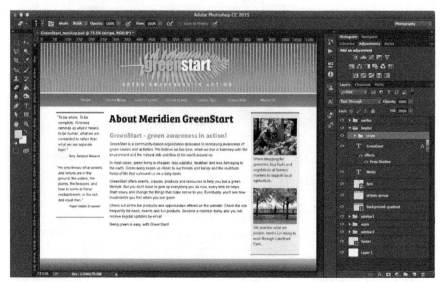

In addition to creating graphical mockups, Photoshop has tricks geared specifically for web designers, like the Adobe Generator feature.

Creating Web Assets using Adobe Generator

Adobe Generator is one of the web-oriented tools that allow you to export web assets from a Photoshop file in a variety of sizes, resolutions, and even file types. Best of all, this feature works in real time, exporting image assets from your file based on user-specified attributes added to the layer name. Let's take a closer look at this great tool.

Working with Adobe Generator

In this exercise, you'll work with an Adobe Photoshop document to prepare assets for your web project.

1 Launch Photoshop CC 2015 or higher.

2 Open **GreenStart_mockup.psd** from the chapter05/resources folder.

The Photoshop file contains a complete mockup of the GreenStart site design, which is composed of various **vector-based design components** as well as image assets stored in separate layers. Note the use of colors and gradients in the design.

3 Choose File > Save As.
Name the file **myGreenStart_mockup_xx.psd** and save it in the location or folder as indicated by your teacher.

4 If necessary, choose Window > Layers to display the Layers panel. Observe the names and contents of the layers and layer groups.

The layers and layer groups are named for the webpage components.

5 Open the header layer group, and observe the contents.

The header group contains two text elements and four graphical elements. Often, it's difficult to understand how a graphic component is built or for what purpose it is intended by looking at the layer names alone.

Note: This exercise requires the installation of Photoshop CC 2015 or higher and the Chapter05 lesson files.

Note: The sample file used in this exercise requires the font Bree Serif, which you can download and install for free from Adobe Typekit. To access this font, and the entire Typekit library, choose Type > Add Fonts from Typekit in Photoshop CC 2015 or higher.

Vector-based design components: Graphics and images that are made up of points, lines or paths, curves, shapes or polygons. Vector graphics are based on mathematical expressions and algorithms for representing the image. Points and paths are based the x and y axes of the workspace.

Tip: It's a good idea to save the file under a different name so you can refer back to the original assets should you make an error.

6   In the GreenStart layer, click the eye icon  to toggle the layer visibility off.

The text "greenstart" disappears from the layer.

7   In the fern layer, click the eye icon 👁 to toggle the layer visibility off.

The image of the fern disappears. Using this method, you can identify each element of the header and see what role it plays in the creation of the overall design. The number and type of layers and the level of detail used here aren't necessary for a mockup that you merely want to use for a client approval. This file was set up specifically to create many of the final assets for the page design.

8   Click the eye icon 👁 to toggle the GreenStart and fern layers back on.

Exporting Assets from Photoshop

web asset

A graphic, image, text, video or audio that has been saved or converted into a file that can be used in a website.

The fern layer will be used to create one component of the header background. Photoshop generates a **web asset** automatically if you add a file extension to the layer name.

1   Double-click the name of the fern layer, type **fern.png** and press Enter/Return to complete the name.

When activated, Generator works in the background exporting assets in real time.

2 Choose File > Generate > Image Assets.

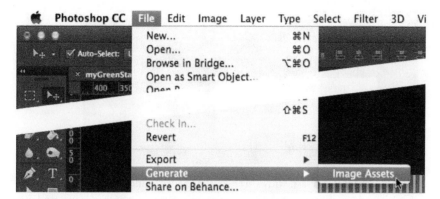

The next time you look at the Generate menu option, a checkmark will appear beside Image Assets, indicating that Generator is active.

3 Choose File > Open.

Navigate to the folder as indicated by your teacher.

A new folder has been created and named **myGreenStart_mockup_xx-assets** by Generator. Whenever you add file extensions to the layer names and enable Generator, it creates a folder and fills it with assets automatically, based on the layer names and settings.

4 Navigate to the **myGreenStart_mockup_xx-assets** folder as instructed by your teacher.

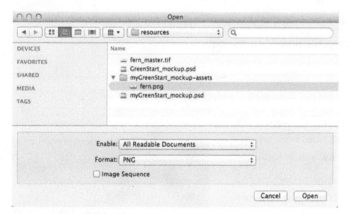

The folder contains a single image: **fern.png**.

5 Open **fern.png**.

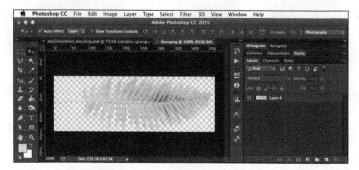

The file contains the fern with a transparent background. Note that the image displays a drop shadow. The shadow is a permanent part of the image, no longer created by a Photoshop effect.

6 Choose Image > Image Size.
Note the dimensions and resolution of the image.

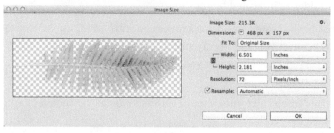

The image is 468 pixels by 157 pixels, at 72 pixels per inch (ppi).

7 Click OK to close the Image Size dialog.
Close **fern.png**.

Creating Multiple Assets using Generator

Generator can also modify the default export specifications and even create multiple assets at multiple resolutions.

Note: If you do not see the images created as described, check to make sure that the command File > Generate > Image Assets is enabled as described in the previous exercise.

1 Change the layer name fern.png to **200% fern.png+fern.jpg** and press Enter/Return to complete the name.

2   Choose File > Open. If necessary, navigate to the **myGreenStart_mockup_xx-assets** folder as instructed by your teacher.

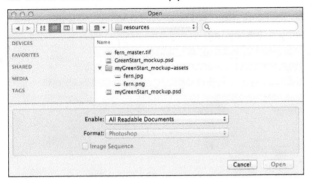

The folder contains two images: **fern.png** and **fern.jpg**, both created by Generator. Older files with the same names are replaced automatically.

3   Select **fern.png** and open the file.

The file contains the fern, but it appears twice as large as the previous image.

4   Open **fern.jpg**.

The file contains the same fern image, but at the original size. JPEGs do not support transparency, so the background is white. There's no need for the JPEG version of the image. Generator can remove assets automatically too.

5   Make the myGreenStart_mockup_xx.psd file active and change the layer name **200% fern.png+fern.jpg** to **150% fern.png** and press Enter/Return to complete the name.

The specification creates a larger, higher-quality image that will display well in regular browsers and on new higher-resolution devices. By removing "fern.jpg" from the layer name, Generator automatically deletes the JPEG version of the file.

6   Choose File > Open. Navigate to the myGreenStart_mockup_xx-assets folder as instructed by your teacher.

The JPEG version of the file is no longer visible in the folder. As you can see, Photoshop generates assets based on the name of the layer. You can create an entire set of images for your site design from the layers in this file.

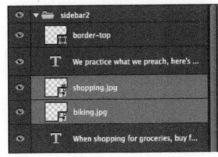

Note: In Photoshop, the background is mocked up using two layers: stripe and stripes-group. You are exporting the web background from the smaller stripe layer group, which looks like a folder icon in the Layers panel.

7 In the Layers panel, open the header layer group. Change the name of the *stripe* layer group to **stripe.png**.

8 Open the sidebar2 layer group. Change the layer shopping to **shopping.jpg**. Change the layer biking to **biking.jpg**.

9 Choose File > Open. Navigate to the myGreenStart_mockup_xx-assets folder as instructed by your teacher.

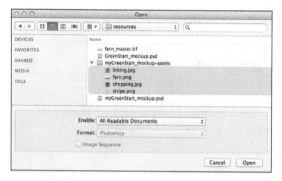

The myGreenStart_mockup_xx-assets folder now contains four image files. These files are identical to the ones you will use to build the site template and populate articles in upcoming chapters. As you can see, Generator offers some handy tools for turning this mockup into real web design assets, but the tricks don't stop there. Photoshop and Dreamweaver have even more collaboration tools to offer, as you will see later.

Check out http://helpx.adobe.com/photoshop/using/generate-assets-layers.html to see a complete explanation of Adobe Generator and how to use it.

Communicating with Customers

No matter if you work for a company or for yourself, communicating with your customers is key to a successful, long-term relationship. Communication requires work and attention. Learning to communicate effectively will create trust and lead to friendship with your customers. This friendship leads to successful, on-time projects. Effective communication helps businesses in numerous ways. It provides:

- Closer ties with your customers and clients

- Opportunities to influence conversations, perceptions, and trends

- Increased productivity and faster problem solving

- Better financial results and higher returns in profit

- Earlier warning of potential problems, from rising project costs to critical safety issues

- Stronger decision making based on timely, reliable information

- Clearer and more persuasive website and marketing messages

- Greater customer engagement with the project, leading to higher customer satisfaction and lower customer turnover

What Makes Business Communication Effective?

Effective communication strengthens the connections between a company and its customers. To make your communication efforts as effective as possible, focus on making them practical, factual, concise, clear, and persuasive:

- **Provide practical information.** Give customers and clients useful information, whether it's to help them perform a desired action or understand the flow of a new website.

- **Give facts rather than vague impressions.** Use concrete language, specific detail, and information that is clear, convincing, accurate, and ethical. Even when an opinion is called for, present compelling evidence to support your conclusion.

- **Present information in a concise, efficient manner.** Concise messages show respect for people's time, and they increase the chances of a positive response. When working in the web design field, creating a plan helps outline the project and how it will be completed.

- **Clarify expectations and responsibilities.** Craft messages to generate a specific response from a specific audience. When appropriate, clearly state what you expect from customer or client and state what you can do for them.

- **Offer compelling, persuasive arguments and recommendations.** Show your readers precisely how they will benefit by responding the way you want them to respond to your website message.

Improving your communication skills could be the single most important thing you do for your career. Effective communication delivers a variety of important benefits. Effective messages are practical, factual, concise, clear, and persuasive.

Create a Plan for the Development of a New Website

Achieving in business requires a plan (or many plans) and this also applies to the development and implementing a website. Use the following list to create a web development project plan.

1. *Identify the website to be made.* Make sure you recognize and understand the choice. Define the decision as a goal—what do I want to achieve with this choice?

2. *Gather website information.* You usually have lots of options for each decision. Try to think of as many as you can, and write them down. Don't just consider

the obvious choice; some of the best options might seem pretty bizarre at first. Consider your available resources and what you are trying to achieve.

3. *Layout the development process in a measurable plan.* Create a project plan that spans from the conception of the website to the design and development of the site, then to the implementation of the site on the World Wide Web. This includes goals and milestones that are easily measured to ensure completion of the project.

4. *Identify all tools required for the completion of the website.* Identify the tools you will need for your website project. This includes the HTML editor program, server hosting platforms, any ecommerce or other application required, personnel required to develop the site.

5. *Evaluate the decision, process, and outcome.* After you completed a project it is a good idea to look back on the process and evaluate how well you did to complete the site within the desired timeframe. Did you achieve the goal you defined in step 1? Did you miss any possible options? Did you correctly identify the consequences? Did you make use of your resources and tools? Was the outcome what you hoped for?

Setting Goals & Milestones

A **goal** is something you are trying to achieve. A goal helps direct your actions and guide your decision-making because they give you something to work toward. It is a good idea to set goals for all your website projects. When you achieve a goal, you can be proud and express satisfaction. There are two types of goals, short-term goals and long-term goals.

Short-Term Goals

When you want to achieve something quickly, you set **short-term goals**. You can accomplish short-term goals in the near future—maybe even today. For example, finishing your homework on time is a short-term goal. It is usually easy to define short-term goals because they are specific and not very complicated. If you keep a to-do list, it is full of short-term goals—meet friends at the mall, call your grandmother, make your bed.

Long-Term Goals

A **long-term goal** is something you want to achieve in the more distant future—maybe a year from now or maybe even more distant than that. Graduating from college is a long-term goal. So is buying a car.

Defining long-term goals may be more difficult than defining short-term goals. You might know you want to get married some day, but you don't know when or to whom. You might know you want to travel, but you don't know where or how.

What Are Milestones?

Sometimes it's harder to stay focused on a long-term goal—it seems so far away. Breaking the long-term goal down into a series of short-term goals—or **milestones**—makes it easier to stay on track.

Becoming a nurse might be a long-term goal. To achieve that goal, you can set a series of realistic and attainable milestones, such as:

- Volunteering at a hospital or senior care center
- Working part-time in a clinic
- Graduating from high school
- Attending college

Five Steps to a Goal

You can use the following process to help identify, assess, and set goals.

- **Identify the goal:** Write down the goal using as much detail as you can. This helps you understand and recognize the goal. Be positive, not negative: "I will attend the FCCLA meeting" rather than "I won't skip the FCCLA meeting."

- **Assess the goal:** Determine if it is something you really want and if it is realistic and attainable. It might be a fad or something that sounds good or even something someone else wants for you.

Note: Setting Goals and Success
If all you do is think about a goal, it's just a dream. You make goals real by deciding what you want to achieve and then planning how to get there. A successful entrepreneur, for example, has a vision of what he or she expects to accomplish. To achieve that vision, it is important to set realistic and attainable goals. Goals help an entrepreneur plan, develop, and grow a business. They let the entrepreneur identify the challenges ahead, so he or she is prepared when problems arise. While you should set goals that are within reach, there is nothing wrong with challenging yourself to push harder.

Goals are not written in stone. As you progress through different stages of your life, you will learn more about yourself, your values, and your standards. Your resources will change. You can change your goals at any time and develop new goals. Most people do.

- **Make an action plan for achieving the goal:** What resources will you need? If you cannot come up with a plan that works, it may mean the goal is not realistic or attainable. If so, you may need to go back to step 1.

- **Write down your action plan:** Be as specific as possible.

- **Reevaluate your goals:** Every once in a while, make sure they are still important to you and, if so, that you are on track to achieve them.

Make a Website Development Project Plan

Just because a goal is short-term doesn't mean you can achieve it without a plan. What if you have a short-term goal to meet friends at the mall?

Where will you meet? What time will you meet? How will you get there? What time should you leave?

Considering all of the factors helps you make decisions and form a realistic plan. The more specific the plan, the easier it will be to achieve your goal.

In most businesses, managers are responsible for keeping projects on time, on track, and on budget. Even small projects may become overwhelming at times. To make the job easier, many use project management software tools for collecting data, tracking tasks, and enabling everyone involved to communicate effectively.

Project management software programs vary in terms of complexity. Most include such features as scheduling, assigning tasks, file storage, file sharing, to-do lists, time tracking, and security.

Make a project plan for all websites that you develop. This typically is in a timeline format and has checkpoints that require customer sign off to show completion of each milestone and goal. Project plans keep the project progressing and places ownership of the development process in the customer's hands. If a goal or milestone, this plan helps you renegotiate the process with the customer so that the plan is realistic and back on schedule with the customer.

Web Site Project for Company XYZ				
Today's Date - 12/29/2016				
Purpose of the Site?:	Create a website for company XYZ that showcases their new product line of environmental widgets			
Who is your Audience?:	Consumers, male and female, 25 - 50yrs old			
How do they get to your site - Browsers?:	Google Chrome			
What type of devices will be connecting to your site?:	Desktop, tablet, mobile phone			
What is the typical Internet speed of your visitors?:	Broadband			
What colors will be used?:	Color Rule: Monochromatic, base color - #307327, supporting colors- #70736F, #ADF5A2, #EBF3EA, #BAC0B9			
Goals	Milestones	Start Date	End Date	Client Milestone Sign Off
Create a website for company XYZ that showcases their new product line of widgets				
	Gather Information & tools	1/6/17	1/20/17	x
	Aquire domain name	1/6/17	1/20/17	x
	Secure web hosting	1/20/17	3/2/17	x
	Develop Thumbnails of site flow	1/20/17	1/31/17	
	Develop Wireframe of page layout	1/20/17	1/31/17	
	Develop mockup of Site	1/20/17	2/5/17	
	HTML development	2/5/17	3/2/17	
	Set up web hosting server	2/20/17	3/5/17	
Post site to World Wide Web	Test website	2/25/17	3/5/17	
	Make changes as needed based on testing	3/5/17	3/10/17	
	Migrate site to web hosting server	3/10/17	3/15/17	

End-of-Chapter Activities

Review Questions

Directions: Choose the correct answer for each question.

1. What is the first question that you should answer when planning a new website?
   a. Who is the audience?
   b. What content or web assets are available?
   c. What is the purpose of the site?
   d. What is the timeline for completion of the site

2. To help plan a new website, it is important to check out the competition.
   a. True
   b. False

3. What are some considerations you need to determine about how visitors get to your site?
   a. Internet connection speed
   b. Browsers used
   c. Type of devices connecting to the site
   d. All of the above
   e. A and C only

4. What is the most popular browser used today?
   a. Google Chrome
   b. Firefox
   c. Internet Explorer
   d. Safari

5. What does responsive web design mean?
   a. The website response instantly to user inquiries
   b. The website reflects user input and progress instantly
   c. The website changes colors frequently
   d. The website automatically adjusts page layout based on the accessing devise screen size.

6. In regards to web design, what is a thumbnail?
   a. A design mockup of the web page created in a graphics package
   b. A sketch of the web page
   c. Graphical shopping list of the pages needed for a web site
   d. Page layout showing header, footer and navigation
   e. A and D only

7. In regards to web design, what is a wireframe?
   a. A design mockup of the web page created in a graphics package
   b. A sketch of the web page
   c. Graphical shopping list of the pages needed for a web site
   d. Page layout showing header, footer and navigation
   e. A and D only

8. In regards to web design, what is a design mockup?
   a. Complete page design created in a graphics package
   b. A sketch of the web page
   c. Graphical shopping list of the pages needed for a web site
   d. Page layout showing header, footer and navigation
   e. A and D only

9. What are some components you can show in a design mockup?
   a. Header
   b. Footer
   c. Sidebars
   d. Navigation
   e. All of the above

10. What is the power position in a web page layout?
    a. The upper right corner
    b. The upper left corner
    c. The lower left corner
    d. Any thing above the fold

Essay Questions

Directions: Respond to each question by writing your answers in complete sentences and paragraphs. Be thorough in your answers.

1. What are the questions should you ask before starting any web design project?

2. What is the purpose of using thumbnails and wireframes?

3. Why is it important to create a design that takes into account smartphones and tablets?

4. Why would you use Adobe Photoshop, Illustrator, or Fireworks to design a website?

5. What are the seven color rules that Adobe Kuler site uses to create color schemes?

6. When evaluating an existing web page what questions are important to answer?

7. List the ways that effective communication helps businesses?

8. What are some tools for planning and creating a website?

9. Describe how goals and milestones can help plan the development of a website.

10. List the five steps to a goal.

Explore Project Management Tools

Use the Internet or magazines or visit a local computer/electronics store to research project management software. Make a list of long-term and short-term goals for yourself. Select one, and use the five-step goal-setting process to develop the goal and make an action plan for achieving the goal. Include a timeframe and assess the plan to make sure it is reasonable and attainable. Add both the list of goals and the action plan to your career portfolio. Present the list to your class.

Online Portfolio Builder — Plan Your Site

Plan your Portfolio website by completing the following.

1. Plan your web site by first researching other portfolio websites. Identify things you like about how other sites present their information and how they navigate through the site. Examine page layout and the location of major website components on the Home page and secondary pages of the site. Save your favorite websites by bookmarking or using Favorites feature of your browser.

2. Use Adobe Kuler to create a color scheme for your site. Write down each color's hexadecimal and/or RGB values. You can use these values to recreate your color scheme in Dreamweaver's color palette.

3. Next identify the number of web pages you need for your site's message and content by creating a sketch showing the thumbnail of all pages in your site. Use lines to link the pages in your site showing the site levels and flow of information. Name each page and briefly detail the content each page will contain. This sketch will serve as a site map of your portfolio site. By thinking through your idea for the site, you will get a sense of how many pages you need, how they are related, and which topics visitors to your site will most want to see.

4. Create a wireframe mockup of your site. Sketch how the home page will look and the secondary level page design.

5. Finally answer the following questions.

Critical Thinking Project – Create a Web Design Project Plan for your Portfolio Site

Create a project plan for your portfolio site. Think about the goals you need to meet to create the site based on the progression of the class. Structure your goals and milestones so that they produce a measurable product or result, like a completed wireframe or thumbnail sketch.

1. Open the projectplan.pdf from the Datafile/Resources folder as instructed by your teacher. Print this document.

2. Record answers to the five questions under Todays Date. Write your answers in the appropriate blank area to the right of each question

3. Define your goals for the site, both short-term and long-term.

4. Break down your long-term goals based on measurable steps and define a timeline for completion. Think about the progression of the class and the class syllabus or outline of topics covered and when provided by your teacher for setting your starting and ending dates. Record this information in your Web Project Plan.

5. As you work through this class you will be the client. Check off the completion of each Milestone or Goal.

6. If you miss a start or end date, reassess your project and timeline, and then adjust the dates to reflect the new timeline schedule.

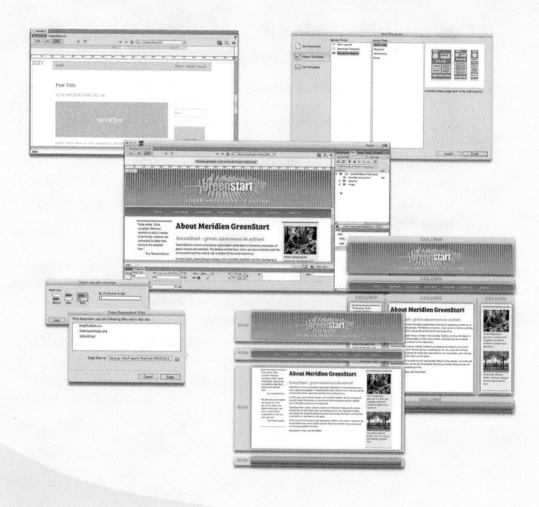

CREATING A PAGE LAYOUT

Whether you are designing a single page or an entire website, Dreamweaver provides all the tools you need to complete the project on time and under budget.

Chapter Overview

In this chapter, you'll learn how to do the following:

- Examine the chosen page design and evaluate the use of the predefined layouts provided by Dreamweaver
- Work with the Visual Media Query interface
- Create a new layout using the BootStrap framework
- Modify the layout structure to use HTML5 semantic elements

Evaluating Page Design Options

In the previous chapters, you went through the process of identifying the pages, components, and structures you would need for a specific website. The selected design balances those needs against a variety of other factors, such as the types of visitors that may come to the site and their means of connecting to it. In this lesson, you will learn how to break down a graphical mockup into actual HTML structures and components and then build that basic layout in code.

Since there are almost unlimited ways to build a particular design, we'll concentrate on building a simple structure that uses the minimum number of HTML5 semantic elements. This will produce a page design that will be the easiest to implement and maintain.

Let's start by taking a look at the mockup created in Lesson 5.

1   Open **GreenStart_mockup.html** from the chapter06/Datafiles folder as instructed by your teacher.

This file contains an image depicting the final mockup of the GreenStart site design. The design can be broken down into basic components, such as header, footer, navigation, main, and sidebar content elements. If you diagrammed this scheme over the mockup, it might look like the following figure.

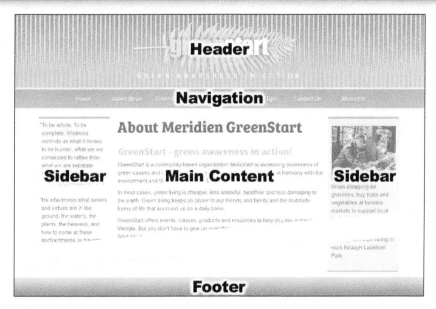

Once you identify the basic page component scheme, you could then break down the diagram into basic HTML elements, like this:

Although the `<div>` element is perfectly acceptable, and still in wide use as a page component, it is a holdover from HTML 4 and comes with some disadvantages. For example, it makes the underlying code more complex by requiring the use of class attributes to help delineate the various components within the design. Today, web designers are instead using the new HTML5 elements to simplify their designs and to add semantic meaning to their code. If you substitute the `<div>` elements for HTML5 structures, it's easy to see how much simpler the layout can be.

Now that the page has been diagrammed and broken down into its components, you could start creating the basic structure right away. But before you spend any time creating the new layout by hand, Dreamweaver may offer some better alternatives.

2   Close **GreenStart_mockup.html**.

Working with Predefined Layouts

Dreamweaver has always tried to offer the latest tools and workflows to all web designers, regardless of their skill level. For example, over the years, the program has provided a selection of predefined templates and various page components to make the task of building and populating webpages fast and easy. Often the first step of building a website was to see if one of these predefined layouts matched your needs, or if your needs could be adapted to one of the available designs.

Dreamweaver CC (2015.1 release) continues this tradition by providing sample CSS layouts and frameworks that you can adapt to many popular types of projects. You can access these samples from the File menu.

1   Choose File > New.

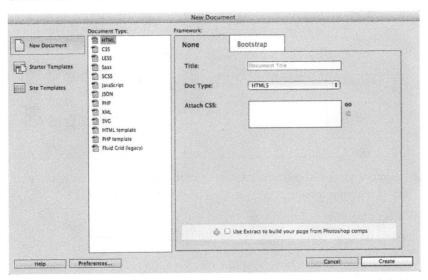

The New Document dialog appears. Dreamweaver allows you to build a wide spectrum of web-compatible documents besides those built using HTML, CSS, and JavaScript. The New Document dialog displays many of these document types, including PHP, XML, and SVG. Predefined layouts, templates, and frameworks can also be accessed from this dialog.

At the time of this writing, Dreamweaver CC (2015.1 release) offers three basic layouts, four responsive starter layouts and six Bootstrap templates. The exact number and features of these layouts may change over time through automatic updates via Creative Cloud. The changes to this list may occur without notice or fanfare, so keep your eyes peeled for new options in this dialog.

All the featured starter layouts are responsive design built using HTML5-compatible structures and will help you gain valuable experience with this evolving standard. Unless you need to support older browsers (such as IE5 and 6), there's little to worry about when using the newer designs. Let's check out these layouts.

2   In the New Document dialog, select Starter Templates > Responsive Starters.

The Starter Templates window of the New Document dialog displays five options: About page, Blog post, eCommerce, Email, and Portfolio.

3 Select **About page**.

Observe the preview image in the dialog.

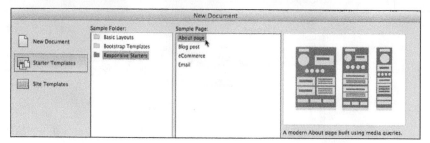

An image appears showing the design of a responsive webpage for desktop, tablet, and smartphone.

4 Select **Blog Post**.

The preview image changes to depict the new design.

5 Select each of the design options in turn.

Observe the preview image in the dialog.

Each template offers a design appropriate for specific applications. None of the templates are identical to our chosen design, but Blog Post is the closest. Let's take a closer look.

6 Select **Blog Post** again.

Click Create.

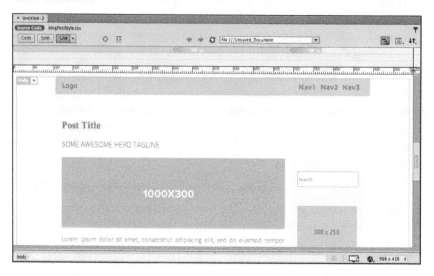

A new, untitled document appears in the workspace based on the starter layout. Before working in any document, it's a good idea to save it.

7   Select File > Save.

The Save As dialog appears.

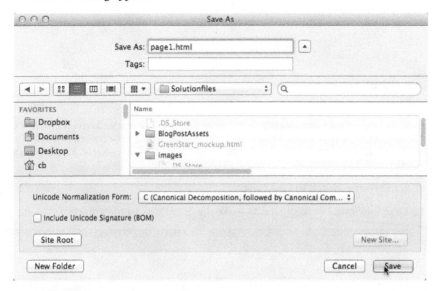

8   Name the page **page1.html**, and click Save to save the page into the root folder for Chapter06 as instructed by your teacher.

The file is saved to the site folder. At the same time Dreamweaver creates a BlogPostAssets folder and copies some files to it to support the starter layout.

Dreamweaver designed this page for use as a blog post. The new page is populated with placeholders for text, images, and even menus. To use it, you simply swap out these placeholders with your own words and pictures.

Another attribute of this layout that is not readily apparent at this moment is that it has been built right out of the box to be fully responsive. Fortunately, you can test this functionality right in Dreamweaver.

Live view is the new default workspace for most functions in Dreamweaver CC (2015.1 release). It offers an accurate display of all page components, styling, and even interactivity. You may still switch to Design or Code view for various operations, but you'll find that Live view provides most of the tools you'll ever need in one place.

Note: The support files may not appear immediately in the Files panel.

Note: Dreamweaver CC 2015 first release for the Macintosh has a bug when creating a new responsive page document. After you click Create in the New Document window, a glitch occurs by the display of the Save Style Sheet File As window displays.

Even though you might set a new CSS style sheet in this window, it is never saved. The only style sheet created is the locked bootstrap.css file which is the correct file to be created to support the new bootstrap document. To solve this problem, upgrade your Dreamweaver CC 2015 to the latest update.

9 If necessary, switch to Live view.

10 Drag the Scrubber to the left to make the document window narrower.

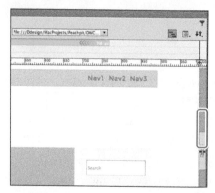 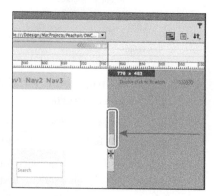

As the document window narrows, some of the components resize or reformat to adapt to the smaller window. Note that some elements actually change positions within the layout. When the window narrows below 480 pixels, the content displays in a single column.

11 Drag the Scrubber to the right to make the document window wider.

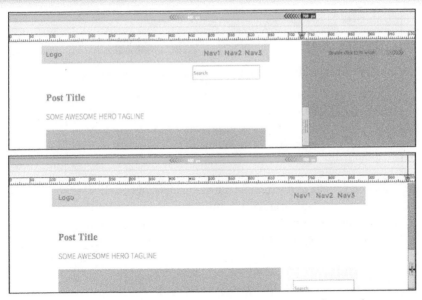

As the window widens, notice that the content continues to adapt to the screen until it resumes its original layout and formatting.

Did you notice that the layout changed abruptly at certain widths? These changes were caused by **media queries** that control the application of the CSS styling. To help you work with media queries, Dreamweaver CC (2015.1 release) offers the new *Visual* Media Queries interface, which should be visible at the top of the document window when you are in Live view.

Introducing the Visual Media Queries Interface

The Visual Media Queries (VMQ) interface allows you to identify and interact with media queries instantly using the cursor.

1 If necessary, click the "Show Visual Media Queries bar" icon at the top of the document window to display the toolbar.

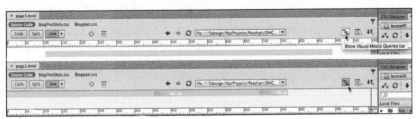

The toolbar displays two media queries settings for this document.

2 Position the insertion point over the first media query.

Media queries

A feature of CSS3 that allow web pages to adapt to the different screen sizes and resolutions of connecting devices like mobile phones, tablets and desktop computers. They are a fundamental feature of responsive websites.

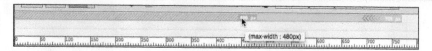

A tooltip appears, identifying that the media query is set for a max-width of 480 pixels.

3 Position the cursor over the second media query.

The second media query is set for a max-width of 769 pixels. The interface displays the existing settings using numbers and colors so you can see the specifications instantly. You can use the insertion point to activate or switch between each media query.

VMQ Enables You to See the Differences

Media queries enable your webpage and its content to adapt to a variety of different types of screens and devices. They do this by loading custom style sheets created just for specific screen sizes, devices, or even orientations. Later, you'll learn more about media queries, how they work, and how to create them. For now, let's just review how the Visual Media Queries (VMQ) interface works.

The VMQ interface identifies all media queries defined on the page or within style sheets linked to it. The media queries are displayed in color based on their specifications.

Media queries that define only a minimum width are displayed in green.

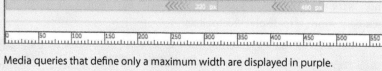

Media queries that define only a maximum width are displayed in purple.

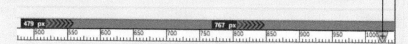

Media queries that define both minimum and maximum widths are displayed in blue.

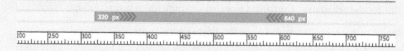

The Dreamweaver workspace is fully responsive and will display all the defined CSS styling appropriate to the screen size and orientation. To display the styling associated with a specific media query, simply double-click its representative display in the VMQ.

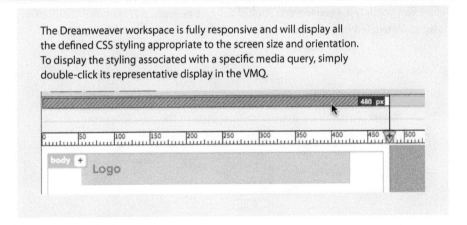

4   Click the Insertion point to the left of the number 480 in the VMQ interface.

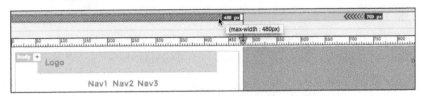

The document window narrows instantly to 480 pixels. The content adapts to the window size based on the applicable CSS styles.

5   Click the Insertion point to the left of the number 769 in the Visual Media Queries interface.

The document window widens to 769 pixels. To return to full size, you can drag the Scrubber to the right edge of the window or double-click in the gray area to the right of the Scrubber.

6   Double-click in the gray area on the right side of the Scrubber.

The document window opens to the full size of the workspace.

Note: Don't click directly on the number itself; Dreamweaver may open an editing window instead.

If you examine the current layout and compare it to our chosen site design, the Blog Post layout is not similar enough to be easily adaptable. The same is true of the other responsive starter layouts. Perhaps the Bootstrap templates offer a closer fit.

Introducing Bootstrap

The Bootstrap templates are predefined layouts using the Bootstrap framework. Bootstrap is a set of open-source tools that help you quickly build websites and web applications that are fully responsive.

Created by Twitter, Bootstrap was released to the public in 2011 and quickly became one of the most popular frameworks in use. It has now been incorporated into Dreamweaver.

Before you begin this exercise, you should define a new site based on the Chapter06 folder as instructed by your teacher. This will be your local root folder for this exercises HTML documents.

1 Select File > New.

The New Document dialog appears.

2 Select Starter Templates > Bootstrap Templates in the New Document dialog.

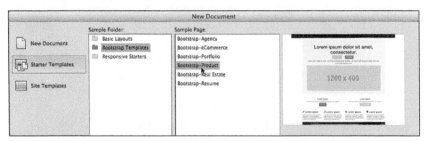

The Sample Page window displays six templates based on the Bootstrap framework. A preview of the layout appears when you select the template name.

3 Select each layout option and compare the preview to the proposed site design.

None of the templates are close enough to the proposed design to warrant trying to use one as the basis for the new site. Instead, you'll see what all the hype about Bootstrap is all about by using it to create your own template from scratch.

4 Select the New Document tab in the New Document dialog.

5 Select HTML in the Document Type window.

6 Select the Bootstrap framework.

7 For Bootstrap CSS, select Create New.

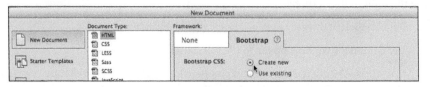

8 Deselect the Design option Include a Pre-built Layout.

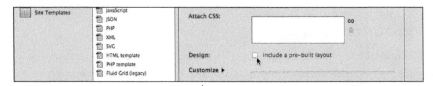

9   Click the triangle beside the Customize option to expand it.

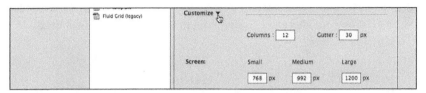

The Customize options allow you to change the number of columns, the gutter width, or the predefined screen sizes. For this layout, you will leave the default settings as they are, but if you use Bootstrap in the future you should make sure these numbers reflect the needs of your site and its visitors.

10 Click Create.

A new, untitled document appears in the document window.

Note: Dreamweaver CC 2015 first release for the Macintosh has a bug when creating a new Bootstrapp document. After you click Create in the New Document window, a glitch occurs by the display of the Save Style Sheet File As window displays.

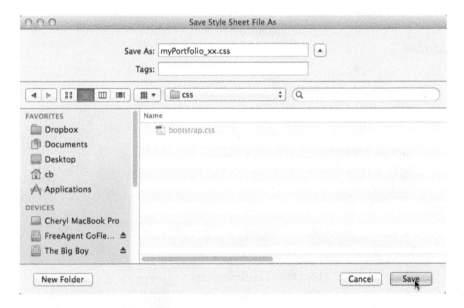

Even though you might set a new CSS style sheet in this window, it is never saved. The only style sheet created is the locked bootstrap.css file which is the correct file to be created to support the new bootstrap document. To solve this problem, upgrade your Dreamweaver CC 2015 to the latest update.

11 The new HTML Bootstrap document displays. Next save this HTML document as mylayout_xx.html in the folder as instructed by your teacher.

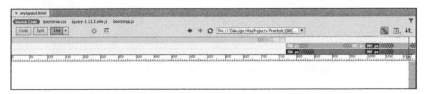

Although the file is entirely empty, lots of things are already going on. You can see that the VMQ interface displays at least six media queries and that the Related files interface shows one CSS and two JavaScript files. The next thing to do is to add some basic structure.

Creating a Layout with Bootstrap

Underlying all the power and flexibility of Bootstrap is a basic grid system of rows and columns. This concept harks back to the earlier days of web design, before the advent of CSS, when we would use tables to cobble together our layouts. The only way to impose order on our webpages was to organize our text and pictures into table rows and cells.

No, we're not going back to the bad old days. Tables were not responsive. Although they could scale up or down in size, they would not automatically adapt to the screen and knew nothing about mobile devices. Instead, the rows and columns of Bootstrap have been carefully engineered to work in most modern browsers and devices.

The first step in Bootstrap is to identify the basic grid structure you need to build, or impose, on the proposed site design. This should be quite easy when you examine the mockup. Start by marking up the content that would be grouped together in rows, as in the following figure.

Next, identify the columns within the content. Remember that the columns are divvied up in the rows you already created.

You will use the Insert panel to build this structure.

1 If necessary, open **mylayout_xx.html** in Split view.
   Click in the Live view window.

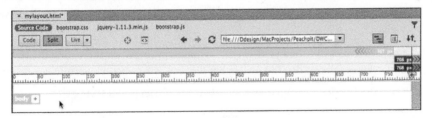

   The <body> element is selected in the window.

2 Display the Insert panel. If it's not visible on the screen, you can select it from the Window menu.

3 In the Insert panel, select **Bootstrap Components** from the drop-down menu.

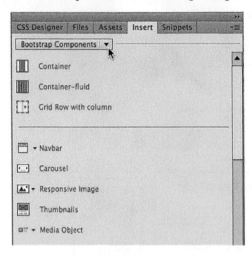

The panel displays a list of 26 main items and over 80 sub-items supported by the framework. Although the list is not exhaustive, it's a good start. Whatever you can't find in the Insert panel can always be added by hand manually in the Code window.

4 Click the **Container** item at the top of the panel.

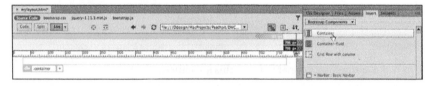

Note: If you instead prefer to create a site that automatically scales to every screen width, use the Container-fluid item in the panel.

This option inserts in the page a fixed-width `<div>` element that in Bootstrap is, by default, 1170 pixels wide in a full-screen browser on a desktop computer. On smaller screens or devices, this container will display at various smaller fixed widths.

Once you've established your overall container, you can start creating the row and column scheme devised earlier, but first you will target the default page width.

Note: To see all the media queries, the document window will have to be at least 1100 pixels in width.

5 Click the *Small* media query (min-width 768 pixels) in the VMQ.

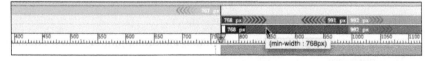

The document window resizes to match the dimensions of the media query. Targeting the width first determines what classes are automatically assigned by the Bootstrap framework when you add columns to your rows.

6   Click the **Grid Row with Column** item in the Insert panel.

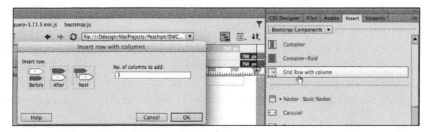

The Insert Row with Columns dialog appears.

7   Click the **Nest** option.
Enter **1** in the No. of Columns to Add field.
Click OK.

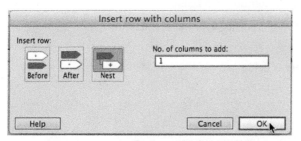

When choosing a position option click the graphic icon above the option name. The icon dark-
ens to indicate that it is selected.

In the Code window, you can see that Dreamweaver inserted two `<div>` elements,
one with a class of `row` and the other with a class of `col-sm-12`, nested one inside
the other in the initial container. Since the *Small* media query is targeted, the class
says `sm`. *Medium* classes will say `md`, and *Large* classes will say `lg`.

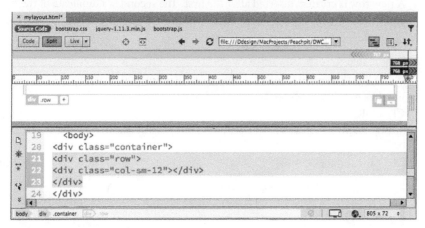

The structure doesn't look very remarkable, but this is the key to the power
of Bootstrap. These classes apply to these elements predefined styles that will

allow them to adapt to different screens and devices. By adding more classes or manipulating the existing ones, you can provide different formatting as desired.

As complex and elaborate as Bootstrap is, one aspect of this scheme is easy to understand. If you remember from the New Document dialog, when you created the page, the Bootstrap specifications called for 12 columns in the grid. The class col-sm-12 speaks to this grid by telling the <div> to be *12 columns* wide on *small* devices. A small device is considered to be a tablet at least 768 pixels wide. But don't let that fool you. It's important to know that some Bootstrap classes, like this one, are inherited and continue to format even on larger devices.

As we work through this layout and the upcoming lessons, you will learn how to add to the main components of other Bootstrap classes that will specify their behavior in each environment you wish to support. Let's add the next row to the structure.

8 Click the **Grid Row with Column** item again.

The Insert Row with Columns dialog appears. The first row should still be selected.

9 Select **After**.
Enter **1** for the number of columns.
Click OK.

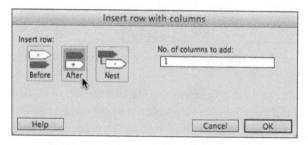

A new row is created, inserted after the first. The second is a duplicate of the first and will eventually hold the navigation menu. You'll add that later, but now let's create the next row.

10 Repeat step 8.
In the Insert Row with Columns dialog, select After, and this time, for the number of columns, enter **3**.
Click OK.

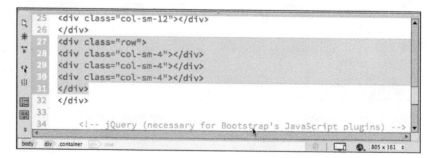

A new row appears with three nested `<div>` elements. The new elements have a class of `col-sm-4`. Because 4 divides into 12 three times, the new elements form three columns that divide the available space into three equal parts. Later, you will modify these classes to change the widths and the relationships of these elements to one another. But let's finish the layout first. There's one more row needed for the page footer.

11 Repeat steps 8 and 9 to create a row with one column.

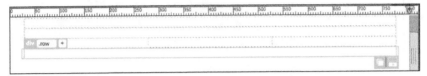

A new row is added for the last row, which will hold the footer. The basic Bootstrap structure has been created for the site design.

12 Save the file. If you are continuing to the next exercise, leave **mylayout_xx.html** open and any of the supporting related files for this page, but close all other open documents.

In the upcoming exercises you will modify the basic layout to add HTML5 elements and content placeholders for the site template.

Adding HTML5 Elements to Bootstrap

As you can see from the previous exercise, Bootstrap relies heavily on the `<div>` element. There's nothing wrong with this technique, since the framework can't understand the purpose of the elements in the rows and columns and automatically add the appropriate tags. But as a generic container, the `<div>` element conveys no semantic value or other information to search engines or other web applications.

Once you have created your basic structure, it makes sense to go back and swap out these generic structures with ones that more closely match your intended usage or content model. Dreamweaver makes it easy to edit structural elements.

1 If necessary, launch Dreamweaver CC (2015.1 release) or later.
Open **mylayout_xx.html** from the folder as instructed by your teacher.

The file has a basic Bootstrap structure containing four rows, three with one column and one with three columns.

2 Select Split view so that the workspace displays the Code and Live view windows at the same time.

The Bootstrap borders, rows, and columns should be visible in the Live view window.

3   Click in the first row of the layout and examine the tag selector at the bottom of the document window.

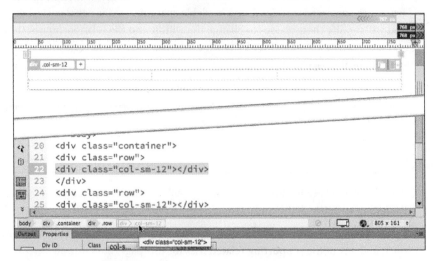

Dreamweaver selects one of the elements in the row and displays the blue heads-up display (HUD) interface.

Depending on where or how you click, you could select the row itself or the column nested within it. You can determine which element is selected by looking at the class name displayed in the HUD or tag selectors: `div.row` indicates that you have selected a row, whereas `div.col-sm-12` means you have a column selected. The selected element will be highlighted in blue in the tag selectors.

4   Click the tag selector for `div.row`.

5   Press Ctrl+T/Cmd+T to activate the Quick Tag Editor.

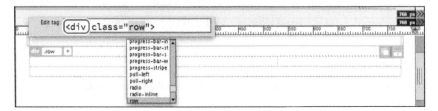

The Quick Tag Editor appears, populated by the code for the row element. If you recall from the original page diagram, this element should be designated as an HTML5 `<header>`.

6 Edit the element code as highlighted:

```
<header class="row">
```

7 Press Enter/Return twice to complete the change.

The structure is now updated to use the new element.

8 Click in the second row, and select the `div.row` tag selector.

9 Press Ctrl+T/Cmd+T.

Edit the element code as highlighted:

```
<nav class="row">
```

10 Press Enter/Return twice to complete the change.

11 Repeat steps 8–10 to edit the third row as highlighted:

```
<article class="row">
```

This row also contains three columns: one main element and two sidebars.

12 Click in the first column of the `article.row`.

The first `div.col-sm-4` element in the row should be selected. We'll refer to this element as Sidebar 1 throughout the book.

13 Press Ctrl+T/Cmd+T.

Edit the element as highlighted:

```
<aside class="col-sm-4">
```

14 Repeat steps 12–13 to edit the second column as highlighted:

```
<section class="col-sm-4">
```

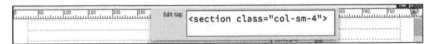

15 Edit the third column as highlighted:

```
<aside class="col-sm-4">
```

We'll refer to this element as Sidebar 2.

16 Edit the fourth row as highlighted:

```
<footer class="row">
```

17 Save the file.

The layout has now been updated to use HTML5 elements. In the next lesson, you'll learn how to add some basic content and to format various elements.

Considerations for Website Content

Many websites, particularly company websites, function as informational reports, offering sections with information about the company and its history, products and services, executive team, and so on. Making this information clear, accessible and understandable requires critical thinking from the designer. The online environment requires some special considerations with the first being communicating the message. Here are some considerations that need to be heeded for an effective website.

- **Web visitors are demanding.** If they can't find what they're looking for in a few minutes, most will click away to another site.

- **Reading online can be difficult.** Studies show that reading speeds are about 25 percent slower on a monitor than on paper. Reading from computer screens can also be exhausting and a source of physical discomfort.

- **The web is a nonlinear, multidimensional medium.** Visitors of online material move around in any order they please; there often is no beginning, middle, or end. In addition, many websites have to perform more than one communication function and therefore have more than one purpose. Each of these individual purposes needs to be carefully defined and then integrated into an overall statement of purpose for the entire website. Moreover, many websites also have multiple target audiences, such as potential employees, customers, investors, and the news media. You need to analyze each group's unique information needs and find a logical way to organize all that material. Website designers use the term **information architecture** to describe the structure and navigational flow of all the parts of a website. As you develop the site architecture, you can begin to simulate how various audiences will enter and explore the site. Accommodating multiple entry points is one of the most difficult tasks in site design.

To organize your site effectively, keep the following advice in mind:

- If you know that a sizable percentage of your target audience will access your site with mobile devices, take a *mobile-first* approach: Design the site to work with tablets and smartphones, then make sure it functions well on conventional computer screens as well.

- Plan your site structure and navigation before you write.

- Let your visitors be in control by creating links and pathways that let them explore on their own.

- Help online visitors scan and absorb information by breaking it into self-contained, easily readable chunks that are linked together logically.

- When planning online reports or other website content, remember that the online reading experience differs from offline reading in several important ways.

- The information architecture of a website is the equivalent of the outline for a paper report, but it tends to be much more complicated than a simple linear outline.

Major sections on websites, particularly those that are fairly static (unlike, say, a blog) function in much the same way as reports. The skills you've developed for report writing adapt easily to this environment, as long as you keep a few points in mind:

- Because visitors can be skeptical of online content, take special care to build trust with your intended audiences. Make sure your content is accurate, current, complete, and authoritative.

- As much as possible, adapt your content for a global audience. Translating content is expensive, so some companies compromise by *localizing* the homepage while keeping the deeper, more detailed content in its original language.

- In an environment that presents many reading challenges, compelling, reader-oriented content is a key to success. Wherever you can, use the *inverted pyramid* style, in which you cover the most important information briefly at first and then gradually reveal successive layers of detail—letting readers choose to see those additional layers if they want to.

- Present your information in a concise, skimmable format. Effective websites use a variety of means to help readers skim pages quickly, including lists, use of color and boldface, informative headings, links to drill down to relevant information and helpful summaries that give readers the option of learning more if they choose to do so.

A-Navigation bar

B-The choices on the right side of the screen are supplemental topics that may be of interest to some readers

C-Navigation bar to advance one article forward or backwards based on search results

D-Drill down to more specific information through text links

- Write effective links that serve for both site navigation and content skimming. Above all, clearly identify where a link will take readers. Don't resort to cute wordplay that obscures the content, and don't force readers to click through and try to figure out where they're going.

- Make your website a "living" document by regularly adding fresh content and deleting content that is out of date or no longer relevant to your target audience. Over time, websites can accumulate many pages of outdated information that get in the way and send a negative message about the company's efforts to stay on top of user needs.

Accessibility and Web Design

Today web designers also need to integrate accessibility standards into a website. Remember that a website can be viewed by people throughout the world. That's a lot of people with different languages, needs, and abilities. These special needs considerations sparked the United States government in June of 2001 to add Section 508 to the Rehabilitation Act of 1973. This Act outlines new accessibility requirements that should be included in all electronic communications, which includes websites. The Section 508 Act provides information on accessibility guidelines to use when creating web pages so that the page is accessible and readable and understandable by all people. It is targeted to help people of all ages, people with disabilities as well as people with English as a second language access to website content, no matter how the content is presented in the website. Also, any website of a government agency or school must meet these requirements or the designer could be liable of breaking this law.

Visit the http://www.section508.gov website for more information about this Act.

Designing for Accessibility

People with special needs require special tools and software to help them understand a digital information and website. For people who are visually challenged there are screen readers that read the content on a web page. Also, most computers have accessibility features built into the operating system to help people with disabilities. For instance, most computers come with Accessibility features that allow their computer interface to be optimized for a particular disability. A common one is the ability to make screen resolutions higher or lower, increase magnification of a computer screen or the ability to have the computer read the text on a screen. People with limited mobility often need voice input software or trackballs that allow them to interact with a website. Web designers need to think critically and apply problem solving skills when creating page layout designs that support accessibility. At the beginning of the web site development process, start planning for accessibility in your site. The Critical Thinking and the Online Portfolio activities at the end of this lesson require that you implement critical thinking and problem solving skills to create a page layout that supports the site message as well as accessibility for all viewers.

- Use backgrounds that are simple and plain so that they do not interfere with the legibility of the information on the page.

- Use fonts that are not too small or ornamental for easy reading. Rule of thumb is never use a font size below 12 points for your information.

- Use a color scheme that promotes good contrast for easily seeing text and content on the page. Do not use colors that clash with each other like red background with green text. Clashing color schemes hurt the eye and it is very difficult to read text that clashes with the background color.

- Consistent navigation and page layout is a must; visitors need to know where the navigation bar is on each page. They should not have to search for the navigation bar on each page that they visit in a site. Also site features like headers, sidebars, and footers need to be laid out in the same locations in the page design.

- Do not use blinking text or images as these can evoke seizures in some people.

- When presenting a speech, presentation or song in a site, make sure you also include a transcription of the message/song.

- Web pages with links, images, video and audio need special considerations and descriptions for tags and techniques are used in the page, these people can understand the content.

- Keep the page design and flow of information simple and clear for each page in a site.

- Text your site with multiple browsers for display, multiple users for ease of use, and use accessibility testing tools to test against Section 508 accessibility standards.

- Present text in no longer than 440 pixel wide blocks. The human eye does not like to read digital text blocks longer than this width.

> **Note: Accessibility testing tools**
> Dreamweaver has a built in tool for testing a website with Section 508 accessibility standards. This is covered in Chapter 15 "Publishing to the Web". You can also visit the following URL for other third party accessibility testing tools.
>
> http://www.w3.org/WAI/ER/tools/

Using HTML Accessibility Tags

When creating a website today, think about how people will access your site. In particular, consider how people that are blind or deaf interact with a website. A fancy video or visual presentation with audio and animation will not be effective for this type of visitor. Sites that rely heavily on sound, images, and graphics will not be understood by a people with visual or hearing challenges. Fortunately, HTML has accessibility features built into it, like the [alt] tag for describing images and the [title] tag for providing information about the webpage. Tags like these can be read by a screen reader and the descriptive text attached to these tags are then read to supplement or replace an HTML element, like an image. The following tags describe metadata and are accessible to a screen readers:

- <title>

- <style>

- <meta>

- <link>
- <script>
- <base>

Visit this page on the W3C website for a quick reference guide for designing for accessibility.

http://www.w3.org/WAI/WCAG20/quickref/#customize

Understanding Design Principles

Another area important area to consider when creating a website is how to use traditional design principles to make your page layout and design really shine. Design principles have been used for years in traditional print to create effective, engaging, and professional advertising and communications. Traditional design principles control how content and page elements interact with each other to help communicate a message more effectively. These design principles are emphasis, contrast, balance, alignment, balance, repetition, flow, consistency, and proximity. Here is an explanation and example of each.

- **Emphasis**: highlights a special importance or significance. Analyze a site's content in order to determine what hierarchy of importance the content should use. The larger or bolder the text or image the more emphasis is placed on it in the design. The human eye is drawn to these larger components on the page first.

Emphasis on the picture immediately communicates what the site is all about.

- **Contrast**: Visual Differentiation of two or more elements. – Stark contrast appear distinct and separate – low contrast elements appear similar and tend to blend together.

Using a black background in the header area provides great contrast for reading the white text and seeing the top navigation bar menu options.

- **Balance**: There are two types of balance principles, symmetrical and asymmetrical.

  Symmetrical: Design of the page is mirrored on some axis and the two halves have identical visual weights.

This design is symmetrical – a line could be drawn down the middle of the page and each half reflects the same layout of information

Asymmetrical: Visual weight of a page is equally distributed on an axis, but the individual elements of these halves are not mirror images.

This design is symmetrical – a line could be drawn down the middle of the page and each half reflects the same layout of information

- **Alignment**: arrangement of elements in such a way that the natural lines (or borders) created by them match up as closely as possible. – Elements become unified and form a greater whole.

This design uses alignment design principle to create natural lines that flow through the design.

- **Repetition**: repetition of design elements throughout a design in varying ways. Examples of this in a web page design is the use of color for headings, typically a Heading 1 color would be the same throughout all pages of the site. The same goes for Heading 2 – 6. The sidebar is in the same location on the page though for each page, different relevant information is communicated.

This design uses the repetition of colors for menu choices and charts to help convey their message.

- **Consistency**: be consistent in the location of design elements on a page. This principle can be reinforced with colors used in a site as well.

This design has a consistent page layout which is reinforced by the colors used for navigation links and the information on the page.

- **Proximity**: the relationship between elements on a page. An element that is by itself on the page stands out. Elements that are next to each can support each other's message.

This design uses proximity between the Heading 2 titles and the images to help communicate the page's message

- **Flow:** The path the user's eye takes through a design. Flow is the results of all other principles put together. Use flow principle to guide the visitor eye though your page and its message, point by point.

The design principle of flow is used in this site to guide your eye through the page layout by guiding your eye from top left to the middle right.

By following these design principles, you can create a cleaner, more interesting and profession page layout and overall design for your website.

Purpose of a Non-disclosure Agreement

Another item that might come up at the very beginning of a website project is a non-disclosure agreement. Typically clients and customers will use these when they have an idea or product that is new and needs to be protected and kept a secret from others until they are ready to release it to the world. As the web designer, you are seeing this idea or product prior to anyone else and helping the client design a website for the launch of the idea or product. The client or customer will provide you with a non-disclosure agreement to help protect the idea or product prior to its release. These Non-disclosures are usually straightforward and outline the agreement to keep the idea or product a secret and consequences if you were the one to leak out information. It is wise to have a lawyer review any non-disclosures prior to signing them. But if you are willing and able to keep the idea or product a secret, do not be afraid to sign the agreement, as it is very common to see this in the web design field.

End-of-Chapter Activities

Review Questions

Directions: Choose the correct answer for each question.

1. What types of new documents can you create using File>New command?
    a. PDF, DOCX and XLSX
    b. HTML, CSS, and JavaScript
    c. PHP, XML, and SVG
    d. None of the above
    e. B and C only

2. How many Bootstrap Starter Templates are available in Dreamweaver?
    a. 5
    b. 3
    c. 4
    d. 6

3. How many Responsive Starter Templates are available in Dreamweaver?
    a. 5
    b. 3
    c. 4
    d. 6

4. What is a placeholder used for in a Starter Template?
    a. To hold a place in the web page layout for future content
    b. To create a section or page break
    c. To create white space in the web page design
    d. To hold CSS formatting code

5. What are some considerations you must think through prior to creating a web page design?
    a. Visitor behavior
    b. Plan the Flow of information well before starting the design
    c. Accessibility
    d. Design Principles to help communicate site message better
    e. All of the above

6. What is the function of a non-disclosure agreement?
   a. To layout the terms of the working relationship between client and service provider.
   b. To layout the terms of the payment schedule between client and service provider.
   c. To protect and keep secret an idea or product prior to its release to the public.
   d. To govern the ownership of the website

7. What is the purpose of a screen reader?
   a. To read the screen to a person who is visually impaired.
   b. To access books online for people who are visually impaired
   c. To read the HTML accessibility tags and descriptions so a website is understood by a visually impaired visitor.
   d. A and C
   e. B and C

8. The design principle of Flow does what?
   a. Uses page elements to guide the eye through the design
   b. Establishes the order of the HTML tags in the document
   c. Establishes the order of the color usage in the design.
   d. None of these above

9. The design principle of Contrast does what?
   a. Makes the page elements easy to see
   b. Makes the text easy to read
   c. Makes the site message stand out better
   d. All of the above

10. What font size is recommend for text?
    a. 10 point
    b. 9 point
    c. 12 point
    d. 14 point

Essay Questions

Directions: Respond to each question by writing your answers in complete sentences and paragraphs. Be thorough in your answers.

1. A webpage layout can be broken down into what common page components that relate to what common HTML elements? List the common page component and set it equal to the related HTML element.

2. What advantages do you get from using a responsive starter layout?

3. What does the Visual Media Queries (VMQ) interface do?

4. What do the colors in the VMQ signify?

5. How does the Scrubber work in conjunction with the VMQ?

6. Why should you consider using Bootstrap for your next website?

7. True or false: You have to use one of the six predefined templates if you want to use Bootstrap.

8. Why should you replace the <div> elements created by Bootstrap with HTML5 semantic elements?

9. List web accessibility HTML tags.

10. List software and tools for special needs people.

Analyze Websites Based on Design Principles

In groups of 3-4 students, evaluate some of the more popular sites on the web today. Look at websites for Apple, Microsoft, CNN, Google, Adobe and other popular sites and break down their designs based on design principles. Base your analysis on how effective the design is for communicating the site message and information and how the design helps bring out or communicate the message. Present your findings to the class with examples of each website analyzed.

Critical Thinking Project – Working with Pre-Defined Layouts

This project has you working with Pre-defined layouts that are included in Dreamweaver to help you get started with a page design.

1. On your computer create a local root folder as directed by your teacher. Name the folder **layouts_xx**. Open this folder and create a new folder. Name the folder **images**.

2. Open Dreamweaver and define a new site.

3. In the Welcome window under New, click HTML Document to open the New Document window. You can also choose File>New from the menu bar to open the New Document window.

4. Click the **Starter Templates**, and then click the **Responsive Starters** option. Click the **About Page** option and then click **Create**.

5. Save the new responsive page as **myAbout_xx.html** as instructed by your teacher. Choose File>Save from the menubar to save the page.

6. If necessary, switch to Live View

7. Drag the Scrubber to the left to make the document window narrower. Notice that the page content resizes to fit the window width.

8. Drag the Scrubber to the right to make the document window wider. Again notice that the document window resizes to fit new wider window size.

9. View the pre-defined Visual Media Queries that are part of this pre-defined responsive layout by first displaying the Visual Media Queries bar. Click the Show Visual Media Queries bar icon in the upper right of the document window.

10. Position your insertion point over the first media query to display the tooltip. This media query is set for a max-width of 480 pixels. Position your insertion point over the second media query. This media query is set to a max-width of 1024 pixels. Position your insertion point over the third media query. This media query is set to a min-width of 1025 pixels.

11. Click to the left of the number 480 in the VMQ interface to make the window narrow instantly to 480 pixels. The page content reformats to this new width.

12. Click to the left of the number 1024 in the VMQ interface to make the window widen instantly to 1024 pixels. Again the page content reformats to this new window size. Now click to the right of the 1025 number in the VMQ interface to make the window expand in width. The page content again reformats to this new window size.

13. Double-click in the gray area on the right side of the Scrubber. The page layout files the document window in Dreamweaver.

14. Next you'll create a Bootstrap web page for a website that promotes Lake Powel. Open the lakepowell_Grid.jpg. Think about how Bootstrap organizes information in rows and columns and examine this web page mockup. Determine where the rows and columns need to be to support this design.

This mockup has 4 rows and one row with three columns.

15. Create a new custom Bootstrap document by choosing File>New and selecting **New Document** and then clicking **HTML** under the Document Type option. Click the **Bootstrap** tab.

16. For the Bootstrap CSS option select **Create New**. Deselect the Design option of Include a pre-built layout. Click the triangle next to the Customize option and review the settings. Keep these as they are set and click Create.

17. In the Save Style Sheet File As window, type **myBootstrap_xx.css** in the Save As field and double-click the CSS folder to designate that as the folder the new style sheet will be located. Click Save to save the style sheet.

18. Save the new Bootstrap document by choosing File>Save. Name the file **myBootstrap_xx.html**.

19. Switch to Split view and make the Insert panel if active by clicking its tab. If it is not opened choose Window>Insert to open this panel.

20. Click the Body tag in the tag selector to focus Dreamweaver on the <body. Tag. In the Insert panel select **Bootstrap Components** from the drop-down menu. Click to the right of the number 1200 in the VMQ interface. Then add a container element to the full width of the page by clicking the **Container fluid** option from the Insert panel. This creates a container for page content to automatically scales to every screen width.

21. With the overall container created, now you can create the row and column scheme for this page. First target the small media query by clicking to the left of the number 767. Then click the **Grid Row with column** option from the Insert panel and then click the **Nest** option to next the new row in the container and change the **No. of columns to add** option to 1.

22. Add another row after the nested row by clicking the Grid Row with column option from the Insert panel. Then click the **After** option and change the **No. of columns to add** option to **1**.

23. Add another row that has 3 columns by clicking the Grid Row with column option by clicking the After option and changing the **No. of columns to add** to **3**.

24. Add another row that as 1 column by repeating step 22.

25. Now rename the default <div> tags that you just created for the rows to HTML5 semantic tags. First switch to the Split view. Then click the first row of the layout and in the tag selector at the bottom of the document window click the div.row tag. Press Ctrl+T/Cmd+T to activate the Quick Tag Editor. Edit the tag to **<header class="row">**.

26. Repeat Step 25 to change the <div> tag to the following HTML5 tags:
    a. Row 2 – change to: nav
    b. Row 3 – change to: article
    c. Row 4 – change to: footer

27. Review your HTML code in the code view. It should look like this figure.

28. Now name the columns in the article row by clicking in the first column of the article. row. The first div.col-sm-4 element in the row should be selected. Press Ctrl+T/ Cmd+T. Edit the element to **<aside class="col-sm-4">**

29. Repeat step 28 and name the other two columns in the article row with the middle column being named **section** and the right column named **aside**. Your code should look like this figure.

30. Save the document by choosing File>Save.

Online Portfolio Builder – Create a Bootstrap Layout for your Portfolio Site

Using the mockup sketch of your site that you created in Lesson 5 Online Portfolio Builder project, create a custom Bootstrap page layout to start converting the mockup to HTML. Think about design principles, in particular Alignment, as you analyze the mockup and determine the rows and columns that occure naturally in the design. These rows and columns will translate to HTML elements and you are building the framework for these elements in this project.

1. Analyze your mockup sketch of your Online Portfolio website's home page that you created in Lesson 5. Draw lines that identify the basic page layout components. Label these on the sketch.

2. Using the same mockup sketch, next identify by writing on the sketch the HTML elements needed to represent each of the basic page layout components used in your home page mockup.

3. Open Dreamweaver and close the Welcome window. Open the File panel if it is not already opened by choosing Window>Files, or if it is open, click the File tab to make this the active panel.

4. Make sure you have defined your site and know where your myPortfolio_xx local root folder is on your computer or external device. As instructed by your teacher, set your Files Panel to this local root folder.

5. Next, create a new document by choosing File>New from the menubar. This opens the New Document window.

6. Explore the predefined responsive Responsive Starters templates by selecting **Starter Templates** and then the **Responsive Starters** folder. Click each of the layout options and compare the preview to your mockup sketches.

7. Explore the predefined Bootstrap Templates by selecting **Starter Templates** and then **Bootstrap Templates** folder. Click each of the layout options and compare the preview to your mockup sketches.

8. Next identify the Bootstrap basic grid structure in your mockup sketches for both the home page and the second level pages by identifying the rows for the page components.

9. Create a new Bootstrap custom page layout for your home page layout by selecting **New Document** category, and then selecting **HTML** option for the Document Type. In the Framework area of the New Document window, click the **Bootstrap** tab.

10. Click the **Create New** option for the Bootstrap CSS. Deselect the Design option **Include a Pre-built Layout**. Then click the **Customize** option to expand it. Preview the default setting. Leave these default settings as set. Click **Create** to create a new Bootstrap page for the home page of your site.

11. It is a good idea to save your new page after your create it. Choose File>Save from the menubar. Type *myHome_xx.html* in the Save As field and click **Save**.

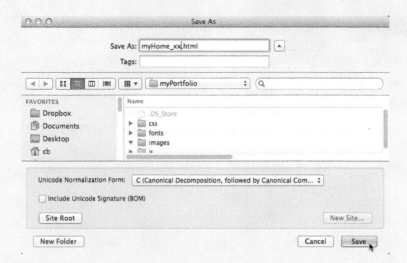

12. The Files panel reflects the new custom Bootstrap page as well as other folders that Dreamweaver created for supporting the new Bootstrap page. Compare your Files panel with the following figure. If it does not reflect these files and folders click the **Refresh** button to refresh the Files Panel display.

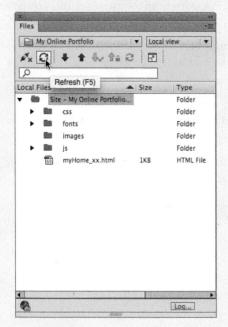

13. Display the Insert panel by clicking its tab. If the Insert panel is not opened choose Windows>Insert to open it.

14. Select Bootstrap components from the drop-down menu.

15. Click the Container item at the top of the panel to insert a fixed width <div> element. This is your overall container for your page layout.

16. Click the Small media query (min-width 768 pixels) in the VMQ to set the page layout size to a tablet sized window.

17. Click the **Grid Row with Column** item from the drop-down menu in the Insert panel. This displays the Insert Row with Columns window. Click the **Nest** option and enter **1** in the **No. of Columns to Add** field. Click **Ok** to nest a row in the overall container for your page layout.

18. Click the **Grid Row with Column** item again from the drop-down menu in the Insert panel. In the Insert Row with Columns window, select **After** and enter **1** for the number of columns. Click OK to create another row after the nested row.

19. Repeat step 19 to recreate your mockup layout for the home page of your site by inserting rows after the previously created row.

20. Now rename the default <div> tags that you just created for the rows to HTML5 semantic tags. First switch to the Split view. Then click the first row of the layout and in the tag selector at the bottom of the document window click the div.row tag. Press Ctrl+T/Cmd+T to activate the Quick Tag Editor. Edit the tag to **<header class="row">**.

21. Repeat Step 25 to change the <div> tags for your portfolio website to HTML5 tags – For instance:
    a. <nav class = "row"> for the navigation bar in your site
    b. <article class = "row"> for the main content area
    c. <footer class = "row"> for the footer

22. The article row has three columns, name each column from left to right these HTML semantic tags- **aside, section, aside.**

23. Save your myHome_xx.html document by choosing File>Save.

24. Close Dreamweaver.

WORKING WITH
A WEB FRAMEWORK

Dreamweaver has incorporated many advanced functions and components from various web frameworks, such as jQuery and Bootstrap, to speed up and simplify the process of developing fully functional, mobile-friendly websites, much of it without having to write a single line of code.

Chapter Overview

In this chapter, you'll learn how to do the following:

- Insert and format new content and components into a Bootstrap-based layout
- Use the CSS Designer to identify applied CSS formatting
- Create advanced CSS background and gradient effects
- Access and use web-hosted fonts

Creating Header Content

If you start at the top of the webpage and work down, the first element to address is the `<header>`. If you follow the site design mockup as your guide, the `<header>` is composed of several components, including the company name, the motto, the logo, and a graphical background.

This effect could be reproduced by using a single image, but that image would have to be quite large. A single image would be the least flexible option, not to mention the least accessible. Instead, we'll stretch your CSS skills by building a composite design combining text and multiple background effects. This technique will allow the design to be more adaptable to various devices, such as cellphones and tablets. This technique also makes the web page more accessible to screen readers and accessibility software. Let's start by adding the text.

1   If necessary, open **mylayout_xx.html** that you created in Chapter 6 or open the **mylayout_xx.html** from the Chapter07/Datafiles folder as instructed by your teacher.

2   Click the first row of the Bootstrap structure.
    Select the `div.col-sm-12` tag selector.

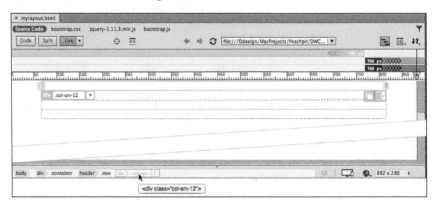

3   Open the Insert panel.
    Select the HTML tab from the drop-down menu.

    The HTML tab provides an easy way to insert all sorts of standard HTML elements.

4   In the Headings drop-down menu, select **H2**.

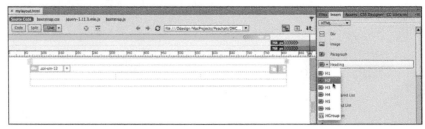

The position-assist interface appears. This interface enables you to choose where the new element will be inserted: before, after, nested within the current selection, or wrapped around the selection.

5   Select **Nest**.

A new <h2> element appears within the <div> filled with placeholder text. Text can now be edited directly in Live view, but you need to know a simple trick to make it editable.

6   Double-click the placeholder text.

The blue HUD disappears and is replaced by a plain orange box, indicating that the content of the <h2> is now in text-editing mode.

7   Select the text and type **greenstart** in all lowercase.

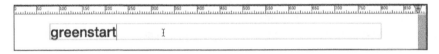

The company name replaces the placeholder text. Now let's add the company motto.

8   Press Enter/Return to create a new line.
Type **GREEN AWARENESS IN ACTION** in all uppercase.

The motto appears in a new <p> element, but the change is not permanent yet. Looking at the Code window you will not see the text you just typed. If you press the ESC key or click in the Code window, the new text may be discarded altogether.

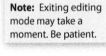
Note: Exiting editing mode may take a moment. Be patient.

9   Click the insertion point just outside the orange editing box.

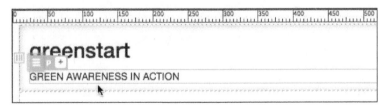

The orange box disappears. The heading and the motto are now a permanent part of the header.

10 Save the file.

The text has been entered but still needs to be formatted. Text and structural elements are formatted using cascading style sheets. The main tool for creating, editing, and troubleshooting these style sheets is the CSS Designer. Before you start styling your new webpage and content, it will help to familiarize yourself with how the CSS Designer functions.

Working with the CSS Designer

In the upcoming exercises in this chapter, you'll learn how to use the CSS Designer to inspect the existing CSS and create new rules to complete the basic site template design. Before you proceed, it's vital to your role as a designer to understand and identify any existing structure and formatting of a page so that you can effectively complete your tasks.

It's always a good idea when using any predefined components or frameworks to take a few minutes to examine the underlying HTML and CSS to understand what role they perform in the current document. It will also be a good opportunity to familiarize yourself with the CSS Designer and how to use it properly.

1 Open **mylayout_xx.html** that you created in Chapter 6 or open the **mylayout_xx.html** from the Chapter07/Datafiles folder as instructed by your teacher.

2 Choose Window > Workspace Layout > Design.
Choose Window > CSS Designer to display it, if necessary.

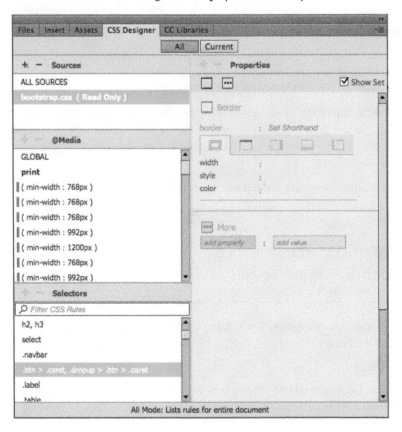

The CSS Designer has four windows that display different aspects of the CSS structure and styling: *Sources, @Media, Selectors,* and *Properties.* The latest version of CSS Designer also features two distinct modes: *All* and *Current.* At this moment you should ensure that the All mode is enabled.

3   Click the All button in the CSS Designer, if necessary.

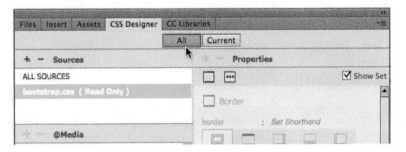

Note: CSS Designer should be a default component of the Design workspace, but sometimes users close panels unintentionally. Dreamweaver will remember any customizations you perform to the interface. If necessary, you can open it by selecting Window > CSS Designer.

The Sources window now displays all style sheets embedded or linked to the page. You should see two notations: ALL SOURCES and bootstrap.css.

4   Select ALL SOURCES in the Sources window.

The @Media and Selectors windows display all the media queries and selector names defined in any listed style sheet. The All mode will be very helpful in tracking down a specific rule and where it's defined. By selecting an item in either window, the CSS Designer will identify its location by highlighting its source in bold.

Note: The Current mode limits the display to only the CSS affecting the element selected in the document window.

5   Select the rule `a:active, a:hover` in the Selectors window.

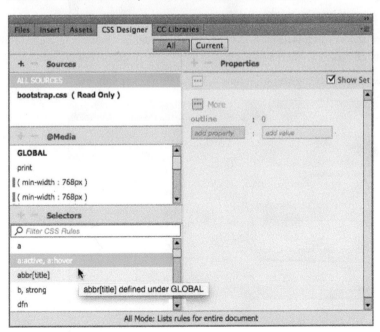

Global Rule

A rule that is accessible for all media queries.

Note that the name bootstrap.css in the Sources window and GLOBAL in the @Media window are now bolded. The bolding indicates that `a:active, a:hover` is defined in the bootstrap.css style sheet as a **global rule**. This behavior works even in the other windows.

6 Select the first (`min-width 768`) media query in the @Media window. Observe the changes in the CSS Designer display.

Note that bootstrap.css is still selected but the Selectors window now shows only one name: `.lead`. This indicates that only one rule is defined within the selected media query.

7 Select the `.lead` rule in the Selectors window.

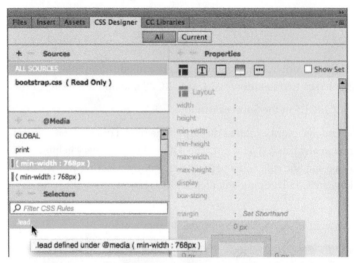

The Properties window displays the CSS properties defined in the rule. Depending on its configuration, you may not see which property or properties are set.

8 If necessary, select the Show Set option in the Properties window.

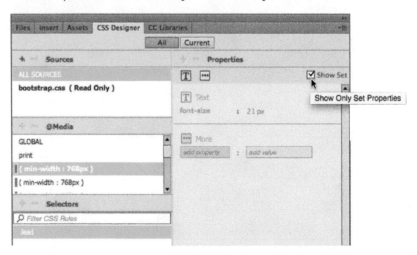

When Show Set is enabled, the Properties window displays only the properties modified by the rule. In this case, the `.lead` rule sets the font-size property to 21 px.

You may also notice that the Properties window has a gray background color. This indicates that the properties are non-editable. If you look at the Sources window, you can see that the **bootstrap.css** style sheet is marked as (`read only`). Since the page is based on the Bootstrap framework, Dreamweaver prevents you from modifying and potentially damaging its predefined styling. The styling contained within it is very complex and full of interdependencies. It's recommended that any changes be made in your own custom style sheet.

At the moment, there is no custom style sheet. Before you can style the structure or content of the new page and site, you'll have to add a new editable style sheet. You can create the style sheet directly in the CSS Designer.

9   Click the Add CSS Source icon ✚ in the CSS Designer.

A drop-down menu appears that allows you to create a new CSS file, attach an existing CSS file, or define a style sheet embedded within the page itself.

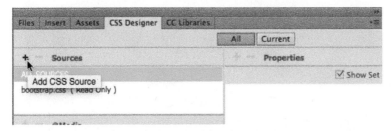

10 Choose **Create A New CSS File** from the drop-down menu.

The Create A New CSS File dialog appears.

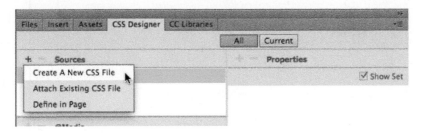

11 Type **green_styles.css** in the Create a New CSS File dialog. Click OK to create the style sheet reference.

When you click OK, a reference to the new style sheet is added to the CSS Designer Sources window. The CSS file has not actually been created yet, but a link has been added to the <head> section of the page and the file will be created automatically as soon as you create your first custom rule.

12 Click **green_styles.css** in the Sources window.

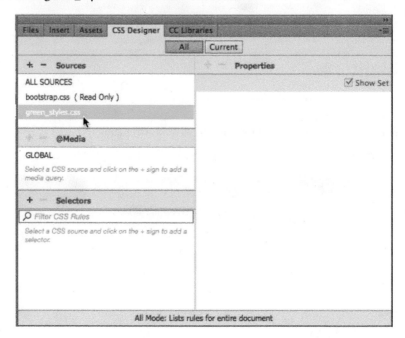

The @Media and the Selectors windows are both empty. This means there are no CSS rules yet. You have a blank slate on which you can make any design additions or modifications. Since you will not change the Bootstrap CSS, this style sheet will be the means you use to make the structure and content bend to your wishes.

13 Select the text "greenstart" in the `<header>` element.

14 Click the Current button.
Observe the CSS Designer.

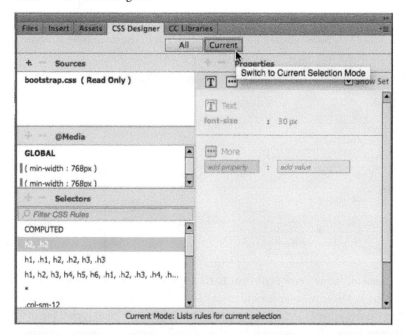

The windows in the CSS Designer change, displaying the media queries and selectors that format the selected element. A close inspection of the Sources window tells you that only the **bootstrap.css** file holds any of these rules. Then, a look at the Selectors window shows you the names of the rules that provide some sort of styling to the `<h2>` element itself or to its surrounding structure.

> **Note:** Remember you learned in Chapter 4, "CSS Basics," that some HTML elements have default styling. Default properties will not be shown in the CSS Designer.

15 Select each rule in the Selectors window, starting at the top of the list. Observe the Properties window as each rule is highlighted, but keep your eyes peeled for other changes in the workspace.

As you inspect each rule, you will see the Properties window change to display the formatting applied by each one. Did you notice that as you clicked each rule Live view highlighted the specific elements affected by the rule within the layout?

As you can see, CSS Designer can be used in a variety of ways to identify the styling applied to a specific element as well as to identify the element affected by a specific rule. It can also help you create and name the CSS rules.

Working with Type

In this exercise, you will learn how to create new selectors that will format text within the `<header>` element.

Note: When the Current button is selected, the CSS Designer allows you to edit only existing properties or add new properties to existing CSS rules.

1   Select the All button again in the CSS Designer.

When All is selected you can create new rules. Since **bootstrap.css** is locked, you need to select a different location for your new rule.

2   Select **green_styles.css** in the Sources window.

3   Make sure you have selected the text - greenstart- in the document window and then click the Add New Selector icon ➕.

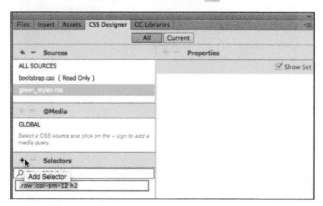

The selector name `.row .col-sm-12 h2` appears in the Selectors window. By default, Dreamweaver tries to create selector names using specific class or id attributes whenever they are present. This might be a good technique in a different layout, but this one is based on Bootstrap grid structures, meaning that the class names are not as useful as they might be in another situation.

For example, a selector written this way would affect <h2> elements inserted into the first, second, and fourth rows. To target the styling more narrowly, a bit of tweaking is required.

4   Edit the selector by double-clicking the selector name and typing as shown:
`header.row h2`
Press Enter/Return twice to complete the selector.

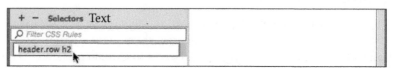

This new name will target only <h2> headings that are inserted into <header> elements with a class of `row`. Note that the Properties window has a white background, indicating that this rule is fully editable.

Note: The Properties window is a list of CSS properties. You can also scroll up or down to the desired category.

5   Deselect the Show Set option in the Properties window.

Only when Show Set is deselected does the Properties window display the list of all available CSS specifications. The list is organized into five categories, which can be accessed quickly by clicking their icons: Layout ⬛, Text Ⓣ, Border ▢, Background ⬛, and More ▪▪▪. To focus the display on a particular category, you can use the category icons at the top of the Properties window.

6   Click the Text category icon [T].

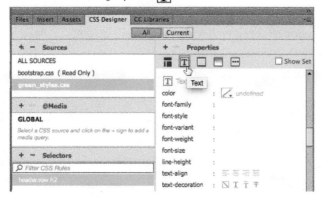

The Properties window focuses on the Text properties. You'll set some basic styling now and come back to this element later when you add more styling to the header.

7   Click the Set Color icon [✏] to open the Color Picker pop-up window.

The color picker enables you to select colors in several ways. You can choose a color by sight by using the various visual tools or by entering the color by number, using RGB, Hex, or HSL values.

8   Select Hex and enter #00FF00 in the color field.
    Press Enter/Return to close the color window.

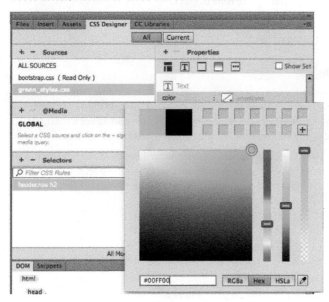

The text changes color to a bright green.

9   Click the value field to the right of the **font-family** property.

A pop-up window appears showing nine groups of typeface names and several design categories, such as **sans-serif** and **monospace**. We'll explore and learn

Note: It does not matter if you use uppercase or lowercase for Hexadecimal text character values but it does matter if you proceed the value with a #. Always use the # before the values, like #00ff00, or Dreamweaver will not recognize it and it then will automatically insert the default color of black -(#000000) as your color choice.

San-serif

A font that does not have small lines or flags at the end or top of the character lines. Examples of san-serif fonts are Arial, Helvetica, Avant Garde. A san-serif font is also called a machine font as it is installed on the computer when it is built and is always accessible to any program.

Monospace font

A font that has the same amount of spacing between each letter of a word. A monospaced font is also called a machine font as it is installed on the computer when it is built and is always accessible to any program.

Font group

A grouping of similar font styles. In web design these font groups are used to indicated the order for font usage by the visitor computer. Due to the fact that everyone can access a web page, designating one font for a page does not work, not everyone will have the font installed on their computer. Therefore, web designers use font groups which tells the browser to look for the first font in the list on the visitors computer first and if it is not there, then to look for the second and so forth through the list. The font group usually ends with a machine font like san-serif.

more about how to use fonts later, but for the moment let's just pick one of the predefined **font groups**.

10 Select the group Impact, Haettenschweiler, "Franklin Gothic Bold", "Arial Black", sans-serif

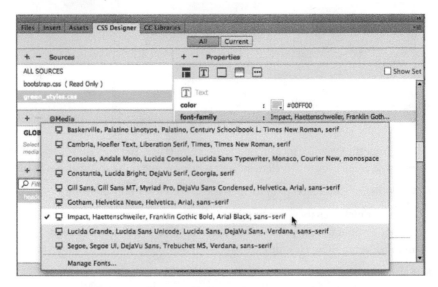

The <h2> is now formatted by the font Impact.

Defining Values

Values can be expressed in one or two parts in the Properties window. When the value comes in two parts, numeric values are entered on the left side and the measurement system (px, em, %) is entered, or selected, on the right. Single-part values (center, left, right, and so on) can be selected from the right side of the field or entered manually.

Predefined values (center, middle, top) or measurement systems can be selected from a hinting menu that pops up when Show Set is deselected. When Show Set is selected, the hinting menu does not appear at all and all values must be entered in full, manually.

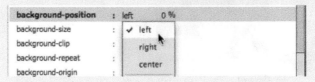

You may enter the value and measurement system all at once at any time by double-clicking the field and typing them in using the keyboard.

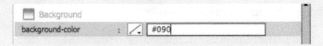

11 Double-click the **font-size** property value field, enter 350%

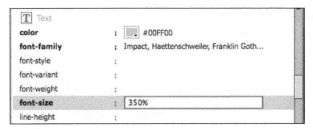

As you learned in Chapter 4, font sizes based on percentage are factored from the size of the body element.

12 In the **text-align** property, select center.

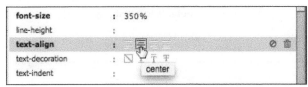

The text moves to the center of the <header>. The text is hard to read in such a bright color, but a drop shadow can improve the legibility.

13 In the **text-shadow** property, enter the following specifications:

```
h-shadow: 0px
v-shadow: 5px
blur: 5px
color: rgba(0,0,0,0.4)
```

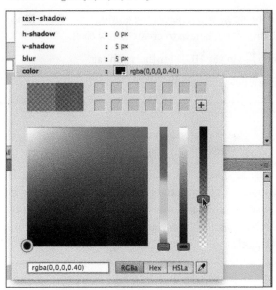

A drop shadow appears behind the heading.

The last task is to format the letters in "start" in white. This will require a custom class.

Creating Custom Classes

CSS styling can be applied to any distinct element, such as div, h1, p, a, and so on. When you want to apply formatting to a string of text that has no tag of its own, you need to use the <span> tag. When the styling can't be targeted using the structure of the code itself, the use of a class attribute is warranted.

In this exercise, you will create a custom class to apply white to a portion of the logo.

1 Double-click the text "greenstart" to enter text-editing mode in Live view.

The blue HUD is replaced by the orange editing box.

2 Select the letters "start".

3 Press Cmd+T/Ctrl+T to activate the Quick Tag Editor.

The Quick Tag Editor appears. It should default to Wrap tag mode.

4 Type <span> and press Enter/Return twice to complete the tag.

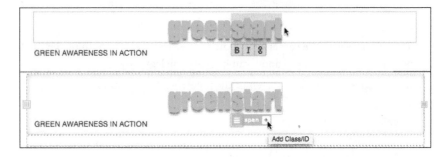

Tip: If you know what class you want to add to the <span> tag, you can also add it directly in the Quick Tag Editor.

The blue HUD, displaying the span tag, replaces the editing box. There is no existing formatting to call on, so you'll have to create a new class.

5 Click the Add Class/ID icon ⊞ in the HUD for the span tag.

6 Type .logowhite to create a new class name.

After you type the leading period (.) to start the class name, Dreamweaver will display a list of existing classes for you to choose from. As you continue to type, the list is filtered to names that match. When you are done typing, the list will disappear, indicating that this class name doesn't already exist.

7   Press Enter/Return to create the class.

A window appears allowing you to pick the style sheet and media query into which you can insert the new class. Since **bootstrap.css** is a read-only file, the menu should default to **green_styles.css**. At the moment, there are no media queries in **green_style.css**, so the class will be entered as a global style.

Note: If green_styles.css does not appear in the source menu, select it manually.

8   Press Enter/Return to complete the creation of the class `logowhite`.

9   Select **green_styles.css** in the Sources window.
Select `.logowhite` in the Selectors window.

10 Select the Text category icon [T] in the Properties window.

11 In the **color** property, enter #FFFFFF

The letters "start" appear in white. The logo is complete. Now, let's format the association motto. As with the heading, the process starts with a selection.

12 Select the text "GREEN AWARENESS IN ACTION" in the <header> element.

The blue HUD should appear around the <p> element in the Code view.

13 If necessary, select the **green_styles.css** file in Sources.

14 Click the Add Selector icon [+].

The name `.row .col-sm-12 p` appears in the Selectors window.

15 Change the selector to `header.row p`
Press Enter/Return twice to complete the name.

The new selector will target only <p> elements in the <header>.

16 Click the Text category in the CSS Designer, if necessary.

17 In the font-family property, select `"Lucida Grande", "Lucida Sans Unicode", "Lucida Sans", "DejaVu Sans", Verdana, sans-serif`.

18 In the **font-weight** property, enter `bold`

19 In the **text-align** property, select `center`.

20 In the **text-shadow** property, enter the following specifications:

```
h-shadow: 0px
v-shadow: 3px
blur: 5px
color: rgba(0,0,0,0.50)
```

21 In the **letter-spacing** property, enter `.5em`

The spacing between the letters expands.

22 In the **color** property, enter `#FFFFFF`

The motto now displays in white with a drop shadow. The styling of the header text is complete.

23 Save **mylayout_xx.html** and leave this open for the next exercise.

Next, you'll learn how to add background effects to the element.

Adding a Background Image

In this exercise, you will add the first background image to the `<header>` element and then use CSS to adjust its size and position.

1 If necessary, **mylayout_xx.html** from the Chapter07/Datafiles folder as instructed by your teacher.

2 Select or open the CSS Designer.

3 Click the first row of the Bootstrap structure.
Select the `header.row` tag selector.

4   Click the All button in the CSS Designer.

5   Select **green_styles.css** in the Sources window.

When **green_styles.css** is selected, the Selectors window displays only the rules that appear in that file.

6   Click the Add Selector icon ➕.

The selector name `.container .row` appears in the Selectors window. As you saw earlier, this name is too generic to be useful here. It would format every element with the class of `row`, which includes all four rows of the layout. In this case, you want to format only the `<header>`.

7   Edit the selector name to say `header.row`
Press Enter/Return as needed to complete the name.

This new selector appears in the CSS Designer and will specifically target only the header row. The first thing you should do is add a little breathing room above and below the header text. In the past, designers would often set a fixed height to elements like this. But the trend is to stay away from hard measurements so that the design can be more responsive and adaptable. One technique is to add padding to an element, which allows it to expand naturally.

8   Click the Layout category icon ▛.

9   In the padding property, enter 20px 0px

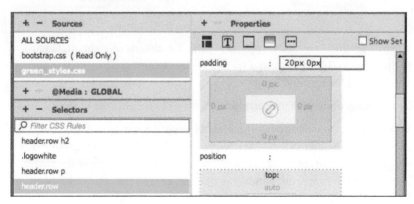

The header increases in height 40 pixels in total.

If you remember from Chapter 4, you can abbreviate CSS values using shorthand. This property applies 20 pixels of padding to the top *and* bottom of the header. Now, let's insert a background image.

10 Click the Background category icon ▧.
In the **background-image** section, click in the URL field.

11 Click the Browse icon ▧ next to the URL field.

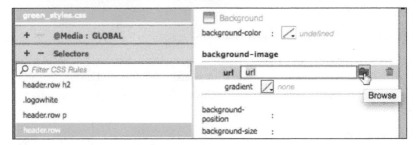

12 In the Select Image Source dialog, navigate to the default images folder.

13 Select **fern.png** and click Choose/Open.

Background images repeat both vertically and horizontally by default. This image is too tall to repeat vertically but, depending on your screen size, two ferns appear left to right.

14 In the **background-repeat** property, choose the no-repeat option.

The background image now appears once in the <header> element, aligned to the left side. The background specifications can also control the size and alignment of background images.

15 In the **background-size** property, select % from the **height** (right side) value field.

When you set the measurement system, the value defaults to zero (0). If only one value is set, the other value is set to auto by default. For the background-size property, a percentage value scales the image based on the size of the parent element. In the Properties window you can enter the value via the keyboard or by using the mouse.

16 Position the insertion point over the height value field.
Drag to the right to increase the value to 80%.

The image will scale to 80 percent of the height of the <header> element.

Tip: If you find the process of dragging to set the values too difficult, you may enter them via the keyboard by double-clicking the field.

17 In the **background-position** property, select `center` from the **horizontal** (left side) and **vertical** (right side) value fields by clicking the value unit field, not the number field.

The image appears centered vertically, but it seems slightly off-center horizontally.

18 In the **background-position** property, select % from the **horizontal** (left side) field.

The field defaults to zero (0).

19 In the left number value field click the field and drag to the right to increase the setting to 47%. You can also drouble-click in the value field on the left and type 47.

The fern image is now visually centered vertically and horizontally in the <header>.

20 Save the file.

In addition to the background image, you can also apply other background effects, such as solid colors and even gradients. Since gradients are a new CSS3 specification, it's recommended that you always add a solid color to the background to support browsers or devices that don't support gradients.

Adding Other Background Effects

In this exercise, you will add both a `background-color` and a `background-gradient` to the <header> element.

Note: Hexadecimal colors can be written in shorthand, like #090, when the numbers are in matched pairs, such as #009900. Be aware, however, that any time you enter such shorthand expressions Dreamweaver may arbitrarily rewrite them in full or swap them with RGB values.

1 If necessary, open **mylayout_xx.html** from the Chapter07/Datafiles folder as instructed by your teacher.

2 Click the All button in the CSS Designer.
Select **green_styles.css** in the Sources window.

3 Select the `header.row` rule.
In the **background-color** property, enter #090

The background color of the header changes to green. This color setting is a fallback option, which will display if the browser doesn't support CSS gradients. Next, let's create the gradient background for the newer applications and devices.

4 In the **background-image** property of the `header.row` rule, click the gradient color picker ⬜.

Note: When you set colors using hexadecimal formats in gradients, Dreamweaver will change them to RGBa notations automatically.

CSS3 gradients are code-intensive effects, but Dreamweaver's gradient color picker makes their specification both fast and easy. The default gradient has two color stops.

5 Click the top gradient color stop and type #060 int he Hex value field.
Then click the bottom gradient color stop and type #0C0 in the Hex value field.
Set the Linerar Gradient Agle to 180.
Press Enter/Return to set the gradient color.

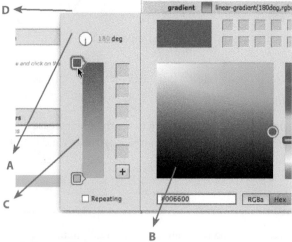

A - Top gradient color stop

B - Hex Value

C - Bottom gradient color stop

D - Linear Gradient Angle

The gradient is applied, but there's a problem. The effect is centered vertically and horizontally behind the fern image but does not fill the entire header from edge to edge. Background gradients are treated as background *images*. Since there's already a background image applied to the element, the gradient uses the same size and positioning specifications that were applied to the fern.

CSS3 allows you to apply multiple background images to an element. It even allows you to apply individual specifications to each effect. Unfortunately, although the CSS Designer can apply both a gradient and an image to the background, it provides only one set of size and positioning specifications. But don't worry. Whenever the CSS Designer lets you down, you can always resort to Code view.

6 Right-click the header.row rule in the Selectors window.
Choose **Go to Code** from the context menu.

Dreamweaver switches to Split view, inserts the insertion point in the Code view window, and focuses on the `header.row` rule in the style sheet. Note that the `background-image` property shows specifications for both the fern image and the gradient in one declaration. A comma separates the two properties.

If you examine the `background-size` and `background-position` properties, you'll see but a single specification in each. To add a second value for the gradient, you just have to add a comma at the end of each declaration and then enter the desired values.

7   Add the following highlighted values to these existing properties:
`background-size: auto 80%, 100% auto;`
`background-position: 47% center, left top;`

8   Select Show Set in the Properties window.
Observe the `header.row` rule and all the specifications displayed in the CSS Designer.

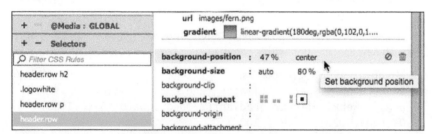

The Properties panel displays the background image and gradient but shows only one set of specifications for the size and position. You can edit the original set using the CSS Designer, but you'll have to continue to edit any others in Code view, manually.

9   Choose File > Save.

The fern remains formatted as before, but the gradient now fills the entire header.

Now that you've learned how to edit the rule manually, there's nothing stopping you from taking this effect one step further by adding a third background effect to create the vertical stripes, as shown in the mockup.

10 Right-click the `header.row` rule.

A context menu appears.

Tip: Don't forget to add the comma (,) between each specification. They won't work properly without it.

Note: CSS properties in your code may appear in a different order than that pictured.

Tip: In some cases, you may need to refresh the document window display manually to see the effects of the CSS.

Incompatible Code

When you finish defining the gradient background for the header, you might see an error message appear above the document window.

Dreamweaver reports when specific code elements are not fully standardized or supported in various browsers or applications. In this case, the program is advising you that CSS gradients have not been fully adopted by all browsers and may display poorly or not at all.

Be sure to read the message and follow the links to learn more. When you are finished, you can clear the message by clicking the ⊗ on the right side of the window.

11 Select Go To Code from the menu.

The Code view window appears in Split view focused on the first header.row rule in the linked style sheet.

The reference to **fern.png** appears first in the background-image property, the gradient in the second. To get the stripes to appear between these two effects, you'll have to insert the new specifications between them. Be sure to separate each new specification with a comma.

> **Note:** The stripe.png image is identical to the one created using Adobe Generator in Chapter 5, "Web Design Basics."

12 Modify the following properties:
```
background-image: url(images/fern.png), url(images/stripe.
png), -webkit-linear-gradient(270deg,rgba(0,102,0,1.00)
0%,rgba(0,204,0,1.00) 100%);
background-image: url(images/fern.png), url(images/stripe.
png), linear-gradient(180deg,rgba(0,102,0,1.00) 0%,
rgba(0,204,0,1.00) 100%);
background-repeat: no-repeat, repeat-x;
background-size: auto 80%, auto auto, 100% auto;
background-position: 47% center, left top, left top;
```

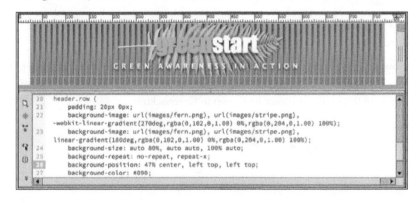

13 Choose File>Save All and leave the file open for the next exercise. The File>Save All command saves all open files. This is your myLaout_xx.html as well as all supporting resource files.

The stripes appear and repeat horizontally across the header. By using a small graphic that repeats across the element, you are minimizing the size of the graphics that must be downloaded to create this effect. Best of all, if the graphic doesn't download at all, the gradient background is still displayed. In the odd chance that neither the graphic nor the gradient is displayed, the header will display the solid green color applied in step 1.

The basic design of the `<header>` element for desktop or GLOBAL environments is now complete. The text, logo, and background effects will require some custom specifications for smaller screens, but we'll address that task in Chapter 8, "Designing for Mobile Devices." Instead, let's turn our attention to the next component on the page: the horizontal navigation menu.

Creating a Navigation Menu

The site mockup we used in Chapter 6 has a horizontal navigation menu with seven links. We don't have seven pages to link to yet, but you can create simple placeholders for the final content; we'll add actual functioning links in Chapter 12, "Working with Navigation." Let's create a menu to match the pages outlined in the thumbnails created in Chapter 5, and then style it to match the site color scheme.

Note: The site design mockup is included in the file set for Chapter 6. Feel free to open GreenStart_mockup.html to refresh your memory of the design and components.

1 If necessary, open **mylayout_xx.html** from the Chapter07/Datafiles folder as instructed by your teacher in Live view.

2 Select the second row of the Bootstrap layout.

The Element HUD appears.

3 Display the Insert panel.
Select the Bootstrap Components category.

The Bootstrap Components category offers two types of navigational elements: complete navigational menubars, or *navbars,* and standalone navigational menu components. In this situation, you'll use one of the complete navbars. Since the component already has its own built-in responsive structure and formatting, one of the existing layout elements will have to be removed to prevent conflicts, along with some other tweaks.

4 Select the `div.col-sm-12` tag selector.

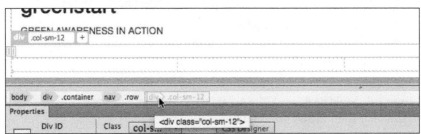

This `<div>` element is inserted as a responsive Bootstrap element. The class `col-sm-12` formats the element to occupy all 12 columns in the grid, or the entire width of the container. The Bootstrap navbars are designed to be responsive, so this element is redundant and may cause undesirable interference with the navbar itself. You will replace this element with the navbar.

5 Click the Navbaritem drop-down menu and then click **Basic Navbar**.

The position-assist dialog appears.

6 Click **Nest**.

A predefined Bootstrap navbar appears nested in the `<div>`, which can now be removed. The easiest way to delete an element is by using the Remove Tag command.

7 Switch to Split view. If necessary, select Source Code in the Referenced File display.

The Remove Tag command works only in Design view or Code view.

8 In Code view, locate and insert the insertion point after the tag `<div class="col-sm-12">`.

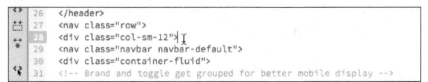

9 Right-click the `div.col-sm-12` tag selector. Select Remove Tag from the context menu.

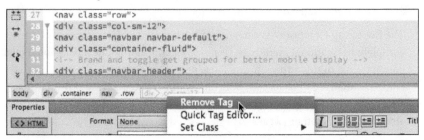

The `<div>` is removed from the layout without affecting the navbar.

The navbar remains composed of two separate navigation menus with drop-down components and a search field with a button. It would be a rare situation that you would want or need all of these items.

In this case, you need only a single set of seven links. Any element that's not needed should be deleted. The safest method to select and delete HTML elements is via the tag selector interface.

10 In Live view, click the Dropdown menu on the right side of the navbar in Live view.

The HUD appears, focusing on the a tag. Observe the tag selector interface. Can you identify the parent element to the right side menu?

11 Select the ul.nav.navbar-nav.navbar-right tag selector.

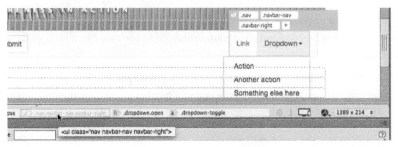

The entire menu on the right side of the navbar is selected, displaying the HUD.

12 Press Delete.

The menu is removed. Next, you'll remove the search field and button.

13 Click the search field or button.

As before, the HUD appears, identifying the selected element. If you examine the tag selectors, you should be able to track down the parent structure. It helps to know that search fields need to be inserted in HTML <form> elements.

14 Select form.navbar-form.navbar-left in the tag selector interface and press Delete.

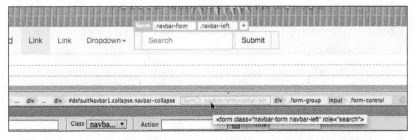

The search field and button are removed. The current design doesn't call for a drop-down menu. If you need one later, it's a simple matter to add one back. Drop-down menus are usually built from a sub-list inserted into an existing menu item.

15 Click the Dropdown menu and observe the tag selectors.

Dreamweaver will focus on the a tag in the parent <li>. In Live view, the drop-down menu should open, displaying the sublinks contained within the menu. Deleting the parent will remove the entire structure.

16 Select li.dropdown.open and press Delete.

The drop-down menu is removed, leaving two links and the word Brand. At first you might think that the word is simply another link in the remaining menu. But a quick look using the tag selectors and you will see the reality.

17 Click one of the Link items in the menu, and then click the word Brand. Examine the tag selectors.

If you compare the structures, you should see that the Link items are contained within nav.nav.navbar-nav, while the word Brand is actually in nav.navbar-header. In Bootstrap, the Brand element is intended to be used as a stand-in for your logo and to provide a handy link back to your home page. Like the other elements, it's unneeded in this layout. You need to remove the text as well as the link markup.

18 Select the a.navbar-brand tag selector and press Delete.

All the unneeded components have now been removed. Next, you will replace the generic link placeholders with ones that match the site design and learn how to make new Link items.

19 Switch to Design view and double-click the first menu item.
Select the text "Link" and change it to **Home.**

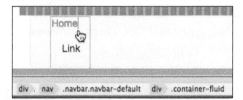

20 Change the remaining Link item to **Green News** and save the file. Leave it open for the next exercise.

The two predefined links now match the menu items from the design mockup, but you still need to create five more items. The good thing about using an unordered list for the menu is that Dreamweaver makes it easy to insert new list items.

Adding New Items to a Navigation Menu

In this exercise, you will learn how to insert new items in the navigation menu. Links can be added in any view mode, although the techniques differ.

1 Use the file from the previous exercise or open **mylayout_xx.html** from the Chapter07/Datafiles folder as instructed by your teacher.
In Live view, click the *Green News* link.
Select the li tag selector.

2 Choose Window > Insert to display the Insert panel.
In the HTML category, click the **List Item** option.

The position-assist interface appears.

3 Click **After**.

A new list item appears with placeholder text.

4 Select the placeholder text *Content for li Goes Here*.
Type **Green Events** to replace it.

The new item appears beside the previous ones, but it's not formatted like the other links. You might be able to figure out what's wrong using Live view, but in this case, the problem can be identified faster in Code view.

5 Click the `<li>` tag selector for the new link item and switch to Code view.
Observe the menu items and compare the first two to the new one.

Can you identify the difference? In fact, there are a few. For one thing, the first item features a class of `active` as well as a `<span>` element containing text intended for screen readers (`class="sr-only"`). But the only thing the first two share that the last item lacks is the hyperlink placeholder markup `<a href="#">`.

Since this is the only meaningful difference between the list items, you can rightly assume that the `<a>` markup is conveying at least part of the menu styling. To make *Green Events* look like the other menu items, you have to add a hyperlink to it, too, or at least a similar placeholder.

6 Select the text "Green Events" in Code view.
In the Property inspector Link field, type # and press Enter/Return.

The `<a href="#">` notation is added to the text so that the menu item now features the same markup as the others.

7   Switch to Split view.

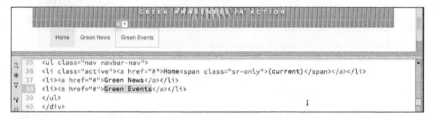

```
35   <ul class="nav navbar-nav">
36   <li class="active"><a href="#">Home<span class="sr-only">(current)</span></a></li>
37   <li><a href="#">Green News</a></li>
38   <li><a href="#">Green Events</a></li>
39   </ul>
40   </div>
```

The new item looks like the others. New menu items can also be added by typing.

8   In Live view, insert the insertion point at the end of the text "Green Events" and press Enter/Return to create a new line.

It may not be apparent in Live view, but Dreamweaver is creating a new `<li>` element in the background. But unlike using the Insert panel, this method doesn't add any placeholder text.

9   Type **Green Travel** and select the text.
Click just outside the orange editing box.

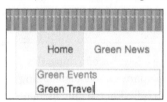
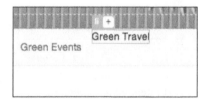

The HUD appears focused on the new *Green Travel* item.

10 In the Property Link field, enter # and press Enter/Return.

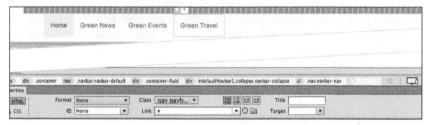

The new *Green Travel* link is complete. You can also add menu items in Code view.

11 Switch to Code view.

In this view, you can choose from several methods for creating a new list item. For example, you can type out the entire element manually, use the Insert panel as in step 2, or use copy and paste.

12 Insert the insertion point in the *Green Travel* link.
Select the li tag selector.

By using the <li> element, Dreamweaver selects the link markup as well as the text.

13 Choose Edit > Copy or press Ctrl+C/Cmd+C.

14 Press the right arrow key.

The insertion point moves to the end and outside the current <li> element. Although there's no need to insert a new line in the code, it keeps the markup consistent and easier to read.

15 Press Enter/Return to insert a new line.
Choose Edit > Paste or press Ctrl+V/Cmd+V.

```
38   <li><a href="#">Green Events</a></li>
39   <li><a href="#">Green Travel </a></li>
40   <li><a href="#">Green Travel </a></li>
41   </ul>
```

A duplicate version of the *Green Travel* list item appears.

16 Select the duplicate text *Green Travel*.
Type **Green Tips** to replace it.

The new menu item is complete and already contains the link # placeholder.

17 Using any of the methods describe above, create two more menu items for the links *Contact Us* and *About Us*.

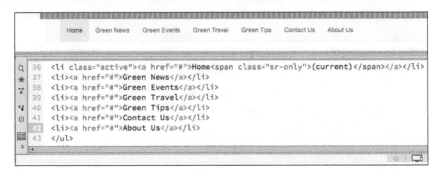

18 Save the file. Leave it open for the next exercise. If necessary, switch to Split view.

There are seven items in the menu now. Before you can format the menu, though, you'll have to correct some inconsistencies in its basic structure. These differences entail the attributes class `active` and the screen reader text (`sr-only`) noted earlier. Let's discard both of them.

Cleaning Up Bootstrap Components

Your newly modified Bootstrap menu has some inconsistent code structures in the new menu. In this exercise, you'll clean up these inconsistencies.

1 Use the file from the previous exercise or if necessary, open **mylayout_xx.html** from the Chapter07/Datafiles folder as instructed by your teacher. Switch to Split view.

2 Examine the code of the horizontal menu.

The menu is constructed using an unordered list with seven list items. In Live view you can see that the *Home* link is formatted differently from the rest. The most obvious difference between this link and the others is the class attribute `active`.

3 Select and delete the attribute ~~class="active"~~ from the first `<li>` element in Code view.

Once the class is deleted from the *Home* link, the formatting of the button will match the others. The last step is to remove the screen reader text.

4 Select and delete the element ~~<span class="sr-only">(current)</span>~~ from the first `<li>` element.

5 Save the file. Leave it open for the next exercise.

All the links in the menu are now formatted identically. It's common when using predefined or third-party components that you will have to modify the original structure and formatting to conform to your own content or project requirements.

Hyperlink Pseudo-Classes

The <a> element (hyperlink) provides five states, or distinct behaviors, that can be modified by CSS using what are known as pseudo-classes. A pseudo-class is a CSS feature that can add special effects or functionality to certain selectors, such as the <a> anchor tag:

- The a:link pseudo-class creates the default display and behavior of the hyperlink, and in many cases is interchangeable with the a selector in CSS rules. But the a:link is *more* specific, and will override specifications assigned to a less-specific selector if both are used in the style sheet.

- The a:visited pseudo-class formats the link after it has been visited by the browser. This resets to default styling whenever the browser cache, or history, is deleted.

- The a:hover pseudo-class formats the link when the insertion point passes over it.

- The a:active pseudo-class formats the link when the mouse clicks it.

- The a:focus pseudo-class formats the link when accessed via keyboard as opposed to mouse interaction.

When used, the pseudo-classes must be declared in the order listed above to be effective. Remember, whether declared in the style sheet or not, each state has a set of default formats and behaviors.

Styling a Navigational Menu

Menus typically exhibit two basic behaviors, or looks: a static, or default, state and a rollover, or hover, state. All the formatting is controlled by CSS.

1   Use the file from the previous exercise or if necessary, open **mylayout_xx.html** from the Chapter07/Datafiles folder as instructed by your teacher and, if necessary, switch to Live view. Maximize the program to fill the computer display. The document window should be wider than 1024 pixels.

The navigation menu was created from a Bootstrap component and comes with basic predefined styling provided by the Bootstrap default style sheet, which is locked. Any styles you create will be added to the **green_styles.css** file. The new styles will reset or override the predefined specifications or create new ones from scratch. The first step is to add a background color to the entire menu.

2   Select any menu item. Examine the tag selectors to identify the structure of the menu.

The menu is built by inserting an <a> element within an unordered list. The list is contained within the nav.row element you created originally using Bootstrap components. But the formatting is coming from some aspect of the menu you inserted. To create a background color for the entire navbar, you first need to identify the rule that applies the current formatting.

Note: You will notice that the row and the navbar feature <nav> elements and classes named "nav," which could create some confusion. When identifying elements for styling, make sure you select the correct one.

3   Click the Current button in the CSS Designer.

The Selectors window displays a list of rules that are applying some sort of styling to the navbar or menu items.

4   Select the Show Set option, if necessary.

5   Start at the top of the Selectors list and click each rule. Examine the properties assigned by each, and look for any that assign background colors or background gradients.

The very first rule applies a background color of `transparent`. Although this is the correct property, you can see that the background of the navbar has some sort of shading or gradient. Keep looking.

Next, you will come across a rule that formats the `a:hover` and `a:focus` states of the menu links. Although this is a valid background property, the `a:hover` and `a:focus` selectors will format only the actual hyperlinks themselves. There still has to be another rule that formats the entire navbar. Keep looking.

Finally, over 20 rules down the list you will find `.navbar-default`, which applies a background color of `#f8f8f8`. To reset the styling and apply a background to match the site design, you have to make a new rule that has equal or greater specificity.

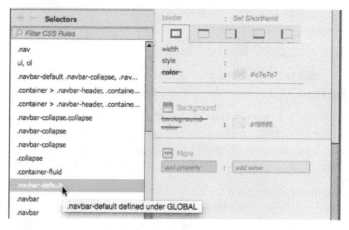

6   Select the `nav.navbar.navbar-default` tag selector.

The HUD appears around the entire navbar.

7   In the CSS Designer, click the All button.
Select **green_styles.css** in the Sources window.
Click the Add Selector icon ➕.

A suggested selector name appears in the window.

8   Edit the name to:

`nav.row .navbar.navbar-default`

Note: Make sure you select the nav.navebar.navbar-default tag in Step 6. If you choose a CSS rule that has the period in front, indicating that it is a class selector, the following steps will not work.

9 Press Enter/Return twice to complete the selector.

10 In the CSS Designer, deselect Show Set.

11 In the Background category, enter #069 in the **background-color** property.

The background color changes from light gray to dark blue. The background-color property covers the older browsers; now let's add some advanced styling.

12 In the **background-image** property, click the gradient color picker.

13 Set #069 as the **top** gradient color stop.
Set #08A as the **bottom** gradient color stop.
Set the Linear Gradient Angle to 180 degrees.
Press Enter/Return to complete and apply the gradient.

The gradient background supersedes the solid background color. The new background color is nice, but it makes the menu buttons hard to distinguish. They could use some definition of their own, like adding some borders.

14 Select one of the menu items.

The HUD displays the a tag.

15 In the CSS Designer, click the Current button and enable the Show Set option again.

Check the list of rules again for ones that set borders. When you are finished, you'll find that there are a few that apply borders to the entire navbar, but none that do so for the menu items themselves. You could apply rules to either the <li> or the <a> element in this structure, but in this case it makes more sense to create a rule to format the <a> element.

16 Click the All button.
In **green_styles.css**, create a new selector named
`nav.row.nav.navbar-nav > li > a`

By adding nav.row to the selector, it will override the default formatting and specifically target only this nav element. It will also preclude the rule from unintentionally formatting other menus you may insert in the layout later.

Note: The greater-than symbols you see in the selector name indicate that the rule is targeting only the immediate children of the preceding element rather than any descendant.

17 Add borders by first deselecting the Show Set option in the CSS Designer. Then click the Border option. Click the Top option from the Border Type area and then set the Border Style options for the top border as indicated below. Set the other border styles by repeating these steps for the bottom, right and left borders as indicated below.

```
border-top: solid 1px #0AE
border-right: solid 1px #037
border-bottom: solid 1px #037
border-left: solid 1px #0AE
```

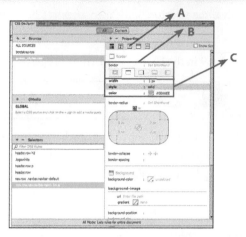

A - Border

B - Border Type

C - Border Style

Click the Show Set option in the CSS Designer and compare your properties to the figure below. Make any changes as needed to match these settings.

By alternating the border colors this way, it produces a three-dimensional effect on the menu buttons.

The main feature of the navigation menu is the hyperlink. It features five distinct states: link, visited, hover, active, and focus, in that order. See the sidebar "Hyperlink pseudo-classes" for a full description of hyperlink behaviors and states.

When links appear in the body of a webpage, the link and visited states are usually formatted separately, but in a menu you want them to be identical. The selector created in step 16 already targets the default a state of the hyperlink. But you'll need to add the *visited* reference to the name to cover both behaviors.

18 Double-click the name `nav.row .nav.navbar-nav > li > a`.

The selector name becomes editable.

19 Select the entire name and copy it.

> **Note:** Don't forget the comma between selectors.

20 Insert the insertion point at the end of the selector, type `:link,` and press Ctrl+V/Cmd+V to paste the copied selector.

21 At the end of the new name, type `:visited` and press Enter/Return as needed to complete the name.

The new selector targets the link and visited states of the menu items. Check your selector name to make sure you did not accidentally add spaces to the pseudo-classes.

22 Deselect the Show Set option.
In the Text category, enter #FFC in the **color** property.

Note: It's not required to add the :link markup to the default link name, but it increases the specificity of the rule.

The link names appear in light yellow.

The :hover pseudo-class is responsible for styling links whenever the insertion point is positioned over them. Normally, you'll see this behavior simply as the insertion point turning into the pointer icon, but for this dynamic menu let's apply different background and text colors to create a rollover effect.

23 Click the Add Selector icon ✚ . Select the new name and press Ctrl+V/Cmd+V to replace it with selector you copied in step 19.

24 At the end of the name, type :hover
Press Enter/Return twice to create the new selector.

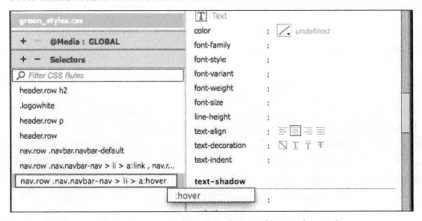

25 In the **background-image** property, click the gradient color picker.

26 Set #069 as the **top** gradient color stop.
Set #08A as the **bottom** gradient color stop.
Set the Linear Gradient Angle to 0 degrees.
Press Enter/Return to complete and apply the gradient.

The new gradient is a mirror image of the one created in step 12.

27 In the Text category, enter #FFF in the **color** property.

You can test the effect in Live view.

28 Position the insertion point over any of the menu items.

The gradient background flips vertically and the link color displays in white, providing a good contrast from the default menu state. Now, let's add the yellow border that divides the header from the menu.

29 Create a new Selector named `nav.row`

In the **border-top** property, enter `5px solid #FD5`

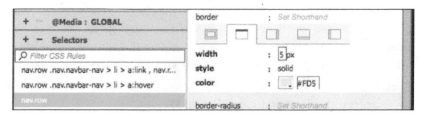

A yellow border appears above the menu.

30 Select File>Save All and then leave the file open for the next exercise.

The navigation menu is nearly complete. The last step is to center the menu horizontally within the navbar itself.

Centering the Navigation Menu

Bootstrap allows you to create complex menu and navigation components with a minimum of effort, but it doesn't offer unlimited styling options. For one thing, the framework offers two basic alignment options for horizontal menus: aligned to the left or justified across the entire structure. Aligning the menu to the center of the navbar, as in our site design, will require you to step away from the framework defaults and create your own custom styling.

The first step is to set a fixed width on the menu.

> **Note:** The menu width is derived from the Bootstrap CSS, which sets a maximum of 750 pixels for the menu before it collapses to an icon. You will work with mobile design in Chapter 8.

1 Create a new selector in **green_styles.css** named
`nav.row .nav.navbar-nav`

2 Under Layout in the CSS Designer, in the **width** property, enter `715px`

This width allows the menu to fit on one line but still function properly in the responsive structure. Now that you have set the element width, you can center it using a simple CSS trick.

3 In the **margin** property, enter the shorthand:
`0px auto`

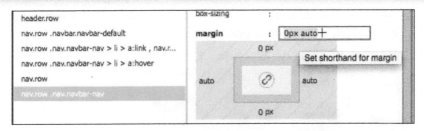

The shorthand applies zero pixels of margin to the top and bottom of the menu and equal amounts of spacing to the left and right. This setting should center the element, but the menu isn't moving. When styling doesn't work as expected, use CSS Designer to identify the issue.

4   Select Show Set and then click the Current button in CSS Designer. Select the COMPUTED option in the Selectors window.

5   Examine the properties styling the menu.

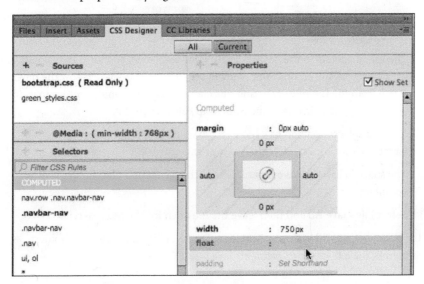

Some properties are displayed in gray and some in white, indicating which items are editable and which are not. One of the uneditable Bootstrap rules sets a float:left property. We can cancel it out using the rule created in step 1.

6   Select the nav.row .nav.navbar-nav rule.

When the Show Set option is enabled you can still edit the properties and values in the CSS Designer or even create new ones. When Show Set is enabled you don't see a list to choose from, so you have to know what property you want to enter in the open field.

7   Insert the insertion point in the empty field in the Properties window.

8   Type float and press the Tab key.

Note how the hinting menu filters as you type. As with the HTML hinting menu, feel free to select the property using your mouse or keyboard.

9   Type or select none in the value field.

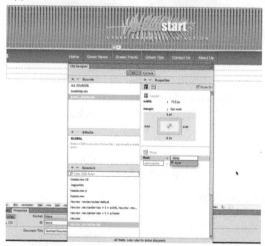

The menu centers in the navbar. There's one last tweak you need to make. If you look closely at the second row, you will see that there is space below the navbar. If you examine the rules affecting this element, you will find a bottom margin of 20 pixels applied via one of the Bootstrap rules: .navbar.

10 Create a selector named nav.row .navbar
    Create a new property **margin-bottom** and enter 0px

The space below the navbar is removed. The navigation placeholder is now complete.

11 Select File>Save All and then leave the file open for the next exercise.

The next task is to fill in the content area. First, you'll insert new placeholder content in the left <aside> element.

Building Semantic Content

The left column of the <article> element will be used for environmentally themed quotations. In the past, you might display quotations like any other paragraph, but to follow web standards under HTML5 you'll want to build these quotations using semantic elements. Unlike normal paragraph text, the value of a quotation is usually based on the perceived reputation of the author or source. HTML provides several elements designed specifically to identify this type of content.

1   Use the file from the previous exercise or if necessary, open **mylayout_xx.html** from the Chapter07/Datafiles folder as instructed by your teacher and, if necessary, switch to Live view.

2   Click the first column of the third row.
    Examine the tag selectors.

    The current structure is based on an **<aside>** element with the class of
    col-sm-4. First, we'll insert the placeholder for the quotation and then wrap it
    with a semantic structure.

3   Open the Insert panel and select the HTML category.

4   Click the **Paragraph** item.
    Select **Nest**.

    A <p> element appears in the column with placeholder text.

5   Select the placeholder text *This is the content for Layout P Tag* and delete it.

6   Type **"Insert quotation here."** and press Enter/Return to create a new paragraph.
    Make sure you type quotation marks around this text for this step.

7   Type **Insert author here** and click outside the orange box to complete the
    elements.

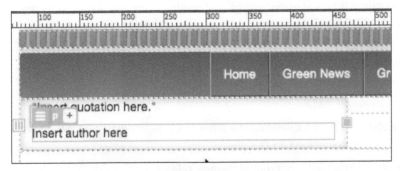

Semantically, quotations should be based on the <blockquote> element. You
need to put both paragraphs into the **blockquote**, but unfortunately, you can't
select two elements at once in Live view.

8   Select the p tag selector for the first paragraph.
    Select Split view.

    The first paragraph is selected entirely.

9   In the Code view window, hold the Shift key and click at the end of the second
    paragraph.

    Both paragraphs are selected in Code view.

10 Press Ctrl+T/Cmd+T to activate the Quick Tag Editor.

    The Quick Tag Editor appears in Wrap tag mode.

11 Type `blockquote`

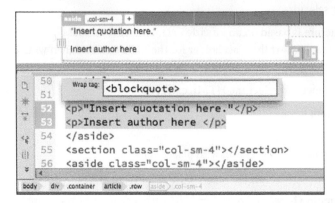

12 Press Enter/Return twice to close the Quick Tag Editor and complete the element.

When it's completed, the default styling of the `<blockquote>` element automatically formats the content, indenting the text on the left and right. Such indentation is typical of material quoted within a term or research paper, and may be desirable in the main content area, but it's totally unnecessary in the `<aside>` element. You'll need to create a new CSS rule to format these elements.

13 If necessary, click the All button.
Create a new selector in **green_styles.css**:

`article.row aside blockquote`

The Show Set option should still be active from the previous exercise. If not, click this option in the CSS Designer.

14 Create the following properties in the new rule:
`margin: 0px 0px 20px 0px`
`padding: 0px`

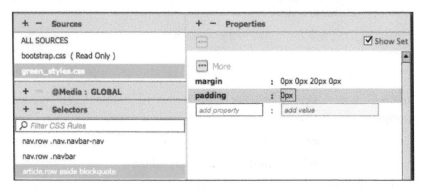

Note: The Quick Tag Editor features three modes: Edit tag, Wrap tag, and Insert HTML. When you select an element using the tag selector, the Quick Tag Editor should default to Edit mode. Press Ctrl+T/Cmd+T again to switch modes.

Typically, a blockquote should contain a quotation, either alone or in one or more paragraphs, and an element providing the source or citation. Like `<blockquote>`, the `<cite>` element provides the correct semantic structure in this application.

15 In Code view, select the second paragraph.

Select the p tag selector.

16 Press Ctrl+T/Cmd+T to edit the tag.

Replace the p tag with `cite` and press Enter/Return twice to complete the edit.

Tip: An alternate method is to right-click the tag selector and access the Quick Tag Editor from the context menu.

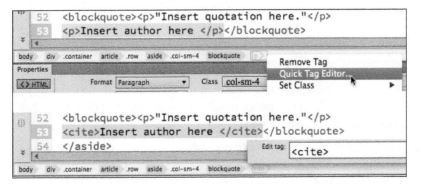

If you look carefully, you can see that the opening quotation mark in the first paragraph is indenting the first line of text slightly, leaving the text in the two paragraphs misaligned. A technique used by professional typesetters actually *outdents* such items to produce a *hanging* quotation mark.

17 Create a new selector in **green_styles.css**:

```
article.row aside blockquote p
```

18 Create the following properties:

```
margin: 0px 0px 5px 0px
padding: 0px .5em
text-indent: -0.5em
```

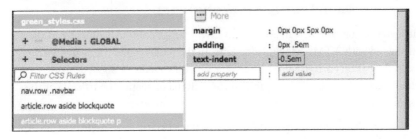

You can see now that the two lines of text are aligned, while the quotation mark is shifted to the left slightly. The effect on multiline quotations will be quite appealing.

Now you'll create a new rule to style the author name.

19 Create a new selector: `article.row aside blockquote cite`

20 Create the following properties in the new rule:

```
display: block
padding: 0px 10px
font-style: italic
text-align: right
```

Note: There are four font units used in Web design, em, percentage, pixel or points. Traditionally points are used for printed designs, like magazines or newspaper articles and advertisements. Pixels are used in graphic design and equate to the resolution of a screen which is made up of pixels per inch. Pixels are often used to set a finite measurement for padding or margins in web design. The two popular choices for web design is em or percentage. The both are similar in usage as they both are based on the default size of the page font. For instance if the default font size for a page is Times 12 point, 1 em would equate to 12 points, 2ems would be 24 points. To make a font size smaller use decimals, like .5em would be equated with 6 points. Percentages work similarly - 100% would be 12 points, 200% would be 24 points. Both em and percentage are scalable across multiple device screens and are great choices for responsive web design.

The quotation placeholder is complete and semantically designed. To remain semantically correct, each new quotation should be inserted into its own <blockquote> element. The last thing you need to do is add the top and bottom borders shown in the site design.

21 Create a new selector: article.row aside

This rule will format both the left and right columns at once.

22 Add the following properties to the new rule:

```
border-top: solid 5px #069
border-bottom: solid 3px #069
margin: 1em 0px
padding: 1em 0px
```

Both <aside> elements display blue borders on the top and bottom.

23 Select File>Save All and then leave the file open for the next exercise.

The placeholder for the first column is complete. Let's address the center section of the <article> element next.

Inserting Main Content Placeholders

The layout will feature the main content in the center column. Content is usually introduced with HTML heading elements. In the past, typically only one <h1> would appear on each page. With the new semantic element, some designers are actually using <h1> elements to introduce each major section or article. For this design, you'll start with one <h1> and use more when warranted.

1 Use the file from the previous exercise or if necessary, open **mylayout_xx.html** from the Chapter07/Datafiles folder as instructed by your teacher and, if necessary, switch to Live view. Click the second column in the third row.

The HUD appears focused on the <section class="col-sm-4"> element.

2 Using the Insert panel under the HTML category, select the Heading, insert an H1 nested in the center column.

3 Select the placeholder text.
Type **Insert main heading here** to replace the text.

4 Press Enter/Return to create a new line.
Type **Insert subheading here** and press Enter/Return.

5   Type **Insert content here** and click outside the orange editing box.

You have now created one heading and two new placeholder paragraphs. You need to make the first paragraph an <h2>.

Tip: If the Property inspector is not visible, you can display it by selecting Window > Properties. Most people like to dock it to the bottom of the document window.

6   Click the first paragraph "Insert subheading here".
The HUD appears focused on the p element.

7   In the Property inspector, select Heading 2 from the Format drop-down menu.

The paragraph is converted to an <h2> element. The placeholders for the center content area are complete. You'll format them later.

8   Select File>Save All and then leave the file open for the next exercise.

Now, let's add placeholders and formatting to the right column.

Creating Custom Element Classes

The right column of the layout will contain materials related to the main content. As you can see from the site design, the element has a background color. You already have a rule that formats both <aside> elements, but in this case, the background will apply only to the right column. When you need to target styling to a specific element and there's no structural difference between it and other similar elements, a custom CSS class is warranted. First, we need to add a class attribute to the element. There are several ways you can do this, but using the HUD in Live view is fast and easy.

1   Use the file from the previous exercise or if necessary, open **mylayout_xx.html** from the Chapter07/Datafiles folder as instructed by your teacher and, if necessary, switch to Live view.

2   Select the third column of the third row.

The HUD appears focused on the aside element with a class of col-sm-4. At the moment, this structure is identical to the column. To change this column format, we need to apply a class selector style rule by creating a class ID and then applying a CSS style rule to the class id.

3   Click the Add Class/ID icon + in the HUD.

A blank text field appears beside the existing class col-sm-4.

4   Type .sidebar2 and press Enter/Return.

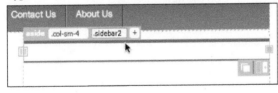

A dialog appears allowing you to insert the new class into an existing style sheet and media query. If **green_styles.css** does not appear in the source menu select it manually.

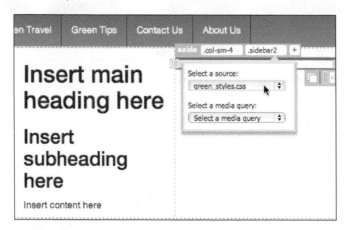

5   Press Enter/Return to complete the operation.

If you look at the **green_styles.css** reference in the CSS Designer, you will see the new class `.sidebar2`. The class will allow you to apply styling to the right column that differs from the left.

6   Select `.sidebar2` in the Selectors window of the CSS Designer. Create the following properties:

```
background-color: #CFC
padding: 0px 10px
```

A light green background color appears in the right column. Let's add the placeholder text.

7   Using the Insert panel, add an <h2> element to the right column using the Nest option.

8   Select the placeholder text.
Type **Insert sidebar heading here** to replace it.

9   Press Enter/Return to create a new paragraph.
Type **Insert sidebar content here** on the new line.

10 Create a new selector, `.sidebar2 h2`

11 Create the following properties in the new rule:

```
margin-top: 10px
margin-bottom: 5px
padding: 0px 10px
font-size: 130%
line-height: 1.4em
```

12 Create a new selector, `.sidebar2 p`

13 Create the following properties in the new rule:

```
margin-bottom: 5px
padding: 0px 10px
line-height: 1.3em
```

14 Select File>Save All and then leave the file open for the next exercise.

The right column is complete. Before we move on to the `<footer>`, we need to adjust the spacing of the three columns in the main content row. Currently, the three columns are equal in width, but in the site design the left and right columns are narrower than the center one. Since the widths are determined by the predefined Bootstrap, changing the relationship of these elements is simply a matter of changing their class names.

Reading No Writing

The Bootstrap style sheet is formatted as a read-only file to prevent you from making any accidental changes to the framework's complex styling. From time to time as you work in your pages, a warning message may appear at the top of the screen indicating that the file is read-only. You can dismiss the message by clicking the ⊗ icon on the right side. It also provides an option to make the file writable. You're advised to resist the temptation.

Managing Bootstrap Component Width

Bootstrap is based on a 12-column vertical grid system. Elements inserted into a layout conform to this grid by occupying some fraction of it. The amount of space an element uses is typically represented by a number that appears in the class attribute. For example, the three columns all have a class of `col-sm-4`. Since 4 divides into 12 three times, each column occupies one-third of the screen. By adjusting these class names, you should be able to change the width of each element.

1   Use the file from the previous exercise or if necessary, open **mylayout_xx.html** from the Chapter07/Datafiles folder as instructed by your teacher and, if necessary, switch to Live view.

At the moment, the three columns have the same class name and are equal in width.

2   Click the first column of row three.

The HUD appears. Depending on where you click, it may focus on any of the elements contained with the first column.

3   If necessary, select the `aside.col-sm-4` tag selector.

You can edit the class name directly in the HUD.

4   Double-click the class name `.col-sm-4` in the HUD.
Change the name to `.col-sm-3`

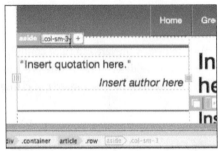

The width of the first column narrows. The other columns shift to the left, leaving open space on the right side of the third row. The right column should be the same width as the left one.

5   Click the third column.
Select the `aside.col-sm-4` tag `.sidebar2` selector.

6   Change the class name to `.col-sm-3`

The right column narrows. In total, the entire row is now occupying only 10 of the 12 columns in the grid. You can leave these settings this way, add more space between the columns, or simply add the space to the main content section.

7   Select the second column.
Select the `section.col-sm-4` tag selector.
Change the class name to `.col-sm-6`

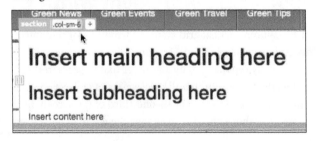

The center column widens to take up the empty space.

8   Select File>Save All and then leave the file open for the next exercise.

Later, you will learn more about how you can control the responsive behavior of your layout using Bootstrap classes. This will enable your layout to adapt to various screen sizes and devices automatically.

The last tasks remaining to complete the basic layout are to insert some new place-holder text and to format the footer.

Inserting HTML Entities

In this exercise, you will insert a generic copyright statement that includes an HTML entity and format the footer.

1   Use the file from the previous exercise or if necessary, open **mylayout_xx.html** from the Chapter07/Datafiles folder as instructed by your teacher and, if necessary, switch to Live view.

The file contains a four-row Bootstrap layout with various placeholder contents and formatting, but the fourth row is still empty.

2   Click the fourth row of the layout.

The HUD appears focused on the `div` element displaying a class of `.col-sm-12`.

The site design shows the footer containing a copyright symbol. This character is one of many that you might want to use in your website but that you can't type directly using the keyboard. To insert a copyright character, you will use an HTML entity. But before you can insert the copyright character, you first need to insert a paragraph element to hold it.

3   Choose Insert > Paragraph to nest a new paragraph into the footer.

Dreamweaver inserts a <p> element into the footer, complete with placeholder text. To insert the entity, you will have to switch to Design or Code view. This particular command does not work in Live view.

4   Switch to Split view.
Locate the `<footer>` element and the new placeholder text in Code view.

5   Select the placeholder text "*This is the content for Layout P Tag*" and delete it.

6   Choose Insert > HTML > Character > Copyright from the menubar.

The copyright symbol © appears at the insertion point. Dreamweaver creates the copyright character using the named entity `&copy;` in the code. Since the insertion point is already inserted in this location, let's finish the footer placeholder text.

Warning: You may discover that you can sometimes insert special characters directly. This is not a recommended practice.

Note: Many entities can be created with named or numbered entities. Some applications do not support named entities. Always check to make sure you can use a specific character.

7 Press the spacebar to insert a space.
Type **2015 Meridien GreenStart. All rights reserved.**

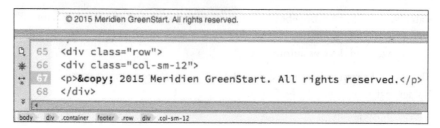

```
65   <div class="row">
66   <div class="col-sm-12">
67   <p>&copy; 2015 Meridien GreenStart. All rights reserved.</p>
68   </div>
```

body   div   .container   footer   .row   div   .col-sm-12

Tip: Modify the copyright date as necessary when you create a new page or update the content.

8 In **green_styles.css** in the CSS Designer, create a new selector named footer

9 Create the following properties:

```
padding: 1em 0px
background-color: #090
```

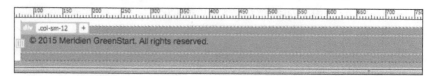

10 Deselect the Show Set option.

11 In the **background-image** property, click the gradient color picker.

12 Set #060 as the **top** gradient color stop.
Set #0C0 as the **bottom** gradient color stop.
Set the Linear Gradient Angle to 0 degrees.
Press Enter/Return to complete the gradient.

The footer displays a gradient that shifts from light to dark green.

13 Change the color property of the font to #FFC in the footer rule.

14 Select File>Save All and then leave the file open for the next exercise.

You've completed the basic structure and added placeholders to all the elements. You've even formatted some of the elements and content. The last task you'll accomplish will be to implement a global theme for the site design that will establish the basic design and usage of type within the site.

Creating Global Type Styles

Most of the content of your site will be represented in text. Text is displayed in the web browser using digitized typefaces. Based on designs developed and used for centuries on the printing press, these typefaces can evoke all sorts of feelings in your visitors, ranging from security to elegance to sheer fun and humor.

Face versus Font: Know the Difference?

People throw the terms *typeface* and *font* around all the time as if they were interchangeable. They are not. Do you know the difference? *Typeface* refers to the design of an entire family of letterforms. *Font* refers to one specific design. In other words, a typeface is usually composed of multiple fonts. Typically, a typeface will feature four basic designs: regular, italic, bold, and bold-italic. When you choose a font in a CSS specification, you usually choose the regular format, or font, by default.

When a CSS specification calls for italic or bold, the browser will normally load the italic or bold versions of the typeface automatically. However, you should be aware that many browsers can actually generate italic or bold effects when these fonts are not present or available. Purists resent this capability and go out of their way to define rules for italic and bold variations with specific calls to italic and bold versions of the typefaces they want to use.

Some designers may use multiple typefaces for different purposes throughout a site. Others select a single base typeface that may match their normal corporate themes or culture. CSS gives you tremendous control over page appearance and the formatting of text. In the last few years, there have been many innovations in the way typefaces are used on the web. The following exercises describe and experiment with these methods.

Using Edge Web Fonts

The first choice for most web designers is selecting the base typeface that will display their content. In this exercise, you will see how easy it is to use web fonts to apply a global site typeface by editing a single rule. There's no need to be intimidated about using web fonts—everything you need to implement this technology is built right into Dreamweaver CC.

Note: Edge Web Fonts and other types of hosted fonts are rendered properly in Dreamweaver only in Live view with an active Internet connection.

1   Use the file from the previous exercise or if necessary, open **mylayout_xx.html** from the Chapter07/Datafiles folder as instructed by your teacher and, if necessary, switch to Live view.

2   In the CSS Designer, select **green_styles.css**.
Create a new selector named body

3 In the Properties window, deselect the Show Set option, if necessary.

The window now displays all CSS specifications.

4 Click the Text category icon $\boxed{\text{T}}$.

The window display focuses on CSS Properties for text.

5 Click to open the **font-family** property.

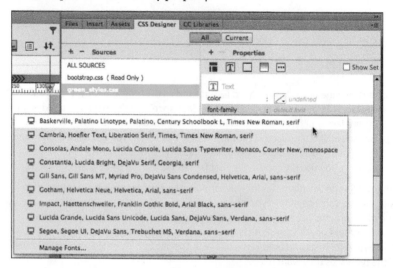

A window appears showing nine predefined Dreamweaver font groups, or *stacks*. You can select one of these or create your own. Are you wondering why you don't see the entire list of fonts installed on your computer?

The answer is a simple but ingenious solution to a problem that has nagged web designers from the very beginning. Until recently, the fonts you see in your browser were not actually part of the webpage or the server; they were supplied by the computer browsing the site.

Although most computers have many fonts in common, they don't always have the same fonts. So, if you choose a specific font and it isn't installed on the visitor's computer, your carefully designed and formatted webpage could immediately and tragically appear in Courier or some other equally undesirable typeface.

For most people, the solution has been to specify fonts in groups which can also be referred to as font families or *stacks*. Giving the browser a second, third, and perhaps fourth (or more) choice to default to before it picks for itself (egads!). Some call this technique *degrading gracefully*. Dreamweaver CC (2015.1 release) offers nine predefined font groups.

As you can see, the predefined font stacks are pretty limited. If you don't see a combination you like, you can click the Manage Fonts option at the bottom of the **Set Font Family** pop-up menu and create your own.

But before you start building your own group, remember this: Go ahead and pick *your* favorite font, but then try to figure out what fonts are installed on your visitors' computers, and add them to the list too. For example, you may prefer the font Hoefelter Allgemeine Bold Condensed, but the majority of web users are unlikely to have it installed on their computers. By all means, select Hoefelter as your first choice; just don't forget to slip in some of the more tried-and-true, or *web-safe*, fonts, such as Arial, Helvetica, Tahoma, Times New Roman, Trebuchet MS, Verdana, and, finally, a design category like serif or sans serif.

In the last few years, a new trend has been gaining momentum to use fonts that are actually hosted on the site or by a third-party service. The reason for the popularity is obvious: Your design choices are no longer limited to the dozen or so fonts from which everyone can choose. You can choose among thousands of designs and develop a unique look and personality that was nearly impossible in the past. But you can't use just *any* font.

Licensing restrictions prohibit many fonts from web-hosted applications altogether. Other fonts have file formats that are incompatible with phones and tablets. So it's important to look for fonts that are designed and licensed for web applications. Today, multiple sources exist for web-compatible fonts. Google and Font Squirrel are two such sources, and they even provide some free fonts for the budget-minded. Luckily, as a subscriber to Adobe Creative Cloud, you have access to two new services: Adobe Typekit and Adobe Edge Web Fonts.

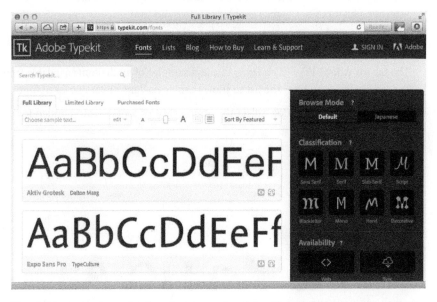

Web-hosted fonts offer a vast variety of design options.

Typekit is a web-hosted subscription service that offers both print and web fonts. You can subscribe to the service even if you don't have Creative Cloud, but as a subscriber you can access many of the available fonts for free. Adobe Edge Web Fonts is a free service that provides only web fonts, hence its name, and is powered by Typekit. The best thing about Edge Web Fonts is that you can access it directly inside Dreamweaver.

6   At the bottom of the font stack window, click Manage Fonts.

The Manage Fonts dialog gives you three options (tabs) for using web fonts: Adobe Edge Web Fonts, Local Web Fonts, and Custom Font Stacks. The first two tabs provide access to a new technique for using custom fonts on the web. Adobe Edge Fonts supports the Edge Web Fonts service to access hundreds of fonts in multiple design categories right inside the program. Local Web Fonts allows you to define the use of fonts that you can buy or find free on the Internet. Custom Font Stacks enables you to build font stacks using either the new web-hosted fonts, various web-safe fonts, or a combination of both. For the site's base font, let's pick one from Edge Web Fonts.

The tab for Adobe Edge Web Fonts displays samples of all the fonts available from the service. You can filter the list to show specific designs or categories of fonts.

7   In the Manage Fonts dialog, select the option "List of fonts recommended for Headings."

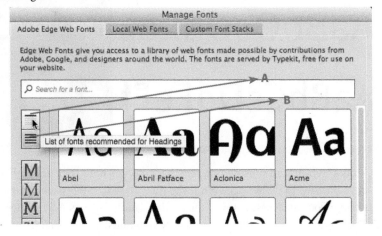

A - List of fonts recommended for Headings

B - List of fonts recommended for Paragraphs

The window shows a list of fonts that are typically used for headings and titles. Some designers like to use the same font for both headings and paragraph text.

8   Select the option "List of fonts recommended for Paragraphs," directly below the option for "Headings."

Only one font is displayed: Source Sans Pro. Since this font works well for headings and paragraph text, it's a perfect choice for the site's base font. By applying it to the body rule, it will automatically be applied to headings and paragraphs throughout the site.

9   Click the font sample displayed in the Manage Fonts dialog. Click Done to close the panel.

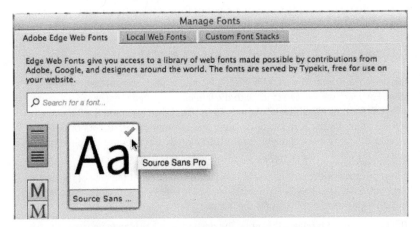

A blue checkmark appears on the sample of Source Sans Pro. Once you click Done, Dreamweaver will add the font to the CSS Designer interface and write any code needed in your page to use it in your CSS specifications.

10 In the CSS Designer, click the **font-family** property again.

When the Font Stack dialog opens you will see source-sans-pro at the bottom of the list.

11 Select source-sans-pro.

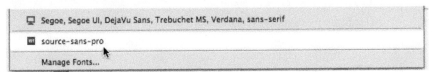

12 In the **font-weight** property, select 400.

Source Sans Pro appears in the font-family property for the body rule. In most cases, the change in the layout will be instantaneous. The entire page, both headings and paragraph text, should now display Source Sans Pro. If you did not see the font style change, Dreamweaver may have not updated the Live view display.

13 If necessary, click the Refresh icon ⟳ above the document window.

If this step doesn't display the new font, you may not have a live connection to the Internet at this moment. Because Edge Web Fonts are hosted on the Internet, you won't be able to see them until you establish a live connection or upload this page to a live web server. You will learn how to upload pages to the Internet in Chapter 15, "Publishing to the Web."

14 Select File>Save All and then leave the file open for the next exercise.

As you can see, using Edge Web Fonts on your website is really easy. But don't be fooled into thinking they're any less problematic than old-fashioned font stacks. In fact, even if you want to use Edge Web Fonts as your primary font source, the best practice would be to include them in a custom font stack of their own.

Introducing Web-hosted Fonts

The latest trend around the Internet is the increasing popularity of custom typefaces. For years, we've been stuck with the familiar but faded presence of the same web-safe fonts gracing most of our websites: Arial, Tahoma, Times New Roman, Trebuchet MS, Verdana, and so on. To use a less common typeface, your options were to chance fate and flirt with font substitution or to render the custom typeface as a graphic (and all that entails).

If the concept of web fonts is new to you, you're not alone. At the time of this writing, "web fonts" had only been in existence a little over five years and only starting to gain widespread popularity for the last two.

The basic concept is relatively simple: The desired font is copied to your website or linked to it from a common web server. Then, the browser loads the font and caches it, as needed.

Here are some handy links to learn more about the new trend in web fonts:

- Adobe Edge Web Fonts: http://html.adobe.com/edge/webfonts
- Adobe Typekit: https://typekit.com

Here are some other font services:

- Google Web Fonts: www.google.com/fonts
- Font Squirrel: www.fontsquirrel.com
- MyFonts.com: www.myfonts.com/search/is_webfont:true/fonts

Building Font Stacks with Web Fonts

If you're lucky, your web-hosted fonts will display every time for every user. But luck can run out and it's better to be safe than sorry. In the last exercise, you accessed and selected an Edge Web Font and applied it to the base font of the body rule. In this exercise, you'll build a custom stack anchored on your chosen web font to provide the necessary fallback support for safety's sake.

1   Use the file from the previous exercise or if necessary, open **mylayout_xx.html** from the Chapter07/Datafiles folder as instructed by your teacher and, if necessary, switch to Live view.

2   In the CSS Designer, select the body rule.

3   In Text category, select the **font-family** property.

The Font stack dialog appears.

4   Choose **Manage Fonts**.

5   In the Manage Fonts dialog, click the Custom Font Stacks tab.

6   In the Available Fonts list, locate **Source Sans Pro**.

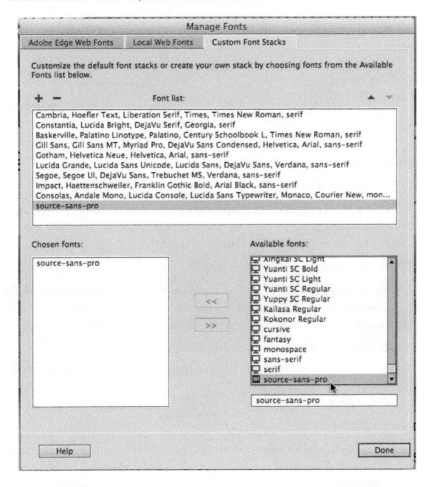

Click the << button to move the font to the Chosen Fonts list. You can also double-click a font which will select and also add it to the Chosen fonts list. If you cannot find the font in the list, you can type the name in the text field at the bottom of the dialog and press the << button.

7 Repeat step 6 to add **Trebuchet MS**, **Verdana**, **Arial**, **Helvetica**, and **sans-serif** to the Chosen Fonts list.

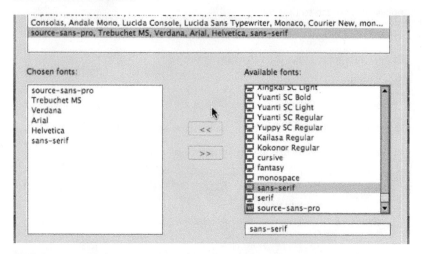

With your teacher's permission, add more web or web-safe fonts to your list as desired. If any fonts you want to use are not installed on your computer, type the names into the text field and then add them to the stack using the << button.

8 Click Done.

9 In the **font-family** property, select your new custom font stack.

The page display should not change; Source Sans Pro is still the primary font in the list. But the new font stack, based on the new Edge Web Font, will ensure that your text will be formatted in all contingencies.

10 In the **font-size** property, enter `14px`

Setting the size of the body rule is a common practice for many web designers. This is designed to reset the base font size to a size that should be optimum. You can adjust the size as necessary using media queries for various devices and screen sizes.

11 Select File>Save All and then leave the file open for the next exercise.

Now you've learned how to specify the look of your text content. Next, you'll learn how to control the size of the text.

Specifying Font Size

Font size can convey the relative importance of the content on the page. Headings are typically larger than the text they introduce. In your working document, the content is divided into three areas: the main content and the two sidebars. In this exercise, you will learn how to manage the size of the text in both areas to add emphasis as desired.

1 Use the file from the previous exercise or if necessary, open **mylayout_xx.html** from the Chapter07/Datafiles folder as instructed by your teacher and, if necessary, switch to Live view.

2 Insert the insertion point in the text "Insert main heading here."

If you look at the Selectors window, you will see that you have not yet created a rule to format this heading. Let's create one now.

3 Create a new selector in **green_styles.css** named
`article.row section h1`

Since the <h1> element is the main heading of the page, you should design it to stand out from the rest of the text and headings. This can be done in a variety of ways, using color, size, or a great typeface.

4 Add the Edge Web Font **Patua One** as you did in the previous exercise.

5 Create the following properties for the h1 rule:

```
margin-top: 0px
margin-bottom: 15px
font-family: patua-one
font-size: 300%
line-height: 1.4em
```

> **Note:** In this rule formatting the h1, you added only a single font. You may think you should have to build a custom font stack, but you don't. That's because the stack created earlier will be inherited by default if this font doesn't display properly.

Insert main heading here

Insert subheading here

Insert content here

The main heading reformats and increases in size.

The sidebars contain text that is related to, but not semantically as important as, the main content. Reducing the size of this content provides a visual distinction to the layout. You created rules earlier in this chapter to format these items.

6 In **green_styles.css,** select the rule `article.row aside.`

7 Create the following property: `font-size: 95%`

The text in the right column has resized, but the quotation placeholder in the left column has not changed. When a rule does not format an element, it means one or more other rules are conflicting with it. This will be a common problem when you use predefined templates or frameworks, like Bootstrap. You can use the CSS Designer to troubleshoot the conflict.

8 Click the text "Insert quotation here" in the left column.

The HUD appears, focused on the p element.

9 In the CSS Designer with the Show Set option selected, examine the list of rules and identify any that format font-size properties.

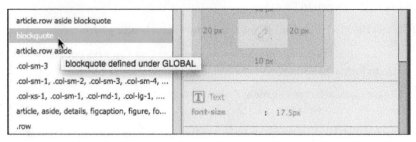

A `blockquote` rule in the **bootstrap.css** file is applying a font-size property of `17.5px` and applied a 5px gray border on the left. To override this rule, you have to create a similar or more specific selector in **green_styles.css**.

10 In **green_styles.css**, create the selector: `article.row blockquote`

11 Create the following property in the new rule:

```
font-size: 100%
border: none
```

The new property resets the size of the blockquote and its contents to the default font size. That means the property you created in step 7 can function properly now. The basic page layout for desktop media is complete.

12 Save all files.

You created a workable basic page layout for your project template and learned how to insert additional components, placeholder text, and headings; modified existing CSS formatting; and created new rules. In upcoming chapters, you will continue to work on this file to tweak the CSS and Bootstrap structure to make it work on all mobile devices and then set it up as the primary site template.

Working with Others

Interpersonal communications

The process of interacting with others, exchanging information with each other and understanding each other.

Emotional intelligence:

The ability to perceive and understand emotions and to use that knowledge to guide your own behavior as well as respond to others.

Unless you work completely by yourself, your success on the job depends on working well—and communicating well— with others: coworkers and teammates, supervisors and managers, vendors and service providers, and customers and clients. This ongoing process of interacting with others, exchanging information and meaning, and achieving understanding is called **interpersonal communication**. People who are good at it typically have what experts call **emotional intelligence**—the ability to perceive and understand emotions and to use that knowledge to guide their own behavior and respond to others. Research by experts such as psychologist Daniel Goldman has shown that emotional intelligence is as important to good leadership and effective teamwork as are more traditionally valued skills and capacities.

Many businesses are concerned that as the world becomes more digital, people spend less time developing their emotional intelligence and interpersonal communication abilities and, as a result, feel more comfortable emailing and texting rather than talking with others in "real-time" conversations and discussions. While no one disputes the value of digital communication, it cannot replace conversations that encourage people to understand each other's point of view more deeply rather than exchange short bursts of information. In a conversation, you learn to listen actively and pay attention to tone, facial expressions, and body language—all of which are critical aspects of emotional intelligence. This kind of synchronous communication—where all the communicators are present at the same time—will help you forge the positive and productive working relationships that are critical to business.

This lesson will help you strengthen your interpersonal communication skills, develop your emotional intelligence, and improve your ability to work well with others. It focuses on developing communication skills to help you work effectively with others. In workplace environments, your work with others will often be accomplished in teams. A team is more than a group of people working together. An effective **team** involves two or more people who recognize and share a commitment to a specific, common goal and who collaborate in their efforts to achieve that goal.

> **Team**
>
> Two or more people who recognize and share a commitment to a specific, common goal and who collaborate in their efforts to achieve that goal.

Teams are integral to an organization's success largely because one individual does not have all the skills needed to compete in today's business world. In addition, if a company needs to bring a product to market before a competitor does, it cannot wait for one or two people to do all the work involved. Instead, the company must rely on a well-coordinated team, with each person doing his or her part to achieve the common goal. Individuals benefit from team- work, too. By working on a team, you will improve your interpersonal skills, expand your personal network, and use your best individual strengths while learning new skills from others. This section suggests six ways you and your teammates can improve team performance and make teamwork an enjoyable and productive experience.

Agreeing on Team Goals and Standards

For a team to be successful, all team members need to agree on key elements at the beginning of the project:

- **Goals.** Good teams are goal-oriented. All members understand their purpose as a team, share a concrete goal and vision for success, and believe that what they are doing is worthwhile. They know their work will make a significant contribution to their organization, their client, the community, or something they care about. In addition, each individual member must be willing to do whatever it takes to make the team successful, including helping each other if the need arises. To promote commitment, teams should make sure that all members get a chance to participate in decisions and feel they are being heard.

- **Expected results.** Good teams are also results-oriented. In other words, the team's success is measured by results, not effort, and the team is organized to achieve those results. Specifically:

- All team members have a clear role and are held accountable for their contributions.

- Workload is divided equitably. Some tasks may require more effort than others, so it is important to discuss the work to ensure that the team is aware of each member's responsibilities and no one is overburdened with too much work.

- The team has an effective communication system to keep all team members informed in a timely way.

- Team members give each other prompt and helpful feedback on their performance so each person can do his or her best work.

- **Team standards.** Finally, good teams have standards and hold each team member accountable for them. You may develop standards about any or all of the following topics: conducting meetings, communicating between meetings, keeping records, making decisions, and managing conflict. Working together to create team standards helps a team get off to a strong start. If conflict begins to arise during a project, the team standards can help a team resolve the conflict.

Pay Attention to Team Development and Dynamics

There is more than one way to approach team dynamics. Different approaches will work better in different contexts. For teams that aim to work together for the long term, it can be productive to give team members time to develop their collaborative working relationship. As the next figure illustrates, a model for understanding team development first proposed by Bruce W. Tuckman. He identified four stages of development in teams that had no formal team training: **forming, storming, norming**, and **performing**. Here is what happens in each stage:

- **Forming.** When a team first begins to form, everyone is usually polite and considerate. You exchange information about your schedules, when and where you can meet, and how you can contact each other. Usually, expectations for the team and its success are high, and conflicts are not evident.

- **Storming.** The team eventually begins to encounter problems that aren't easily resolved. Members begin to feel tense and anxious about the success of the project. Some team members may begin to feel disillusioned and discouraged. As you experience conflict, try to identify the reasons for the conflict to help the group move to the next stage of development.

- **Norming.** Norming begins when team members start to manage conflict and establish a consensus about how to work together efficiently. This is the stage at which many teams decide to create standards about communication and accountability.

- **Performing.** At the performing stage of team development, team members have learned how to work collaboratively and are able to use their differences as a source of strength, not weak- ness. Although problems will continue to arise, a performing team feels comfortable confronting and resolving the problems that might jeopardize the success of the project. Members begin to enjoy working together and are glad they don't have to complete the project alone. They often get so involved and excited about what they are doing that they lose track of time, and the success of the project becomes more important than individual goals.

FORMING	STORMING	NORMING	PERFORMING
Exchange vital information	Experience conflict and tension	Discuss and resolve problems	Work collaboratively
Learn about each other	Feel disillusioned and discouraged	Create standards for communicating	Use individual differences as a source of strength
Have high expectations for success		Plan regular meetings	Put project above individual goals
Act politely and considerately	Identify reasons for conflict	Hold members accountable	Achieve high level of productivity

Stages of Team Development: What Team Members Do at Each Stage

One reason to study teamwork in a business communication course is so that you can move more quickly to the performing stage. A performing team may also evolve into a *high-performing team:* a team whose members are deeply committed to each other's growth and success.

Harvard Business School professor Amy Edmondson provides an alternative model for achieving high performance in short-term teams that don't have time to progress through Tuckman's four stages. Because teams often come together and dissolve so quickly, she argues that the concept of a stable "team" should be replaced by that of a fluid process: teaming. "Teaming is a verb," she maintains. "It is a dynamic activity, not a bounded, static entity." This shift reflects the needs of a complex contemporary work environment, where businesses must be flexible enough to shift gears quickly and effectively. Because people are often grouped together only temporarily for specific projects, they often don't have the opportunity to "gel" over time and develop stable structures and relationships. Working in these dynamic conditions requires team members to communicate frequently in order to learn collectively, fix issues quickly as they arise, and ensure that the best ideas are put into action. To achieve these goals, Edmondson recommends that participants do the following:

- Ask for help and clarification early and often

- Share information quickly and broadly

- Discuss mistakes

- Try out new strategies and ideas
- Continuously seek out feedback to improve ideas and processes

Develop Good Leadership Practices

While different team development strategies fit different needs, both Tuckman and Edmondson emphasize that successful teamwork depends on the vision and guidance that can be provided only by effective *leadership*. A team leader may not be the team member who has the most creative ideas. An effective leader is the person who has the skills to motivate people, manage work processes, and help the team succeed. A team can establish leadership in a number of ways. One person can serve as leader, leadership can rotate during phases of the project, or different leaders can take responsibility for different aspects of the project. It is not crucial for the team to have one single leader. However, it is crucial for the team to have capable leadership that keeps the good of the team in mind. Remember that if you volunteer to be a team leader, that role does not put you in charge of the team. Instead, it puts you in service of the team. Here is a partial list of ways that a leader can serve the team and help it succeed:

- **Establish and maintain a vision of the future.** One of the most valuable roles for any leader is to keep the team focused on the ultimate goal and remind the team why that goal is valuable. Teams can easily get bogged down in the details of the work and forget why the project is worthwhile. A good leader will reenergize team members, refocus them on the goal, and make the team believe in itself.

- **Create a supportive climate.** Teams work best when team members feel that they can take risks and that they will be listened to and respected. A team leader can set the tone for the team by encouraging creativity and being respectful to everyone.

- **Delegate responsibility and assign tasks equitably.** Delegating responsibility and assigning tasks is a balancing act. On the one hand, the team needs to take full advantage of its human resources and assign people tasks that call on their strengths. On the other hand, teams need to provide members with opportunities to learn, stretch, and develop new skills. A good leader can help maintain this balance by considering each individual's talents and goals. In addition, a good team leader can help ensure that workloads are shared equitably. As a project progresses, work assignments may need to shift: Some tasks may prove to be bigger than anticipated, some may be smaller, and new tasks may arise.

- **Establish a timeline.** Once the team collaboratively determines a plan for the project, a team leader can oversee the creation of a timeline to help the team progress and ensure deadlines will be met. Then, throughout the process, a leader can help the team reevaluate and reassess the plan. One project scheduling tool that teams often use to establish a timeline and track the project is a Gantt chart (named after its inventor, Henry Gantt). As the following shows, one advantage of a Gantt chart is that it helps you manage time by identifying tasks that can take place simultaneously versus those that need to be completed sequentially.

Gantt Chart

Assignment Key

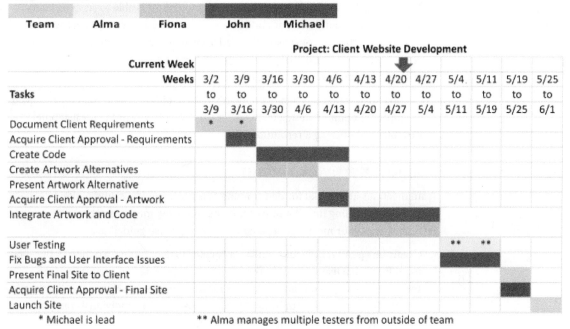

Gantt Chart

- **Keep the project on track.** Although individual members of the team may work on separate tasks, a good leader will bring the team together throughout the project to discuss progress, encourage group feedback, and share ideas. Scheduling regular meetings keeps the project on track to meet established deadlines while also allowing for changes in the plan based on continual input and feedback.

- **Manage meetings effectively and encourage positive collaboration.** A good leader will use effective listening, questioning, and restating techniques to ensure that all members of the team participate in meetings and provide input. Leaders also encourage positive collaboration among team members and referee any unconstructive feedback or personality conflicts.

- **Ensure effective decision-making.** Although teams can take many approaches to decision making, important decisions should never be made by giving in to the team member who is the loudest and most assertive. A team leader can ensure that the team makes fact-based judgments and is able to support all its decisions with sound evidence and reasoning. Although a good leader will help a team work toward consensus, the leader must also protect the team against engaging in groupthink, the practice of achieving unanimity by eliminating all critical thinking that threatens consensus.

- **Resolve differences.** When team members have differences of opinion and need an impartial point of view, a team leader can take responsibility for listening carefully and offering a resolution.

Plan for Effective Meetings

Team meetings are crucial for determining tasks, sharing ideas, and making decisions. To avoid falling into the trap of holding too many meetings where not enough gets done, plan your meetings in advance following these guidelines:

- **Create an agenda.** Base the agenda—a detailed plan or outline for the meeting—on input from each team member. The following figure shows an agenda for a team that is developing an on- line handbook for summer interns. Notice that the agenda provides the list of topics to be discussed, the names of the individuals responsible for each item, and the amount of time to spend discussing each item.

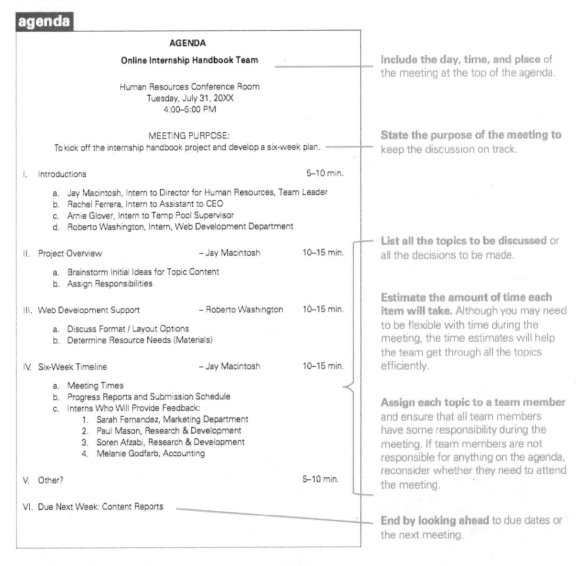

agenda

AGENDA

Online Internship Handbook Team

Human Resources Conference Room
Tuesday, July 31, 20XX
4:00–5:00 PM

MEETING PURPOSE:
To kick off the internship handbook project and develop a six-week plan.

I. Introductions   5–10 min.

    a. Jay Macintosh, Intern to Director for Human Resources, Team Leader
    b. Rachel Ferrera, Intern to Assistant to CEO
    c. Arnie Glover, Intern to Temp Pool Supervisor
    d. Roberto Washington, Intern, Web Development Department

II. Project Overview   – Jay Macintosh   10–15 min.

    a. Brainstorm Initial Ideas for Topic Content
    b. Assign Responsibilities

III. Web Development Support   – Roberto Washington   10–15 min.

    a. Discuss Format / Layout Options
    b. Determine Resource Needs (Materials)

IV. Six-Week Timeline   – Jay Macintosh   10–15 min.

    a. Meeting Times
    b. Progress Reports and Submission Schedule
    c. Interns Who Will Provide Feedback:
        1. Sarah Fernandez, Marketing Department
        2. Paul Mason, Research & Development
        3. Soren Afzabi, Research & Development
        4. Melanie Godfarb, Accounting

V. Other?   5–10 min.

VI. Due Next Week: Content Reports

Include the day, time, and place of the meeting at the top of the agenda.

State the purpose of the meeting to keep the discussion on track.

List all the topics to be discussed or all the decisions to be made.

Estimate the amount of time each item will take. Although you may need to be flexible with time during the meeting, the time estimates will help the team get through all the topics efficiently.

Assign each topic to a team member and ensure that all team members have some responsibility during the meeting. If team members are not responsible for anything on the agenda, reconsider whether they need to attend the meeting.

End by looking ahead to due dates or the next meeting.

How to Create a Meeting Agenda

- **Distribute the agenda sufficiently in advance.** Distributing the agenda before the meeting ensures that all the team members know what will be expected, who is responsible, and what their roles will be during the meeting.

- **Assign someone to serve as a timekeeper during the meeting.** The timekeeper can keep track of how well the meeting follows the agenda. If the meeting becomes sidetracked on unrelated matters or if participants get stuck on unproductive tangents, the timekeeper can bring the conversation back to the necessary topic.

- **Assign someone to serve as a note taker during the meeting.** The note taker will produce meeting minutes, a written description of what was discussed, what was decided, and what actions will follow. The following figure shows the minutes of the online handbook team's meeting.

- **Plan for follow-up.** Include a wrap-up as the last item on your agenda. This reminds you to end the meeting by reviewing the actions and deadlines that everyone agreed upon and scheduling the next meeting's time and place.

minutes

MINUTES

Online Internship Handbook Team

Human Resources Conference Room
July 31, 20XX

Include the day, time, and place of the meeting at the top of the agenda.

Present: Jay Macintosh, Intern to Director for Human Resources, Team Leader
Rachel Ferrera, Intern to Assistant to CEO
Arnie Glover, Intern for Temp Pool Supervisor
Roberto Washington, Intern, Web Development Department

Include a list of who attended.

I. **Introductions:** Jay Macintosh called the meeting to order, introduced himself, and asked the others to state their department, experience, and skills.

II. **Project Overview:** Jay Macintosh explained the project goals. The team brainstormed ideas for topics and assigned content as follows:

   a. Welcome to the Company   - Rachel Ferrera
      1. History of the Organization
      2. Mission / Vision Statements
      3. Organizational Chart
      4. Your Role as an Intern

   b. Policies and Procedures   - Arnie Glover
      1. Maintaining Work Hours and Reporting Absences
      2. Sending and Responding to Email
      3. Logging Telephone Calls
      4. Using the Internet
      5. Using Social Media
      6. Submitting Reimbursement Requests

Organize content by categories. If possible, match the agenda.

   c. Human Resources   - Jay Macintosh
      1. Salary and Payroll Procedures
      2. Health Benefits
      3. Educational Resources
      4. Applying for Permanent Employment

III. **Web Development Support:** Roberto Washington explained company policies about website format, layout, and design options. The team discussed where on the current company website the internship handbook should be located. Decision: Roberto will check with his supervisor about content and resource needs and report to the team by email before the end of the week.

Focus on what the team decided and do not repeat everything that was said.

IV. **Six-Week Timeline: Decisions:**
      1. We will meet on Tuesdays from 3–5 PM. Between meetings we will update each other by email.
      2. Jay will send our weekly meeting minutes to his supervisor as our progress reports.
      3. We will send the completed version of our first draft to the other interns who volunteered for this project to get their feedback by Week 3.
      4. We will submit a draft to the Director of Human Resources by Week 4.
      5. Roberto will begin putting the material on the web in Week 5.

Include assignments (who agreed to do what) and deadlines (when you agreed to submit deliverables).

V. **Next Meeting:** The team will meet on August 7 to discuss the content reports.

End with decisions about the next meeting.

How to Create a Meeting Agenda

Be a Good Team Member

Although a team works together to achieve a common goal, it is still made up of individuals.

Each individual needs to take responsibility for his or her own tasks and also contribute to a productive working relationship with others. To be a good team member, follow these guidelines:

- **Make a commitment to the team and its goals.** At times, it may be tempting to do minimal work for the team and assume that others will take up the slack. But a team will succeed only if everyone shares a similar level of commitment. Every member must be reliable and pull his or her own weight. In addition, every team member must be willing to do whatever it takes to make the team successful, including helping each other if the need arises.

- **Create a collaborative working climate.** To work well together, team members need to trust each other and believe that everyone is working in the team's best interests. This means that, as a good team member, you need to be worthy of that trust. Listen to your teammates without criticism or judgment and give everyone a chance to participate in decision-making. Respond constructively to feedback from others, and address conflicts when they arise rather than let- ting them grow silently and weaken team cohesion.

- **Support and encourage your teammates.** Individuals appreciate recognition, even when they are working as a team. A good team member will show gratitude for the efforts of others and identify how individual contributions support the larger team effort.

- **Support team decisions.** Even if the team has made a decision that differs from what you wanted, once the decision is made, support that decision and work toward implementing it. If you have concern about the decision or believe it may cause problems, voice your concerns to the team. Do not try to undermine the decision.

- **Focus on continuous quality improvement.** No matter how well your team is performing, individual team members may see ways that the team can do better. By making productive suggestions, you can help improve the team and its results.

Using Social Media to Collaborate

Most of the conversation about social media in business focuses on public social media—for example, using Facebook and Twitter to reach new customers and maintain customer satisfaction, or using LinkedIn to recruit job candidates. But companies are increasingly investing in social media for internal communication and collaboration. The terms *social collaboration and internal social media (ISM)* are sometimes used to describe this use of technology to enhance communication and teamwork within an organization.

How do companies use social media and collaboration tools?

- **File sharing and real-time collaborative writing.** When teammates need to work on the same document or spread- sheet, file-sharing tools such as Google Docs ensure that everyone can access the most up-to-date version available. Team members who are working in different offices, or even on different sides of the world, can access a document and write or edit at the same time. Many companies use wikis such as ThoughtFarmer for this purpose. In a global survey on social collaboration, sponsored by Microsoft, half of the 10,000 respondents indicated they use social tools for document collaboration.

- **Brainstorming and getting feedback on ideas.** Companies that value innovation encourage employees to share ideas and engage in discussions that develop new ideas. Whiteboards, blogs, and microblogs, such as Twitter or Yammer, help people communicate their ideas.

- **Sharing knowledge.** Wikis have proven to be a great collaboration tool for sales teams. Sales representatives need the newest and best product information available at all times to understand and sell the goods and services their companies offer. Wikis ensure everyone has access to up-to-date information.

Because organizations adopt internal social media to support information sharing and collaboration, they often encourage employees to suggest ideas for making social media more effective and functional. As Lisa Bonner, assistant vice president of contemporary work practices at The Hartford, an insurance company, attests, developing the best collaborative tools is in itself a collaborative effort: "After launching weConnect, The Hartford's professional social network, many of the ideas came from our users. We incorporated their ideas, AND invited them to join our team!"

End-of-Chapter Activities

Review Questions

Directions: Choose the correct answer for each question.

1. What is the typical layout of a mockup webpage design?
   a. Nav, Header, Content, Footer
   b. Content, Header, Nav, Footer
   c. Header, Nav, Content, Footer
   d. Header, Content, Nav, Footer

2. The position-assist interface does what?
   a. Determines whether the element is inserted before, after, or nested in the page or HTML element.
   b. Quickly access the HTML code of the active element.
   c. Makes placeholder text editable.
   d. Shows the CSS style rules attached to an element.

3. True of false: Dreamweaver will remember any customizations your make to the work-space interface.
   a. True
   b. False

4. The CSS Designer is very useful for what?
   a. Creating and linking style sheets
   b. Creating style rules
   c. Troubleshooting CSS rule conflicts
   d. All of the above

5. How many link properties are there for formatting hypertext links in a webpage?
   a. 4
   b. 5
   c. 3
   d. 6

6. In the CSS Designer, how do you know which style sheet contains the active style rule?
   a. The aMedia window displays the style sheet in red.
   b. The Selectors window displays the style sheet in a blue highlight.
   c. The Show Set option displays the style sheet in bold.
   d. The Sources window displays the style sheet in bold.

7. When selected, the Show Set option of the CSS Designer displays what?
   a. The active style sheet
   b. The active media queries
   c. The active style rule properties
   d. All properties available to a style rule

8. What hexadecimal number does this shorthand representation indicate, #0FC
   a. #0FC0FC
   b. #0000FC
   c. #0FFCCC
   d. #00FFCC

9. After you have a mockup of your portfolio site, as well as a wireframe and thumbnails of the site, the next step is to do what?
   a. Post the site to the Internet
   b. Create an HTML document that recreates the Portfolio mockup design through HTML elements and CSS style rules.
   c. Create a template for the site
   d. None of these above

10. What is a font group?
   a. A group of fonts that are similar in typeface style
   b. A group of fonts that dictate the order of display based on the fonts installed on the visitor's computer
   c. An online third party site that allows access to their library of fonts.
   d. None of these above
   e. A and B only

Essay Questions

Directions: Respond to each question by writing your answers in complete sentences and paragraphs. Be thorough in your answers.

1. Why should you insert images into the element as a background property?

2. What is the advantage of using Bootstrap components in your layout?

3. Can you edit the properties of style rules in the bootstrap.css default style sheet?

4. How does the CSS Designer assist in troubleshooting your website layout?

5. If a character does not appear on your keyboard, such as a copyright symbol, how is it possible to use this element on your webpage?

6. Can you use any font to create a font stack?

7. Why should you consider using web-hosted fonts?

8. Can digital communications like texting and instant messaging replace verbal communications between people? List examples to support your answer.

9. What do all team members need to commit to for the team to be successful?

10. Teams work best when members each fulfill different roles. Your role is Team Leader. Write about why it is important for you to plan items and tasks for team meetings, and why this planning will help meetings be successful.

Critical Thinking Project – Work in teams to develop the Bootstrap Layout of the Lake Powell Site

Working together in teams of 2 or 3 students, develop the design of the mockup website for Lake Powell into HTML elements that are formatted with CSS style rules. This project will take 2-3 days to complete.

Working in Groups

As instructed by your teacher, identify groups and group members. Work together to create the Lake Powell website page layout.

1. In your group, designate who will be the leader of your group. Also designate who will take meeting notes and who will time the meeting.

2. As a group plan your first meeting by creating an agenda of how to proceed with the development of the Lake Powell website. In your agenda identify the roles and duties of the group members. Review the following exercise steps for website development and identify measurable results of the development of the site. Develop a project timeline for completing the steps. Identify group skills and dynamics and assign roles for the development of the site. Plan the follow-up meeting.

Developing the Lake Powell Website

Now that your group has a plan to start creating the Lake Powell Website. Use the following steps to guide you through the development of the site mockup into HTML document and HTML elements with CSS rules for formatting. Based on the identified skills and roles of each person in the group, tackle this project by breaking down the development by each group member taking into consideration each members strengths. For example, typing might be a strength of a group member, another might have a good grip on how to create and use CSS for formatting. Work through these steps to convert the site mockup into a HTML document.

1. Open the lakepowell.jpg file located in the Chapter07/Datafiles/lakepowell_xx/ resources/lakepowell.jpg as instructed by your teacher.

2. On your computer create a local root folder as directed by your teacher. Name the folder **lakepowell_xx**. Copy the class data files from the Chapter07/Datafiles/lakepowell_xx directory as instructed by your teacher.

3. Open Dreamweaver CC 2015 and define a new Lake Powell website.

4. Open the **lakepowell_xx.html** file.

5. Attach another style sheet that will contain all the CSS style rules you will create in this project. Open the CSS Designer and click the Add CSS Source. Choose **Create a New CSS File**. Name the new style sheet **lakepowell.css**.

6. First develop the header of the design. Click in the header row (first row) and open the Insert panel. Choose **HTML** tab from the dropdown menu and then select **H1** from the Headings drop-down menu that displays. Click the **Nest** option for the position assist interface.

7. Select the placeholder text and then type **Lake Powell**. Press Enter/Return. Click outside the first row to set this text.

8. Save the file.

9. Choose Window>Workspace Layout>Design to make sure you are working in the Design workspace. Then open the CSS Designer.

10. Focus Dreamweaver on the <header> element the by clicking anywhere in row 1. In the CSS Designer, select **lakepowell.css** and then click the **All** mode button.

11. To apply format we need to create a CSS rule. Add a new selector to this <header> element by clicking **Add Selector** in the Selectors window. A new selector displays. Double-click the default selector and name it **header.row h1** to focus Dreamweaver on any <h1> element in the <header> element.

12. In the CSS Designer, if necessary deselect **Show Set** to turn this feature off. Format the <h1> element text by setting rule properties. Click the **Text** category icon. Click the color property field and set the color to #633. Set the font to **Impact, Haettenschweiler, "Franklin Gothic Bold", "Arial Black", sans-serif** font group. Set the font-size to **575%**.

13. Add a drop shadow by setting the **text-shadow** properties to:
    a. h-shadow: 5px
    b. v-shadow: 5px
    c. Blur: 5px
    d. Color: #CC9933

14. Set the **letter-spacing** property to **.2em**

15. Next at a top border to the header element by selecting the **header.row** selector and then in the Border category option, set the top border to **40px, solid #990000.**

Adding a Graphic as a Background Image

Next add a background image to the <header> element.

1. In the CSS Designer, make sure the lakepowell.css style sheet is selected and add a new selector. Rename the selector to **header.row** and press enter/return twice.

2. Click the Layout category icon and set the padding property to **40px** for the top and bottom padding. You can also use shorthand field and type **40px 0px** for this setting.

3. Click the **Background** category icon and set the background color to #cc9933. Then set a graphic for the background image by clicking in the **URL** field and then click the **Browse For** folder. Browse to the **images** folder and open the **header.jpg** graphic.

4. Set the background-repeat property to no-repeat option. Set the background-size property to **100%** for both the size value field – height and width. Set the **background-position** property for both values to **center**.

5. Save all files by choosing File>Save All.

Developing a Navigation Menu

Next add a pre-built navigation menu to the <nav> element in the second row of the Lakepowell.html document.

1. In the lakepowell.html document, open the Insert panel. Click in the <nav> element in the second row.

2. In the Insert panel select the **Bootstrap components** drop-down menu and then select the **Navbar: Basic Navbar**. Click Nest in the position assist dialog. This inserts the Basic Navbar Bootstrap component in the second row. It is nested in its own <div> tag, which will be deleted next.

3. Delete the extra <div> tag by switching to Code view and then click to set your cursor after the code <div class="col-sm-12"> which is the new line of code under the <nav class="row"> line of code.

```
18      </head>
19      <body>
20        <div class="container">
21          <header class="row">
22            <div class="col-sm-12">
23              <h1>Lake Powell</h1>
24              <p>Heaven on Earth! </p>
25            </div>
26          </header>
27          <nav class="row">
28            <div class="col-sm-12">    I
29              <nav class="navbar navbar-default">
30                <div class="container-fluid">
31                  <!-- Brand and toggle get grouped for better mobile
      display -->
32                  <div class="navbar-header">
33                    <button type="button" class="navbar-toggle collapsed"
      data-toggle="collapse" data-target="#defaultNavbar1" aria-expanded=
      "false"><span class="sr-only">Toggle navigation</span><span class=
      "icon-bar"></span><span class="icon-bar"></span><span class="icon-bar"
```

This focuses Dreamweaver on this line of code. To delete it, in the tag selector right-click the **div.col-sm-12** tag and choose **Remove Tag** from the Context menu.

4. Now edit the Navbar so that there are less options and it only reflects the menus as show in the Lake Powell mockup design. Make sure Live view is active. Then click the Dropdown menu on the right side of the Navbar. In the tag selector, select the parent element **ul.nav.navbar-nav.navbar-right** from the tag selector and delete it by pressing Delete from your keyboard.

5. Delete the other Drop-down menu on the left by selecting it in the menu bar to focus Dreamweaver on this element. To delete it, in the tag selector click the **li.dropdown** tag and press Delete.

6. Now delete the Search field from the Navbar by selecting it in the Navbar and then delete the parent element of **form.navbar-form.navbar-left** in the tag selector.

7. One more item to delete from the Navbar and that is the Brand menu option. Click to select it in the Navbar. Then delete the parent element by clicking the **a.navbar-brand** tag selector and pressing delete.

8. With the extra elements delete from the bar, now create the menu options as shown in the Lake Powell mockup of the site. Double-click the first **Link** menu option and rename it to **Home**. Do the same for the second **Link** and rename it **Houseboats**.

9. Add three more menu options by first selecting Houseboats menu option and then select the **li** tag selector. In the Insert panel, select the HTML category and then click the List item option. In the position-assist interface, click **After**. Change the place-holder text to **Jet skis**. Click outside of the menu option to set the new menu and name. To get this new menu to format with the CSS for the Navbar, you need to make it a link. Click to select the menu option again and then click the **li** tag selector and make the Property inspector active and type a # in the Link field. Repeat this step to add these other menu options: **Hiking** and **Contact Us**.

10. Next clean up some of the inconsistent code structures in the new menu bar. Notice that the Home option is formatted different than the other menu options. Click to the Home option, and then in Çode view, delete the attribute **class-"active"** from the first <li> element. Next remove the screen reader text by selecting the **<span class="sr-only">(current)</span>** from the first <li> element.

11. The Navbar element needs formatting to make it match the Lake Powell mockup. Size the Dreamweaver workspace area so that your document window is larger than 1024px in width. Click any menu in the Navbar to focus Dreamweaver on this Navbar. Open the CSS Designer and select the Current mode and then select the Show Set option.

12. Now find the **nav.navbar.navbar-default** tag selector and click it. Add a new selector in the CSS Designer and name it **nav.row .navbar.navbar-default**. Deselect the Show Set option in the CSS Designer. Click the Background category option and set the **background-color** to **#990000**

13. Create a new tag selector for controlling the format of the menu options by adding a new tag selector to the lakepowell.css style sheet. Name this new selector **nav.row.nav. navbar-nav>li>a**. This new selector targets the <nav> element and will override the default formatting. Click the Border category option and add the following properties to the new rule:
    a. Border-top: solid 1px #633
    b. Border-right: solid 1px #C93
    c. Border-bottom: solid 1px #633
    d. Border-left: solid 1px #C93

14. Now target the Hyperlink pseudo-classes with format by double-clicking the **nav.row .nav.navbar-nav>li>a** selector in the CSS Designer. Select the entire name and then copy it. Click to set the insertion point at the end of this selector name and type **:link,** (don't forget the comma) and then paste the name again after the **:link,**. At the end of this new selector type **:visited** and press Enter/Return twice to set this new group selector.

15. Deselect the **Show Set** option in the CSS Designer. Click the Text category option and set the following Font category properties:
    a. color: #CC9933
    b. font-size: 14px
    c. font-weight: bold

16. Create a hover state for the menu options by creating a new selector in the CSS Designer and rename it by pasting the copied selector name from the previous step. Add **:hover** to the end of this new selector. In the CSS Designer, click the Background category option and under background-image click the **gradient** property. Create a gradient by setting the top color stop to **#990000** and the bottom color stop to **#663333**. Click the Text category option and set the following:
    a. color: #FFFFFF
    b. font-size: 14px
    c. font-weight: bold

17. Test your menu bar by positioning the insertion point over a menu option and test the different button states by clicking the option.

18. Now add a border between the header image and the menu bar by adding a top and bottom gold border. Create a new selector named **nav.row** and set the border-top property to **5px, solid #CC9933**.

19. Finally, center the menu bar by creating a new selector in the CSS Designer. Name it **nav.row .nav.navbar-nav.** In the Layout category option, set the width property to **432px**. In the margin property enter the shorthand: **0px auto**. To get the menu bar to center a Float property needs to be cancelled out. Make sure the **nav. row .nav.navbar-nav** selector is selected and click the Show Set option in the CSS Designer. Insert the insertion point in the empty Properties window. Type **float** and then press the tab key. Select **none** from the value field. The menu bar centers in the site design.

20. Finally delete the extra space below the menu bar in the second row by creating a new selector named **nav.row .navbar**. With the Show Set option selected, click in the Properties window and type margin-bottom and enter 0px.

21. Save all files by choosing File>Save All.

Create Placeholder Content

Next you'll develop the content <article> area. This element is comprised of two <aside> elements, one on the left and one on the right, as well as a <section> element. All are used to present information about Lake Powell for the website.

1. Insert an HTML paragraph element in the left <aside> element by clicking in this column to focus Dreamweaver on this element. From the Insert panel, choose the HTML category and then click the H2 item. Click Nest from the position-assist interface. Select the placeholder text and delete it. Type **Relevant News About Lake Powell**. Click outside this column to set the text. Repeat this process for the right aside so that both <aside> elements contain a H2 element.

2. Format this <aside> element by creating a new selector in the lakepowell.css style sheet. Name the selector **article.row aside**. Create the following properties for this new rule:
   a. margin: 0px 0px 20px 0px
   b. padding: left - 10px, right – 10px
   c. border-top: 5px solid #CC9933

3. Create another selector to format the H2 tag in the <aside> elements. Name this rule **article.row aside h2**. Set the following Font category properties:
   a. color: #633
   b. font family: "Lucida Grande", "Lucida Sans Unicode", "Lucida Sans", "DejaVu Sans", Verdana, sans-serif
   c. font-weight: Bold

4. Now develop the center content by clicking in the second column and use the Insert panel to nest a H1 in this <section> element.

5. Format this <section> element by creating a new selector targeted at the <section>element. Create a new selector for the lakepowell.css and name it **article.row section**. Set the following format:
   a. margin: 0px 0px 20px 0px
   b. padding: left - 10px, right – 10px
   c. border-top: 5px solid #CC9933

6. Next format the nested H1 tag in the <section> element by creating another selector named **article.row section H1**. Set the following Font category properties:
   a. color: #900
   b. font family: Impact, Haettenschweiler, "Franklin Gothic Bold", "Arial Black", sans-serif
   c. line-height: 1.2em
   d. letter-spacing: .1em

7. Add a paragraph element to each all three columns under the headings that you just created by using the Insert panel and selecting the **HTML** category and then clicking the **paragraph** item. Click the **After** option from the position-assist interface.

8. Create a new selector to format the <aside> element paragraph for both <aside> elements. Name it **article.row aside p**. Set the Text category format to the following:
   a. color: #000
   b. line-height: 1.1em

9. Create a new selector to format the <aside> element paragraph for both <aside> elements. Name it **article.row section p**. Set the Text category format to the following:
   a. color: #000
   b. line-height: 1.1em

10. Save all files by choosing File>Save All.

Format the Footer

Next format the footer for the Lake Powell site.

1. Click in the fourth row. which contains the <footer> element.

2. Nest a <paragraph> element in this row. Delete the placeholder text and insert a copyright symbol by choosing Insert>HTML>Copyright. Then type a space and **2017 by Lake Powell Adventures. All rights reserved. Come to Lake Powell to experience Heaven on Earth!**.

3. Create a new selector rule and name it **footer**.

4. Create the following properties:
   a. padding: 10px 0px
   b. background-color: #900
   c. background-gradient: top color stop - #633, bottom color stop - #900
   d. color: #off (Font category option)

5. Save your work by choosing File>Save As.

Working with Adobe Edge Web Fonts

To add a little more pizzazz to the site you'll add a new Adobe Edge Font to the site using the Font Manager.

1. Add a new Adobe Edge Web Font to be used in the Lake Powell website. In the CSS Designer, select green_styles.css and create a new selector named body. In the Properties window, if necessary deselect the Show Set option. Click the text category icon and click to open the **font-family** property.

2. Click Manage Fonts at the bottom of the font stack window. Click the **List of fonts recommended for Headings**. Click the **Copper Black Std** to select it and then click Custom Font Stacks.

3. Create a new Font Stack by clicking the (**Add fonts in list below**) option. In the search field below the list of **Available fonts** type **Cooper**. The Manage Font window highlights the Cooper Black Std font. Click the << button to add the font to the top position in the list. Repeat this process to add the following fonts to this new font stack.
    a. Impact
    b. Haettenschweiler
    c. Franklin Gothic Book
    d. Arial Black
    e. sans-serif

4. The new Font stack displays in the Font list. Click Done when you have the new font stack created.

5. Now add this new font stack for the H1 tags used in the site. In the CSS Designer, click the lakepowell.css style sheet and then click the header.row h1 selector. Click the Font category option and then click the font-family field. Click to select the new font stack that you created in step 3. Repeat this process to change the article.row section h1 selector to this same font stack.

6. To view the new font, save all documents by choosing File>Save All and then Preview the web page in a browser by choosing File>Preview in Browser and then select your browser from the submenu list.

7. Now set a default font to be used for your page by creating a new selector named **body**. Click the Font category option and in the font-family field select **Gotham, "Helvetica Neue", Helvetica, Arial, sans-serif**. Set the font-size to 14px and the line-height to 1.1em.

8. Save all files and preview the page in a browser.

Adjusting Bootstrap Columns

The final modification to make on this web page is to adjust the column spans and widths for the page.

1. If necessary switch to the Split view. In the Code view find the code for the <article> element row. Change the two references to the <aside> code to match the following:

```
<article class="row">

        <aside class="col-sm-3">

                <h2>Relevant News About Lake Powell</h2>

                <p>This is the content for Layout P Tag</p>

        </aside>

        <section class="col-sm-6">

                <h1>H1 Heading Here </h1>

        <p>This is the content for Layout P Tag</p>

        </section>

        <aside class="col-sm-3">

                <h2 class="text-capitalize">Relevant News About Lake
                Powell</h2>

                <p>This is the content for Layout P Tag</p>

        </aside>

</article>
```

2. Save all files and preview this page in a browser.

3. Begin building accessibility for the site by creating a document title tag. Click anywhere in a blank area of the page and if necessary display the Property inspector by choosing Window>Properties. Click the Properties tab and in the Document Title field. Delete the default text and then type **Lake Powell Adventures – Heaven on Earth.**

4. Again, save all files and preview the page in a browser.

Follow up Meeting: Evaluate Group Performance

It is always good to evaluate a project upon completion.

1. As a group, discuss your group's dynamics and progress through this exercise. Identify areas that were performed well. Answer these questions:
   a. How did people interact in your group?
   b. What could have been done better and how?
   c. Did you meet the measurable results as planned?
   d. Did you stick with your project timeline?

2. Then pat yourself on the back and congratulate your team members.

Online Portfolio Builder – Create a Bootstrap Webpage to Serve as the Template Page for your Online Portfolio Website

Develop the Bootstrap layout of your portfolio site created in Chapter 6 Bootstrap Page Layout project to reflect the page design of the Portfolio site mockup created in Chapter 5 Portfolio project.

1. If necessary, create a local root directory and copy any files or folders over to the new local root directory. Define your site as instructed by your teacher.

2. Using your Bootstrap layout created in Chapter 6 and your site mockup created in Chapter 5 develop each HTML element using CSS style rules.

3. Create placeholder text in the design to create general areas in your design that will contain content based on the site mockup design.

4. Use the preceding Critical Thinking Project that developed the Lake Powell site as well as the chapter exercises to help guide you through the development of your portfolio site with HTML elements and CSS style rules.

Chapter 8

DESIGNING FOR
MOBILE DEVICES

The trend toward designing sites to respond automatically to mobile devices and smartphones continues to grow exponentially. Dreamweaver has powerful tools to get your site mobile-ready.

Chapter Overview

In this chapter, you'll edit and adapt cascading style sheets (CSS) and CSS3 media queries in Dreamweaver for mobile devices and learn how to:

- Edit and manipulate a Bootstrap framework to adapt to different types of mobile devices
- Create and edit a media query for mobile and handheld devices, such as tablets and smartphones
- Select and target CSS rules within specific media queries
- Configure page components to work with mobile devices
- Preview this page in Dreamweaver

Responsive Design

The Internet was never conceived for smartphones and tablets. For the first decade, the most difficult challenge a programmer or developer had to worry about was the size and resolution differences between 13- and 15-inch computer monitors. For years, resolutions and screens sizes only got *larger*.

Today, the chances that some or all of your visitors are using a smartphone or tablet to access your site are increasing day by day. Statistics show that in 2014, more people were using mobile devices to access the Internet than using desktop computers, and that number has been increasing steadily ever since.

Mobile-first Design

One concept that is starting to gain traction today is known as "mobile-first" design. It assumes that sites that aren't optimized for phones and tablets will shed users and traffic in this new environment.

This technique actually starts with a design for mobile devices, such as smartphones, and then adds content and structure for larger devices and computers. In some cases, the site content is actually minimized so that it loads and performs in an optimal fashion, then other content can be injected using JavaScript and databases for computers and more powerful devices. In the end, the decision to design for desktop or mobile first should be based on your site's demographics and analytics.

How your site deals with smartphones and mobile devices depends on whether you're adapting an existing site or developing a new one from scratch. For an existing site, you first have to create a basic design for the site's main components. Then, you have to work through each page, one at a time, to individually assess existing components—like images and tables—that do not inherently adapt to the specific environment.

For new websites, the typical approach is to build in the adaptability as you create the overall design, and then build each page to achieve maximum flexibility. In either case, to support a truly mobile design, be aware that some site components may need to be replaced, left out of the final design altogether, or swapped out live by JavaScript or by the media query itself. For the time being, there is no single solution to all responsive issues, and many solutions are still in development.

Whether you design for desktop or mobile first, you still need to learn how to build designs that respond to all devices. To help web designers adapt pages and content to this changing landscape, two basic tools were created: *media type* and *media query*. These functions enable browsers to identify what size and type of device is accessing the webpage and then load the appropriate style sheet, if one exists.

Media Type Properties

The media type property was added to the **CSS2 specifications** and adopted in 1998. It was intended to address the proliferation of non-computer devices that were able to access the web and web-based resources at that time. The media type is used to target customized formatting to reformat or optimize web content for different media or output.

In all, CSS includes ten individually defined media types, as shown in **Table 7.1**.

Note: In Chapters 5 and 6, you created the basic design for the website as it should appear on a standard desktop computer display based on the screen media type.

Table 7.1 Media Type Properties

PROPERTY	INTENDED USE
all	All devices
aural	Speech and sound synthesizers
braille	Braille tactile feedback devices
embossed	Braille printers
handheld	Handheld devices (small screen, monochrome, limited bandwidth)
print	Documents viewed onscreen in print preview mode and for printing applications
projection	Projected presentations
screen	Primarily for color computer screens
tty	Media using a fixed-pitch character grid, such as teletypes, terminals, or portable
tv	Television-type devices (low resolution, color, limited-scrollability screens, sound available)

CSS2 Specifications

Standards and specifications for Cascading Style Sheets or CSS. W3C released CSS2 specifications in 1998, CSS3 new properties and specifications augment ed and, in some cases, replaced CSS2 properties.

Although the media type property works fine for desktop screens, it never really caught on with browsers used on cellphones and other mobile devices. Part of the problem is the sheer variety of devices in all shapes and sizes. Add to this smorgasbord an equally diverse list of hardware and software capabilities, and you've produced a nightmare environment for the modern web designer. But all is not lost.

Media Queries

A media query is a newer CSS development that provides code in the webpage that allows it to interactively determine what formatting to use based on not only what kind of device (media type) is displaying the page, but also on what dimensions and orientation it's using. Once the browser knows the type or size of the device it has encountered, it reads the media query to know what resources to load to format the webpage and content. This process is as fluid and continuous as a precision dance routine, even allowing the user to switch orientations during a session and have the page and content adapt seamlessly without other intervention. The key to this ballet is the development of style sheets optimized for specific browsers, specific devices, or both.

Media Query Syntax

Like the CSS it controls, a media query requires a specific syntax to work properly in the browser. It consists of one or more media types and one or more expressions, or media features, which a browser must test as true before it applies the styles it contains. Currently, Dreamweaver supports 22 media features. Others are being tested or are still under development and may not appear in the interface, but you can add them manually to the code, if necessary.

The media query creates a set of criteria to determine whether or not a specific set of rules contained within it is applied in a webpage.

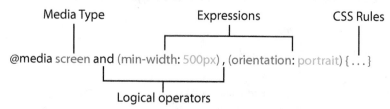

You can create media queries in a variety of ways. For example, they can be designed to work exclusively—by completely resetting the existing styling—or in tandem—by inheriting some styles and modifying specifications only as necessary. The latter method requires less CSS code and is typically more efficient. We will favor that method in the upcoming exercises and for the sample site design.

To learn more about media queries and how they work, check out www.w3schools.com/cssref/css3_pr_mediaquery.asp.

Adapting Bootstrap Layouts to Different Screen Sizes

The GreenStart site design was based on a predefined Bootstrap layout that was created to be responsive out of the box. The Bootstrap framework provides a very complex style sheet complete with numerous media queries and CSS rules to accommodate a wide variety of browsers and devices. Using a framework like Bootstrap shortens the development time and allows you to concentrate on your content, instead of on technical issues.

In Chapter 7, you fleshed out a Bootstrap layout with placeholder content based on your site design. This content will form the foundation of the site template, which you will use later to build pages for your site. At the moment, the page is partially responsive. In this exercise, you will learn how to tap into Bootstrap's built-in styles and media queries to make the page fully responsive.

Working with the Responsive Scrubber

Before you can learn how to manipulate the Bootstrap framework for various screen sizes, it helps to identify how the current layout responds to changing screen sizes. New to Dreamweaver CC (2015.1 release) is the Scrubber tool. It enables you to change the width of your document viewport so you can interact with the style sheets and media queries defined in the page and actually simulate different device widths right inside Dreamweaver. In the past, to change the viewport you had to manipulate the whole program interface, dragging the edge of the document window or program to see a reaction in the page.

1 If necessary, define a site based on the Chapter 8 folder as instructed by your teacher.

2 Open **mylayout_xx.html** from the Chapter 8 folder in Live view.

3 Maximize the program to fill the entire display; the program window should be displayed at a minimum of 1200 pixels in width to display and test all the media queries contained in the Bootstrap CSS.

The page displays the basic site design, complete with text placeholders and graphical treatments for the header and footer.

4 Drag the Scrubber to the left to decrease the width of the document window.

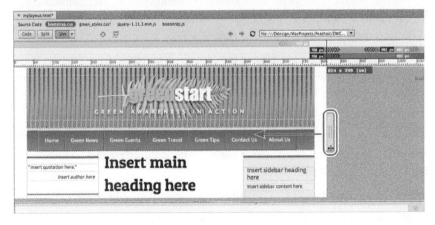

Tip: Dreamweaver displays the current screen size just below the VMQ interface as you drag the Scrubber.

As the window narrows, the layout adapts to the changes. At first, the columns in the main content area share the row side by side. When the screen narrows below 767 pixels, the layout completely changes and all the elements stack vertically one atop the other and the navigation menu collapses to an icon. The collapse coincides with the beginning of the final media query displayed in the Visual Media Queries or VMQ interface at the top of the document window.

5 Stop dragging the Scrubber when the width reaches 320 pixels. Observe how the structure and content reacts to this screen width.

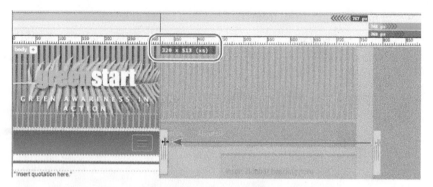

This is the width of the original iPhone and one of the narrowest phone screens you will want to support.

6 Drag the Scrubber to the right to increase the width of the document window.

As the window widens, the content and structure resume their original styling. As you can see, the Bootstrap structure that you created is already fairly responsive, although there are a few things you will probably want to tweak.

For example, as the page narrows the content continues to divide the space into the three-column layout. When the page narrows below 900 pixels, it gets unappealingly tight. Although the columns adjust properly for the tighter space, you may want to change the basic structure or content. One technique designers use in this situation is to hide content when there's no room for it or when it doesn't make sense to show it in a specific way or in a specific screen size.

Since the first column is intended for quotations and other inspiring messages, it's not essential to the purpose of the page or the site. Hiding it is one solution to the issue. Luckily, Bootstrap provides a simple solution.

Hiding Bootstrap Elements

In this exercise, you will learn how to use predefined Bootstrap styles to hide unwanted content on small screens.

1 If necessary, open **mylayout_xx.html** as instructed by your teacher.

2 Make sure the Scrubber is positioned fully to the right side of the document window and the Dreamweaver workspace is wider than 900 pixels.

The change can be made when the screen is at any width, but displaying the correct window size makes it easier to select the desired elements and styling.

3   Click the Small media query in the VMQ.

The Scrubber jumps to the media query displayed in the VMQ. The three columns appear very tight at this width; headlines and text break into short lines, which may adversely affect readability.

4   Click the first column of the third row.
    Select the `aside.col-sm-3` tag selector.

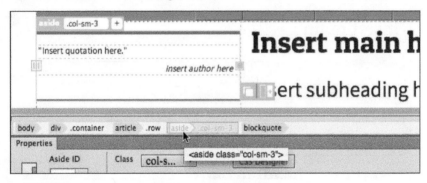

The HUD appears focused on the `<aside>` element.

Bootstrap provides various CSS styles to format elements at specific screen sizes. The framework classifies these sizes as *large* (desktop screens larger than 1200 pixels), *medium* (screens from 992 to 1199 pixels), *small* (screens from 768 to 991 pixels), and *extra-small* (screens 767 pixels and below).

The class assigned to the `<aside>` (`col-sm-3`) styles the element for small screens. The styling will be inherited for larger screen sizes, but for smaller screen sizes there is no styling applied so the elements revert to CSS defaults. To hide the element on small screens, you need to add a second predefined Bootstrap class.

5   Click the Add Class/ID icon in the HUD.

    A text field appears in the HUD.

6   Type `.hidden-sm` and press Enter/Return to complete the class.

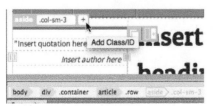
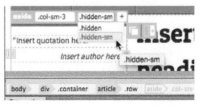

Note: As you type the class, a hinting menu will appear. This hinting menu is responsive to the screen width and the media query selected and may not show classes pertinent to other media queries.

A hinting list appears as you type. After you select the class, Dreamweaver assigns it to the element. The element disappears from the layout.

7   Drag the Scrubber to the right to the Medium Bootstrap media query (992 to 1199 pixels).

The `<aside>` element reappears. A second class appears on the element. This class is designed to hide elements on small screens. If the document width is from 768 to 991 pixels, the first column will disappear from the row. At 992 pixels, it reappears. Let's see what happens on extra-small screens.

8   Drag the Scrubber to the left until the document window is less than 767 pixels wide.

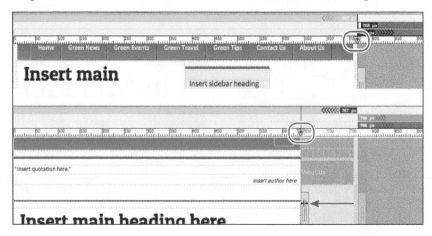

The `<aside>` disappears and then reappears back in the layout when the page drops below 767 pixels in width. Did you notice how the quotations reappeared at the top of the document in the Extra Small media query? The class `hidden-sm` hides the element only on small screens.

Hiding the element on small screens solves the original spacing issue when you have three columns. But on extra-small screens, the position of the element creates a new problem. It appears at the top of the page, pushing the main content down the screen where it may not even be visible on smaller devices. You could hide the element again on extra-small screens, but this is a problem that calls for a more imaginative solution.

Mobile-ready vs. Mobile-optimized

Hiding elements, such as the first sidebar, is not an ideal solution in all situations. If you find yourself hiding an inordinate amount of content, or you see that you have a large number of visitors via phones and tablets, you may want to consider creating a separate, mobile-*optimized* site.

A mobile-optimized site is often hosted on a subdomain, such as *mobile .yourdomain.com*, and contains pages designed specifically for mobile devices. These sites not only reduce page size, they may also select, or filter, content appropriate for the specific device. For example, some sites remove images, tables, video, and other large elements that don't scale down very well.

Obviously, producing two or more completely different sites can drastically increase design and maintenance costs, especially if the content changes on a regular basis. It's also not the best plan for optimizing your search engine ranking.

Instead, another option is to create your website based on an online database or content management system (CMS), such as Drupal, Joomla, or WordPress. A CMS can dynamically create pages as needed based on a template and style sheets with no additional effort. These systems enable you to design mobile-optimized templates that can automatically adapt to various devices and be programmed to deliver only content appropriate for those devices.

On sites that aren't made with a CMS, you may have to figure out a different solution. Hiding elements is good in some situations. But hiding an element doesn't prevent it from downloading. A hidden video or image still takes up valuable bandwidth on your visitors' devices and may cost them in minutes or data charges. Some designers take a mobile-first strategy and actually remove the undesirable content entirely from the page, making the pages and site work optimally on mobile devices. Then, they use JavaScript or other techniques to *inject* videos or large images into the layout but only on screens or devices that can handle it.

In this case, the quotations are not too large or unwieldy to display; they just appear in the wrong place at the wrong time, or screen size.

In situations like this, Bootstrap may offer a better alternative than hiding the element: You can *move* it. To learn how to rearrange the elements in your layout you'll first have to remove the `hidden-sm` class.

9 Select the `aside.col-sm-3.hidden-sm` tag selector.

The HUD appears focused on the `<aside>` element.

10 Hover your insertion point in the `.hidden-sm` class and then click the Remove Class/ID icon ✖ for the `hidden-sm` class.

The class is removed from the element.

11 Drag the Scrubber to the Small Media Query stop and double check that the hidden element is now displayed. Save the file.

Before you can solve this "mobile" design challenge, you'll have to adjust the way you think about how elements are ordered and structured. You have to discard old-fashioned notions of form and function.

Creating a mobile-first Structure

In this exercise, you will change the basic structure of the layout to create a mobile-first structure.

1 If necessary, open **mylayout_xx.html** as instructed by your teacher.

2 Make sure the document window is wider than 767 pixels and that the Scrubber is positioned at the right side of the window.

3 Drag the Scrubber to the Extra Small media query (767 pixels or less).

The content of the layout stacks vertically. The quotations appear at the top.

To build the mobile-first scheme, you have to adjust the current layout by moving the quotations to a location that will be more appropriate on extra-small screens. Then, by using a Bootstrap function, you will adjust the display of the elements for small screens before finally restoring the original design for larger screens and devices.

The process starts by moving the first column to a different position in the code structure. You could move the elements in Code view, but in this case you'll use a new tool: the DOM viewer.

4 If necessary, open the DOM viewer by selecting Window > DOM. Resize the window as necessary to see the document structure.

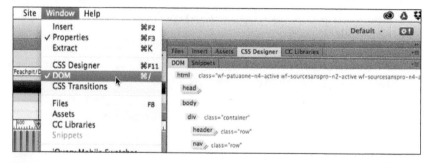

DOM stands for Document Object Model. It offers a schematic view of your HTML code, displaying the elements that compose its structure in a graphical interface. But it's not just a pretty picture. You can also use the DOM viewer to insert, delete, and move elements.

5   Select the `aside.col-sm-3` tag selector.
Observe the DOM panel display.

Note: Notice that if an element has nested elements it has a different display in the DOM panel. the DOM arrow icon displays in a stack of arrow. You can expand that stack by clicking it. Click it again to collapse it back.

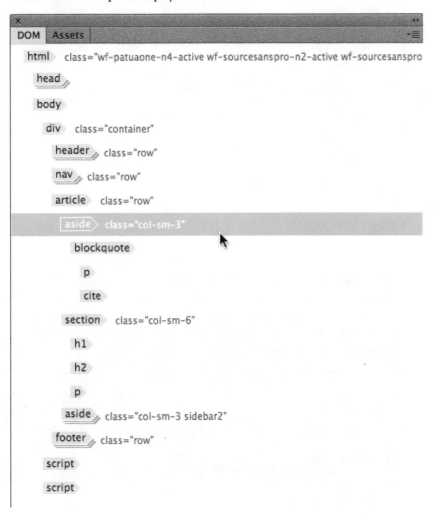

The `<aside>` element is highlighted. The diagram shows the parent `<article>` element and its three children. Notice that the child elements are indented in the structure. To move an element, simply drag it to the proper location.

6 Drag the first `<aside>` element below the `<section>` element.

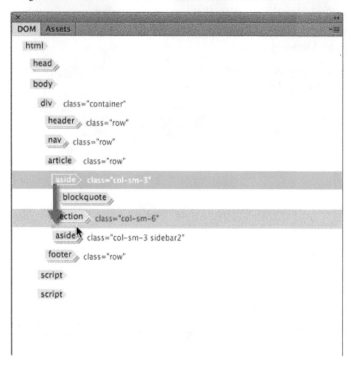

Note: Dragging elements in the DOM viewer requires a careful eye and a steady hand. It's easy to mess up the first few times you try. Take your time and check the code to make sure you put the element in the right spot. You can undo any errors by pressing Ctrl+Z/ Cmd+Z.

A green line appears indicating where the element will be inserted. If done properly, the element will appear below the `<section>` and indented at the same level. The quotations now appear below the main content. The new arrangement puts the important content where it belongs on extra-small screens, but it has created a new problem on larger screens.

7 Drag the Scrubber to, or click, the Small media query (768 to 991 pixels).

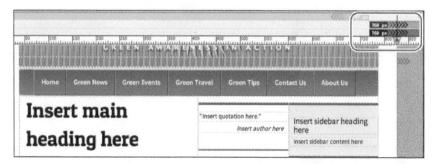

When the Scrubber moves into the Small media query, the three-column layout reappears, but now the quotations are displayed to the right of the main content. To restore the original look of the layout, you have to use a special Bootstrap function that is supplied within the predefined CSS.

8 If necessary, select the `aside.col-sm-3` tag selector for the quotations' column in the Tag Selector bar.

9 Using the HUD, add the following class:

`.col-sm-pull-6`

Note: When working in the HUD, make sure you press Enter/Return to set the edit you made to a class or to create a new class.

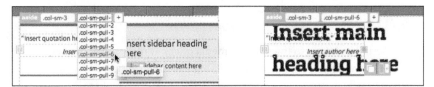

The `pull` function shifts the quotations back to the left side of the row, but it's overlapping the main content. To correct this problem, you can use a `push` function to move the main content back to the right.

10 Click the `<h1>` element nested in the `<section>` element.
Select the `section.col-sm-6` tag selector.
Add the class `.col-sm-push-3`

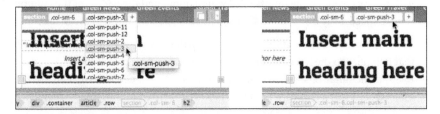

The main content section moves back to the center. All three columns are back in their original locations, but with an important *mobile-first* difference.

11 Drag the Scrubber to the left until the document window is narrower than 767 pixels.

Below 767 pixels the content displays in a single column again. The quotations appear below the main content. Through some Bootstrap magic you have created a layout that automatically adapts to mobile screens by shifting elements to more appropriate positions depending on the size of the screen.

12 Save the file.

Although you have solved one of the original challenges, the three columns still look a bit too tight on small screens. It would look better and less crowded in a two-column layout.

Manipulating Column Widths in Bootstrap

The great thing about Bootstrap is that it makes it easy to change the widths of columns at different screen sizes. In this exercise, you will create a two-column layout on small screens and then switch back to three columns at larger sizes.

1 If necessary, open **mylayout_xx.html** as instructed by your teacher.

2 Click the Medium screen media query (992 to 1199 pixels) in the VMQ.

The Scrubber jumps to the selected media query. It may stop at the beginning or end of the screen range, but the CSS applies to the entire range, so it doesn't really matter where it stops. The important concept here is that setting the screen to the correct size before you begin allows you to see the results immediately.

Before you can change the layout, you have to understand how it was created in the first place. In Chapter 6, "Creating a Page Layout," you built the three-column layout by manipulating the default Bootstrap class `col-sm-4` applied to each element in the row. The number indicates how many grid columns the element will use. By changing the number "4," you manipulated the widths of the columns to take space away from the `<aside>` elements and give more to the main content.

You may have noticed that the class has the letters `sm` in the name. This indicates that it applies to the Small media query. Some Bootstrap classes limit styling to a specific range of screen sizes, while others are designed to have their styles inherited. In this instance, column widths are inherited in the larger screens sizes.

To change the number of columns displayed in different screen sizes, you simply have to change the existing classes or add additional ones. Since you want to keep the current layout on larger screens, the first change will be a minor one.

Tip: Press Enter/Return to complete each new class.

3 Click the quotation placeholder.
Select the `aside.col-sm-3 .col-sm-pull-6` tag selector for the first column.

4 In the HUD, edit the class name as highlighted:

`.col-md-3`

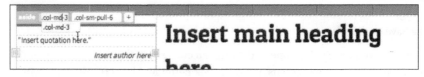

This change makes the class start formatting on Medium screens. You'll have to change the `pull` function too.

5 In the HUD, edit the class name as highlighted:

`.col-md-pull-6`

This change pulls the element into the first column for medium screens. You need to make the same changes for the other columns.

6   Change the classes for the main content element to:

.col-md-6 and .col-md-push-3

7   Change the class for Sidebar 2 to:

.col-md-3

Nothing changes. The layout remains the same as before, which means the new classes are doing their job. The layout is ready now for medium and larger screens. But let's check out what happens on smaller screens.

8   Click the Small screen media query.

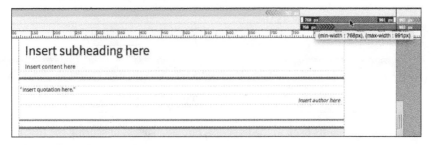

The document window resizes. The layout reformats into a single column, as it had done for the extra-small screens. This is because none of the Bootstrap classes are currently formatting these elements. To create the new column layout, you'll need to add new classes to each element.

9   Click in the main content window.
Select the section.col-md-6.col-md-push-3 tag selector.

On small screens, you want two columns on the first line and Sidebar 2 on the second line. You'll split the first line, with one-third for the quotations and two-thirds for the main content.

10 Add a new class to the section:

.col-sm-8

The main content section resizes to two-thirds of the screen width. Let's push the column to the right side of the row.

11 Add a new class to the `section`:

`.col-sm-push-4`

The column shifts to the right side of the row. Next, you'll deal with the quotations column.

12 Select the tag selector `aside.col-md-3.col-md-pull-6` for Sidebar 1. Add a new class to the `aside`:

`.col-sm-4`

The column occupies four column grids but is still aligned to the right.

13 Add a new class to the `aside`:

`.col-sm-pull-8`

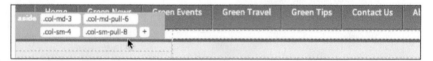

The column shifts back to the left edge, but Sidebar 2 is obscuring the first row. Nothing is formatting this column, and since it isn't floating it's trying to rise up to take the place of the other two elements. You can get it back into the mix by adding the proper class.

14 Select the `aside.col-md-3.sidebar2` tag selector and add the following class:

`.col-sm-8`

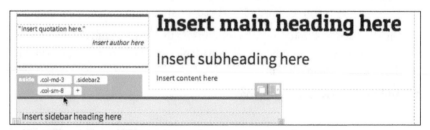

The new class resizes the column. It now matches the width of the main content area and has shifted below it. The column is aligned to the left. Let's match the alignment of the main content column.

15 Add the following class:

`.col-sm-push-4`

Sidebar 2 aligns to the main content section. The styling of the new structure is complete. Let's see how it responds now to different screen sizes.

16 Drag the Scrubber left and right to test the styling at different screen widths.

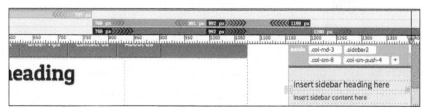

On small and extra-small screens, the layout looks fine. When the Scrubber hits the medium media query, the elements shift back to one row, but there's a problem. Sidebar 2 was OK originally, but now it appears far to the right edge of the screen. To get it back into the layout, you need to add a push function.

17 Add the following class to Sidebar 2:

`.col-md-push-0`

Sidebar 2 now fits back into the layout.

18 Drag the Scrubber left and right and observe the layout.

The layout shifts from one, to two, to three columns interactively as you change the width of the window. The layout works perfectly now, responding to all screen sizes smoothly. Overall, the structure looks fine, but the content could use a few tweaks on smaller screens. When the screen width gets to the smallest size, the logo in the header seems too big and actually extends beyond the edges of the screen.

19 Save the file.

In the remaining exercises, you will learn how to style elements at different screen sizes by creating a custom media query and adding CSS rules to it.

Working with Media Queries

As you learned earlier, a media query is a method you can use to target styling to specific screen sizes, orientations, and devices. The Bootstrap framework provides predefined style sheets and JavaScript to make the underlying page structure responsive out of the box with these scripting languages. In most cases, you only have to add your own style sheets and media queries to deal with conflicts with your page content or with specific design requirements. Whenever you start a project with predefined resources, it's a good idea to inspect the basic structure and the elements that format it.

Identifying Media Queries

The `<header>` is made up of several elements and CSS effects. Take a moment to identify the styling that has already been created for mobile devices and what it does.

1   If necessary, launch Dreamweaver CC (2015.1 release) or later.
    Maximize the program to fill the entire screen.

2   In Live view, open **mylayout_xx.html** from the Chapter08/Datafiles folder as instructed by your teacher.

3   Choose Window > CSS Designer, if necessary, to display the panel.
    Click the All button.

Note: If your screen is too small to display the CSS Designer in two columns, you will still be able complete the exercise.

4   Adjust the CSS Designer to display in two columns while maintaining a screen width of 1024 pixels or wider, if possible.

    Setting up the CSS Designer in two columns makes working with and editing CSS easier.

5   Select ALL SOURCES.

6   Examine the @Media window and note the existing media queries.

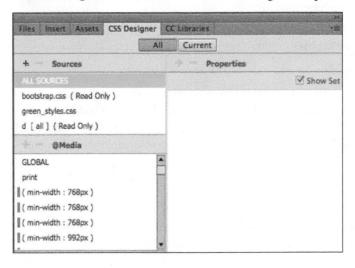

The window shows a list of media queries for a variety of screen sizes and applications.

7 Click the first few media queries and observe the Sources window display.

The bootstrap.css file is highlighted in bold, indicating that the selected media query is defined within that file. In fact, there are over 60 media queries defined. The nature of a predefined framework is to anticipate all the needs and usage of basic HTML elements as well as any provided components and format them to work in any foreseeable environment or application. The rest is up to you.

8 Click in the <header> element.
Click the Current button.

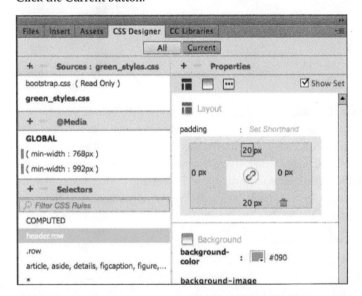

The list of media queries is shorter, showing only the styles affecting the <header> element.

9 Drag the Scrubber to the left. Observe the text "Green Awareness in Action." When the words break to two lines, stop dragging the Scrubber.

The motto breaks to two lines at approximately 425 pixels. Also note that the logo is filling the screen from left to right. If you added a new rule to adjust the formatting of this element, it would apply to the element at all screen sizes. That's because CSS rules are applied to all screen states unless limited by a media query. Since the Bootstrap media queries are locked, you'll need to create a new one in the **green_styles.css** file.

Note: If your text doesn't display on one line, keep dragging to the right until it does and then adjust the media query accordingly.

10 Drag the Scrubber to the right until the motto appears on one line, approximately between 426 to 438 pixels.

The motto should still be displayed on one line. Dreamweaver allows you to create a new media query right in the document window.

11 Click the Add Media Query icon at the top of the Scrubber.

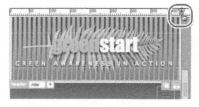

| Mac | Windows |

Note: If *green_styles.css* does not appear in the pull-down menu automatically, select it manually.

A Media Query Definition dialog appears. The max-width field is already populated with the pixel position of your Scrubber, between 426 to 438 pixels. The min-width field is empty. That means this media query will apply to screens starting at this width and smaller. Using the minimum-width property means that none of the styles contained within it will affect any devices wider than that designated. Make sure that the file name **green_styles.css** appears in the source pull-down menu.

12 Click OK to create the media query.
If necessary, open the CSS Designer.

13 Click the All button.
Click **green_styles.css** in the Sources panel.

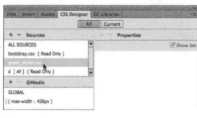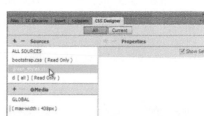

Mac   Windows

Note: The purpose of the media query is to keep the motto on one line. Your pixel position may differ from the one described here or pictured in subsequent screen shots. Substitute your measurement in the following exercises, as necessary.

A new (max-width) media query has been added to the style sheet. Your max-width media query might be a different number between 426 – 445 based on the size of your monitor screen. You will use this media query to tweak the header and other elements on small screens.

14 Save all files.

Adding Rules to a Media Query

CSS rules contained within a media query are used to reset or reformat elements based on the size, orientation, or type of device displaying your webpage. In this exercise, you will add rules to the new media query.

1 If necessary, open **mylayout_xx.html** as instructed by your teacher.

2 Ensure the Dreamweaver workspace is maximized to the full extent of the computer display.

3 Adjust the CSS Designer to display in two columns while maintaining a screen width of 1024 pixels or wider, if possible.
Click the All button.

4 Click the new media query displayed in the VMQ interface (max-width 426 pixels).

The Scrubber repositions to 426 pixels. The motto should display in one line.

5 Drag the Scrubber to 320 pixels.

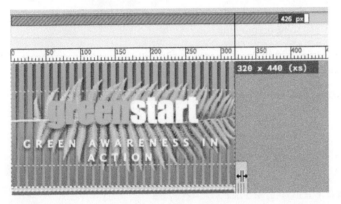

This is the width of the iPhone classic and probably the smallest device you will have to support. The motto breaks to two lines.

6 Click the motto "GREEN AWARENESS IN ACTION."

The motto is highlighted, displaying the HUD focused on the p tag. When adding new rules, it's vital that the rule be inserted into the correct style sheet and media query. The following technique will ensure that your rules get into the proper location every time in the CSS Designer.

7 Select **green_styles.css** in Sources.
Select (max-width:426px) in @Media.
Click the Add Selector icon ✚ in Selectors.

The selector .row .col-sm-12 p appears in the Selectors window.

8   Edit the selector name to `header.row p` and press Enter/Return as needed to complete the name.

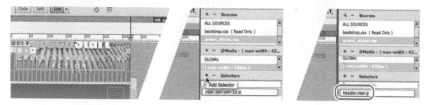

9   Add the following property to the new rule:

```
letter-spacing: .1em
```

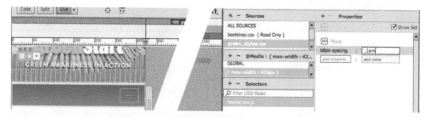

The motto narrows to fit on one line.

10 Drag the Scrubber to the right.
Observe the header.

The motto remains narrow until the screen width exceeds 426 pixels. Then it expands to its original settings.

11 Save all files.

Now you can adjust the logo.

Copying and Pasting CSS Properties

In this exercise, you will learn how to create CSS styling by copying and pasting properties from one rule to another.

1   Drag the Scrubber to 320 pixels.
Click in the `<header>` element and select the `header.row` tag selector.

2   Click the All button in the CSS Designer, if necessary.

The `<header>` has a complex set of properties creating the background effects. Writing a new rule to tweak the `<header>` on small devices might be a challenge for some designers. But instead of writing the new rule from scratch, you'll use a feature of the CSS Designer that will make the job fast and simple.

3   Select **green_styles.css** in Sources.

The Selectors window shows all the rules contained in the file. To narrow down the list to the rules affecting the `<header>`, use the Current button.

4 Click the Current button.

The selectors list shows only the rules affecting the `<header>` in **green_style.css**. The `header.row` rule is at the top of the list.

5 Select `header.row` in Selectors.

When the rule is selected, **green_styles.css** is bolded, indicating where the rule is located. The Properties window displays the current settings. The CSS Designer enables you to copy some or all of the styles within one rule and paste them into a new or existing rule.

6 Right-click the `header.row` rule.

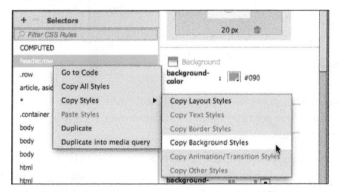

A context menu appears. Note the options for copying some or all of the properties in the rule.

7 Select Copy Styles > Copy Background Styles.

8 Click the All button.

The All button must be selected to create new rules.

9 Select **green_styles.css** in Sources.
Select (`max-width:426px`) in @Media.
Click the Add Selector icon ✚ in Selectors.
The name `.container .row` appears in the Selectors window.

10 Edit the name to `header.row` and press Enter/Return as needed to complete the selector.

The new selector appears in the window. The Properties window is empty. The new rule has no styling applied to it.

11 Right-click `header.row` in Selectors.
In the context menu, select **Paste Styles**. If necessary, in the CSS Designer select Show Set to see the pasted styles.

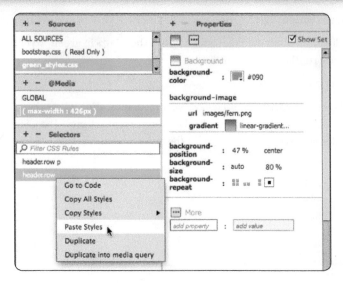

The background styles you copied in **step 6 and 7** are pasted into the new rule. The Properties window is populated with the background styling from the original `header.row` rule.

There are now two rules formatting the `<header>`. Since the original rule still formats the element even at the smaller sizes, there's no need to keep any property that isn't going to change. You need only the ones that will reset the logo's size. Let's delete the redundant properties.

12 Select the new `header.row` rule and select the Show Set option in Properties, if necessary.

The Properties window displays the background specifications that were copied and pasted into the new rule. Beside the fields that allow you to add or edit CSS properties, each setting in the window also provides options to disable or delete the value.

13 Position the insertion point over the **background-color** property.

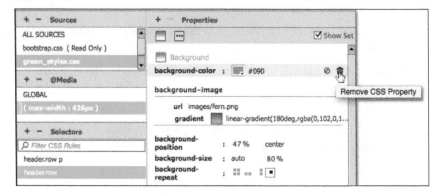

When the insertion point moves over the property, Dreamweaver highlights it. The Disable icon and the Delete icon 🗑 appear to the right.

14 Click the Delete icon 🗑.

The background-color property is removed.

15 Delete all background properties except **background-size**.

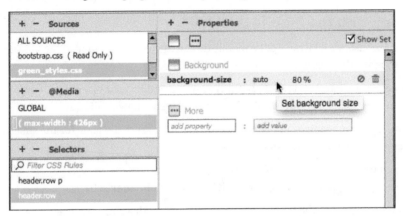

The new rule now styles only the background size. At the moment, the setting is still identical to the one in the original rule. You can use this last property to reformat the <header> on extra-small screens, but remember that it contains multiple settings to format the different parts of the background.

16 Right-click the rule `header.row`.
Select **Go to Code** from the context menu.

Dreamweaver switches to Split view and loads **green_style.css** in the Code window. The window is focused on the `header.row` rule in the media query `@media (max-width: 426px)`.

17 Edit the declaration as highlighted:

`background-size: 95% auto, auto auto, 100% auto;`

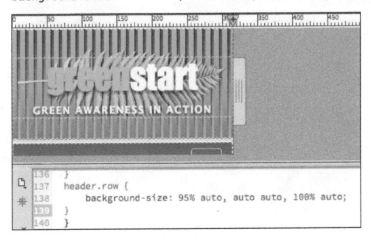

Note: Switching the emphasis of the settings to the width instead of the height allows the logo to adapt better to the narrowing screen width.

Live view updates the `<header>` display, scaling the logo to fit the width of the screen. The new settings will prevent the logo from getting too big on the smaller screens.

18 Save all files.

The last step is to tweak the text styles to fit the content better on smaller screens.

Completing the Mobile Design

In this exercise, you'll wrap up the mobile design by overriding some of the existing rules to make the text fit better on the smaller window.

1 If necessary, open **mylayout_xx.html** as instructed by your teacher.
Adjust the screen width to 400 pixels to activate the new media query.

The logo and headings in the `<article>` element seem too large for the smaller screen. They take up too much space.

2 Open the CSS Designer, if necessary.
Select **green_styles.css** > (max-width:426px) > `header.row`

You can adjust all the text sizes in the `<header>` with a single property.

3 Create the following properties:

```
padding: 10px 0px
font-size: 80%
```

The logo text and motto scale down in size along with the height of the `<header>`.

4 Create a new rule: `article.row section h1`
Add the following properties:

```
padding-top: 15px
font-size: 185%
line-height: 1.1em
text-align: center
```

5 Create a new rule: `article.row section h2`
Add the following properties:

```
font-size: 150%
line-height: 1.1em
```

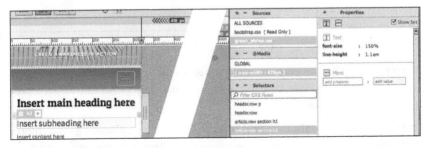

The h1 and h2 headings now fit the smaller screens better.

6 Save all files.

The layout is complete and adapted to mobile screens. In the next chapter, you will turn this layout into a Dreamweaver template, which will allow you to create pages based on the site design quickly and easily.

More Information on Media Queries

To learn more about media queries and how to work with them, visit the following links:

- Adobe: http://tinyurl.com/adobe-media-queries
- W3C Consortium: http://tinyurl.com/w3c-media-queries
- Smashing Magazine: http://tinyurl.com/media-queries-smashing

You've now successfully modified a predefined mobile-ready layout and adapted it to your site design requirements. Although it's hard to imagine what amazing new features may come along, one thing you can be sure of is that Dreamweaver will continue to be at the forefront of web development. With support for media queries and other responsive techniques, the program continues to innovate and be a leader in the industry.

Computers and Safety

Computers are tools and, like other tools, they are controlled by the person using them. People can use computers to learn, to communicate, and to have fun. However, people can also use computers to snoop into another person's private life or to commit crimes. Careless computer users can pass computer viruses from their machines to those of other users. What can make computers dangerous is the same thing that makes them helpful: They can store vast amounts of data.

When people learn to use tools, they learn to use them with care and to protect themselves and others from harm. Computer users need to learn ways to protect themselves, too.

Privacy in Cyberspace

Many consumers share personal information about themselves, their habits, and their finances. Sometimes, however, such information is gathered without a person's knowledge or approval.

How Businesses Obtain Personal Information Some businesses gather information from public records kept by the government. They may also access information that people volunteer about themselves in several ways:

- Website registration—Many websites require visitors to fill out registration forms.

- Online purchases—Some websites gather information about people who buy their goods or services.

- Warranty registration—To take advantage of a product warranty, you usually must register with the manufacturer. Some warranty registrations ask for a lot of personal information.

- Sweepstakes entries—Many people fill out sweepstakes entry forms hoping to win a prize. In doing so, they provide important personal information.

- Social networking sites—These sites gather information about their users from their profiles and posts, including where they live, what they like, and products they use.

- Search engines and messaging services—Some of these sites collect data about users and their online search history to learn what interests them.

Companies that gather personal information often sell it to other organizations, such as marketing companies, whose job is to sell products and services to consumers. As a result, marketing companies have access to enormous quantities of data about people. This information is stored in large computerized databases.

Protecting Privacy Some people say that individuals should have the right to refuse to provide information about themselves, as well as the right to have information about themselves removed from a database. Although such a guarantee does not yet exist in the United States, you can protect your privacy by being careful to whom you give out personal information about yourself. You can also select privacy settings on websites and social networks that limit who can access your personal information or view your posts. For example, you can select to only share your personal information with friends, or set your social networking status to invisible so other people do not know you are online.

The web is not the only way others can learn about you on the Internet. Visitors to newsgroups can reveal facts about themselves to other visitors.

Think About It!

Think about what you might say in a newsgroup or on social media sites. Which statement(s) below might reveal too much personal information?

- "In my town, people often leave their doors unlocked."

- "We always go to the shore on weekends in the summer."

- "I don't like being alone."

- "Our porch light doesn't work."

- "My parents get home an hour after I arrive from school."

Respecting Others' Privacy You also need to make sure not to infringe or interfere with the privacy and rights of others. Do not post personal information about others online, via texts, or in e-mails.

Expectations of Privacy Remember that everything you post online or send by e-mail is on record. Employees of a company have no right of privacy for their e-mail when they use their employer's computer system. Although the employer may not say so, every message might be read by someone who alerts management if anything seems amiss. Employees may face serious consequences if they disclose inside information to competitors, threaten or harass other employees, or tell jokes.

In addition, when you apply to a college or university, or to a job, you should expect that the school or potential employer will look for you online. A simple search will let them see a history of what you have posted on almost every Internet site. These are strong reasons why you should always be respectful and polite online, and why you should never post items that may be embarrassing to you in the future.

New Technology and Your Privacy

The Internet has generated new methods for tracking what people do. Even if you do not buy anything online, outsiders can use different hardware and software to learn about your habits and interests. Some people worry that these technologies— and your personal information—can be misused.

Cookies A cookie is a small file that is saved to your hard drive when you visit some websites. Cookies give websites a way of storing information about you so it is available when you return. Cookies are meant to make your web experience more pleasurable by personalizing what you see. However, they can also be used to gather data on your browsing and shopping habits without your consent.

If you wish, you can set your browser to reject cookies or warn you about them. Several programs and web browsers let users see what the purpose of a cookie is. Then you can decide whether or not to accept the cookie.

Global Unique Identifiers A global unique identifier, or GUID, is a unique identification number that is generated by a piece of hardware or by a program. Companies that place GUIDs in their products generally do not say so openly. Some people worry that GUIDs can be used to follow a person's online activity, invading his or her privacy.

Cybercrime Techniques

Many cybercrimes are based on the ability of people to tap illegally into computer networks. They may create a **virus**, **worm**, or **Trojan horse** program to infiltrate computers and damage or delete data. Or, they may use a variety of other criminal techniques.

Virus

A computer virus is a small software program designed to spread between computers. Every virus has a purpose with most designed to interfere with a computer's operation. Most viruses need to attach to an existing program on the infected computer.

Worm

A computer worm is a standalone software program that is designed to replicate itself in order to spread to other computers.It spreads through computer networks and targets security failures on a computer to access it. This type of virus can be very harmful to your computer and information on the computer. A worm does not need to attach itself to an existing program like a virus.

Trojan horse

A malicious computer program that tricks the user into installing it on their computer. This type of virus misrepresents itself to appear useful, routine, or interesting so that the user is persuaded to installing it.

Scanning Some intruders develop programs that try many different passwords until one works. This is called scanning, or probing. Networks can be blocked from scanners by limiting the number of failed attempts to log onto the system. After three password failures, for instance, the network can refuse access.

Superzapping A program called a superzapper allows authorized users to access a network in an emergency situation by skipping security measures. In the hands of an intruder, a super- zapper opens the possibility of damage to the system.

Spoofing Some intruders spoof, or use a false Internet Protocol (IP) or e-mail address to gain access. Intruders assume the IP address of a trusted source to enter a secure network and distribute e-mails containing viruses.

Phishing Phishing criminals try to lure victims into giving them user names, passwords, bank account numbers, or credit card details, usually by using an e-mail that looks like it comes from an official and legitimate source. For example, in a typical phishing scam, a thief sends an e-mail message that looks as if it is from your bank, asking you to verify or update your account information. The thief captures the information you enter and can then steal from your account.

Time Bombs A time bomb is a program that sits on a system until a certain event or set of circumstances activates the program. For example, an employee could create a time bomb designed to activate on a certain date after he or she resigns from the company. Although a time bomb is not necessarily a virus, these malicious programs are often categorized or described as viruses.

Trap Doors Some employees may create a trap door, or a secret way into the system. Once they quit working for the employer, they can use this to access the system and damage it. Not all trap doors are viruses, but some viruses are trap doors. Many Trojan horse programs, for example, act as trapdoors.

Scams Some criminals use advertisements and e-mail messages to scam you into sending them money. For example, they might claim you have won a lottery, and if you pay a tax or fee, they will send you the winnings.

Social Engineering A common criminal tactic is to use social engineering to trick you into clicking a link that will install a virus or capture your personal information. Social engineering is not technical. It relies on human nature and manipulation to convince someone to do something. A common social engineering hack would be an official-looking e-mail notifying you about a problem with your bank account. When you click a link you are sent to a fake bank web site.

Types of Cybercrime

Crimes using the Internet can take many different forms. They affect individuals, businesses, and government agencies.

Fraud When someone steals your personal information, he or she can impersonate you and make credit card purchases in your name or access your bank accounts.

This is called identity theft. The criminal leaves you with bills and a damaged credit rating.

Piracy Software piracy is the illegal copying of computer programs. It is estimated that about one third of all software in use is pirated. Most programs that people buy are licensed only to the purchaser. In other words, it is illegal for you to copy such a program and give it to a friend. It is also illegal to accept a copy of software from someone else.

Software piracy affects software publishers. They lose money when people use illegal copies of pro- grams to avoid paying for legitimate copies.

Theft The vast majority of computer thefts occur "on the inside" (by employees), leaving no signs of forced entry. The hardest crime to detect is memory shaving. In this act, a thief steals some of a computer's memory chips but leaves enough so the computer will start. The crime might go unnoticed for days or weeks.

Vandalism Some web servers are not properly secured. As a result, intruders can vandalize a website by placing prank material on it.

The High Cost of Computer Crime

The Internet has opened the door to new kinds of crime and new ways of carrying out traditional crimes. Computer crime is any act that violates state or federal laws and involves using a computer. The term cybercrime often refers specifically to crimes carried out by means of the Internet. Computer crime causes businesses to lose money in the following ways.

Staff Time Even if intruders steal nothing from a business, they still cost companies money. Staff must make the network secure again and consider how to stop security breaches.

Downtime Security breaches also cost a company in terms of downtime, or a temporary stop to work. System administrators sometimes shut a network down to prevent the loss of data. While the system is down, workers cannot do their jobs. A company can lose business if customers are affected by downtime.

Bad Publicity When security problems become known, the public image of a company may suffer. Even if no personal information is lost, customers lose confidence that the company's security is trustworthy. Customers then take their business elsewhere.

Fighting Cybercrime

Law enforcement officials are using technology to catch cybercriminals. Several groups have taken part in this effort.

Computer Crime and Intellectual Property Section (CCIPS)

The Department of Justice created a special group known as CCIPS to advise and train federal prosecutors and local law enforcement on cybercrime. They review and

Did You Know?

Spyware is software that sends information about you and your web-surfing habits back to companies from whom you downloaded freeware or shareware, or for whom you completed online registrations.

Spyware programs install themselves on your system without your knowledge. Most spyware claims that it tracks habits anonymously; that is, without naming specific individuals. Its goal is to gather data and then draw conclusions about a group's web habits.

You can protect your computer from spyware by installing and using virus and malware protection software.

propose new laws. They coordinate international efforts to combat computer crime and prosecute offenders.

Computer Hacking and Intellectual Property Project (CHIP)

In the CHIP project, law enforcement officials and prosecutors work closely together to pursue cybercrime. CHIP offices are in areas with a heavy concentration of computer companies.

National Infrastructure Protection Center (NIPC)

In 1998, government officials became worried about terrorist attacks on U.S. computer systems. Staffed by people from intelligence agencies and private companies such as Internet service providers, the NIPC ensures that the nation's computer system could continue to operate in the case of an attack.

Avoiding Cybercrime

One way companies generate mailing lists for spam messages is by checking the addresses of people in chat rooms and in web discussion groups. If you use these services, you can minimize spam at your primary e-mail address by using a secondary e-mail address for these chats. You can then trash the spam when you want.

Think About It!

Which contacts listed below would you give your secondary e-mail address to?

- friend
- movie promotional site
- website from which you ordered a DVD
- chat room
- website where you receive support for your computer

Many computer crimes start when an unauthorized user hacks, or gains unauthorized entry, into a computer network. This of- ten happens when the intruder learns the password to access the victim's computer and the network. Following are ways such criminals learn passwords.

Guessing Too often, computer users choose passwords that are easy for them to remember, such as birthdates, names of pets, names of celebrities, and names of family members. Unfortunately, these passwords are also easy for intruders to guess. Surprisingly, the most common passwords used are "password" and "123456," both of which are extremely weak.

Finding Sometimes people keep passwords written on pieces of paper near their computer. Other times, criminals simply look over someone's shoulder as he or she types the password and use it later. An intruder can also search the trash in the hopes of finding user IDs and passwords.

"Sniffing" Some criminals may use packet sniffers. A packet sniffer is a program that examines data streams on networks to try to find information, such as passwords and credit card numbers.

Pretending Some intruders pretend to be network administrators. They call network users and ask for their passwords, claiming that the passwords are needed to solve a problem in the system.

Modifying Network software makes the people who administer a system into superusers. Intruders who have superuser access can modify virtually any file on the network. They also may change user passwords to ones they know.

Protecting Your Personal Data

It is in your best interest to protect your computer and its data. Here are some ways to help protect personal information.

Use Strong Passwords Whenever you create a password, don't use things like family names, nicknames, or birth dates. Random passwords are often the strongest, like S3nD3v. Use a combination of at least six upper- and lowercase letters, numbers, and symbols. Often the site will let you know if your password is strong enough. Remember to change your password every so often. Do not keep a record of your passwords on your computer or on a piece of paper near your computer. Never give out your passwords to anyone, and never type a password while someone is watching.

Browse Anonymously When you go online, surf from sites that protect your identity. Anonymizer and IDZap are two sites offering this service.

Use a Different E-mail Address Although you may not be able to do this at school, on a home computer you can sign up for a free e-mail account from a website such as Hotmail or gmail. Use that address when you register at websites or participate in other public Internet spaces. This will protect you from receiving unwanted mail, or spam, at your primary e-mail address.

Avoid Site Registration Be careful of websites that require you to register. Do not fill out a registration form unless the site clearly says that the data will not be shared with other people without your approval

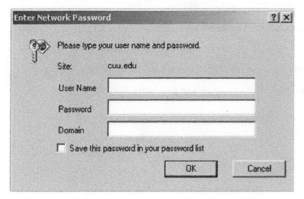

You may be required to provide a user name and password before accessing a computer network. Be sure to use a "strong" password.

Be Smart Online

You can avoid most computer crime simply by being a smart computer user. You can make sure your Internet browser settings are at the highest level for security and privacy, you can delete e-mail from unknown senders without opening it, and you can be wary of offers that seem too good to be true. Make sure you do business only with established companies that you know and trust. No reputable company or bank will ever ask you to send your username, password, account information, or social security number. You should never reveal financial or other personal information, even if the request sounds legitimate.

Safe Social Networking

Here are some safety tips for online social networking.

- Do not add just anyone as a "friend." This person will see everything you post, including pictures and status updates.
- Check your settings. If you don't understand how to manage your account, get an adult to help you make sure you maintain your privacy.
- Learn how to change your status to invisible, so others do not know you are online, or visible, so they do know you are online.
- Give your parents or other trusted adult access to monitor your social networking activity.
- Remember that your posts and profiles can be easily tracked online. Don't write or post anything online that you would not want your grandparents or teachers to see or that you would not want posted about yourself.
- Never give out private information such as your phone number or address.
- Never agree to meet a new online friend in person.
- If you feel uncomfortable about an online experience, immediately tell a trusted adult.
- Don't download or install programs without parental permission.

Where did all the unusual names for destructive software come from?

- A computer virus is named for the kind of virus that causes infectious diseases like the cold and the flu.
- A worm is named for a tapeworm, a kind of organism that lives in the intestines of another creature and lives off the food that creature eats.
- A Trojan horse takes its name from an ancient Greek story about soldiers who entered a fortress by hiding inside the body of a giant replica of a horse, which the defenders allowed in. The soldiers hidden inside the horse attacked and defeated the defenders.

End-of-Chapter Activities

Review Questions

Directions: Choose the correct answer for each question.

1. What has helped web designers adapt pages and content to the mobile first design?
   a. Media type functions
   b. Media query functions
   c. JavaScript, CSS, and HTML5
   d. All of the above
   e. A & B only

2. How many individually defined media types are there in CSS?
   a. 6
   b. 10
   c. 12
   d. 8

3. How many media features does Dreamweaver support?
   a. 10
   b. 12
   c. 22
   d. 30

4. The Scrubber in Dreamweaver CC 2015 does what?
   a. Quickly adjusts the screen size to help preview your media query displays of your webpage.
   b. Sets CSS style rules
   c. Displays the DOM structure of a webpage
   d. Displays elements and attached class CSS rules

5. What is the correct code for hiding an aside class selector for the extra small framework screen size?
   a. .hidden-sm
   b. .hide-xs
   c. .hidden-xs
   d. .hide-sm

6. True or False: When you hide an element this prevents the hidden data from down-loading to the users computer or device.
   a. True
   b. False

7. What is the DOM viewer used for in Dreamweaver?
   a. Quickly adjusts the screen size to help preview your media query displays of your web page.
   b. Sets CSS style rules
   c. Displays the Document Object Structure of a web page
   d. Displays elements and attached class CSS rules

8. What does this class code do in a Bootstrap web page - **.col-xs-push-4**?
   a. Pushes the active extra small column 4 column widths to the right in the page design
   b. Pushes the active small column 4 column widths to the right in the page design
   c. Pushes the active extra small column 4 column widths to the left in the page design
   d. None of the above

9. What does this class code do in a Bootstrap web page - **.col-md-pull-4**?
   a. Pulls the active small column 4 column widths to the right in the page design
   b. Pulls the active medium column 4 column widths to the left in the page design
   c. Pulls the active small column 4 column widths to the right in the page design
   d. None of the above

10. Which of the following are examples of computer malware?
    a. Computer Virus
    b. Trojan Horse
    c. Worms
    d. All of the above
    e. None of the above

Essay Questions

Directions: Respond to each question by writing your answers in complete sentences and paragraphs. Be thorough in your answers.

1. What's the purpose of a media type?

2. What are media queries?

3. How do media queries target a specific device or screen size?

4. What's the difference between a mobile-ready and mobile-optimized site design?

5. Do you have to worry about CSS inheritance when using media queries?

6. In a mobile device, what happens to the webpage display if you rotate the device?

7. List how businesses can gather information about people.

8. What are privacy expectations when you are job hunting and when you work for a company?

9. List cybercrime techniques that are used to gather information from your computer or mobile device.

10. What is the process to copy CSS properties from one rule to another?

Critical Thinking Project – Develop a Mobile-First Design for the Lake Powell Website

Further develop the Lake Powell website to respond to all devices that access it to create a mobile-first responsive design. Use media queries and media type functions to create this type of responsive design.

Hide an Element in the Design

1. On your computer create a local root folder as directed by your teacher. Name the folder **lakepowell_xx**. Copy the class data files from the Chapter08/Datafiles/lakepowell_xx directory as instructed by your teacher.

2. Open Dreamweaver CC 2015 and define a new Lake Powell website.

3. Open the **lakepowell_xx.html** file and switch to Live view. Open or access the CSS Designer.

4. Preview the site design and how it currently responds to the various screen sizes by dragging the scrubber to the left and right.

5. Focus first on the extra small screen media query by clicking the Extra Small media query stop in the VMQ. Then in the CSS Designer, click the lakepowell.css style sheet.

6. Click the second <aside> element that is at the bottom of the element stack in the <article> element. Then select the **aside.col-xs-3** tag selector in the Tag Selector bar. Click the Add Class/ID icon in the HUD. In the text field type **.hidden-xs** and press Enter/Return.

7. The second <aside> element disappears. Drag the scrubber to the Small media query and the <aside> element reappears.

8. Save all documents by choosing File>Save All.

Create a Mobile-first Page Structure

Next create a mobile-first page structure by developing the page layout based on the media queries that are automatically set when you create a new page from the Bootstrap Custom starter page.

1. In the **lakepowell_xx.html** document, move the Scrubber to the Extra Small media query. Open the DOM viewer by choosing Window>DOM and then resize it to see all the document structure. If necessary, expand the **article** element in the DOM viewer by clicking it once.

2. The layout for the extra small media query, is not in the correct order for this screen display. It would be better to have the <section> element with the main content at the top of the <aside> element. To rearrange these two elements, select the **aside** element in the DOM view and drag it below the **section** element.

3. Next, develop the small media query display by clicking the Small Media query in the VMQ. Again, hide the second <aside> element that displays on the right of the design by selecting the **aside.col-sm-3** tag selector. In the HUD click the Add Class/ID icon. In the text field type **.hidden-sm**

4. Adjust the column span of the <section> element by first clicking in the <section> element and then select the **section.col-sm-6** tag selector. In the HUD, edit the class to **.col-sm-8**. The section area expands to cover 8 column-widths. Repeat this process to resize the visible <aside> element by clicking it and in the HUD edit the class to **.col-sm-4**.

5. Test your Mobile-first design by dragging the Scrubber into the extra small media query and then back to the small media query.

6. Now develop the medium media query by first switching to the Live view so that entire screen shows just the page and the Live view fills the entire screen with the document.

7. Next, click the Medium media query in the VMQ to display the page layout. All sorts of things are going on now in this layout due to the other classes we have created to support the smaller screen sizes. Fix this layout by first clicking in the <section> element and then clicking the section.col-sm-8 tag selector. In the HUD create a new class and in the text field type .col-md-6 to reset this element for a 6 column display in the Medium media query display. Using this process adjust the right <aside> element to a 3 column display.

8. Rearrange the elements so that the <section> element is in the center of the page with the two asides positioned on each site by using the push and pull properties. Click in the <section> element and then click the **section.col-sm-8.col-md-6** tag selector. In the HUD add a Class/ID and in the text field, type **.col-md-push-3**

9. Move the first <aside> element in the current display to the far left by first clicking in this element and then select the **aside.col-sm-4.col-md-3 tag** selector. In the HUD, add another Class/ID and in the text field type **.col-md-pull-6**

10. Save all documents.

Working with Media Queries

You now have the three media query layouts set but some of the page assets, like the header image need to adjust better in size to the smaller screens. Next you'll add rules to the media queries to adjust page content for smaller screen displays.

1. In the **lakepowell_xx.html** document, move the Scrubber to the left until you see the <header> element text "Lake Powell" breaks into two lines. This should be around 628px. This number will differ based on whether you are using a Macintosh or a Windows computer – regardless, note this number.

2. Then create a new media query stop by clicking the new media query button on the VMQ interface. In the New Media Query dialog set the dropdown menu at the top of the dialog to **Max-Width**, then set the next field below this to a max-width of **628** (this width will be the one that you identified in step 1), set the next dropdown menu to **lakepowell.css**. Click OK to create a new media query stop. Double-check that the new media query is displayed in the CSS Designer by clicking the **lakepowell.css** style sheet and you should see this new media query listed in the @media window.

3. In the CSS Designer, click the **lakepowell.css** style sheet and in the @media window, click the new media query **max-width:628** (this width will be the one that you identified in step 1). Create a new rule and edit the selector name to **header.row h1** and press Enter/Return as needed to complete the name. Use the Scrubber to view the effects of this rule by dragging it to the Extra Small media query and then back to the custom media query that you created.

4. Next adjust the text "Lake Powell" in the <header> element so that it is smaller in size when the custom media query is active. Start by dragging the Scrubber to 500px width. Click the text in the <header> element then select the **header.row** tag selector.

5. In the CSS Designer, click the All button and then click the **lakepowell.css** style sheet. Click the **Current** button and select the **header.row h1** selector. Right-click the **header.row h1** rule and in the context menu choose Copy>Styles>Copy Text Styles.

6. Click the **All** button so you can create a new rule. Select the **lakepowell.css** in Sources and then click the **(max-width:628px)** in @media. Add a new selector rule and name it **header.row h1**. Press Enter/Return as needed.

7. Paste the previously copied background properties into the new **header.row h1** selector rule by right-clicking this rule and then choose **Paste Styles** from the context menu.

8. Next delete two of the text properties from the new rule so that they are inherited from the other **header.row h1** rule that was copied. Select the new **header.row h1** rule and then click the **Show Set** option in the CSS Designer. Hover the insertion point over the **color** property and then delete this rule by clicking the Delete icon. Repeat this process to delete the font-family property. Leave the other settings asset.

9. The **font-size** property needs to be adjusted for the smaller screen size. Click in the font-size field and change this to 350%. Test the new properties by dragging the Scrubber to the left and then to the right and watch the <h1> text element reformat based on the media queries that are set.

10. This change causes the other heading elements in the <article> element to look too big. Adjust them in the design by creating a new rule. In the CSS Designer, select the lakepowell.css style sheet. Click the (max-width:628px) in the @Media window and then create a new rule named **article. Row section h1** rule. Adjust the properties to the following:

    > padding-top: 15px
    > font-size: 195%
    > line-height: 1.1em
    > text-align: center

11. Repeat step 10 to create a new rule named **article.row aside h2** targeted at the <article> element <h2> tag. Set the following properties:

    > padding-top: 15px
    > font-size: 145%
    > line-height: 1.1em
    > text-align: center

12. Test your new properties for the custom media query by dragging the Scrubber left and right to see the screen displays.

13. Save all documents.

Online Portfolio Builder – Develop Your On-line Portfolio Page to be a Mobile-First Layout

Use the chapter exercises as well as the Critical Thinking Project to develop your portfolio website page. The following steps provide general instructions to help guide you through this process.

1. If necessary, create a local root directory and copy any files or folders over to the new local root directory. Define your site as instructed by your teacher.

2. Identify the device that your audience will use the most to access your site. This device will guide the development of your Mobile-first design.

3. Use the Scrubber to see the pre-set media queries in your portfolio page. Think about how you can rearrange or hide certain elements in the three different media queries.

4. Focus Dreamweaver on the media query for the device you identified in step 2 by clicking this media query from the VMQ interface.

5. Hide any elements in this media query page layout.

6. Use the DOM viewer to rearrange any elements in the page layout.

7. Add Class/ID in the HUD as needed to increase or decrease the column layout of your elements in the Bootstrap page.

8. Create a custom media query for a very small screen and adjust the size of your background images and headings/text to fit the smaller screen size.

9. Save your documents.

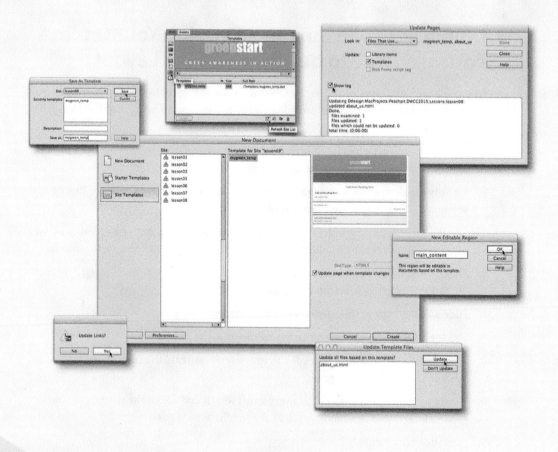

WORKING WITH TEMPLATES

Dreamweaver's productivity tools and site-manage-
ment capabilities are among its most useful features
for a busy designer.

Chapter Overview

In this chapter, you'll learn how to work faster, make updating easier, and be more productive. You'll learn how to do the following:

- Create a Dreamweaver template
- Insert editable regions
- Produce child pages
- Update templates and child pages
- Use proper webpage naming conventions for new webpages
- Explain the quality assurance process
- Develop and implement a quality assurance plan
- Develop a website test plan for usability

Note: Create a new site based on the Chapter09 folder before beginning the chapter.

Creating a Template from an Existing Layout

A template is a type of master page from which you can create related child pages. Templates are useful for setting up and maintaining the overall look and feel of a website while providing a means for quickly and easily producing site content. A template is different from your completed pages; it contains areas that are editable and other areas that are not. Templates enable a workgroup environment in which page content is created and edited by several team members while the web designer controls the page design and the specific elements that must remain unchanged.

Although you can create a template from a blank page, converting an existing page into a template is far more practical and also far more common. In this exercise, you'll create a template from your existing layout.

1   Launch Dreamweaver CC (2015.1 release) or later.

2   Open **mylayout_xx.html** from the Chapter09 folder. Switch to Design view.

Note: Design view will often not display the layout accurately in the document window, and some of the responsive styling may not work as expected.

The first step in converting an existing page to a template is to save the page as a template. Most of the work creating a template must be completed in Design or Code view. The template options will not be accessible within Live view.

3   With Design view active, choose. File > Save as Template.

The Save As Template dialog appears.

4   If necessary, choose Chapter09 from the Site pop-up menu. Leave the Description field empty. Type **mygreen_temp_xx** in the Save As field. Click Save.

Tip: Adding the suffix "temp" to the filename helps to visually distinguish this file from others in the site folder display, but it's not a requirement.

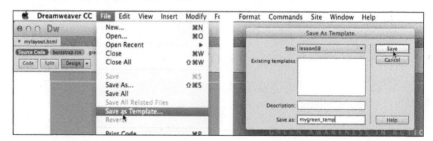

An untitled dialog appears, asking whether you want to update links.

Templates are stored in their own folder, Templates, which Dreamweaver automatically creates at the site root level.

Note: A dialog may appear, asking about saving the file without defining editable regions; just click Yes to save anyway. You'll create editable regions in the next exercise.

5   Click Yes to update the links.

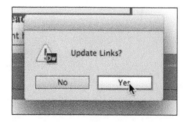

Since the template is saved in a subfolder, updating the links in the code is necessary so that they will continue to work properly when you create child pages later. Dreamweaver automatically resolves and rewrites links as necessary when you save files anywhere in the site.

Although the page still looks exactly the same, you can identify that it's a template by the file extension **.dwt** displayed in the document tab, which stands for Dreamweaver template.

A Dreamweaver template is *dynamic*, meaning that the program maintains a connection to all pages within the site that are derived from the template. Whenever you add or change content within the dynamic regions of the template and save it, Dreamweaver passes those changes to all the child pages automatically, keeping them up-to-date. But a template shouldn't be completely dynamic. Some sections of the page should contain areas where you can insert unique content. Dreamweaver allows you to designate these areas of the page as *editable*.

Inserting Editable Regions

When you create a template, Dreamweaver treats all the existing content as part of the master design. Child pages created from the template would be exact duplicates, and all the content would be locked and uneditable. This setup is great for repetitive features of the design, such as the navigation components, logos, copyright, contact information, and so on, but the downside is that it stops you from adding unique content to each child page. You get around this barrier by defining *editable regions* in the template. Dreamweaver creates two editable regions automatically, one for the `<title>` element and another for metadata or scripts that need to be loaded in the `<head>` section of the page; you have to create the rest.

First, give some thought to which areas of the page should be part of the template and which should be open for editing. At the moment, three sections of your current layout need to be editable: both `<aside>` elements and the main content area.

1   Open **mygreen_temp_xx.dwt** from the Chapter08 templates folder in Design view, if necessary. Maximize the program window to fill the entire screen.

2   Insert the insertion point in the heading text *Insert main heading here*. Click the `section` tag selector.

    Dreamweaver selects the entire `<section>` element.

3   Choose Insert > Template > Editable Region.

> **Note:** The template workflow currently works only in Design and Code views. You will not be able to perform any of these tasks in Live view.

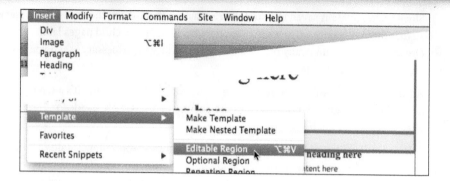

4 In the New Editable Region dialog, type **main_content** in the Name field. Click OK.

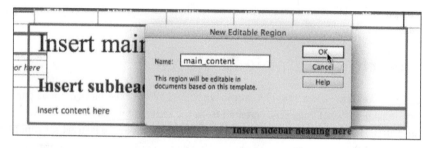

Each editable region must have a unique name, but no other special conventions apply. However, keeping the name short and descriptive is a good practice. The name is used solely within Dreamweaver and has no other bearing on the HTML code. In Design view, you will see the new region name in a blue tab above the designated area identifying it as an editable region. In Live view, the tabs are orange.

You also need to add an editable region to Sidebar 1 and Sidebar 2. Each of these sidebar regions contains text placeholders that you can customize on each page.

5 Insert the insertion point in the left column. Click the `aside` tag selector.

6 Choose Insert > Template > Editable Region.

7 In the New Editable Region dialog, type **side_region1** in the Name field. Click OK.

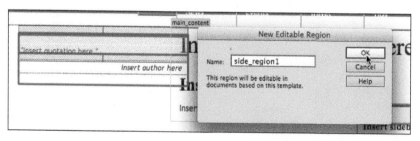

8   Insert the insertion point in the right column.
    Click the `aside` tag selector.

9   Choose Insert > Template > Editable Region.

10 In the New Editable Region dialog, type **side_region2** in the Name field.
    Click OK.

11 Save the file.

Once you have set up the visible components of the template, you should turn your attention to areas that are hidden from most visitors.

Inserting Metadata

A well-designed webpage includes several important components that users may never see. One such item is the *metadata* that is often added to the `<head>` section of each page. Metadata is descriptive information about your webpage or the contents it contains that is often used by other applications, like the browser or a search engine.

Adding metadata—for instance, a piece of data such as *title*—is not only a good practice, it's vital to your ranking and presence in the various search engines. Each title should reflect the specific content or purpose of the page. But many designers also append the name of the company or organization to help build more corporate or organizational awareness. By adding a title placeholder with the company name in the template, you will save time typing it in each child page later.

1   If necessary, open **mygreen_temp_xx.dwt** in Design view.

2   In the Document Title field of the Property inspector, select the placeholder text *Untitled Document*.

    Many search engines use the page title in the listings of a search result. If you don't supply one, the search engine will pick one of its own. Let's replace the generic placeholder with one geared for this website.

3   Type **Meridien GreenStart Association - Add Title Here** to replace the text. Press Enter/Return to complete the title.

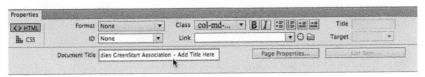

> **Tip:** The Document Title field is available in the Property inspector only when you are in Design or Code views.

> **Tip:** If the Property inspector is not visible, you can display it by selecting Window > Properties.

Along with the title, the other piece of metadata that usually appears in these search results is the page *description*. A description is a type of summary of a page that succinctly describes the contents in 25 words or less. Over the years, web developers have tried to drive more traffic to their sites by writing misleading titles and descriptions or outright lies. But be forewarned—most search engines have become wise to such tricks and will actually demote sites that use these tactics.

To achieve the highest ranking with the search engines, make the description of the page as accurate as possible. In many cases, the contents of the title and the description metadata will appear verbatim in the results page of a search.

4 Choose Insert > HTML > Description.

An empty Description dialog appears.

5 Type **Meridien GreenStart Association - add description here**. Click OK.

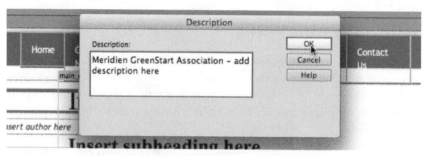

Dreamweaver has added the two metadata elements to the page. Unfortunately, only one of them was implemented properly in the template.

6 Switch to Code view. Locate and examine the `<title>` tag in the code and the surrounding markup.

```
7   <!-- TemplateBeginEditable name="doctitle" -->
8   <title>Meridien GreenStart Association - Add Title Here</title>
9   <!-- TemplateEndEditable -->
```

In most cases, the `<title>` will appear around line 8. Notice how the title appears between two comments that delineate an "editable" portion of the template named `"doctitle"`.

7 Locate and examine the `<meta>` tag containing the `"description"` and the surrounding markup.

```
21  <!-- TemplateBeginEditable name="head" -->
22  <!-- TemplateEndEditable -->
23  <meta name="description" content="Meridien GreenStart Association - add description here">
24  </head>
25    <body>
```

You should find the description near the end of the `<head>` section, around line 23. This element is not contained in an *editable* section of the template. This means that this metadata will be locked on all child pages, and you will not be able to customize it for that page.

Luckily, Dreamweaver comes to the rescue by providing an editable section designed for metadata just like this. In this case, it can't even get any more convenient—you'll find it just above the description delineated by the HTML comment markup `<!-- TemplateBeginEditable name="head" -->`. To make the description metadata editable, you'll need to move it into this section.

8   Click the line number containing the entire description, or select the entire `<meta>` element using the insertion point.

The `<meta>` tag and its contents should occupy a single line of the markup.

9   Press Ctrl+X/Cmd+X to cut this code into memory.

10 Insert the insertion point at the end of the comment `<!--TemplateBeginEditable name="head"-->` (around line 21).

11 Press Enter/Return to insert a new line.

12 Click the line number of the new blank line.
    Press Ctrl+V/Cmd+V to paste the description `<meta>` element.

> **Note:** The new line is simply intended to make the markup easier to read. It's otherwise unnecessary.

```
21   <!-- TemplateBeginEditable name="head" -->
22   <meta name="description" content="Meridien GreenStart Association - add description here">
23   <!-- TemplateEndEditable -->
```

The description is now contained within the editable template region named "head".

13 Choose File > Save.

You now have three editable regions—plus editable metadata for title and description—that you can change as needed when you create new child pages using this template.

14 Choose File > Close All.

Now it's time to learn how to use your new template.

Producing Child Pages

Dreamweaver templates are used to create child pages. Once a child page has been created from a template, only the content within the editable regions can be modified in the child page. The rest of the page remains locked within Dreamweaver. It's important to remember that this behavior is supported only within Dreamweaver and a few other HTML editors. Be aware: If you open the page in a text editor, like Notepad or TextEdit, the code is fully editable.

Creating a New Page

The decision to use Dreamweaver templates for a site should be made at the beginning of the design process so that all the pages in the site can be made as child pages of the template. In fact, that was the purpose of the layout you've built up to this point: to create the basic structure of your site template.

1   Launch Dreamweaver CC (2015.1 release) or later, if necessary.

The template workflow functions only in Design and Code views. You can also access site templates from the New Document dialog.

2   Choose File > New, or press Ctrl+N/Cmd+N.

The New Document dialog appears.

3   In the New Document dialog, select the Site Templates option.
Select Chapter09 in the Site list, if necessary.
Select **mygreen_temp_xx** in the Template For Site "Chapter09" list.

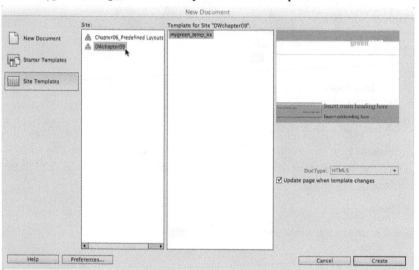

4   Select the Update Page When Template Changes option, if necessary.
Click Create.

Dreamweaver creates a new page based on the template.

5   If necessary, switch to Design view.

Typically, Dreamweaver defaults to the last document view (Code, Design, or Live) you were using for the new document. In Design view, you will see the name of the template file displayed in the upper-right corner of the document window. Before modifying the page, you should save it.

6   Choose File > Save.

The Save As dialog appears.

7   In the Save As dialog, navigate to the site root folder.
    Name the file **about_us.html**, and click Save.

The child page has been created. When you save the document in the site root folder, Dreamweaver updates all links and references to external files. The template makes it easy to add new content.

Tip: The Save As dialog provides a handy button, the Site Root button, to take you to the site root with a single click. Feel free to use it in any exercise, as needed.

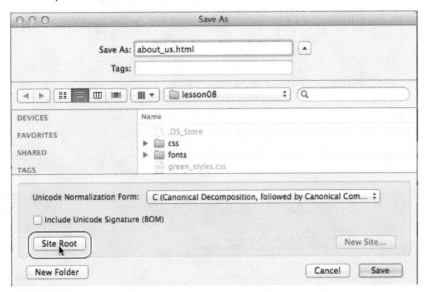

Adding Content to Child Pages

When you create a page from a template, only the editable regions can be modified.

1   Open **about_us.html** in Design view, if necessary.

You'll find that many of the features and functionality of templates work properly only in Design view, although you should be able to add or edit content in the editable regions from Live view.

2   Position the insertion point over each area of the page.

Warning: If you open a template in a text editor like Note Pad (Window) or TextEdit (Mac), all the code is editable, including the code for the non-editable regions of the page.

When the insertion point moves over certain areas of the page, such as the header, horizontal menu, and footer, the Locked icon ⊘ appears. These areas are uneditable regions that are locked and cannot be modified within the child page inside Dreamweaver. Other areas, like side_region1 and the main content section, can be changed.

3   Open the Property inspector, if necessary.
    In the Title field, select the placeholder text *Add Title Here.*
    Type **About Meridien GreenStart** and press Enter/Return.

4   In the `main_content` region, select the placeholder text *Insert main heading here.* Type **About Meridien GreenStart** to replace the text.

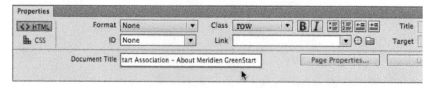

5   Select the placeholder text *Insert subheading here.*
    Type **GreenStart - green awareness in action!** to replace the text.

6   In the Files panel, double-click **aboutus-text.rtf** in the Chapter08 resources folder to open the file.

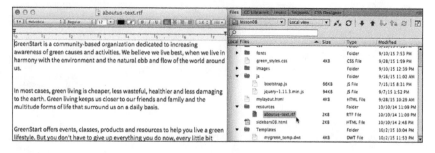

Tip: To add a little editorial flair, use the command Insert > HTML > Character > Em Dash to replace the hyphen in the heading with a long dash.

Dreamweaver opens only simple, text-based file formats, such as .html, .css, .txt, .xml, .xslt, and a few others. When Dreamweaver can't open the file, it passes the file to a compatible program, such as Word, Excel, WordPad, TextEdit, and so on. The file contains content for the main content section.

7   Press Ctrl+A/Cmd+A to select all the text. Press Ctrl+C/Cmd+C to copy the text.

8   Switch back to Dreamweaver.

9   Insert the insertion point in the placeholder text *Insert content here.*
    Select the p tag selector.

10 Press Ctrl+V/Cmd+V to paste the text.

GreenStart - green awareness in action!

GreenStart is a community-based organization dedicated to increasing awareness of green

causes and activities. We believe we live best, when ~~Insert sidebar heading here~~ vironment

and the natural ebb and flow of the world around us. Insert sidebar content here

In most cases, green living is cheaper, less wasteful, healthier and less damaging to the earth. Green living keeps us closer to our friends and family and the multitude forms of life that surround us on a daily basis.

GreenStart offers events, classes, products and resources to help you live a green lifestyle. But you don't have to give up everything you do now, every little bit helps. Start slowly and change the things that make sense to you. Eventually, you'll see how much better you feel when you live green.

Check out all the fun products and opportunities offered on the website. Check the site frequently for news, events and fun products. Become a member today and you will receive

The placeholder text is replaced by the new content. You can also add content to the sidebar elements.

11 Open **sidebars08.html** in Design view from the site root folder.

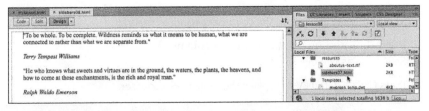

The file contains content for each sidebar. The top half is composed of three environmentally themed quotations and the bottom half of environmental tips and news.

12 Insert the insertion point in the first paragraph, and examine the tag selectors.

The tag selectors indicate a structure identical to what you created for the quotations column in Chapter 7, "Working with a Web Framework," but unformatted by the CSS. Now you will use this content to replace the existing sidebar.

13 Click the `aside` tag selector.

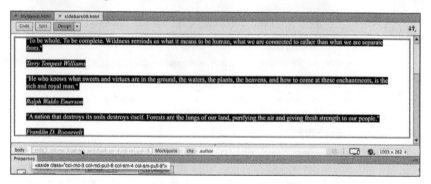

The tag selector shows the same Bootstrap class structure used in the template.

14 Press Ctrl+X/Cmd+X to cut the entire element into memory.

15 Select the **about_us.html** document tab.

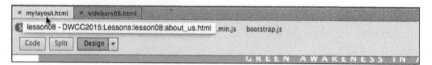

The child page appears in the document window again.

16 Insert the insertion point into the first column.
Select the `aside` tag selector.

17 Press Ctrl+V/Cmd+V to replace the sidebar placeholder.

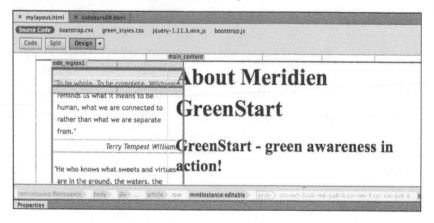

Tip: You may find it difficult to identify and select Sidebar 2 because of the inaccurate way Design view renders the page. To achieve success, be sure to use the correct tag selectors.

The replacement content appears, formatted somewhat by the external CSS file.

18 Select the **sidebars08.html** document tab.

19 Repeat steps 12–17 to replace the Sidebar 2 placeholder.

All three editable regions have now been populated with content.

20 Close **sidebars08.html**.
Do not save the changes.

By not saving the changes, you preserve the content in the file if you want to
repeat the exercise later.

21 Switch to Live view to preview the page.

The CSS styling kicks in again and the page design and columns now render
properly. Although you can't see the template name in the upper-right corner
any more, the names of the editable regions now display in orange tabs above
their corresponding element.

22 Save the file.

You have populated the editable regions with text and pictures, but they can hold
any type of web-compatible content, including tables, video, banner ads, and more.
From time to time, content inserted into a template will require some additional
styling via CSS.

For example, notice that the images and text in the right column are touching the
left and right edges of the column. If the element had no background color, this
would not be an issue. But normally you would want the text and other content to
be moved slightly off these edges.

Formatting Content in Editable Regions

Often content inserted into the editable regions will need to have custom styling
created for it to help it adapt to the layout itself or to various screen sizes that
may be encountered. In this exercise, you will create some new rules to format
the picture and text in Sidebar 2.

1 Open **about_us.html** in Live view, if necessary. Maximize the program window
to the full size of the computer display. Ensure that the document window and
Scrubber show the page at least 1024 pixels in width.

Before you create any CSS rules, you should examine the structure of the
element you want to style.

2   Select the first image in Sidebar 2.

The HUD appears focused on the `img` tag. The image appears in a semantic structure using the `<section>` and `<figure>` elements.

3   In the CSS Designer, select the All button.
Select **green_styles.css** > GLOBAL.
Click the Add Selector icon ➕.

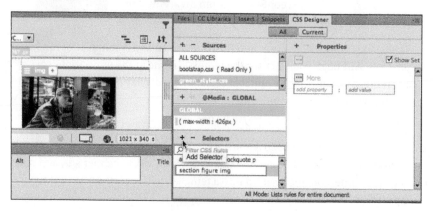

The selector `section figure img` appears in the Selectors window. This selector would format the image, but you'll want to limit the effect to Sidebar 2 to prevent unintended consequences.

4   Edit the selector name to say:

`.sidebar2 section figure img`

By adding the class `sidebar2` to the selector name, only images appearing in this specific structure will be targeted.

5   Create the following properties in the new rule:

```
margin: 0px auto
display: block
```

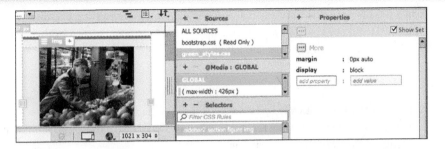

The images in Sidebar 2 align to the center of the column. Setting *auto* margins on the left and right forces elements toward the center. But this alone will not achieve the desired result. Images are considered inline elements, which ignore margin settings. Setting display: block allows images to honor the specifications.

6 Click in the caption below the first image in Sidebar 2.

The HUD appears focused on the figcaption element.

7 Select **green_styles.css** > GLOBAL.
Click the Add Selector icon ✚.

The selector section figure figcaption appears in the Selectors window. Let's limit this selector as you did the previous one.

8 Edit the selector name to say:

.sidebar2 section figure figcaption

9 Create the following property:

margin: 5px 10px 15px 10px

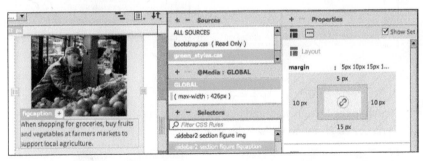

The captions are now indented on the left and right and exhibit more space at the top and bottom. Other custom styling may be needed as you create more pages, but for now you're finished.

10 Save all files.

11 Choose File > Close All.

Once you have created child pages and added content, there will come a time when you need to add or change a menu item, update the header or footer, or otherwise modify the content in the base template.

Updating a Template

Templates can automatically update any child pages made from that template. But only areas outside the editable regions will be updated. Let's make some changes in the template to learn how templates work.

1 If the Assets panel is not opened, open it by choosing Window>Assets, otherwise click the Assets panel tab.

The Assets panel appears. If it appears floating freely in the document window, you can dock it with the CSS Designer panel. The Assets panel gives you immediate access to a variety of components and content available to your website.

Tip: The Template category in the Assets panel does not appear when a document is open in Live view. Switch to Design or Code view, if necessary, to access this category.

2 In the Assets panel, click the Templates category icon 📄. If no templates appear in the list, click the refresh icon **C**.

The panel displays a list of site templates and a preview window. The name of your template appears in the list.

3 Right-click **mygreen_temp** and choose Edit from the context menu.

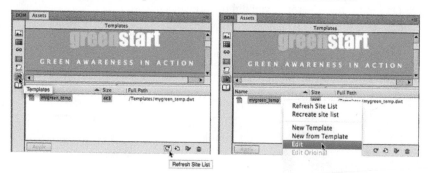

The template opens.

4 Switch to the Design view and in the navbar, select the text *Home*. Type **Green Home** to replace the text.

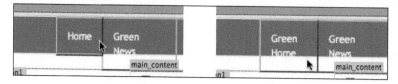

5 In the navbar, select the text *Green News*. Type **Headlines** to replace the text.

6 Select and replace the text *Insert* with the word **Add** wherever it appears in the main_content, side_region1, and side_region2 editable regions.

7 Switch to Live view.

You can now clearly see the changes to the menu and content areas. In the template, the entire page is editable.

8 Save the file.

The Update Template Files dialog appears. The filename **about_us.html** appears in the update list.

9 Click Update.

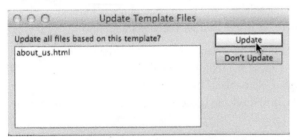

The Update Pages dialog appears.

10 Select the Show Log option.

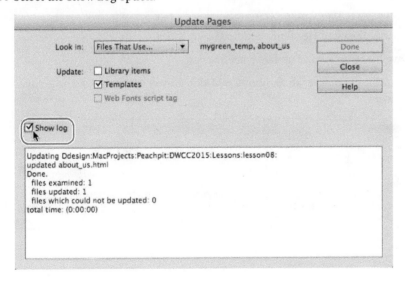

The window displays a report detailing which pages were successfully updated and which ones were not.

11 Close the Update Pages dialog.

12 Choose File > Open Recent > **about_us.html**. Observe the page, and note any changes.

Tip: If an open page has been changed during the update, it will be updated by Dreamweaver and show an asterisk in the document tab by its name.

The changes made to the horizontal menu in the template are reflected in this file, but the changes to the sidebars and main content areas were ignored, and the content you added to both areas earlier remains unaltered.

As you can see, you can safely make changes and add content to the editable regions without worrying that the template will delete all your hard work. At the same time, the boilerplate elements of the header, footer, and horizontal menu all remain consistently formatted and up-to-date, based on the status of the template.

13 Click the document tab for **mygreen_temp_xx.html** to switch to the template file.

14 Switch to Design view.

15 Delete the word *Green* from the Green Home link in the horizontal menu. Change the word Headlines back to **Green News**.

16 Save the template and update related files.

17 Click the document tab for **about_us.html**. Observe the page and note any changes.

The horizontal menu has been updated. Dreamweaver even updates linked documents that are open at the time. The only concern is that the changes have not been saved; the document tab shows an asterisk, which means the file has been changed but not saved.

If Dreamweaver or your computer were to crash at this moment, the changes would be lost; you would have to update the page manually or wait until the next time you make changes to the template to take advantage of the automatic update feature.

18 Save and close all files.

Dreamweaver's templates help you build and automatically update pages quickly and easily. In the upcoming chapters. You will use the newly completed template to create files for the project site. Although choosing to use templates is a decision you should make when first creating a new site, it's never too late to use them to speed up your workflow and make site maintenance faster and easier.

Tip: Always use the Save All command whenever you have multiple files open that have been updated by a template. In most cases, it's better to update when your files are closed so that they are saved automatically.

Naming Webpages

It is important to name your webpages correctly. There are webpage naming conventions that need to be heeded to ensure that your pages open when accessed from the hosting server. The basic rule to following is to name your pages in lowercase letters and not to use any special symbols except for the dash (-) or underslash (_). Do not use the #, $, period or comma, or add any extra spaces. Also avoid using Uppercase letters. Here are some proper webpage naming examples:

- lakepowell_xx.html
- about-us.html
- contact.html

Here are improper webpage naming examples:

- lakePowell.html
- lake.powell.html
- lake powell.html
- lakepowell_#2.html

The home page is a specially named page that needs to be one of the following naming conventions:

- home.html
- index.html
- default.html

Test Plan

In web design, a test plan is a high level summary that outlines the various areas of the web development process that need to be tested. This plan covers different scenarios modeling how the visitor navigates the site, page by page as well as area by area on the page.

Quality assurance process

The quality assurance process, or QA process, is a very important part of any business and also very important in the Information Technology field. The quality of a product or service reflects directly on the company and because of this, time and effort needs to be given to the process of the development of the product or the service.

Quality assurance plan

In regards to the web design, the quality assurance plan, or QA plan, implements the QA process. This plan is divided into different stages and processes of web development and is unique based on the website. This QA plan test usability and outlines each process or step with a predefined measurable result.

The most common naming convention for the home is the index.html as it is recognized by most web hosting servers. The home.html is also recognized by most web hosting servers but used less frequently. The default.html naming convention is used by Microsoft web hosting servers.

Aside from following the naming conventions for pages, you also need to think about SEO or Search Engine Optimization too. What common keywords and keyword phrases should be used in your page names. Search engines use the page name to help index your site for keyword searches. For example, if your site promotes furniture you definitely want to have pages named based on furniture, like sofas.html, loveseats.html, kitchen_tables.html, etc. Following naming conventions and thinking about SEO keywords when naming your pages ensures that they will be searchable and pull up properly when accessed by a visitor to the site.

Test Plans and Quality Assurance

When you create a template for a website, you are at the point in the web development process that you should implement a test plan for usability of the site. This **test plan** is made up of the **quality assurance process** and a predefined **quality assurance plan**.

Quality Assurance Process in Web Design

The QA process focuses on improving the development of a website from start to finish so that future web projects can be completed quickly and accurately. This is accomplished by focusing on quality control standards. The QA process helps a website with better functionality, usability and performance. The QA process can be related to the voice of the user, how they perceive the site. It ensures that they have a quality experience with the site content and site functionality. Many things can effect a user's experience with a website like broken links, faulty scripts, images that do not display or display poorly, misspelled words or poor grammar, and inconsistent or faulty navigation. Ensuring the quality of your website and the visitor experience requires a QA test plan.

Using QA Plans

Every website is unique in its information and how it is presented. The QA test plan catered to the website project and is used to test the usability of the site.

A QA plan is made up of two areas, how to address errors and how to improve the process to limit these errors. Here are common elements of the web design process that need to be covered in the QA plan:

- Content
- Graphics
- Layout

- Navigation
- Scripts
- Browser compatibility
- Mobile device viewing
- Accessibility
- Usability
- Process documentation and revision

Implementing a Test Plan

A QA testing plan should be laid out for the sites you develop. Chapter 5 discussed a Web Design Project Plan. The Web Design Project Plan is the beginning of the quality assurance plan as it identifies the process guiding the development of a website. Use this plan to define the web project and then identify the QA process and measurable results. Break the test plan into the phases of web develop and then define the results in measurable terms. Here are common areas that require a QA process and should be outlined in the test plan.

- Definition of the web project
- Functionality of Scripts
- Functionality of website
- Graphic display for image quality and download time
- Page layout for overall design, alignment of elements, window size displays, and color accuracy
- Review of site content for relevance, spelling and grammar errors
- Implementation of the web design and development process
- Validation of code based on W3C standards
- Browser compatibility
- Accessibility
- Usability studies
- Correction of any areas that have problems
- Revision of QA plan for future projects

Once you have gone through a test plan with a website, revise your quality assurance process from the test results. Quality assurance never ends and is always an ongoing process.

To learn more about quality assurance and testing visit:

http://www.oregon.gov/Pharmacy/Imports/Compliance/QA_plan_design.pdf

http://www.usabilityfirst.com/usability-methods/quality-assurance-testing/

> **Note: Usability Study** Another effective test that many web designers use for assessing the quality of a website is to engage a usability study. A usability study is a sampling of people that test the website by working through it. The study records how they interact with the site. This includes how they navigate through the site as well as their opinions on the site overall, its content, design, and functionality. A lot can be learned from an outsider's thoughts, critiques and recommendations for improving the website experience.

End-of-Chapter Activities

Review Questions

Directions: Choose the correct answer for each question.

1. What are templates useful for in web design?
   a. Setting a master page
   b. Maintaining the overall look and feel of a website
   c. Quickly produce pages and page content
   d. All of the above
   e. A & C only

2. True or False: Design view will often not display the layout accurately in the document window, and some of the responsive styling may not work as expected.
   a. True
   b. False

3. Templates let you create what?
   a. Graphics
   b. Video
   c. Child pages
   d. Parent pages

4. A template is made up of what?
   a. Fixed area of site that cannot be edited
   b. Fixed area of the site that can be edited
   c. Both A and B
   d. None of the above

5. All templates in Dreamweaver automatically include what editable regions?
   a. <section> and <article> elements
   b. <title> element and metadata or scripts
   c. <head> and <aside> elements
   d. <nav> and <header> elements

6. The Dreamweaver template workflow only works in what views?
   a. Design view
   b. Live view
   c. Code view
   d. A and C only

7. What is Metadata?
   a. Descriptive information about your webpage
   b. Page title
   c. Placeholder for page content
   d. Link

8. True or False: a quality assurance test plan is a high level summary that outlines the various areas of the web development process that need to be tested.
   a. True
   b. False

9. Usability studies test what?
   a. Functionality of the website
   b. How people perceive a website
   c. The message and content of the site
   d. All of these above

10. What happens to a child page when a template is updated?
    a. Nothing
    b. It updates with the changes and edits
    c. Existing content in the editable areas in the child page is deleted and need to be re-created.
    d. B & C only
    e. None of the above

Essay Questions

Directions: Respond to each question by writing your answers in complete sentences and paragraphs. Be thorough in your answers.

1. How do you create a template from an existing page?

2. Why is a template "dynamic"?

3. What must you add to a template to make it useful in a workflow?

4. How do you create a child page from a template?

5. Can templates update pages that are open?

6. Explain the quality assurance process for web design

7. Define areas that are addressed in a QA plan.

8. What is the main purpose of the QA process.

9. What are common naming conventions for webpages?

10. What are the three names for the home page of a website?

Critical Thinking — Create and Implement a Quality Assurance Test plan for your portfolio site

In Chapter 5, Web Design Basics, you created a Web Design Project Plan for your portfolio website. Use this Web Design Project Plan and develop a quality assurance plan by defining the web project and the QA process for your online portfolio web project. Break the test plan into the phases of web development and then define the results in measurable terms. Focus on these common areas of web design that require a QA process.

- Definition of the web project
- Functionality of Scripts
- Functionality of website
- Graphic display for image quality and download time
- Page layout for overall design, alignment of elements, window size displays, and color accuracy
- Review of site content for relevance, spelling and grammar errors
- Implementation of the web design and development process
- Validation of code based on W3C standards
- Browser compatibility
- Accessibility
- Usability studies
- Correction of any areas that have problems
- Revision of QA plan for future projects

Develop a test plan for your website. Remember to revise any quality assurance processes in the test plan that might need to be updated as your work through the plan. Remember, quality assurance never ends and is an ongoing process.

Critical Thinking Project — Create a Master Template for the Lake Powell Website

Further develop the Lake Powell website by developing a master template and then create child pages for the second level pages of the site.

1. On your computer, create a local root folder as directed by your teacher. Name the folder **lakepowell_xx**. Copy the class data files from the Chapter09/Data files/lakepowell_xx directory as instructed by your teacher.

2. Open the **lakepowell_xx**.html page and switch to the Design view. Maximize the Dreamweaver workspace to fill the to fill the entire screen.

3. Convert the page to a master template by choosing File>Save as Template. In the Save As Template dialog, name the page **lakepowell_temp.dwt**. Click Yes to update the links.

4. Insert editable regions in the two <aside> elements containing the text Relevant News About Lake Powell, and the <section> element for the main content. Do this by clicking in the element that you want to insert the editable region and then clicking the element tag selector to select the area. Choose Insert>Template>Editable Region. Name the region as follows:
   a. Name the left <aside> in the page layout – **weather**
   b. Name the right <aside> in the page layout – **facts**
   c. Name the center <section> in the page layout – **content**

5. Now add metadata to the site. Click the **lakepowell_temp.html** page to make it active. Add a metadata description to the site by choosing Insert>HTML>Description from the menu bar. In the Description dialog type **Lake Powell Adventures – add description here**.

6. Switch to Code View. Locate and examine the <title> tag in the code in line 8. This code is contained in the <head> element. Search this element to find the new meta description. Highlight this line of code by clicking the line number. Then cut it by pressing Ctr+X/Cmd+X. Insert the insertion point at the end of the code **<!--TemplateBeginEditable name="head" -->** and press Enter/Return. Then paste the meta description code in the new line by pressing Ctrl+V/Cmd+V.

7. Save all documents by choosing File>Save All.

8. Next create a home page for the site by choosing File> New and then clicking the **Site Templates** option on the left of the New Document window and then select the site that you defined in step 1 from the Site area and select **lakepowell_temp**. Click **Create** to create a new page based on the master template.

9. Save this home page as **index.html** by choosing File>Save. In the Save As dialog, click the Site Root button to make sure you are in the local root directory and then type **index.html** in the Save As field. Click Save to save the page.

10. Create four other child pages by repeating steps 8-9. Name the **pages houseboats. html, jetskis.html, hiking.html, and contact.html**. After saving these four pages, close them leaving only the **index.html** page and the **lakepowell_temp.dwt** open.

11. Next add some content to the home page. In the Files panel, open the **facts.txt** file in the **resources** folder by double clicking the **facts.txt** file. Copy just the monthly weather information from January to December.

12. If necessary, switch to the Design view and click the **index.html** page tab. Select the "Relevant News About Lake Powell" text in the **weather** editable area – it is formatted by a <h2> element. Type **Lake Powell Average Monthly Temperatures**. Then highlight the placeholder text "This is the content for Layout P Tag" and paste the copied text.

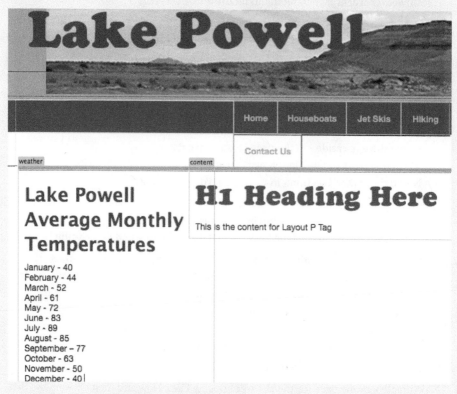

13. Again access the **facts.txt** file in the Files panel by clicking its tab, and then copy the paragraph below the Home Page Info. Click the **index.html** tab to make this the active document. In the **content** editable area, highlight the placeholder text "This is the content for Layout P Tag" and then paste the copied paragraph. Change the heading in the content editable area by highlighting the heading text "H1 Heading Here". Type **Lake Powell – Heaven on Earth**.

14. Next add content to the **facts** editable area by copying the five facts from the Lake Powell Facts section of the **facts.txt** file and pasting it into the placeholder text "This is the content for Layout P Tag". Highlight the "Relevant News About Lake Powell" heading and type **Lake Powell Facts**.

15. Switch to the Live view. Your home page should look like this figure. Save all files. Close **facts.txt**.

16. Save all files.

17. Next update the template file so that the navigation menu options are more descriptive. Click the **lakepowell_temp.dwt** tab to make this the active document. Switch to the Design view. Click the Houseboats menu and set your insertion point. Change this menu to Houseboat Rentals. Do the same for the other menu options and change them to the following:
    a. Home – change to Lake Powell Home
    b. Jet Skis – change to Jet Ski Rentals
    c. Hiking – Scenic Hikes

18. Switch to Live view and notice that the new menu names are longer than a CSS width rule setting we set in the previous chapter so they are stacked. Open the CSS Designer and click the lakepowell.css and then click the **nav.row .nav.navbar-nav** selector rule. Click the **Show Set** option and change the width property to **700px**.

19. Now propagate these new menu names to the child pages by choosing File>Save. The Update Template Files dialog displays. Click the Update button. Examine the Update Pages dialog that displays to confirm that your child pages where all updated and then click Close.

20. Notice that the index.html file that is still opened now has an * after the name in the tab. This indicates that it needs to be saved. Choose File>Save All to save all files.

21. Finally add individual meta descriptions for each child page. Change the index.html page first by clicking its tab to make it active and then switch to the Code view. In the <head> element at the top of the page find the meta description placeholder that was added to the Editable <head> section of the page earlier in this exercise, <meta name="description" content="Lake Powell Adventures - add description here">

22. Change this line of code by highlighting the "add description here" to **Lake Powell Adventures – Heaven on Earth!**. Open the other four child pages and change their meta descriptions to the following

    a. Houseboats.html – <meta name="description" content="Lake Powell houseboat rentals">

    b. jetskis.html – <meta name="description" content="Lake Powell jet ski rentals">

    c. hiking.html – <meta name="description" content="Lake Powell scenic and historical hikes">

    d. contact.html – <meta name="description" content="Contact us to set up your awe-some Lake Powell adventure!">

23. Save and close all files.

Online Portfolio Builder — Create a Bootstrap Page Representing Your Portfolio Site Home Page

Convert your online portfolio page to a template page and create child pages based on the template. Follow the steps below to create this template and develop your portfolio site pages with meta descriptions and basic text and verbiage.

1. If necessary, create a local root directory and copy any files or folders over to the new local root directory. Define your site as instructed by your teacher.

2. Open your portfolio page that you have developed up to this point in the class. Switch to the Design view. Maximize the Dreamweaver workspace to fill the to fill the entire screen.

3. Convert the page to a master template by choosing File>Save as Template. In the Save As Template dialog, name the page **portfolio_temp.dwt**. Click **Yes** to update the links.

4. Insert editable regions in the areas of the page that you want to be able to edit. Name them appropriately.

5. Now add metadata to the site. Click the **portfolio_temp.html** page to make it active. Add a metadata description to the site by choosing Insert>HTML>Description from the menu bar. In the Description dialog type a generic description that you can customize for each page of your site.

6. Switch to Code View. Locate and examine the <title> tag in the code in line 8. This code is contained in the <head> element. Search this element to find the new meta description. Highlight this line of code by clicking the line number. Then cut it by pressing Ctrl+X/Cmd+X. Insert the insertion point at the end of the code **<!-- TemplateBeginEditable name="head" -->** and press Enter/Return. Then paste the meta description code in the new line by pressing Ctrl+V/Cmd+V.

7. Save all documents by choosing File>Save All.

8. Next create a home page for the site by choosing File> New and then clicking the **Site Templates** option on the left of the New Document window and then select the site that you defined in step 1 from the Site area and select **portfolio_temp**. Click **Create** to create a new page based on the master template.

9. Save this home page as **index.html** by choosing File>Save. In the Save As dialog, click the Site Root button to make sure you are in the local root directory and then type **index.html** in the Save As field. Click Save to save the page.

10. Create other child pages by repeating steps 8-9. Name the pages appropriately following the webpage naming conventions covered in this chapter. After saving these pages, close them leaving only the **index.html** page and the **portfolio_temp.dwt** open.

11. Next add some content to the home page by changing the headings and placeholder text. Just add textual data at this time.

12. Switch to the Live view to preview your home page. Save all files.

13. Apply an update to the template by changing any of the text in the <header> or <footer> non-editable areas.

14. Switch to Live view and preview your site. Adjust any CSS rules to fix any page layout issues that might occur due to the new information in the template.

15. Now propagate these changes to the child pages by choosing File>Save. The Update Template Files dialog displays. Click the Update button. Examine the Update Pages dialog that displays to confirm that your child pages where all updated and then click Close.

16. Notice that the index.html file that is still opened now has an * after the name in the tab. This indicates that it needs to be saved. Choose File>Save All to save all files.

17. Finally add individual meta descriptions for each child page. Change the index.html page first by clicking its tab to make it active and then switch to the Code view. In the <head> element at the top of the page find the meta description placeholder that was added to the Editable <head> section of the page.

18. Change this line of code by highlighting it and typing new meta description text. Think about SEO and try to make each description unique but use the previously identified keywords and keyword phrases in the descriptions. Open the other child pages and change their meta descriptions as well.

19. Save and close all files.

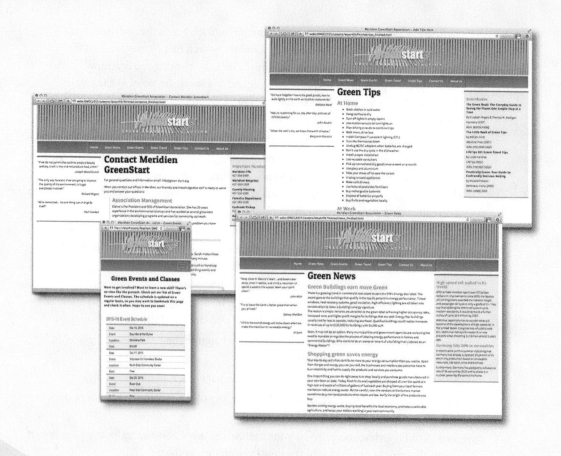

WORKING WITH TEXT, LISTS, AND TABLES

Dreamweaver provides numerous tools for creating, editing, and formatting web content, whether it's created within the program or imported from other applications.

Chapter Overview

In this chapter, you'll create several webpages from your new template and work with headings, paragraphs, and other text elements to do the following:

- Enter heading and paragraph text
- Insert text from another source
- Create bulleted lists
- Create indented text
- Insert and modify tables
- Spellcheck your website
- Search and replace text

Creating and Styling text

Most websites are composed of large blocks of text with a few images sprinkled in for visual interest. Dreamweaver provides a variety of means for creating, importing, and styling text to meet any need. In the following exercises, you will learn a variety of techniques for working with and formatting text.

Importing Text

In this exercise, you'll create a new page from the site template and then insert heading and paragraph text from a text document.

1 Launch Adobe Dreamweaver CC (2015.1 release) or later, if necessary. If Dreamweaver is already running, close any open files.

2 Define a new site for chapter10 folder as instructed by your teacher. Name the new site **Chapter 10**.

3 Choose Window > Assets to display the Assets panel. Select the Templates category icon ▤. Right-click **mygreen_temp**, and choose New From Template from the context menu.

A new page is created based on the site template.

4 Save the file as **news.html** in the site root folder.

5 If necessary, choose Window > Properties to display the Property inspector. In the Document Title field, select the placeholder text *Add Title Here*. Type **Green News** and press Enter/Return to complete the title.

4   In the Files panel, double-click **green_news.rtf** in the Chapter10/resources folder.

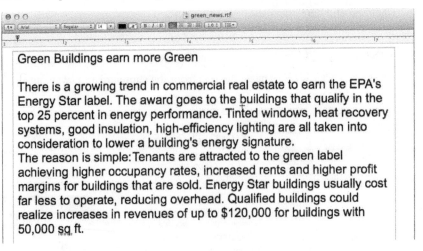

Dreamweaver automatically launches a program compatible to the file type selected. The text is unformatted and features extra lines between each paragraph. These extra lines are intentional. For some reason, Dreamweaver swaps out single paragraph returns for <br> tags when you copy and paste them from another program. Adding a second return forces Dreamweaver to use paragraph tags instead.

This file contains four news stories. When you move the stories to the webpage, you're going to create semantic structures, as you did for the quotation placeholders. As explained earlier, semantic web design attempts to provide a context for your web content so that it will be easier for users and web applications to find information and reuse it, as necessary.

5   In the text editor or word-processing program, insert the insertion point at the beginning of the text *Green Buildings earn more Green*. Press Ctrl+A/Cmd+A.

    All the text is highlighted.

6   Press Ctrl+C/Cmd+C to copy the text.
    Close **green_news.rtf**.
    Do not save any changes.

7   Switch back to Dreamweaver.
    Switch to Design view.
    Select the text *Add main heading here*.
    Type **Green News** to replace it.

> **Tip:** When you use the clipboard to bring text into Dreamweaver from other programs, you must be in Design view if you want to honor the paragraph returns and other formatting.

8   Insert the insertion point in the placeholder heading *Add subheading here.*

9   Click the <h2> tag selector.
    Press Delete.

10 Select the text *Add content here.*

11 Press Ctrl+V/Cmd+V to paste the text from the clipboard and swap out the
    placeholder text.

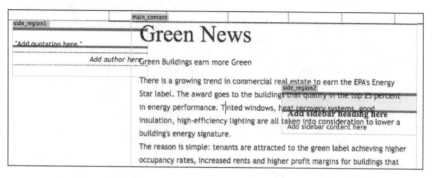

The text from **green_news.rtf** appears in the layout.

12 Save the file.

The four news stories were inserted as individual <p> elements. Although a human
visitor would be able to distinguish where one story ends and another begins, there
is no differentiation between them within the code. Adding semantic structures
should be your goal whenever possible. This is encouraged not only to support
accessibility standards but also to improve your SEO ranking at the same time.

Creating Semantic Structures

In this exercise, you will insert HTML5 <article> elements to contain the news
stories.

1   If necessary, open **news.html** in Design view.
    Click in the text *Green Buildings earn more Green.*
    Select the p tag selector.

    The entire <p> element is selected.

2   Hold the Shift key and click at the end of the text *Energy Waster?*

    The first news story is selected.

3   Choose Insert > Article.

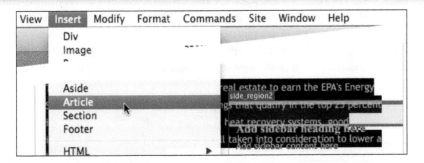

The Insert Article dialog appears. The dialog should default to the Wrap Around Selection mode. If it doesn't, select the option from the Insert drop-down menu in the dialog.

This dialog allows you to add custom IDs and classes to your element. At the moment, we don't have the need for one, so you can insert the new element as is.

4 Click OK to insert a new `<article>` element.

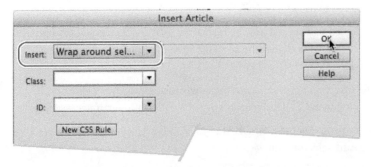

The new element appears in the tag selector interface wrapping the first news story.

5 Repeat steps 1–4 to create new `<article>` elements for the remaining three news stories.

When you're finished, you should have four new `<article>` elements, one for each news story.

6 Save **news.html**.

Creating Headings

In HTML, the tags `<h1>`, `<h2>`, `<h3>`, `<h4>`, `<h5>`, and `<h6>` create headings. Any browsing device, whether it is a computer, a Braille reader, or a cellphone, interprets text formatted with any of these tags as a heading. On the web, headings are used to introduce distinct sections with helpful titles, just as they do in books, magazine articles, and term papers.

You are using one <h1> element per page as the primary page title. Any other headings used on the page should descend in order from the <h1>. Since each news story has equal importance, they all can begin with a second-level heading, or <h2>. At the moment, all the pasted text is formatted as <p> elements. Let's format the news headings as <h2> elements.

Tip: If the Format menu is not visible, select the HTML mode of the Property inspector.

1 In Design view, select the text *Green Buildings earn more Green.*
Choose **Heading 2** from the Format menu in the Property inspector, or press Ctrl+2/Cmd+2.

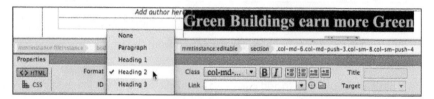

The text is formatted as an <h2> element.

2 Repeat step 1 with the text *Shopping green saves energy, Recycling isn't always Green,* and *Fireplace: Fun or Folly?*

All the selected text should now be formatted as <h2> elements. Let's create a custom rule for this element to set it off from the other headings with a unique style.

3 Insert the insertion point in any of the newly formatted <h2> elements. Choose Window > CSS Designer to open the CSS Designer, if necessary.

4 Choose **green_styles.css** > GLOBAL.
Click the Add Selector icon ➕.

A new selector appears that targets the <h2> element but contains all the Bootstrap classes styling the parent elements too. There's no need for such a complex selector, so you should simplify these names whenever they appear.

5 Edit the selector to say:

```
article h2
```

This name will target only <h2> elements used in the main content area.

Note: By default, each heading tag—<h1>, <h2>, <h3>, and so on—is formatted smaller than the preceding tag. This formatting reinforces the semantic importance of each tag. Although size is an obvious method of indicating hierarchy, it's not a requirement; feel free to experiment with other styling techniques, such as color, indenting, borders, and background shading, to create your own hierarchical structure.

6 Deselect the Show Set option if necessary. Create the following specifications:

```
margin-top: 15px
margin-bottom: 5px
color: #090
font-size: 170%
font-weight: bold
```

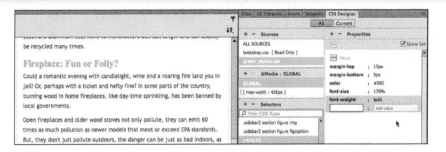

7 Save all files.

Adding Other HTML Structures

Descendant selectors are often sufficient for styling most elements and structures in a webpage. But not all the structural elements are available from the Insert menu or panel. In this exercise, you will learn how to build a custom HTML structure for a quotation and an attribute using the Quick Tag Editor.

1 Open **news.html** in Design view, if necessary.

2 In the Files panel, open **quotes10.txt**.

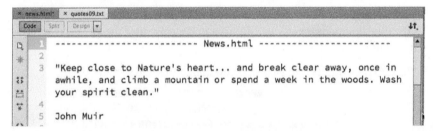

Since this is a plain-text file, Dreamweaver can open it. The file contains quotations you will insert in the pages that will be created in this chapter.

3 Select the text of the first quotation, excluding the author name.
   Press Ctrl+X/Cmd+X to cut the text.

4 Switch to **news.html**.
   Select the first quotation placeholder.
   Press Ctrl+V/Cmd+V.

Note: When pasting text into existing HTML structures, it is important not to accidentally delete or damage these structures.

The quotation has replaced the placeholder.

5   Switch to **quotes10.txt**. Select and cut the author name, John Muir.

6   Switch to **news.html**. Select the *Add Author Name* placeholder text and paste the text.

John Muir has replaced the author name placeholder. Since there was only one quotation placeholder in the template, you'll have to create the other quotation structures from scratch.

7   Switch to **quotes10.txt**. Select and cut the next two quotations and authors.

8   In **news.html**, insert the insertion point anywhere in the first quotation. Click the `blockquote` tag selector. Press the right arrow key.

The insertion point moves to a position in the code after the `<blockquote>` element.

9   Press Ctrl+V/Cmd+V to paste the new quotations and authors.

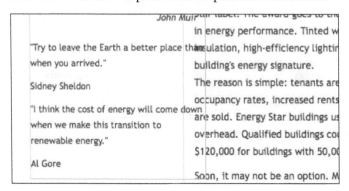

The text appears, but it is not styled properly.

10   Using the insertion point and the tag selector interface, compare the structure of the three quotations, and note the differences.

The new quotations and author names appear in two separate p elements. Part of the styling problem is due to the missing parent `blockquote` element. Dreamweaver has no menu option for adding this specific tag, but you can use the Quick Tag Editor to build all types of custom structures in a pinch.

11 Select the second quotation, including the author name, Sidney Sheldon.

12 Press Ctrl+T/Cmd+T to activate the Quick Tag Editor.

The Quick Tag Editor appears. Since you have more than one element selected, it should default to Wrap mode.

Tip: Press Ctrl+T/Cmd+T to toggle between modes in the Quick Tag Editor, if necessary.

13 Type `blockquote` and press Enter/Return twice to add the element as a parent to the two paragraphs.

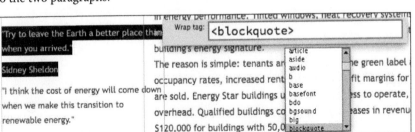

The quotation text is now formatted properly, but the author name needs one more tweak: You need to change the tag applied to it. As with `blockquote`, there's no menu option for the `<cite>` tag.

14 Insert the insertion point in the author name, Sidney Sheldon. Select the tag selector for the `<p>` element. Press Ctrl+T/Cmd+T to activate the Quick Tag Editor.

The Quick Tag Editor appears. Since you have only one element selected, it should default to Edit mode. If the correct mode is not visible, press Ctrl+T/Cmd+T until it is.

15 Press the Backspace key to delete "p" from the selected tag. Type `cite`, and press Enter/Return twice to complete the change.

Note: In HTML5, the *cite* element is used to identify the attribution of a quotation.

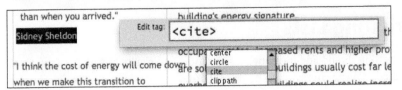

The author name now appears in a `<cite>` element and is styled identically to the other author.

16 Repeat steps 11–15 to create the blockquote structure for the third quotation in **news.html**.

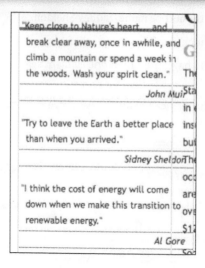

All three quotations are now structured properly in the first column.

17 Save and close **news.html**.

When you close **news.html**, Dreamweaver may prompt you to save **green_styles.css**. It is vital that you remember to save changes to the style sheet, especially when the file itself is not open. If you forget, you will lose any styling that was created in the previous exercises.

18 Click Save if necessary.

19 Close **quotes09.txt**. Do not save changes.

Closing the text file without saving the changes will preserve the original content in case you want to repeat this exercise later.

Creating Lists

Formatting should add meaning, organization, and clarity to your content. One method of doing this is to use the HTML list elements. Lists are the workhorses of the web because they are easier to read than blocks of dense text; they also help users find information quickly.

In this exercise, you will learn how to make an HTML list.

1   Choose Window > Assets to bring the Assets panel to the front.
    In the Template category, right-click **mygreen_temp**.
    From the context menu, choose New From Template.

    A new page is created based on the template.

2   Save the file as **tips.html** in the site root folder. Switch to Design view, if
    necessary.

3   In the Property inspector, select the placeholder text *Add Title Here* in the
    Document Title field. Type **Green Tips** to replace the text and press Enter/
    Return.

4   In the Files panel, double-click **green_tips.rtf** in the resources folder of
    Chapter10.

Note: The Template
category is not
visible in Live view.
To create, edit or
use Dreamweaver
templates, you must
switch to Design or
Code view.

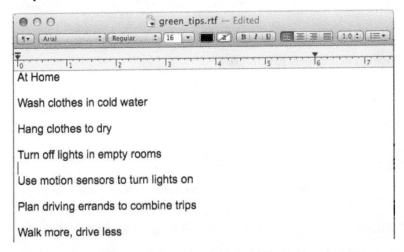

The file will open outside Dreamweaver. The content consists of three
individual lists of tips on how to save energy and money at home, at work, and
in the community. As in the news page, you will insert each list into its own
`<article>` element.

5   In **green_tips.rtf**, press Ctrl+A/Cmd+A.
    Press Ctrl+X/Cmd+X to cut the text. Close but do not save changes to
    green_tips.rtf.

    You have selected and cut all the text.

6   Switch back to Dreamweaver.
    Select *Add main heading here.*
    Type **Green Tips** to replace it.

7   Select and delete the `<h2>` *Add subheading here.*
    Select *Add content here.*
    Press Ctrl+V/Cmd+V.

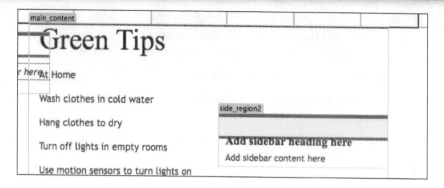

The text for all three lists appears.

8　Select the text starting at *At Home* and ending with *Buy fruits and vegetables locally.*

9　Choose Insert > Article.
Click OK in the Insert Article dialog.

The `<article>` element appears, wrapping the new list.

10　Select the text starting at *At Work* and ending with *Buy natural cleaning products.*

11　Choose Insert > Article.
Click OK in the Insert Article dialog.

12　In Dreamweaver, repeat steps 10 and 11 to create the third list and `article` structure.

All three lists now appear in their own `<article>` elements.

As you did with the titles of the news stories, apply HTML headings to introduce the list categories.

13　Apply `<h2>` formatting to the text *At Home*, *At Work*, and *In the Community.*

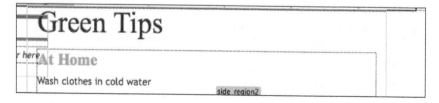

The remaining text is currently formatted entirely as HTML paragraphs. Dreamweaver makes it easy to convert this text into an HTML list. Lists come in two flavors: ordered and unordered.

14　Select all the `<p>` elements under the heading *At Home.*
In the Property inspector, click the Ordered List icon ▤.

An ordered list adds numbers automatically to the entire selection. Semantically, it prioritizes each item, giving them intrinsic values relative to one another. This list doesn't seem to be in any particular order; each item is more or less equal to the next one, so it's a good candidate for an unordered list—used when the items are in no particular order. Before you change the formatting, let's take a look at the markup.

15 Switch to Split view. Observe the list markup in the Code section of the document window.

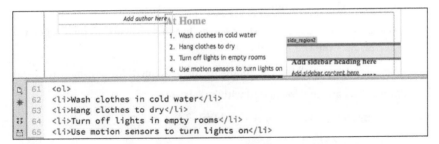

```
61  <ol>
62  <li>Wash clothes in cold water</li>
63  <li>Hang clothes to dry</li>
64  <li>Turn off lights in empty rooms</li>
65  <li>Use motion sensors to turn lights on</li>
```

The markup consists of two elements: `<ol>` and `<li>`. Note that each line is formatted as an `<li>` (list item). The `<ol>` parent element begins and ends the list and designates it as an ordered list. Changing the formatting from numbers to bullets is simple and can be done in Code or Design view.

Before changing the format, ensure that the formatted list is still entirely selected. You can use the `<ol>` tag selector, if necessary.

16 In the Property inspector, click the Unordered List icon 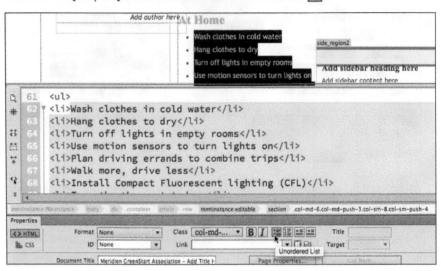.

All the items are now formatted as bullets.

If you observe the list markup, you'll notice that the only thing that has changed is the parent element. It now says `<ul>`, for *un*ordered list.

17 Select all the `<p>` formatted text under the heading *At Work*. In the Property inspector, click the Unordered List icon .

18 Repeat step 17 with all the text following the heading *In the Community*.

All three lists are now formatted with bullets.

19 In Dreamweaver, save and close **tips.html**.

> **Tip:** The easiest way to select the entire list is to use the `<ol>` tag selector.

> **Tip:** You could also change the formatting by editing the markup manually in the Code view window. But don't forget to change both the opening and the closing parent elements.

Creating Indented Text

Some designers still use the `<blockquote>` element in Dreamweaver, and elsewhere, as an easy way to indent headings and paragraph text. Semantically, the `<blockquote>` element is intended to identify whole sections of text quoted from other sources as in Sidebar 1. Visually, text formatted this way will appear indented and set off from the regular paragraph text and headings. But if you want to comply with web standards, you should leave this element for its intended purpose and instead use custom CSS classes when you want to indent text, as you will in this exercise.

1 Create a new page from the template **mygreen_temp**.
Save the file as **contact_us.html** in the site root folder.

2 Switch to Design view, if necessary.
In the Property inspector, add a document title by entering **Contact Meridien GreenStart** to replace the placeholder text *Add Title Here*.

3   In the Files panel, open **contact_us.rtf** from the Chapter10/resources folder.

The text consists of five department sections, including headings, descriptions, and email addresses for the managing staff of GreenStart. You will insert each department into its own `<article>` element.

4   In **contact_us.rtf**, select all the text and cut it.
Close the file and do not save the changes.

5   In Dreamweaver, enter **Contact Meridien GreenStart** to replace the placeholder heading *Add main heading here.*

6   Select and delete the heading *Add subheading here.*

7   Select the text *Add content here* and press Ctrl+V/Cmd+V to paste the content.

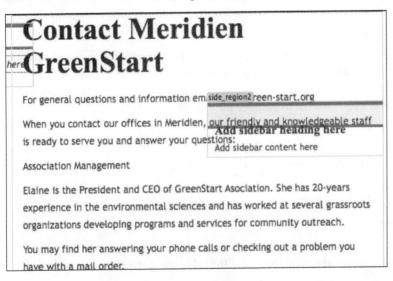

All the content cut from **contact_us.rtf** appears.

8   Format the text *Association Management* as a Heading 2.

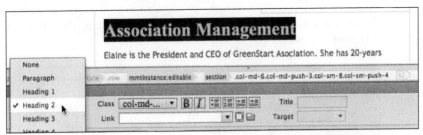

As before, you need to wrap each content group in an `<article>` element.

9   Click the h2 tag selector.
Hold the Shift key and select the rest of the text for this section.

10 Select Insert > Article.

Press Enter/Return in the Insert Article dialog to create the element.

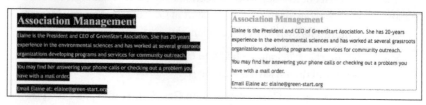

When the `<article>` element is created, the `<h2>` element formats in green as specified by the rule you created earlier.

11 Repeat steps 8–10 to structure and format the content for the *Education and Events, Transportation Analysis, Research and Development*, and *Information Systems* sections.

With all the text in place, you're ready to create the indent styling. If you wanted to indent a single paragraph, you would probably create and apply a custom class to the individual `<p>` element. In this instance, we want to indent the entire `<article>` element to produce the desired graphical effect.

First, let's assign a `class` attribute to the element. Since the class we want to use does not exist yet, you'll have to create it manually. This can be done in any view. In Design view it's best done in the Quick Tag Editor.

12 Insert the insertion point anywhere in the *Association Management* `<article>` element. Click the `<article>` tag selector.

Press Ctrl+T/Cmd+T.

The Quick Tag Editor appears, displaying the `<article>` tag. The insertion point should appear at the end of the tag name, but within the brackets.

13 Press the spacebar to insert a space.

The Code Hinting window appears, displaying the appropriate attributes for the `<article>` element.

14 Type **class** and press Enter/Return, or double-click the `class` attribute in the Code Hinting window.

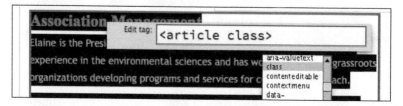

Note how Dreamweaver automatically creates the attribute markup and provides a list of any existing `class` attributes as you type. Since the class you want to use doesn't exist yet, you'll type the entire name yourself.

15 Type **profile** as the class name.

Press Enter/Return as necessary to complete the attribute and close the Quick Tag Editor.

Note: Typically you have to press Enter/Return twice to close the Quick Tag Editor.

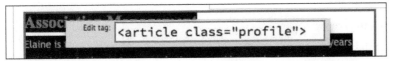

16 Select the `article.profile` tag selector. Choose **green_styles.css** > GLOBAL in the CSS Designer.

17 Click the Add Selector icon ✚.

A new selector name appears.

18 Edit the name to say:

`article.profile`

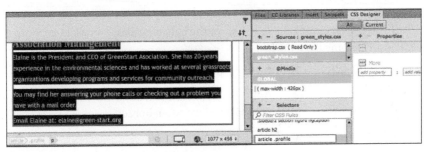

19 Enable the Show Set option, if necessary.

Enter the following property in the Properties window:

`margin: 0px 25px 15px 25px`
`padding-left: 10px`

As with margins, border specifications can be entered individually or all at once.

20 Enter the following specifications for the left and bottom borders:

`border-left: solid 2px #CADAAF`
`border-bottom: solid 10px #CADAAF`

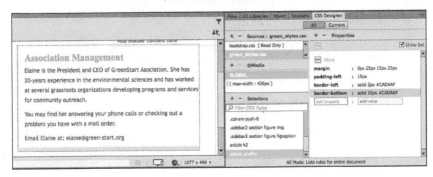

Tip: When creating specifications manually, enter the property name in the field and press Tab. A value field will appear to the right. When Show Set is enabled, hinting may not appear in the values field.

Although the display is not as accurate as in Live view, you can still see the borders appear on the left and bottom of the article element. The borders help to visually group the indented text under its heading. In Live view the display is more accurate.

21 Switch to Live view.

22 Insert the insertion point anywhere in the *Education and Events* section. Click the <article> tag selector.

The HUD appears focused on the article element.

23 In the HUD, click the Add Class/ID icon ⊞ and type **.profile** in the text field.

As you type, a hinting menu will show the matching class names. Feel free to select the name from the list.

24 Repeat steps 22 and 23 to apply the profile class to the remaining <article> elements.

Each section is indented and displays the custom border.

25 Save all files.

Whenever you add new components or styling to a site, you need to make sure the elements and styling work well on all screen sizes and devices.

Making Elements Responsive

In this exercise, you will test the new *profile* elements at multiple screen sizes and adapt them as needed.

1 If necessary, switch to Live view.

2 Drag the Scrubber to the left to make the document window narrower. Observe how the new components respond to the changing widths.

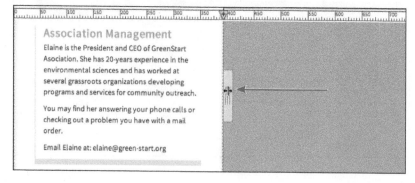

The `.profile` section looks fine until you get down to widths less than 450 pixels. At those sizes the left indent and border wastes too much space. You can fix this situation easily by simply adding alternate styling in the appropriate media query.

3   Restore the document window to its full width.

4   In the CSS Designer, choose **green_styles.css** > (`max-width: 426px`). Create the following selector:

```
article .profile
```

Note: Insert the new rule in the custom media query you created in Chapter 8, if it is different than the one described in step 4.

5   Create the following properties in the new rule:

```
padding: 5px 0px
margin: 5px 0px
border-top: solid 10px #CADAAF
border-bottom: solid 4px #CADAAF
border-left-style: none
```

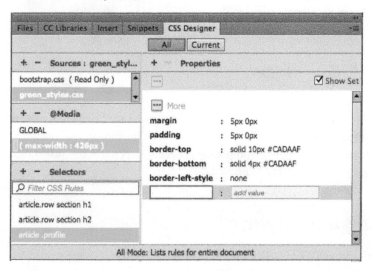

6   Save all files.

Repeat step 2 to test the new styling. Click the Refresh button in the document toolbar to refresh Live view if you do not see any new formatting for the max-width: 426 media query.

Note: You may need to click the Refresh button to see the changes in the layout properly.

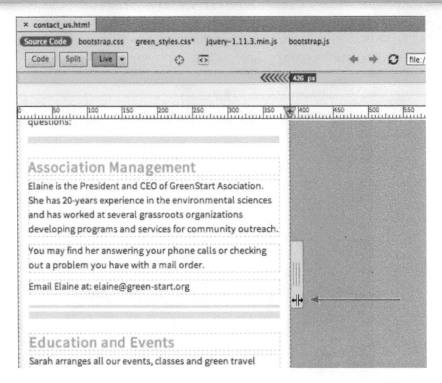

When the screen drops down to your custom media query, the `.profile` section expands nearly to the full width of the screen and drops the indents and the left border. Remember to test all new components at every screen size and orientation and make changes to the styling as needed.

Creating and Styling Tables

Before the advent of CSS, HTML tables were often used to create page layouts. Although tables are not good for page layout, they are very good, and necessary, for displaying many types of data, such as product lists, personnel directories, and timetables, to name a few.

Dreamweaver enables you to create tables from scratch, to copy and paste them from other applications, or to create them instantly from data supplied from other sources, such as database or spreadsheet programs, like Microsoft Access or Microsoft Excel.

Creating Tables from Scratch

Dreamweaver makes it easy to create tables from scratch. In this exercise, you will learn how to create an HTML table.

1   Create a new page from the **mygreen_temp** template.
    Save the file as **events.html** in the site root folder.

2   Enter **Green Events and Classes** to replace the *Title* placeholder text in the
    Property inspector.

3   In Design view, select the *Add main heading here* placeholder heading and type
    Green Events and Classes to replace it.

4   Select the *Add subheading here* placeholder heading and click the h2 tag selector.
    Press Delete.

5   Select the text *Add content here.*

6   Type the following text: **Want to get involved? Want to learn a new skill?
    There's no time like the present. Check out our list of Green Events and
    Classes. The schedule is updated on a regular basis, so you may want to
    bookmark this page and check it often. Hope to see you soon!**

Tip: Whenever
you need to select
complete elements,
it's a good practice to
use the tag selectors.

7   Without moving the insertion point position from step 6, choose Insert > Table.

    The Table dialog appears.

    Some aspects of the table may be controlled and formatted by HTML attributes,
    but others can be controlled entirely by CSS. Whenever possible, avoid using
    HTML to format tables. As with text formatting, HTML formatting is neither
    efficient nor flexible.

    The only advantage HTML has is that the attributes continue to be well
    supported by all popular browsers, both old and new. When you enter values in
    this dialog, Dreamweaver still applies them via HTML attributes.

8   Enter the following specification for the table:

    Rows: **2**
    Columns: **4**
    Width: **100%**
    Border thickness: **1**

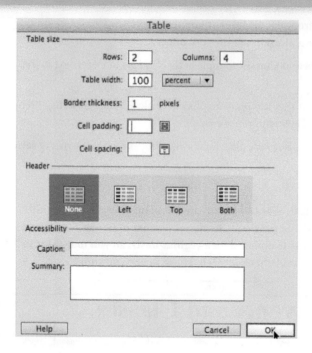

9 Click OK to create the table.

A four-column, two-row table appears below the main heading and content text you just typed. Note that it fills the column from left to right. Let's wrap it in an `<article>` element.

10 Select Insert > Article.

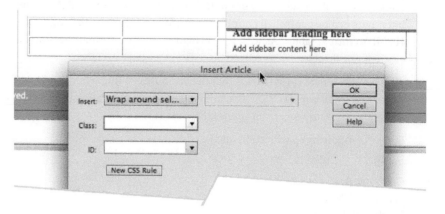

The Insert Article dialog appears. The Insert drop-down menu should default to Wrap Around Selection.

11 Click OK to create the `<article>` element.

The table is ready to accept input.

12 Insert the insertion point in the first cell of the table.

Type **Date** and press Tab to move into the next cell in the first row.

13 In the second cell, type **Event** and press Tab. Type **Location** and press Tab. Type **Cost** and press Tab.

Tip: While in a table cell in Design view, pressing the Tab key moves the insertion point to the next cell on the right. Hold the Shift key when pressing the Tab key to move to the left, or backward, through the table.

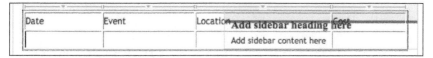

The insertion point moves to the first cell of the second row.

14 In the second row, type **May 1** (in cell 1), **May Day Parade** (in cell 2), **City Hall** (in cell 3), and **Free** (in cell 4).

When the insertion point is in the last cell, inserting additional rows in the table is easy.

15 Press Tab.

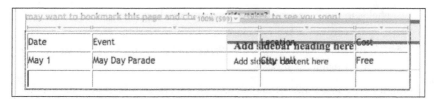

A new blank row appears at the bottom of the table. Dreamweaver also allows you to insert multiple new rows at once.

16 Select the `<table>` tag selector at the bottom of the document window.

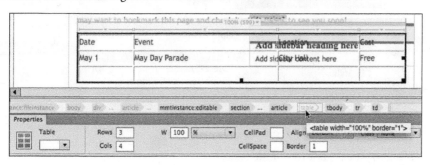

The Property inspector displays the properties of the current table, including the total number of rows and columns.

17 Select the number 3 in the Rows field.

Type **5** and press Enter/Return to complete the change.

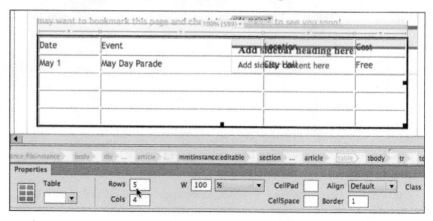

Dreamweaver adds two new rows to the table.

The fields in the Property inspector create HTML attributes to control various aspects of the table, including table width, width and height of cells, text alignment, and so on. You can also add rows and columns to the table interactively using the mouse.

18 Right-click the last row of the table.

Choose Table > Insert Row from the context menu.

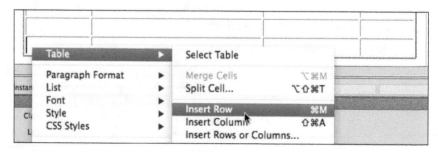

Another row is added to the table. The context menu can also insert multiple rows and/or columns at once.

19 Right-click the last row of the table.

Choose Table > Insert Rows or Columns from the context menu.

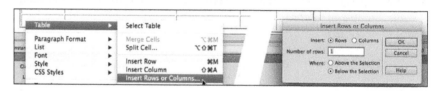

The Insert Rows or Columns dialog appears.

20 Insert 4 rows below the selection and click OK.

Four more rows are added to the table, for a total of 10 rows.

21 Save all files.

Copying and Pasting Tables

Although Dreamweaver allows you to create tables manually inside the program, you can also move tables from other HTML files or even other programs by using copy and paste.

1 Open the Files panel and double-click **calendar.html** in the Chapter10/resources folder to open it.

Date	Event	Location	Cost
Oct 19, 2015	Day hike at the Dunes	Shoreline Park	$10.00
Oct 17, 2015	Volunteer for Homeless Shelter	North Side Community Center	Free
Oct 23, 2015	Book Club	West Side Community Center	Free
Oct 24, 2015	Halloween Haunted Hike	West Side Park	$10.00

Note: Dreamweaver allows you to copy and paste tables from some other programs, such as Microsoft Word. Unfortunately, it doesn't work with every program.

This HTML file opens in its own tab in Dreamweaver. Note the table structure—it has four columns and numerous rows.

When moving content from one file to another, it's important to match views in both documents. Since you were working in Design view in **events.html**, you should use Design view in this file too.

2 Switch to Design view, if necessary.

3 Insert the insertion point in the table.
Click the `<table>` tag selector.
Press Ctrl+C/Cmd+C to copy the table.

4 Click the **events.html** document tab.

5 Insert the insertion point in the table.
Select the `<table>` tag selector.
Press Ctrl+V/Cmd+V to paste the table.

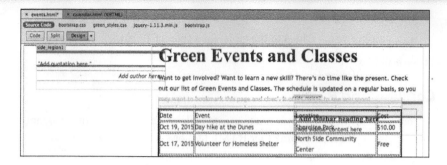

The new table element completely replaces the existing table. This workflow will work in Design and Code views. But you must match views in both documents before you copy and paste.

6   Save the file.

Styling Tables with CSS

Currently, the formatting for the table is a mixed bag. Some is being supplied by HTML defaults and some by the Bootstrap framework. Whenever CSS styles conflict with HTML attributes, CSS wins. In the following exercise, you will create CSS rules to override any HTML styling.

1   If necessary, insert the insertion point in the table. Select the `table` tag selector.

2   In the CSS Designer, choose **green_styles.css** > GLOBAL.
Create a new selector:

```
article table
```

3   In the CSS Designer Properties window, deselect the option Show Set, if necessary.

4   In the Type category, click to open the font-family property.
Select Manage Fonts, and create the following custom font stack:

```
Arial Narrow, Arial, Verdana, sans-serif
```

5   Create the following specifications for the new rule:

```
font-family: Arial Narrow, Arial, Verdana, sans-serif
font-size: 90%
width: 95%
border-bottom: 3px solid #060
margin-bottom: 2em
```

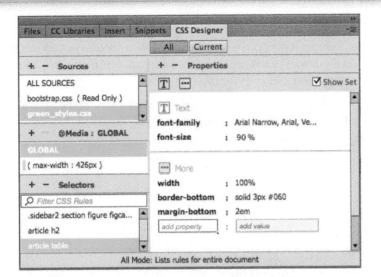

Note: You may want to enable the Show Set option when creating these specifications, as shown.

The table displays a dark green border at the bottom, and the content has been reduced in size and styled with Arial Narrow.

You have applied styling to one aspect of the table properties, but there are plenty of things you still need to address within this element. It's hard to see what's actually happening using Design view. It's a good idea to preview the page in Live view from time to time.

Tip: Table styling may not appear properly in Design view. Switch to Live view to see the full effect of your CSS.

6   Save all files.

7   Switch to Live view and examine the page content.

In Live view everything looks better, but the data in the table appears a bit crowded, and if your screen is narrower than the one shown, the content may wrap to two lines. It could use some extra spacing and other highlighting. The rule `article table` you just created formats only the overall structure of the table. It can't control or format the individual rows and columns. In the next exercise, you will turn your attention to the inner workings of the table.

Styling Table Cells

Just as for tables, column styling can be applied by HTML attributes or CSS rules. Formatting for columns can be applied via two elements that create the individual cells: `<th>` for table header and `<td>` for table data.

It's a good idea to create a generic rule to reset the default formats of the `<th>` and `<td>` elements. Later, you will create custom rules to apply more specific settings.

1   Insert the insertion point into the table.
    In the CSS Designer, choose **green_styles.css** > GLOBAL.

2   Create a new selector:

```
article td, article th
```

This simplified selector will work fine. Since `td` and `th` elements have to be in tables anyway, there's really no need to put `table` in the selector name.

3   In the Properties window, select the Show Set option.

4   Create the following properties for the new rule:

```
padding: 4px
text-align: left
border-top: solid 1px #090
```

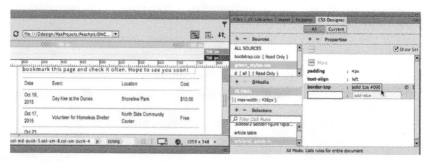

A thin green border appears above each row of the table, making the data easier to read. You may not be able to see the border properly unless you use Live view.

Long columns and rows of undifferentiated data can be tedious to read and hard to decipher. Headers are often used to help the reader identify data. By default, the text in header cells is formatted in bold and centered to help it stand out from the normal cells, but some browsers do not honor this default styling. So don't count on it. You can make the headers stand out by giving them a touch of color of your own.

5   Choose **green_styles.css** > GLOBAL.
    Create a new rule: `article th`

6   Create the following properties in the `article th` rule:
```
color: #FFC
text-align: center
border-bottom: solid 6px #060
background-color: #090
```

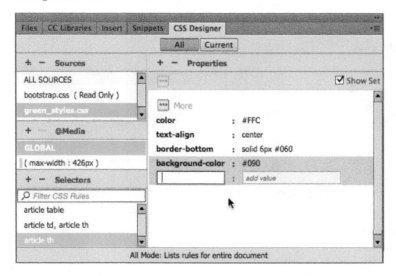

The rule is created, but it still needs to be applied. Dreamweaver makes it easy to convert existing <td> elements into <th> elements.

7   Click once to insert the insertion point into the first cell of the first row of the table. In the Property inspector, select the Header option. Note the tag selector.

> **Note:** You cannot select more than one cell at a time in Live view.

The cell background is filled with green.

When you click the Header checkbox, Dreamweaver automatically rewrites the markup, converting the existing <td> tags to <th> and thereby applying the CSS formatting. This functionality will save you lots of time over editing the code manually. If you switch to Design view, you can also convert multiple cells at one time.

8   Switch to Design view.

9   Click the second cell of the first row and drag to select the remaining cells in the first row. Or you can select an entire row at once by positioning the insertion point at the left edge of the table row and clicking when you see the black selection arrow appear to the left of the row.

10 In the Property inspector, select the Header option to convert the table cells to header cells.

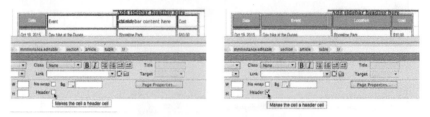

The whole first row is filled with green as the table cells are converted to header cells.

11 Save all files.

Controlling Table Display

Unless you specify otherwise, empty table columns will divide the available space between them equally. But once you start adding content to the cells, all bets are off—tables seem to get a mind of their own and divvy up the space in a different way. In most cases, they'll award more space to columns that contain more data, but that's not guaranteed to happen.

To provide the highest level of control, you'll assign unique classes to the cells in each column. But first you have to create the CSS rules. You can create them one at a time or all at once. If the rules already exist in the style sheet it makes it easier to assign them to the various elements later.

1 Choose **green_styles.css** > GLOBAL. Create the following new selectors:

```
article .date
article .event
article .location
article .cost
```

Note: In HTML 4, rule names can't start with numerals or punctuation characters. In HTML5, these restrictions have been mostly relaxed. But it's probably still a good idea not to use such characters in your selector names.

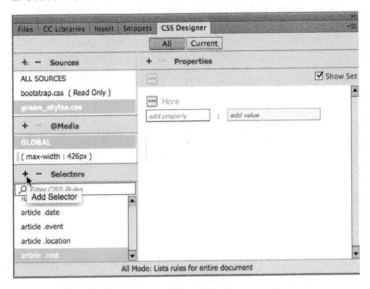

Four new rules appear in the Selectors window but contain no styling information. Even without styling, the classes can be assigned to each column. Dreamweaver makes it easy to apply classes to an entire column.

2 In Design view, position the insertion point above the first column of the table until you see a black arrow. Click to select the entire column.

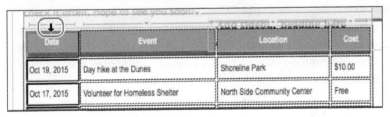

3 Choose `date` from the Class menu in the Property inspector.

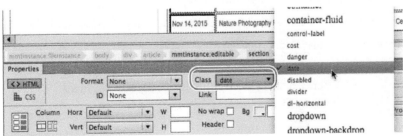

The cells in the first column should display th.date or td.date in the tag selector interface.

4   Repeat steps 2 and 3 to apply the appropriate classes to each column.

Controlling the width of a column is quite simple. Since the entire column must be the same width, you only have to apply a width specification to one cell. If cells in a column have conflicting specifications, typically the largest width wins. Since you just applied a class to the entire Date column, settings will affect every cell at once. This will make it easier to get the table to adapt to any screen.

Note: Even if you apply a width that's too narrow for the existing content, by default a cell can't be any smaller than the largest word or graphic element contained within it.

5   Add the following property to the rule article .date:

```
width: 6em
```

The Date column resizes, although the change may not be visible in Design view. The remaining columns automatically divvy up the space left over. Column styling can also specify text alignment as well as width. Let's apply styling to the contents of the Cost column.

Note: The event and location will be used later in the chapter.

6   Add the following properties to the rule article .cost:

```
width: 4em
text-align: center
```

The Cost column resizes to a width of 4 ems, and the text aligns to the center. Now if you want to control the styling of the columns individually, you have the ability to do so. Note that the tag selector shows the class names with each element, such as th.cost or td.cost.

7   Save all files.

Inserting Tables from Other Sources

In addition to creating tables by hand, you can also create them from data exported from databases and spreadsheets. In this exercise, you will create a table from data that was exported from Microsoft Excel to a comma-separated values (CSV) file. As with the other content models, you will first create an <article> element in which to insert the new table.

1   In Design view, insert the insertion point anywhere in the existing Events table. Select the <article> tag selector. Press the right arrow key.

The insertion point moves after the closing </article> tag.

2   Without moving the insertion point, choose File > Import > Tabular Data.

The Import Tabular Data dialog appears.

3   Click the Browse button and select classes.csv from the Chapter10/resources folder. Click Open. Comma should be automatically selected in the Delimiter menu.

4   Select the following options in the Import Tabular Data dialog:
Table width: **100%**
Border: **0**

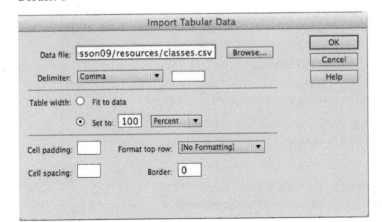

The table width will actually be controlled by the table rule created earlier, but HTML attributes will be honored in browsers or devices that do not support CSS. Because this is the case, make sure that the HTML attributes you use don't break the layout.

5   Click OK.

A new table—containing a class (course) schedule—appears below the first. To conform to the structure you created for the first table, you should insert the new one into an **<article>** element.

6   Select the **table** tag selector for the new table.

7   Select Insert > Article.
Click OK to insert the **<article>** element.

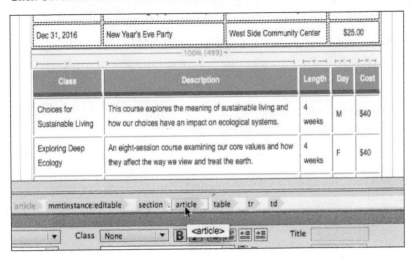

The new table is inserted into the `<article>` element. Green lines appear between the rows, but the header cells are not styled the same as in the first table.

8   Select the first row of the Class schedule.
    In the Property inspector, select the Header option.

    The header cells now display in green with reversed text.

    The new table has an extra column, and the text is wrapping awkwardly in the last three columns. You will fix this display by using the `.cost` class created earlier and by creating additional custom classes too.

9   Select the entire Cost column as you did in the previous exercise.
    In the Property inspector, choose `cost` from the Class menu.

    The two Cost columns are now the same width.

10 In the CSS Designer, right-click the rule `article .cost`.
    Choose Copy All Styles from the context menu.

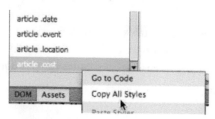

11 Create a new selector: `article .day`
    Right-click the new selector and select Paste Styles from the context menu.

    The new rule now has the same styling as the `article .cost` rule.

12 Repeat step 9 to apply the day class to the Day column in the Classes table.

    Dreamweaver also provides an option for duplicating rules.

13 Right-click the rule `article .cost`.
    Choose Duplicate from the context menu.
    Enter `article .length` as the new selector.

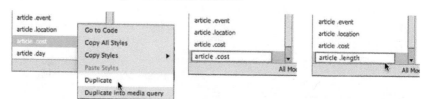

14 Apply the `.length` class to the Length column in the Classes table, as in step 9.

By creating and applying custom classes to each column, you have the means to modify each column individually. We need to make two more rules: one to format the Class column and the other to format the Description column.

15 Duplicate the rule `article .date`. Enter `article .class` as the new rule name. Change the width to `10em`.

16 Duplicate the rule `article .event`.
Enter `article .description` as the new name.

17 Apply the `.class` class to the Class column.
Apply the `.description` class to the Description column.

All columns in both tables now have classes assigned to them.

18 Save all files.

Adding and Formatting Caption Elements

The two tables you inserted on the page contain different information but don't feature any differentiating labels or titles. To help users distinguish between the two sets of data, let's add a title to each and a bit of extra spacing. The `<caption>` element was designed to identify the content of HTML tables. This element is inserted as a child of the `<table>` element itself.

1 Open **events.html** in Design view, if necessary.

2 Insert the insertion point in the first table.
Select the `<table>` tag selector.
Switch to Code view.

By selecting the table first, Dreamweaver automatically highlights the code in Code view, making it easier to find.

3 Locate the opening `<table>` tag.
Insert the insertion point directly after this tag.
Type `<caption>` or select it from the code-hinting menu when it appears.

4 Type **2015-16 Event Schedule** and then type </ to close the element.

```
60    <article>
61      <table width="100%" border="1"><caption>2015-16
      Event Schedule</caption></table>
62        <tr>
```

5 Switch to Design view.

The caption is complete and inserted as a child element of the table.

6 Repeat steps 1 and 2 for the Classes table.
Type **2015-16 Class Schedule.**
Then, type </ to close the element.

7 Switch to Live view.

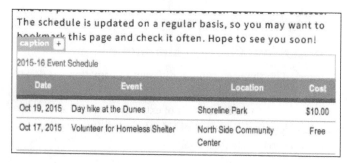

The captions are relatively small, and they're lost against the color and formatting of the table. Let's beef them up a bit with a custom CSS rule.

8 Choose **green_styles.css** > GLOBAL.
Create a new selector: `article caption`

9 Create the following properties for the rule `article caption`:

```
margin-top: 20px
padding-bottom: 10px
color: #090
font-weight: bold
font-size: 160%
line-height: 1.2em
```

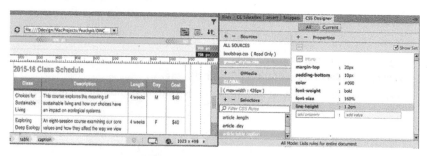

The captions now appear sufficiently large and impressive above each table.

10 Save all files.

Formatting the tables and the captions with CSS has made them much easier to read and understand. Feel free to experiment with the size and placement of the caption and specifications affecting the tables.

Making Tables Responsive

The tables are finished and ready to go. They work fine for normal desktop displays and larger tablets, but the underlying page design is built to work seamlessly all the way down to smartphones. On the other hand, tables are notoriously ill-suited to smaller screens because they don't naturally adapt to them. To understand this concept, let's see how the current elements function on smaller screens.

1 If necessary, open **events.html** in Dreamweaver CC (2015.1 release) or later.

Design view doesn't provide an accurate rendition of the tables. Live view is a better choice, but the best option is to view the page in a browser.

2 Choose File > Preview in Browser.
Choose your favorite browser from the list.

The page opens in the browser, displaying all the colors, fonts, background images, and other CSS specifications set by the style sheet. To see how the tables will react to a smaller screen, just resize the browser window.

3 Drag the right edge of the browser window to the left to make it narrower. Watch carefully how the tables respond, or don't respond, to the changing environment.

As the screen becomes narrower, the media queries will kick in and reformat the page and components to adapt to the smaller screen. Since the table widths are set to 95%, they mostly scale down with the page. But at the smallest sizes, the text within the table is trying to fit by wrapping in very narrow columns.

We need to rethink the whole concept of table design and display. You need to change the basic nature of the elements that compose tables so you can display them in a completely different way. During this process, you may sometimes find it easier to work in the CSS Designer; at other times you may want to enter the settings directly in Code view. Feel free to use whichever method feels more comfortable to you.

4   In Dreamweaver, switch to Live view and open the CSS Designer, if necessary. Click the custom media query in the VMQ you created in Chapter 8.

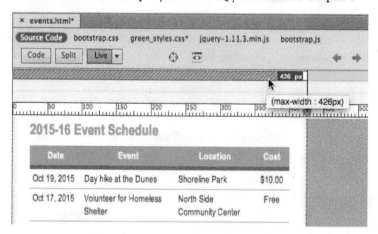

5   Choose **green_styles.css** > (max-width:426px) in the CSS Designer.

Your media query may differ from the one described. Choose the one you created in **green_styles.css**.

6   Create a new selector: `article th, article td`

7   Add the `display: block` property to the new rule.

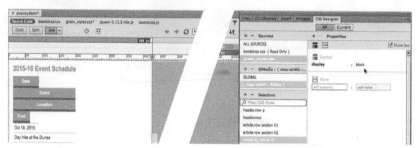

Drag the Scrubber to resize the display to the 426px media query. The cells are now displayed vertically, stacking one atop the other. You might need to refresh Live view to see this new format.

Note: Be sure that all subsequent rules and properties are added only to the custom media query.

This rule resets the default behavior of the table elements so that you can control their appearance on smaller screens. Some cells appear narrower than others because formatting is still being inherited from other parts of the style sheet. You'll have to create additional rules to override these specifications.

8 Create a new rule: `article table`
   Give the new rule the following properties:

   ```
   margin-right: auto
   margin-left: auto
   ```

   With the data stacking vertically, it doesn't make much sense now to have a header row. We could set the header row to the `display:none` property to hide it, but that's not recommended for accessibility standards. The next best thing would be to simply format it to take up no space.

9 Create a new rule: `article th`
   Give the new rule the following properties:

   ```
   height: 0
   margin: 0
   padding: 0
   font-size: 0
   border: none
   overflow: hidden
   ```

The header rows disappear visually but are still accessible to visitors using screen readers or other assistive devices. But now that they are invisible, you have to address the fact that there are no headers describing the data being displayed.

For this purpose, we'll resort to a new CSS3 property that can actually create labels based on the CSS class applied to the cell. Some of the latest CSS3 properties are not directly supported in the CSS Designer, but you can enter them manually in the Properties window or in Code view, and Dreamweaver may provide hinting support for them as well.

10 Create a new rule: `td.date:before`

11 Enable the Show Set option.
    Enter the following property:value combo:

    ```
    content: "Date: "
    ```

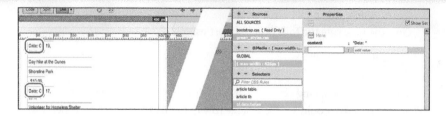

Notice that the label "Date: " appears in all the cells styled by the `date` class. You need to make a similar rule for each of the data elements.

12 Repeat steps 10 and 11 to create the following rules and properties:

Rule	Property: Value
`td.event:before`	`content: "Event: "`
`td.location:before`	`content: "Location: "`
`td.cost:before`	`content: "Cost: "`
`td.class:before`	`content: "Class: "`
`td.description:before`	`content: "Description: "`
`td.day:before`	`content: "Day: "`
`td.length:before`	`content: "Length: "`

Each data cell now shows the appropriate labels. CSS can also style the data and labels.

13 Create the following rule:

```
article .date,
article .event,
article .location,
article .cost,
article .class,
article .description,
article .length,
article .day
```

Tip: Creating long selectors may be easier to do in Code view. You can access the **green_styles. css** file by clicking its name in the Referenced file interface at the top of the document window.

We typed this rule on multiple lines to make it easier to read, but you can enter it as one long string. As long as the styling for all the data cells is identical, you can combine all the selectors into a single rule, separated by commas. Remember to mind the punctuation and spelling carefully. Even a tiny error in the code can cause the formatting to fail. If you want the styling to be different in one or more of the elements, then create seven separate rules.

Next, let's apply some styling to the labels themselves to help make them stand out more distinctly.

14 Apply the following properties to the new rule or in each of the separate rules:

```
width: 100%
padding-left: 30%
position: relative
text-align: left
```

Note: Although the formatting is identical for these classes at this point, you may want to adjust the styling for one or more items later. Making separate rules can add flexibility even though it adds to the amount of code that has to be downloaded.

```
250   article .date,
251   article .event,
252   article .location,
253   article .cost,
254   article .class,
255   article .description,
256   article .length,
257   article .day {
258       width: 100%;
259       padding-left: 30%;
260       position: relative;
261       text-align: left;
262   }
```

2015-16 Event Schedule

Date: Oct 19, 2015

Event: Day hike at the Dunes

Location: Shoreline Park

Cost: $10.00

Date: Oct 17, 2015

Event: Volunteer for Homeless Shelter

Location: North Side Community Center

Cost: Free

The event and class entries are now indented, and all appear at the same width.

15 Create a new rule: `td:before`

Give the new rule the following properties:

```
width: 25%
display: block
padding-right: 10px
position: absolute
top: 6px
left: 1em
color: #060
font-weight: bold
white-space: nowrap
```

```
264   td:before {
265       width: 25%;
266       display: block;
267       padding-right: 10px;
268       position: absolute;
269       top: 6px;
270       left: 1em;
271       color: #060;
272       font-weight: bold;
273       white-space: nowrap;
274   }
```

2015-16 Event Schedule

Date:	Oct 19, 2015
Event:	Day hike at the Dunes
Location:	Shoreline Park
Cost:	$10.00
Date:	Oct 17, 2015
Event:	Volunteer for Homeless Shelter
Location:	North Side Community Center
Cost:	Free

The labels now appear separately from the data and are styled in boldface and dark green. The only thing left to do now is to differentiate one record from the next. One way is to simply add a darker border between each table row.

16 Create a new rule: `article tr`

Give the new rule the following property:

`border-bottom: solid 2px #060`

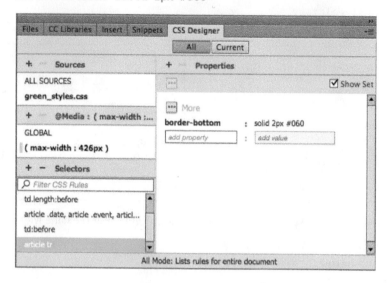

Using a CSS3 selector will add a little more pizzazz to the table.

Warning: Advanced selectors like nth-of-type(even) may not be supported by older browsers.

17 Create a new rule: `tr:nth-of-type(even)`

Give the new rule the following property:

`background-color: #D4EAD4`

This CSS3-based selector actually applies the background only on even rows of the table.

Both tables are now slickly styled and responsive to any changes in the screen size. Although they look good in Live view, don't get complacent; it's vital to test the design in a variety of browsers and mobile devices too.

18 Save all files. Preview the page in the default browser. Test the media queries and the responsive table styling by changing the size of the browser window.

You've learned not only how to insert HTML tables into your web pages but also how to make them adapt to almost any screen environment. It's very likely that everything you tried in this exercise worked perfectly in both Dreamweaver and any browser you tested it in. But you have to remember that CSS3 is still fairly new and has not been fully adopted within the industry.

Spellchecking Web Pages

It's important to ensure that the content you post to the web is error free. Dreamweaver includes a robust spellchecker capable of identifying commonly misspelled words and creating a custom dictionary for nonstandard terms that you might use on a regular basis.

1 Open **contact_us.html**, if necessary.

2 Switch to Design view.
Insert the insertion point at the beginning of the heading *Contact Meridien GreenStart*.
Choose Commands > Check Spelling.

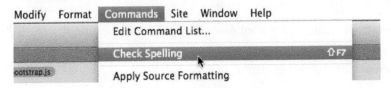

> **Note:** Spellcheck runs only in Design view. If you are in Code view, Dreamweaver will switch to Design view automatically. If you are in Live view, the command will be unavailable.

Spellchecking starts wherever the insertion point has been inserted. If the insertion point is located lower on the page, you will have to restart the spellcheck at least once to examine the entire page. It also does not check content locked in noneditable template regions.

The Check Spelling dialog highlights the word *Meridien*, which is the name of the fictional city where our GreenStart association is located. You could click the option Add To Personal to insert the word into your custom dictionary, but for now we will skip over other occurrences of the name during this check.

3   Click Ignore All.

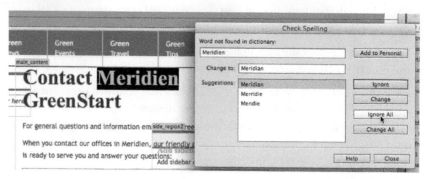

Dreamweaver's spellchecker highlights the word *GreenStart*, which is the name of the association. If GreenStart were the name of your own company, you'd want to add it to your custom dictionary. However, you don't want to add a fictional company name to your dictionary.

4   Click Ignore All again.

Dreamweaver highlights the domain for the email address info@greenstart.org.

5   Click Ignore All.

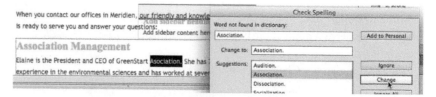

Dreamweaver highlights the word *Asociation*, which is missing an *"s."*

6   To correct the spelling, locate the correctly spelled word (Association) in the Suggestions list and double-click it.

7   Continue the spellcheck to the end. Correct any misspelled words and ignore proper names, as necessary. If a dialog prompts you to start the check from the beginning, click Yes.

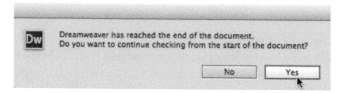

Dreamweaver will start spellchecking from the top of the file to catch any words it may have missed.

8   Click OK when the spellcheck is complete. Save the file.

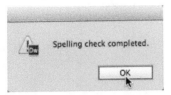

It's important to point out that spellcheck is designed to find only words that are *spelled* incorrectly. It will not find words that are *used* incorrectly. In those instances, nothing takes the place of a careful reading of the content.

Finding and Replacing Text

The ability to find and replace text is one of Dreamweaver's most powerful features. Unlike other programs, Dreamweaver can find almost anything, anywhere in your site, including text, code, and any type of whitespace that can be created in the program. You can search the entire markup, or you can limit the search to just the rendered text in Design view or to just the underlying tags. Advanced users can enlist powerful pattern-matching algorithms known as *regular expressions* to perform sophisticated find-and-replace operations. And then Dreamweaver takes it one step further by allowing you to replace the targeted text or code with similar amounts of text, code, and whitespace.

In this exercise, you'll learn some important techniques for using the Find and Replace feature.

1   Select the **events.html** document tab, if necessary, or open it from the site root folder.

There are several ways to identify the text or code you want to find. One way is to simply type it in the Find field. In the Events table, the name *Meridien* was spelled incorrectly as *Meridian*. Since *Meridian* is an actual word, the spellchecker won't flag it as an error and give you the opportunity to correct it. So you'll use find and replace to make the change instead.

2   Switch to Design view, if necessary. Insert the insertion point in the *Green Events and Classes* heading. Choose Edit > Find and Replace.

The Find and Replace dialog appears. The Find field is empty.

3   Type **Meridian** in the Find field.
Type **Meridien** in the Replace field.
Choose Current Document from the Find In menu, and choose Text from the Search menu.

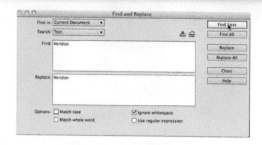

4   Click Find Next.

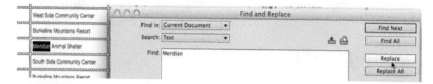

Dreamweaver finds the first occurrence of *Meridian*.

5   Click Replace.

Dreamweaver replaces the first instance of *Meridian* and immediately searches for the next instance. You can continue to replace the words one at a time, or you can choose to replace all occurrences.

6   Click Replace All.

If you replace the words one at a time, Dreamweaver inserts a one-line notice at the bottom of the dialog that tells you how many items were found and how many were replaced. When you click Replace All, Dreamweaver closes the Find and Replace dialog and opens the Search report panel, which lists all the changes made.

7   Right-click the Search report tab and select Close Tab Group from the context menu.

Another method for targeting text and code is to select it *before* activating the command. This method can be used in either Design or Code view.

8   In Design view, locate and select the first occurrence of the text *Burkeline Mountains Resort* in the Location column of the Events table.
Choose Edit > Find and Replace.

The Find and Replace dialog appears. The selected text is automatically entered into the Find field by Dreamweaver. This technique is even more powerful when used in Code view.

9   Close the Find and Replace dialog. Switch to Code view.

10 With the insertion point still inserted in the *Burkeline Mountains Resort* text, click the `<tr>` tag selector at the bottom of the document window.

11 Choose Edit > Find and Replace. The Find and Replace dialog appears.

Observe the Find field. The selected code is automatically entered into the Find field in its entirety by Dreamweaver, including the line breaks and other whitespace. The reason this is so amazing is that there's no way to enter this type of markup in the dialog manually.

12 Select the code in the Find field. Press Delete to remove it.
Type `<tr>` and press Enter/Return to insert a line break. Observe what happens.

Pressing Enter/Return did not insert a line break; instead, it activated the Find command, which finds the first occurrence of the `<tr>` element. In fact, you can't manually insert any type of line break within the dialog.

You probably don't think this is much of a problem, since you've already seen that Dreamweaver inserts text or code when it's selected first. Unfortunately, the method used in steps 8 and 10 don't work with large amounts of text or code.

13 Close the Find and Replace dialog box. Click the `<table>` tag selector.

The entire markup for the table is selected.

14 Choose Edit > Find and Replace. Observe the Find field.

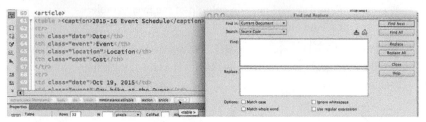

This time, Dreamweaver didn't transfer the selected code into the Find field. To get larger amounts of text or code into the Find field, and to enter large amounts of replacement text and code, you need to use copy and paste.

15 Close the Find and Replace dialog. Select the table again, if necessary. Right-click the selected code and choose Copy from the context menu.

16 Press Ctrl+F/Cmd+F to activate the Find and Replace command. Right-click the Find field, and choose Paste from the context menu.

The entire `<table>` selection is pasted into the Find field.

17 Insert the insertion point into the Replace field, and press Ctrl+V/Cmd+V.

The entire selection is pasted into the Replace field. Obviously, the two fields contain identical markup, but it illustrates how easy it would be to change or replace large amounts of code.

18 Close the Find and Replace dialog. Save all files.

In this chapter, you created four new pages and learned how to import text from multiple sources. You formatted text as headings and lists and then styled it using CSS. You inserted and formatted two tables, added captions to each one, and styled them to make them responsive. And you reviewed and corrected text using Dreamweaver's spellcheck and Find and Replace tools.

Find In and Search

Note the options in the Find In and Search menus. The power and flexibility of Dreamweaver shines brightest here. The Find and Replace command can search in selected text, in the current document, in all open documents, in a specific folder, in selected files of the site, or the entire current local site. But as if those options weren't enough, Dreamweaver also allows you to target the search to the source code, text, advanced text, or even a specific tag.

End-of-Chapter Activities

Review Questions

Directions: Choose the correct answer for each question.

1. What tool lets you add a <title> element in Dreamweaver?
   a. CSS Designer
   b. Property Inspector
   c. Files panel
   d. Insert panel

2. What advantages does semantic structures offer in web design?
   a. Supports accessibility standards
   b. Increases page download times
   c. Improves SEO ranking
   d. A and C only
   e. None of the above

3. How many heading tags are there in HTML?
   a. 6
   b. 4
   c. 7
   d. 5

4. The <cite> element is used to identify what in HTML5?
   a. Blocks of text
   b. Attribution of a quotation
   c. Font colors
   d. Author names

5. The <0l> element creates what type of list?
   a. Unordered list
   b. Bulleted list
   c. Numbered list
   d. A & B only
   e. None of the above

6. The <ul> element creates what type of list?
   a. Unordered list
   b. Bulleted list
   c. Numbered list
   d. A & B only
   e. None of the above

7. True or False: Whenever possible, avoid using HTML to format tables.
   a. True
   b. False

8. When using HTML attributes to make a table responsive you need do what?
   a. Set the columns to a percentage (%)
   b. Set the Rows to percentage (%)
   c. Set the Width to percentage (%)
   d. Tables cannot be responsive

9. When styling tables if a CSS style conficts with an HTML attribute what happens?
   a. Nothing
   b. The CSS style overrides the HTML attribute
   c. The HTML attribute overrides the CSS style
   d. All style properties and HTML attributes display together

10. To cause a HTML element to not display on the screen but to be still be accessible to a screen reader you need to do what?
    a. Hide the element
    b. Set the element CSS styles to a property of zero - "0"
    c. This cannot be done
    d. None of these above

Essay Questions

Directions: Respond to each question by writing your answers in complete sentences and paragraphs. Be thorough in your answers.

1. How do you format text to be an HTML heading?

2. Explain how to turn paragraph text into an ordered list and then an unordered list.

3. Describe two methods for inserting HTML tables into a webpage.

4. What element controls the width of a table column?

5. What items will not be found by Dreamweaver's spellcheck command?

6. Describe three ways to insert content in the Find field.

7. What type spreadsheet files can be imported into Dreamweaver?

8. What type of files can be opened by Dreamweaver?

9. Explain the process of creating and applying a class selector.

10. Explain how you can create one CSS style rule that formats many selectors.

Add Lists and Tables to the Lake Powell Website

Its time to add some information to the Lake Powell website. You'll do this by adding lists and tables to help organize the display of the information.

Creating and Formatting Lists

The home page could use some more work. In this exercise you'll add both ordered and unordered lists to the two <aside> elements. Then format the lists with CSS.

1. On your computer create a local root folder as directed by your teacher. Name the folder **lakepowell_xx**. Copy the class data files from the Chapter10/Data files/ lakepowell_xx directory as instructed by your teacher.

2. From the Files panel open index.html. Switch to Design view. Make the page more semantically correct by wrapping the weather information in the left <aside> element with the <article> element. Do this by highlighting all text in the aside. Choose Insert>article from the menu bar.

3. Repeat step 2 and wrap the facts information in the right <aside> element in an <article> element.

4. Wrap the main content information contained in the <section> element in an <article> element as well.

5. The two <aside> elements contain information that would look better in a list format. Apply an unordered or bulleted list to weather information in the left <aside> by selecting the weather statistics starting with January through December. Then click the Unordered List button in the Property inspector.

6. Now create an ordered or numbered list for the right <aside> content. Highlight the facts and click the Ordered List button in the Property inspector.

7. This looks better but it needs more formatting. Next apply a Class/ID to the <article> element and then format it with CSS. Click any where in the facts information and then select the <article> tag selector. Open the Quick Tag Editor by pressing Ctrl+T / Cmd+T and then typing **<article class="facts">**

8. In the CSS Designer, create a selector rule for the **article.facts** class by selecting the **lakepowell.css>GLOBAL** and then clicking New Selector. Name the class selector **article.facts**. Set the following properties:
    a. margin: 0px 15px 15px 15px
    b. padding: 0px 10px 10px 10px
    c. border-bottom: solid 2px #900

9. Repeat steps 7 and 8 to create a Class/ID for the <article> element for the Weather information. Name it **<article class="weather">**. Then create a CSS rule named **article.weather** and set the following properties:
   a. margin: 0px 15px 15px 15px
   b. padding: 0px 10px 10px 10px
   c. border-bottom: solid 2px #900

10. Save all files and then switch to Live view. Test the page by dragging the Scrubber to the left. Notice that we need to adjust the display of the custom media query max-width: 628px. Create another rule in the CSS Designer by selecting the **lakepowell. css>(max-width: 628px)** and then create a new selector named **article .facts**

11. Create the following properties.
    a. margin: 5px 0px
    b. padding: 5px 0px
    c. border-bottom: solid 4px #900

12. Repeat steps 10 and 11 to adjust the weather information area with the same format. Name the new selector, **article .weather**. Make sure you are targeting the **lakepowell. css>(max-width: 628px)**.

13. Save all files and preview the site in a browser.

Creating and Formatting Tables

Next we'll add a table to the home page that replaces the Weather information with a more robust table of temperature and water depth averages.

1. Switch to the Design view, then highlight the temperature data and delete it. Press Enter/Return to create a new line under the Lake Powell Averages <h2> element.

2. Create a new table by choosing Insert>Table from the menu bar. In the Table dialog set the Row field to 12, Columns to 4, Table Width to 100%, Border Thickness to 0px. Click OK to create the table.

3. Next wrap an article tag around the table by choosing **Insert>Article**. The table is ready for content.

4. Click in the first cell on the left in the first row and type **Month**. Press Tab on the keyboard and then add the label **High**. Press Tab again and add the following column labels in the first row: **Low** and **Water**. Click in the first cell in the second row and type **January**. Notice that you are shy one row to contain the remaining months February-December. Click in the last row and then right-click the row and choose **Table>Insert Row** from the context menu and add a new row.

5. Add the months February through December below January.

6. This table is shaping up. Next import tabular .csv data into the new table by first select-ing the table and then clicking the <table> selector. Then choose **File>Import>Tabular data**.

7. The table is looking better. Next designate the first row of the table as a header row. Highlight the first row by either clicking and then dragging through all the cells, or by positioning your cursor to the left of the row so that an arrow displays and then click to select the entire row. In the Property Inspector, click the Header option.

8. Now format the table by first creating CSS rules to cancel out any HTML formatting. In the CSS Designer, choose lakepowell.css>GLOBAL. Create a new selector named **article table**

9. In the CSS Designer Properties window, deselect the Show Set option and set the fol-lowing properties:
   a. font-family: Arial Narrow, Arial, Verdana, san-serif
   b. font-size: 95%
   c. width: 100%
   d. margin-bottom: 2em

10. Switch to Live view and view the new table format.

11. Switch back to Design view. Add a little more format to the rows and columns in the table. Insert your cursor in the table in any cell and then create a new selector in the CSS Designer for lakepowell.css>GLOBAL. Name the selector **article td, article th**.

12. In the Properties window select the Show Set option. Create the following properties for the new rule:
   a. padding: 4px
   b. text-align: left
   c. border-top: solid 1px #C93

13. Add a background color to the header row by creating a new selector for the lakepow-ell.css>GLOBAL. Name the rule **article th**. Add the following:
   a. background-color: #633
   b. color: #C93
   c. border-bottom: solid 1px #900
   d. text-align: center

14. Next format the individual columns for the table by creating three selectors in the lake-powell.css>GLOBAL. Name the selectors:
   a. article .month
   b. article .temp

15. Add properties for the **article .month** class selector rule as indicated below.
    a. width: 7em

16. Add properties for the **article .temp** class selector rule as indicated below.
    a. width: 4em
    b. text-align: center

17. Select the entire Month column and apply the **.month** class selector rule by selecting it from the Class dropdown menu in the Property inspector. Repeat this step to apply the **.temp** to the High, Low and Water columns.

18. Add a caption to the table. Switch to Split view and click any cell in the table. Then select the <table> selector. In the Code view find the opening <table> tag and set your insertion point at the end of the tag. Type <caption>Average Temperatures</caption>

19. Apply format to this caption by creating a new selector rule for the lakepowell. css>GLOBAL and name it **article caption**. Set the following properties:
    a. margin-top: 10px
    b. padding-bottom: 5px
    c. color: #900
    d. font-weight: bold
    e. font-size: 150%
    f. line-height: 1.1em

20. Save all files and preview the site in a browser.

Make the Table Responsive

Next you'll make a table responsive so that it displays better at a smaller screen size.

1. Switch to Live view and open the houseboat.html page. Move the Scrubber to the left to reduce the display width. The table data is really cramped at a 400px width. At the smaller window size, table needs to show less information in the Season column. Next you'll make this table responsive.

2. First define a new media query for the smaller screen size. Set the window screen size at 400px by dragging the Scrubber to the left to this size setting. In the CSS Designer choose lakepowell.css and in the @Media window, create a new media query. In the Define Media Query dialog, set the conditions to **max-width** and the unit value field to **400px** and then click OK.

3. If necessary choose lakepowell.css>(max-width:400px). Create a new selector named **article th, article td** and add the **display: block** property.

4. Create a new selector rule named **article table** with the following properties
   a. margin-right: auto
   b. margin-left: auto

5. Next hide the <th> element from the table display. This hides the header row but it is still there keeping the table accessible to screen readers and other assistive devices. Create another new selector rule named **article th** with the following properties:
   a. height: 0px
   b. margin: 0px
   c. padding: 0px
   d. font-size: 0px
   e. border: none
   f. overflow: hidden

6. To save time and effort, this table already has the class selector for each column applied. You did this earlier in this exercise. Click in the first column and switch to the Split view. Notice that the code reflects the Class/ID that has been assigned to that column as well as the Property inspector.

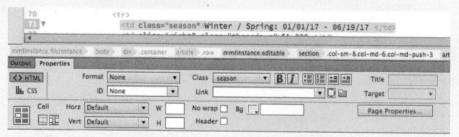

A – Class/ID

You need to create the class selector rules and properties to format these Class selectors applied to the columns. Choose lakepowell.css>(max-width:400px) and then create another new rule named **td.season:before** and set the following property:value combo:
   a. content: "Season: "

7. Repeat steps 6 and 7 to create the following rules and property:value combo:
   a. td.threedays:before   content: "3 Days: "
   b. td.fourdays:before   content: "4 Days: "
   c. td.fivedays:before   content: "5 Days: "
   d. td.sixdays:before   content: "6 Days: "
   e. td.sevendays:before   content: "7 Days: "

8. Create the following group selector rule:

```
article .season, article .threedays, article .fourdays,
article .fivedays, article .sixdays, article .sevendays
```

9. Indent the season and rental days and set them to the same width by applying the following properties to the new group selector rule you just created or in each of the separate rules:
   a. width: 100%
   b. padding-left: 30%
   c. position: relative
   d. text-align: left

10. Next make the labels displays separately from the data and in boldface in the tan color. Create a new rule named **td:before** and add the following properties:
    a. width: 25%
    b. display: block
    c. padding-right: 10px
    d. position: absolute
    e. top: 6px
    f. left: 1em
    g. color: #C93
    h. font-weight: bold
    i. white-space: nowrap

11. Add a bottom border by creating another rule named **article tr** and set the following properties:
    a. border-bottom: solid 1px #633

12. Finally to add more style for the table, apply a new CSS3 selector by creating a new rule named **tr:nth-of-type(even)** and set the following property:
    a. background-color: #F4ECDD

    Note: Remember that older browsers will not understand the new CSS3 styles and therefore might not display the responsive table styles correctly.

13. Save all pages and preview the page in a browser. Resize the browser window to the smallest size to see the new responsive format of the table.

Spellcheck the Lake Powell Site

Spellcheck the Lake Powell site for spelling errors.

1. If necessary, open the houseboat.html page. Switch to Design view.

2. Spellcheck the page by choosing Command>Check Spelling.

3. In the Check Spelling dialog, Dreamweaver identifies *Wahweap* as a possible misspelling. Click the Ignore All button. Dreamweaver indicates that all is spelled correctly on the page.

4. Repeat steps 2 and 3 to spell check the index.html.

5. Save all files.

Online Portfolio Builder – Develop Your Online Portfolio Website by Adding Content, Lists, and Tables

Develop your online portfolio website by adding more content relevant to each page you created in Chapter 9. Focus on the textual content at this point in the development of each page. Develop by added addition content to the each page. Review the content and convert or recreate any verbiage that would be better presented in a list or a table. Examples of lists for a portfolio site can be schools or classes attended, honors, awards, and special accomplishments. Examples of where a table should be used to present information would be complex but related data like a table showing software you use, years in use and projects created with the software. Format these elements so that they display nice and are responsive to all window sizes. Follow the basic steps below to create and format these elements.

1. If necessary, create a local root directory and copy any files or folders over to the new local root directory. Define your site as instructed by your teacher.

2. Open your site pages that you have developed up to this point in the class. Switch to the Design view. Maximize the Dreamweaver workspace to fill the entire screen.

3. Add any new content to each page.

4. Review content and identify areas that need to be a list or a table.

5. Convert information identified as a list to a list.

6. Make the list semantically correct by wrapping it in an <article> element.

7. Format with CSS your lists by creating Class/IDs with appropriate properties. Pay attention to your identified color palette and use these colors for your properties.

8. Convert information identified as a table to a table. You can copy existing tables or import any table you create in a spreadsheet application by saving the spreadsheet in .csv format. Then import the .csv file into the webpage.

9. Make the table semantically correct by wrapping it in an <article> element.

10. Format with CSS your tables by creating Class/IDs with appropriate properties. Pay attention to your identified color palette and use these colors for your properties.

11. Develop a responsive table by creating a new media query for smaller screen sizes – you can also edit the media query you created in Chapter 8 to make it responsive to tables.

12. Spellcheck the pages in your Online Portfolio website.

13. Save all files often and preview your site in at least two of browsers often.

Chapter 11

WORKING WITH IMAGES

Dreamweaver provides many ways to insert and adjust graphics, both within the program and in tandem with other Creative Suite tools, such as Adobe Fireworks and Adobe Photoshop.

Chapter Overview

In this chapter, you'll learn how to work with images to include them in your webpages in the following ways:

- Inserting an image
- Using Photoshop Smart Objects
- Copying and pasting an image from Photoshop and Fireworks
- Evaluate the various input, processing, output, and storage devices and storage services
- Explain and demonstrate ethical use of technology and online resources
- Differentiate between copyright and trademarks;
- Explain the concept of intellectual property laws, including copyright, trademarks, and patents and consequences of violating each type of law;
- Examine the consequences of plagiarism;
- Adhere to copyright and trademark intellectual property laws and regulations, including demonstrating correct acquisition and citation of sources;
- Discuss the process of acquiring rights to use copyrighted and trademarked content in a website;
- Demonstrate appropriate behavior and adherence to acceptable use policies when accessing and using online resources;

Web Image Basics

The web is not so much a place as it is an experience. And essential to that experience are the images and graphics—both still and animated—that populate most websites. In the computer world, graphics fall into two main categories: vector and raster.

Vector graphic formats excel in line art, drawings, and logo art. Raster technology works better for storing photographic images.

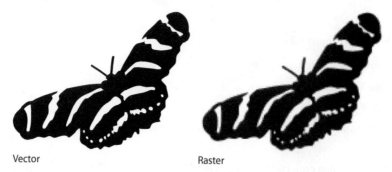

Vector   Raster

Vector Graphics

Vector graphics are created by math. They act like discrete objects, which you can reposition and resize as many times as you want without affecting or diminishing their output quality. The best application of vector art is wherever geometric shapes and text are used to create artistic effects. For example, most company logos are built from vector shapes.

Vector graphics are typically stored in the AI, EPS, PICT, or WMF file formats. Unfortunately, most web browsers don't support these formats. The vector format that is supported is SVG (scalable vector graphic). The simplest way to get started with SVG is to create a graphic in your favorite vector-drawing program—such as Adobe Illustrator or CorelDRAW—and then export it to this format. If you are a good programmer, you may want to try creating SVG graphics using XML (Extensible Markup Language). To find out more about creating SVG graphics, check out www.w3schools.com/svg.

Raster Graphics

Although SVG has definite advantages, web designers primarily use raster-based images in their web designs. Raster images are built from *pixels,* which stands for *picture elements.* Pixels have three basic characteristics:

- They are perfectly square in shape.
- They are all the same size.
- They display only one color at a time.

Raster-based images are composed of thousands, even millions, of pixels arranged in rows and columns, in patterns that create the illusion of an actual photo, painting, or drawing. It's an illusion, because there is no real photo on the screen, just a bunch of pixels that fool your eyes into seeing an image. And, as the quality of the image increases, the more realistic the illusion becomes. Raster image quality is based on three factors: resolution, size, and color.

The inset image shows an enlargement of the flowers, revealing the pixels that compose the image itself.

Resolution

Resolution is the most well known of the factors affecting raster image quality. It is the expression of image quality, measured in the number of pixels that fit in one inch (ppi). The more pixels you can fit in one inch, the more detail you can depict in the image. But better quality comes at a price. An unfortunate by product of higher resolution is larger file size. That's because each pixel must be stored as bytes of information within the image file—information that has real overhead in computer terms. More pixels means more information, which means larger files.

Note: Printers and printing presses use round "dots" to create photographic images. Quality on a printer is measured in dots per inch, or dpi. The process of converting the square pixels used in your computer into the round dots used on the printer is called screening.

72 ppi   300 ppi

Resolution has a dramatic effect on image output. The web image on the left looks fine in the browser but doesn't have enough quality for printing.

Luckily, web images have to appear and look their best only on computer screens, which are based mostly on a resolution of 72 ppi. This is low compared to other applications or output—like printing—where 300 dpi is considered the lowest acceptable quality. The lower resolution of the computer screen is an important factor in keeping most web image files down to a reasonable size for downloading from the Internet.

Size

Size refers to the vertical and horizontal dimensions of the image. As image size increases, more pixels are required to create it, and therefore the file becomes larger. Since graphics take more time to download than HTML code, many designers in recent years have replaced graphical components with CSS formatting to speed up the web experience for their visitors. But if you need or want to use images, one method to ensure snappy downloads is to keep image size small. Even today, with the proliferation of high-speed Internet service, you won't find too many websites that depend on full-page graphics.

Although these two images share the identical resolution and color depth, you can see how image dimensions can affect file size

500KB

1.6MB

Color

Color refers to the color space, or *palette*, that describes each image. Most computer screens display only a fraction of the colors that the human eye can see. And different computers and applications display varying levels of color, expressed by the term *bit depth*. Monochrome, or 1-bit color, is the smallest color space, displaying only black and white, with no shades of gray. Monochrome is used mostly for line-art illustrations, for blueprints, and to reproduce handwriting.

The 4-bit color space describes up to 16 colors. Additional colors can be simulated by a process known as *dithering*, where the available colors are interspersed and juxtaposed to create an illusion of more colors. This color space was created for the first color computer systems and game consoles. Because of its limitations, this palette is seldom used today.

The 8-bit palette offers up to 256 colors or 256 shades of gray. This is the basic color system of all computers, mobile phones, game systems, and handheld devices. This color space also includes what is known as the *web-safe* color palette. Web-safe refers to a subset of 8-bit colors that are supported on both Mac and Windows computers. Most computers, game consoles, handheld devices, and even phones now support higher color palettes, so 8-bit is not as important any more. Unless you need to support non-computer devices, you can probably disregard the web-safe palette altogether.

Today, a few older cellphones and handheld games support the 16-bit color space. This palette is named *high color* and sports a grand total of 65,000 colors. Although this sounds like a lot, 16-bit color is not considered good enough for most graphic design purposes or professional printing.

The highest color space is 24-bit color, which is named *true color*. This system generates up to 16.7 million colors. It is the gold standard for graphic design and professional printing. Several years ago, a new color space was added to the mix: 32-bit color. It doesn't offer any additional colors, but it provides an additional 8 bits of data for an attribute called *alpha transparency*.

Alpha transparency enables you to designate parts of an image or graphic as fully or even partially transparent. This trick allows you to create graphics that seem to have rounded corners or curves, and can even eliminate the white bounding box typical of raster graphics.

24-bit color

8-bit color

4-bit color

Here you can see a dramatic comparison of three color spaces and what the total number of available colors means to image quality.

As with size and resolution, color depth can dramatically affect image file size. With all other aspects being equal, an 8-bit image is over seven times larger than a monochrome image. And the 24-bit version is over three times larger than the 8-bit image. The key to effective use of images on a website is finding the balance of resolution, size, and color to achieve the desired optimal quality.

Raster Image File Formats

Raster images can be stored in a multitude of file formats, but web designers have to be concerned with only three: GIF, JPEG, and PNG. These three formats are optimized for use on the Internet and compatible with most browsers. However, they are not equal in capability.

GIF

GIF (graphic interchange format) was one of the first raster image file formats designed specifically for the web. It has changed only a little in the last 20 years. GIF supports a maximum of 256 colors (8-bit palette) and 72 ppi, so it's used mainly for web interfaces—buttons and graphical borders and such. But it does have two interesting features that keep it pertinent for today's web designers: index transparency and support for simple animation.

JPEG

JPEG, also written JPG, is named for the Joint Photographic Experts Group that created the image standard back in 1992 as a direct reaction to the limitations of the GIF file format. JPEG is a powerful format that supports unlimited resolution, image dimensions, and color depth. Because of this, most digital cameras use JPEG as their default file type for image storage. It's also the reason most designers use JPEG on their websites for images that must be displayed in high quality.

This may sound odd to you, since "high quality" (as described earlier) usually means large file size. Large files take longer to download to your browser. So why is this format so popular on the web? The JPEG format's claim to fame comes from its patented user-selectable image compression algorithm, which can reduce file size as much as 95 percent. JPEG images are compressed each time they are saved and then decompressed as they are opened and displayed.

Unfortunately, all this compression has a downside. Too much compression damages image quality. This type of compression is called *lossy*, because it loses quality. In fact, the loss in quality is great enough that it can potentially render the image totally useless. Each time designers save a JPEG image, they face a trade-off between image quality and file size.

Here you see the effects of different amounts of compression on the file size and quality of an image.

Low Quality
High compression 130K

Medium Quality
Medium compression 150K

High Quality
Low compression 260K

PNG

PNG (portable network graphics) was developed in 1995 because of a looming patent dispute involving the GIF format. At the time, it looked as if designers and developers would have to pay a royalty for using the .gif file extension. Although that issue blew over, PNG has found many adherents and a home on the Internet because of its capabilities.

PNG combines many of the features of GIF and JPEG and adds a few of its own. For example, it offers support for unlimited resolution, 32-bit color, and full alpha and index transparency. It also provides lossless compression, which means you can save an image in PNG format and not worry about losing any quality when you save the file.

The only downside to PNG is that its most important feature—alpha transparency—is not fully supported in older browsers. As these browsers are retired year after year, this issue is not much of a concern to most web designers.

But as with everything on the web, your own needs may vary from the general trend. Before using any specific technology, it's always a good idea to check your site analytics and confirm which browsers your visitors are actually using.

Computer Hardware, Storage Devices, and Storage Services

When you think about a computer, you probably picture its **hardware**, the computer's physical parts. You use hardware devices such as a keyboard or mouse to input data. The processor is a hardware **device** that turns the raw data into usable information. Hardware devices such as a monitor or a disk drive show output and store data for later access.

Much of a computer's hardware is found inside the computer case, hidden from view. Most of this hardware is used for processing and storing data.

Computer Basics

A **computer** is a machine that changes information from one form into another by performing four basic actions. Those actions are input, processing, output, and storage. Together, these actions make up the information processing cycle. By following a set of instructions, called a program, the computer turns raw data into organized information that people can use. Creation of usable information is the primary benefit of computer technology. There are two kinds of computers:

- Analog computers measure data on a scale with many values. Think of the scales on a mercury thermometer or on the gas gauge of a car.

- Digital computers work with data that has a fixed value. They use data in digital, or number, form. The computers that run programs for playing games or searching the Internet are digital computers.

Hardware

The physical parts of a computer.

Device

A hardware component installed for use with a computer system.

Computer

A machine that changes information from one form into another by performing input, processing, output, and storage.

Input

Input

Raw information, or data, that is entered into a computer; also, to enter data into a computer.

Input is the raw information, or **data**, that is entered into a computer. This data can be as simple as letters and numbers or as complex as color photographs, videos, or songs. You input data by using a device such as a keyboard or digital camera. The data that you input can be stored on an external storage device or internal hard drive, as well as through a data input storage service like the Cloud as is discussed later in this lesson.

Data

Raw, or unprocessed, information.

Data is entered into a computer in a coded language. The building blocks of that language are units called **bits**. *Bit* is short for *binary digit*. Each bit is a number, or a digit. A bit can have only two possible values—0 or 1.

Bit

The smallest unit of information with values of either 0 or 1; a number that is a building block for computer languages; short for *binary digit*.

Every letter, number, or picture is entered into the computer as a combination of bits, or 0s and 1s. The bits are combined into groups of eight or more. Each group is called a **byte**. Each letter or number has a unique combination of bits. For instance, on most personal computers, the letter *A* is coded as 01000001. The number *1* is 00110001.

Images are formed by combinations of bytes. Those combinations tell the computer what colors to display and where to put them.

Byte

A group of bits combined into groups of eight or more.

Color can be represented by a three-byte combination where each byte represents the red, green, or blue (RGB) component of the displayed color. The intensity of each component is measured on a scale from 0 to 256 since there are 256 possible combinations of 1 or 0 in each group of eight bits. To represent a color, the three-byte RGB codes are simplified into a 6-digit **hexadecimal value** where the first two digits represent the intensity of red, the second two are green, and the last two are blue.

Hexadecimal value

A six-digit code that uses the hexadecimal system to represent color; the first two digits represent the intensity of red, the second two represent the intensity of green, and the last two represent the intensity of blue.

A hexadecimal number has sixteen possible values, so the RGB values are assigned a number from 0 to 15. But since 10 through 15 are two digit numbers they are expressed with the letters A through F, where A equals 10 and F equals 15. In this way, the 256 possible combinations of each byte can be expressed in two digits. For example, the hexadecimal value for pure, intense red is FF0000 since red has highest intensity and both green and blue are at zero. The hexadecimal for white is FFFFFF, or complete intensity of all three colors, and black is 0000000.

Processing

Processing

A task a computer carries out with data in response to a command.

The second step of the information processing cycle is called **processing**. In this step, the computer does something to the data.

Program

The coded instructions that tell a computer what to do; also to write the code for a program.

What the computer does depends on the instructions, or **program**, given to the computer. The instructions are also written in binary code, using combinations of 0s and 1s. They might tell the computer to add two numbers, or they might have the computer compare two numbers to see which is larger

Computers can process data very rapidly, performing millions of operations every second. The ability to process data with lightning speed is another reason computers are so valuable. After data is processed, it can be stored on a external or internal storage device, as well as a processed storage service like FTP or in the Cloud as is discussed later in this chapter.

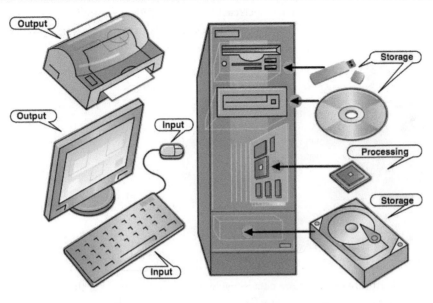

Each computer component plays a role in one of the system's four primary functions.

Output

The third step shows what happens after the computer processes the data. This is the **output** step. If the program tells the computer to add two numbers, the output stage displays the result. To create output, the computer takes the bytes and turns them back into a form you can understand, such as an image on the screen or a printed document.

Output can take many forms. A program might convert the 0s and 1s into a report. It might become an image you are drawing on the computer. If you are playing a game, the output might be a car zooming along a road and the sound of its engine. A computer provides output through a device such as a monitor, speaker, or printer. The output data can then be stored on an external or internal storage device, as well as a output storage service like FTP or in the Cloud as is discussed later in this chapter.

Storage

The fourth operation is **storage**, in which the computer saves the information. Without storage, all the work you do on the computer would be lost. Computers have a temporary memory that is used during the processing stage. When the computer is turned off, however, any data in that temporary memory is lost.

By storing the data in a permanent form, you can access the information over and over. This is another great advantage of computers—what you do one day can be saved and reused on another day.

Inside the Case

Perhaps the most important piece of hardware in a computer is the **central processing unit**, or **CPU**. This is the device that processes data. The CPU is a small,

In some schools, students' work is collected over the year in electronic portfolios. These portfolios reflect a range of the students' work on many projects during the school year. The computer's ability to store this information is perfect for portfolio work.

Think About It!

Think about how an electronic portfolio might be used. Which items below do you think could be in an electronic portfolio?

multimedia presentations maps paper-and-pencil homework poetry lab report

Output

The result of a computer's processing, displayed on-screen, printed on paper, or heard through a speaker.

Storage

The action by which a computer saves information so the information is available for use and reuse.

Central processing unit (CPU)

A piece of the computer's hardware that processes and compares data, and completes arithmetic and logical operations.

Circuit board

An insulated board on which microchips and other components are mounted or etched.

Circuit

In electronics, a path between two or more points along which an electrical current can be carried; in telecommunications a specific path between two or more points along which signals can be carried.

Random access memory (RAM)

Special chips that store data and instructions while the computer is working.

Secondary storage

Computer disk drives such as the hard drive and CD-ROM drive used to store large amounts of data.

Universal serial bus (USB)

A standard that allows communication between devices, such as between a flash drive and a computer.

Note: Computer hardware sometimes fails. When that happens, people call service technicians. These people work for computer companies. They might work in the offices of the company that employs them, or they might travel to business sites to fix machines. Technicians need to know about software and hardware because problems are sometimes caused by a computer's programs and not by its equipment.

thin piece of silicon attached to a **circuit board**. The CPU is covered with tiny electrical **circuits**. By moving data along these circuits in specific ways, the CPU can do arithmetic and compare data very quickly.

The CPU fits in a socket on a circuit board.

Some hardware used to store data is inside the computer case near the CPU. The computer uses **random access memory**, or **RAM**, to store data and instructions while the computer is working. In this way, the CPU can quickly find the data it works with. This type of storage is called primary storage. RAM is volatile memory, which means data in RAM is lost when the computer is turned off.

Other pieces of storage hardware are **secondary storage**. The following devices let you store data permanently—even when the computer is turned off.

- Hard drives use a stack of disk platters to store large amounts of information permanently on the computer. External hard drives, which are plugged into the computer, are used to store back-ups of your data. They can be desktop or portable devices. They usually connect to the computer via a **universal serial bus**, or **USB**, port.

Today, nearly all computers feature a built-in hard drive. Some have capacities of 4 terabytes or more. Some external hard drives are able to store 30 terabytes of data.

- **Flash, jump, thumb,** or **pen drives**—all names for the same kind of storage device—connect to the computer through a USB port. They hold anywhere from 4 gigabytes to as many as 32 gigabytes or more.

- **Compact Discs (CDs), Digital Video Discs (DVDs),** and **Blu-ray Discs (BDs)** are optical storage devices. You insert the CD or DVD into your computer through the disc drive. A CD can store 650 to 700 megabytes of data. DVDs can store anywhere from 4.7 gigabytes to double that amount if the DVD is double-sided. Blu-ray Discs hold from 25 gigabytes to 128 gigabytes.

- **"Cloud" storage** is online storage offered on various Web sites. Most of them will give you a few gigabytes for free, but then require you to pay for more space. Cloud storage is a popular solution for many people and businesses as it is a storage service where you as the customer do not have to upkeep any of the computer hardware for the storage devices and typically the storage service handles backups of the data. There are many companies jumping into this area and sell their storage services by a set amount of space for a monthly fee. Apple offers the iCloud and another popular service is Dropbox for cloud storage solutions. See this URL for more information about Cloud storage: http://www.thetop10bestonlinebackup.com/cloud-storage

- **Memory cards** store data for mobile devices like smart phones and digital cameras. Some memory cards can store 256 gigabytes.

Hard disk drives hold the most data. Many computers now have hard drives that can store several hundred gigabytes. A gigabyte is just over a billion bytes. Some external hard drives can store more than 30 **terabytes** (tb). A terabyte is about 1,000 gigabytes. Thumb or flash drives hold the next largest amount of data, sometimes going over 128 gigabytes. CDs and DVDs hold the least amount of data—from around 700 megabytes to almost 10 gigabytes. A megabyte is just over a million bytes, but still several hundred of them on a CD can store entire encyclopedias, including images, maps, and sound.

File Transfer Protocol (FTP) lets you transfer files on the Internet. With an FTP client, you can transfer files from an FTP server to your computer in an operation called **downloading**. In **uploading**, you transfer files from the client to the server. FTP can transfer both text files and binary files. Binary files are program files, graphics, pictures, music or video clips, and documents. Once you've stored a file on an FTP server, you can share the URL so that others can download the file from the server, as well. The file remains on the server until you delete it. When you transfer a file as an e-mail attachment you must save the file on your computer or it will be deleted when you delete the message. E-mail is considered a more secure method, however, because only the recipient of the e-mail message has access to the attached files.

Flash, jump, thumb, or drive

A small storage device that uses flash memory and connects to the computer through a USB port.

Compact Discs (CDs), Digital Video Discs (DVDs), and Blu-ray Discs (BDs)

These are all optical storage devices.

Terabyte

A unit of measure equal to 1024 gigabytes.

Download

To transfer copies of files from a remote computer to a local computer by means of a modem or network.

Upload

To send data from a client computer to a server computer through a network or Internet connection.

Note: When you upload or download files you are transferring them between your computer and an Internet, or cloud, server. Most Web sites have buttons or links to make it easy to upload and download files, or you may use your browser's File > Open and File > Save As commands.

Peripherals

For most desktop systems, input devices, such as the keyboard and mouse, are separate from the case. So are output devices, such as monitors and printers. Hardware that is separate but can be connected to the case is called a **peripheral**.

> **Peripheral**
>
> Separate input, output, and storage hardware.

Not all computers have all this equipment as peripherals. Apple's iMac° computers include the monitor as a physical part of the main system. Other computers may have built-in storage devices. Portable computers have the keyboard, a type of mouse, and a monitor all attached to the main unit.

Peripherals need to be connected to the computer so that data can be moved back and forth. Some use a wireless connection and some are linked to the computer by a cable. Both wire- less connections and cables connect to the computer with a plug. Most plugs join the computer at a connector on the computer case, but some are installed internally. Connectors can be unique for the peripheral. Monitors have specific plugs designed for transferring image data. Speakers and microphones have unique plugs as well. Many devices such as keyboards, printers, and mice use USB ports.

> **Note:** One problem with computer hardware is the tangle of cables that can result from lots of peripherals. BluetoothTM is a wireless way of communicating that uses radio waves to communicate between electronic devices.
>
> Many cell phones and other portable devices use Bluetooth to send signals to each other. For example, many people use Bluetooth to send photos from their cell phones to their computers. These users may also use Bluetooth to send commands from their telephones and computers to DVD players, data video recorders, refrigerators, and other computer-controlled appliances.

Connectors

There are several main types of connectors, or ports:

- Serial ports move data one bit at a time. For example, they connect computers to modems for Internet access.

- Parallel ports move data in groups.

- Multiple device ports, such as Small Computer Systems Interface (SCSI) and Universal Serial Bus (USB) ports, connect several peripherals to a computer at one time. They all move data faster than serial ports can.

Equipment for Web Development

As you can see, in today's world, there is a lot of choice when it comes to computers hardware, additional storage devices, or storage services. As a web developer, you will need to move and access images and data from many different places and from many different people and locations. You'll want to have a few different ways to transfer data as you go forward. Many web developers have multiple monitors as you will work between many software applications like Dreamweaver, a browser, and an image editing software.

Inserting an Image

Images are key components of any webpage, both for developing visual interest and for telling stories. Dreamweaver provides numerous ways to populate your pages with images, using built-in commands and even using copy and paste from other Adobe apps. Let's start with some of the tools built into Dreamweaver itself, such as the Assets panel.

1   Launch Adobe Dreamweaver CC (2015.1 release) or later. Define a new site for Chapter11 folder as instructed by your teacher. In the Files panel, open **contact_us.html** in Live view.

2   Click the first paragraph under the heading *Association Management*.

The HUD appears focused on the p element.

3   Choose Window > Assets to display the Assets panel, if necessary. Click the Images category icon ⊡ to display a list of all images stored within the site.

4   Locate and select **elaine.jpg** in the list.

A preview of **elaine.jpg** appears in the Assets panel. The panel lists the image's name, dimensions in pixels, size in kilo- or megabytes, and file type, as well as its full directory path.

5   Note the dimensions of the image: 150 pixels by 150 pixels.

6   At the bottom of the panel, click the Insert button.

Note: When working with images in Dreamweaver, you should be sure that your site's default images folder is designated as the images folder in your defined site.

Note: The Images window shows all images stored anywhere in the defined site—even ones outside the site's default images folder—so you may see listings for images stored in the chapter subfolder's, too.

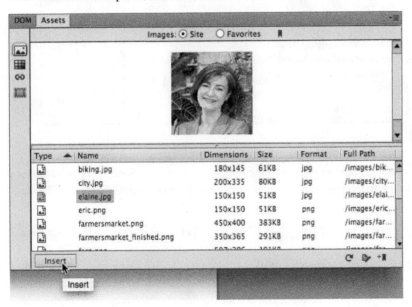

The position assist dialog appears.

7 Click Nest.

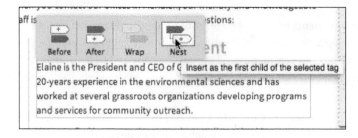

The image appears at the beginning of the paragraph. The HUD now focuses on the img element. You can use the HUD to add alt text to the image.

8 Click the Edit HTML Attribute icon ▤ .

The HTML Attribute dialog appears.

Note: Alt text provides descriptive metadata about images; alt text may be seen if the image doesn't load properly in the browser, or it may be accessed by individuals with visual disabilities.

9 In the Alt text field in the Element HUD, enter **Elaine, Meridien GreenStart President and CEO** as the alternate text.

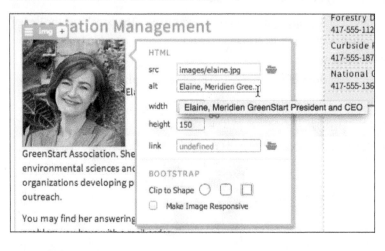

10 Choose File > Save.

You inserted Elaine's picture in the text, but it doesn't look very nice at its current position. In the next exercise, you will adjust the image position using a CSS class.

Adjusting Image Positions with CSS Classes

The <img> element is an inline element by default. That's why you can insert images into paragraphs and other elements. When the image is taller than the font size, the image will increase the vertical space for the line in which it appears. In the past, you could adjust its position using either HTML attributes or CSS, but many of the HTML-based attributes have been deprecated from the language as well as from Dreamweaver. Now you must rely completely on CSS-based techniques.

If you want all the images to align in a certain fashion, you can create a custom rule for the <img> tag to apply specific styling. In this instance, the employee photos will alternate from right to left going down the page and have the text wrap around the image to use the space more effectively. To do this, you'll create a custom class to provide options for left and right alignment. You can use the HUD to create and apply the new class all at once.

1 If necessary, open **contact_us.html** in Live view.

2 Click the image for Elaine in the first paragraph of the *Association Management* section. The HUD appears focused on the img element.

3 Click the Add Class/ID icon +.

4 Type `.flt_rgt` in the text field.

The new class name is short for "float right," hinting at what CSS command you're going to use to style the images.

5 Press Enter/Return.

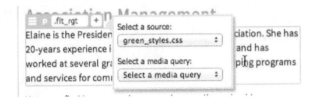

The CSS Source HUD appears.

6 If necessary, select **green_styles.css** from the source drop-down menu. Leave the media query drop-down menu empty.

7 Press Enter/Return to complete the class.
In the CSS Designer, select **green_styles.css** > GLOBAL > `.flt_rgt`.

The new rule appears at the bottom of the list of selectors. No properties are defined yet.

8 Create the following properties:

```
float: right
margin-left: 10px
```

As you learned in Chapter 4, applying a float to the image removes it from the normal flow of the HTML elements, although it still maintains its width and height. The image moves to the right side of the `section` element; the text wraps around on the left. The margin setting keeps the text from touching the edge of the image itself. You will create a similar rule to align images to the left in the next exercise.

Working with the Insert Panel

The Insert panel duplicates key menu commands and makes inserting images and other code elements both quick and easy.

1 In Live view, click the first paragraph under the heading *Education and Events*.

2 Choose Window > Insert to display the Insert panel, if necessary.

3 In the Insert panel, choose the HTML category.

4 Click Image.

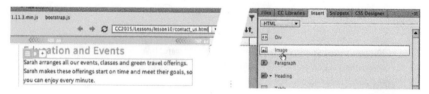

The position assist HUD appears.

5 Click Nest.

The Select Image Source dialog appears.

6 Select **sarah.jpg** from the site images folder. Click OK/Open.

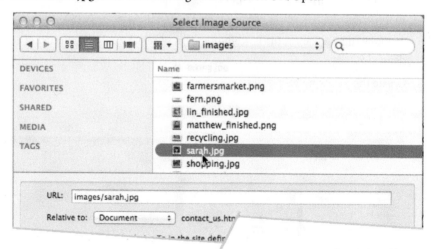

7   In the Property inspector, enter **Sarah, GreenStart Events Coordinator**
    in the Alt text field.

8   In the HUD for the image, click the Add Class/ID icon ⊞.
    Type `.flt_lft` and press Enter/Return.

    The name is short for "float left."

9   Use the CSS Source HUD to add the class to **green_styles.css**.
    No media query should be selected.

10 In the CSS Designer, create the following properties in the new rule:

```
float: left
margin-right: 10px.
```

    The image drops down into the paragraph on the left side, with the text
    wrapping to its right.

11 Save the file.

Another way to insert images in your webpage is by using the Insert menu.

Using the Insert Menu

The Insert menu duplicates all the commands you'll find in the Insert panel. Some
users find the menu faster and easier to use. Others prefer the ready nature of the
panel, which allows you to focus on one element and quickly insert multiple copies
of it at once. Feel free to alternate between the two methods as desired or even
create your own custom keyboard shortcuts. In this exercise, you will use the Insert
menu to add images.

1   Click the first paragraph under the heading *Transportation Analysis*.

2   Choose Insert > Image, or press Ctrl+Alt+I/Cmd+Option+I.

The position assist dialog appears.

3   Click Nest.

The Select Image Source dialog appears.

4   Navigate to the images folder in Chapter 11.
Select the file **eric.png** and click Open.

The **eric.png** image appears in the Dreamweaver layout. Once the classes have been created and defined, you simply have to add the appropriate class using the HUD.

5   Click the Add Class/ID icon and type: `.flt_rgt`

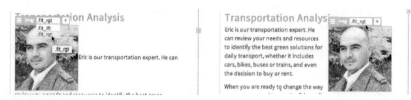

As you type, the class will appear in the hinting menu. You can click the name or use the arrow keys to highlight it, and you can press Enter/Return to select it. As soon as the class is selected, the image floats to the right side of the paragraph.

6   In the Property inspector, type **Eric, Transportation Research Coordinator** in the Alt text field.

7   Save all files.

So far, you have inserted web-compatible image formats. But Dreamweaver is not limited to the file types GIF, JPEG, and PNG; it can work with other file types too. In the next exercise, you will learn how to insert a Photoshop document (PSD) into a webpage.

Inserting Non-web File Types

Although most browsers will display only the **web-compliant** image formats described earlier, Dreamweaver also allows you to use other formats; the program will then automatically convert the file to a compatible format on the fly.

Web Compliant

Compatible with webpages. Web-compliant assets can be insert into a web-page and displayed in a browser.

1   Click the first paragraph under the heading *Research and Development*.

2   Choose Insert > Image.
Nest the image in the first paragraph.
Navigate to the Chapter 11/resources folder.
Select **lin.psd**.

3   Click OK/Open to insert the image.

The image appears in the layout, and the Image Optimization dialog opens; it acts as an intermediary that allows you to specify how and to what format the image will be converted.

4   Observe the options in the Preset and Format menus.

The presets allow you to select predetermined options that have a proven track record for web-based images. The Format menu allows you to specify your own custom settings from among five options: GIF, JPEG, PNG 8, PNG 24, and PNG 32.

5   Choose JPEG High For Maximum Compatibility from the Presets menu. Note the Quality setting.

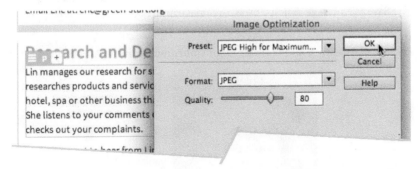

Note: The Image Optimization dialog displays the final file size of the image, indicating how much compression is being applied.

This Quality setting produces a high-quality image with a moderate amount of compression. If you lower the Quality setting, you automatically increase the compression level and reduce the file size; increase the Quality setting for the opposite effect. The secret to effective design is to select a good balance between quality and compression. The default setting for the JPEG High preset is 80, which is sufficient for your purposes.

6 Click OK to convert the image.

Note: When an image has to be converted this way, Dreamweaver usually saves the converted image into the site's default images folder. This is not the case when the images inserted are web-compatible. So before you insert an image, you should be aware of its current location in the site and move it to the proper folder first, if necessary.

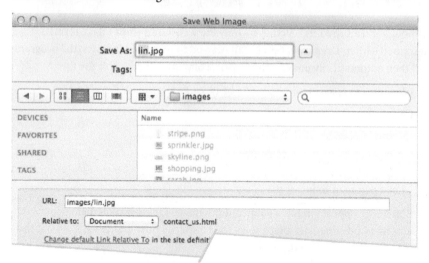

The Save Web Image dialog appears with the name lin entered in the Save As field. Dreamweaver will add the .jpg extension to the file automatically. Be sure to save the file to the default site images folder. If Dreamweaver does not automatically point to this folder, navigate to it before saving the file.

7 Click Save.

The Save Web Image dialog closes. The image in the layout is now linked to the JPEG file saved in the default images folder.

8 Enter **Lin, Research and Development Coordinator** in the Alt text field.

Tip: The image HUD and the Property inspector can be used interchangeably to enter alt text.

The image appears in Dreamweaver at the insertion point position. The image has been resampled to 72 ppi but still appears at its original dimensions, so it's larger than the other images in the layout. You can resize the image in the Property inspector.

9 If necessary, click the Toggle Size Constrain icon 🔒 to display the closed lock. Change the Width value to **150px** and press Enter/Return.

Note: Whenever you change HTML or CSS properties, you may need to press Enter/Return to complete the modification.

When the lock icon appears closed, the relationship between width and height is constrained, and the two change proportionally to each other: Change one and they both change. The change to the image size is only temporary at the moment, as indicated by the Reset ⊘ and Commit ✔ icons. In other words, the HTML attributes specify the size of the image as 150 pixels by 150 pixels, but the JPEG file holds an image that's still 300 pixels by 300 pixels—four times as many pixels as it needs to have.

10 Click the Commit icon ✔ .

The image is now resized to 150 by 150 pixels permanently.

11 Apply the `flt_lft` class to this image using the HUD. Save all files.

In Live view, the image now appears like the others in the layout; however, this image has a difference. But you can't see it in Live view.

12 Switch to Design view.

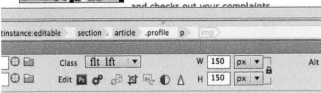

In Design view you can now see an icon in the upper-left corner of the image that identifies this image as a Photoshop Smart Object.

Right Size, Wrong Size

Until the latest mobile devices appeared on the scene, deciding what size and resolution to use for web images was pretty simple. You picked a specific width and height, and saved the image at 72 pixels per inch. That's all you needed to do.

But today, web designers want their sites to work well for all visitors, no matter what type or size device they want to use. So the days of picking one size and one resolution may be gone forever. But what's the answer? At the moment, there isn't one perfect solution.

One trend simply inserts an image that is larger or higher resolution, and resizes it using CSS. This allows the image to display more clearly on high-resolution screens, like Apple's Retina display. The downside is that lower-resolution devices are stuck downloading an image that's larger than they need. This not only slows the loading of the page for no reason, but it can incur higher data charges for smartphone users.

Another idea is to provide multiple images optimized for different devices and resolutions and to use JavaScript to load the proper image as needed. But many users object to using scripts for such basic resources as images. Others want a standardized solution.

So W3C is working on a technique that uses a new element named `<picture>`, which will not require JavaScript at all. Using this new element you would select several images and declare how they should be used and then the browser would load the appropriate image. Unfortunately, this element is so new that Dreamweaver doesn't support it yet, and few browsers even know what it is.

Implementing a responsive workflow for images is outside the scope of this course. For the purposes of these chapters, you will simply learn how to adapt standard web images to the current responsive template using CSS and media queries.

Working with Photoshop Smart Objects

Note: Dreamweaver and Photoshop can work only with the existing quality of an image. If your initial image quality is unacceptable you may not be able to fix it in Photoshop. You will have to re-create the image or pick another.

Unlike other images, Smart Objects maintain a connection to their original Photoshop (PSD) file. If the PSD file is altered in any manner and then saved, Dreamweaver identifies those changes and provides the means to update the web image used in the layout. The following exercise can be completed only if you have Photoshop installed on your computer along with Dreamweaver.

1 If necessary, open **contact_us.html** in Design view.
Scroll down to the **lin.jpg** image in the *Research and Development* section. Observe the icon in the upper-left corner of the image.

The icon indicates that the image is a Smart Object. The icon appears only within Dreamweaver itself; visitors see the normal image in the browser as you saw originally in Live view. If you want to edit or optimize the image, you can simply right-click the image and choose the appropriate option from the context menu.

To make substantive changes to the image, you will have to open it in Photoshop. (If you don't have Photoshop installed, copy Chapter 11/resources/smartobject/ **lin.psd** into the Chapter 11/resources folder to replace the original image, and then skip to step 6.) In this exercise, you will edit the image background using Photoshop.

2   Right-click the **lin.jpg** image.

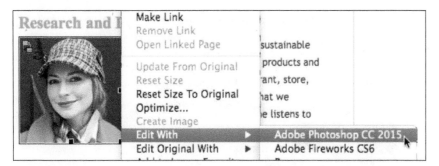

Note: The exact name of the apps appearing in the menu may differ depending on what version of Photoshop you have installed and your operating system. If Photoshop is not installed at all, you may see no program listed.

Choose Edit Original With > Adobe Photoshop CC 2015 from the context menu.

Photoshop CC 2015 launches—if it is installed on your computer—and loads the file.

3   In Photoshop, choose Window > Layers to display the Layers panel, if necessary. Observe the names and states of any existing layers.

The image has two layers: Lin and New Background. New Background is turned off.

4   Click the eye icon 👁 for the New Background layer to display its contents.

The background of the image changes to show a scene from a park.

5   Save the Photoshop file.

6   Switch back to Dreamweaver.
Position the insertion point over the Smart Object icon.

A tool tip appears indicating that the original image has been changed. You don't have to update the image at this time, and you can leave the out-of-date image in the layout for as long as you want. Dreamweaver will continue to monitor its status as long as it's in the layout. But for this exercise, let's update the image.

7   Right-click the image and choose Update From Original from the context menu.

This Smart Object, and any other instances of it, changes to reflect the new background. You can check the status of the Smart Object by positioning the pointer over the image. A tool tip will appear showing that the image is synced. You can also insert the same original PSD image multiple times in the site using different dimensions and image settings under different filenames. All the Smart Objects will stay connected to the PSD and will allow you to update them as the PSD changes.

8 Save the file.

As you can see, Smart Objects have several advantages over a typical image work-flow. For frequently changed or updated images, using a Smart Object can simplify updates to the website in the future.

Copying and Pasting Images from Photoshop

As you build your website, you will need to edit and optimize many images before you use them in your site. Adobe Photoshop is an excellent program for performing these tasks. A common workflow is to make the needed changes to the images and then manually export the optimized GIF, JPEG, or PNG files to the default images folder in your website. But sometimes simply copying images and pasting them directly into your layout is faster and easier.

1 Launch Adobe Photoshop, if necessary.
Open **matthew.tif** from the Chapter 11/resources folder.
Observe the Layers panel.

Note: You should be able to use any version of Photoshop for this exercise. But Creative Cloud subscribers can download and install the latest version at any time.

The image has only one layer. In Photoshop, by default you can copy only one layer at a time to paste into Dreamweaver. To copy multiple layers, you have to merge or flatten the image first, or you have to use the command Edit > Copy Merged to copy images with multiple active layers.

2   Choose Select > All, or press Ctrl+A/Cmd+A, to select the entire image.

3   Select Edit > Copy, or press Ctrl+C/Cmd+C, to copy the image.

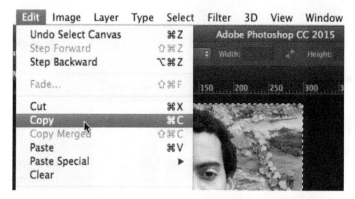

4   Switch to Dreamweaver. Scroll down to the Information Systems section in **contact_us.html**. Insert the insertion point at the beginning of the first paragraph in this section and before the name *Matthew*.

5   Press Ctrl+V/Cmd+V to paste the image from the clipboard.

The image appears in the layout, and the Image Optimization dialog opens.

6   Choose the preset PNG24 for Photos (Sharp Details), and choose PNG 24 from the Format menu. Click OK.

The Save Image dialog appears.

7   Name the image **matthew.png** and select the default site images folder, if necessary. Click Save.

8   If necessary, select the image for Matthew and enter **Matthew, Information Systems Manager** in the Alt text field in the Property inspector.

The **matthew.png** image appears in the layout. As in the earlier exercise, the PNG image is larger than the other images.

9   In the Property inspector, change the image dimensions to **150px** by **150px**. Click the Commit icon ✔ to apply the change. Click OK in the dialog that appears acknowledging that the change is permanent.

Note: Raster images can be scaled down in size without losing quality, but the opposite is not true. Unless a graphic has a resolution higher than 72 ppi, scaling it larger without noticeable degradation may not be possible.

10 Apply the `flt_rgt` class to **matthew.png** using the Class menu in the Properties inspector.

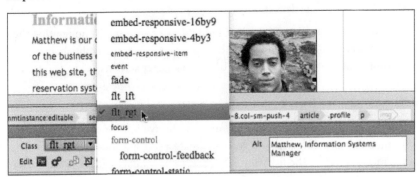

The image appears in the layout at the same size as the other images and aligned to the right. Although this image came from Photoshop, it's not "smart" like a Photoshop Smart Object and can't be updated automatically. It does, however, give you an easy way to load the image into Photoshop or another image editor to perform any modifications.

Tip: If no image-editor program is displayed, you may need to browse for a compatible editor. The executable program file is usually stored in the Program Files folder in Windows and in the Applications folder on a Mac.

11 In the layout, right-click **matthew.png**. Choose Edit With > Photoshop CC 2015 from the context menu.

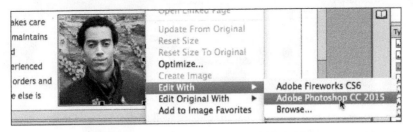

The program launches and displays the PNG file from the site images folder. If you make changes to this image, you merely have to save the file to update the image in Dreamweaver.

Note: The exact name displayed in the menu may differ depending on the program version or operating system installed.

12 In Photoshop, press Ctrl+L/Cmd+L to open the Levels dialog. Adjust the brightness and contrast. Save and close the image.

Note: This exercise is geared specifically to Photoshop, but the changes can be made in most image editors.

Note: Although Dreamweaver automatically reloads any modified file, most browsers won't. You will have to refresh the browser display before you see any changes.

13 Switch back to Dreamweaver. Scroll down to view the **matthew.png** image in the Information Systems section.

The image should be updated in the layout automatically. Since you saved the changes under the original filename, no other action is necessary. This method saves you several steps and avoids any potential typing errors.

14 Save all the files.

Today, the modern web designer has to contend with a multitude of visitors using different browsers and devices. Depending on the size of the images and how they are inserted, you may need to use several different strategies to get them to work effectively in your page design.

For example, the images used on the *Contact Us* page are small enough that they should be usable all the way down to the size needed on a smartphone, but they'll need some work to make them adapt better to smaller screens.

Adapting Images to Smaller Screens

To get the current images to make the most of the available space as the pages respond to the size of the screen, you can create a few specific rules in the appropriate media queries. The first step is to observe how images adapt to the current design, and then you'll create an effective strategy for reformatting them.

1 Open **contact_us.html**.
Preview the page in the default browser.

2 Resize the width of the browser window as necessary to engage each of the existing media queries. Observe how the images adapt to the different designs.

The images are small enough that they adapt well to desktop and tablet screen sizes. On the smallest screens, the text is starting to get crowded, wrapping around the edges of the images. One fix would be to remove the float and center the images.

3 In Dreamweaver, switch to Live view if necessary and click your custom media query (max-width: 426px).

4 In CSS Designer, choose **green_styles.css** > (max-width:426px).
Create a new rule: .flt_lft, .flt_rgt

5   Add the following properties to the new rule:

```
max-width: 95%
display: block
margin: 0px auto
float: none
```

Tip: For this new rule to work, it must appear within the media query markup and after the rules it is designed to reset. If your layout does not look like the screen shot, check the structure and order of your CSS rules.

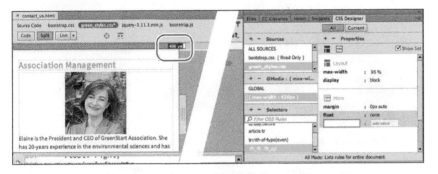

These new settings put the images on their own line and center them. The `max-width` property makes sure that larger images automatically scale down with the screen. In the next exercise, you will insert a much larger image that will have to use a different responsive strategy.

Inserting Images by Drag-and-Drop

Most of the programs in the Creative Suite offer drag-and-drop capabilities. Dreamweaver is no exception.

1   Open **news.html** from the site root folder in Live view.

2   Choose Window > Assets to display the Assets panel, if necessary.

The Assets panel is no longer opened by default in the Dreamweaver workspace. You can leave it as a floating dialog or dock it to keep it out of the way.

3   Drag the Assets panel to dock it beside the Files tab, if necessary.

4   In the Assets panel, click the Images icon 🖾.

5   Drag **skyline.png** from the panel, and position the insertion point between the first paragraph and the heading *Green Buildings earn more Green*.

Tip: If you don't see specific image files listed in the Assets panel, click the Refresh icon ↻ to reload site images.

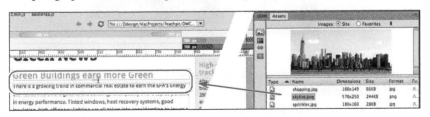

If you position the insertion point correctly, you will see a green line between the heading and the paragraph, indicating where the image will be inserted.

Unlike the images used in the previous exercises, **skyline.png** was inserted between the <h2> and the <p> elements. The image is also too large for the column. Part of it is obscured behind Sidebar 2. Luckily, Dreamweaver has a new built-in way to deal with just this situation.

6 Click the Edit HTML Attributes icon ⊟ on the new image.

The HTML Attributes HUD appears.

7 Select the Make Image Responsive checkbox.

The image now conforms to the width of the column. But what happens when the screen gets smaller? You can check the behavior in Live view, or you can preview the page in a browser window.

8 Enter **Green buildings are top earners** in the Property inspector's Alt text field.

9 Save all files.

10 Drag the Scrubber to the left, and observe how the image adapts to the changes to the layout.

The image scales automatically as the document window changes sizes. The option in the HTML Attributes HUD applies the Bootstrap `.img-responsive` class to the image. This class forces the image to fit within the existing element and scale as needed.

Optimizing Images with the Property Inspector

Optimized web images try to balance image dimensions and quality against file size. Sometimes you may need to optimize graphics that have already been placed on the page. Dreamweaver has built-in features that can help you achieve the smallest possible file size while preserving image quality. In this exercise, you'll use tools in Dreamweaver to scale, optimize, and crop an image for the web.

1   If necessary, open **news.html** in Design view or switch to it.

2   Insert the insertion point at the beginning of the paragraph under the heading "Shopping green saves energy".
    Choose Insert > Image.
    Insert **farmersmarket.png** from the site images folder.

3   Enter **Buy local to save energy** in the Alt text field.

4   Apply the f1t_rgt class to the image.

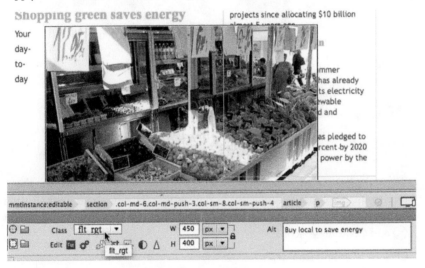

The image is too large. There is barely any room for the image in the column. It could really use some cropping. To save time, you can use tools in Dreamweaver to fix the image composition.

5   If necessary, choose Window > Properties to display the Property inspector.

Whenever an image is selected, image-editing options appear to the right of the image source field in the Property inspector. The buttons here allow you to edit the image in Photoshop or Fireworks or to adjust various settings in place. See the sidebar "Dreamweaver's graphic tools" at the end of the chapter for an explanation of each button.

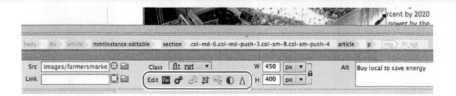

There are two ways to reduce the dimensions of an image in Dreamweaver. The first method changes the size of the image temporarily by imposing user-defined dimensions.

6   Select **farmersmarket.png**. If necessary, click the Toggle Size Constrain icon 🔒 in the Property inspector to lock the image proportions.
Change the image width to **350 pixels** and press the Tab key.

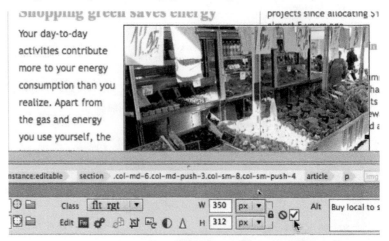

Tip: Dimensions may also be entered manually if you know the final proportions.

When the size constraint is locked, the height automatically conforms to the new width. Note that Dreamweaver indicates that the new size is not permanent by displaying the current specifications in bold and also by displaying the Reset ⊘ and Commit ✔ icons.

7   Click the Commit icon ✔.

A dialog appears that indicates the change will be permanent.

8   Click OK.

Dreamweaver can also crop images.

9   With the image still selected, click the Crop icon ⊠ in the Property inspector.

A dialog appears indicating that the action will permanently change the image.

10 Click OK.

Crop handles appear slightly inset from the edges of the image. We want to crop the width but not the height.

11 Drag the crop handles to set the image to a width of 300 pixels and a height of 312 pixels.

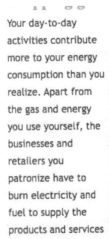

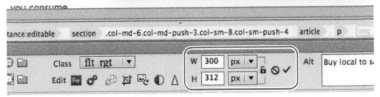

12 Press Enter/Return to apply the change.

13 Save all files.

Most designers will edit and resize images prior to bringing them into Dreamweaver, but it's nice to know that these tools are available for any last-minute changes or fast turnarounds.

In this chapter, you learned how to insert images and Smart Objects into a Dreamweaver page, copy and paste from Photoshop, and use the Property inspector to edit images.

There are numerous ways to create and edit images for the web. The methods examined in this chapter show but a few of them and are not meant to recommend or endorse one method over another. Feel free to use whatever methods and workflow you desire based on your own situation and expertise.

Dreamweaver's Graphic Tools

All Dreamweaver's graphic tools appear in the Property inspector when an image is selected in Design view. Here are the seven tools:

Edit—Opens the selected image in the defined external graphics editor if you have one installed. You can assign a graphics-editing program to any given file type in the File Types/Editors category of the Preferences dialog. The button's image changes according to the program chosen. For example, if Fireworks is the designated editor for the image type, a Fireworks icon **Fw** is shown; if Photoshop is the editor, you'll see a Photoshop icon **Ps**. If neither app is installed you will see a generic edit icon ✎.

Edit Image Settings—Opens the Image Optimization dialog, allowing you to apply user-defined optimization specifications to the selected image.

Update from Original—Updates any placed Smart Object to match any changes to the original source file.

Crop—Permanently removes unwanted portions of an image. When the Crop tool is active, a bounding box with a series of control handles appears within the selected image. You can adjust the bounding box size by dragging the handles or by entering the final dimensions. When the box outlines the desired portion of the image, double-click the graphic to apply the cropping.

Resample—Permanently resizes an image. The Resample tool is active only when an image has been resized.

Brightness and Contrast—Offers user-selectable adjustments to an image's brightness and contrast; a dialog presents, for each value, sliders that can be adjusted independently. A live preview is available so that you can evaluate adjustments before committing to them.

Sharpen—Affects the enhancement of image details by raising or lowering the contrast of pixels on a scale from 0 to 10. As with the Brightness and Contrast tool, Sharpen offers a real-time preview.

You can undo most graphics operations by choosing Edit > Undo

The Web and Ethics

When you present information that you gather from research in a website, business report or proposal, your audience has the right to expect that the information is reliable, accurate, and complete. To meet those expectations, as a researcher you have ethical responsibilities. The following six guidelines address both how to gather information and how to report it.

- **Use reputable sources.** If you use **secondary sources**, take responsibility to ensure that those sources are credible using the criteria of authorship, accuracy, and age. Also, ensure the information can be verified. For example, imagine you are conducting research to help your company decide whether or not to use direct mail advertising sent through the U.S. mail. You want to be able to report on the environmental impact of mail that people discard. What would be the best source to cite: Wikipedia, a company that is marketing software for electronic direct mail, or the United States Environmental Protection Agency? If you originally found useful information in Wikipedia, look at the reference list at the end of the article and see if you can verify the information in a more credible source. Then cite the more credible source.

> **Secondary sources**
>
> Research that some-one else has already collected and made available.

- **Cite all sources.** In business research, just as in academic research, you are responsible for citing sources for all ideas and opinions that are not your own by giving credit to the original writers. In addition, you are responsible for citing facts that are not general knowledge. Source citations for statistics and other facts help your audience evaluate the accuracy of the information. Imagine, for example, that you want to report the unemployment rate in the United States. The credibility of that "fact" may differ depending on whether you got the information from a blog on the web or from the Bureau of Labor Statistics.

- **Ensure that all interview and survey sources provide informed consent.** When you interview or survey people—especially when the survey is not anonymous—let those people know how you plan to use the information and if they may experience any negative consequences from the way you use the data. For example, imagine you are interviewing residents of a town to identify opinions for and against building a new shopping mall. In conducting this research, you need to ensure that people know you will be quoting them in a report to the city council. They also need to know that the city council will use the results to help decide whether to provide a zoning variance for a shopping mall. Once your interview subjects have this information, you need to be sure that they consent to their responses being used this way.

- **Report research accurately.** Be sure that you understand the intention of a source before reporting it. Do not take quotations out of context, report data in a misleading way, or make claims that your research cannot support. For example, if your research consisted of interviewing 10 customers about to enter a coffee store, you cannot say "According to our interviews, consumers prefer coffee over tea." You have data from only 10 people. You do not have enough data to support the larger conclusion. In addition, your sample may be biased as you are interviewing people who are likely to be coffee drinkers. Similarly, if your data about economic growth came from a reputable source published in 2002, you cannot say, "According to the International Economics Statistics Database, Equatorial Guinea has the fastest-growing economy in the world." That was true in 2002, but is it true now? It would be more accurate and ethical to say, "In 2002, Equatorial Guinea had the fastest-growing economy in the world."

- **Include all relevant information.** You may find it tempting to report only research that supports the position you want to argue. However, if you find information that contradicts your position, you have an ethical responsibility to address it in your report. For example, suppose you plan to argue that your company should not advertise through direct mail but instead use email advertising. You'd like to be able to show that direct mail is not environmentally friendly because it contributes significantly to the municipal solid waste stream. In researching, however, you find this fact, showing that the contribution is not as significant as you originally believed. The most recent research by the U.S. Environmental Protection Agency showed that standard mail, which includes direct bulk mailing, comprised only 1.9 percent of municipal solid waste. Instead of ignoring this fact and maintaining your original position, choose one of these other options:

1. Concede the fact and explain why it does not undermine your position. "Although direct mail advertising represents only a small percentage of our solid waste stream, every bit of extra solid waste costs money for disposal and takes up valuable space in landfills."

2. Eliminate this environmental argument from your report and stress other arguments against direct mail advertising.

3. Modify your position. You may not expect to find information that convinces you to change your point of view, but this routinely happens when people conduct thorough research.

Ethical Computer Use

Ethics
Moral principles.

How people use computers, including networks and e-mail, can affect other people. People who practice **ethics** behave morally. Ethical computer users respect others, and make sure their actions do not harm anyone.

Acceptable Use Policies

One way you can act ethically is to follow your school district's **acceptable use policy,** or **AUP.** These policies identify the responsibilities of Internet use. They spell out certain rules of behavior and explain the consequences of breaking those rules. Many businesses use AUPs, too, to govern the way workers use company-owned computers. An AUP may include the following ethical guidelines:

- Do not visit Web sites that contain content that does not meet community standards.

- Do not use language that is profane, abusive, or impolite.

- Do not copy copyrighted material or damage computer equipment belonging to the school.

- Do respect the privacy of other people. Schools and businesses may restrict the content that users can access from internal computers. For example, they may **censor**, or block, specific sites that they determine are inappropriate.

They may also use a **filter** to block access to sites. Disabling the filters or otherwise accessing blocked sites is considered breaking the AUP, and may result in punishment.

Possible Penalties

People who do not follow these rules may face consequences. They might lose privileges or be suspended from school activities. Very serious violations, such as using a school computer to threaten someone, may require police involvement.

Accessing Data from the Web

The Web provides access to a wide array of files and information. You can find pictures, text, videos, and audio files available for the taking. Downloading content from the Web can be risky. Viruses and malware may be transmitted through a webpage or a downloaded file. Before downloading any content to your computer or smart phone you should use an antivirus or antimalware program to check the file. You should also check the copyright for the file to make sure you have legal permission to download it.

Copyright Laws

Copyright is the legal right to make copies, license, and otherwise use a literary, musical, or artistic work. Copyright protects a person's work like songs, paintings, and books. Copyright laws protect people from the misuse of their intellectual property by others. Someone who pretends that another person's work is his or her own has broken the law by committing copyright infringement. He or she has stolen another person's work.

Acceptable use policy (AUP)

A policy—published by a school district, business, or other organization—that identifies rules of behavior that must be followed by anyone using that organization's telecommunications equipment, computers, network, or Internet connection

Censor

To ban or block.

Filter

To select or display items based on whether they meet or match specific criteria; also, a feature in some e-mail programs that can delete certain messages or file messages in folders.

Copyright

The right to control use of creative, literary, or artistic work.

Intellectual property

Someone's creative, literary, or artistic work.

Federal laws that involve **copyright** protect individuals and companies from the theft or misuse of their **intellectual property**, such as creative, literary, or artistic work. Copyright exists as soon as a work is created, but the creator can register it with the U.S. Copyright Office. It is a crime to copy this kind of work without the permission of the person who owns the copyright to it.

Copyright Your Work

Basically, anytime you create something, it is copyrighted the moment you create it. You can strengthen this by providing a copyright notice that doing one of the following copyrights your intellectual work.

- Attach a copyright notice by using the copyright symbol @ followed by the word Copyright, i.e. @Copyright.

- Strengthen this basic copyright even more by applying a year of publication and author, i.e. @Copyright 2017 by Lake Powell Adventures, LLC

- Complete required forms and process for officially copyrighting your work with the U.S. Government. Visit their website at http://www.copyright.gov. This process can take many years to complete due to the complexity of the process as well as the number of backlogged filings from others.

- Mail a copy of the work to yourself so that it goes through the public mail system and gets a date stamp of when it was mailed. Do not open this mail, as it is official proof that you created the work prior to the date stamp of the mail. This is often called the poor man's copyright.

Copyright work is protected from the moment of creation through the owner's life and then for an addition 70 years after the owner's death. This varies slightly for any works for hire, which are work you create for someone else that is paying you. Work for hire copyright protection is slightly longer, 95 years from the publication date or 120 years after the creation date - whichever one is shorter.

Fair Use Doctrine

The use of copyrighted material in a review, in research, in schoolwork, or in a professional publication, which does not necessarily require permission from the material's owner.

Copyright and Fair Use Doctrine

If the content is protected by copyright, you must have permission from the copyright holder to use the work. However, part of copyright law called the **Fair Use Doctrine** allows you to use a limited amount of copyrighted material without permission for educational purposes. For example, you can quote a few lines of a song or a passage from a book. Similarly, an author may issue a creative commons license allowing others to use the work.

Respect intellectual property and "fair use" of other people's material. Under U.S. copyright law and the doctrine of fair use, you may include brief quotations from others' work in your reports and presentations. However, you cannot quote substantial portions of another work in your own, even if you cite that work, because you are benefitting from that person's intellectual property. If you plan to draw heavily from someone else's text, it is safest to receive written permission from the copyright owner.

There is no such thing as an International copyright though there are agreements among various countries to honor any copyrighted work and therefore allow for prosecution if someone breaks the law. Breaking a copyright is stealing and can be prosecuted in court for monetary damages. Each case is different and the justice system assesses the case and awards damages. Many cases settle out of court due to the complexities of this type of law and the difficulty in determining the monetary damages.

Creative Commons License

A content owner, such as an author, composer, or software developer may provide a **creative commons license** so others may share, use, or even modify the work. The owner may set limitations on the usage, such as allowing students or teacher's unlimited use, but restricting commercial use. Some software developers create **open-source software**, which means they make the source code for their programs available to the public so users can change the way it works.

Trademarks and Patents

Some intellectual property is protected by trademark or patent. Trademarks are created to protect words, names, sounds, colors, and symbols that are used to distinguish goods and/or services that are sold by others. A **trademark** is a symbol that indicates that a brand or brand name is legally protected and cannot be used by other businesses.

There are different ways to trademark your work. If you want to trademark a name, logo, graphic or design, just like with copyright, you can use a ™ symbol in the upper right corner of your work, i.e. Lake Powell Adventures™. You can apply for a Federal Registration Certificate form the United States Patent and Trademark office. This lets you use the ® symbol after the work name.

If you use someone's trademark or a trademark that is confusingly similar as your own, this is called trademark infringement and you can be liable for a civil action or lawsuit in either federal or state court. If the trademark owner can prove infringement you might need to pay the them money for damages sustained. Typically the process begins with a court order or "cease and desist injunction" requesting that you stop using the trademark and then can be followed with a lawsuit.

Trademarks are only valid in the country that they are registered. You need to register for a trademark with a lawyer through the U.S. Patent and Trademark Office. Once granted you can use the official trademark symbol - ® after the trademark symbol to establish official ownership of the trademark. If you use someone else's trademark in a web site, you must ask them for permission in writing.

A **patent** is the exclusive right to make, use, or sell a device or process. Many types of inventions can be patented. You must apply for a patent through the United

---

Creative commons license

A license that enable the free distribution of an otherwise copyrighted work.

Open-source software

Software for which the source code is made available to the public.

Trademark

A symbol that indicates that a brand or brand name is legally protected and cannot be used by other businesses.

Patent

The exclusive right to make, use, or sell a device or process.

Citation

A reference to a source that gives credit to the source and provides the tools a reader needs to locate the source on his or her own.

Plagiarism

Illegal copying of creative material owned by another person

Get Clear Answers to Murky Copyright Questions

Find out what is covered by copyright, what isn't, and how to secure a copyright for your own work. Go to copyright.gov/help/faq/ for answers to common copyright questions.

States Patent and Trademark Office. A patent is an intellectual property right that the U.S. grants an inventor. It protects the invention of a product or of a new process. Patent infringement consists of using someone else's invention as your own and is settled much like a patent infringement with a "cease and desist injunction" followed by a lawsuit in federal court. Patents are not recognized worldwide and are only valid in the country that they are filed. If you want to use someone else's patent, you can contact them and try and secure a license to grant you the right to use the patent in your product or service.

Cite Your Source

If you use information you find on the Web in your work, you must give credit to the source. You do this by inserting a reference to the source, called a **citation**, in a footnote, endnote, or bibliography. A proper citation gives credit to the source, and provides the tools a reader needs to locate the source on his or her own. Some Web sites have features that automatically generate the citation information for you.

Plagiarism

If you do not cite your sources you are guilty of **plagiarism**, which is the unauthorized use of another person's idea's or creative work without giving that person credit. Plagiarism is equivalent to stealing another person's work and passing it off as your own. The consequences of plagiarism can be quite significant. If you plagiarize work in school, you may have to redo the assignment or lose credit all together. Your school may also take disciplinarian actions, like detention. In the professional world, the consequences of plagiarism are even more significant. A professional who plagiarizes work suffers a loss to his or her reputation and may face legal ramifications, such as a lawsuit.

To avoid plagiarism you just need to properly cite your source. You should insert a citation when you quote, summarize, or paraphrase someone else, use someone else's idea, or reference someone else's work. In a works cited section or footnote, you tell the reader the source of your credited information.

Avoiding the Problem

Fair use

The use of copyrighted material in a review, in research, in schoolwork, or in a professional publication, which does not necessarily require permission from the material's owner.

Public domain

Without a copyright.

If you want to quote someone, or use content created by someone else, such as a song or picture, make sure that you identify the source of the quotation or owner of the content. Placing a quote in a school assignment is usually considered **fair use**, or acceptable with the correct citation. Written permission may be required for long quotes or if you use content for commercial use, such as advertising. You may also quote or use content that is in the **public domain**, meaning the copyright has expired, or is no longer valid.

Taking Responsibility for Your Actions

As a web designer, you may not always easily identify the best and most ethical course of action to take. However, a ethical businessperson recognizes the responsibility to try. Jeff Bezos, the CEO of Amazon.com, illustrated this characteristic in handling an ethical and public relations crisis. Amazon realized it was inadvertently acting unethically by selling electronic access to books that it did not own the digital copyrights to sell, including George Orwell's novel *1984*. To correct that ethical mistake, Amazon deleted the book from customers' online libraries and returned the purchase price to the customers.

Amazon thought this was the ethical thing to do, but customers who had purchased the book were angry. What right did Amazon have to delete the book from their libraries without any warning or communication? Imagine how you would feel if you needed a book from your electronic library to study for an exam the next day and the book had simply disappeared. Customers did not expect this type of treatment from a company that presents itself as customer-centric. While Bezos could easily have explained or defended his actions, instead he posted an apology on the Amazon discussion forum, taking responsibility for a decision that hurt customers, acknowledging that the company deserved the criticism it received, and vowing to make better decisions moving forward. Customer response in the discussion forum was overwhelmingly positive, and the media picked up the story, praising Bezos for taking responsibility for the company's actions.

Practicing Netiquette

The Internet has an informal set of rules for expected behavior called **netiquette**. As an ethical computer user, you have a responsibility to use netiquette at all times. Some ways to practice netiquette include:

Netiquette

An informal set of rules for how to behave online.

- Send e-mails only to people who really need to see a message.
- Keep e-mail messages short.
- Avoid sending extremely large files via e-mail.
- Do not use impolite or rude language when communicating online.
- Do not pretend to be someone else when communicating online.
- Do not use someone else's work without citing the source.
- Do not share files illegally. The rules of netiquette are similar to general standards for good behavior. If you go to a search engine and type "netiquette," you will find many Web sites on the topic.

Brand

An image or identity assigned to a person or product based on how they are perceived by others.

Managing Your Online Identity

Online, people learn about you by what you post and what sites you frequent. You can use your online profile to both promote a positive image, or **brand**, of yourself, and to protect your identity. Building your brand means making sure everything you post or display online supports the reputation and character you want people to associate with you. You can protect your identity by making sure you effectively manage all of your online profiles, including on gaming sites and on social networking sites such as Twitter, LinkedIn, and Face- book. Be sure to set privacy settings and to never give out your personal information in your profiles. You might also maintain both a professional and a personal identity. For example, you might have two e-mail accounts; one you use for professional and business communication such as a job search, and one you use for personal communication with your friends and family.

Cybercriminal

Someone who uses the Internet or private networks to violate state or federal laws.

Cyberbullying

To use electronic communications to threaten or harass someone.

Don't Be a Cybercriminal

When you use the Internet it can feel as if no one can identify who you really are. As a result, behavior online can often turn inappropriate, rude, and even illegal. Some users are Internet trolls, which means they go on sites specifically to post rude, mean comments intended to upset people. Remember, you can be tracked; someone will figure out who you are.

Whether you are playing a game online or posting a comment on a web site, it is important to behave in the online space as you would in the real world. Always be courteous and respectful. If you post a negative review of a product or service, make sure it is true and accurate and not mean or spiteful. Poor reviews can be damaging to a business. Never insult or bully an individual, or post comments that are untrue. **Cyberbullying** is a crime.

Sometimes it is not mean comments that can get you into trouble. Many people flirt using electronic communications. Messages can be forwarded or posted on social networking sites for all to see. Sending inappropriate text and pictures electronically is called sexing, and in some circumstances it is illegal.

End-of-Chapter Activities

Review Questions

Directions: Choose the correct answer for each question.

1. What are the three factors that determine raster image quality?
   a. Resolution, image dimensions, and color depth.
   b. Resolution, image compression and color depth
   c. Pixels per inch, color depth and image compression
   d. None of the above

2. What file format(s) are specifically designed for use on the web?
   a. GIF and JPEG
   b. PNG, and SVG Property Inspector
   c. PSD, JPG and GIF
   d. A and B
   e. All of the above

3. PPI stands for what?
   a. Photographic Picture Information
   b. Pixels Per Inch
   c. Pre-Photographic Image
   d. Pixels Per Image

4. When optimizing pictures for Web what file format creates the best image with the lowest file size?
   a. JPG
   b. GIF
   c. PNG
   d. SVG

5. When optimizing vector images for web what file format creates the best image with the lowest file size
   a. JPG
   b. GIF
   c. PNG
   d. SVG

6. What panel lets you quickly view and insert graphic images?
   a. Files panel
   b. Property inspector
   c. CSS Designer
   d. Assets panel

7. What devices would be good to use as a Web developer
   a. Computer with lots of processing power and primary storage
   b. Secondary storage devices
   c. Flash, jump, thumb, pen drives, and memory cards
   d. Cloud storage and FTP site access
   e. All of the above

8. When adding images to a webpage, what tag is important to use for making the image accessible to screen readers and other assistive technology?
   a. <h1> tag
   b. <alt> tag
   c. <p> tag
   d. <article> tag

9. True or False: If your initial image quality is not acceptable, you can increase the size of the image in both physical size and in PPI to make it better
   a. True
   b. False

10. What image correction and edits can you make directly in Dreamweaver?
    a. Crop
    b. Resample
    c. Brightness & Contrast
    d. Sharpening
    e. All of these above

Essay Questions

Directions: Respond to each question by writing your answers in complete sentences and paragraphs. Be thorough in your answers.

1. Describe at least two methods for inserting an image into a webpage using Dreamweaver.

2. True or false: All graphics have to be optimized outside of Dreamweaver. Explain your answer.

3. What is the advantage of using a Photoshop Smart Object over copying and pasting an image from Photoshop?

4. Describe appropriate behavior and adherence to acceptable use policies when accessing and using online resources

5. Explain and demonstrate ethical use of technology and online resources;

6. Explain the difference between copyright and trademarks

7. Explain the concept of intellectual property laws, including copyright, trademarks, and patents and consequences of violating each type of law.

8. List the consequences of plagiarism.

9. Describe copyright and trademark intellectual property laws and regulations, including demonstrating correct acquisition and citation of sources.

10. Describe Fair Use and Creative Commons Licenses as well as describe appropriate behavior and adherence to Acceptable Use Policies when accessing and using online resources.

11. Describe cloud storage services for computer input, processed and output data. List examples of vendors offering these services.

Critical Thinking Project-Insert Images into the Lake Powell Website

Next you'll add images to the Lake Powell web site as well as develop the page layout further.

Insert an Image on the Home Page

The home page could use some more work. In this exercise add an image and make it accessible and responsive.

1. On your computer create a local root folder as directed by your teacher. Name the folder **lakepowell_xx**. Copy the class data files from the Chapter11/Data files/lakepowell_xx directory as instructed by your teacher.

2. Open the index.html webpage. Switch to Live view.

3. Insert a picture under the main content area by double-clicking at the end of the second paragraph. The orange box replaces the blue HUD indicating that you are in text-editing mode. Press Enter/Return to create a new line. Open the Asset panel by selecting its tab from either the panel group or, if it is not opened, choosing Window>Assets. Locate the **lp_view3.jpg** file and select it. Click the Insert button. In the Position Assist, click the Nest option.

4. Add text to the <alt> element to make this image accessible by clicking the Edit HTML Attribute icon in the upper-left corner of the image HUD. Type **Lake Powell offers many spectacular views, there's something new around every bend!**

5. Make the image responsive so that it sizes to smaller screen sizes by clicking the Make Image Responsive option.

6. Save all files and preview the page in a browser. Adjust the browser window size to see the image resize.

Format Images with CSS

The Contact Us page could use some images to make it more friendly and inviting for the visitor to use. Personalize this page with images of the Lake Powell Adventure staff. You'll also add a background image to the .sidebarRt class rule that is applied to the Sign Up for Our Newsletter <article> element and then a non-web Photoshop image to the left Weather sidebar.

1. Open the **contact.html** webpage. Switch to Design view.

2. First insert the staff images. Click at the beginning of the first paragraph under the heading Lake Powell General Questions. Choose Insert>Image and in the Insert dialog locate and click the **mike.jpg** file. Click Open and the image is inserted into the paragraph.

3. Repeat step 2 to insert the **jim.jpg** at the beginning of the first paragraph under the Houseboat & Jet Ski Rentals heading. Next insert the image joanne.jpg by dragging from the Assets panel and then dropping it beginning of the first paragraph under the Hiking and Rock Climbing heading. As you can see there are many different techniques to add images to your webpages in Dreamweaver.

4. Add Alternate text to all three images by clicking the image and then in the Property inspector, click in the Alt field and type the following respectively:
   a. mike.jpg–Mike Brown, Owner and CEO of Lake Powell Adventures
   b. jim.jpg–Jim Owen, Captain and Booking Agent
   c. joanne.jpg–Joanne Weatherby, Outdoor enthusiast

5. Apply CSS by creating two new class rules to float the staff images left and right. Click the image of Mike in the first paragraph under the Lake Powell General Questions heading. Create a class CSS rule by clicking the Add Class/ID icon and typing **flt_left** in the text field. Press Enter/Return. In the CSS Source HUD, if necessary select **lakepowell.css** from the source drop-down menu and leave the Select a media query setting. Press Enter/Return to complete the class.

6. Set CSS properties for the new rule in the CSS Designer. If necessary click lakepowell. css>GLOBAL and then locate the rule in the Selector window and click it. Create the following properties:
   a. float: left
   b. margin-right: 10px
   c. margin-bottom: 10px
   d. border: solid 2px #900

7. Float the image of Jim to the right by creating a new rule. Repeat steps 5-6 and create a class rule named **flt_right**. Set the properties to the following:
   a. float: right
   b. margin-left: 10px
   c. margin-bottom: 10px
   d. border: solid 2px #900

8. Apply the **flt_left** class rule to the image of Joanne by clicking this image and then in the Property inspector click the Class dropdown menu and select **flt_left**.

9. Next add a new CSS3 property to these three images by clicking to select the image and then clicking the Edit HTML Attribute icon in the upper-left corner of the image HUD. Select the **rounded corner clipping** option from **Clip to space**.

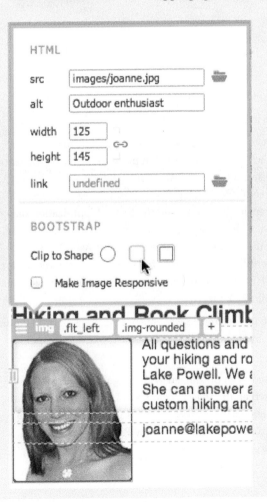

10. Repeat step 9 and apply the rounded corner clipping option to the other two images.

11. Add a background image to the Sign Up for Our Newsletter by adding properties to the **.sidebarRt** class assigned to the <article> element. In the CSS Designer if necessary click lakepowell.css>GLOBAL and then add a new rule. Add a background image by clicking the Background category icon. Click in the URL field and then click the Browse folder icon. In the Select Image Source dialog, click to select the **lizards.jpg** file. Click Open to set this image as the background image. Also set a background-color property for this rule to #C93.

12. Add a few more properties to the **.sidebarRt** class rule. Set the following additional properties to this rule:
   a. color: #fff
   b. padding-top: 0px
   c. padding-bottom: 100px
   d. padding-right: 10px
   e. padding-left: 10px
   f. text-align: center
   g. text-shadow: 5px 5px 10px #663333

13. Save all files and preview the page in a browser.

14. Finally add a non-web image to the contact.html page. This image will go under the We Are Here To Help heading. Click to set your insertion point to the left of the text of the first bullet point. Choose Insert > Image. Nest the image in the first paragraph. Navigate to the Chapter11/resources folder. Select lp_view2.psd. Click OK/Open to insert the image. The image appears in the layout, and the Image Optimization dialog opens; it acts as an intermediary that allows you to specify how and to what format the image will be converted. Observe the options in the Preset and Format menus. The presets allow you to select predetermined options that have a proven track record for web-based images. Choose JPEG High For Maximum Compatibility from the Presets menu. Set the Quality setting to 80. Click Ok.

15. In the Save Web Image dialog save the optimized web image as lp_view2.jpg. Make sure you are in the local root directory by clicking the Site Root button and then opening the images folder. Click Save.

16. The image is converted and inserted as an optimized Web image. Notice, that in the Design view this image is off the screen to the left. Switch to Live view to see the image in the page layout. It is nested in a bullet, to correct this click to the left of the image to set your insertion point before the image and then in the Property inspector click to deselect the Unordered Bullet button.

17. The image is also too large. You can manually adjust the size of the image by first clicking the image. Then in the Property inspector make sure the Toggle Size Constraint is locked for the Width and Height field and then click the Width (W) field and type **300**. The height changes due to the dimensions being constrained. Click the **Confirm** option to confirm this edit. The original file has been altered to a smaller size.

18. Add Alternate text to the image by clicking in the Alt field and typing **Lake Powell spectacular view**.

19. Save all files and preview in a browser.

20. Create a new CSS rule to format this image through the parent .left_background class rule that is applied to the <article> element. In the CSS Designer create a new selector class rule named **.left_background**. Set the following properties:
    a. background-color: #C93
    b. padding-bottom: 15px
    c. padding-left: 10px
    d. padding-right: 10px
    e. border: solid 2px #900
    f. padding-top: 15px
    g. text-align: center

21. Make the **lp_view2.jpg** image responsive by clicking the image and then click the Edit HTML Attribute icon in the upper-left corner of the image HUD and then click the Make Image Responsive option. Attach a class rule to this image to create some space below the image and the first by clicking the image and then click **Add Class/ID** in the image HUD. Type **.viewImage** and press Enter/Return. Check that the lakepowell.css is select in the first dropdown menu and then press Enter/Return again to set this new class. Find this new class rule in the CSS Designer and set the following property:
    a. padding-bottom: 10px
    b. margin: auto

22. Save all file and preview in a browser.

Resizing Images for a Smaller Screen

You might have notice that has you resize a browser window and watch the images display in the smaller screen area, that the images on the contact.html page would look better centered in the layout. You can control this through CSS.

1. Open the **contact.html** webpage. Switch to Live view and click the max-width: 400px custom media query created in Chapter 10.

2. In the CSS Designer, choose lakepowell.css>(max width: 400px). Create a new group rule named **.flt_left, .flt_right** and add the following properties.
   a. display:block
   b. margin: 0px auto
   c. float: none

3. Save all files and preview in a browser. Resize the browser window to see the images display in the center of the page layout when it reaches the max-width of 628px and 400px.

Edit Image Quality Using Dreamweaver Image Edit Tools

The Houseboat Rentals page could also benefit with the use of images to make it more appealing. Insert a houseboat image and the edit the image right in Dreamweaver.

1. Open the **houseboats.html** webpage. Switch to Design view.

2. Click to set your insertion point at the end of the paragraph in the right <aside> element with **Explore Lake Powell by Boat** heading. Press Enter/Return to create a new line. Choose Insert>Image from the menu bar.

3. In the Select Image Source select **houseboat.jpg** and click Open. In the Property inspector, click in the Alt field and type **Houseboating Lake Powell is fun**.

4. Switch to Live view. If necessary click the **houseboat.jpg** image and make it responsive by clicking the **Edit HTML Attribute** icon in the upper-left corner of the image HUD. Select the **Make image responsive** option.

5. Switch to the Design view and perform some image edits right in Dreamweaver. In the Property inspector click the Crop icon to edit the image. In the message box that displays warning that changes are permanent, click OK. Adjust the cropping outline by clicking and dragging the borders to show less water and foliage. When you have it how you want, double-click in the middle of the cropping outline to apply the crop. The original image is cropped and automatically saved.

6. Click the Brightness and Contrast icon to adjust the brightness of the image. Click OK in the message dialog that displays. In the Brightness and Contrast dialog, lower the brightness by dragging the brightness slider to the left so the image is a little less bright. Click OK when you have the level you want.

7. Finally click the Sharpen icon and click OK to the message dialog. In the Sharpen dialog, drag the slider to the right to increase the sharpness of the image. Click OK to set this level.

8. Save all files and preview in the browser.

Online Portfolio Builder—Develop Your Online Portfolio Website by Adding Images

Develop your online portfolio website by adding images to your pages. Format these elements so that they display nice and are responsive to all window sizes. Follow the basic steps below to create and format these elements.

1. If necessary, create a local root directory and copy any files or folders over to the new local root directory. Define your site as instructed by your teacher.

2. If necessary copy all Web optimized images into the local root directory **images** folder.

3. Open your website pages that you have developed up to this point in the class. Switch to the Design view. Maximize the Dreamweaver workspace to fill the entire screen.

4. Using any of the insert image techniques, Insert>Image from the menu bar, Assets panel or the Insert panel, insert images into your pages.

5. Add text to all <alt> tags for each image to make the accessible.

6. Make any image responsive by clicking the image and then clicking the **Edit HTML Attribute** icon in the upper-left corner of the image HUD

7. Use CSS and Class/ID attributes to format the images so that they display well in all screen sizes.

8. Use Dreamweaver image edit tools to make quick edits to image quality. Make sure you are in Design view to use these tools.

9. Save all files and preview in a browser.

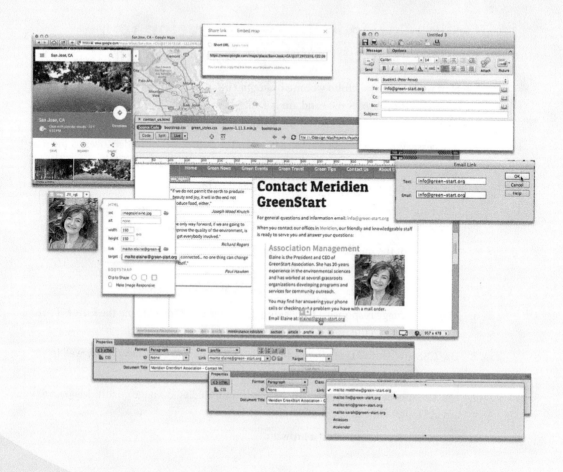

WORKING WITH NAVIGATION

Dreamweaver can create and edit many types of links—from text-based links to image-based links—and does so with ease and flexibility.

Chapter Overview

In this chapter, you'll apply several kinds of links to page elements by doing the following:

- Creating a text link to a page within the same site
- Creating a link to a page on another website
- Creating an email link
- Creating an image-based link
- Creating a link to a location within a page

Hyperlink Basics

The World Wide Web, and the Internet in general, would be a far different place without the hyperlink. Without hyperlinks, HTML would simply be ML (markup language). The *hypertext* in the name refers to the functionality of the hyperlink. So what is a hyperlink?

A hyperlink, or *link*, is an HTML-based reference to a resource available on the Internet or within the computer hosting a web document. The resource can be anything that can be stored on and displayed by a computer, such as a webpage, an image, a movie, a sound file, a PDF—in fact, almost any type of computer file. A hyperlink creates an interactive behavior specified by HTML and CSS, or by the programming language you're using, and is enabled by a browser or other application.

An HTML hyperlink consists of the anchor <a> element and one or more attributes.

Internal and External Hyperlinks

The simplest hyperlink—an internal hyperlink—takes the user to another part of the same document or to another document stored in the same folder or hard drive on the web server that hosts the site. An external hyperlink is designed to take the user to a document or resource outside your hard drive, website, or web host.

Internal and external hyperlinks may work differently, but they have one thing in common: They are enabled in HTML by the <a> *anchor* element. This element designates the address of the destination, or *target*, of the hyperlink, and can then specify how it functions using several attributes. You'll learn how to create and modify the <a> element in the exercises that follow.

Relative vs. Absolute Hyperlinks

A hyperlink address can be written in two ways. When you refer to a target by where it is stored in relation to the current document, it is known as a **relative link**. This is like telling someone that you live next door to the blue house. If she were driving down your street and saw the blue house, she would know where you live. But those directions don't really tell her how to get to your house or even to your neighborhood. A relative link frequently will consist of the resource name and perhaps the folder it is stored within, such as `logo.jpg` or `images/logo.jpg`.

Relative hyperlink

A link to a file, folder, or document that is relative to the current domain or location in the current site.

Sometimes, you need to spell out precisely where a resource is located. In those instances, you need an **absolute hyperlink**. This is like telling someone you live at 123 Main Street in Meridien. This is typically how you refer to resources outside your website. An absolute link includes the entire uniform resource locator, or URL, of the target, and may even include a filename—such as http://forums.adobe.com/index.html—or just a folder within the site.

Both types of links have advantages and disadvantages. Relative hyperlinks are faster and easier to write, but they may not work if the document containing them is saved in a different folder or location in the website. Absolute links always work no matter where the containing document is saved, but they can fail if the targets are moved or renamed. A simple rule that most web designers follow is to use relative links for resources within a site and absolute links for resources outside the site. Of course, whether you follow this rule or not, it's important to test all links before deploying the page or site.

> **Absolute hyperlink**
>
> The complete address to a file or folder. In web design, absolute hyperlinks are used to link to pages outside of the current website to a page, file, or folder in a website with a different domain name.

Creating Internal Hyperlinks

Creating hyperlinks of all types is easy with Dreamweaver. In this exercise, you'll create relative text-based links to pages in the same site, using a variety of methods. You can create links in Design view, Live view, and Code view.

Creating relative links

Dreamweaver provides several methods for creating and editing links. Links can be created in all three program views.

1 Launch Adobe Dreamweaver CC (2015.1 release) or later. If necessary, press F8 to open the Files panel. In the Files panel, expand the Chapter 12 folder as instructed by your teacher. Open **about_us.html** from the site root folder in Live view.

2 In the horizontal menu, position the insertion point over any of the horizontal menu items. Observe the type of insertion point that appears.

The pointer indicates that the menu item is structured as a hyperlink. The styling changes as you position the insertion point over each link and then move it away. The links in the horizontal menu are not editable in the normal way. But this is something you can actually see only in Design view.

3 Switch to Design view.

Position the insertion point over any item of the horizontal menu again.

The "slash" icon ⊘ appears indicating that this section of the page is uneditable. The horizontal menu was not part of one of the editable regions you created in Chapter 9, "Working with Templates." That means it's considered part of the template and is locked with Dreamweaver. To add hyperlinks to this menu, you'll have to first open the template.

4 Choose Window > Assets. In the Assets panel Template category, right-click **mygreen_temp**, and choose Edit from the context menu.

Tip: When editing or removing an existing hyperlink, you don't need to select the entire link; you can just insert the insertion point anywhere in the link text. Dreamweaver assumes you want to change the entire link by default.

5 Switch to Design view, if necessary.

In the horizontal menu, insert the insertion point into the *Green News* link.

The horizontal menu is editable in the template.

6 If necessary, choose Window > Properties to open the Property inspector. Examine the contents of the Link field in the Property inspector.

To create links, the HTML tab must be selected in the Property inspector. The Link field shows a hyperlink placeholder (#). The home page doesn't exist yet, but the link can be created by typing the name of the file or resource into this field.

7   In the Link field, click the Browse for File icon 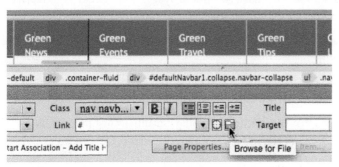.

> **Note:** The link won't have the typical hyperlink appearance—a blue underscore—because of the special formatting you applied to this menu in Chapter 5.

The Select File dialog appears.

8   Navigate to the site root folder, if necessary.
    Select **news.html** from the site root folder. Click Open.

    The link `../news.html` appears in the Link field in the Property inspector.

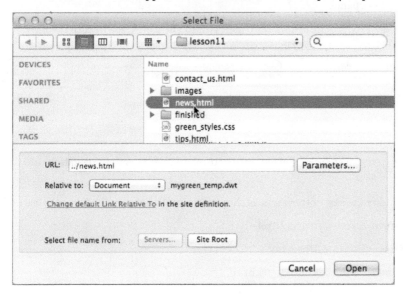

You've created your first text-based hyperlink. Since the template is saved in a subfolder, Dreamweaver adds the path element notation (../) to the filename so that the link properly resolves once the template pages are updated. This notation tells the browser or operating system to look in the parent directory of the current folder. Dreamweaver then rewrites the link simply to "news.html" when the template is applied to a page that is modified automatically based on where the pages are saved. If necessary, you can type links in the field manually too.

9 Insert the insertion point in the *Home* link.

The home page does not exist yet. But that doesn't stop you from entering the link text by hand.

10 In the Link field, select the hash (#) symbol, type `../index.html` to replace the placeholder and press Enter/Return.

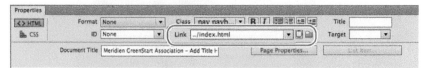

At any time, you may insert a link by typing it manually just this way. But, entering links by hand can introduce a variety of errors that can break the very link you are trying to create. If you want to link to a file that already exists, Dreamweaver offers other interactive ways to create links.

11 Insert the insertion point in the *Green Events* link.

Tip: If a folder in the Files panel contains a page you want to link to but the folder is not open, drag the Point to File icon over the folder, and hold it in place to expand that folder so that you can point to the desired file.

12 Click the Files tab to bring the panel to the top, or choose Window > Files.

You need to make sure you can see the Property inspector and the target file in the Files panel.

13 In the Property inspector, drag the Point to File icon ⊕ —next to the Link field—to **events.html** in the site root folder displayed in the Files panel.

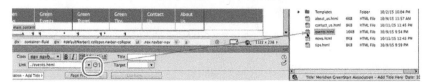

Dreamweaver enters the filename and any necessary path information into the Link field.

Note: The **index. html** and **travel.html** pages will be created later. Just type the page name and path into the Property inspector Link field for these pages.

14 Modify the rest of the menu as shown using any of the methods you've learned:

Green Travel: **../travel.html**

Green Tips: **../tips.html**

Contact Us: **../contact_us.html**

About Us: **../about_us.html**

For files that have not been created, you will always have to enter the link manually. Remember that all the links added to the template pointing to files in the site root folder must include the **../** notation so that the link resolves properly. Remember also that Dreamweaver will modify the link as needed once the template is applied to the child page.

Creating a Home Link

Most websites display a logo or company name, and this site is no different. The GreenStart logo appears in the header element—a product of two background graphics, a gradient, and some text. Frequently, such logos are used to create a link back to the site home page. In fact, this practice has become a virtual standard on the web. Since the template is still open, it's easy to add such a link to the GreenStart logo.

1   Select the *GreenStart* text in the `<header>` element.

The text component of the logo is highlighted. Dreamweaver keeps track of links you create in each editing session until you close the program. You can access these previously created links from the Property inspector.

2   In the Property inspector Link field, choose `../index.html` from the drop-down menu.

Note: You can select any range of text to create a link—from one character to an entire paragraph or more; Dreamweaver will add the necessary markup to the selection.

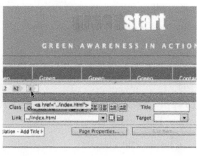

This selection will create a link to the home page you will create later. The `<a>` tag now appears in the tag selector interface, and the logo has changed color to match the default styling of hyperlinks. Although you may want normal hyperlinks to be styled this way, the logo is not supposed to be blue. It's a simple fix with CSS.

3   In the CSS Designer, choose **green_styles.css** > GLOBAL. Create the following selector:

```
header h2 a:link, header h2 a:visited
```

This selector will target the "default" and "visited" states of the link within the logo.

Note: Design view
will not render all
the styling properly,
but it will appear
correctly in Live view
and in a browser.

4 Add the following properties to the rule:

```
color: inherit
text-decoration: none
```

5 Switch to Live view.

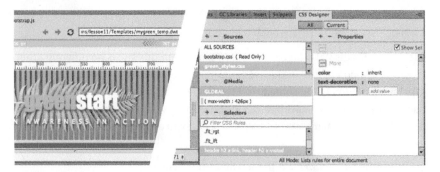

These properties will cancel the hyperlink styling and return the text to its original appearance. By using `inherit` for the color value, the color applied by the `header h2` rule will be passed automatically to the text. That way, any time the color in the `header h2` rule changes, the hyperlink will be styled in turn without any additional work or redundant code.

So far, all the links you've created and the changes you've made are only on the template. The whole purpose of using the template is to make updating pages in your site easy.

Updating Links in Child Pages

To apply the links you've created to all the existing pages based on this template, all you have to do is save it.

1 Choose File > Save.

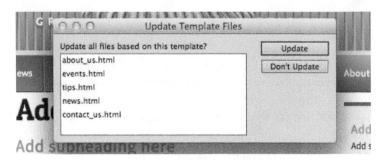

The Update Template Files dialog appears. You can choose to update pages now or wait until later. You can even update the template files manually, if desired.

2 Click Update.

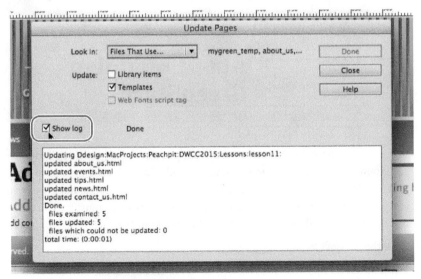

Dreamweaver updates all pages created by this template. The Update Pages dialog appears, and displays a report listing the updated pages. If you don't see the list of updated pages, click the Show Log option in the dialog.

3 Close the Update Pages dialog.
Close **mygreen_temp.dwt**.

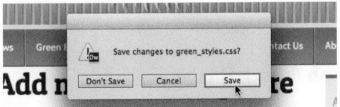

Dreamweaver prompts you to save **green_styles.css**.

4 Click Save.

The file **about_us.html** is still open. Note the asterisk in the document tab; this indicates that the page has been changed but not saved.

5 Save **about_us.html** and preview it in a browser.
Position the insertion point over the *Home* and *Green News* links.

Note: When you close templates or web pages, Dreamweaver may ask you to save changes to **green_styles.css**. Whenever you see these warnings, always save the changes; otherwise you could lose all your newly created rules and properties.

Tip: Thoroughly test every link you create on every page. Remember that the index.html and travel.html pages have not been created yet so when you test the GreenStart navigation bar, these links display a file not found page.

If you display the status bar in your browser, you can see the links applied to each item. When the template was saved, it updated the locked regions of the page, adding the hyperlinks to the horizontal menu. Child pages that are closed at the time of updating are automatically saved. Open pages must be saved manually or you will lose changes applied by the template.

6   Click the *Contact Us* link.

The *Contact Us* page loads to replace the *About Us* page in the browser.

7   Click the *About Us* link.

The *About Us* page loads to replace the *Contact Us* page. The links were added even to pages that weren't open at the time.

8   Close the browser.

You learned three methods for creating hyperlinks with the Property inspector: typing the link manually, using the Browse for File function, and using the Point to File tool.

Creating an External Link

The pages you linked to in the previous exercise were stored within the current site. You can also link to any page—or other resource—stored on the web if you know the URL.

Creating an Absolute Link in Live View

In the previous exercise, you used Design view to build all your links. As you build pages and format content, you'll use Live view frequently to preview the styling and appearance of your elements. Although some aspects of content creation and editing are limited in Live view, you can still create and edit hyperlinks. In this exercise, you'll apply an external link to some text using Live view.

1   Open **contact_us.html** from the site root folder in Live view.

2   In the second <p> element in the main_content region, note the word *Meridien*.

You'll link this text to the Google Maps site.

3   Launch your favorite browser. In the URL field, type **maps.google.com** and press Enter/Return.

Google Maps appears in the browser window.

4   Type **San Jose, CA** into the search field and press Enter/Return.

Tip: For this exercise, you can use any search engine or web-based mapping application.

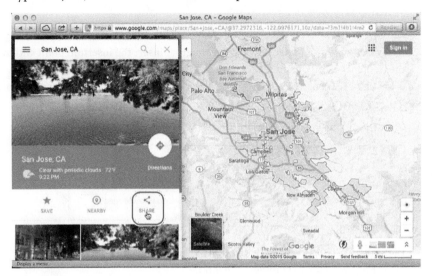

Note: In some browsers, you can type the search phrase directly in the URL field.

Note: We're using Adobe's headquarters in place of the fictional city of Meridien. Feel free to use another search term.

San Jose appears on a map in the browser. In Google Maps, somewhere on the screen you should see a settings or share icon.

5   Open the settings interface as appropriate for your chosen mapping application.

Search engines and browsers may display their link-sharing and embedding interface slightly differently than the one pictured. Google Maps, MapQuest, and Bing usually offer at least two separate code snippets: one for use within a hyperlink and the other to generate an actual map that you can embed in your site.

Note: The technique for sharing map links is implemented differently in various browsers and search engines and may change over time.

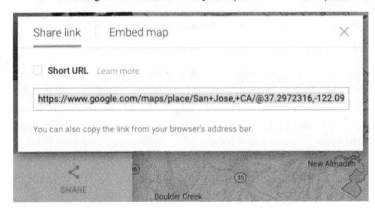

Note how the link contains the entire URL of the map, making it an *absolute* link. The advantage of using absolute links is that you can copy and paste them anywhere in the site without worrying whether the link will resolve properly.

6 Select and copy the link.

Tip: Double-click to select text in Live view.

7 Switch to Live view in Dreamweaver.
Select the word *Meridien*.

In Live view, you can select an entire element or insert the insertion point within the element to edit or add text or apply hyperlinks, as desired. When an element or section of text is selected, a HUD will appear. The Text HUD allows you to apply `<strong>` or `<em>` tags to the selection, or (as in this case) to apply hyperlinks.

8 Click the Hyperlink icon 🔗 in the Text HUD.

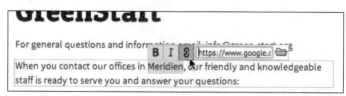

Press Ctrl+V/Cmd+V to paste the link in the Link field.
Press Enter/Return to complete the link.

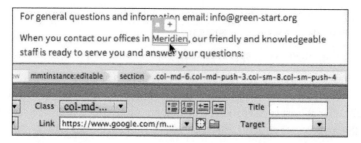

The selected text displays the default formatting for a hyperlink.

9 Save the file and preview it in the default browser. Test the link.

When you click the link, the browser takes you to the opening page of Google Maps, assuming you have a connection to the Internet. But there is a problem: Clicking the link replaced the *Contact Us* page in the browser; it didn't open a new window as when you previewed the page at the beginning of the chapter. To make the browser open a new window, you need to add a simple HTML attribute to the link.

10 Switch to Dreamweaver.
Click the *Meridien* link in Live view.

The Element HUD appears. The Property inspector displays the value of the existing link.

11 Choose _blank from the Target field menu in the Property inspector.

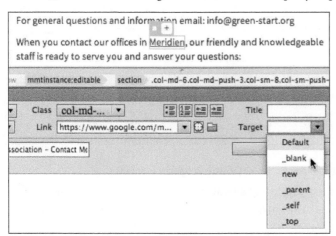

Tip: You can access the Target attribute in the Property inspector in Live, Design, and Code views whenever a link is selected.

12 Save the file, and preview the page in the default browser again. Test the link.

This time when you click the link, the browser opens a new window or document tab.

13 Close the browser windows, and switch back to Dreamweaver.

As you can see, Dreamweaver makes it easy to create links to internal or external resources.

Setting up Email Links

Another type of link doesn't take the visitor to another page; rather, it opens the visitor's email program. Email links can create automatic, pre-addressed email messages from your visitors for customer feedback, product orders, or other important communications. The code for an email link is slightly different from the normal hyperlink, and—as you probably guessed already—Dreamweaver can create the proper code for you automatically.

1 If necessary, open **contact_us.html** in Design view.

2 Select the email address (info@green-start.org) in the first paragraph underneath the heading and press Ctrl+C/Cmd+C to copy the text.

3 Choose Insert > HTML > Email Link.

The Email Link dialog appears. The text selected in the document window is automatically entered into the Text field.

Note: Many web visitors don't use email programs installed on their computers. They use web-based services like AOL, Gmail, Hotmail, and so on. For these visitors, email links like the one you tested won't work. The best option is to create a web-hosted form on your site that sends the email to you via your own server.

Tip: The Email Link menu cannot be accessed in Live view. But you can use the menu in Design view or Code view or just create the links by hand in any view.

Tip: If you select the text before you access the dialog, Dreamweaver enters the text in the field for you automatically.

4 Insert the insertion point in the Email field and press Ctrl+V/Cmd+V to paste the email address, if necessary.

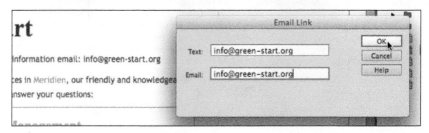

5 Click OK. Examine the Link field in the Property inspector.

Dreamweaver inserts the email address into the Link field and also enters the `mailto:` notation, which tells the browser to automatically launch the visitor's default email program.

6 Save the file and preview it in the default browser. Test the email link.

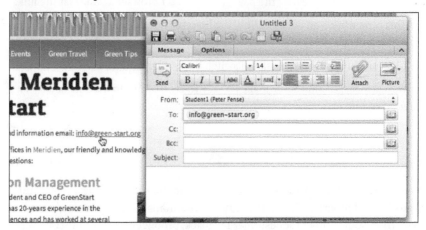

If your computer has a default email program installed, it will launch and create a new email message using the email address provided in the link. If there is no default email program, your computer's operating system may ask you to identify one.

7 Close any open email program, related dialogs, or wizards. Switch to Dreamweaver.

You can also create email links by hand.

8 Select and copy the email address for Elaine.

9   Type `mailto:` in the Property inspector link field.
    Paste Elaine's email address directly after the colon.
    Press Enter/Return to complete the link.

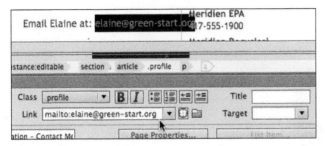

10 Save the file.

    The text `mailto:elaine@green-start.org` appears in the Text HUD link
    field in Live view. You can use the HUD to add links to images too.

Creating an Image-Based Link

Image-based links work like any other hyperlink and can direct users to internal or
external resources. You can use the Insert menu in Design or Code views or apply
links and other attributes using the HUD interface in Live view.

Creating Image-Based Links Using the Element HUD

In this exercise, you will create and format an image-based link using the email
addresses of each GreenStart employee via the Element HUD.

1   If necessary, open **contact_us.html** in Live view from the site root folder.

2   Select the image of Elaine in the *Association Management* section.

    To access the hyperlink option, you must open the Edit HTML Attributes menu.

3   In the Element HUD, click the Edit HTML Attributes icon ▤ .

    The menu opens and displays options for the image attributes `src`, `alt`, `link`,
    `target`, `width`, and `height`.

> **Note:** Normally, an
> image formatted with
> a hyperlink displays a
> blue border, similar to
> the blue underscore
> that text links get.
> But the predefined
> Bootstrap CSS turns
> this styling off. In
> non-Bootstrap sites,
> you may want to
> create a similar rule.

> **Tip:** Make sure there
> is no space after the
> colon or the link will
> not work properly.

4 If the email address is still in memory from the previous exercise, simply enter `mailto:` and paste the address in the Link field.

Otherwise, enter `mailto:elaine@green-start.org` in the link field after the colon.

Press the ESC key to close the HUD.

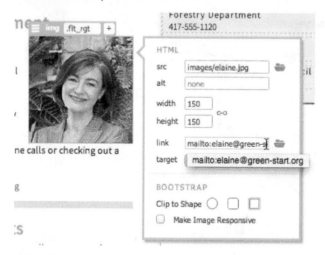

The hyperlink that is applied to the image will launch the default email program in the same fashion as it did with the text-based link earlier.

5 Select and copy the email address for Sarah.

Repeat steps 2–4 to create an email link for Sarah's image.

6 Create image links for the remaining employees using the appropriate email address for each.

All the image-based links on the page are complete. You can also create text-based links using the Text HUD.

Creating Text Links Using the Text HUD

In this exercise, you will create text-based email links as needed for the remaining employees.

1 If necessary, open **contact_us.html** in Live view.

2 Select and copy the email address for Sarah.

The Text HUD appears around the selected text.

3 Click the Link icon 🔗.

A link field appears. A folder icon displays on the right side of the link field. If you were linking to a file on the website, you could click the folder to target the file. In this case, we're creating an email link.

4   Insert the insertion point in the link field, if necessary.
    Enter `mailto:` and paste Sarah's email address and press Enter/Return.

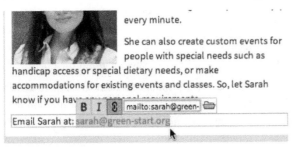

5   Using the Text HUD, create email links for the remaining email addresses
    displayed on the page.

6   Save all files.

Attack of the Killer Robots

Although on the surface it sounds like a good idea to add email links to make it easier for your
customers and visitors to communicate with you and your staff, email links are a double-edged sword.
The Internet is awash in bad actors and unethical companies that use intelligent programs, or robots,
to constantly search for live email addresses that they can flood with unsolicited email and spam.
Putting a plain email address on your site as shown in these exercises is like putting a sign on your
back that says "kick me."

In place of active email links, many sites use a variety of methods for limiting the amount of spam
they receive. One technique uses images to display the email addresses, since robots can't read data
stored in pixels (yet). Another leaves off the hyperlink attribute and types the address with extra
spaces, like this:

```
elaine @ green-start .org
```

However, both of these techniques have drawbacks; if visitors try to use copy and paste it forces them
to go out of their way to remove the extra spaces or try to type your email address from memory.
Either way, the chances of you receiving any communication decreases with each step the user has to
accomplish without additional help.

At this time, there is no foolproof way to prevent someone from using an email address for dishonest
purposes. Coupled with the fact that fewer users actually have a mail program installed on their
computers anymore, the best method for enabling communication for your visitors is to provide
a means built into the site itself. Many sites create web-hosted forms that collect the visitor's
information and message and then pass it along using server-based email functionality.

Targeting Page Elements

As you add more content, the pages get longer and navigating to that content gets more difficult. Typically, when you click a link to a page, the browser window loads the page and displays it starting at the very top. But it can be very helpful when you provide convenient methods for users to link to a specific point on a page.

HTML 4.01 provided two methods to target specific content or page structures: a *named anchor* and an *id* attribute. In HTML5, the named anchor method has been deprecated in favor of ids. If you have used named anchors in the past, don't worry, they won't suddenly cease to function. But from this point on, you should start using ids exclusively.

Creating Internal Targeted Links

In this exercise, you'll work with id attributes to create the target of an internal link. You can add ids in Live, Design, or Code view.

1 Open **events.html** in Live view.

2 Scroll down to the table containing the class schedule.

   When users move down this far on the page, the navigation menus are out of sight and unusable. The farther down the page they read, the farther they are from the primary navigation. Before users can navigate to another page, they have to use the browser scroll bars or the mouse scroll wheel to get back to the top of the page. Adding a link to take users back to the top can vastly improve their experience on your site. Let's call this type of link an *internal targeted* link.

   Internal targeted links have two parts: the link itself and the target. Which one you create first doesn't matter.

3 Click the Class table.
   Click the `article` tag selector.

   The HUD appears focused on the `article` element.

4 Open the Insert panel.
   Select the HTML category.
   Click the Paragraph item.

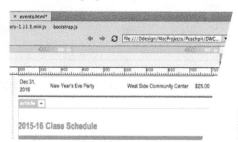
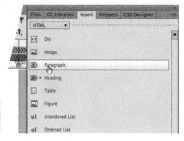

The position assist interface opens.

5 Click Before.

A new paragraph element appears in the layout, with the placeholder text *This is the content for Layout P Tag*.

6 Select the placeholder text.
Type **Return to top** to replace it.

The text is inserted between the two tables, formatted as a <p> element. The text would look better centered.

7 In the CSS Designer, choose **green_styles.css** > GLOBAL.
Create a new selector: `.ctr`

8 Create the following property for `.ctr`:
`text-align: center`

9 Click the Add Class/ID icon $\boxed{+}$ for the selected <p> element.

10 Type `.ctr` in the text field, or choose `.ctr` from the hinting menu and press Enter/Return.

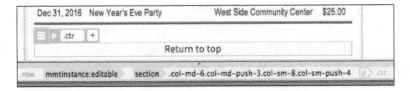

The *Return to top* text is aligned to the center. The tag selector now displays `p.ctr`.

11 Select the text *Return to top*.
Click the Link icon ☍ and type #top in the Link field.
Press Enter/Return to complete the link.

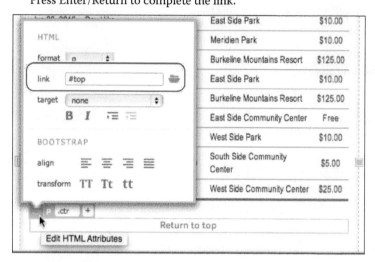

By using #top, you have created a link to a target within the current page. When users click the *Return to top* link, the browser window jumps to the position of the target. This target doesn't exist yet. For this link to work properly, you need to insert the destination as high on the page as possible.

12 Save all files. Switch to Design view.

13 Scroll to the top of **events.html**.
Position the insertion point over the header element.

The mouse icon indicates that this part of the page (and its related code) is uneditable, because the header and horizontal navigation menu are based on the site template. Putting the target at the very top is important, or a portion of the page may be obscured when the browser jumps to it. Since the top of the page is part of an uneditable region, the best solution is to add the target directly to the template.

Creating a Link Destination Using an Id

By adding a unique id to the template, you will be able to access it automatically throughout the site wherever you want to add a link back to the top of a page.

1   Open the template **mygreen_temp.dwt** from the Templates folder in
    Design view.

2   Click in the text *greenstart* in the `<header>`.
    Select the h2 tag selector.
    In the Property inspector, type **top** in the id field and press Enter/Return.

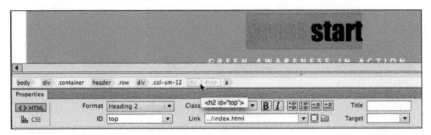

The tag selector changes to h2#top; otherwise, the page shows no visible
difference. The big difference is in how the page reacts to the internal hyperlink.

3   Save the file and update all template child pages. Close the template.

4   Switch to or open **events.html**, if necessary.
    Save the file, and preview it in a browser.

5   Scroll down to the Class table.
    Click the *Return to top* link.

    The browser jumps back to the top of the page.

    Now that the id has been inserted in every page of the site by the template, you
    can copy the *Return to top* link and paste it anywhere in the site you want to add
    this functionality.

6   In Dreamweaver, switch to Live view.
    Select and copy the `<p>` element containing the text *Return to top* and its link.

7   Insert the insertion point in the Class table.
    Using the tag selector, select the `<article>` element.
    Press Ctrl+V/Cmd+V to paste.

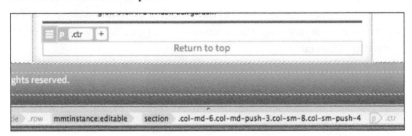

A new `p.ctr` element and link appear at the bottom of the page.

8   Save the file and preview it in the browser. Test both *Return to top* links.

Both links can be used to jump back to the top of the document. In the next exercise, you'll learn how to create link targets using element attributes.

Creating a Destination Link in the Element HUD

There's no need to add any extra elements to create hyperlink destinations when you can simply add an id attribute to a handy element nearby. In this exercise, you will use the Element HUD to add an id.

1 Open **events.html** in Live view.
Insert the insertion point in the Events table.
Click the `table` tag selector.

The Element HUD and the Property inspector display the attributes currently applied to the Events table. You can add an id using either tool.

Note: When creating ids, remember that they need to have names that are used only once per page. They are case sensitive, so look out for typos.

2 Click the Add Class/ID icon ⊞ .
Type a hash mark (#).

If any ids were defined in the style sheet but unused on the page, a list would appear. Since nothing appears, it means that there are no unused ids. Creating a new one is easy.

Note: If you add the id to the wrong element, simply delete it and try again.

3 Type `calendar` and press Enter/Return.

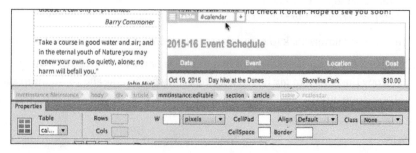

The CSS Source HUD appears. We do not need the id in any style sheet.

4 Press ESC to close the HUD.

The tag selector now displays `table#calendar`. Since ids are unique identifiers, they are perfect for targeting specific content on a page. We also need to create an id for the Class table.

5   Repeat steps 1–4 to add the id `#classes` to the Class table.

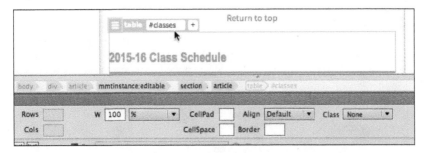

The tag selector now displays `table#classes`.

6   Save all files.

You'll learn how to link to these ids in the next exercise.

Targeting Id-Based Link Destinations

By adding unique ids to both tables, you have provided an ideal target for internal hyperlinks to navigate to a specific section of your webpage. In this exercise, you will create a link to each table.

1   If necessary, open **contact_us.html** in Live view.
    Scroll down to the *Education and Events* section.

2   Select the word *events* in the first paragraph of the section.

3   Using the Text HUD, create a link to the file **events.html**.

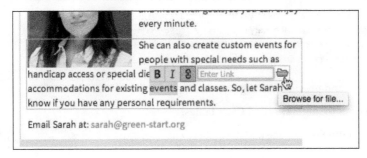

> **Tip:** You can select single words by double-clicking them.

This link will open the file, but you're not finished. You now have to direct the browser to navigate down to the Events table.

Note: Hyperlinks cannot contain spaces; make sure the id reference follows the filename immediately.

4   Type `#calendar` at the end of the filename to complete the link and press Enter/Return.

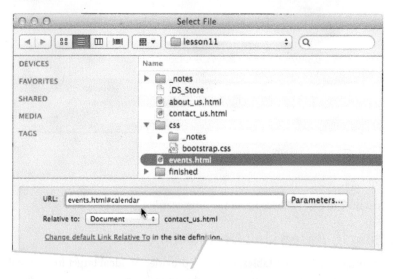

The word *events* is now a link targeting the Events table in the **events.html** file.

5   Select the word *classes*.

Create a link to the **events.html** file.

Type `#classes` to complete the link and press Enter/Return.

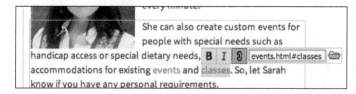

6   Save the file and preview the page in a browser.

Test the links to the *Events* and *Class* tables.

The links open the *Events* page and navigate to the appropriate tables.

Checking Your Page

Dreamweaver can check your page automatically for valid HTML, accessibility, and broken links. In this exercise, you'll check your links and learn what you can do in case of a browser compatibility problem.

1   If necessary, open **contact_us.html** in Design view.

2   Choose Site > Check Links Sitewide.

 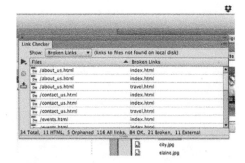

A Link Checker panel opens. The Link Checker panel reports broken links to the files **index.html** and **travel.html** you created for nonexistent pages. You'll make these pages later, so you don't need to worry about fixing these broken links now. The Link Checker will find broken links to external sites, should you have any.

3   Right-click the Link Checker tab, and choose Close Tab Group from the context menu.

You've made big changes to the pages in this chapter by creating the main navigation menu, links to specific positions on a page, to email, and to an external site. You also applied links to images. Finally, you checked your page for broken links.

Note: The Link Checker may find some suspicious links in a Bootstrap JavaScript file. Ignore any of these errors.

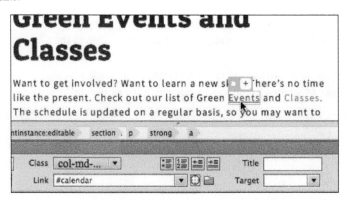

End-of-Chapter Activities

Review Questions

Directions: Choose the correct answer for each question.

1. What is an internal hyperlink?
   a. A link in a webpage that links to another webpage in the same site
   b. A link in a webpage that links to a webpage in the another site
   c. A link in a webpage that links to an area in the same webpage in the same site
   d. A and C
   e. None of the above

2. What is an external hyperlink?
   a. A link in a webpage that links to another webpage in the same site
   b. A link in a webpage that links to a webpage in the another site
   c. A link in a webpage that links to an area in the same webpage in the same site
   d. A and B
   e. None of the above

3. What is a relative link?
   a. The path to a link that references where the target page is stored in relation to the current document
   b. The full path that precisely spells out where the target document is located
   c. A link in a webpage that links to an area in the same webpage in the same site
   d. A and C
   e. None of the above

4. What is an absolute link?
   a. The path to a link that references where the target page is stored in relation to the current document
   b. The full path that precisely spells out where the target document is located
   c. A link in a webpage that links to an area in the same webpage in the same site
   d. B and C
   e. None of the above

5. In most browsers, when you hover your insertion point over a link where can you see the destination of the link?
   a. Address bar
   b. Tooltip
   c. Menu bar
   d. Status bar

6. When working in Dreamweaver and what does it mean when you hover your insertion point over a page element and you see the slash icon [slash].
   a. You need to switch to Design view to access the element
   b. You need to switch to Live view to access the element
   c. The element is part of the non-editable areas of the template and must be edited in the template file
   d. You need to use the Property inspector to access the element

7. True or False: When working in Dreamweaver, you need to select the entire text on the webpage to attach a hyperlink to it.
   a. True
   b. False

8. If you double-click a word what happens?
   a. The entire word is selected
   b. Nothing
   c. The entire paragraph is selected
   d. A hyperlink is attached

9. What code creates a target for a link to open in a new browser window?
   a. _blank
   b. _top
   c. _parent
   d. _self

10. Which of the following is correct syntax for an email link?
    a. email=info@lakepowell.com
    b. emailto=info@lakepowell.com
    c. emailto:info@lakepowell.com
    d. emailMe:info@lakepowell.com

Essay Questions

Directions: Respond to each question by writing your answers in complete sentences and paragraphs. Be thorough in your answers.

1. Describe two ways to insert a link into a page.

2. What information is required to create a link to an external webpage?

3. What's the difference between standard page links and email links?

4. What attribute is used to create destination links?

5. What limits the usefulness of email links?

6. Can links be applied to images?

7. How can you check to see whether your links will work properly?

8. Break down the following link by specifying the various parts of a hyperlinks, i.e. HTML elements, URLS, attributes, values, and visible text.

   <a href=http://www.greenstart.org/events.html target="_blank">GreenStart</a>

9. When working in Dreamweaver, describe the process required to attach a hyperlink to an image in a webpage.

10. What is the advantage of creating a link target in the template for a site.

Critical Thinking Project—Develop Site Navigation for the Lake Powell Website

Its time to develop the navigation for the Lake Powell website. Next you develop the main navigation bar and then create both internal and external links as well as use IDs to jump to different sections of a page.

Develop the Navigation Bar

First add links to the menu in the main navigation bar. Since these are part of a non-editable area of the template, you need to make the changes in the template.

1. On your computer create a local root folder as directed by your teacher. Name the folder **lakepowell_xx**. Copy the class data files from the Chapter12/Data files/lakepowell_xx directory as instructed by your teacher.

2. Open the lakepowell_temp.dwt webpage. Switch to Design view.

3. Create a link for the **Lake Powell Home** menu in the navigation bar by clicking in the menu name. In the Property inspector click the Browse button to the right of the Link field. If necessary, click Site Root to make sure you are in the local root directory. Find the **index.html** page and select it. Click Open. The home menu is now linked to the **index.html** page.

4. Now create a link for the Houseboats Rental menu. You'll use the Point To File icon for this link. Open the Files panel first and then click the **Houseboats Rental** menu. In the Property inspector click the Point To File icon and drag the pointer arrow to **houseboats.html**.

5. Use either step 3 or 4 to create the following menu links in the navigation bar:
   a. Jet Ski Rentals – jetski.html
   b. Scenic Hikes – hiking.html
   c. Contact Us – contact.html

6. Save the **lakepowell_temp.dwt** file. In the Update Template Files dialog click Update to update all files. Then in the Update Pages dialog select the Show Log option if necessary and review the log to make sure all files updated. Click Close to close the dialog.

7. Save all files and preview in a browser. Check all navigation bar menus to ensure all links are working.

Link the Company Name in the <header> Element

Next add a link to the home page from the company name "Lake Powell Adventures" in the <header>element. Then format the new link so that it does not have the default This is again in a non-editable area of the web site so you need to edit the template file for creating the link.

1. Open the **lakepowell_temp.dwt** template. Switch to Design view.

2. Highlight the words "Lake Powell Adventures" and then click the Link dropdown menu. Select **../index.html** from the list.

3. Next create a CSS rule to turn the hyperlink color off for the default state of a link and default underline off for the hyperlink in the visited state. In the CSS Designer, choose lakepowell.css>GLOBAL and then create the following selector.
   a. header h1 a:link, header h1 a:visited

4. Add the following properties to the new rule:
   a. color: inherit
   b. text-decoration: none

5. Save the template file and update all other pages of the site.

6. Save all files and then preview in a browser. Test the new link.

Creating External Links

Next you'll create external links to other website pages and resources.

1. Open jetski.html and switch to Live view.

2. In the right **<aside>** element select the words **WaterCraft.com**. In the HUD that displays click the Hyperlink icon. Type **http://www.personalwatercraft.com/** in the Hyperlink field. Set the link to target a new blank browser window by clicking the Target field and choosing _blank from the dropdown menu. Press Enter/Return.

3. Repeat step 2 to create these external links to the other two boating references.
   a. Lake Powell Boating Safety Rules: http://www.lakepowelllife.com/boating-on-lake-powell-safety-rules/
   b. American Watercraft Association: http://www.awahq.org/

4. Save all files and test your links in a browser.

5. Next create an external link to a Lake Powell map generated by Google Maps. Go to Google Maps in your browser by type **maps.google.com** in the Address field. In the Search Google Maps field, type **Lake Powell, UT**. A map of Lake Powell is displayed, click the Share or Settings button and in the dialog that displays select and copy the link. You can also copy the URL in the browser's Address field.

6. Switch back to Dreamweaver and open the **hiking.html** webpage. In Live view, select the image of the map of Lake Powell. Click the Edit HTML Attributes menu in the HUD and then click in the Link field. Paste the copied URL link and press Enter/Return. Click in the Target field and choose _blank from the dropdown menu. Press ESC to exit the HUD.

7. Save all files and preview the hiking.html page in a browser.

Set Email Links

Next add email links to the email address that you have set up for the Contact.html page.

1. Open the **contact.html** webpage. Switch to Design view.

2. In the main content section highlight Mike's email address at the bottom of the Lake Powell General Questions section. Copy this by pressing Ctrl+C/Cmd+C. Click in the Link field in the Property inspector and type **mailto:mike@lakepowelladventures.com**.

3. Highlight Jim's email address in the **Houseboat and Jet Ski Rentals** section of the page and again copy the address. With the address still selected, choose Insert>HTML>Email Link. In the Email Link dialog if needed click in the Text field and press Ctrl+V/Cmd+V to paste the email address. Click in the Email field and again paste the address. Press Ok.

4. Using either step 2 or 3 create an email link for Joanne's email address in the **Hiking and Rock Climbing** section

5. Save all files and text your email links in a browser.

6. Close the Email application after you are done testing.

Create a Link for Text

Next add email links text in the Sign Up for Our Newsletter section of the contact.html page.

1. Switch to Live view. If necessary open the contact.html page.

2. In the Sign Up for Our Newsletter section, highlight the Mike's email address. The HUD displays around the selected text. Click the Hyperlink icon and Link field type mailto: and then paste the copied email address for mike. Press Enter/Return and then press ESC to exit the HUD.

3. Save all files and test the new link in a browser.

4. Close the Email application after you are done testing.

Target Page Elements

The Jet Ski Rental page is quite long and it would be nice to have a menu bar that jumps to the individual <h3> subheadings. You'll do this by creating a menu bar and then setting up **id** attributes for each of the subheadings and then linking to that **id** attribute.

1. Switch to Live view. If necessary open the jetski.html page.

2. Click the <h1> element in the main content section and then choose Insert>Paragraph. In the position assist interface click **After**.

3. Select the placeholder text in the new <p> element and delete it. Type **Operating Tips** and press the spacebar 10 times to insert ten spaces, then type **Safety Equipment**. Again insert 10 spaces and type **Riding Practices**

4. Add a class attribute to this <p> element by clicking the <p> element in the HUD click the Add Class/ID button. Type **jetskimenu** as the class name. Press Enter/Return and make sure the new class is being created in the lakepowell.css style sheet. Press ESC to exit the HUD.

5. Set up the **ids** for the <h3> elements in the main content section by selecting the first <h3> element by clicking in the text **Jet Ski Rental Operating Tips** and then click the <h3> selector. In the Property inspector click in the ID field and type **operating**.

6. Repeat this for the other two <h3> elements and set the following ids for these elements:
   a. Jet Ski Rental Safety Equipment – **equipment**
   b. Safety Riding Practices for Jet Ski Rentals – **practices**

7. Save all files and test the links in a browser. Notice that you need to manually scroll up to the top of the page to test another **id** link. It would be nice to have a "Back to Top" link for the visitor to click to return to the top of the page so they can access the menu options again.

8. Next you'll create this Back to Top functionality in the template page so that this functionality is available to all pages of the site. Open the **lakepowell_temp.dwt** page. Switch to Design view.

9. Select the text Lake Powell Adventures in the <header> element. Then click the <h1> tag selector. In the Property inspector click in the ID filed and type **top**. Press Enter/Return.

10. Save the page and update all other pages. Save all files.

11. Switch to the jetski.html page and switch to Live view.

12. Click the heading Jet Ski Rental Safety Equipment and then click the **<h3>#equipment** tag selector. Choose Insert >Paragraph and in the position assist interface click Before to insert a new paragraph before this heading.

13. Select the placeholder text for the new paragraph and delete it by typing **Back to Top**.

14. Highlight the Back to Top text and in the HUD, click in the Hyperlink icon and type **#top**. Press Enter/Return.

15. Repeat steps 12–14 to create the "Back to Top" functionality for the second <h3> heading.

16. For the third <h3> element heading click in the last line item for the <ol> element. Click the <ol> tag selector and choose Insert>Paragraph. In the position assist interface, click After. Then select the placeholder text in the new paragraph and click the Hyperlink icon in the HUD. Type **#top** in the field and press Enter/Return.

17. Save all files and test your page.

18. Next center the new menu bar by applying CSS to the class attribute you created for the <p> element that contains the menu options. In the CSS Designer select lakepowell. css>GLOBAL, then locate the **.jetskimenu** selector rule and create the following property:
    a. text-align: center

19. The final touch is to set text link colors for the different states of a link for the main content section so that the new links match the site color palette. In the CSS Designer create a new selector for the lakepowell.css>GLOBAL style sheet and name it **article. row p a:link, article.row p a:visited**. Create the following properties for the new rule:
    a. color: #900

20. Save all files and test the page in a browser.

Check the Webpage and Links

Next you'll double check that all links are set up correctly and link to a page or resource by checking the validity of the HTML, accessibility and for broken links.

1. Switch to Design view. If necessary open the jetski.html page.

2. Choose Site>Check Links Sitewide.

3. Review the results in the Link Checker panel at the bottom of your workspace. Fix any broken links.

4. Right-click the Link Checker tab, and choose Close Tab Group.

5. Save all files and test your site again in a browser

6. Close all files.

> **Note:** When you test your links sitewide, you'll see three links from the Bootstrap JavaScript file. Ignore these broken links.

Online Portfolio Builder—Develop your Online Portfolio Website by Creating Links for Navigation

Develop your online portfolio website by adding images to your pages. Format these elements so that they display nice and are responsive to all window sizes. Follow the basic steps below to create and format these elements.

1. If necessary, create a local root directory and copy any files or folders over to the new local root directory. Define your site as instructed by your teacher.

2. Open your website pages that you have developed up to this point in the class.

3. Create links for your email addresses in your pages.

4. Create links for your navigation bar to all pages of the site respectively.

5. Create menu bars and ids any pages that have lots of content so the visitor can jump to the section of the page that they are interested in. Develop the "Back to Top" functionality so that the visitor can quickly jump back up to the top of the page.

6. Apply links to any images that you want to open an additional resources or pages.

7. Create any external links to pages on other websites. Make sure you are creating the rules for the lakepowell.css>GLOBAL style sheet.

8. Create any CSS rules to center your menus and to format the text link states so that they use your sites color palette.

9. Test your pages and links often by saving all files and previewing the page in a browser.

ADDING INTERACTIVITY

Dreamweaver can create sophisticated interactive effects with behaviors and accordion panels using Adobe's Bootstrap and jQuery frameworks.

Chapter Overview

In this chapter, you'll add Web 2.0 functionality to your webpages by doing the following:

- Use Dreamweaver behaviors to create an image rollover effect
- Insert a Bootstrap Accordion widget

Exploring Advanced Web Design Tools

To create some of the dramatic effects you see on the web, designers use advanced design tools and upgraded browsers to display the pages as they intended. Advances like DHTML (Dynamic Hypertext Markup Language), JavaScript, and others have made it possible to have internal search engines, animation, downloadable audio and video clips, and streaming audio and video on the Web.

Some designers use JavaScript, a cross-platform programming language, to create applets, or small applications for the Web. JavaScript works with HTML and CSS for creating its functionality. JavaScript can be placed in the <body> and <head> elements of an HTML document. CSS is used to format the JavaScript as well as the HTML. The following figure shows an example of JavaScript placed in the <head> and <body> elements of an HTML document.

```
<!DOCTYPE html>
<html>

<head>
<script>
function myFunction() {
    document.getElementById("demo").innerHTML = "Paragraph changed.";
}
</script>
</head>

<body>                                    A

<h1>My Web Page</h1>

<p id="demo">A Paragraph</p>

<button type="button" onclick="myFunction()">Try it</button>

</body>                                   B
</html>
```

A – JavaScript in the <head> element – Consists of a function that changes a button name to "Paragraph changed"

B – Trigger for the Javascript – when the button is clicked, it calls the function **"myFunction()"**

This JavaScript has a function that changes the name of a button when the visitor clicks the button.

Advanced Design Tools Designers can also use Dynamic Hypertext Markup Language, or DHTML, to add interactivity to Web pages. You might see butterflies flying across a screen or a personal greeting when you visit an online store. These are examples of DHTML functionality. DHTML combines HTML, JavaScript, CSS and the DOM (Document Object Model) to create this advanced functionality for a

Web page. Here is an example of DHTML code that opens an extra paragraph when the visitor requests it.

```html
<!doctype html>
<html lang="en">
    <head>
        <meta charset="utf-8">
        <title>Using a DOM function</title>
        <style>
            a {background-color:#eee;}
            a:hover {background:#ff0;}
            #toggleMe {background:#cfc; display:none; margin:30px 0; padding:1em;}
        </style>
    </head>
    <body>
        <h1>Using a DOM function</h1>

        <h2><a id="showhide" href="#">Show paragraph</a></h2>

        <p id="toggleMe">This is the paragraph that is only displayed on request.</p>

        <p>The general flow of the document continues.</p>

        <script>
            changeDisplayState = function (id) {
                var d = document.getElementById('showhide'),
                    e = document.getElementById(id);
                if (e.style.display === 'none' || e.style.display === '') {
                    e.style.display = 'block';
                    d.innerHTML = 'Hide paragraph';
                } else {
                    e.style.display = 'none';
                    d.innerHTML = 'Show paragraph';
                }
            };
            document.getElementById('showhide').onclick = function () {
                changeDisplayState('toggleMe');
                return false;
            };
        </script>
    </body>
</html>
```

DHTML resides in the <body> element of an HTML page.

Browser Support for Advanced Design Tools

Web users may like to access splashy features, but their browsers must be able to process them. Browsers can be upgraded with plug-in programs— small, download-able programs that add new features to an application. RealPlayer® and Windows Media® Player play streaming media. Shockwave®/Flash™ supports interactive documents and animation. Sometimes sites are created all in Adobe® Flash, but the main drawback is that they are not as searchable and take longer to load than sites done in HTML. Finally, Adobe® Acrobat® Reader makes it possible to view documents on-screen in the same format as they appear when printed.

Note: Visit the w3schools.com website for complete examples of advanced design tools for web development: www.w3schools.com/js/default.asp. This site presents the code and then allow you to see the code in action.

Note: To access Dreamweaver Behaviors, you must have a file open.

JavaScript

A text-based programming language that can be executed without any need for conversions and it does not need to be compiled. Javascript is used often in web design. To use JavaScript in web design, you can do one of two techniques. You can add the code directly to an HTML page as long as it is inside a <script> element. The second technique is to create a JavaScript file, with a .js extension. This JavaScript file is is then referenced in the HTML document by an empty <script> element with a src attribute. For instance this code is wrapped in the <script> element and calls the html5shiv. min.js file:

<script src="https:// oss.maxcdn.com/ html5shiv/3.7.2/ html5shiv.min.js"></ script>

Widget

A widget is composed of HTML code that defines the widget's structure, JavaScript that controls the interaction between a visitor's actions and the object, and CSS coding used to format the widget.

Learning About Dreamweaver Behaviors

The term *Web 2.0* was coined to describe a major change in the user experience on the Internet—from mostly static pages, featuring text, graphics, and simple links, to a new model of dynamic webpages filled with video, animation, and interactive content. Dreamweaver has always led the industry in providing a variety of tools to drive this movement, from its tried-and-true collection of **JavaScript** behaviors, jQuery, and Bootstrap widgets to the latest support for jQuery Mobile. This chapter explores two of these capabilities: Dreamweaver behaviors and Bootstrap **widgets**.

A Dreamweaver *behavior* is predefined JavaScript code that performs an action—such as opening a browser window or showing or hiding a page element—when it is triggered by an event, such as a mouse click. Applying a behavior is a three-step process:

1 Create or select the page element that you want to trigger the behavior.

2 Choose the behavior to apply.

3 Specify the settings or parameters of the behavior.

The triggering element often involves a hyperlink applied to a range of text or to an image. In some cases, the behavior is not intended to load a new page, so it employs a dummy link enabled by the hash sign (#), similar to ones that you used in Chapter 12, "Working with Navigation." The Swap Image behavior you will use in this chapter does not require a link to function, but keep this in mind when you work with other behaviors.

Dreamweaver offers more than 16 built-in behaviors, all accessed from the Behaviors panel (Window > Behaviors). Hundreds of other useful behaviors can be downloaded from the Internet for free or a small fee. Some are available from the online Adobe Add-ons website, which can be added to the program by clicking the Add Behavior icon ➕ in the Behaviors panel and choosing Get More Behaviors from the pop-up menu or by choosing Window > Browse Add-ons.

When the Adobe Add-ons page loads in the browser, click the link to download the plug-in, extension, or other add-on. Often you can simply double-click the add-on to install it.

The following are some examples of the functionality available to you using the built-in Dreamweaver behaviors:

- Opening a browser window
- Swapping one image for another to create what is known as a *rollover effect*
- Fading images or page areas in and out
- Growing or shrinking graphics
- Displaying pop-up messages

- Changing the text or other HTML content within a given area
- Showing or hiding sections of the page
- Calling a custom-defined JavaScript function

Not all behaviors are available all the time. Certain behaviors become available only in the presence and selection of certain page elements, such as images or hyperlinks. For example, the Swap Image behavior must be applied to an image.

Each behavior invokes a unique dialog that provides relevant options and specifications. For instance, the dialog for the Open Browser Window behavior enables you to open a new browser window; set its width, height, and other attributes; and set the URL of the displayed resource. After the behavior is defined, it is listed in the Behaviors panel with its chosen triggering action. As with other behaviors, these specifications can be modified at any time.

Behaviors are extremely flexible, and multiple behaviors can be applied to the same trigger. For example, you could swap one image for another and change the text of the accompanying image caption—and do it all with one click. Although some effects may appear to happen simultaneously, behaviors are actually triggered in sequence. When multiple behaviors are applied, you can choose the order in which the behaviors are processed. To learn more about Adobe Add Ons, visit creative.adobe.com/addons.

Working with Dreamweaver Behaviors

Adding Dreamweaver behaviors to your layout is a simple point-and-click operation. But before you can add the behaviors, you have to create the travel page.

1 Launch Adobe Dreamweaver CC (2015.1 release) or later. If necessary, define a site based on the Lesson13 folder. Name the site Lesson13 as instructed by your teacher.

2 Create a new page from **mygreen_temp**.

3 Save the file as **travel.html** in the site root folder.
Switch to Design view, if necessary.

4   Open **sidebars12.html** in Design view from the Chapter13_Exercise/resources folder. Insert the insertion point into the first paragraph.
Examine the tag selectors.

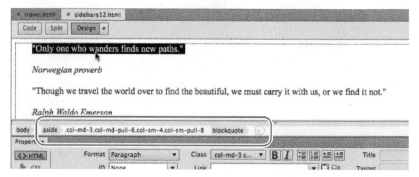

The paragraph is a child of a `<blockquote>` within an `aside` element. The classes and structure in the new file are identical to Sidebar 1 in the site template.

5   Select the `aside` tag selector.

6   Copy the `aside` element from **sidebars12.html**.

7   Switch to **travel.html**.
Insert the insertion point into the first quotation.
Select the `aside` tag selector.

8   Paste the new content.

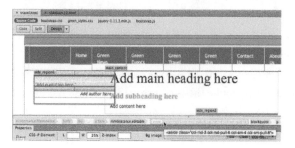 

The new content replaces the placeholder.

9   Close **sidebars12.html**.

10 Open **travel-text.html** in Design view from the Chapter13_Exercise/resources folder.

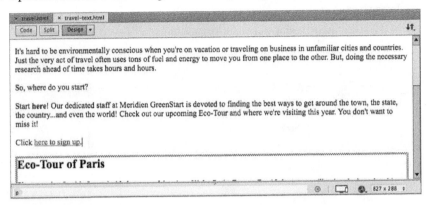

The **travel-text.html** file contains content in some paragraphs and a table for the travel page. Note that the text and table are unformatted.

11 Press Ctrl+A/Cmd+A to select all the text, and press Ctrl+C/Cmd+C to copy the contents of **travel-text.html**.
Close the file.

12 In **travel.html**, select the placeholder *Add main heading here*.
Type **Green Travel** to replace the text.

13 Select the heading placeholder *Add subheading here*.
Type **Eco-Touring** to replace it.

14 Select the p tag selector for the *Add content here* text.
Press Ctrl+V/Cmd+V to paste.

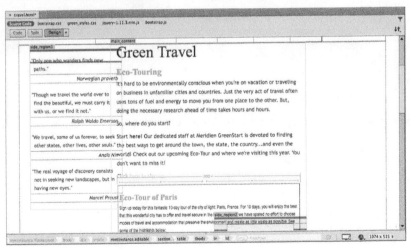

The content from **travel-text.html** appears, replacing the placeholder text. It assumes the default formatting for text and tables applied by the style sheet you created in Chapter 10, "Working with Text, Lists, and Tables."

Next, let's insert the Eco-Tour ad, which will be the base image for the Swap Image behavior.

15 In the table, double-click the *SideAd* placeholder.
Select **ecotour.png** from the images folder.
Click OK/Open.

The placeholder is replaced by the Eco-Tour ad. But before you can apply the Swap Image behavior, you have to identify the image you want to swap. You do this by giving the image an id.

16 Select **ecotour.png** in the layout.
In the Property inspector, select the existing id SideAd.
Type ecotour and press Enter/Return.
Enter Eco-Tour of Paris in the Alt field.

Tip: Although it takes more time, giving all your images, unique ids is a good practice.

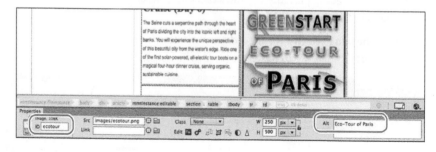

17 Save the file.

Next, you'll create a Swap Image behavior for **ecotour.png**.

Applying a Behavior

As described earlier, many behaviors are context sensitive, based on the elements or structure present. A Swap Image behavior can be triggered by any document element, but it affects only images displayed within the page.

Note: Feel free to dock the Behaviors panel with the other panels in the interface.

1 Choose Window > Behaviors to open the Behaviors panel.

2 Insert the insertion point in the *Tour Eiffel* text, and select the <h3> tag selector.

3 Click the Add Behavior icon ➕.
Choose Swap Image from the behavior menu.

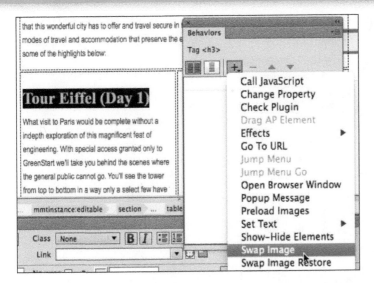

The Swap Image dialog lists any images on the page that are available for this behavior. This behavior can replace one or more of these images at a time.

4   Select the `image` "ecotour" item and click Browse.

5   In the Select Image Source dialog, select **tower.jpg** from the site images folder. Click OK/Open.

Note: Items listed as unnamed <img> are images without id attributes. If you wish to swap them too, you'll have to first give them ids.

6   In the Swap Image dialog, select the Preload Images option, if necessary, and click OK.

Note: The Preload Images option forces the browser to download all images necessary for the behavior when the page loads. That way, when the user clicks the trigger, the image swap occurs without any lags or glitches.

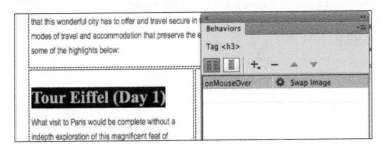

A Swap Image behavior is added to the Behaviors panel with an attribute of `onMouseOver`. Attributes can be changed, if desired, using the Behaviors panel.

7 Click the onMouseOver attribute to open the pop-up menu, and examine the other available options.

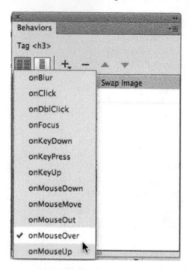

The menu provides a list of trigger events, most of which are self-explanatory. For now, however, leave the attribute as onMouseOver.

8 Save the file.

Switch to Live view to test the behavior.

Position the insertion point over the *Tour Eiffel* text.

When the insertion point passes over the text, the Eco-Tour ad is replaced by the image of the Eiffel Tower. But there is a small problem. When the insertion point moves away from the text, the original image doesn't return. The reason is simple: You didn't tell it to. To bring back the original image, you have to add another command—Swap Image Restore—to the same element.

Applying a Swap Image Restore Behavior

In some instances, a specific action requires more than one behavior. To bring back the Eco-Tour ad once the mouse moves off the trigger, you have to add a restore function.

1 Switch to Design view.

Insert the insertion point in the *Tour Eiffel* heading and examine the Behaviors panel.

The inspector displays the currently assigned behavior. You don't need to select the element completely; Dreamweaver assumes you want to modify the entire trigger.

2   Click the Add Behavior icon ⊕.

Choose Swap Image Restore from the drop-down menu.

Click OK in the Swap Image Restore dialog to complete the command.

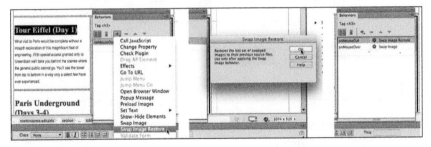

The Swap Image Restore behavior appears in the Behaviors panel with an attribute of onMouseOut.

3   Switch to Code view and examine the markup for the *Tour Eiffel* text.

```
95   <td scope="col">
96   <h3 onMouseOver="MM_swapImage('SideAd','','images/ecotour.png',1)"
97   onMouseOut="MM_swapImgRestore()">Tour Eiffel (Day 1)</h3>
98   <p>What visit to Paris would be complete without a indepth exploration
```

The trigger events—onMouseOver and onMouseOut—were added as attributes to the <h3> element. The rest of the JavaScript code was inserted in the document's <head> section.

4   Scroll to the top of the code and find the JavaScript code in the <head> element around line 23. The <script> element is used to declare the Javascript with a type of text. Javascript makes use of functions and logic to create many different types of effects and functionality.

```
23   <script type="text/javascript">
24   function MM_preloadImages() { //v3.0
25     var d=document; if(d.images){ if(!d.MM_p) d.MM_p=new Array();
26       var i,j=d.MM_p.length,a=MM_preloadImages.arguments; for(i=0; i<a.
     length; i++)
27       if (a[i].indexOf("#")!=0){ d.MM_p[j]=new Image; d.MM_p[j++].src=a[i];
     }}
28   }
29   function MM_swapImgRestore() { //v3.0
30     var i,x,a=document.MM_sr; for(i=0;a&&i<a.length&&(x=a[i])&&x.oSrc;i++) x
     .src=x.oSrc;
31   }
32
33   function MM_findObj(n, d) { //v4.01
34     var p,i,x;  if(!d) d=document; if((p=n.indexOf("?"))>0&&parent.frames.
     length) {
35       d=parent.frames[n.substring(p+1)].document; n=n.substring(0,p);}
36     if(!(x=d[n])&&d.all) x=d.all[n]; for (i=0;!x&&i<d.forms.length;i++) x=d.
     forms[i][n];
37     for(i=0;!x&&d.layers&&i<d.layers.length;i++) x=MM_findObj(n,d.layers[i]
     .document);
```

```
38      if(!x && d.getElementById) x=d.getElementById(n); return x;
39    }
40
41    function MM_swapImage() { //v3.0
42      var i,j=0,x,a=MM_swapImage.arguments; document.MM_sr=new Array; for(i=
      0;i<(a.length-2);i+=3)
43        if ((x=MM_findObj(a[i]))!=null){document.MM_sr[j++]=x; if(!x.oSrc) x.
      oSrc=x.src; x.src=a[i+2];}
44    }
45    </script>
46    <!-- InstanceEndEditable -->
47    </head>
48      <body
```

5   Save the file and switch to Live view to test the behavior.

Test the text trigger *Tour Eiffel*.

When the pointer passes over the text, the Eco-Tour image is replaced by the one of the Eiffel Tower, and then reappears when the pointer is withdrawn. The behavior functions as desired, but nothing is visibly "different" about the text. There is nothing here to prompt a user to roll their pointer over the heading. The result will be that many users will miss the swap image effect altogether.

Users sometimes need to be encouraged or directed to these types of effects. Many designers use hyperlinks for this purpose, since users are already familiar with how they function. Let's replace the current effect with one based on a hyperlink.

Removing Applied Behaviors

Before you can apply a behavior to a hyperlink, you need to remove the current Swap Image and Swap Image Restore behaviors.

1   Switch to Design view.

Open the Behaviors panel, if necessary.

Insert the insertion point in the *Tour Eiffel* text.

The Behaviors panel displays the two applied events. Which one you delete first doesn't matter.

2   Select the Swap Image event in the Behaviors panel.

Click the Remove Event icon [—].

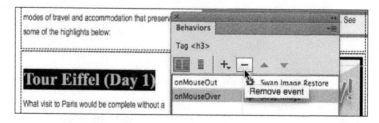

3   Select the Swap Image Restore event.

In the Behaviors panel, click the Remove Event icon.

Both events are now removed. Dreamweaver also removes any unneeded JavaScript code.

4   Save the file and check the text in Live view again.

The text no longer triggers the Swap Image behavior. To reapply the behavior, you need to add a link or link placeholder to the heading.

Adding Behaviors to Hyperlinks

Behaviors can be added to hyperlinks even if the link doesn't load a new document. For this exercise, you'll add a link placeholder (#) to the heading to support the desired behavior.

1   Select only the text *Tour Eiffel* in the <h3> element.
    Type # in the Property inspector Link field.
    Press Enter/Return to create the link placeholder.

The text displays with the default hyperlink styling. The tag selector for the a tag appears.

2   Insert the insertion point in the *Tour Eiffel* link.
    Click the Add Behavior icon ![+].
    Choose Swap Image from the pop-up menu.

As long as the insertion point is still inserted anywhere in the link, the behavior will be applied to the entire link markup.

3   In the Swap Image dialog, select the item `image "ecotour"`.
    Browse and select **tower.jpg** from the images folder.
    Click OK/Open.

4   In the Swap Image dialog, select the **Preload Images** option and the **Restore Images onMouseOut** option, if necessary, and click OK.

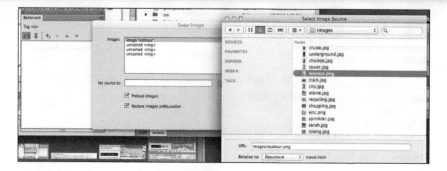

The Swap Image event appears in the Behaviors panel along with a Swap Image Restore event. Since the behavior was applied all at once, Dreamweaver provides the restore functionality as a productivity enhancement.

5   Apply a link placeholder (#) to the text *Paris Underground*.
Apply the Swap Image behavior to the link.
Use **underground.jpg** from the images folder.

6   Repeat step 5 for the *Seine Dinner Cruise* text.
Select the image **cruise.jpg**.

7   Repeat step 5 for the *Champs Élysées* text.
Select the image **champs.jpg**.

The Swap Image behaviors are now complete, but the text and link appearances don't match the site's color scheme. Let's create custom CSS rules to format them accordingly. You will create two rules: one for the heading element and another for the link itself.

8   In the CSS Designer, select **green_styles.css** > GLOBAL.
Create the new selector: `article table h3`

9   Create the following properties in the new rule:

```
margin-top: 0px
margin-bottom: 5px
font-size: 130%
font-family: "Arial Narrow", Verdana, sans-serif
```

10 Select **green_styles.css** > GLOBAL.
Create a new selector:

```
table h3 a:link, table h3 a:visited
```

11 Create the following properties in the new rule:

```
color: #090
font-weight: bold
```

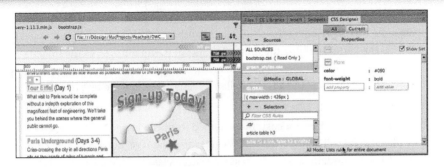

The headings are now more prominent and styled to match the site theme.

12 Save all files.

Test the behaviors in Live view.

Note how the links are underlined when the mouse moves over them. The Swap Image behavior should work successfully on all links. If one or more of the links do not function, check to make sure the behavior was assigned to the link successfully.

Making It Responsive

Once you're satisfied that all the rollover effects are functioning properly, you should check to make sure that the new components adapt properly to the responsive page design too. You can check the functionality in Dreamweaver or in any modern browser installed on your computer.

1 If necessary, open **travel.html**.

Switch to Live view.

2 Drag the Scrubber to the left to test how the new table responds to the existing set of media queries.

The table adapts to the changing screen in a fashion similar to the tables created and styled in Chapter 10. Everything seems to display fine, although the Eco-Tour ad does not scale or resize in any way.

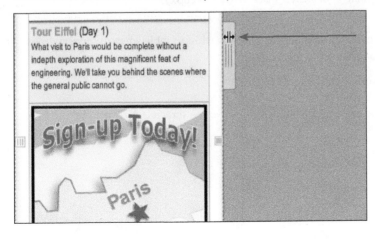

At a width of 426 pixels, the two columns merge and the cells begin to stack one atop the other, including the cell containing the ad. The image does not appear beside the text describing the tours. At this point, the purpose of the rollover effect will be lost completely, as does the need for the ad itself. The simplest plan would be just to hide the ad on smaller screens and allow the text to speak for itself.

At this moment, there's a custom id applied to the ad image but nothing applied to the cell containing it. CSS can hide the image, but it will leave the blank cell behind. Instead, let's create a custom class to hide the cell and its contents.

3   Drag the Scrubber all the way to the right to restore the table layout to two columns.

4   Select the Eco-Tour image.

5   Select the `td` tag selector.

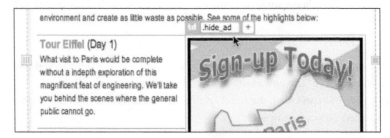

The HUD appears focused on the `td` element.

6   Click the Add Class/ID icon [+].

7   Enter `.hide_ad` in the HUD text field. If the CSS Source HUD appears press the ESC key to close it.

8   If necessary, open the CSS Designer.
Select **green_styles.css** > (max-width: 426px).
Create a new selector: `table .hide_ad`

This rule limits the styling to elements within a table when the screen drops down to the smallest media query.

9   Create the following property:
`display: none`
The table cell and ad will hide whenever the screen is 426 pixels or narrower.

10 Drag the Scrubber to the left until it is narrower than 426 pixels. Observe the changes to the table and its content.

The Eco-Tour ad hides once the screen is narrower than 426 pixels. It reappears as soon as the screen gets wider than 426 pixels.

11 Save all files.

12 Close **travel.html**.

In addition to eye-catching effects such as the dynamic behaviors you've just been learning about, Dreamweaver also provides structural components—such as jQuery and Bootstrap widgets—that conserve space and add more interactive flair to your website.

Working with Bootstrap Accordion Widgets

The Bootstrap Accordion widget allows you to organize a lot of content into a compact space. In the Accordion widget, the tabs are stacked, and when opened, they expand vertically rather than side by side. Let's preview the completed layout.

1 In the Files panel, select **tips_finished.html** from the Chapter13_Exercise folder and preview it in your primary browser.

The page content is divided among three panels using the Bootstrap Accordion widget.

2 Click each panel in turn to open and close each.

When you click a tab, the panel slides open with a smooth action. The panels are set to a specific height; if the content is taller than the default panel size, the panel adjusts its height automatically. When the panels open and close, the bulleted lists of green tips are revealed. The accordion allows you to display more content in a smaller, more efficient footprint.

3 Close your browser and return to Dreamweaver.
Close **tips_finished.html**.

Inserting a Bootstrap Accordion Widget

In this exercise, you'll incorporate a Bootstrap Accordion widget into one of your existing layouts.

1 Open **tips.html** in Live view.

The page consists of three bulleted lists separated by <h2> headings. These lists take up a lot of vertical space on the page, requiring the user to scroll down two or more screens to read them. Keeping content on one screen as much as possible will make it easier to access and read.

One technique to maximize screen real estate is using tabbed or accordion panels. Dreamweaver offers both types of components in jQuery and Bootstrap frameworks. Since we're using a Bootstrap layout, let's use a Bootstrap Accordion.

2 Insert the insertion point in the *At Home* heading, and select the <h2> tag selector.

3 Open the Insert panel.
Select the Bootstrap Components category.
Click the Accordion item.

The position assist HUD appears.

4   Click Before.

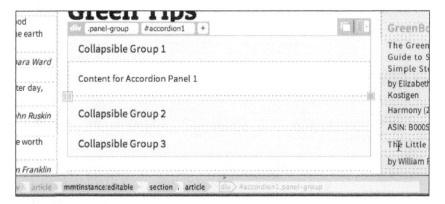

Dreamweaver inserts the Bootstrap Accordion widget element above the heading, but inside the `<article>` element. The default element is a three-panel Accordion widget that appears with the top panel (*Collapsible Group 1*) open. The HUD appears above the new object, focused on a `div` element with a class of `.panel-group` and an id of `#accordion1`.

The next step is to move the existing lists into the panel. Since two of the panels are hidden by default, the easiest way to work with the content will be in Code view.

5   Switch to Code view.

6   Scroll down, and insert the insertion point in the first bullet:
    `<li>Wash clothes in cold water.</li>` (approximately line 87).

7   Select the `ul` tag selector.
    Press Ctrl+X/Cmd+X to cut the whole list.

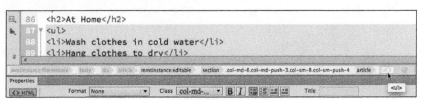

8   Delete the code `<h2>At Home</h2>`.

9   Scroll up and select the heading *Collapsible Group 1* (approximately line 63).
    Edit the heading to say: At Home

```
62  <div class="panel-heading" role="tab">
63  <h4 class="panel-title"><a data-toggle="collapse" data-parent="#accordion1" href=
    "#collapseOne1">At Home</a></h4>
64  </div>
65  <div id="collapseOne1" class="panel-collapse collapse in">
66  <div class="panel-body">Content for Accordion Panel 1</div>
67  </div>
```

The new heading structure is based on an `<h4>` element.

Tip: As you work in Code view, you may need to click the Refresh button from time to time in the Property inspector to see the tag selectors.

10 Select and delete the text placeholder *Content for Accordion Panel 1* (approximately line 66).

```
62   <div class="panel-heading" role="tab">
63   <h4 class="panel-title"><a data-toggle="collapse" data-parent="#accordion1" href=
     "#collapseOne1">Collapsible Group 1</a></h4>
64   </div>
65   <div id="collapseOne1" class="panel-collapse collapse in">
66   <div class="panel-body">Content for Accordion Panel 1</div>
67   </div>
```

The text appears in the `<div>` without any other structure. Make sure you do not delete the `<div>`.

11 Press Ctrl+V/Cmd+V to paste the list.

```
63   <h4 class="panel-title"><a data-toggle="collapse" data-parent="#accordion1" href=
     "#collapseOne1">Collapsible Group 1</a></h4>
64   </div>
65   <div id="collapseOne1" class="panel-collapse collapse in">
66   <div class="panel-body"><ul>
67   <li>Wash clothes in cold water</li>
68   <li>Hang clothes to dry</li>
69   <li>Turn off lights in empty rooms</li>
70   <li>Use motion sensors to turn lights on</li>
71   <li>Plan driving errands to combine trips</li>
72   <li>Walk more, drive less</li>
73   <li>Install Compact Fluorescent lighting (CFL)</li>
```

The list markup appears in `<div class="panel-body">`. The first Accordion panel group is complete. You have to repeat this process for the other two lists.

12 Scroll down and select the "At Work" tip list (approximately line 112).

13 Using the `ul` tag selector as in step 7, press Ctrl+X/Cmd+X to cut the list.

14 Click the `<article>` tag selector.
Press Delete.

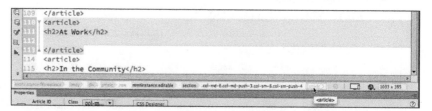

The `<article>` and the heading *At Work* are deleted.

15 Select the heading *Collapsible Group 2* and type **At Work** to replace it (approximately line 93).

```
91   <div class="panel panel-default">
92   <div class="panel-heading">
93   <h4 class="panel-title"><a data-toggle="collapse" data-parent="#accordion1" href=
     "#collapseTwo1">At Work</a></h4>
94   </div>
95   <div id="collapseTwo1" class="panel-collapse collapse">
96   <div class="panel-body">Content for Accordion Panel 2</div>
97   </div>
```

16 Delete the placeholder text *Content for Accordion Panel 2* and paste the list you cut from step 13 (approximately line 96).

```
92  <div class="panel-heading">
93  <h4 class="panel-title"><a data-toggle="collapse" data-parent="#accordion1" href=
    "#collapseTwo1">At Work</a></h4>
94  </div>
95  <div id="collapseTwo1" class="panel-collapse collapse">
96  <div class="panel-body"><ul>
97  <li>Use recycled paper.</li>
98  <li>Print on both sides of the paper</li>
99  <li>Turn your computer screen off when you leave your desk</li>
```

17 Repeat steps 12–16 to create the content section for *In the Community*.

When you're finished, all three lists are now contained within Accordion 1, and all the empty `<article>` elements have been deleted.

18 Switch to Live view.

You inserted a Bootstrap Accordion and added content to it.

19 Test the panels by clicking each heading.

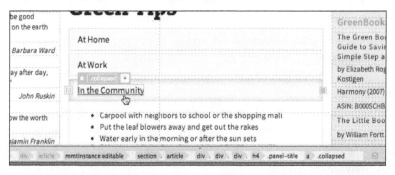

When clicked, the panel should open, revealing the list contained within. When you click a different heading, the new panel opens, closing the old one.

20 Save all files.

In the next exercise, you'll learn how to apply the site color scheme to the Accordion widget.

Styling a Bootstrap Accordion

As with the basic layout and the other Bootstrap components created by Dreamweaver, the accordion is formatted by the Bootstrap CSS and JavaScript files. You should avoid editing these files directly unless you know what you are doing. Instead, you'll apply the site design theme to Accordion 1 using your own custom style sheet as before. Let's start with the tabs.

1 Click the *At Home* tab.

Examine the tag selectors.

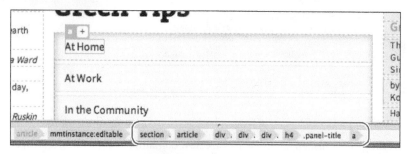

The tab is composed of three main elements: `<div.panel-heading>`, `<h4.panel-title>`, and `<a>`. But that's only on the surface. Behind the scenes, the Bootstrap JavaScript and CSS functions are manipulating the HTML and CSS to produce the various behaviors controlling the accordion. As you move your mouse over the tabs and click them, class attributes are being changed on the fly to produce the hover effects and animated panels.

As you learned earlier, hyperlinks exhibit four basic behaviors: link, visited, hover, and active. The Bootstrap framework is taking advantage of these default states to apply the various effects you see when interacting with Accordion 1 for the *At Home* list.

Your job will be to create several new rules that will override the default styling and apply the GreenStart theme instead. The first step is to format the default state of the tabs. Since only one tab can be open at a time, the closed state is considered the default state.

2 Click the *At Home* tab heading to close the tab content.

The tabs are currently styled a light gray. You need to identify any rules that format the background color of the Accordion tab. Be aware that there may be more than one rule affecting these properties.

One trick that can help you identify rules that are styling a specific element is to notice how the selected element is displayed in the document window. For example, when you clicked the heading initially, only the `<a>` element was selected, as shown below.

You can see how the HUD outlines the heading text.

3 Click the h4 tag selector for the closed tab.

When you click the h4 tag selector, the HUD outlines the <h4> element but does not extend to the entire tab.

The outline is a literal indication of how far the styling of the heading extends. That means you can ignore rules styling the a and h4 elements if you want to set the background of the entire tab.

4 Click the next element in the tag selector interface.

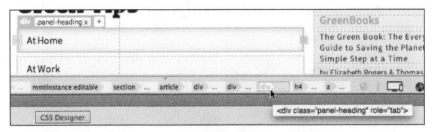

The element <div.panel-heading> is selected. Note how the HUD outlines the entire tab.

5 Click the Current button in the CSS Designer.
Examine the rules and properties applied to this element.

The very first rule displayed in the Selectors window, .panel-default > .panel-heading, applies a background color. To apply the site color theme, you need to override this rule.

6 Click the All button.
Choose **green_styles.css** > GLOBAL.
Create a new selector:

```
article .panel-default > .panel-heading
```

Since some elements already feature the site theme, it's a simple matter to grab this styling using the CSS Designer. Let's format the tabs the same way the footer is styled.

7 Select the footer rule in **green_styles.css** in the Selectors window.

8 Right-click the `footer` rule.
Select Copy Styles > Copy Background Styles from the context menu.

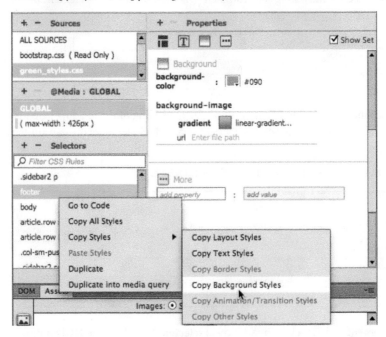

9 Right-click the rule `article .panel-default > .panel-heading` and select Paste Styles from the context menu.

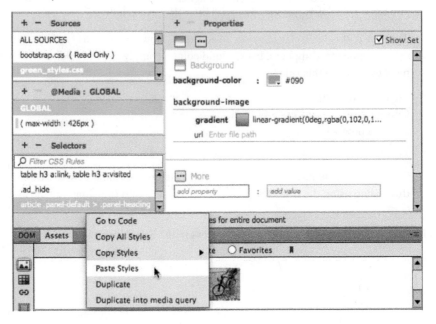

The background color and gradient properties are added to the new rule.

10 Add the following property:

`color: #FFC`

This styling will apply to the default state of the Accordion tabs. We'll add some interactive styling later, but first let's flesh out the styling of the accordion.

11 Choose **green_styles.css** > GLOBAL.
Create a new selector:
`article #accordion1`

12 Create the following properties:

`border: solid 1px #060`
`border-radius: 5px`

This new rule defines a border around the entire accordion.

13 Create a new selector: `article .panel-body`
Create the following property: `background-color: #CFC`

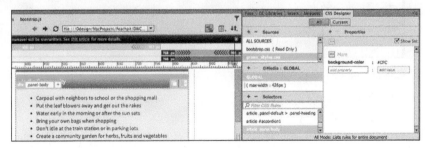

This rule adds a background color to the content panels.

Finally, let's give the accordion a little flair by adding a rollover behavior to the tabs. Although it's mainly used for links, the `:hover` pseudo-class can be used anytime you want to create interactive effects.

14 Right-click the rule
article .panel-default > .panel-heading.
Select Duplicate from the context menu.

A duplicate of the rule appears in the Selectors window, complete with the same styling.

15 Edit the new selector by adding the highlighted markup:
article .panel-default > .panel-heading:hover

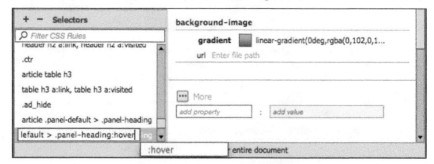

The new rule will format the tabs whenever you position the insertion point over the tab. But at the moment, the styling is identical to the original.

16 Edit the background gradient property of the top color stop.
Change the angle to 180

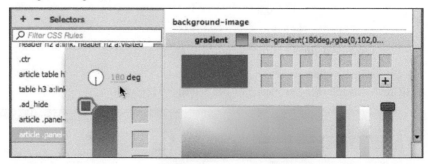

17 Change the color property to #FFF

18 Save all files.

19 Position the insertion point over each tab to test the new behavior.

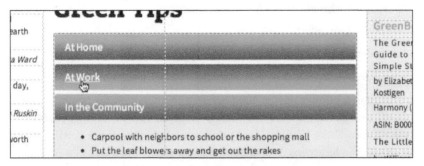

The gradient background inverts as the insertion point moves over and away from each tab. There is only one distraction in the overall effect. The default hyperlink styling adds an underline to the heading when the insertion point passes over it.

Although this may be an acceptable behavior in a normal text-based link, it's rather distracting in the Accordion tab. To turn this effect off, you first have to find the rule that's responsible for creating it.

20 Select the Current button in the CSS Designer.

21 Click the heading *At Home* in the first tab. Examine the rules listed in the Selectors window. Try to identify any rules adding the underline effect.

The third rule, `a:hover, a:focus`, applies the underline effect. We don't want to turn this styling off for all hyperlinks, just for links in the Accordion tabs.

22 Create a new selector in **green_styles.css** > GLOBAL.

The name `.panel-heading .panel-title a` appears in the window.

23 Press the up arrow key to make the selector less specific.

24 Add the highlighted markup to the name:
`.panel-title a:hover,`
`.panel-title a:focus`

This rule will style the hover state of the tab heading.

25 Create the following property:

```
text-decoration: none
```

26 Test the rollover effect.

The underline no longer appears in the Accordion tabs.

27 Save all files.

The accordion is just one of over 100 Bootstrap and jQuery widgets and components offered by Dreamweaver. They allow you to incorporate advanced functionality into your website, while requiring little or no programming skill. All of these components can be accessed via either the Insert menu or panel.

Adding interactivity to your webpages opens new possibilities of interest and excitement for your visitors, engaging them in new ways. It can easily be overdone, but a wise use of interactivity can help bring in new visitors and keep your frequent visitors coming back for more.

End-of-Chapter Activities

Review Questions

Directions: Choose the correct answer for each question.

1. The Swap Image behavior can only be applied to what?
   a. Text in an HTML document
   b. A hyperlink in an HTML document
   c. An image in an HTML document
   d. A and C only
   e. None of the above

2. True or False, You can only apply one behavior to an HTML element.
   a. True
   b. False

3. The Preload Images option does what when applying the Swap Image behavior.
   a. Loads the images controlled by the behavior only when the visitor initiates the behavior
   b. Loads the images controlled by the behavior after the page loads in the browser
   c. Loads the images controlled by the behavior as the page loads in the browser
   d. A and B only

4. The trigger event of **onKeyDown** initiates a behavior when the user does what?
   a. Presses a key down on their keyboard]
   b. Letting up on a key that has been pressed down
   c. Clicking the mouse button
   d. Letting up on the mouse button.

5. The trigger event of **onMouseUp** initiates a behavior when the user does what?
   a. Presses a key down on their keyboard
   b. Lets up on a key that has been pressed down
   c. Clicks the mouse button
   d. Lets up on the mouse button

6. The Swap Image Restore behavior does what?
   a. Replaces the image controlled by the behavior with a high-resolution image.
   b. Restores the initial image that what swapped with a new image in the Swap Image behavior.
   c. Restores an image to its original image size when it has been resized.
   d. None of the above

7. True or False: Once your create a behavior in Dreamweaver you cannot remove it.
   a. True
   b. False

8. If you want to hide an element in an HTML web page you can control what CSS property?
   a. Set the **Display** property to **None**
   b. Set the **Background-Color** property to the **none**
   c. Set the **width** and **height** properties to **none**
   d. Set the **Display** property to **hidden**

9. Bootstrap Accordion Widgets are makeup of what?
   a. HTML
   b. JavaScript
   c. CSS
   d. All of the above
   e. B & C only

10. What CSS Designer feature helps you figure out what CSS selectors rules that were applied to an HTML element?
    a. All button
    b. Current button
    c. Show Set button
    d. New Selector button

Essay Questions

Directions: Respond to each question by writing your answers in complete sentences and paragraphs. Be thorough in your answers.

1. What is a benefit of using Dreamweaver behaviors?

2. What three steps must be used to create a Dreamweaver behavior?

3. What's the purpose of assigning an id to an image before applying a behavior?

4. What does a Bootstrap Accordion widget do?

5. What Dreamweaver tools are helpful in troubleshooting CSS styling on dynamic elements?

6. Describe the process to copy the properties of a CSS selector rule to another CSS selector rule.

7. What are the four states of a link?

8. Describe what the term Web 2.0 means?

9. List the behaviors that come with Dreamweaver CC 2015.

10. List the Bootstrap Widgets that are available in the Dreamweaver CC 2015?

Critical Thinking Project—Develop the Lake Powell Hiking Page with Interactivity

Using Dreamweaver's built in advanced web design tools, add interactivity and special effects to the Lake Powell website. You'll use Bootstrap widgets and Dreamweaver Behaviors to create this Web 2.0 functionality for the site.

Add the Accordion Bootstrap Widget

The **hiking.html** page of the Lake Powell site needs to be developed. The Bootstrap Accordion widget is a great feature to display multiple hiking adventures and trails for the site.

1. On your computer create a local root folder as directed by your teacher. Name the folder **lakepowell_xx**. Copy the class data files from the **Chapter13/Data files/lakepowell_xx** directory as instructed by your teacher.

2. Open the **hiking.html** webpage. Switch to Live view. Select the text in the <h1> element of the main content area. Type **Hiking Trails of Lake Powell**

3. Next you copy content from a basic HTML page. Open the Files panel and then in the resource folder open the **trails.html** file. Select the first paragraph on the page and copy it.

4. Make the **hiking.html** page active and select the <p> element that contains the first paragraph under heading **Hiking Trails of Lake Powell**. Paste the copied text. Double-click in a blank area on exit the <p> element you just edited.

5. Next add a Bootstrap Accordion panel under the paragraph by first selecting the <p> selector. Then open the Insert panel and choose the Bootstrap Components category. Locate the Accordion widget and select it. In the position assist interface that displays, click **After**.

6. The Accordion widget displays with three panels. Switch to Design view and then switch to Split view so you can see the code. Select the **Collapsible Group 1** heading. Double check in code view that you only have selected the default text in the link text.

```
59            <div class="panel-group" id="accordion1" role="tablist"
     aria-multiselectable="true">
60              <div class="panel panel-default">
61                <div class="panel-heading" role="tab">
62                  <h4 class="panel-title"><a data-toggle="collapse"
     ▼ data-parent="#accordion1" href="#collapseOne1">Collapsible Group 1</a>
     </h4>
63                </div>
64                <div id="collapseOne1" class="panel-collapse collapse
     in">
65                  <div class="panel-body">Content for Accordion Panel 1
     </div>
66                </div>
67              </div>
68              <div class="panel panel-default">
69                <div class="panel-heading">
70                  <h4 class="panel-title"><a data-toggle="collapse"
     data-parent="#accordion1" href="#collapseTwo1">Collapsible Group 2</a>
     </h4>
71                </div>
72                <div id="collapseTwo1" class="panel-collapse collapse">
73                  <div class="panel-body">Content for Accordion Panel 2
     </div>
74                </div>
75              </div>
76              <div class="panel panel-default">
77                <div class="panel-heading">
78                  <h4 class="panel-title"><a data-toggle="collapse"
     data-parent="#accordion1" href="#collapseThree1">Collapsible Group 3</
     a></h4>
79                </div>
80                <div id="collapseThree1" class="panel-collapse collapse"
     >
81                  <div class="panel-body">Content for Accordion Panel 3
     </div>
82                </div>
83              </div>
84            </div>
85          </section>
```

7. Change this to **Rainbow Bridge – Easy**. Repeat this step to change the other two headings to the following:
   a. Collapsible Group 2 – **Antelope Canyon - Moderate**
   b. Collapsible Group 3 – **West Canyon – Difficult**

8. Make the **trails.html** document the active document and copy the paragraph below the **Rainbow Bridge – Easy** heading. Switch back to the **hiking.html** document and in Code view select the default text in the <div class="panel-body"> element.

```
60          <div class="panel panel-default">
61              <div class="panel-heading" role="tab">
62                  <h4 class="panel-title"><a data-toggle="collapse" data-parent=
   "#accordion1" href="#collapseOne1">Rainbow Bridge - Easy</a></h4>
63              </div>
64              <div id="collapseOne1" class="panel-collapse collapse in">
65                  <div class="panel-body">Content for Accordion Panel 1</div>
66              </div>
67          </div>
68          <div class="panel panel-default">
69              <div class="panel-heading">
70                  <h4 class="panel-title"><a data-toggle="collapse" data-parent=
   "#accordion1" href="#collapseTwo1"> Antelope Canyon</a></h4>
71              </div>
72              <div id="collapseTwo1" class="panel-collapse collapse">
73                  <div class="panel-body">Content for Accordion Panel 2</div>
74              </div>
75          </div>
76          <div class="panel panel-default">
77              <div class="panel-heading">
78                  <h4 class="panel-title"><a data-toggle="collapse" data-parent=
   "#accordion1" href="#collapseThree1">West Canyon</a></h4>
79              </div>
80              <div id="collapseThree1" class="panel-collapse collapse">
81                  <div class="panel-body">Content for Accordion Panel 3</div>
82              </div>
83          </div>
84      </div>
85    </section>
```

9. Paste the copied paragraph. Repeat steps 8-9 to replace the other panel body default text with the appropriate paragraph from the trails.html page.

10. Save all files and test the **hiking.html** page and the new accordion panel in a browser. Make sure you click the panel headings to expand and collapse the panel description area of the widget.

11. Close the trails.html page.

> **Tip:** As you work in Code view, you may need to click the Refresh button from time to time in the Property inspector to see the tag selectors.

Add the Swap Image Behavior of Dreamweaver

Take the Hiking page farther by adding the Swap Image behavior of Dreamweaver to the information in the accordion panel.

1. If necessary open the **hiking.html** page. Switch to Design view.

2. First create an ID for the image of the Lake Powell map in the left <aside> element by selecting the image. Apply an ID by clicking in the ID field in the Property inspector and typing **map**. Press Enter/Return.

3. Now develop the right <aside> element. Select the default heading and type **Hiking Trails**. Replace the paragraph below the heading with **Take a break from the boat and hike the land, canyons, and plateaus of Lake Powell**. Press Enter/Return to create a new paragraph.

4. Insert an image by choosing Insert>Image. Insert the hiking_top.html image. Attach an ID to the image by clicking in the ID field in the Property Inspector and typing **hiking**. Add the <alt> text by typing **Lake Powell offers miles of hiking and land adventures**

5. Switch to Live view. Drag the Scrubber to the left to see how the image response to a smaller screen. It stays the same size and displays too large for the smaller screens. It needs to be responsive.

6. Since this image has a custom **id** assigned to it already, an alternate technique needs to be used to make it responsive. Click the image and in the Property inspector change the Width field to **100%**. This uses HTML code to make the image fit the <aside> element width no matter what size the screen ,and all swapped images adhere to the width as well.

7. Save all files and test the page in a browser. Resize the Browser window to see the responsiveness of the image. Switch back to Dreamweaver.

8. Next add interactivity to the panel headings so that when a visitor hovers their insertion point over a heading the hiking picture changes to reflect that tour. Apply the Swap Image behavior to the first heading by selecting the **Rainbow Bridge – Easy** heading. Open the Behaviors panel and click the **Add behavior** button. Select **Swap Image** from the dropdown list.

9. In the Swap Image dialog, select the **image "hiking"** from the Images field and then click the Browse button to identify the image that this behavior will switch to. In the Select Image Source dialog, click the **hiking_rocks.jpg** image. Click Open. Then in the Swap Image dialog select the options **Preload images** and **Restore images onMouse-Out**. Click OK to close the dialog.

10. Repeat step 9 to add the Swap Image behavior to the other two panel headings. Add the following image to the Swap Image headings.
    a. Antelope Canyon – Moderate: **hikes.jpg**
    b. West Canyon – Difficult: **hiking_2.jpg**

11. Save all files and test your page in a browser. Make sure you hover your mouse over the panel headings.

Format the Accordion Widget

The Accordion widget that was created needs to be formatted with CSS. It comes designed with a default format created by existing CSS rules. Alter these rules to make it reflect the website color palette and sites color theme by creating new CSS rules for the four states of a link.

1. If necessary open the **hiking.html** page. Switch to Live view.

2. Click the **Rainbow Bridge - Easy** tab heading to close the tab content. The tabs are currently styled a light gray. Next identify any CSS rules that format the background color of the Accordion tab. There is more than one rule affecting these properties. Click the **h4** tag selector for the closed tab. This rule does not extend to the entire tab so you can ignore these rules styling the **a** and **h4** elements in order to set the background of the entire tab.

3. Click the next element in the tag selector interface. The element **<div.panel-heading>** is selected. The HUD outlines the entire tab. Click the Current button in the CSS Designer. Examine the rules and properties applied to this element. The very first rule displayed in the Selectors window, **.panel-default > .panel-heading**, applies a background color. A new CSS rule needs to be created to override this rule.

4. Click the All button. Choose lakepowell.css > GLOBAL. Create a new selector:
   a. article .panel-default > .panel-heading

5. The Lake Powell site already has elements formatted with the site color theme. You can format the tabs the same way the footer is styled by copying the background style applied to the footer CSS rule. Select the **footer** rule in **lakepowell.css** in the Selectors window. Right-click the **footer** rule. Select Copy Styles > Copy Background Styles from the context menu.

6. Next, right-click the **rule article .panel-default > .panel-heading** and select Paste Styles from the context menu. The background color and gradient properties are added to the new rule.

7. Add the another property to this rule:
   a. color: #C93

8. Next create another selector to define the border around the entire accordion. Choose lakepowell.css > GLOBAL and create a new selector named **article #accordion1** and set the following properties:
   a. border: **solid 1px #060**
   b. border-radius: **5px**

9. Now create a rule that adds a background color to the content panel by creating a new selector: **article .panel-body** with the following property:
   a. background-color: #F9F9DE

10. Finally, add a rollover behavior to the tabs by targeting the :hover pseudo-for link hover state. Right-click the rule **article .panel-default > .panel-heading**. Select Duplicate from the context menu. A duplicate of the rule appears in the Selectors window, complete with the same styling. Edit the new selector to be named **article .panel-default > .panel-heading:hover**

11. The styling is identical to the original and needs to be changed to reflect the color theme of the site. Edit the background gradient property by changing the angle to **0** and the color property to **#FFF** .

12. Save all files and position the insertion point over each tab to test the new behavior. Notice that the default hyperlink styling adds an underline to the heading when the cursor passes over it. Turn this effect off by finding the rule that's responsible for creating it.

13. Select the Current button in the CSS Designer and click the heading **Rainbow Bridge - Easy** in the first tab. Examine the rules listed in the Selectors window. Identify any rules adding the underline effect. The rule, **a:hover, a:focus**, applies the underline effect. Turn this styling off for links in the Accordion tabs.

14. Click the All button in the CSS Designer and create a new selector in lakepowell.css > GLOBAL. The name **.panel-heading .panel-title a** displays in the window. Press the up arrow key to make the selector less specific. Edit this rule name to add the highlighted markup to the name:
   a. **.panel-title a:hover, .panel-title** a: focus

15. Create the following property:
   a. text-decoration: none

16. The underline no longer appears in the Accordion tabs. Save all files and test the rollover effect in a browser.

Online Portfolio Builder—Develop your Online Portfolio Website by Adding Interactivity and Web 2.0 functionality

Develop your online portfolio website by adding Dreamweaver behaviors and Bootstrap widgets to your pages. Follow the following basic steps to add this functionality.

1. If necessary, create a local root directory and copy any files or folders over to the new local root directory. Define your site as instructed by your teacher.

2. Open your website pages that you have developed up to this point in the class.

3. Add a Dreamweaver behavior to the pages that need advanced interactivity to help add flare to the site. You will need to plan ahead and identify the pages you want to edit and create any images that you might use with the Swap Image Behavior. If you swap images, they need to be the same physical dimensions in both height and width. Access the Behaviors panel and set up your Behavior. Remember to assign an **id** to your images.

4. Make any new images responsive and if needed, create a Class ID for any images that you want to hide in smaller screen sizes. Do this by targeting the smaller screen media query in the CSS Designer. Then create a new class selector with the **Display** property of **None** for these elements.

5. Next add one of the Bootstrap widgets by accessing the Insert panel and choosing the Bootstrap Components category and then add your content for the widget. An Accordion widget is a great way to show multiple examples of your work while keeping the page length shorter.

6. Use CSS to format the Bootstrap Accordion widget so that it matches your sites color theme and identified color palette.

7. Create any other CSS rules to format the pages of your site.

8. Test your pages often as you develop the advanced interactivity by saving all files and previewing each page in a browser.

Chapter 14

WORKING WITH WEB ANIMATION AND VIDEO

Dreamweaver allows you to integrate HTML5-compatible animation and video.

Chapter Overview

In this chapter, you'll learn how to incorporate web-compatible animation and video components into your webpage and do the following:

- Insert web-compatible animation
- Insert web-compatible video

Adobe Flash

A software product that is part of Adobe's Creative Suite of software. Flash is used to create animation and interactivity for the web and for games. It also has ActionScript built into it for creating programming that controls vector graphics and other assets. Flash uses SWF or FLV format for web display.

coder-decoders (codecs)

A computer program that can encode and decode a video. Encoding compresses and standardizes the video so it is smaller in size and transmitted quicker over the Internet. Decoding uncompresses and interprets the video for display purposes.

proprietary players

Video or audio software player developed for just one product or file type.

SWF

Acronym for Small Web Format. Adobe Flash creates files in this format for web display.

FLV

Acronym for Flash Video which is a streaming video format for Web display. Adobe Flash creates this type of streaming video format.

Understanding Web Animation and Video

The web can provide a variety of experiences to the average user. One second, you are downloading and reading a best-selling novel. Next, you're listening to your favorite radio station or performing artist. Then, you're watching live television coverage or a feature-length movie. Before **Adobe Flash**, animation and video were hard to incorporate onto websites. That's because HTML was invented at a time when even static images were difficult to use on the Internet; video was a dream far off in the future.

Video and animation content was eventually provided in a variety of formats using a hodgepodge of applications, plug-ins, and **coder-decoders (codecs)** that could transfer data across the Internet to your computer and browser. Often this was accomplished with enormous difficulties and incompatibilities. Frequently, a format that worked in one browser was incompatible with another. Applications that worked in Windows didn't work on the Mac. Most formats required their own **proprietary players** or plug-ins.

For a time, Adobe Flash brought order to this chaos. It provided a single platform for creating both animation and video. Flash started as an animation program and changed the web for everyone. A few years ago, it revolutionized the industry again by making it a simple task to add video to a site. By inserting a video into Flash and saving the file as a **SWF** or **FLV** file, web designers and developers were able to take advantage of the almost universal distribution of the Flash Player (installed on over 90 percent of all desktop computers). No more worries over formats and codecs—Flash Player took care of all that.

With the invention and rise in popularity of smartphones and tablet devices over the last decade, Flash has fallen on hard times. For most manufacturers, the power and capability of Flash were too difficult to support on these devices, and it was abandoned. Flash is not dead. It's still unmatched for its multimedia power and functionality. But today, all bets are off when it comes to animation and video. The techniques for creating web-based media are being reinvented. As you may have guessed, this trend away from Flash is ringing in a new era of chaos on the web media front. Half a dozen or more codecs are competing to become the "be-all, end-all" format for video distribution and playback for the web.

The only ray of sunshine in this morass is that HTML5 was developed with built-in support for both animation and video. Great strides have already been made to replace much of the capability of Flash-based animation using native HTML5 and CSS3 functionality. The status of video is not as clear. So far, a single standard has not yet emerged, which means that to support all the popular desktop and mobile browsers, you'll have to produce several different video files. In this chapter, you'll learn how to incorporate different types of web animation and video into your site.

Adobe Edge Animate

The animation used in this chapter was built in Edge Animate—a program developed by Adobe not to replace Flash but to create web animation and interactive content natively using HTML5, CSS3, and JavaScript. Edge Animate is available to all Creative Cloud subscribers.

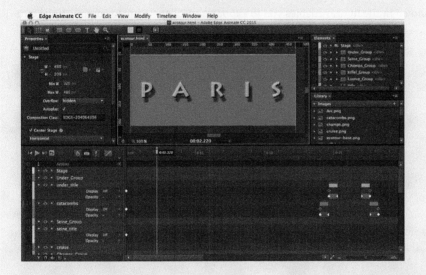

Visit www.adobe.com/products/edge-animate.html for more information about Edge Animate.

Note: Each browser supports different video and audio formats. IOS devices also support different video and audio formats. Check out Wikipedia for more informaiton on the current browser support for the various video and audio file formats: https://en.wikipedia.org/wiki/HTML5_video#Browser_support

Adding Web Animation to a Page

Dreamweaver has a built-in and simplified workflow for inserting Edge Animate compositions, making the process a point-and-click operation. Dreamweaver takes advantage of a feature in Edge Animate designed to assist in deploying compositions to other programs and workflows, such as Adobe InDesign, Adobe Dreamweaver, and Apple's iBooks Author. The File > Publish Settings command (shown in the figure) enables you to export your Edge Animate compositions into a single file or folder.

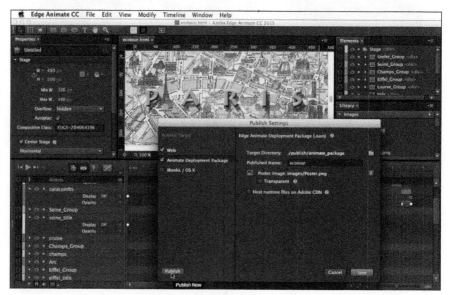

By defining your Publish settings appropriately, you can create a complete set of files that are compatible with these applications. For the purposes of this exercise, we published an OAM file for you, which is an archive file format that contains all the constituent elements needed to support the animation in Dreamweaver.

1 Launch Adobe Dreamweaver CC (2015.1 release) or later. If necessary, define a site based on the Chapter 14 as instructed by your teacher. Open **travel.html** from the Chapter14 site root folder in Live view.

The banner will be inserted above the main heading. But we have to take an interim step to get it into this page. At the time of this writing, Dreamweaver can't insert OAM files into child pages still connected to a template. So you will have to insert the animation into an empty page and then manually transfer the code to the travel page.

2 Select File > New.

The New Document dialog appears.

3 Choose HTML in the Document Type section of the dialog.

4 Choose None in the Framework section.

5 Click Create.

A new blank document appears. Before you can insert the banner, you have to save the file.

6 Save the file as **animation_transfer.html**.
If necessary, switch to Live view.

7 Choose Insert > HTML > Animated Composition. You may also use the Animated Composition option in the Insert panel's HTML category.

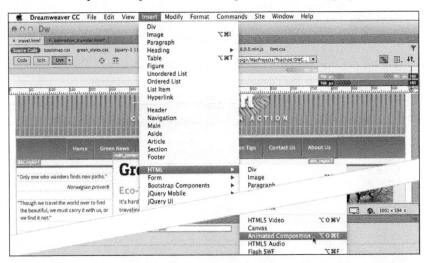

8 Navigate to the Chapter14/resources folder.
Select **ecotour.oam**.

9 Click OK/Open to insert the composition.

The banner should appear and begin to play. It is designed to loop over and over.

10 Save the file and switch to Code view.

11 Examine the HTML code.

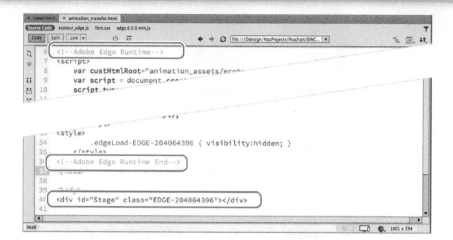

Tip: When selecting large amounts of code, click or drag the line numbers.

The file contains the structure of a basic webpage, including <head> and <body> sections, as well as the Edge Animate stage and support code.

12 In the Code view window, select and copy all the markup contained between the <!--Adobe Edge Runtime--> and <!--Adobe Edge Runtime End--> comments.

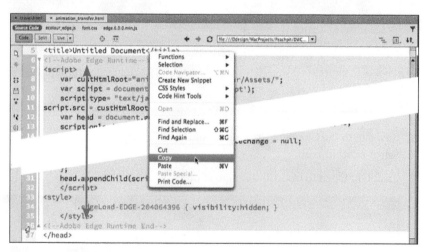

13 Click the **travel.html** document tab and switch to Code view.

14 In the Code view window, scroll to the <head> section. Insert the insertion point at the end of the notation <!-- InstanceBeginEditable name="doctitle" --> and press Enter/Return to create a new line (approximately line 7).

15 Paste the runtime markup copied in step 12.

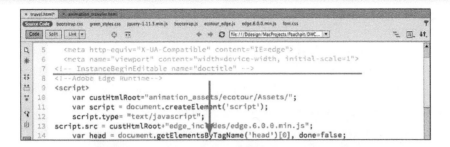

The next step is to transfer the composition stage.

16 Switch to **animation_transfer.html**.

17 In Code view, select the markup
`<div id="Stage" class="EDGE-204064396"> </div>` and copy it
(approximately line 40).

Note: When
selecting the stage,
don't forget the
closing `</div>` tag.

```
39 ▼ <body>
40 ▼   <div id="Stage" class="EDGE-204064396"></div>
41
42     </body>
```

18 Switch to **travel.html**.

19 In the Code view window, scroll to the `<body>` section. Insert the insertion point before the markup `<h1>Green Travel</h1>` (approximately line 114) and paste the stage.

20 Press Return/Enter to move the heading to a new line, if necessary.

```
112   <article class="row"><!-- InstanceBeginEditable name="main_content" -->
113   <section class="col-md-6 col-md-push-3 col-sm-8 col-sm-push-4">
114   <div id="Stage" class="EDGE-204064396"></div>
115   <h1>Green Travel</h1>
116   <h2>Eco-Touring</h2>
```

21 Switch to Live view.

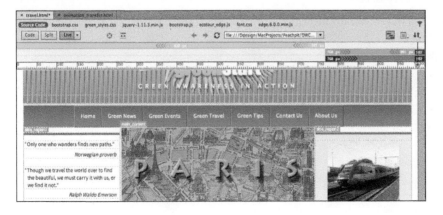

The banner animation plays automatically in Live view once the code is processed.

It may seem like a miracle that this amazing banner animation was created by one simple file, but what you cannot see is that Dreamweaver just created in the site root directory a new folder that is populated by more than a dozen files.

22 Open the Files panel and examine the list of folders in the site root.

Warning:
Dreamweaver will not automatically upload all the support files needed for the Edge Animate composition. Be sure to upload the entire contents of the **animation_assets** folder when publishing the site to the web.

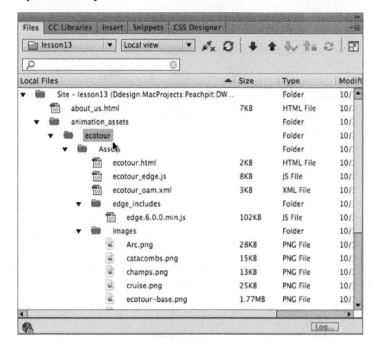

The folder named **animation_assets** now appears in the root directory. The folder was generated automatically and contains all the files needed to support the composition. The entire folder must be uploaded to the web host when **travel.html** is posted.

23 Save all files.

You've successfully incorporated an HTML5- and CSS3-based animation in your page.

Poster Child

The widespread popularity and support of HTML5 should mean that your animation will run in most browsers and mobile devices. But there's a very small possibility that the animation may be incompatible with older computers and software. Edge Animate can include either a down-level stage or a static poster image that will be viewed in these circumstances.

To add or create a down-level stage or poster within Edge Animate, select the project stage and then add the appropriate content using the Properties panel.

Adding Web Video to a Page

Implementing HTML5-compatible video in your site is a bit more involved than it was when you had to insert only a single Flash-based file. Unfortunately, no single video format is supported by all browsers in use today. To make sure your video content plays everywhere, you'll have to supply several different formats. Dreamweaver CC now provides a built-in technique to add multiple video files so you won't have to do all the coding yourself. In this exercise, you will learn how to insert HTML5-compatible video on a page in your site.

1 If necessary, open **travel.html** in Live view.

You will insert the video in the `main_content` section of the page.

2 Click the paragraph *Click here to sign up.*

The HUD appears focused on the p tag.

3 Choose Insert > HTML > HTML5 Video.

The Position Assist HUD appears.

Note: Open the Property inspector and dock it to the bottom of the document window, if necessary.

4   Click Before.

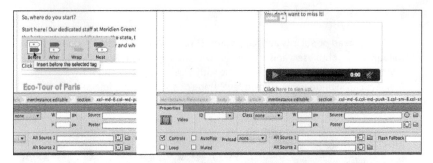

An HTML5-compatible video placeholder appears on the page, and the Property inspector displays new options for targeting the video source files. Note that this interface enables you to specify up to three video source files and one Flash fallback file. The first step is to select your primary video source.

5   In the Property inspector, click the Browse icon ▨ in the Source field. Navigate to the **movies** folder and select the **paris.mp4** file. Click OK/Open.

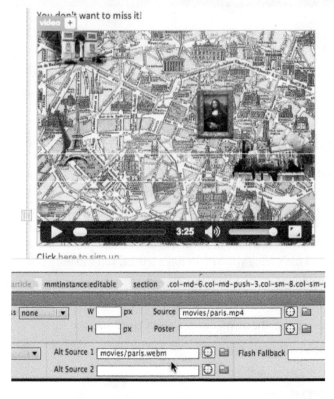

The MP4 video replaces the video placeholder. Note that Alt Source 1 is automatically populated with a WebM version of the movie.

The MP4 file format will be the primary video format loaded. MP4, also known as MPEG-4, is a video format based on Apple's QuickTime standard. It is supported natively by iOS-compatible devices, such as the iPhone and iPad, as well as by Apple's Safari browser. Many experts advise loading MP4 files first; otherwise, iOS devices may ignore the video element altogether.

WebM is an open-source, royalty-free video format sponsored by Google. It is compatible with Firefox 4, Chrome 6, Opera 10.6, and Internet Explorer 9 and later.

To round out our HTML5 video selections, the next format you'll load is a lossy, open-source multimedia format: Ogg. It is designed for the distribution of multimedia content that is free of copyright and other media restrictions.

Note: Ogg is a container format. When the container contains a video, it uses the extension .ogv.

6   Click the Browse icon ▨ for the Alt Source 2 field. Select the file **paris.theora. ogv** from the **movies** folder and click OK/Open.

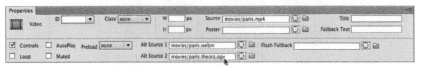

These three formats support all the modern desktop and mobile browsers. But to support older software and devices, using a stalwart old friend—Flash video—may be necessary. By adding it last, you ensure that only browsers that don't support the other three formats will load the Flash content. Although many are abandoning Flash, Dreamweaver still provides support for inserting both FLV and SWF files.

7   Click the Browse icon to the right of the Flash Fallback field.

Select the **paris.flv** file from the **movies** folder and click OK/Open.

8   Save the file.

9   If necessary, switch to Live view.

In some browsers, the <video> element won't generate a preview of the video content. You can add an image placeholder by using the Poster field in the Property inspector.

10 If necessary, select the `<video>` tag selector.
In the Property inspector, click Browse in the Poster field.

11 In the **movies** folder, select **paris-poster.png** and click OK/Open.

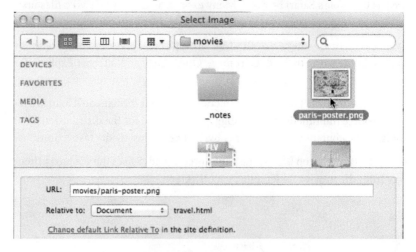

A preview image has been applied to the `<video>` element. It won't be visible in Dreamweaver, but you may see the poster in the browser. The advantage of using a poster is that something will always appear on the page, even in the rare browsers that do not support HTML5 or Flash video formats.

12 Save all files.

Video controls appear below the poster depending on what video format is displayed. In the next exercise, you will learn how to configure these controls and how the video will respond to the user.

Buggy Video

At this point, you would normally be finished and ready to test your video configuration in multiple browsers. Unfortunately, the Flash fallback using an FLV source file is missing some essential support files and will not play the FLV correctly as is. Dreamweaver has a bug affecting the proper support of both FLV and SWF video using the new HTML5 video workflow described in this section.

The Dreamweaver engineers promised to fix this issue in a subsequent cloud update, but until then you can correct the issue yourself by simply replacing the new code element using the legacy Flash video workflow, like this:

1 Select the <video> tag selector.

2 Switch to Code view. If necessary, select Source Code in the Related Files interface.

3 Select the entire <embed> element containing the reference to **paris.flv** and delete it.

4 Choose Insert > HTML > Flash Video.

5 In the Insert FLV dialog, click the Browse icon. Select **paris.flv** from the **movies** folder and click OK/Open.

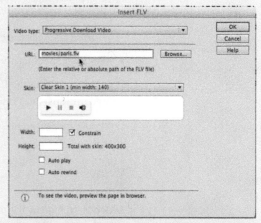

The filename **paris.flv** appears in the URL field of the dialog. Flash video supplies its own controls via a **SWF skin interface**. You can choose your own skin design in this dialog.

6 Choose **Corona Skin 2** from the Skin pop-up menu.

Before you can insert the file, you have to specify the dimensions of the video.

7 In the Width field, enter: **400**
In the Height field, enter: **300**

You can use the options below these fields to specify whether you want the video to autoplay and autorewind.

8 Click OK to insert the FLV video.

The <embed> element is now replaced by an <object> tag, along with all the code necessary to run the Flash video and even detect the presence and version of the needed Flash Player. This is the simplest method to insert FLV-compatible video so that it will play properly in all browsers that don't support HTML5 video.

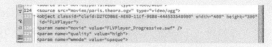

SWF skin interface

This applies to a SWF file and what format, placement and style to display the video/audio controls.

Choosing HTML5 Video Options

The final step for configuring the video is to decide what other HTML5-supported options to specify. The options are displayed within the Property inspector whenever the `<video>` element is chosen. The options are selectable in all views.

1   If necessary, open **travel.html** in Live view.
    Select the `<video>` tag selector.
    Observe the left side of the Property inspector.

    • **Controls** displays visible video controls.

    • **AutoPlay** starts the video automatically after the webpage loads.

    • **Loop** causes the video to replay from the beginning automatically once it finishes.

    • **Muted** silences the audio.

    • **Preload** specifies the method in which the video loads.

2   If necessary, select the Controls option and deselect the AutoPlay, Loop, and Muted options. Set Preload to **none**.

Video is very memory- and bandwidth-intensive. This is especially true for phones and tablets. Setting Preload to none prevents any video resources from downloading until the user actually clicks the video. It may take the video a few more seconds to download when launched, but your visitors will appreciate that you are respectful of their minutes and data plan.

The `<video>` element is now complete, but it's not responsive. Adding a simple rule can take care of that issue.

3   Select the `video` tag selector, if necessary.

4   In the CSS Designer, select **green_styles.css** > GLOBAL.
    Create a new selector: `video`

5   Create the following properties:
    `max-width: 100%`
    `height: auto`

6   Preview the page in Live view or in a browser. If the video controls are not visible, move your insertion point over the still image to display them. Click the Play button to view the movie.

Note: In Microsoft Internet Explorer, a notice may appear notifying you that the active content was blocked. Click the Allow Blocked Content button to play the video.

Chrome

Firefox

Safari

Depending on where you preview the page, you will see one of the four video formats. For example, in Live view you will see the MP4-based video. The controls will appear differently depending on what format is displayed. This movie has no sound, but the controls will often include a speaker button to adjust the volume or mute the audio.

7   Drag the Scrubber to the left to check the display of the video at various screen widths.

The video resizes as needed to fit the available space.

You've embedded three HTML5-compatible videos and an FLV fallback, which gives you support for most browsers and devices that can access the Internet. But you've learned only one possible technique for supporting this evolving standard. To learn more about HTML5 video and how to implement it, visit the following links:

*   http://tinyurl.com/video-HTML5-1
*   http://tinyurl.com/video-HTML5-2
*   http://tinyurl.com/video-HTML5-3

To learn more about implementing video for mobile devices, visit these links:

*   http://tinyurl.com/fluid-video
*   http://tinyurl.com/fluid-video-1

End-of-Chapter Activities

Review Questions

Directions: Choose the correct answer for each question.

1. In the past, video and animation content was added to a webpage through what techniques?
   a. Applications
   b. Plug-ins
   c. Coder-decoders
   d. SWF files
   e. All of the above

2. The Flash Player was installed on over what percentage of browser?
   a. 80%
   b. 90%
   c. 75%
   d. 50%

3. What caused Flash to not be used today for adding video to webpages?
   a. HTML5 <video> element
   b. SWF and FLV files are not supported in mobile devices
   c. A and B only
   d. None of the above

4. What is the single standard today for adding video to a webpage?
   a. Plug-ins
   b. JW Player
   c. Adobe Edge
   d. There is no standard yet

5. What are the video file formats required for viewing video in a browsers?
   a. MP4
   b. WebM
   c. Ogg
   d. SWF or FLV
   e. All of the above
   f. None of the above

6. What web video file formats does Chrome support?
   a. MP4
   b. WebM
   c. Ogg
   d. All of the above
   e. None of the above

7. What web video file formats does Firefox support?
   a. MP4
   b. WebM
   c. Ogg
   d. All of the above
   e. None of the above

8. What web video file formats does Internet Explorer support?
   a. MP4
   b. WebM
   c. Ogg
   d. All of the above
   e. None of the above

9. What web video file formats does Microsoft Edge support?
   a. MP4
   b. WebM
   c. Ogg
   d. All of the above
   e. None of the above

10. Adobe Edge Animate creates web animation through what technologies?
    a. HTML5
    b. HTML5 and CSS3
    c. HTML5, CSS3 and JavaScript
    d. HTML5, CSS3, JavaScript and Flash

Essay Questions

Directions: Respond to each question by writing your answers in complete sentences and paragraphs. Be thorough in your answers.

1. What advantage does HTML5 have over HTML 4 regarding web-based media?

2. What programming language(s) created the HTML5-compatible animation used in this chapter?

3. True or false: To support all web browsers, you can select a single video format.

4. In browsers or devices that do not support video, what can you do to provide some form of content to these users?

5. What video format is recommended to support older browsers?

6. What file format was designed to support workflows in other programs and workflows like Adobe InDesign? Describe this format.

7. Describe the best practice for selecting large amounts of code in Dreamweaver?

8. When working with Edge Animate composition files, what do you need to do to ensure that the animation is viewable on the web?

9. What is a static poster image?

10. In Dreamweaver, where can you find other HTML5 video supported features, like automatically playing the video or turning the video controls on or off?

Critical Thinking Project—Add Web Video to the Lake Powell Website

Lake Powell is an HTML5 website and this project takes advantage of this language by adding HTML5 video through the <video> element of HTML5.

Add a Web Image to the Home Page

Take the Lake Powell site further by adding web video to the site's home page to add a little more flare to the site.

1. On your computer create a local root folder as directed by your teacher. Name the folder **lakepowell_xx**. Copy the class data files from the **Chapter14/Data files/lake-powell_xx** directory as instructed by your teacher.

2. Open the index.html webpage. Switch to Live view.

3. The video will be inserted in place of the image at the bottom of the main content area. Select the **lp_view3.jpg** image and press Delete to delete it. Then delete the **<p>** element that contained the image by selecting the **<p>** selector and again pressing delete.

4. To insert the web video, click the second paragraph of the main content area. The HUD appears focused on the p tag. Choose Insert > HTML > HTML5 Video. The Position Assist HUD displays, click **After**.

5. An HTML5-compatible video placeholder appears on the page. In the Property inspector new options display for targeting the video source files. Select your primary video source by clicking the Browse icon in the Source field. Navigate to the videos folder and select the **lakepowell.mp4** file. Click OK/Open.

6. Note that the Property Inspector now displays target files in the Alt Source 1 and 2 fields. Alt Source 1 is set to **lakepowell.webm** and Alt Source 2 is set to **lakepowell.ogv**. These three formats support all the modern desktop and mobile browsers.

7. Finally add a FLV file for very old browsers. Click Browse in the Flash Fallback field and select the **lakepowell.flv** file from the videos folder and click OK/Open.

8. Save all files. If necessary, switch to Live view.

Add a Poster Image for Video

In some browsers, the <video> element won't generate a preview of the video content. Next you'll add an image placeholder by using the Poster field in the Property inspector.

1. If necessary open the **index.html** page. Switch to Design view.

2. If necessary, select the **<video>** tag selector. In the Property inspector, click Browse in the Poster field.

3. In the **videos** folder, select imges/lp_view3.jpg and click OK/Open.

4. A preview image has been applied to the **<video>** element. It won't be visible in Dreamweaver, but you may see the poster in the browser. The advantage of using a poster is that something will always appear on the page, even in the rare browsers that do not support HTML5 or Flash video formats.

5. Save all files and preview the page in a browser.

Fix a Flash FLV Bug in Dreamweaver

Dreamweaver has a bug affecting the proper support of both FLV and SWF video using the new HTML5 video workflow described in this chapter. The Flash fallback using an FLV source file is missing some essential support files and will not play the FLV correctly. You can fix this yourself by editing the code.

1. If necessary open the **index.html** page. Switch to Live view.

2. Select the **<video>** tag selector.

3. Switch to Code view. If necessary, select Source Code in the Related Files interface.

4. Select the entire <embed> element containing the reference to lakepowell.flv and delete it.

5. Choose Insert > HTML > Flash Video.

6. In the Insert FLV dialog, click the Browse icon. Select **lakepowell.flv** from the **videos** folder and click OK/Open. The filename **lakepowell.flv** appears in the URL field of the dialog. Flash video supplies its own controls via a SWF skin interface. You can choose your own skin design in this dialog. Choose **Halo Skin 1** from the Skin pop-up menu. Before you can insert the file, you have to specify the dimensions of the video. In the **Width** field enter **600** and then in the Height field enter **343**. You can use the options below these fields to specify whether you want the video to **autoplay** and **autorewind**.

7. Click OK to insert the FLV video.

8. Save all files and preview in a browser. Test how the page displays at a smaller size.

Format the Web Video with CSS

The video is needs to be responsive. This can be done through CSS.

1. If necessary open the **index.html** page. Switch to Live view.

2. In the CSS Designer, select lakepowell.css>GLOBAL and then create a new selector. Name the selector **video**

3. Set the following properties for the new selector:
   a. max-width: 100%
   b. height: auto

4. Save all files and preview in a browser. Again, test how the page displays at a smaller size.

Set HTML5 Video Options

Finally configure the video to set other HTML5-supported options.

1. If necessary open the **index.html** page. Switch to Live view.

2. Select the video on the page and then select the **<video>** tag selector.

3. Now set the video to automatically play upon loading in the browser. In the Property inspector click the AutoPlay option.

4. Save all files and preview in a browser.

Online Portfolio Builder—Add Web Video to Your Portfolio Website

Develop your online portfolio website by adding web video. Follow the following basic steps to add this functionality.

1. If necessary, create a local root directory and copy any files or folders over to the new local root directory. Define your site as instructed by your teacher.

2. Open your website pages that you have developed up to this point in the class.

3. You need to create web video to insert into your site. You can do this through a variety of programs that allow you to save as .mp4 or .webm or .ogv. Programs like iMovie, Powerpoint, Adobe Edge, etc. You can also use other third party software to convert an .mp4 file into .webm or .ogv. Examples of these are Mira Video Converter or Wonders Video Converter Ultimate.

4. To insert your web video, use Insert>HTML>HTML5 Video. Then set the target source files to the appropriate video files.

5. Set a Poster file for the video by clicking the Browse icon to the right of the Poster field and selecting the image you want to use.

6. If you set a target SWF, you will want to edit the HTML code to correct the bug that exists. In Code view, select the <embed> line of code for the .flv file and delete it. Then choose Insert>HTML>Flash Video.

7. Choose a SWF Skin for the video controls and set the appropriate video options.

8. Create any CSS rules to make your video responsive by creating a new CSS selector rule that targets the <video> element. Then create the following properties:
   a. max-width: 100%
   b. height: auto

9. Save all files and test your pages in a browser.

PUBLISHING TO THE WEB

The goal of all the preceding chapters is to design, develop, and build pages for a remote website. But Dreamweaver doesn't abandon you there. It also provides powerful tools to upload and maintain any size website over time.

Chapter Overview

In this chapter, you'll publish your website to the Internet and do the following:

- Define a remote site
- Define a testing server
- Put files on the web
- Cloak files and folders
- Update out-of-date links sitewide

Computers, Servers, and Networks

Companies and other organizations use the full range of computers. Large organizations can afford the largest and most expensive machines, and such companies are more likely to need all the processing power that these huge machines have. Many companies also want some of their workers, such as salespeople, to have small handheld computers.

Supercomputers

The largest and most powerful computers can process huge amounts of data very quickly. These superfast scientific computers are called supercomputers. Where most CPUs can perform millions of calculations a second, supercomputers can perform millions upon millions of calculations a second. The organizations using supercomputers do very complex work, such as forecasting the weather or creating detailed models of nuclear reactions. Supercomputers are not only the largest and most powerful type of computer, they are also the most expensive. A single supercomputer can cost hundreds of thousands of dollars or tens of millions of dollars. They are also extremely rugged and dependable systems, so users place constant heavy workloads on them.

Some organizations use very large computer systems and house them in their own special environments.

Mainframes

The mainframe is another type of computer used by government agencies and large corporations. Mainframe computers are used in centralized computing systems as the storage location for all or most of the data. Other, less powerful computers connect to the mainframe so users can access the data. For example, airline company employees use mainframes to store and process reservations. In this way, reservations agents and travel agents all around the world can locate and use the same information at the same time. The trend now is to replace mainframes with servers. Even many government agencies have reduced the amount they rely on mainframes.

Servers

Most organizations connect their computers together in a network. All the computers that are part of the network are connected to a computer called a server. The server holds data and programs that people on the network can use on their personal computers. A computer connected to a network, called the host, uses a special program called the client to contact the server and get data from it. Unlike terminals, computers on a network can have their own disk storage, but the main source of data for the network is still the server. Servers can be host- or client-based. If the server is host-based, the server runs the programs and receives directions from the client computers. In a client-based server the programs and processing are split between the client and host computers. The networking found in servers can also be found in peer-to-peer networks, where computers in a system share resources and there is no host computer.

Computer Network

A computer network is two or more computers connected to one another to share resources. Networks allow users to access files and programs. They also let users share printers and other equipment. They allow people to work together, too. A network may be small, with just a few computers, or it may be large, with thousands of workstations. The network functions the same way, no matter how many workstations are connected.

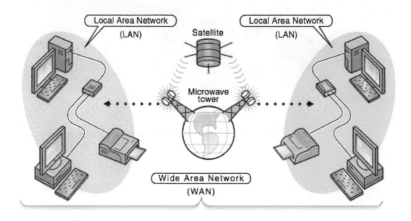

Introducing Computer Networks

In the simplest terms, a computer network is a group of computers and devices connected to each other so they can exchange data. The smallest network may only connect two computers; the largest—the Internet—connects millions. All computer networks are made up of the following components, physical media like a computer, cables, routers, network interface cards, storage devices both internal and external.

Physical Media

To create a computer network, each workstation and device must be able to communicate with the network. This requires establishing the connection using physical media or wirelessly. The physical media can be any type of telecommunications connector: twisted pair telephone lines, coaxial cable, fiber-optic cable, or a microwave, radio, or infrared system. Working together, the network media and the computers determine how much data can be sent through the connector. Wireless networks usually aren't as fast as wired networks.

Network Interface Cards

Some computers are designed with the ability to connect to networks. Others need a network interface card, or NIC, which handles the flow of data to and from the computer in both wired and wireless networks. If the network is put together by actual cables, those cables connect to the NIC. NICs often have a light that blinks green and amber to alert you to activity it's experiencing.

Network interface cards enable PCs to connect to a network.

Wireless Networks

Cell phones are one form of wireless communication. In addition, wireless networks allow computers to communicate through radio signals. Many hospitals, college campuses, businesses, hotels, and even cafes use wireless networks or "Wi-Fi." Wi-Fi is a short-range network with high-bandwidth for data transfer. Multi-computer households may also use wireless networks, allowing family members to share equipment and exchange data. Wireless networks can be secured or unsecured. An unsecured network can be accessed by anyone within range, which puts information at risk. You can secure a wireless network by using an encryption protocol such as Wired Equivalent Privacy (WEP) or Wi-Fi Protected Access2 (WPA2).

With the advent of smart phones there is need for networks designed for use with cell phone technology. These networks, called 3G or 4G, provide layered transmission of data, allowing for increased network capacity, a wider range of services, and faster upload and download speeds.

Kinds of Protocols

Once a network is created, the computers and other connected equipment can communicate with one another. The communication on a network is called network traffic. Network traffic is the electronic pulses of information sent by the network cards to carry data through the network wires to its destination. Specifically, computers communicate with languages called protocols.

A protocol sets a standard format for data and rules for handling it. There are many different protocols available to use on networks. For computers to speak with one another, they must use the same protocol.

There are two protocol categories: open and proprietary. An open protocol is available for anyone to use. For example, the most common open protocol is the Transmission Control Protocol/Internet Protocol (TCP/IP), which is used by computers on the Internet.

> **Connections Note – Literature**
>
> With e-books, your next reading selection could come from a network instead of a bookstore! Today, readers download their selections onto PDAs or special reading devices. Aside from convenience, there are practical advantages to e-books. Many schools are making textbooks available as e-books, so students don't have to lug around heavy backpacks filled with books. And, seniors and people with disabilities can buy books or borrow them from the public library without leaving home.

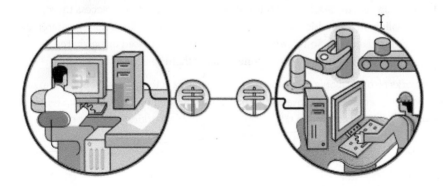

Computers in different locations can communicate as long as they use the same network protocols.

A proprietary protocol, however, is not open to everyone. Instead, only people who buy certain equipment, services, or computers can use it. Some personal digital assistants, digital cameras, and even dial-up Internet services use proprietary protocols. Overall, however, open protocols are more common. Both manufacturers and consumers benefit from open protocols that allow a broad range of connections.

The protocols networks use to communicate are often called a protocol suite. A protocol suite is the stack, or collection, of individual protocols that determines how the network operates. For example, TCP/IP is not just one network language, but many smaller ones. Each small protocol in this suite has a specific job to do in a specific order. Working together, protocols allow computers to communicate.

Internet Protocols

The Internet uses different protocols than a typical business network. Here are the more common protocols for the Internet:

- TCP/IP: Short for Transmission Control Protocol (TCP) and Internet Protocol (IP), this protocol controls the end-to-end connectivity of Internet data between the requestor and the host.

- HTTP: Short for Hypertext Transfer Protocol is used for the distribution and transmission of webpages and hypertext media.

- HTTPS: Secure connection using HTTP.

- FTP: Short for File Transfer Protocol and is the standard network protocol for transferring computer files between local computer and the web server.

- SFTP: Secure connection using FTP.

Working with Others

Everyone on a network has the ability to access programs and data stored anywhere on the network. You might use an application like Google docs which is stored on a network rather than on your own computer, or you might print a document on a printer that is located on a different floor than your computer. Of course, for security, you can specify sharing levels for folders to control who can access the stored data. Publicly shared folders allow anyone access. Shared folders may be shared only with authorized users. Sometimes, shared folders are accessed using shared links. That means you send a link to someone to allow them to access the folder.

Networks also let people work together in new and exciting ways. People on a network can collaborate more easily than those working on standalone systems. Synergy is the effect a group effort can create. People working together on a network can accomplish more than people working alone on unconnected computers.

Types of Networks

There are two main types of networks, Large Area Networks or LANs and Wide Area Networks or WANs. A LAN is a network in which all the workstations and other equipment are near one another. A school lab with its ten computers networked together is an example of a LAN. LANs can be set up in any defined area, such as a home, a school, an office building, or even a cluster of shops.

A WAN connects computers and other resources that are miles or even continents apart. A business with offices in many places can use a WAN to link its LANs in different cities. Then, users from any of the locations can, with the proper permissions, access the network. Each user can access files, printers, and other resources as if they were local. As far as users are concerned, a WAN "feels like" one giant LAN.

Often, a WAN connects two or more LANs into one large network. Suppose a company has networks in Chicago, Illinois; Indianapolis, Indiana; and St. Louis, Missouri. A high-speed data line between Chicago and Indianapolis can connect those two networks. From Indianapolis, another high-speed data line is connected to St. Louis. Now, all three networks are connected, and the company has a WAN.

Introducing LANs

A LAN can have just a few or several hundred users. Small or large, a LAN lets its members share equipment and information, resulting in lower costs. There are three key ways to share information: sharing files, using collaborative software, and sharing peripherals.

Sharing Files: Through a computer's operating system, people connected to a LAN can participate in file sharing. File sharing is making files available to more than one user on the network. The file is stored on a network server so anyone with permission rights may access the file from any location.

Using Collaborative Software: Collaborative software enables the network to help people work together more closely. With collaborative software, users can share calendars, work on a document together, or even hold meetings through the network. Collaborative software is also called groupware.

Sharing Peripherals: In addition to sharing files and software, a LAN allows users to access remote resources such as printers, fax machines, or any other equipment that is not connected directly to your computer, but is connected to the network.

Introducing WANs

A WAN is a very large network that can connect millions of people. A WAN is a client/server network. You are likely exposed to Wide Area Networks-WANs every day. Many of the retail stores you visit, such as grocery stores, shoe stores, or video stores, use WANs to track sales, inventory, and profits. You are also involved with WANs every time you use the Internet.

Organizing Users

If you have more than one computer at home, you probably identify them by each user's name—your computer, Mom's computer, and so on. In businesses, schools, and other organizations, a network is organized into workstations, each with its own name and address. In both home and larger networks, pieces of equipment connected together must be able to understand one another.

Career Connection: LAN Administrator

LAN administrators design, install, and maintain the LANs in organizations. They must understand the needs of the network users, stay up-to-date on new technology, and continue to learn about software choices. They should pay special attention to new ways to improve network security to keep the LAN safe from trespassers and viruses.

Once a WAN is created, users may not even realize the files they are sharing are remote. And that's the way it should be. Users should not worry about the physical location of the shared files, just that the files are available.

The Internet is the most common example of a WAN. You and others access the Internet through an Internet service provider (ISP). The ISP is connected to a backbone in order to reach other networks where Web servers are located.

The POS System

One example of a WAN in action is a **point-of-sale** system or POS. Here's how it works:

- The cashier at a retail outlet, such as a grocery store, scans the bar code on the item you purchase. That bar code is linked to a central database.

- The POS system allows the store to order more of the product automatically, learn which day of the week customers are likely to buy the item, and compare its sales with other stores.

- Once a store has collected information on its sales, it can predict trends. Knowing these trends lets the store managers stock the shelves and set prices sensibly.

Protecting a Network

A network can be secured or unsecured. On an unsecured network, there are no barriers to access and anyone within the network can access information. These networks allow for free flow of information but leave little protection from hacking for the individual computers. Secured networks, however, limit access and protect the computers and users. One way secured networks prevent unauthorized access is by requiring users to enter an ID and password.

Computing in a network can be private or public, as well. When you use the computers in your local library, you are on a public network that anyone can access. The networks in your school or home, however, are private and usually require an ID and password for access.

There are also public and private IP addresses. Public IP addresses are used by all computers connected to the Internet by a modem, including your home network computers. Private IP addresses are used on internal networks, such as a company intranet. Private IP addresses cannot be contacted directly over the Internet the way a computer with a public IP address can be. This provides an extra layer of security for the internal network.

Networks also use firewalls as a level of security. A firewall is a filtering system that opens or blocks programs and ports to keep outside data from entering the network. Firewalls are usually located on a gateway, such as a router that lets a network access the Internet. From that location the firewall can examine the packets trying to get into the network and determine whether or not to let them through. Some firewalls are built into a computer's operating system, such as Windows. You, or the system administrator, can control what the firewall blocks and what it lets through by maintaining lists of allowed or blocked programs and ports.

Use the Windows Firewall Allowed Apps settings to allow or block programs and ports.

Using a Network

The steps you use to access network resources are basically the same as those you use to work on your own computer. Your actions may seem simple enough, but behind the scenes, the network's hardware and software are performing complex tasks. Some tasks you can accomplish using a network include:

- Scheduling a meeting
- Instant messaging
- Sending e-mail
- Video conferencing
- Exchanging documents
- Playing games

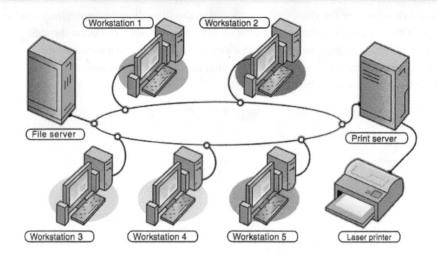

In a client/server network, users can share files stored on the file server and access a common printer, too.

Cloud Computing

A recent network trend is cloud computing. Cloud computing is the use of remote network servers to store data and resources, such as applications. Cloud resources are shared, so users do not actually own them. Instead, they pay to use server space. Cloud computing is a cost-effective option for many businesses, because they do not have to build and maintain their own network. With cloud computing, users with access to the cloud can retrieve data from multiple computers. Multiple users can also retrieve the same information, allowing for easy collaboration. Another benefit is that cloud-based applications such as Microsoft Office 365 and Adobe Creative Cloud are updated automatically. Users always have access to the most current software.

Web Servers

A web server is a computer on the Internet that hosts websites and functions as a client/server network. It has a unique IP or Internet Protocol address that lets other computers on the Internet know where to find it. Its main role is to serve up webpages upon user request. This service is referred to as web hosting. A web server offers these services and advantages.

- They offer a central location for files.
- Data is easy to back up and easy to recover.
- Servers are faster than workstations.
- Servers usually are powered on.
- Security is easier to maintain.

Using Web Apps

Web apps, which are sometimes called Cloud apps, are applications that are stored on cloud servers so you do not have to install them on your computer. Usually, you must register with a website to use a Web app. Some common Web apps include online e-mail services such as Gmail and Yahoo mail, social networking sites such as Facebook and Twitter, and productivity suites, such as Google Docs and Office 365.

As a client/server network, a web server does have a few disadvantages like congestion in the network caused by too many request from clients. This leads to overload and breakdown of the server. Also, if a server fails, the whole network goes down. A client/server network requires IT people to administer it and to upgrade the hardware and software which can be expensive.

There are security threats that can occur to both the server and client. Client and server are vulnerable to malicious viruses, trojan horses, worms and other deviant code and data. Servers are vulnerable to data overloading caused by someone sending a very large file very few seconds to the server message box. As a web designer, you can add a test question on a web site form that can only be answered by a human, not a computer BOT as a solution to server overloading. Learn more about Captcha at http://www.captcha.net/.

Web server requires a computer with Internet connection and special software for using the HTTP network protocol. It is comprised of a computer with ample internal storage and a fast processor, broadband Internet connection, additional external storage and hard drives, as well as routers, power supplies and connecting cables.

A web server needs a basic network protocol for processing HTTP request between the website visitor and the web server. It needs to process the HTTP request and then serve up the page for display in the browser. Therefore, special software needs to be installed on a web server. Due to the different server platforms, like windows or UNIX, there is software designed for each platform. Here is a list of the more popular software designed for web servers such as Microsoft IIS (Internet Information Server), IBM HTTP Server, Apache HTTP Server, Oracle HTTP Server Individual Scripts and applications for extra server functionality.

You can find a detailed list of web server types and server software at this URL:

https://en.wikipedia.org/wiki/Comparison_of_web_server_software

Secure Transaction Interfaces

Have you ever wondered how your purchase on an online store is secure and safe? A common problem when administering a web server is how to secure the data that is being transmitted. A solution used for authenticated servers and clients is TLS/SSL. TLS stands for Transport Layer Security protocol and SSL is short for Secure Socket Layer. Both technologies are used in creating a secure area on a web server that cannot be seen by others unless they have the right login.

Here's how the process works, when a visitor to your site sends a request to the web server that is stored in a secure area on the server, the server needs to be authenticate. This means that the client and server communicate additional information to complete the authentication. The client confirms the authentication of the server's credentials by accessing a trusted root certification authority's (CA's) certificates that is loaded on the server. Then the SSL-secured communication between the client and the server can begin. This communication is encrypted ensuring that it is safe from others.

It is a good idea to physically layout and record your security measure to help ensure the correct setup of your TLS/SSL area of the web server. Think about the various areas that your web site might be venerable or open to a hacker. Visit this site for a guide on cyber threats and how to protect your server.

https://transition.fcc.gov/cyber/cyberplanner.pdf

Backing Up and Restoring Data on a Web Server

All servers have addition administration software that you can install on them to administer the server. This software can be propriety to the server that you are using or an open source or public software that works on many servers. An example of common web server administration software is cPanel. cPanel lets you administer a server. Visit this link to learn more about cPanel:

http://www.cpanel.com/

Web server administration software lets you back up the server, or just a file or folder with a simple command or by a button click. You can also set up users and set user rights in the administration software. Restore an old backup of the entire server or just a file with a simple command and/or a click. The administration software is designed to make the complex tasks of server administration much easier.

Third Party Web Hosting Companies

Evaluate Third Party Web server Providers

There are many different web server providers. In groups or two or three students, research local and national web hosting service providers. Make a list of the vendors that and the services that they offer. Present your findings to the class.

There are third party companies that offer hosting packages for websites. These packages range from an individual site up to Virtual Private Server – VPS. VPS is a web server that virtually simulates an individual server. It is virtual space created through partitioning hard drive space on the third party company's web server. They rent out space based on the amount of Gigabytes needed for a web developer. This allows the web developer to have their own web server and they are in control of the web server. The web developer is responsible for server software upgrades and server administration. The third party company providing the VPS is responsible for the physical hardware, overall security, and storage capacity. Many web designers go this route for hosting their clients' websites as it offers the most flexibility and control for web server management.

Managing User Accounts

Computers are used for many different tasks, from playing games to writing reports and calculating numbers, businesses may want to restrict the use of some programs and files to designated users. This also is true for web servers as well as in schools, homes, and other settings where several people can use the same computer. A web server can be set with user accounts to allow the administrator and others to access the server.

Usernames and Passwords

One way to protect data or to allow a web client access to their website is to setup user accounts that identify who can access a computer. Each user is assigned a username and a password that he or she must provide in order to gain access. User accounts are set up using a system tool provided by the operating system. The system administrator is the person responsible for maintaining the computer system and for setting up user accounts. He or she has permission to customize and configure all aspects of the system for all users. System administrators should create documentation of user, user rights and software versions to help administer the network .

User Rights

User accounts may also have specific user rights assigned to them to limit or allow access, including:

- file access rights that specify which files a user can access and whether he or she can only read files or has access to read and write (edit) them
- installation rights that specify whether a user can install or remove programs
- hardware rights that specify whether a user can add or remove hardware
- configuration rights that specify whether a user can change operating system settings
- group policy rights that specify configuration and policy settings for a group of users on computers and mobile devices

Logging On and Off

To access your account, you log on to the system. When you are finished, you should always log off so no one else can access your data and account information. Most operating systems also let you switch users without logging off. This closes your account and switches to the account for the other user.

Enterprise Storage

As computer use increases, the need also grows for faster, more reliable, and higher capacity storage. In a network environment, computers can share data using an enterprise storage system. This technology allows networked computers to access storage devices linked to the network, such as servers, RAID systems, tapes, and optical disc systems.

Cloud Computing and Virtualization

Both cloud computing and virtualization make computers more efficient by using centralized storage, memory, and processing. Cloud computing uses the Internet and central remote servers to host data and applications.

Career Connection: Computer Security Specialist

Today, security specialists are in demand to work with various computer storage systems, such as tape warehouses and online storage companies.

Computer security specialists study ways of improving the overall security of their systems. For example, some goals include improving recording or access time or the safety of the protected information in case of a natural disaster.

Online Storage

Many online—or cloud—storage sites such as Google Drive, Dropbox, Microsoft OneDrive, and Apple iCloud, are available where you can store files on a network server at a remote location. You access your data by logging in through the Internet using a secure password. Some programs, including Microsoft Office, come with free online storage space. You can also pay a storage service provider (SSP) for space. Online storage offers these three benefits:

1 it is expandable;

2 it allows you to share files with others;

3 data stored in a remote location is protected if your computer is stolen or damaged.

Virtualization and SANs

Virtualization is when physical storage is pooled from multiple network storage devices into what seems to be one single storage device managed from a central console. Storage virtualization is usually used in a storage area network (SAN), a network of storage devices that can be accessed by multiple computers. Many businesses use virtualization to consolidate many different servers onto one piece of physical hardware that then provides a simulated set of hardware to two or more operating systems. While cloud computing and virtualization are two distinct storage options, many cloud computing providers use virtualization in their data centers.

New Magnetic Media

In the future, by manipulating molecules and atoms, magnetic hard drives will store as much as 1 terabyte (TB) per square inch of disk space. That's an increase of 100 times the 10 gigabytes per square inch of current hard drives.

New Optical Media

DMDs, or digital multilayer discs, contain multiple layers of a fluorescent material that stores information on each layer. A disc can hold 1 terabyte of data.

Holographic Media

A holographic data storage system, or HDSS, stores data in images called holograms on optical cubes the size of a sugar cube. These devices will hold more than 1 terabyte of storage and will be ten times faster than today's hard drives.

Introducing Bandwidth

People always want faster, better, and less expensive telecommunications choices. Twisted pair copper wiring in many homes and businesses in the United States at first made it hard to increase bandwidth. Then telephone, cable, and satellite television companies began to compete in offering higher speed communications. Now, more than eight out of ten homes and businesses are using high-speed connections for Internet access.

Understanding Bandwidth

Bandwidth is the amount of data that can be sent through a modem or network connection. The more bandwidth, the faster the connection. It is usually measured in bits per second (bps) or in Megabits per second (Mbps). The more bandwidth, the more information can be transferred in a given amount of time.

Imagine several people on different computers connecting to the Internet to visit Web pages, participate in video chats, or send e-mail. These users need a lot of bandwidth. That's why there is always a race to find a technology that offers services that transmit data faster. Currently the fastest technology is broadband transmission.

Working with Broadband Transmission

Broadband is the general term for all high-speed digital connections that transmit at least 1.5 megabits per second (Mbps), though current broadband services transmit between 10 and 30 Mbps. Mobile phones use mobile broadband which transmits around 10 Mbps. Current phones use the fourth generation of technology, or 4G. Broadband technology is able to send multiple signals at the same time through the medium. Unlike broadband, baseband technology uses the entire bandwidth to send one signal. Several broadband technologies are available, and more are always on the drawing board. This high transmission speed is required for videoconferencing, video-on-demand, digital television services, and high-speed Internet connectivity in general.

When broadband uses twisted pairs, the twisted pairs are categorized by the amount of data the wires can carry. Category 3 wires (Cat 3) are used in Ethernet at about 10 Mbps. Cat 5e wires can support 1 Gigabit Ethernet.

DSL

Digital Subscriber Line, or DSL, uses the same copper wires telephones use, but it transmits data in digital form rather than analog. Voice calls and DSL can exist simultaneously on copper lines, because each service has its own

Career Connection: Sales and Service Technician

Cable and satellite companies hire many sales and service technicians. These employees sell broadband services to customers and try to get current customers to upgrade their existing service. They also install and test the equipment.

Experience with technology is desirable, as is hands-on training specific to this industry. As more homes accept cable and satellite offerings, the need for sales and service technicians will grow to meet the demand.

frequency band. Unlike the old dial-up, DSL allows for very fast connections to the Internet and features an "always-on" connection. DSL service also requires a modem, which translates the computer's digital signals into voltage sent across phone lines to a central hub. There is one drawback to DSL: A user must be within a few miles of a local telephone switching station for a connection to be made.

Different companies offer DSL at different levels of service and price. For instance, asymmetric DSL (ADSL) allows download speeds of up to 1.5 Mbps and upload speeds of 128 kilobits per second (Kbps). This means you can receive data (download) faster than you can send it (upload) with ADSL. Subscribers to a Symmetric Digital Subscriber Line (SDSL) can send data at the same speed at which they receive it. These are used usually by businesses that need to send large files, data, and programs.

SONET

Telephone companies that offer DSL and other Internet connection methods rely on a digital network called SONET. SONET stands for *Synchronous Optical Network*. It uses fiber optics to provide faster connections and greater bandwidth—from 52 Mbps to up to a whopping 40 gigabits per second (Gbps).

In a video-conference, users in different locations transmit and receive audio, video, and computer data in real time. This kind of activity requires a great deal of bandwidth.

Cable and Satellite TV Connections

Most cable and digital television companies offer high-speed Internet connection through a cable modem. Satellite television companies also offer a similar service with signals sent through the customer's satellite dish. A cable modem connects your computer to the local cable TV line and supports data transfer rates of up to 30 Mbps— over 500 times faster than the old dial-up modem. However, this number can be misleading, because most Internet Service Providers (ISPs) cap subscribers' transfer rates to less than 6 Mbps to conserve bandwidth. However, this is more than enough for the average home computer user.

Voice Over Internet Protocol

Just as you can use your telephone to send and receive messages over the Internet, you can use the Internet to send and receive messages over the telephone. Voice over Internet Protocol (VoIP) technology allows you to have a telephone connection over the Internet. VoIP uses data sent digitally, with the Internet Protocol (IP), instead of analog telephone lines. People use VoIP to talk to each other from across the globe, sometimes without having to pay a cent. With Webcams callers can also see each other during their calls.

The Future of Bandwidth

The demand for bandwidth is growing. People want increased bandwidth for video-on-demand, meetings via the Internet, and web-based learning. Thus, telephone and other high-tech companies continue to look for new ways to improve telecommunications services and data transmission.

Validate, Test, and Analyze the Website

Before you post a site to the Internet and take it live to the world, you need to perform routine tests on your sites pages to validate each page based on W3C standards, site usage, spelling, broken links, and HTML errors like missing ALT tags or empty and redundant tags.

Validate Site Pages with W3C Standards

Dreamweaver makes this easy to validate your site's web pages with recommended W3C standards by including the Validation panel in the Results panel group. This panel lets you check your pages and the code with W3C

Making Communication Possible

It's not just governments and huge companies that put communications satellites into orbit. Students are doing it, too.

In 2001, for example, six students at the U.S. Naval Academy built a satellite with equipment anybody could buy: A tape measure was used as the antenna, and 24 AA batteries provided the power. Both a sailor in the Atlantic Ocean and some hikers in New Zealand used signals from the students' satellite to contact family at home.

How might students fund the cost of their experiments?

Career Connection: Telematics

Blending telecommunications technology with computers to control the electric, electronic, and mechanical tools we use is a relatively new field known as telematics.

Requirements for success in this industry include programming, engineering, and telecommunications training and experience.

Telematics professionals will find a growing demand for their services as the field develops.

standards. You run a report that identifies potential issues, errors or warnings for compliancy with W2C standards. You access this panel by choosing Window>Results>Validation.

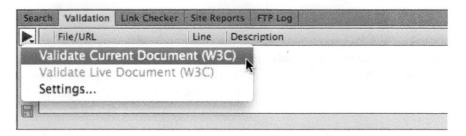

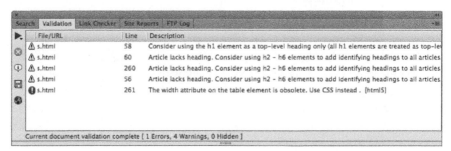

Test Website for Accessibility and Generate Usage Reports

Dreamweaver also offers another way to test your site for problems with the site content and to check accessibility for all site visitors. You can test for site accessibility issues and site usage. This is all done through the Site Reports panel, which is included in the Results panel group.

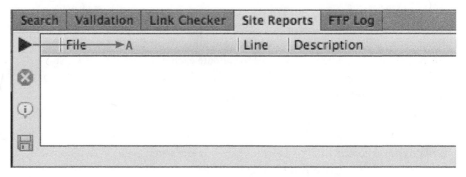

A – Reports

Tip: If you click the Checked Out by option in the Reports dialog, you must have Check in/Out option enabled in the Site Definitions dialog for the defined site.

To run a report, click the Report button. This opens the Reports dialog. Click the **Report on** dropdown menu and select whether to run a report on the current page, the entire site, or just certain files in the site, as well as a folder. You can run multiple reports at the same time by checking the Workflow and HTML Report options that you need. The Workflow folder provides usage reports for sites that have multiple editors and designers, and HTML Reports folder provides information about HTML content.

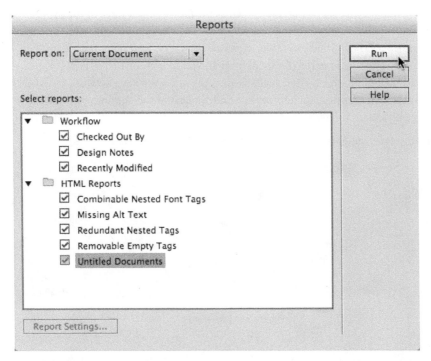

The Site Reports panel displays the errors and warnings that it found.

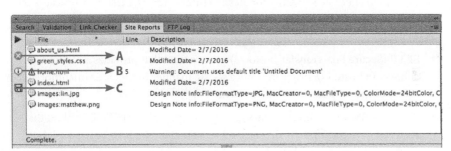

A – Delete

B – More Info

C – Save Report

You can double-click an error or warning and Dreamweaver takes you to the content in the site that has been identified and you can revise the content. Sometimes you might want to just ignore the issue as the report identifies some issues that might be a problem for older browsers or might be depreciated code that will still work with current browsers. The Site Report panel also has buttons for deleting issue or to get more information on the issue. You can also save the report.

Defining a Remote Site

Dreamweaver's workflow is based on a two-site system. One site is in a folder on your computer's hard drive and is known as the *local site*. All work in the previous chapters has been performed on your local site. The second site, known as the *remote site*, is established in a folder on a web server, typically running on another computer, and is connected to the Internet and publicly available. In large companies, the remote site is often available only to employees via a network-based intranet. Such sites provide information and applications to support corporate programs and products.

Dreamweaver supports several methods for connecting to a remote site:

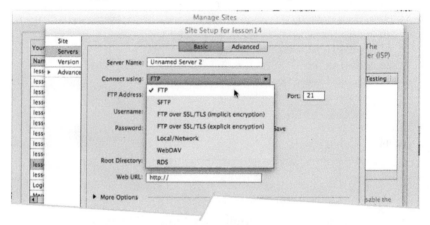

- **FTP** (File Transfer Protocol)—The standard method for connecting to hosted websites.

- **SFTP** (Secure File Transfer Protocol)—A protocol that provides a method to connect to hosted websites in a more secure manner to preclude unauthorized access or interception of online content.

- **FTP over SSL/TLS** (implicit encryption)—A secure FTP (FTPS) method that requires all clients of the FTPS server be aware that SSL is to be used on the session. It is incompatible with non-FTPS-aware clients.

- **FTP over SSL/TLS** (explicit encryption)—A legacy-compatible, secure FTP method where FTPS-aware clients can invoke security with an FTPS-aware server without breaking overall FTP functionality with non-FTPS-aware clients.

- **Local/network**—A local or network connection is most frequently used with an intermediate web server, known as a *staging server*. Staging servers are typically used to test sites before they go live. Files from the staging server are eventually published to an Internet-connected web server.

- **WebDav** (Web Distributed Authoring and Versioning)—A web-based system also known to Windows users as Web Folders and to Mac users as iDisk.

- **RDS** (Remote Development Services)—Developed by Adobe for ColdFusion and primarily used when working with ColdFusion-based sites.

Dreamweaver now can upload larger files faster and more efficiently and as a background activity, allowing you to return to work more quickly. In the following exercises, you'll set up a remote site using the two most common methods: FTP and Local/Network.

Setting up a Remote FTP Site

The vast majority of web developers rely on FTP to publish and maintain their sites. FTP is a well-established protocol, and many variations of the protocol are used on the web—most of which are supported by Dreamweaver.

Warning: To complete the following exercise, you must have a remote server already established. Remote servers can be hosted by your own company or contracted from a third-party web-hosting service.

1 Launch Adobe Dreamweaver CC (2015.1 release) or later.

2 Choose Site > Manage Sites or choose Manage Sites from the site list drop-down menu in the Files panel.

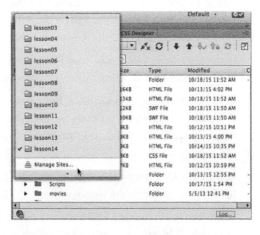

3 In the Manage Sites dialog is a list of all the sites you may have defined.

Make sure that the current site, chapter 15, is selected.

Click the Edit icon ✎.

4 In the Site Setup dialog for chapter 15, click the Servers category.

The Site Setup dialog allows you to set up multiple servers, so you can test several types of installations, if desired.

5 Click the Add New Server icon ➕.
Enter **GreenStart Server** in the Server Name field.

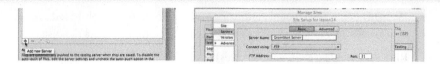

6 From the Connect Using pop-up menu, choose FTP.

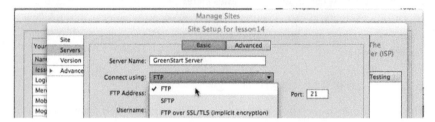

7 In the FTP Address field, type the URL or IP (Internet protocol) address of your FTP server.

If you contract a third-party service as a web host, you will be assigned an FTP address. This address may come in the form of an IP address, such as 192.168.1.100. Enter this number into the field exactly as it was sent to you. Frequently, the FTP address will be the domain name of your site, such as **ftp.green-start.org**. But don't enter the characters *ftp* into the field.

8 In the Username field, enter your FTP user name.
In the Password field, enter your FTP password.

Usernames may be case sensitive, but password fields almost always are; be sure you enter them correctly. Often, the easiest way to enter them is to copy them from the confirmation email from your hosting company and paste them into the appropriate fields.

9 In the Root Directory field, type the name of the folder that contains documents publicly accessible to the web, if any.

Some web hosts provide FTP access to a root-level folder that might contain nonpublic folders—such as cgi-bin, which is used to store common gateway interface (CGI) or binary scripts—as well as a public folder. In these cases, type the public folder name—such as public, public_html, www, or wwwroot—in the Root Directory field. In many web host configurations, the FTP address is the same as the public folder, and the Root Directory field should be left blank.

10 Select the Save option if you don't want to re-enter your username and password every time Dreamweaver connects to your site.

11 Click Test to verify that your FTP connection works properly.

Tip: If you are in the process of moving an existing site to a new Internet Service Provider (ISP), you may not be able to use the domain name to upload files to the new server. In that case, the IP address can be used to upload files initially.

Tip: Check with your web-hosting service or IS/IT manager to obtain the root directory name, if any.

Tip: If Dreamweaver does not connect to your host, first check the username and password, as well as the FTP address and root directory for any errors.

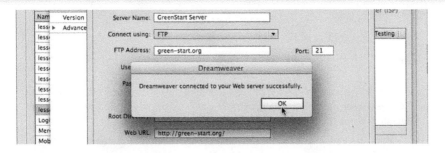

Dreamweaver displays an alert to notify you that the connection was successful or unsuccessful.

12 Click OK to dismiss the alert.

If Dreamweaver connects properly to the webhost, skip to step 14. If you received an error message, your web server may require additional configuration options.

13 Click the More Options triangle to reveal additional server options.

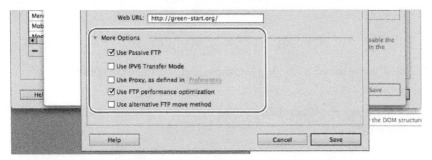

Consult the instructions from your hosting company to select the appropriate options for your specific FTP server:

- **Use Passive FTP**—Allows your computer to connect to the host computer and bypass a firewall restraint. Many web hosts require this setting.

- **Use IPV6 Transfer Mode**—Enables connection to IPV6-based servers, which use the most recent version of the Internet transfer protocol.

- **Use Proxy**—Identifies a secondary proxy host connection as defined in your Dreamweaver preferences.

- **Use FTP Performance Optimization**—Optimizes the FTP connection. Deselect this option if Dreamweaver can't connect to your server.

- **Use Alternative FTP Move Method**—Provides an additional method to resolve FTP conflicts, especially when rollbacks are enabled or when moving files.

Troubleshooting Your FTP Connection

Connecting to your remote site can be frustrating the first time you attempt it. You can experience numerous pitfalls, many of which are out of your control. Here are a few steps to take if you have issues connecting:

- If you can't connect to your FTP server, double-check your username and password and re-enter them carefully. Remember that usernames may be case sensitive on some servers, while passwords frequently are. (This is the most common error.)

- Select Use Passive FTP and test the connection again.

- If you still can't connect to your FTP server, deselect the Use FTP Performance Optimization option and click Test again.

- If none of these steps enable you to connect to your remote site, check with your IS/IT manager or your remote site administrator or web-hosting service.

Once you establish a working connection, you may need to configure some advanced options.

14 Click the Advanced tab. Select among the following options for working with your remote site:

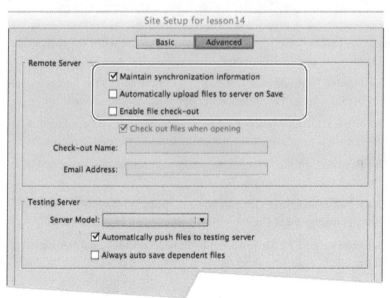

- **Maintain Synchronization Information**—Automatically notes the files that have been changed on the local and remote sites so that they can be easily synchronized. This feature helps you keep track of your changes and can be helpful if you change multiple pages before you upload. You may want to use cloaking with this feature. You'll learn about cloaking in an upcoming exercise. This feature is usually selected by default.

- **Automatically Upload Files To Server On Save**—Transfers files from the local to the remote site when they are saved. This option can become annoying if you save often and aren't yet ready for a page to go public.

- **Enable File Check-Out**—Starts the check-in/check-out system for collaborative website building in a workgroup environment. If you choose this option, you'll need to enter a check-out name and, optionally, an email address. If you're working by yourself, you do not need to select this option.

It is acceptable to leave any or all these options unselected, but for the purposes of this exercise, select the Maintain Synchronization Information option, if necessary.

15 Click Save to finalize the settings in the open dialogs.

The server setup dialog closes, revealing the Servers category in the Site Setup dialog. Your newly defined server is displayed in the window.

16 Click the Remote radio button to the right of the server name if necessary.

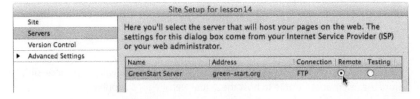

17 Click Save to finish setting up your new server.

A dialog appears, informing you that the cache will be re-created because you changed the site settings.

18 Click OK to build the cache. When Dreamweaver finishes updating the cache, click Done to close the Manage Sites dialog.

You have established a connection to your remote server. If you don't currently have a remote server, you can substitute a local testing server instead as your remote server.

Installing a Testing Server

When you produce sites with dynamic content, you need to test functionality before the pages go live on the Internet. A testing server can fit that need nicely. Depending on the applications you need to test, the testing server can simply be a subfolder on your actual web server, or you can use a local web server such as Apache or Internet Information Services (IIS) from Microsoft.

For detailed information about installing and configuring a local web server, check out the following links:

- Apache/ColdFusion—http://tinyurl.com/setup-coldfusion
- Apache/PHP—http://tinyurl.com/setup-apachephp
- IIS/ASP—http://tinyurl.com/setup-asp

Once you set up the local web server, you can use it to upload the completed files and test your remote site. In most cases, your local web server will not be accessible from the Internet or be able to host the actual website for the public.

Establishing a Remote Site on a Local or Network Web Server

Warning: To complete the following exercise, you must have already installed and configured a local or network web server as described in the sidebar "Installing a testing server."

If your company or organization uses a staging server as a "middleman" between web designers and the live website, it's likely you'll need to connect to your remote site through a local or network web server. Local/network servers are often used as testing servers to check dynamic functions before pages are uploaded to the Internet.

1 Launch Adobe Dreamweaver CC (2015.1 release) or later.

2 Choose Site > Manage Sites.

3　In the Manage Sites dialog, make sure that Chapter 15 is selected. Click the Edit icon ✐.

4　In the Site Setup for Chapter 15 dialog, select the Servers category.

5　Click the Add New Server icon ⊞ if you have already installed a local testing server.
In the Server Name field, enter **GreenStart Local**.

6　From the Connect Using pop-up menu, choose Local/Network.

7　In the Server Folder field, click the Browse icon ▨.

Select the local web server's HTML folder, such as C:\wamp\www\chapter 15.

8　In the Web URL field, enter the appropriate URL for your local web server. If you are using WAMP or MAMP local servers, your web URL will be something like http://localhost:8888/chapter 15 or http://localhost/chapter15.

You must enter the correct URL, or Dreamweaver's FTP and testing features may not function properly.

Note: The paths you enter here are contingent on how you installed your local web server and may not be the same as the ones displayed.

9　Click the Advanced tab, and as with the actual web server, select the appropriate options for working with your remote site: Maintain Synchronization Information, Automatically Upload Files To Server On Save, and/or Enable File Check-Out.

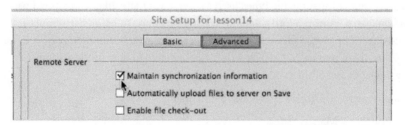

Although leaving these three options unselected is acceptable, for the purposes of this exercise, select the Maintain Synchronization Information option if necessary.

10　If you'd like to use the local web server as the testing server too, select the server model in the Advanced section of the dialog. If you are creating a dynamic site using a specific programming language, like ASP, ColdFusion, or PHP, select the matching Server Model from the drop-down menu so you'll be able to test the pages of your site properly.

11 Click Save to complete the remote server setup.

12 In the Site Setup dialog for Chapter 15, select Remote. If you want to use the local server as a testing server too, select Testing. Click Save.

13 In the Manage Sites dialog, click Done. If necessary, click OK to rebuild the cache.

Only one remote and one testing server can be active at one time, but you may have multiple servers defined. One server can be used for both roles, if desired. Before you upload files for the remote site, you may need to cloak certain folders and files in the local site.

Cloaking Folders and Files

Not all the files in your site root folder may need to be transferred to the remote server. For example, there's no point in filling the remote site with files that won't be accessed or that will remain inaccessible to website users. Minimizing files stored on the remote server may also pay financial dividends, since many hosting services base part of their fee on how much disk space your site occupies. If you selected Maintain Synchronization Information for a remote site using FTP or a network server, you may want to cloak some of your local materials to prevent them from being uploaded. *Cloaking* is a Dreamweaver feature that allows you to designate certain folders and files that will not be uploaded to or synchronized with the remote site.

Tip: You might consider uploading the template files to the server as means of creating a backup.

Folders you don't want to upload include the Templates and resource folders. Some other non-web-compatible file types used to create your site, like Photoshop (.psd), Flash (.fla), or Microsoft Word (.doc) files, also don't need to be on the remote server. Although cloaked files will not upload or synchronize automatically, you may still upload them manually, if desired. Some people like to upload these items to keep a backup copy of them off-site.

The cloaking process begins in the Site Setup dialog.

1 Choose Site > Manage Sites.

2 Select Chapter 15 in the site list, and click the Edit icon ✎ .

3 Expand the Advanced Settings category and select the Cloaking category. Select the Enable Cloaking and Cloak Files Ending With checkboxes, if necessary.

The field below the checkboxes displays the extensions .fla and .psd.

4 Insert the insertion point after *.psd,* and insert a space, if necessary. Type **.doc .txt .rtf**

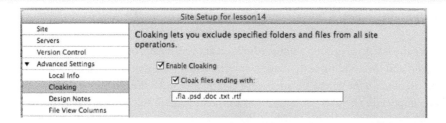

Be sure to insert a space between each extension. By specifying the extensions of file types that don't contain desired web content, you prevent Dreamweaver from uploading and synchronizing these file types automatically no matter where they appear in the site.

5 Click Save. If Dreamweaver prompts you to update the cache, click OK. Then, click Done to close the Manage Sites dialog.

Although you have cloaked several file types automatically, you can also cloak specific files or folders manually from the File panel.

6 Open the Files panel.
The Files panel appears.

7 Right-click the resources folder.
From the context menu, choose Cloaking > Cloak.

The Templates folder is not needed on the remote site because your webpages do not reference these assets in any way. But if you work in a team environment, it may be handy to upload and synchronize these folders so that each team member has up-to-date versions of each on their own computers. For this exercise, let's assume you work alone.

8 Apply cloaking to the Templates folder.

9 In the warning dialog that appears, click OK.

Using the Site Setup dialog and the Cloaking context menu, you cloaked file types, folders, and files. The synchronization process will ignore cloaked items and will not upload or download them automatically.

Wrapping Things Up

Over the last 15 chapters, you have built an entire website, beginning with a starter layout and then adding text, images, movies, and interactive content, but a few loose strings remain for you to tie up. Before you publish your site, you'll need to create one important webpage and make some crucial updates to your site navigation.

The file you need to create is one that is essential to every site: a home page. The home page is usually the first page most users see on your site. It is the page that loads automatically when a user enters your site's domain name into the browser window. Since the page loads automatically, there are a few restrictions on the name and extension you can use.

Basically, the name and extension depend on the hosting server and the type of applications running on the home page, if any. Today, the majority of home pages will simply be named *index*. But *default*, *start*, and *iisstart* are also used.

Extensions identify the specific types of programming languages used within a page. A normal HTML home page will use an extension of .htm or .html. Extensions like .asp, .cfm, and .php, among others, are required if the home page contains any dynamic applications specific to that server model. You may still use one of these extensions—if they are compatible with your server model—even if the page contains no dynamic applications or content. But be careful—in some instances, using the wrong extension may prevent the page from loading altogether. Whenever you're in doubt, use .html, because it's supported in all environments.

The specific home page name or names honored by the server are normally configured by the server administrator and can be changed, if desired. Most servers are configured to honor several names and a variety of extensions. Check with your IS/IT manager or web server support team to ascertain the recommended name and extension for your home page.

1   Create a new page from the site template.
    Save the file as **index.html**, or use a filename and extension compatible with your server model.

2   Open **home.html** from the Chapter 15 site root folder in Design view.

    The file contains content for the new home page.

3   Insert the insertion point in the heading *Welcome to Meridien GreenStart*. Select the `section` tag selector, and copy the content.

4   In **index.html**, select Design view.
    Click the heading *Add main heading here*.
    Select the `section` tag selector and paste.

> **Note:** Pasting to replace an element works only in Design and Code views.

5   Replace the quotation placeholder with the first `<aside>` element in **home.html**.

6   Replace Sidebar 2 with the second `<aside>` element in **home.html**.

    Note the hyperlink placeholders in the `main_content` region.

7   Insert the insertion point in the *News* link and click the a tag selector.
    In the Property inspector, browse and connect the link to **news.html**.

8   Repeat step 2 with each link.
    Connect the links to the appropriate pages in your site root folder.

9   Save and close all files.

The home page is complete. Let's assume you want to upload the site at its current state of completion even though some pages have yet to be created. This happens in the course of any site development. Pages are added and deleted over time; missing pages will be completed and uploaded at a later date. Before you can upload the site to a live server, you should always update any out-of-date links and remove dead ones.

Prelaunch Checklist

Take this opportunity to review all your site pages before publishing them to see if they are ready for prime time. In an actual workflow, you should perform most or all the following actions, which you learned in previous chapters, before uploading a single page:

• Spellcheck (Chapter 10, "Working with Text, Lists, and Tables")

• Site-wide link check (Chapter 12, "Working with Navigation")

Fix any problems you find and then proceed to the next exercise.

Putting Your Site Online

For the most part, the local site and the remote site are mirror images, containing the same HTML files, images, and assets in identical folder structures. When you transfer a webpage from your local site to your remote site, you are publishing, or *putting*, that page. If you *put* a file stored in a folder on your local site, Dreamweaver transfers the file to the equivalent folder on the remote site. It will even automatically create the remote folder or folders if they do not already exist. The same is true when you download files.

Using Dreamweaver, you can publish anything—from one file to a complete site—in a single operation. When you publish a webpage, by default Dreamweaver asks if you would also like to put the dependent files too. Dependent files are the images, CSS, HTML5 movies, JavaScript files, server-side includes (SSI), and all other files necessary to complete the page.

You can upload one file at a time or the entire site at once. In this exercise, you will upload one webpage and its dependent files.

1 Open the Files panel and click the Expand icon 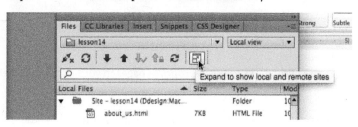, if necessary.

2   Click the Connect To Remote Server icon ⚡ to connect to the remote site.

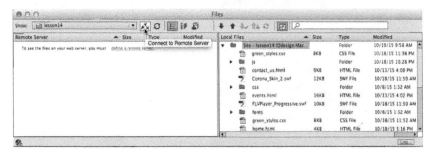

If your remote site is properly configured, the Files panel will connect to the site and display its contents on the left half of the panel. When you first upload files, the remote site may be empty or mostly empty. If you are connecting to your Internet host, specific files and folders created by the hosting company may appear. Do not delete these items unless you check to see whether they are essential to the operation of the server or your own applications.

3   In the local file list, select **index.html**.
In the Document toolbar, click the Put icon ⬆.

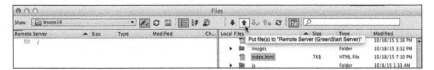

By default, Dreamweaver will prompt you to upload dependent files. If a dependent file already exists on the server and your changes did not affect it, you can click No. Otherwise, for new files or files that have had any changes, click Yes.

4   Click Yes.

Dreamweaver uploads **index.html** and all images, CSS, JavaScript, server-side includes, and other dependent files needed to properly render the selected HTML file.

The Files panel enables you to upload multiple files as well as the entire site at once.

5   Select the site root folder for the local site, and then click the Put icon ⬆ in the Files panel.

Note: Dependent files include but are not limited to images, style sheets, and JavaScript used within a specific page and are essential to the proper display and function of the page.

Dialogs appear, asking you to confirm that you want to upload dependent files and the entire site.

6 Click Yes and OK as appropriate.

Dreamweaver begins to upload the site. It will re-create your local site structure on the remote server. Dreamweaver uploads pages in the background so that you can continue to work in the meantime. If you want to see the progress of the upload, click the Log button in the lower-right corner of the Files panel.

7 Click the Log button.

Tip: If you are using a third-party web-hosting service, be aware that they often create placeholder pages on your domain. If your home page does not automatically appear when you access your site, check to make sure that there is no conflict with the web-host's placeholder pages.

If you click the Log button before all the files have been uploaded, you will see a list featuring the filenames and the status of the selected operation. When the upload is finished, the dialog provides a report.

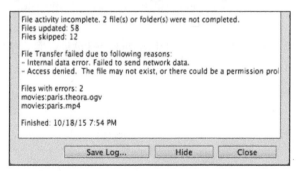

Note that none of the cloaked chapter folders were uploaded. Dreamweaver will automatically ignore all cloaked items when putting a folder or an entire site. If desired, you can manually select and upload individually cloaked items.

8 Right-click the Templates folder and choose Put from the context menu.

Note: A file that is uploaded or downloaded will automatically overwrite any version of the file at the destination.

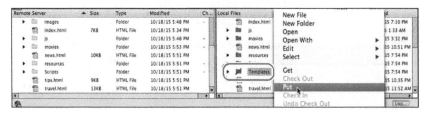

Dreamweaver prompts you to upload dependent files for the Templates folder.

9 Click Yes to upload dependent files.

The Templates folder is uploaded to the remote server. The log report shows that Dreamweaver checked for dependent files but did not upload the files that had not changed.

Note that the remote Templates folder displays a red slash, indicating that it, too, is cloaked. At times, you will want to cloak local and remote files and folders to prevent these items from being replaced or accidentally overwritten. A cloaked file will not be uploaded or downloaded automatically. But you can manually select any specific files and perform the same action.

The opposite of the Put command is Get, which downloads any selected file or folder to the local site. You can get any file from the remote site by selecting it in the Remote or Local pane and clicking the Get icon ⬇. Alternatively, you can drag the file from the Remote pane to the Local pane.

10 If you were able to successfully upload your site, use a browser to connect to the remote site on your network server or the Internet. Type the appropriate address in the URL field—depending on whether you are connecting to the local web server or to the actual Internet site—such as http://localhost/*domain_name* or http://www.*domain_name*.com.

Note: When accessing Put and Get, it doesn't matter whether you use the Local or Remote pane of the Files panel. Put always uploads to Remote; Get always downloads to Local.

The GreenStart site appears in the browser.

11 Click to test the hyperlinks to view each of the completed pages for the site.

Once the site is uploaded, keeping it up-to-date is an easy task. As files change, you can upload them one at a time or synchronize the whole site with the remote server.

Synchronization is especially important in workgroup environments where files are changed and uploaded by several individuals. You can easily download or upload files that are older, overwriting files that are newer in the process. Synchronization can ensure that you are working with only the latest versions of each file.

Synchronizing Local and Remote Sites

Synchronization in Dreamweaver keeps the files on your server and your local computer up to date. It's an essential tool when you work from multiple locations or with one or more coworkers. Used properly, it can prevent you from accidentally uploading or working on out-of-date files.

At the moment, your local and remote sites are identical. To better illustrate the capabilities of synchronization, let's make a change to one of the site pages.

1 Open **about_us.html** in Design view.

2 Collapse the Files panel.

Clicking the collapse button re-docks the panel on the right side of the program.

3 In the CSS Designer, select **green_styles.css** > GLOBAL.
   Create a new selector: `.green`

4 Add the following property to the new rule:
   `color: #090`

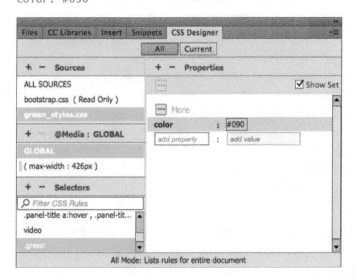

5 In the main heading, select the characters *Green* in the heading *About Meridien GreenStart.*

6 Apply the green class to this text.

7 Apply the green class to each occurrence of the word *"green"* anywhere on the page where the text is not already green in color.

8 Save all files and close the page.

9 Open and expand the Files panel. In the Document toolbar, click the Synchronize icon ⟳.

The Synchronize Files dialog appears.

Note: The Synchronize icon looks similar to the Refresh icon but is located on the right side of the Files panel.

10 From the Synchronize pop-up menu, choose the option Entire 'Chapter 15' Site. From the Direction menu, choose the Get And Put Newer Files option.

Choose specific options in this dialog that meet your needs and workflow.

11 Click Preview.

Note: Synchronize does not compare cloaked files or folders.

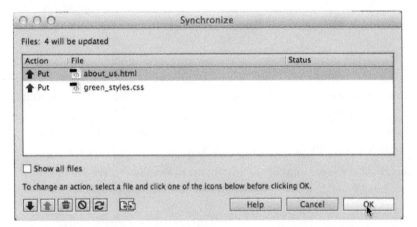

The Synchronize dialog appears, reporting what files have changed and whether you need to get or put them. Since you just uploaded the entire site, only the files you modified—**about_us.html** and **green_styles.css**—appear in the list, which indicates that Dreamweaver wants to put them to the remote site.

Synchronization Options

During synchronization, you can choose to accept the suggested action or override it by selecting one of the other options in the dialog. Options can be applied to one or more files at a time.

⬇ **Get**—Downloads the selected file(s) from the remote site

⬆ **Put**—Uploads the selected file(s) to the remote site

🗑 **Delete**—Marks the selected file(s) for deletion

🚫 **Ignore**—Ignores the selected file(s) during synchronization

🔃 **Synchronized**—Identifies the selected file(s) as already synchronized

▦ **Compare**—Uses a third-party utility to compare the local and remote versions of a selected file

12 Click OK to put the two files.

If other people access and update files on your site, remember to run synchronization *before* you work on any files to be certain you are working on the most current versions of each file in your site. Another technique is to set up the Check-out/Check-in functionality in the advanced options of the server's setup dialog.

In this chapter, you set up your site to connect to a remote server and uploaded files to that remote site. You also cloaked files and folders and then synchronized the local and remote sites.

Congratulations! You've designed, developed, and built an entire website. By finishing all the exercises in this book, you have gained experience in all aspects of the design and development of a standard website compatible with desktop computers and mobile devices. Now you are ready to build and publish a site of your own.

End-of-Chapter Activities

Review Questions

Directions: Choose the correct answer for each question.

1. True or false: You have to manually publish every file and associated image, JavaScript file, and server-side include that are linked to pages in your site.
   a. True
   b. False

2. What kind of machine is more powerful than a server?
   a. desktop computer
   b. portable computer
   c. mainframe
   d. handheld computer

3. What features does Dreamweaver offer for testing your webpages based W3C standards, site usage, accessibility and HTML errors?
   a. Results panel
   b. Site Report panel
   c. Validation panel
   d. All of the above

4. Which of the following is **NOT** an example of a physical medium used to connect a network?
   a. telephone wires
   b. electric cords
   c. fiber-optic cables
   d. radio signals

5. Which of the following are server administration tasks?
   a. Backup and Restore files and folders
   b. Setup and manage users
   c. Install software and scripts
   d. All of the above

6. A network that covers vast distances is called what?
   a. LAN
   b. WAN
   c. HTTP
   d. groupware

7. Which of the following are Internet protocols?
   a. TCP/IP
   b. FTP
   c. SFTP
   d. SHTTP
   e. All of the above
   f. A and B only

8. A secure transaction interface is comprised of what?
   a. TLS/SSL
   b. Trusted Root Certification
   c. Super computer
   d. A and B Only
   e. All of the above

9. What panel lets you identify and analyze site usage statistics, accessibility and HTML errors?
   a. Files panel
   b. Site Report panel
   c. Search panel
   d. Insert panel

10. True or False: It is important to maintain documentation of the server environment specifications, passwords and software versions.
    a. True
    b. False

11. What three options are available in the Site Reports feature for the site usage report?
    a. Checked Out By, Design Notes, Recently Modified
    b. Missing Alt Text, Removable Empty Tags, Untitled Documents
    c. Spell Report, Clean Up HTML, Clean up Word HTML
    d. None of the above

Essay Questions

Directions: Respond to each question by writing your answers in complete sentences and paragraphs. Be thorough in your answers.

1. What is a remote site?

2. Name two types of file transfer protocols supported in Dreamweaver.

3. How can you configure Dreamweaver so that it does not post or synchronize certain files in your local site with the remote site?

4. What service does synchronization perform?

5. Identify networking components, hardware and software requirements for a web server and define the impact of networking components on web development.

6. Describe how to backup or restore a file on a web server as well as an overview of setting up user access. Discuss the advantages of having a document that outlines users, user rights, and software for the network.

7. Describe the process to post and get files from the local root directory and the web server.

8. Identify current and future Internet protocols and their use in client/server networks. Discuss security measure required for these protocols.

9. Describe the process to validate a site based on W3C standards.

10. What are the advantages and disadvantages of running a personal server versus using a server provider?

11. List the advantages and disadvantages of a client/server network as well as security threats for both.

Critical Thinking Project—Finalize and Post the Lake Powell Website

The final step in any website is to validate all pages in the site for compliance with the W3C standards, as check the site for accessibility and HTML code issues. The Results panel group also has the Search and Link Checker panels, which were covered earlier in the book. Finalize your site pages and content by using the panels in this panel group to check your content.

With you site content finalized, you can publish the site to the Internet so that it is live to the world. The following exercise has you simulate publishing the Lake Powell website by defining a location on your computer to be the server and then using the Local/Network connection option for your server.

Validate the Lake Powell Site Pages with W3C Standards

Before posting the site Lake Powell site to the remote hosting server, validate the pages of the site for compliance with W3C standards.

1. Open the **lakepowell_temp.dwt** page and then open the Validate panel by choosing Window>Results>Validate

2. To run the report, click the Report button and choose **Validate Current Document (W3C)** to run the validation test. In the W3C Validation Notification dialog, click OK.

3. Dreamweaver checks your document with the W3C standards and lists errors and warnings that might need to be fixed to make the document compliant with W3C Standards.

4. Double-click one of the errors or warnings and Dreamweaver identifies the page content that has this error. You can make your edits to your document to fix these errors or warnings.

5. Save the template page and update all pages of the site with the new changes to the template.

6. Open all other pages of the site and run another validation test on them by repeating steps 2 – 4.

7. Save all pages.

Test Website for Accessibility and Other Issues

Test the Lake Powell site accessibility issues and other problems with the HTML code. This is all done through the Site Reports panel, which is included in the Results panel group.

1. If necessary, open the Site Report panel by choosing Window>Results>Site Report. To run the report, click the Report button. This opens the Reports dialog. Click the **Report on** dropdown menu and select whether to run a report on the current page, the entire site, or just certain files in the site, as well as a folder. Then select all the reporting options except for the **Check Out By** option. Click Run to run the report.

2. Due to having the Recently Modified option selected, your browser should activate and the page displays listing the files that where recently modified. Review the site usage of modified files list.

3. Switch back to Dreamweaver and review the results in the Site Reports panel. Select an issue and click the More Info button to see more information about the issue. Double-click an issue to go directly to that page content. Make any edits and modifications as needed.

4. Save all pages and preview the site in a browser.

Setup a Local/Network Folder as the Server

To simulate a FTP Server, you'll create a folder on your computer to serve as the FTP Server and then practice uploading and downloading files between your local root director and this server folder.

1. If necessary create a local root directory for your online portfolio site and copy your site files and folders into this directory as instructed by your teacher.

2. Define the local root directory as instructed by your teacher.

3. On your computer create a remote hosting server folder as instructed by your teacher. Name the folder **lakepowell_server**.

4. Create a local root directory for the Lake Powell website and then copy the class data files from the Chapter15/Data files/lakepowell_xx directory as instructed by your teacher.

5. Define a new site for the Lake Powell site. Leave the Site Setup for lakepowell_xx dialog open for the next step.

6. Now set up the server folder **lakepowell_server_xx** as the hosting server. In the Site Setup for lakepowell_xx dialog, click the **Server** category. Click the **Add New Server** icon and in the **Server Name** field, enter **LakePowell Local**. Then, from the **Connect Using** pop-up menu, choose **Local/Network**. In the **Server Folder** field, click the Browse icon. Select the local **lakepowell_server** folder on your computer.

7. In the **Web URL** field, enter **http://www.lakepowelladventures.com** for your local web server.

8. Click the Advanced tab, and select the **Maintain Synchronization Information** option, if necessary. Click Save to complete the remote server setup.

9. Using a Word Processor, open a new document. Use your Site Setup dialog to review the options that you set and then create the Web Server Overview document that outlines the following settings. Save the document and then print it for a hard copy of your Web server and settings.
   a. Name of server
   b. Connection Type and connection URL and Port
   c. User Login and Password
   d. Enabled More Options
   e. Local Root Directory

f. Web URL

g. Any options set in More options

h. Any Advanced Remote Server options

10. Click Save to complete the remote server setup. In the Manage Sites dialog, click Done/ Save. If necessary, click OK to rebuild the cache.

Cloak Files and Folders

Before you upload your Lake Powell site files and folders, you need to cloak files and the folders so that they are not uploaded to the hosting server.

1. Open the Manage Sites dialog and double-click the lakepowell_xx site. In the Site Setup dialog, click the Advanced Settings category to expand the Advanced Setting categories and click the Cloaking category. Click the **Cloak files ending with** option and insert the cursor after *.psd*, and type **.doc .txt .rtf**. with one space between each extension.

2. Click Save. If Dreamweaver prompts you to update the cache, click OK. Then, click Done to close the Manage Sites dialog.

3. Next cloak specific files or folders manually from the File panel. Open the Files panel. The Files panel appears. Right-click the resources folder and choose Cloaking > Cloak. Repeat this process to cloak the Templates folder. In the warning dialog, click OK.

Post and Get Files from the Server

Upload the files in the local root folder to the lakepowell_server_xx hosting server.

1. Using the Files panel post your local root directory to the lakepowell_server_xx local server by opening the Files panel and clicking the **Expand to show local and remote files** icon, if necessary. Then click the **Connect To Remote Server** icon to connect to the remote hosting site.

2. Since you have not uploaded your site yet, the lakepowell_server_xx displays with nothing listed under it. Post the Lake Powell site by selecting all the files and folders listed in the local root directory and then clicking the Put icon.

3. The site files and folders upload to the remote hosting server. When the Background File Activity dialog displays letting you know that the files where uploaded successfully, click Close.

4. You want your template folder to be posted to the server and Dreamweaver ignores all cloaked items when posting the entire site. You can post this folder manually by right-clicking the Templates folder and choose Put from the context menu. Dreamweaver prompts you to upload dependent files for the Templates folder. Click Yes to upload dependent files.

5. Collapse the Files panel by clicking the **Collapse to show only local or remote files** icon.

Syncing Files between Local Root Directory and the Hosting Server

Next you'll modify the on footer in **lakepowell_temp.dwt** and update the entire Lake Powell site with the change. Then by syncing the local site with the lakepowell_server_xx hosting server site, you'll upload these modified files to the server.

1. Open the template file for the Lake Powell site. Click in the footer area and change the footer text in the second sentence to read: Come **one and all** to Lake Powell and Experience Heaven on Earth!

2. Save the template and update the site files.

3. Next sync your local root directory files with the hosting server by clicking the Synchronize with Remote Server icon in the Files Panel. In the Synchronize with Remote Service dialog, click Preview. Dreamweaver checks the files on the server with the local root directory files for any changes and then opens the Synchronize dialog. Review the files that have been identified and then Click OK to upload these files to the server.

Online Portfolio Builder—Post your Online Portfolio Site to a Server

If you have a remote hosting provider you'll need to get the login information from them to set up the FTP connection for posting your site. If you do not have a hosting provider, simulate this process by creating a folder on your computer that will be the server. Post your online portfolio site the hosting server by following these general instructions.

1. If necessary, create a local root directory and copy your online portfolio site files or folders to the new local root directory as instructed by your teacher. Define your site.

2. If you have a remote hosting server, skip this step. If you do not, you need to create a folder on your computer that will serve as your remote server. Create and name this server as instructed by your teacher.

3. Run reports on your web site by accessing the Results panel group. Choose Window>Results>Validate to check your sites HTML with the W3C standards. Spell check and check our links as well through the Spell Check menu command and the Link Checker panel. Then check the code for errors through the Site Reports panel.

4. Open the Site Management dialog by choosing Site>Manage sites and double-clicking your online portfolio site.

5. Set up your hosting server by click the Server category and then click the **Add New Server** button. Type a name for your hosting server in the Server Name field. Then do one of the following:
   a. If you have a remote hosting server, choose FTP as the Connect Using option. Then fill in the other fields with the information provided by your remote hosting server provider. Click the Test button to test your connection. When you have a successful connection click Save and then click Save again to close the Site Setup dialog. Click Done to close the Manage Site dialog. Proceed to the next step.
   b. If you have a simulated remote hosting server, choose Local/Network option from the Connect Using dropdown menu. Set the location to the folder you created for your remote hosting server by clicking the Browse button and navigating to this folder. Add a web URL as instructed by your teacher. Click Save.

6. Cloak the files that do not need to be uploaded to the remote hosting server by expanding the Advanced Settings option and clicking the Advanced Settings category to expand the Advanced Setting categories and click the Cloaking category. Click the **Cloak files ending with** option and insert the cursor after *.psd*, and type **.doc .txt .rtf**. with one space between each extension.

7. Click Save. If Dreamweaver prompts you to update the cache, click OK. Then click Save again to close the Site Setup dialog. Then, click Done to close the Manage Sites dialog.

8. Next cloak specific files or folders manually from the File panel. Open the Files panel. The Files panel appears. Right-click the **resources** folder and choose Cloaking > Cloak. Repeat this process to cloak the Templates folder. In the warning dialog, click OK.

9. Post your site by opening the Files panel if necessary. Then click the **Expand to show local and remote sites** icon. Make a connection with the remote hosting server by clicking the **Connect to Remote** icon. Then select all the files in your local root directory and click Put icon.

10. Congratulations, you have uploaded your site to the remote hosting server. If you have a web hosting server provider, preview your live site, by typing your URL for your site in a Browser.

11. You have created a online portfolio site from scratch and then posted it to the Internet and it's live. This site will be a great resource for you as you go forward with your studies and your future career!

INDEX

comma-separated values (CSV), 412
common gateway interface (CGI), 608
Compact Discs (CDs), 451
company brand, 156
Compare command, 624
complementary color rule, 158
compound color rule, 159
COMPUTED option, 57–58
computer basics, 447–452
    analog computers, 447
    bits, 448
    bytes, 448
    central processing unit, 449–450
    circuit board, 450
    circuits, 450
    connectors or ports, 452
    device, 447
    digital computers, 447
    ethics in using, 476–477
    hardware, 447
    hexadecimal value, 448
    input, 448
    output, 449
    peripherals, 452
    processing, 448–449
    program, 447, 448
    random access memory, 450
    secondary storage, 450–451
    software for web development, 452
    storage, 449
    Universal Serial Bus, 450, 452
Computer Crime and Intellectual Property
    Section (CCIPS), 339–340
Computer Hacking and Intellectual
    Property Project (CHIP), 340
computer networks, 589–596
    cloud computing, 596
    LANs, 593
    network interface cards, 590
    network traffic, 591
    organizing users, 592, 593
    overview of, 589
    physical media, 590
    POS system, 594
    protecting, 594–595
    protocols, 591–592
    using, 595–596
    WANs, 593–594
    wireless networks, 591
computer safety, 335–342
    cybercrime, 337–340
    privacy in cyberspace, 336–337
    protecting personal data, 341

    security and privacy measures,
        341–342
    social networking, 342
computer security specialists, 599
computing research centers, 9
connectors, 452
consistency, 213
container format, 575
content management system (CMS), 317
context-driven, 51
contrast, 211
cookies, 337
copying and pasting
    CSS properties, 330–334
    Photoshop images, 465–469
    tables, 405–406
copyright
    Fair Use Doctrine and, 478–479
    of intellectual work, 478
    laws, 477–479
CorelDRAW, 442
cover letter, 68
Create tab, 29–30
Creative Cloud account folder, 46
creative commons license, 479
Critical Thinking
    client-server architecture, 24
    create and implement QA test plan for
        portfolio site, 374
    review project, 80–87
Critical Thinking Project
    add web video to website, 582–585
    create master template for website,
        375–378
    create web design project plan for
        portfolio site, 183
    CSS in practice, 145–149
    develop Mobile first design for website,
        345–348
    develop site navigation for website,
        520–525
    develop webpage with interactivity,
        557–562
    finalize and post website, 627–631
    insert images into website, 485–490
    using HTML5 to create webpage,
        102–107
    working with pre-defined layouts,
        218–222
    work in teams to develop Bootstrap
        layout of site, 297–307
Crop tool, 474
cross browser compatibility, 115

digital computers, 447
Digital Subscriber Line (DSL), 601–602
Digital Video Discs (DVDs), 451
disseminate, 94
dithering, 444
<div> tag, 92, 95
.doc extension, 614
docking panels, 39, 42–43
Document Object Model (DOM), 60, 528–529
Document tab, 28
Document Title field, 355
Document toolbar, 28, 47, 111
domain extensions, 16
domain name, 15–17
   acquiring, 16
   defined, 16
   Domain Name System, 16
   IP address, 15
   top-level, 16
   WHOIS database, 16–17
Domain Name System (DNS), 16
down-level stage, 573
download, 12, 451
drag-and-drop to insert images, 469–470
dragging panels, 41, 42
Dreamweaver. *See* Adobe Dreamweaver CC
Dropbox, 451, 600
drop zone, 42
DSL (Digital Subscriber Line), 601–602
.dwt extension, 353
dynamic effects, 35
Dynamic Hypertext Markup Language (DHTML), 528–529

E

e-books, 591
Edge Web Fonts, 275–280
editable regions
   formatting content in, 363–366
   inserting, 353–355
Edit Image Settings tool, 474
Edit tool, 474
Edmondson, Amy, 287–488
efficacy, 111
Element HUD, 61, 507–508
element references, 3
elements, 92–93
   attributes, 37
   caption, adding and formatting, 415–417
   child element, 53, 127
   custom classes, 269–271
   defined, 35, 91

HTML character entities, 93
HTML tags, 92–93
   nested, 53, 118, 127, 319
   overt styling information, 113
   page, targeting (*See* targeting page elements)
   parent element, 53, 124
   rendering, 115
   responsive, 398–400
   triggering, 530
em (font unit), 267
<em> tag, 92
e-mail
   addresses, 341
   links, setting up, 505–507
   pros and cons, 12
   spam, 509
   web-based services, 505
embedded style, 118
Emmet, 62–64
emotional intelligence, 284–285
emphasis, 210
employment trends, 70–71
enterprise storage, 599–600
   cloud computing, 599
   holographic media, 600
   magnetic media, 600
   online storage, 600
   optical media, 600
   storage area network, 600
   virtualization, 600
entities, HTML, 93, 273–274
ethics, 475–482
   acceptable use policies, 477
   avoiding problems, 480
   citing sources, 475, 480
   in computer use, 476–477
   copyright laws, 477–479
   creative commons license, 479
   defined, 476
   fair use, 480
   include relevant information, 472
   informed consent, 475
   netiquette, 481–482
   patents, 479–480
   penalties for violations, 477
   plagiarism, 480
   public domain, 480
   report research accurately, 475–476
   responsibility for actions, taking, 481
   secondary sources, 475
   trademarks, 479
   web and, 475–481

Hypertext Markup Language (HTML). *See* HTML (Hypertext Markup Language)

hypertext transfer protocol (HTTP), 14, 592, 597

I

IBM HTTP Server, 597

id attribute
  added to wrong element, correcting, 514
  applied to images, 534, 535
  CSS to create, 140
  link destinations, 512–516
  named anchor method deprecated in favor of, 510
  names, 513, 514

identity theft, 339

iDisk, 607

ids in CSS, 35

<iframe> tag, 92

Ignore command, 624

image-based links
  creating, 507–509
  Element HUD to create, 507–508

Image HUD, 61

images, 440–491
  adapting to smaller screens, 468–469
  background, 242–245
  copying and pasting from Photoshop, 465–469
  CSS to position, 454–456
  drag-and-drop to insert, 469–470
  id attributes applied to, 534, 535
  inserting, 453–454
  inserting non-web file types, 459–461
  inserting right/wrong size, 462
  Insert menu, 457–458
  Insert panel, 456–457
  properties, in Property inspector, 52
  Property inspector to optimize, 471–473
  raster graphics, 442–447
  Smart Objects, 462–465
  vector graphics, 442

<img> tag, 92

importing, 382–384

incompatible code, 248

indented text, 394–398

index.html, 369–370

index page. *See* home page

informed consent, 475

inheritance theory, 118, 123–126

inline elements, 92

inline style, 118

input, 448

<input> tag, 92

Insert menu, 457–458

Insert panel, 28, 456–457

Inspect mode, 38

intellectual property, 478

interactivity, 526–563
  Bootstrap Accordion widgets, working with, 543–554
  Dreamweaver behaviors, 530–543
  web design tools, advanced, 528–529

internal links
  creating, 495–502
  defined, 494

internal social media (ISM), 294

Internet
  e-mail, 12
  file transfer on, 12–13
  freedom of, 10
  history of, 9
  management, 10
  organization of, 9
  pitfalls of, 10
  protocols, 592
  voting on, 11
  WAN compared to, 10
  World Wide Web compared to, 8

Internet Corporation for Assigned Names and Numbers (ICANN), 10

Internet Engineering Task Force (IETF), 10

Internet Information Services (IIS) from Microsoft, 597, 612

Internet Protocol (IP) address, 15, 594, 596

Internet Service Provider (ISP), 14, 594

InterNIC, 16, 17

interpersonal communication, 284–294. *See also* team
  defined, 284
  emotional intelligence in, 284–285

IP (Internet Protocol) address, 15, 594, 596

IPV6 Transfer Mode, 609

ISP (Internet Service Provider), 14, 594

J

JavaScript, 3. *See also* Adobe Dreamweaver behaviors
  defined, 530
  file extension for (.js), 530
  overview of, 528

job interview, 68

Joint Photographic Experts Group (JPEG or JPG), 446, 447

JPEG or JPG (Joint Photographic Experts Group), 446, 447

targeting page elements
    Element HUD to create link destination, 514–515
    id-based link destinations, targeting, 515–516
    id to create link destination, 512–514
    internal targeted links, creating, 510–512
TCP/IP (Transmission Control Protocol/Internet Protocol), 591–592
`<td>` tag, 93
team, 285–293
    agenda, 290–292
    defined, 285
    development, stages of, 286–288
    expected results, 285–286
    goals, 285
    high-performing, 287
    individual responsibility in, 293
    leadership practices, 288–290
    meetings, 290–292
    standards, 286
telematics, 603
Telnet, 12, 14
templates, 350–379
    Bootstrap, 195–198
    creating from existing layout, 352–353
    file extension for (.dwt), 353
    inserting editable regions, 353–355
    inserting metadata, 355–357
    naming webpages, 369–370
    producing child pages, 357–369
    test plans and quality assurance, 370–371
    view for creating, editing, or using, 391
tenet, 117
terabyte (TB), 451, 600
testing server, 612
test plans, 370–371
    defined, 370
    implementing, 371
    QA plans, 370–371
    QA process, 370
    usability study, 371
text, 382–390
    creating and styling, 382–390
    finding and replacing, 425–429
    Find In menu, 429
    formatting (*See* CSS rules)
    headings, creating, 385–387
    HTML structures, adding other, 387–390
    importing, 382–384
    indented, 394–398
    Search menu, 429
    semantic structures, creating, 384–385
text-align property, 239, 242

`<textarea>` tag, 93
text-based links, Text HUD to create, 508–509
text files, 12
Text HUD, 61, 508–509
text-shadow property, 239, 242
`<th>` tag, 93
theft, 339
third-party web hosting service, 598, 607, 608, 620
3G network, 591
thumb drives, 451
thumbnails in web design, 161–162
time bombs, 338
TinyURLs, 2
Tips & Techniques tab, 31–32
`<title>` tag, 93
TLS/SSL (Transport Layer Security/Secure Socket Layer), 597–598
toolbars, 47
top-level domain name, 16
`<tr>` tag, 93
trademark infringement, 479
trademarks, 479
Transmission Control Protocol/Internet Protocol (TCP/IP), 591–592
Transport Layer Security/Secure Socket Layer (TLS/SSL), 597–598
trap doors, 338
travel page, 531–534
trends, employment, 70–71
triad color rule, 158
Trojan horse, 337, 338, 342
true color, 445
Tuckman, Bruce W., 286
TV connections, cable and satellite, 603
Twitter, 195, 294, 482, 596
type
    global styles, 275–284
    in header content, 235–239
typeface, font *vs.*, 275

U

`<ul>` tag, 93
uniform resource locators (URLs)
    defined, 2
    hyperlinks and, 11
    parts of, 14–15
United States Military, 9
Universal Serial Bus (USB), 450, 452
university researchers, 9
UNIX, 597
unsecured networks, 594
Update from Original tool, 474